# Developing and Utilizing E-Learning Applications

Fotis Lazarinis
*University of Teesside, UK*

Steve Green
*Teesside University, UK*

Elaine Pearson
*Teesside University, UK*

Information Science REFERENCE

**INFORMATION SCIENCE REFERENCE**
Hershey · New York

Director of Editorial Content: Kristin Klinger
Director of Book Publications: Julia Mosemann
Acquisitions Editor: Lindsay Johnston
Development Editor: Joel Gamon
Publishing Assistant: Milan Vracarich, Jr.
Typesetter: Deanna Jo Zombro
Production Editor: Jamie Snavely
Cover Design: Lisa Tosheff

Published in the United States of America by
Information Science Reference (an imprint of IGI Global)
701 E. Chocolate Avenue
Hershey PA 17033
Tel: 717-533-8845
Fax: 717-533-8661
E-mail: cust@igi-global.com
Web site: http://www.igi-global.com



Library of Congress Cataloging-in-Publication Data

Developing and utilizing E-learning applications / Fotis Lazarinis, Steve Green and Elaine Pearson, Editors.
p. cm.
Includes bibliographical references and index.
Summary: "This book augments the expanding e-learning industry by offering methods and tools necessary to create and maintain e-learning applications"--
Provided by publisher.
ISBN 978-1-61692-791-2 (hardcover) -- ISBN (invalid) 978-1-61520-793-6 (ebook)
1. Internet in education. 2. Computer-assisted instruction. 3. Instructional systems--Design. 4. Human-computer interaction. I. Lazarinis, Fotis. II. Green, Steve, 1957- III. Pearson, Elaine, 1957-
LB1044.87.D493 2011
371.33'44678--dc22

2009052435

British Cataloguing in Publication Data
A Cataloguing in Publication record for this book is available from the British Library.

## Editorial Advisory Board



## List of Reviewers

# Table of Contents

# Detailed Table of Contents

The work reported in this chapter relates to the importance of e-learning in the European Lifelong Learning Program 2007 – 2013, and presents the Romanian case as a comparative study with the EU and US standards in higher education.



For three consecutive years, the authors have surveyed bachelors and masters students who were enrolled in online courses at a Japanese university, in order to study learners' behavior while they are engaged in online courses. It was also their goal in this study to identify learning strategies and instructional design techniques that can contribute to the development of e-learning standards and can be applied to online course design and management. This book chapter will discuss how these issues were addressed using the survey data collected over three years, and based on the results of data analyses, provide a discussion of some guiding principles for the design and implementation of online learning.



This chapter describes the authors' experience in designing E-learning methodologies for the teaching of accountancy in the Business Administration Degree Course at the Polytechnic University of Valencia. The methodology designed for teaching accounting, is based on PBL (Problem Based Learning).



This chapter focuses on learning methods in entrepreneurial and managerial training. ICT changed the role of entrepreneurs and managers and as a consequence, targets, contents and methodologies of entrepreneurial and managerial training need to be revised and inter-active teaching methods have to be adopted: learning by doing, by playing and dramatization.

# Preface

E-learning is a field at the crossroads of different scientific areas bringing together technologists and instructors. E-learning is the unifying term to describe the fields of online learning, web-based training, distance learning and technology-delivered instruction. More terms have been devised in the past to reflect the different views of people working in the broad area of computer supported learning.

Being such a broad field, it has advanced at a very fast pace; practitioners and scientists from different disciplines work together to deliver a wide range of educational tools. While the interdisciplinary nature of e-learning yields specific tools and solutions, designed on pedagogical principles, new, more intelligent and adaptive tools are needed to satisfy the needs of different groups of students and different instructional aims. A deeper understanding of the implications of e-learning for students and for learning is another demand, if we are to improve the quality of the services on offer.

Therefore, although there are a number of scholarly publications related to e-learning, there is always a need for alternative applications and viewpoints. Hence, the main aim of this publication is to present specific tools and discuss issues related to the development and utilization of e-learning tools. A number of tools and use cases are presented, some of which relate to specific educational systems and topics. Adaptivity, utilization of new technologies in informal learning, engineering and accounting, are among the discussed topics.

Chapter 1, by Sabrina Leone and Giuliana Guazzaroni, discusses the pedagogical sustainability of interoperable formal and informal learning environments. Advantages and drawbacks are highlighted, in terms of technological and pedagogical effectiveness.

Valeria Pandolfini in Chapter 2 analyzes how it is possible to integrate teaching models and use of new technologies in an adult blended course, and to adapt training experiences to the target group, in order to offer a personalized course.

Chapter 3 by Luis Payá, Oscar Reinoso, David Úbeda, Luis M. Jiménez and José M. Marín presents the implementation of an interactive tool so that students can monitor and control the evolution of a team of mobile robots through the Internet. This platform is designed for a computer vision and robotics taught subject and it allows students to learn and practice the basic concepts on those fields and their relationships.

Chapter 4 written by Bob Barrett surveys current online teacher training standards and trends, in terms of what is required of new online instructors. It focuses on the use of the online learning environment as a vehicle to help instructors to prepare for online teaching.

Kevin Downing, Kristina Shin and Flora Ning in Chapter 5 describe a case study which examines detailed data related to student and tutor usage of an asynchronous discussion board as an interactive communication forum.

Chapter 6, written by Yasushige Ishikawa, Mutsumi Kondo and Craig Smith, reports on the development of an innovative interoperable Information and Communication Technology (ICT) application for English teaching in primary schools in Japan. An investigation into the use of the ICT application during a four month period at two primary schools is also described.

Lea Kuznik in Chapter 7, discusses the potentials and the new challenges in the educational field of virtual worlds for adults, youth and children.

Chapter 8 by Cristina Barna, Manuela Epure and Ruxandra Vasilescu, relates to the importance of e-learning in the European Lifelong Learning Program 2007 – 2013, and presents the Romanian case as a comparative study with the EU and US standards in higher education.

Chapter 9 by Minoru Nakayama, Hiroh Yamamoto and Rowena Santiago surveyed bachelors and masters students who were enrolled in online courses at a Japanese university for a period of three years, in order to study learners' behavior while they are engaged in online courses.

Chapter 10 by Alicia Mateos- Ronco and Mª del Mar Marín- Sánchez, describes the authors' experience in designing e-learning methodologies for the teaching of accountancy in the Business Administration Degree Course at the Polytechnic University of Valencia. The methodology designed for teaching accounting, is based on PBL (Problem Based Learning).

Mario G.R. Pagliacci in Chapter 11, focuses on learning methods in entrepreneurial and managerial training. ICT changed the role of entrepreneurs and managers and as a consequence the study claims that, targets, contents and methodologies of entrepreneurial and managerial training need to be revised and inter-active teaching methods have to be adopted.

Ugo Barchetti, Alberto Bucciero and Luca Mainetti in Chapter 12, present the design of a solution for Computer-Supported Cooperative Learning (CSCL) that is able to connect both stationary and mobile users in live shared-learning sessions. The authors started from experiences that were mainly technology-driven to arrive at the development of two subsystems, OpenWebTalk and MobileWebTalk in which users cooperate to perform the same learning task.

Chapter 13 by Anthonia Maduekwe and Adeola Adeosun, presents a survey aimed at identifying the level of usability and applicability of interoperable educational tools in Nigeria language teacher education.

Chapter 14 by Jocene Vallack, formulates how subphenomenology uses intuition to access unconscious knowing, and reveal an archetypal image of the research in question. Subphenomenology is a formula, which can be applied to any weblog data, or indeed any creative work, to enable researchers to understand more about the universal implications of their most subjective reflections.

The last Chapter 15 by Peter Neema-Abooki and Alfred Kitawi aims at highlighting and proposing an e-learning fourfold strategy in the management of universities based on Ideological, Methodological, Output, and Ecological factors.

These studies discuss various aspects related to the development and utilization of learning technology applications. Researchers and lecturers of tertiary education shared their experiences in engaging with learning technology tools. Innovative approaches to the use of virtual world tools in education and to teaching with learning tools have been presented. Overall, this research publication focuses on the utilization and adoption of e-learning tools by educators and presents a number of current studies of best practice.

*Fotis Lazarinis, Steve Green, Elaine Pearson*
*Editors*

# Chapter 1
# Pedagogical Sustainability of Interoperable Formal and Informal Learning Environments

**Sabrina Leone**
*Università Politecnica delle Marche, Italy*

**Giuliana Guazzaroni**
*Università Politecnica delle Marche, Italy*

## ABSTRACT

*Nowadays interaction and networks appear to be crucial. The impact that new technologies have had in every field has flowed into a rethinking of knowledge, knowledge management, teaching and learning, networks and the individual. Formal, non-formal and informal learning have become key words of this age. New technologies and the revolution of Web 2.0 social tools have deeply influenced learning approaches. However, the effectiveness of Web 2.0 educational tools depends on the pedagogical sustainability beneath and on internationally shared standards to facilitate interoperability. This chapter aims to discuss the pedagogical sustainability of interoperable formal and informal learning environments. Advantages and drawbacks will be highlighted, in terms of technological and pedagogical effectiveness and appropriateness, through two case studies illustrating respectively the combined use of Moodle (LMS) and Elgg (PLE) at the University of Florence to facilitate lifelong learning, and a recent experience of integration of Moodle, Mediawiki and De.li.cious that we have carried out as PhD students in elearning at the Università Politecnica delle Marche.*

## INTRODUCTION

The revolution that new technologies have brought about in every field is urging a new vision: knowledge and knowledge management, teaching and learning, social relations and the individual need to be reconsidered in the light of the current importance of interaction and networks. The knowledge society requires new roles and skills, and a new awareness as "active citizens" (Demetrio, 2002; Leone, 2009). Learning to learn has turned out to be a key skill to actively participate in society along life. Formal, non-formal and informal learning have become key words of this age; in particular, there is an increasing understanding

DOI: 10.4018/978-1-61692-791-2.ch001

that learning occurs for the most part outside the traditional formal situations.

Few years ago knowledge was a matter of categorization and hierarchies; today it is represented through networks and "ecologies" (Morin, 2008), it is diffused and distributed. As a whole, life is both a learning and a knowledge-based process.

Knowledge, people, and technology nodes represent useful resources. In this view, human mind, too, is a network, an ecology. It adapts to the environment and, accordingly, learning has become chaotic, continual, co-created and complex. Learning is an integrated process where changes with one element alter the entire ecology of the network. As a result, knowledge is subject to complex and adaptive systems (Siemens, 2006).

In this scenario, the changing role of education systems into networked organizations, into "ecologies", is decisive in order to support learners in constructing various personal learning networks to deeply understand complex fields (Fini, 2008; Sclater, 2008).

Over next years, teaching and learning will go through essential changes. Massive use of new technologies and the revolution of Web 2.0 social tools are only two of the elements that have deeply influenced learning approaches, for three main reasons:

1. many web services are free and easy to use by a connection to the Internet;
2. people may access nodes of information and create knowledge;
3. learners are becoming technically proficient, networked, multi-tasking and lifelong learners (Seely-Brown, 2009; Siemens & Tittenberger, 2009).

The effectiveness of Web 2.0 educational tools depends on the pedagogical sustainability beneath and on internationally shared standards to facilitate interoperability.

In this regard, over recent years research literature has underlined a need for a new theoretical interpretation of teaching and learning methods in education (Catarsi, 2007; Conole, 2008a; Marconato, 2003) to support the new educational models that are being introduced in the light of the lifelong learning paradigm. Emphasis on the shift from formal to informal e-learning through knowledge management and sharing (Leone, 2009; Sclater, 2008; Trentin, 2005) has been placed, with particular attention to Personal Learning Environments (PLE) as learner-centred spaces.

Researchers (Annacontini, 2007; Varisco, 2002) have highlighted the necessity to look at the learning paradigm (Barr & Tagg, 1995; Jonassen & Land, 2000; von Glasersfeld, 1998) as the suitable framework to support an effective implementation of lifelong learning policies. The passage from the traditional instruction paradigm to the learning paradigm allows to give prominence to the learner's needs and to the learning process, rather than to the teacher as a repository of knowledge and to teaching itself. The mission of the education system is to generate learning, to build meaningful learning environments and to bring forth student's construction of knowledge (Leone, 2008a; Marconato, 2003; Trentin, 2001). Success is measured by student learning and achievement outcomes, learning growth and the quality of arousing students' interest and engagement (Leone, 2008a).

In this view, information overload, diversity and distribution highlight the necessity for content and infrastructure applications to interoperate and exchange data in order to better support learners' and educators' needs.

Technology plays an important role in e-learning through the use of many systems relating to specific net-pedagogies (Stojanovic & Handschuh, 2002; Varlamis & Apostolakis, 2007; Trentin, 2004). In the late 1990's, Learning Management Systems (LMS)/Virtual Learning Environments (VLE) were the main protagonists of e-learning with their clear boundaries. Nevertheless, boundaries don't fit a complex society where different educational tools may be used with specific pedagogical aims. Social technologies may provide sets of different tools as an effective alternative to LMS/VLE. Blogs, Wikis, podcasts, Google Docs, YouTube, Del.icio.us, Elgg, for example, represent powerful educational tools to learn in a networked era.

Networked knowledge environments may expose learners to information overload and interoperable systems help users to avoid it.

This chapter aims to discuss the pedagogical sustainability of interoperable formal and informal learning environments.

Advantages and drawbacks of interoperable learning environments will be highlighted, in terms of technological and pedagogical effectiveness and appropriateness.

Starting point of this analysis will be the growth of *digital ecologies* to support cooperative interaction, *connective knowledge* and learning networks. Definitions of formal and informal learning environment within research literature will be commented, with particular attention to PLE as the emerging learner-centred learning environments.

Models, approaches and theories about LMS/VLE and PLE will be explored. In particular, the differences and peculiarities of the two learning paradigms applied to LMS/VLE and PLE will be highlighted.

The second section will be focused on the main issues of interoperability of educational tools at present, through a comparison between SCORM 1.3 and IMS Common Cartridge 1.1.

The final section will illustrate two case studies. The first one consists in the combined use of Moodle (LMS) and Elgg (PLE) at the University of Florence to facilitate lifelong learning. In January 2007 the Laboratorio di Tecnologie dell'Educazione (Laboratory of Technologies for Education – LTE) started out an experience of combination of the University's existing LMS – Moodle – with LTEver – Elgg -, which is a virtual community for staff, students, alumni, contributors and teachers.

The second case study reports a recent experience of integration of Moodle, Mediawiki and De.li.cious to build up a community of practice, that we have carried out as PhD students in e-learning at the Università Politecnica delle Marche.

## THEORETICAL FRAMEWORK

### Networks and Ecologies

The emergence of Web 2.0 has changed the use of the Internet and has deeply affected society and education (Downes, 2005; Levine *et al.*, 2009). Virtual "ecologies" and digitally networked "ecosystems" (Siemens, 2007) are the result of this ongoing evolution.

By the term "ecology" we define the space or environment in which cooperation takes place and the socially organized modes by which the environment facilitates collaboration (Crabtree & Rodden, 2008).

Over the years the development of *digital ecologies* to support cooperative interaction has been investigated. Researchers have deepened three main areas: models of face-to-face collaboration, in which media spaces (Bly *et al.*, 1993), dual ecologies (Kuzouka *et al.*, 2004), and mixed ecologies (Kirk *et al.*, 2005) have emerged; secondly, spatial forms of collaboration, which have encompassed collaborative virtual environments (Benford & Fahlén, 1993), mixed reality environments (Koleva *et al.*, 2000), and graphical interfaces that exploit spatial metaphors (Sawyer & Mariani, 1995); finally, *hybrid ecologies* which match mixed reality environments with ubiquitous computing environments to join the physical-digital dimensions.

Within these dynamic spaces, knowing and learning are shaped and fed by connections.

*Connective knowledge* (Downes, 2005; Siemens, 2006), which is characterized by diversity, autonomy, interactivity and openness, is co-created by individuals sharing and participating in one or more specific cultural systems, in ecosystems. As nowadays human beings live integrated experiences, and as life represents a rich and interconnected occurrence, knowledge is enriched by the integrations of different perspectives (Downes, 2005; Downes, 2006). A continuous dialogue may generate a *forum*, an always renewed conversational space that may constantly re-invent knowledge and action (Mapelli & Margiotta, 2009).

Knowledge should reveal the following factors to be adequate to the post-modern complex world:

- the context (information and data must be considered in their context);
- the global (containing various different parts of reality);
- the multidimensional (human beings are considered biologically, psychologically, socially, emotionally, rationally, as well as societies include historical, economic, sociologic, religious dimensions);
- the complex (relevant knowledge is involved with complexity) (Morin, 1999).

Indeed, *complexification* is an essential aspect of knowledge (Weinberger, 2005). As a consequence, technology plays an important role as a device for knowledge management, as a vehicle for knowledge sharing and as a tool for augmented learning environments.

A traditional and static view of knowledge is being substituted by a more dynamic and multi-faceted vision. Knowledge is becoming increasingly fluid (Downes, 2006; Siemens, 2006). The well-organized blocks of knowledge are turning into a flux (Siemens, 2008).

Concurrently, significant changes are occurring in social spaces and structures. Governments, corporations and schools are urged to replace directive relationships with a different approach to promote, nurture and connect by knowledge.

Since knowledge dissemination facilitates dynamic, adaptive and personalized experiences, individuals, in their numerous roles (as citizens, customers, students and Internet users), no longer accept pre-packaged "products".

"Digital Natives", "the Net Generation", or "the Google Generation", as the new Internet users are labelled, are approaching work and learning differently. Today's learners are digitally literate and constantly connected. They use the Internet socially to communicate, interact and cooperate with peers, globally. On these premises, contemporary mainstream education seems inadequate to grasp global realities seen as transnational, multidimensional, polydisciplinary and planetary. Today's students learn differently, through massive connections to other people and resources. As a result, learners are getting accustomed to meet and share in "tribes" (Maffesoli, 2004).

In this sense, learning networks resemble ecologies. Developing learning ecologies (Siemens, 2006), or learning habitats (Cormier, 2008), atelier learning (Seely-Brown, 2009), studio learning (Fisher, 2008), is a first, important step toward a more general culture of learning (Seely-Brown, 1999) and, thus, toward lifelong learning. Learning might be seen as a learner-centred, holistic experience which involves a complex, continual, chaotic and co-creative process.

## VLE vs. PLE: Toward the Merging of Formal and Informal Learning

The terms "learning society" and "lifelong learning" represent the labels of the change in society and education that has taken place over the last two decades, concurrently with pervading technological development.

Rapid economical, political and social evolution urge "all learning activity" to be "undertaken throughout life, with the aim of improving knowledge, skills and competencies within a personal, civic, social and/or employment-related perspective." (European Commission, 2002).

Lifelong learning denotes "a new paradigm", "a shift away from the notion of provider-driven 'education' toward individualised learning." (UNESCO, 1999).

Protagonist of the learning society is the "active citizen", that is an autonomous individual who is capable of self-learning and who participates in both civil and civic society. He/she is engaged "in the active development of citizenship dimensions, not just knowledge and understanding, but skills development and behaviours picked up through experience of participation in a range of contexts" (Nelson & Kerr, 2006, p.11).

The stress on active citizenship is strengthened by the key role given to education. The education system is increasingly considered as a crucial social change agent. Educational policy should aim at preparing the youth and at supporting the adults to keep the pace of change in modern society, but also to develop the necessary knowledge, skills and attitudes to make the most of the challenges individuals face in their lifetime. Education is now seen as much more holistic and flexible than in the past, taking place in a wider range of contexts and intending to increase personalisation and autonomy for the learner.

Jacques Delors, in the UNESCO report *Learning: The Treasure Within* by the International Commission on Education for 21st Century (1996), defines education as being grounded on four pillars: learning to know, learning to do, learning to live together and learning to be.

UNESCO's (1999) definition of the educational process encompasses formal, informal and non-formal learning. Formal learning consists in the hierarchically structured, chronologically graded educational system running from primary through to tertiary institutions; informal learning allows persons to acquire attitudes, values, skills and knowledge from daily experience, within the individual's environment (such as family, friends, peer groups, the media and other influences); non-formal learning takes place through education organized for specific learners with specific learning objectives, outside the formal established system.

However, when a society becomes pedagogical, when a lifelong learning process is started by the media, at work, in the street, in education, and within associations, the definite distinction between initial education and lifelong education fades away.

In this scenario, the ability of learning to learn appears strategic. Learning to learn means getting the necessary skills to arrange one's own knowledge and learning, selecting and exploiting various resources and tools among those formal, non-formal and informal environments which offer the learner adequate flexibility and tailored solutions in terms of learning goals and strategies.

Moreover, information overload, the necessary solutions for knowledge management and the growing knowledge sharing emphasise the importance of interaction and networks.

In this regard, Web 2.0 technologies and tools facilitate learning ecologies and a society in which people can learn any subject, any way, anywhere, anytime, a society that will enable the citizens of the world to live a fuller life, that is a lifelong learning society.

E-learning 2.0, in particular, is mediating the shift from formal to informal e-learning (Leone, 2009; Sclater, 2008; Trentin, 2005), from Virtual Learning Environments (VLE), which are organization-centred spaces (Bonaiuti, 2007), to Personal Learning Environments (PLE) as emerging learner-centred spaces (Rogers, 1983; Vygotsky, 1986).

A decade ago, VLEs were the main setting of e-learning. Over recent years, however, as a result of the growing adoption of a lifelong learning approach, traditional VLE has shown the following weaknesses:

- rigid schemes and blocks, which cause the lack of social interaction and sharing;
- asymmetric relations (teachers/learners, on the model "I teach, you learn");
- no adoption of open and simple standards (e.g., RSS);

- closeness within the learning environment and term;
- consequent poor visibility of the learning outcomes, no access to the contents of the environment, dequalification of the learning community and lack of interrelation among different education contexts;
- impeded construction of the individual's virtual identity (crucial aim in lifelong learning policies).

The ongoing change of perspective has brought attention on the framework of the learner-centred approach as a new alternative to traditional VLE (Giovannella, 2008):

- the web used as a platform or an environment, where various tools (like Flickr, De.licio.us, e-portfolio) and contents can be aggregated for the construction of a PLE;
- socially constructed educational materials;
- symmetric relations (active role for all the participants);
- open source, open content, open society and, as a result, adoption of open "machine-readable" standards interconnected with proprietary ones;
- the learner's capability of managing his/her learning processes and of configurating his/her e-portfolio as aggregator of personal knowledge and competences (Lubesky, 2006);
- social interaction as a means to learn, to co-construct knowledge and to communicate.

It's no more the user who adapts to the learning environment, but it's the education system that designs learning environments on the learner's needs and prior knowledge. Besides, individuals are more and more oriented to build their own PLE, that is to say an open system, interconnected with other PLEs and external services; an activity-based learning environment, user-managed and learner-centred. A PLE is a concept, rather than specific software, which is nurtured by autonomy, pragmatic, relevance, building on prior knowledge, goal-directed approach.

Motschnig-Pitrik & Mallich (2004) refer to PLE as Person-Centred e-Learning (PCeL).

Downes (2006) defines a PLE as a tool that enables anyone to "engage in a distributed environment" made up of "a network of people, services and resources". It does not consist of "just Web 2.0, but it is certainly Web 2.0" since "it is a read-write application".

A PLE conveys the image of the subject as a landscape as well as individual pieces of information and knowledge; it facilitates the creation of a personal repository of resources and relationships huddled together around a common topic or concept; it allows to document, reflect, communicate and collaborate (Leone, 2009).

For all these reasons, a VLE is much less flexible than a PLE, which is more adherent to the users' expectations of flexibility, active participation and individualisation of a learning environment (Calvani, Buonaiuti, Fini & Ranieri, 2007; Downes, 2005).

Nevertheless, the two settings can be interconnected through sharing-knowledge technologies, like RSS.

Anderson (2006) is convinced that VLEs may endure if the learner-centred model will be adopted. In Attwell's view (2007), since e-portfolio, a basic tool of PLE, is the future of learning systems, PLE is the new learning setting to look at. Buonaiuti (2007) sketches out hypothetical scenerios for the school of the future in which learning has the informal features of PLE.

According to Giovannella (2008), a third alternative between organization-centred VLE and user-centred PLE could be Learning Places (LP), settings that are opened to the interaction with the outside and attentive to the development of individuals' virtual identity.

We are witnessing the passage from a Cartesian view of learning (knowledge as substance and pedagogy as knowledge transfer) to a social view of learning (understanding is socially constructed and participating builds up identity) (Seely-Brown, 2009).

## Interoperability and Integration: Critical Definitions

It is evident that in a networked society which interacts as an ecology, interoperability and integration are significant issues.

People may use the Internet thanks to common information protocols and exchanging architectures facilitated by common standards, to exchange information, to connect hardware with different devices, to establish business nets or to share knowledge.

Also, in the online education field the adoption of internationally recognized standards is crucial to make diverse relevant knowledge nodes intercommunicate effectively and to overcome information overload, diversity and distribution, in order to better support learners' and educators' needs.

Further, learners actively interact and access useful information, instead of passively consuming knowledge distributed by the teacher (Siemens & Tittenberger, 2009). To sustain such proactive students, complex learning systems may simultaneously integrate and make interoperate as much as possible a wide variety of tools.

Various definitions of interoperability and interaction exist in literature. The IEEE (2000) defines interoperability as "the ability of two or more systems or components to exchange information and to use the information that has been exchanged."

The Oxford English Dictionary similarly defines the word "interoperable" as "(of computer systems or software) able to exchange and make use of information." Wikipedia proposes a broader definition: "Interoperability is a property referring to the ability of diverse systems and organizations to work together (inter-operate). The term is often used in a technical systems engineering sense, or alternatively in a broad sense, taking into account social, political, and organizational factors that impact system to system performance."

In Merriman's (2008) view, interoperability is "the measure of ease of integration between two systems or software components to achieve a functional goal. A highly interoperable integration is one that can be easily achieved by the individual who requires the result." And integration is "the act of making two systems work together to achieve a functional goal, regardless of how difficult or expensive that task might be."

In our view, interoperability is the construction of an upper layer of technical specifications, which allow to produce, memorise, search and utilise available educational resources and tools coherently.

We concur that it is possible to distinguish three types of interoperability, all needed to achieve an effective interoperable system (GridWise, 2007):

- technical interoperability (physical devices that make systems communicate);
- informational interoperability (relating to the content, the semantics for data or instructions flow);
- organizational interoperability (relationship between organizations and individuals including business and legal relationships).

On this background, for us integration between different learning tools means "making two systems work together to achieve a functional goal. Systems can be integrated through manipulation of each other's functionality. Interoperability means making these kinds of integrations as simple as technologically possible in pursuit of that goal." (Merriman, 2008).

## PEDAGOGICAL SUSTAINABILITY OF INTEROPERABLE FORMAL AND INFORMAL LEARNING ENVIRONMENTS

This second section aims to examine the main pedagogical issues of interoperable educational tools and platforms at present. Advantages and drawbacks will be highlighted, in terms of technological and pedagogical effectiveness (i.e., success, usefulness and value) and appropriateness (i.e., suitability for and compatibility with the context) through a comparison between the standards SCORM 1.3 and IMS Common Cartridge 1.1.

Two case studies will illustrate examples of interoperable formal and informal learning environments: the first one consists in the combined use of Moodle (LMS) and Elgg (PLE) at the University of Florence to facilitate lifelong learning; the second case study reports a recent experience of integration of Moodle, Mediawiki and De.li.cious that we have carried out as PhD students in e-learning at the Università Politecnica delle Marche.

The following discussion aims to evaluate the pedagogical sustainability beneath Web 2.0 interoperable educational tools and platforms and their role in a lifelong learning vision.

### Current Issues of Interoperable Educational Tools and Platforms

Educational tools can be defined as every device able to provide knowledge and development in a particular learning context. Didactic toys are an example of traditional educational tools. In ICT, a computer game (e.g., Boolify, to learn Boolean operators) or high-level interaction tools (e.g., Bayesiannetworks) may be instructive devices.

The revolution brought about by Web 2.0 has turned many Internet services (e.g., Twitter, Facebook, wikis, blogs, podcasts, Google Docs, YouTube, Del.icio.us, Elgg, etc.) into powerful, aggregable (Wilson, 2005) educational tools that allow the learner to personalise his/her learning environment autonomously and to learn in a networked era.

AllWords.com defines educational technology as follows:

1. "the use of technology to improve teaching and learning;
2. the treatment of the process by which people learn, as a systematic process based on objectives, with strategies and systems to achieve them;
3. a set of expensive tools sold to schools purporting to improve learning but not actually proven to do so."

Current pedagogical debate is on personalised tools versus institutional tools (Calvani, 2006; Downes, 2005; Trentin, 2004; Wilson, 2005; Attwell, 2006; Buonaiuti, 2007; Fini e Vanni, 2004; Ranieri 2005), on implementing integrated institutional systems or loosely coupled systems, and on the issue of what teachers should manage and what students should manage. The implications are profound, for institutional structures and processes, for individual roles and identities, for the way in which learning and teaching are viewed (Conole, 2008b).

In technological systems for education a change of direction of technology is evident: technology is not only a means of social exchange, but it turns into the joint design of learning and organizational strategies, and into the growth of learning communities. This approach arises the strong social, pedagogical and technological relation between lifelong learning, e-learning and knowledge management.

A rethinking of education as a whole should be grounded on strategic openness of contents, actors (user empowerment) and processes (Recchioni *et al.*, 2008).

The interoperability between VLEs and PLEs requires that VLEs make secure software gateways (eg., APIs) available. A vision for learning which promotes pedagogies consistent with social constructivism contrasts with the political and commercial inertia of the technological status quo.

It is unlikely that commercial VLEs are willing to distribute their control of the learning environment and provide flexibility, preferring instead to keep users within their proprietary range (Lubesky, 2006). At the same time, users must be able to export their PLE repository in some generic format for safekeeping, especially if the PLE is a web service.

Moreover, intellectual property and the management of digital rights are relevant issues to be addressed.

Finally, one of the drawbacks of the massive use of integrated educational tools is that they require multiple login names and passwords. More tools a learner uses to compose his/her PLE, more authentications are needed, with resulting information overload.

A more extensive use of standards for a unique authentication of different set of tools (e.g., SSO - Single Sign On, Open id) is crucial.

## Standards

An evident parallel effect of the evolution of the Web is increasing questioning about the standards which have been applied to uselessly delimit learning and teaching processes in the name of interoperability of contents, that is Learning Objects (LO), or "any digital resource that can be used to support learning" (Wiley, 2000).

Standardized technologies have several merits that protect and nurture an e-learning investment: interoperability, content and code re-usability, manageability (tracking of data on learners and contents), content accessibility, content durability (transplantable many times in different platforms with minimum effort), scalability (expansion in functionality in order to serve broader populations and organizational purposes) (Varlamis & Apostolakis, 2007).

A strong barrier is that existing standards usually fit to the needs of specific applications and are inadequate for supporting the interoperability of e-learning.

An e-learning process encompasses conceptual and physical features that should be both standardized in terms of procedures and technologies.

Conceptual features of an e-learning system are the design of the e-learning process, the definition of learners' competencies, the framework for the co-operation among teachers and students.

The physical features are the learning content and its packaging and deployment, the learners' profile, assessment activities, the metadata structure (i.e., structured data that describe, manage and organize Internet resources) and the system architecture.

The most important issues arising from the interoperability of e-learning tools and technologies are content description (metadata) and packaging, learner management and communication of the educational process results (Varlamis & Apostolakis, 2007).

At present, the most diffused sets of metadata standards are:

- the Dublin Core Metadata Initiative, which was the first to describe data on the web. Its version 1.1 (1999) foresees 15 elements of description and 10 attributes for each element. The limit of this metadata set is that it was designed to describe any kind of resource, and not specifically online resources; moreover, only a few elements are dedicated to education;
- the IEEE LOM (Learning Object Metadata) 1484.12.1-2002 standard describes each LO by 9 categories containing various attributes, which cover technical and educational aspects, property rights, learning object lifecycle and relation to other LO, and classification. The limit of this metadata set consists in its complexity: some of the nearly 70 camps are subjective and trigger difficulties of conceptual interoperability.

International organizations have worked out the following technical specifications to standardise e-learning environments:

- SCORM 1.3 2004 (Sharable Content Object Reference Model);
- IMS Common Cartridge 1.1;
- ISO/IEC JTC1 SC36, which is the official chapter of the ISO (International Organization for Standardization) that deals with *Standards For: Information Technology for Learning, Education and Training* internationally. To this day, 26 countries are participants, 8 countries are observers, 27 projects are being developed and 12 standards have been issued since 2004.

SCORM was developed by the US Department of Defence as "a collection of standards and specifications adapted from multiple sources to provide a comprehensive suite of e-learning capabilities that enable interoperability, accessibility and reusability of Web-based learning content". It defines communications between client computer, usually a PC using a browser, and a host system server operating the run-time environment. SCORM also defines how content may be packaged into a ZIP file that can be transferred between different VLEs.

The most recent version SCORM 1.3 2004 (3rd edition) includes sequencing, a set of rules that specify the order in which learners may experience content objects. The standard uses XML for interoperability between systems.

The issue is that SCORM focuses on interface points between instructional content and the VLE, and is silent about the specific features and capabilities provided within a particular VLE. This allows individual vendors to provide different instruction management services, and an array of competitive alternatives, while maintaining the important SCORM goal of interoperability. The same resource material can be used in many different ways.

The structure of a SCORM package consists in the Content Package, which is made up of the Manifest File (imsmanifest.xml) and the Content (the actual content, media, assessment and other files).

The Manifest (Metadata, Organizations, Resources, (sub)Manifest(s), an essential part of the SCORM Content Packages, is similar in many ways to a "packing slip". It lists the contents of the package and may include an optional description of the content structure. It is, in effect, an index to the subsequent content and resources. SCORM packages operate in a run-time environment within a Web browser.

The origins of SCORM were in the defence training industry, where more didactic approaches to learning are acceptable (a fairly fixed syllabus and pre-determined sessions that can be repeated many times). This is not universal practice in education, where learners' needs may be quite different. This has led to advice a more flexible approach that does not use all the features of the standard.

The future development of SCORM has moved from ADL (Advanced Distributed Learning) to LETSI (Learning, Education, and Training Systems Interoperability), an international non-profit federation dedicated to improving individual and organizational learning and performance. SCORM 2.0 should be available this year and include standards for Web 2.0 components, which will mark the passage from "sequencing" of SCORM 1.3 2004 to "orchestration" of SCORM 2.0. "Orchestration refers to the way in which LET activities and resources are selected and combined for the purpose of use." (https://letsi.org).

## SCORM 1.3 vs. Common Cartridge 1.1

IMS Common Cartridge (CC) 1.1 is a new standard by IMS Global Learning Consortium (October 2008) dedicated to organization and distribution of educational resources. It is the first of three new standards planned for the learning technologies of the next generation; the other two, which are still specifications, are *Learning Tools Interoperability – LTI*, for systems, applications and mash-up, and *Learning Information Services – LIS* for data about learners' authorizations and performance.

At the origin of this initiative in 2006, IMS Global Learning Consortium aimed at solving the problem of content sharing between different LMSs; interoperability between LMSs Blackboard, WebCT, Angel and Sakai was tested.

At present, it is not possible to deliver contents from different platforms, given the large number of LMSs and their own proprietary format to save data. The lack of a common format for the delivery of a course creates hurdles to content providers since they have to design, test and publish the course for any possible platform. This triggers work overload and costs boost.

CC 1.1 aims at simplifying content production, at creating more complete catalogues and at encouraging the access to the market of new small groups' contents.

In particular, CC aims to standardize six aspects:

1. a format of interchange for educational contents where contents and their organization are described through a file manifest (like in SCORM). Differently from SCORM, the contents in the cartridge can also be external to the data package (URL);
2. the management of license access to contents;
3. a set of metadata for contents based on Dublin Core;
4. the management and submission of tests and exercises;
5. the use of external applications and data exchange with them (social network, wiki, repository, etc);
6. the management of on-line discussion forums.

The comparison between CC 1.1 and the more diffused standard SCORM shows some features in common (Table 1).

Basically, CC, is grounded on the idea of packing learning contents as SCORM is. Differently from SCORM, which considers learning packages as self-sufficient entities, CC packages allow to keep the context through links to external resources and applications. CC's designers sustain that SCORM is obsolete because it is focused on content portability for computer based self-learning. CC, instead, addresses a different educational environment, that is an online or a

*Table 1. Comparison between common cartridge and SCORM*

| Characteristics | SCORM specifications | Common Cartridge specifications |
|---|---|---|
| Packaging | IMS Content Packaging | IMS Content Packaging |
| Metadata | IEEE LOM | Dublin Core via IEEE LOM |
| Sequencing | IMS Simple Sequencing | none |
| Tracking | AICC | IMS QTI and IMS LTI |
| Assessment | none | IMS QTI |
| Applications integration | none | IMS LTI |
| Authorizations | none | IMS authorization web service |
| Collaborative forums | none | IMS Forum initiation |
| Curriculum | none | IMS RDCEO and IMS VDEX |
| Performance | none | |
| Accessibility | none | IMS Access for All |

blended course developed on cooperative learning, facilitated by one or more teachers. Learning resources can be online, offline or both, provided that the choice is stressed in the cartridge. Among the learning resources foreseen, "digital text books" are explicitly mentioned.

SCOs (Sharable Content Objects, i.e., SCORM packages) can be included in the cartridges as any other content and their management is attributed to the LCMS. SCORM, however, is not necessary for the compliance of CC.

Besides, CC renounces to the tracking of the contents proposed by SCORM run-time and relies instead on the implementation of the IMS QTI (Question & Test Interoperability) standard to track and evaluate students' performance, living the management to compliant platforms.

Finally, CC does not implement content sequencing like SCORM does, but it employs external sequencing applications (which are not limited to specific solutions) through the specifications *LTI - Learning Tools Interoperability*.

## Case Study 1: *LTEver*, University of Florence, Italy

This case study represents an example of possible coexistence of formal and informal learning. At the University of Florence the combination of Moodle (open sorce LMS) and Elgg (open source PLE) started in January 2007, when the Laboratorio di Tecnologie dell'Educazione (Laboratory of Technologies for Education – LTE) launched LTEver (http://lte-unifi.it/elgg), as a virtual community (to last (for) "ever") for staff, students, alumni, contributors and teachers.

The learning experience described underneath draws from my (Leone, 2009) personal path as a student at the University of Florence, started in 2002 with a post-graduate course on e-learning and continued in 2007 as an alumna and a professional in LTEver (of which Giuliana is a member, too). The course I attended was delivered in a blended environment (LMS and face-to-face); in the latest editions the University has adopted Moodle and has kept the same methodological approach illustrated below.

In 2002 the post-graduate course on e-learning delivered by LMS aimed to provide the participants with the fundamental planning, organizational and relational skills to effectively exploit the Internet in an educational project.

The course lasted five months over an average of 150 hours of work and it encompassed three face-to-face classes. The participants admitted were 250 (expert teachers and professionals), who were subdivided into ten sub-areas of specialization and subsequently into cooperative work groups (8-10 people).

The tutor-supervisor coordinated and scheduled activities, answered to technical and organizational doubts, emotionally supported the tutors of sub-groups in their challenging role.

Educational resources and guide-lines were delivered at the very beginning. The course was articulated on four steps: individual technological warm-up, personal documentation, sharing and socialization activities, cooperative project work. Online activity was developed in three stages: documentation (individual), sharing (tutor-groups) and collaboration/cooperation (collaborative/cooperative groups).

The course was metacognitive, project-oriented, and focussed on relational dynamics. The general theoretical background was grounded on the constructivist model of dispersed learning (Calvani, 2006) (situated and co-constructed knowledge, authentic and "spendable" learning). ICTs were used as a tool to support the development of the learning community, rather than as a means to deliver contents. Basic technological facilities and tools were proposed to make the interaction between participants simpler.

The organizers chose not to adopt groupware platforms nor proprietary environments. The technologies employed were gradually introduced: web pages in the documentation phase, emails for support and communication with the tutor, web forum and mailing-list in the phases of sharing and collaboration.

Area forum and mailing-list were used for the collection of materials and tasks assigned by the tutor- supervisor, for discussions about general questions and for interaction between sub-groups.

Later, each sub-group adopted a platform for autonomous communication (for example a YahooGroups mailing-list) and other tools (Nicenet) for collaborative work.

At the end of the course, I was gratified, motivated and enriched. I appreciated the usefulness of metacognitiveness and the challenge of being for most of the time involved in cooperative, hands-on activities. My colleagues and I promised to keep in touch and build a community. As a matter of fact, none of us took up any initiative in this sense and our collaboration faded away.

A few years later (2007), I was more than glad to find out that the University of Florence had launched LTEver, an informal continuation of its formal learning environments and a "learning landscape", as Elgg's (http://elgg.org) authors (Tosh & Werdmüller, 2004) have defined this open source system. LTEver offers basic elements, such as blogs, e-portfolio, social networking, tags, and a totally self-managed personal space to promote reflection and socialization in learning communities.

Further, this system is a connection to the courses that some members have attended and attend within Moodle, through links and RSS.

The compatibility between Elgg and Moodle consented to implement an e-portfolio for current students. This outcome is an example of informational and organizational interoperativity between "personal" and "institutional" systems, as learning ecologies.

Freedom of action and symmetric relations characterize Elgg and are vital for the development of LTEver. Once users are logged in, they can configure their personal space by completing or updating their profile, adding RSS feeds from other sites, building communities, sharing files and inviting new users to join the community. Moreover, attention to privacy and confidentiality is ensured through a simple user-controlled level of access (Fini, 2008).

Recent studies have highlighted some weaknesses and strengths of LTEver. The environment suffers from information overload, mainly due to the originally muddled aggregation of the informal blogs; secondly, some problems of usability of the system arose (Rigutti *et al.*, 2008); finally, active participation seems to come from a relatively small number of users, a threat in the case of a small and highly focused professional context (Calvani *et al.*, 2007); the majority of social media have evidenced this trend, though.

On the other hand, positive aspects are: high-quality contributions, thanks to low "level of noise" (i.e., the quantity of not pertinent posts); steadily increasing trend of users and posts; take-up of some spontaneous initiatives (e.i., participation in the online course "Introduction to Open Education"), principally within consolidated communities (Fini, 2008).

## Case Study 2: "CdP per la produzione di conoscenza", Università Politecnica delle Marche, Ancona, Italy

Between April and June 2009 the 6 (2 males and 4 females) PhD students in e-learning at the Università Politecnica delle Marche carried out the course "Comunità di pratica per la produzione di conoscenza" ("Communities of Practice - CoP - for knowledge construction", teacher prof. Patrizia Ghislandi and e-tutor dott. Carla Falsetti). This hands-on learning experience was focused on the construction and the management of a distributed CoP, in blended learning (initial face-to-face meeting, five-week development online, final meeting in videoconferencing), over 6 weeks/150 hours. Objectives were the acknowledgement of cooperative learning as relevant approach for the participants' empowerment, through the experimentation of the dynamics of a CoP, the students' engagement in team work, the acquisition of new learning tools for collaborative writing, the stimulation of peer-to-peer scaffolding, the principles of online communication and of e-tutoring (Ghislandi *et al.*, 2008).

The tasks assigned (analysis and discussion of the first six chapters of the essay *Cultivating communities of practice* by Wenger, Mc Dermott & Snyder, 2007) and the scheduling of the activities tracked this metacognitive experience.

The adopted methodology drew on activism, constructivism and socio-constructivism (Barr & Tagg, 1995; Jonassen & Land, 2000; Varisco, 2002; von Glasersfeld, 1998; Vygotsky, 1986) and on e-learning pedagogy (Calvani, 2006; Hannon, 2009; Trentin, 2004; Wasson, 2007).

Work groups (2 to 3 students) were freely formed by the participants during the initial meeting; the roles were defines by the teacher, chosen by the participants, but turned at the beginning of every week. Tests and assessment were *in itinere* (interaction and participation), formative (weekly group essay, self and peer assessment) and summative (final written essay and individual interview).

During the initial face-to-face meeting, the teacher and the e-tutor illustrated objectives, contents, methodology and tools available, while students worked in groups to set up the CoP in Moodle, added with Mediawiki and De.li.cious; these two tools were integrated by RSS, while Moodle required a separate access.

Four of the participants already used Moodle; all of them had already experienced a CoP and cooperative learning and had already worked together, both face-to-face and online.

## Discussion

Current pedagogical debate is on personalised tools versus institutional tools (Calvani, 2006; Downes, 2005; Trentin, 2004; Wilson, 2005; Attwell, 2006; Buonaiuti, 2007; Fini e Vanni, 2004; Ranieri 2005), on implementing integrated institutional systems or loosely coupled systems, and on the issue of what teachers should manage and what students should manage. The implications are profound, for institutional structures and processes, for individual roles and identities, for the way in which learning and teaching are viewed (Conole, 2008b).

E-learning 2.0 offers a wide range of scenarios simultaneously characterised by different approaches. In this sense, formal and informal e-learning can interoperate. A broader interpretation of interoperability is that exemplified in the combination of Moodle and LTEver (case study 1) as informational and organizational interoperability between two different learning systems (institutional and personal, respectively) which turn out to be learning ecologies, actually. A more complete connotation of interoperability can be extracted from the experience of CoP built up within our formal learning path as PhD students (case study 2); in this case technical, informational and organizational interoperability (GridWise, 2007) characterize the environment.

Although full interoperability is far from being realized, we concur that the border line between formal and informal learning environments is not always well defined and gives space to a continuity which allows the individual to identify the most suitable mix of learning tools and contexts. Formal e-learning is one of the possible means for the members of a professional community to acquire new knowledge. Knowledge management/sharing tools and approaches (informal learning) can be added progressively to complete institution-driven learning spaces with the opportunity for the individual to personalize learning (Trentin, 2005).

The two case studies illustrated above are examples of successful interaction of formal and informal learning environments. In particular, the CoP at the Università Politecnica delle Marche produced value and gratification, and strengthened the participants' vision as e-learning professionals.

The divide between formal and informal learning in this scenario was nearly vanished by the focus on the practice and by the support of integrated Web 2.0 tools. Beyond the light track of contents and methodology to use (formal learning), this experience was characterized by collaborative construction of knowledge, self-learning, personalization of the learning environment, flexibility. Results are empowerment and consequent contribution within the organization where we operate as PhD students, that is university. Empowerment has to be considered as the success key of the relation between CoP and the organization to which it is linked. The "double link" described by Wenger & Mc Dermott & Snyder (2007) is crucial for the survival and the development of both, CoP and organization: the first conducts the improvement of its members' expertise through informal interaction and learning; the second relies on experts grown in the CoP to identify and implement business strategies, to focus on objectives and outcomes of its business units, thus on performance and clients. As an evidence, the synergy between a CoP and the organization as a whole activates the cycle plan-do-check-act in all the business processes and naturally leads to continuous improvement policy, that closes the circle on human resources as fulcrum and added value of the organization. In this sense we can talk about learning organization. Then, possible horizon, not too far, could be considering universities as learning organizations. Educate to knowledge sharing and to empowerment toward lifelong learning is not simple, especially because the change should start from the actors of the educational system, which is still largely teacher-centred (apart from few exceptions). Nevertheless, the two case studies show that the endevour is not impossible. All change, in all contexts, is often perceived as a threat by structured organizations. Change requires tact and sensitive authority, openness to bottom-up processes, sensitiveness, strategy and leadership.

Finally, what kind of learning is in tune with the net-generation? A culture of participation, building, tinkering, remixing and sharing. Rather than paying attention to the digital gap, we should think of the participation gap. A semantic model of design of e-learning contents could be a suitable strategy. The model could be based on an ontological structure characterised by the integration of hierarchical relations with networked associations. This model should respect the following pedagogical and technological main requisites (Adorni *et al.*, 2008):

- pedagogical expressivity of the knowledge representation independent from the pedagogical approach adopted (Fini, 2005);
- learner-centred design of contents, in terms of learners' learning needs and objectives;
- flexibility and personalization of resources and tools;
- moulding of the contents independent from their different domain;
- reusability, as the capability of the model to formulate exportable maps of learning resources in different contexts;
- interoperability, as the possible implementation of the model in diverse applications and e-learning systems;
- neutrality, as the capability of designing contents of various formats, delivered through different media (Koper, 2001);
- compatibility of the design model with the most diffused standards for e-learning resources (Fini, 2005).

Folksonomies can become the key factor for the development of Semantic Web, or Web 3.0, as "an extension of the current one" where information is attributed "well-defined meaning, better enabling computers and people to work in cooperation" (Berners-Lee & Handler & Lassila, 2001).

A step further is the Social Semantic Web, the combination of technologies, strategies and methodologies from the Web 2.0 and the Semantic Web. The Social Semantic Web will encompass the creation of explicit and semantically rich knowledge representations as a result of developments in social interactions. The core of a social semantic system is a continuous process of eliciting key knowledge of a field through semi-formal ontologies, taxonomies or folksonomies. A broader use of folksonomies can be a valid alternative to traditional ontologies in the development of semantic or relational search engines.

The role of the new Web would thus consist in facilitating a personalised access to knowledge, through repositories of Learning Objects (LO) easily accessible by intelligent software developed within the Semantic Web. As a result, ontologies would allow inferences through software agents and would support the design of much more flexible LMSs, in terms of learning goals and of navigation among collections of Web and LO resources, among "relational and meaningful" links (Acquaviva & Benini, 2004).

It seems high time to go beyond the concept of knowledge offered in compact blocks of contents, difficult to modify. It is high time to develop the design of modular educational resources which can be structured in smaller aggregable and combinable elements, suitable for diverse learning paths and needs.

LO appear as the best format to transfer targeted knowledge.

However, every LO designer impresses his/her own educational strategy which will characterize each resource. Consequently, the description of LO through metadata should not be limited to their external features (self-consistency, modularity, granularity), but it should be extended to internal ones (the teaching strategy within, the learning models proposed, kind of interaction with the context, levels of self-learning and of social learning allowed). An analysis of this kind would certainly emphasize that the "Lego blocks" (Wiley, 2000) do not fit in as expected.

Degrading e-learning to a container of electronic resources that do not interact with the context would be a regress to the idea of e-learning systems based on the economic paradigm, according to which distance education is essentially a low-cost and efficient way to reach and train a large number of people geographically dispersed (Fagioli, 2005). This gap has to become the starting point for the design of new e-learning environments which can deal with the issue of interoperability and of the exchange of LO in a more realistic and operable dimension.

The following steps should be the definition of the modalities to promote learning by doing, as tool of "learn to do", one of the four pillars of lifelong learning education; the creation of models of integration of face-to-face and online cooperative learning (blended learning); the development of communities of practice open to both learners and external professionals.

## FUTURE RESEARCH DIRECTIONS

Education systems traditionally separate subjects and consequently knowledge. Complex fields, though, are always global and *transdisciplinarity* is central to recreate integrated knowledge (Morin, 2008) and to construct global thinking,. In this regard, ecology is the science that may serve as a model, and ecosystems, as complex systems developing on conflict and cooperation, can be considered as the representation of future educational models. The future will see more and more self-directing and self-motivated learners, more and more learner-centred ubiquitous learning environments, facilitated by online instructors and experts based around the world.

"This will be the last generation in which education is the practice of authority, and the first where it becomes an act of liberty" (Downes, 2008). In the future, the learner will be increasingly a proactive and aware citizen who builds his/her PLE and moves toward *Personal Learning Networks* (PLN) to dynamically interact in the co-construction of his/her individual knowledge. The "cloudworker", the prototypical information worker of tomorrow, will virtually collaborate, work and learn in a long-tail micro-market defined by his/her own talents (Venkatesh, 2008). The information worker of tomorrow will be at ease in a knowledge society based on networked ecologies.

In the future, education systems will be more and more focused on innovation and on active participation to build new perspectives for the knowledge society (Mapelli & Margiotta, 2009). Over time, the VLEs implemented by educational institutions will develop into educational delivery systems usable by PLEs, seen as devices to create networks with multiple services: educational delivery systems will recognize the learner's identity and will organize flexible learning, with other online services, open resource repositories or additional student records.

People will be able to study, work and socially interact from different places, without being physically present. Only mind will move in liquid virtual environments, in ubiquitous learning landscapes.

These trends and our past experiences illustrated in the two case studies, let us foresee that integrated formal and informal learning environments will be increasingly adopted.

Furthermore, learning technology is evolving to contain knowledge as a flow (Jarche, 2005). RSS will be one of the most important ways for PLEs to connect with remote systems. A massive use of PLEs will allow people to immerse in flows of conversations (Downes, 2008); on the other hand, growing and continuous conversation flows will make individuals suffer information overload.

Interoperable and pervasive architectures that share and integrate collaborators, contents and services will have to be explored (Yang, 2006). Ubiquitous environments may contribute to tackle information overload, through a more attentive use of information streams. "Lifestreaming" or "learning streaming" activities seem to be key concepts to future networked ecologies of learners and may urge a more helpful use of the Open id protocol to simplify access to set personal learning spaces.

## CONCLUSION

The widespread adoption of new technologies, the knowledge society, the age of active citizenship and lifelong learning have flowed into a rethinking of knowledge, knowledge management, teaching and learning, networks and the individual. Teaching and learning roles, environments and approaches urge to be re-mediated accordingly in this era of virtual ecologies and digitally networked ecosystems.

"Learning ecology", "habitat", "atelier learning" "studio learning" foster connections. Connective knowledge is co-created by individuals sharing and participating in various cultural systems. The new learner is the aware protagonist and author of his/her own lifelong learning process, through networked and distributed relations, through "tribes". Learning might be seen as a learner-centred, holistic experience which involves a complex, continual, chaotic and co-creative process. Flexibility, modularization and personalization characterize the new learning environments. Formal, non-formal and informal learning cross and, more and more often, merge; as a consequence learning to learn becomes crucial.

If e-learning 2.0 becomes strategic to keep the pace of the ongoing change and to amalgamate formal and informal learning, that is VLEs and PLEs, then information overload, integration and interoperability are current issues.

The role that technology has assumed arises the strong social, pedagogical and technological relation between lifelong learning, e-learning and knowledge management. A rethinking of education as a whole should be grounded on strategic openness of contents, actors and processes. A possible horizon could be considering universities as learning organizations, to allow the net-generation for a culture of participation, building, tinkering, remixing and sharing.

Semantic Web and, further, Social Semantic Web will encompass the creation of explicit and semantically rich knowledge representations through semi-formal ontologies, taxonomies or folksonomies, as a result of developments in social interactions. This change would support the design of much more flexible LMSs, in terms of learning goals and of relational and meaningful navigation among collections of Web and LO resources. Consequently, the starting point for the design of new e-learning environments which can deal with the issue of interoperability and of the exchange of LO in a more realistic and operable dimension consists in the description of LO through metadata including their external and internal features.

The following steps should be the definition of the modalities to promote learning by doing, as tool of "learn to do", one of the four pillars of lifelong learning education; the creation of models of integration of face-to-face and online cooperative learning (blended learning); the development of communities of practice open to both learners and external professionals.

## REFERENCES

Acquaviva, M., & Benini, M. (2004). VICE: E-Learning nell'era del Semantic Web. *Proceedings Nat. Conf. EXPO E-learning 04*.

Adorni, G., Coccoli, M., Vercelli, G. & Vivant, G. (2008). Un modello semantico di progettazione di contenuti didattici in ambienti di e-learning. *Atti del V convegno SieL*.

Anderson, P. (2006). What is Web 2.0? Ideas, technologies and implications for education. *JISC*. Retrieved May 12, 2007 from http://www.ukoln.ac.uk/terminolgy/JISC-review2006.html.

Annacontini, G. (2007). Adulti in rete: tecnologie didattiche e formazione universitaria. In A. Alberici (Ed.), *Adulti e Università. Sfide ed innovazioni nella formazione universitaria e continua*. Milano: Franco Angeli

Attwell, G. (2006). Personal Learning Environments. *The Wales Wide Web*. Retrieved June 30, 2008 from http://www.knownet.com/writing/weblogs/Graham_Attwell/entries/6521819364.

Barr, R., & Tagg, J. (1995). From Teaching to Learning: A New Paradigm for Undergraduate Education. *Change Magazine, 2*(12), 8-12. Retrieved January 11, 2008 from www.cic.uiuc.edu/resources/deo/paradigm.html

Benford, S., & Fahlén, L. (1993). A spatial model of interaction in large virtual environments. *Proc, of ECSCW '93*, pp. 107-132, Milano: Kluwer.

Berners-Lee, T., Handler, J., & Lassila, O. (2001). The Semantic Web. *Scientific American*. Retrieved September 23, 2008 from http://www.ryerson.ca/~dgrimsha/courses/cps720_02/resources/Scientific%20American%20The%20Semantic%20Web.htm

Bly, S. (1993). Media spaces: bringing people together in a video, audio, and computing environment. *Communications of the ACM, 36*(1), 28–46. doi:10.1145/151233.151235

Bonaiuti, G. (2007). I learning object nella prospettiva dell'eLearning 2.0. In *Atti del IV congresso Sie-l*. Macerata: EUM.

Calvani, A. (2006). *Rete, comunità e conoscenza. Costruire e gestire dinamiche collaborative*. Trento: Erickson.

Calvani, A., Buonaiuti, G., Fini, A., & Ranieri, M. (2007). I Personal Learning Environment: una chiave di volta per il Lifelong Learning? *Atti del IV congresso* Sie-l. Macerata: EUM.

Catarsi, C. (2007). La formazione di terza generazione: necessaria rifinitura di un paradigma", in A. Alberici (Ed.), *Adulti e Università. Sfide ed innovazioni nella formazione universitaria e continua*. Milano: Franco Angeli

Conole, G. (2008a). Stepping over the edge: the implications of new technologies for education. In Lee, M. J. W., & McLoughlin, C. (Eds.), *Web 2.0-Based E-Learning: Applying Social Informatics for Tertiary Teaching*. Hershey, PA: IGI Global.

Conole, G. (2008b). New Schemas for Mapping Pedagogies and Technologies. In *Ariadne* Issue 56. Retrieved June, 13 2009 from http://www.ariadne.ac.uk/issue56/conole/

Cormier, D. (2008). Rhizomatic knowledge communities: Edtechtalk, Webcast Academy. *Dave's Educational Blog*. Retrieved May, 27 2009 from http://davecormier.com/edblog/2008/02/29/rhizomatic-knowledge-communities-edtechtalk-webcast-academy/.

Crabtree, A., & Rodden, T. (2008). Hybrid Ecologies: Understanding Cooperative Interaction in Emerging Physical-Digital Environments. In *Personal and Ubiquitous Computing, 12* (7) 481-493. Retrieved June, 15 2009 from http://www.mrl.nott.ac.uk/~axc/DReSS_Outputs/PUC_2007.pdf

Demetrio, D. (2002). Cittadini in formazione. In Baratelli, M. (Eds.), *F.A.Re. Formazione con gli adulti. Esperienze a confronto*. Milano: Franco Angeli.

Downes, S. (2005, October 16). *E-Learning 2.0 in eLearn Magazine October 16, 2005*. Retrieved January 20, 2009 from http://www.downes.ca/post/31741

Downes, S. (2005, December 12). *An introduction to connective knowledge*. Retrieved November 12, 2006 from http://www.downes.ca/cgi-bin/page.cgi?post=33034

Downes, S. (2006). *Learning networks and connective knowledge*. Retrieved November 12, 2006 from http://it.coe.uga.edu/itforum/paper92/paper92.html

Downes, S. (2008). *The future of learning 10 years on*. Retrieved August 1, 2008 from http://www.downes.ca/presentation/193

European Commission. (2002). *European Report on Quality Indicators of Lifelong Learning*. Brussels: European Commission.

Fagioli, M. (2005). Learning Object: dal dire al fare. Retrieved June, 20 2009 from http://www.indire.it/content/index.php?action=read&id=1183

Fini, A. (2005). Dai Learning Object al Learning Design. In *Journal of e-Learning and Knowledge Society*.

Fini, A. (2008). 2.0. A case study on a growing community. In *Journal of e-Learning and Knowledge Society, 4, (3), September 2008* (pp. 167–175). E-Learning.

Fini, A., & Vanni, L. (2004). *Learning Objects e metadati. I quaderni di Form@re, n. 2*. Trento: Erickson.

Fisher, C. (2008). *Networks and Studios*. Retrieved June, 16 2009 from http://learning2cn.ning.com/profile/ClarenceFisher

Ghislandi, P., Mattei, A., Paolino, D., Pedroni, A., & Franceschini, D. (2008). Progettare una comunità di apprendimento online per un insegnamento accademico: potenzialità e limiti di Moodle. *Atti del convegno "SIeL-Società Italiana eLearning"*. Trento, 8-11 ottobre 2008. Retrieved May, 2 2009 from http://siel08.cs.unitn.it/Atti/index.html.

Giovannella, C. (2008). Learning 2.0? *Atti del V congresso* Sie-l. Macerata: EUM.

GridWise. (2007). *GridWise Architecture Council Interoperability Context-Setting Framework Draft* (January 2007). Retrieved June, 28 2009 from http://www.gridwiseac.org/pdfs/interopframework_v05%20070129.pdf

Hannon, J. (2009). Breaking down online teaching: Innovation and resistance. *Australasian Journal of Educational Technology, 25*(1), 14-29. Retrieved May, 10 2009 from http://www.ascilite.org.au/ajet/ajet25/hannon.html

Jarche, H. (2005). *Learning is Conversation*. Retrieved June 10, 2009 from http://www.jarche.com/2005/12/OLD651/

Jonassen, D. H., & Land, S. M. (2000). *Theoretical Foundations of Learning Environment*. New Jersey: Lawrence Erlbaum Associates.

JTCL. accessed April, 18 2009 at http://jtc1sc36.org/

Kirk, D., et al. (2005). Ways of the hands. *Proc. of ECSCW '05*, pp. 1-21. Paris: Springer.

Koleva, B. (2000). Traversable interfaces between real and virtual worlds. [The Hague: ACM.]. *Proc. Of CHI*, *00*, 233–240.

Koper, R. (2001). *Modelling units of study from a pedagogical perspective. The pedagogical meta-model behind*. EML Educational Technology Expertise Centre, Open University of the Netherlands.

Kuzouka, H., et al. (2004). Mediating dual ecologies. *Proc. of CSCW '04*, p. 477-486. Chicago: ACM. IEEE, (2000). *IEEE 100 – 2000. The Authoritative Dictionary of IEEE Standards Terms, Seventh Edition.* New York.

Leone, S. (2008a). The use of new technologies in advanced Italian classes. In I. Olney, G. Lefoe, J. Mantei, & J. Herrington (Eds.), *Proceedings of the Second Emerging Technologies Conference 2008* (pp. 120-129). Wollongong: University of Wollongong.

Leone, S. (2009). PLE: a brick in the construction of a lifelong learning society. In O'Donoghue, J. (Ed.), *Technology Supported Environment for Personalised Learning: Methods and Case Studies*. Hershey, PA: IGI-Publisher.

Levine, R., Locke, C., Searls, D., Weinberger, D., & McKee, J. (2009). *The Cluetrain Manifesto: 10th Anniversary Edition*. New York: Perseus Publishing. Retrieved June, 26 2009, from http://www.cluetrain.com/

LTSC. *(Learning Technology Standards Committee)*.Retrieved from http://ltsc.ieee.org/wg12/index.html

Lubesky, R. (2006). *The present and future of Personal Learning Environments (PLE). Optusnet*. Retrieved June 14, 2008 from http://members.optusnet.com.au/rlubensky/2006/12/present-and-future-ofpersonal-learning.html

Maffesoli, M. (2004). *Il tempo delle tribù. Il declino dell'individualismo nelle società postmoderne*. Milano: Guerini e Associati.

Mapelli, M., & Margiotta, U. (Eds.). (2009). *Dai blog ai social network. Arti della connessione nel virtuale*. Milano: Mimesis.

Marconato, G. (2003). Oltre l'e-learning. *Sviluppo & Organizzazione*, *200*(12), 7–11.

Merriman, J. (2008). *Redefining Interoperability (or why the IEEE and Oxford English Dictionary have it Wrong)*. Retrieved July, 10 2009 from http://www.okiproject.org/view/html/site/oki/node/2872

Morin, E. (1999). *Seven Complex lessons in Education for the Future*. Paris: United Nations Educational, Scientific and Cultural Organization.

Morin, E. (2008). *La Méthode. Opus*. Paris: Le Seuil.

Motschnig-Pitrik, R., & Mallich, K. (2004). Effects of Person-Centered Attitudes on Professional and Social Competence in a Blended Learning Paradigm. *Journal of Educational Technology & Society*, *7*(4), 176–192.

Nelson, J., & Kerr, D. (2006). *Active citizenship in INCA countries: definitions, policies, practices and outcomes. Final report.* Retrieved June, 30 2009 from http://www.inca.org.uk/pdf/Active_Citizenship_Report.pdf

Ranieri, M. (2005). *E-learning: modelli e strategie didattiche*. Trento: Erickson.

Recchioni, M., Castello, V., Dell'Aiuto, V. & Sancin, C. (2008). Strumenti collaborativi, intermodalità e life long learning. dove vanno le innovazioni? *Atti del V convegno SieL*. Macerata: EUM.

Rigutti, S., Paletti, G., & Morandini, A. (2008). Lifelong Learning e e-learning 2.0: il contributo degli studi sull'usabilità. *Je-LKS - Journal of e-Learning and Knowledge Society,* 4 (1), 91-100.

Rogers, C. R. (1983). *Freedom to Learn for the 80's*. Columbus, OH: Charles E. Merrill Publishing.

Sawyer, P., & Mariani, J. (1995). Database systems: challenges and opportunities for graphical HCI. *Interacting with Computers*, *7*(1), 273–303. doi:10.1016/0953-5438(95)93605-5

Sclater, N. (2008). *Web 2.0, Personal Learning Environments, and the Future of Learning Management Systems* (Research Bulletin, Issue 13). Boulder, CO: EDUCAUSE Center for Applied Research. Retrieved June, 23 2008 from http://www.educause.edu/ecar.

Seely-Brown, J. (1999). Learning, Working and Playing in the Digital Age. *AAHE Conference on Higher Education*, March 1999. Retrieved June, 15 2009 from http://serendip.brynmawr.edu/sci_edu/seelybrown/

Seely-Brown, J. (2009). Learning in the Digital Age (Indiana University, April 2009) Retrieved June, 15 2009 from http://www.johnseelybrown.com/

Siemens, G. (2006). *Connectivism: Learning Theory or Pastime of the Self-Amused?* Retrieved June, 6, 2009 from http://www.elearnspace.org/Articles/connectivism_self-amused.htm

Siemens, G., & Tittenberger, P. (2009). *Handbook of Emerging Technologies for Learning*. Retrieved April, 20 2009 from http://www.umanitoba.ca/learning_technologies/cetl/HETL.pdf

Stojanovic, N., & Handschuh, S. (2002). *A framework for knowledge management on the semantic web*. Retrieved February, 28 2008, from http://www2002.org/CDROM/poster/130.pdf

Tosh, D., & Werdmuller, B. (2004). *Creation of a learning landscape: weblogging and social networking in the context of e-portfolios*. Retrieved September 24, 2008 from http://elgg.net/bwerdmuller/files/61/179/Learning_landscape.pdf

Trentin, G. (2001). *Dalla formazione a distanza all'apprendimento in rete*. Milano: Franco Angeli.

Trentin, G. (2004). *Apprendimento in rete e condivisione delle conoscenze: ruolo, dinamiche e tecnologie delle comunità professionali online*. Milano: Franco Angeli.

Trentin, G. (2005). From "formal" to "informal" e-Learning through knowledge management and sharing. *Journal of e-Learning and Knowledge Society*, 1(2), 209-217.

UNESCO. (1996). *Learning: The Treasure Within. International Commission on Education for 21st Century*. Paris: UNESCO.

UNESCO. (1999). *The World Declaration on Higher Education for the Twenty-first Century: Vision and Action*. Paris: UNESCO.

Varisco, B. M. (2002). *Costruttivismo socio-culturale. Genesi filosofiche, sviluppi psico-pedagogici, applicazioni didattiche*. Roma: Carocci.

Varlamis, I. & Apostolakis, I. (2007). The Present and Future of Standards for E-Learning Technologies. *Interdisciplinary Journal of Knowledge and Learning Objects*, Volume 2.

Venkatesh, R. (2008, October 23). *The Cloudworker's Creed.* Retrieved October 28, 2008 from Ribbonfarm: http://www.ribbonfarm.com/2008/10/23/the-cloudworkers-creed/

Von Glasersfeld, E. (1998). *Il costruttivismo radicale. Una via per conoscere ed apprendere.* Roma: Società Stampa Sportiva.

Vygotsky, L. S. (1986). *Thought and Language.* Cambridge, MA: MIT Press.

Wasson, B. (2007). Design and Use of Collaborative Network Learning Scenarios: The DoCTA Experience. *Journal of Educational Technology & Society*, *10*(4), 3–16.

Weinberger, D. (2005, June 27). *The new shape of knowledge.* Retrieved on June, 26 2009 from http://www.hyperorg.com/blogger/mtarchive/004153.html

Wenger, E., McDermott, R., & Snyder, W. M. (2007). *Coltivare comunità di pratica.* Milano: Guerini e Associati S.p.A.

Wiley, D. A. (2000). *Learning object design and sequencing theory.* Unpublished doctoral dissertation, Brigham Young University. Retrieved August 11, 2003 from: http://davidwiley.com/papers/dissertation/dissertation.pdf

Wilson, S. (2005). *Future VLE – The Visual Vision.* Retrieved September 18, 2008 from http://www.cetis.ac.uk/members/scott/blogview?entry=20050125170206.

Yang, S. J. H. (2006). Context Aware Ubiquitous Learning Environments for Peer-to-Peer Collaborative Learning. *Journal of Educational Technology & Society*, *9*(1), 188–201.

## ADDITIONAL READING

A.A.V.V. (April 2009). *The Global Online Media Landscape.* Nielsen. Retrieved July 2, 2009 from www.nielsen-online.com/.../nielsen-online-global-lanscapefinal1.pdf

Alvino, S., & Sarti, L. (2004). *Learning Objects e Costruttivismo.* Ferrara: Atti Didamatica.

Catalano, D. (2000). Da un utilizzatore critico dei nuovi media. In Biolghini, D., & Cenarle, M. (Eds.), *Net learning. Imparare insieme attraverso la rete.* Milano: ETAS.

Doolittle, P. E. (2001). *Multimedia Learning: Empirical Results and Practical Applications.* Retrieved April, 30 2009 from http://www.ipfw.edu/as/tohe/2001/Papers/doo.htm

European Commission. (2000). *E-learning – Designing Tomorrow's Education.* Brussels: European Commission.

European Commission – DG XXII. (1995). *Teaching and learning: towards a learning society.* Luxembourg: Office of Official Publications of the European Communities.

Gardner, H. (1991). *Educare al comprendere.* Milano: Feltrinelli.

Gill, T. (2001). *Metadata and the World Wide Web.* Retrieved May, 20 2009 from http://www.getty.edu/research/institute/standards/intrometadata/pdf/gill.pdf

Knowles, M. (1996). *Quando l'adulto impara.* Milano: Franco Angeli.

Landriscina, F. (2005). Simulazioni e apprendimento: aspetti metodologici e concettuali. In *Journal of e-Learning and Knowledge Society*, Issue 3 - No. 3.

Leone, S. (2008). Lifelong learning and tertiary education in Italy. *The International Journal of Interdisciplinary Social Sciences.*, *3*(Issue 2), 7–14.

Levy, P. (2002). *L'intelligenza collettiva. Per un'antropologia del cyberspazio*. Milano: Feltrinelli.

Malhotra, Y. (2002). Information ecology and knowledge management: toward knowledge ecology for hyperturbolent organizational environments. In *Encyclopedia of Life support Systems (EOLSS)*. Oxford, UK: UNESCO/Eolss Publishers.

Marconato, G., & Litturi, P. (2005). Conversazione con David Jonassen. *Sistemi & Impresa*, *9*(12), 15–18.

Merrill, D. (2000). Knowledge objects and mental models. In David Wiley (Ed.), *The Instructional Use of Learning Objects*. Retrieved April, 28 2009 from http://www.id2.usu.edu/Papers/KOMM.PDF

Merrill, D. (2001). *First Principles of Instruction*. Retrieved April, 28 from www.id2.usu.edu/Papers/5FirstPrinciples.PDF

Norris, D. M., Mason, J., Robson, R., Lefrere, P. & Collier, G. (2003). A revolution in knowledge sharing. *EDUCAUSE Review*, 15-16-26.

Panzavolta, S. (2006). Metadatazione e interoperabilità. In *AIDA informazioni*, Anno 24, gennaio-giugno, Numero 1-2/2006.

Petrucco, C. (2002). Learning Objects: un nuovo supporto all'eLearning? In *IS - Informatica & Scuola*, Rivista trimestrale di Didattica & Nuove Tecnologie, Anno X - N. 3- Novembre 2002. Retrieved April, 20 2009 from http://www.edscuola.it/archivio/software/learning_objects.pdf

Policaro, C., & Mangione, G. R. (2009). *Dai Learning Objects ai Knowledge Object. Cosa produce la RETE?* Retrieved April, 28 2009 from http://www.catepol.net/dai-learning-objects-ai-knowledge-object-cosa-produce-la-rete/

Prensky, M. (2001). Digital Natives, Digital Immigrants. *Horizon NCB University Press*, Vol. 9 No. 5. Retrieved April, 15 2009 from www.twitchspeed.com/site/Prensky%20-%20Digital%20Natives,%20Digital%20Immigrants%20-%20Part1.htm

Quinn, C., & Hobbs, S. (2000). Learning objects and instructional components. *Educational Technology and Society*. 3(2), 2000. Retrieved on 10th March 2009 from http://ifets.ieee.org/periodical/vol_2_2000/discuss_summary_0200.html

Ridi, R. (1999). Metadata e metatag: l'indicizzatore a metà strada fra l'autore e il lettore. Presentation at the conference *The digital library: challenges and solutions for the new millenium*, Bologna, 17-18 giugno 1999. Retrieved April, 10 2009 from http://www.aib.it/aib/commiss/cnur/dltridi.htm

Salis, S., Depietro, L., Fiotto, V., Lao, F., & Marras, S. (2002). *Comunità di pratiche, di apprendimento e professionali: una metodologia per la progettazione. Strumenti Formez n. 10, Area Editoria e Documentazione*. Roma: Formez.

Sfard, A. (1998). On two metaphors for learning and the dangers of choosing just one. *Educational Researcher*, *27*(2), 4–13.

Siemens, G. (2004). Connectivism: A learning theory for the digital age. *International Journal of Instructional Technology and Distance Learning*. Retrieved November, 9 2008 from http://www.itdl.org/Journal/Jan_05/article01.htm

Siemens, G. (2006). *Knowing Knowledge*. Paperback. Retrieved October, 28 2008 from http://www.knowingknowledge.com/book.php

Siemens, G. (2008). A brief history of networked learning. In *Connectivism and Connective Knowledge Online Course*. Retrieved July, 1 2009 from http://ltc.umanitoba.ca/wiki/Connectivism#Week_3:_Properties_of_Networks_.28September_22-28.29

Tammaro, A. M. (2002). Meta-Data per le risorse didattiche: una breve nota. In *form@re - newsletter per la formazione in rete*.

Tapscott, D., & Williams, A. (2006). *Wikinomics 2.0. How Mass Collaboration Changes Everything*. USA: Penguin.

Warwick, C. (1997). *Metadata: an overview*. Services to Libraries Division at the Standards Australia Seminar «Matching Discovery and Recovery». Retrieved April, 10 2009 from http://www.nla.gov.au/nla/staffpaper/cathro3.html

Wenger, E. (1998). *Communities of practice*. Cambridge, UK: Cambridge University Press.

Wiley, D. (2000). Connecting learning objects to instructional design theory: A definition, a metaphor, and a taxonomy. In D.A. Wiley (Ed.), *The Instructional Use of Learning Objects*. Retrieved April, 20 2009 from http://reusability.org/read/chapters/wiley.doc

## KEY TERMS AND DEFINITIONS

**Ecology:** The space or environment in which cooperation takes place and the socially organized modes by which the environment facilitates collaboration.

**Formal Learning Environments:** Hierarchically structured, chronologically graded educational settings, mainly represented by VLEs in e-learning.

**Informal Learning Environments:** Individuals' daily environment (i e., family, friends, peer groups, etc.) where attitudes, values, skills and knowledge are acquired, and PLEs in e-learning.

**Interoperability:** The construction of an upper layer of technical specifications to produce, memorise, search and utilise available educational resources and tools coherently; in a broad sense it is a property referring to the ability of diverse systems and organizations to work together.

**Interoperable Learning Environments:** Educational platforms that work together to achieve a functional goal.

**Lifestreaming:** An online record of a person's daily digital activities, like as documents in progress or new emails, photos, movies, voice mail, reminders, blog posts, social network updates, software.

**Pedagogical Sustainability:** The possibility to sustain the field of technology enhanced leaning by a consistent pedagogical /andragogical framework.

**Web Syndication:** Managing many sources or streams using feed reader technology (i.e., RSS and Atom.)

# Chapter 2
# Customizing and Personalizing an Adult Blended Course:
## An Italian Experience on Lifelong Learning

**Valeria Pandolfini**
*University of Genoa, Italy*

## ABSTRACT

*This chapter, by combining research-based results and theoretical principles, analyzes how it is possible to integrate teaching models and use of new technologies in an adult blended course, and to adapt training experiences to the target group, in order to offer a course that may prove personalized as much as possible. Basing on the results of an evaluative study, some improvement factors and best practices are discussed at the end of the chapter, as well as some identified weaknesses, with a view to learning environments that, making use of specific strategies, online tools, and educational contents, are capable to reach high levels of accessibility, adaptability and personalization in training paths specifically tailored on students' actual training requirements.*

## INTRODUCTION

In the last few years, Information and Communication Technologies (ICTs) have allowed testing new methods in teaching and learning process organization, especially in terms of time and space independence (Stigmar & Sundberg, 2001). These changes depend on the way in which educational contents, online tools and environments are designed, developed and provided to those who wish to learn.

DOI: 10.4018/978-1-61692-791-2.ch002

This chapter is particularly focused on the main characteristics of the "PuntoEdu ATA" blended adult training course, an online platform devised and developed by the National Agency for School Autonomy Development in cooperation with the Public Education Department, and presents the main results achieved through evaluation activities. In particular, the chapter describes the PuntoEdu pattern, its educational contents and available online tools, and reports e-tutors' and learners' opinions (obtained through a web-survey and online focus groups) concerning both its technical and training characteristics.

The chapter mentions the main theories developed in the last few years within the pedagogical mainstream which have influenced learning environments design, regardless of their setting (whether real or virtual). Particular attention is paid to those related to the constructivist approach (Vygotsky, 1978) and to the learner-centred model (Ardito et al., 2006), deeply analyzing the elements characterizing a Personal Learning Environment (Tosh, 2005). Basing on PuntoEdu learners' characteristics (i.e. adult workers) the chapter aims at underlining two important issues stressed by andragogy (Knowles, 1984): on one side, the influence of the context (whether social, cultural, organizational, or professional) in defining the learning process (Barab and Duffy, 2000); on the other hand, the necessity to adopt particular strategies and methods to include in it specific situations where learners can face real problems (Alvino and Sarti, 2006). This leads to determine the aspects to be developed in order to establish a flexible learning model (Holmberg, 2006). This should be capable to allow each student conforming his/her training path to his/her personal requirements. In order to make this model effective, it is necessary to enable each student to choose among different subjects and various online tools. This would help student to succeed in managing his/her own learning process in a variety of contexts throughout his/her lifetime (Bentley, 1998).

This chapter aims at verifying how far these theoretical principles can be applied in a real blended course, in order to provide a training path that may result as much as possible accessible, adaptable and customized. In particular, the purpose is to investigate different aspects. First of all, it has to be explored the different chances in combining technology and teaching opportunities (how). Still, it has to be defined the contents (what) and the pursued objectives (for what), while, at the same time, explicating the reasons (why), and the timing sequence of the educational path (when). Lastly, it has to be considered the resources (how) and the agents (who) involved in the process (Moreno and Bailly-Bailliere, 2002).

## BACKGROUND

In the field of the latest studies dealing with the ever-increasing use of new technologies in teaching and learning processes, we can note a growing interest in combining specific technical aspects with pedagogical perspectives. In particular, those who plan training courses supported by new technologies seem to centre their efforts on an analysis of how educational contents, as well as their related tools and environments, should be designed to conform to the particular needs of each student.

This requirement results from an awareness that - as the constructivist approach (Piaget, 1970; Vygotsky, 1978) has widely underlined - when the educational content is far-away from personal interests and a subjects' involvement in the proposed tasks is limited, learners have no motivation to build their own knowledge and to transfer it to new situations. This is connected with three basic characteristics shared with the constructivist theory, which prove that learning is a social and personal phenomenon (Jarvis, 1987): (a) knowledge is not a product to be accumulated, but an active process where the learner attempts to make sense out of the world (Alexander, 1999); (b) people adapt their knowledge in a personal way, that is, they acquire knowledge in "*forms that enable them to use that knowledge later*" (Grabinger, 1996, p. 669); (c) the construction of knowledge is based on the collaboration and social negotiation of meaning, so that "*common understandings and shared meanings are developed through interaction among peers and teachers*" (Grabinger, 1996, pp. 669-670).

The Soviet psychologist Vygotsky, developing the concept of the proximal development zone (ZPD) in 1934, is considered the founding father of the socio-anthropological constructivist approach. He defined the ZPD notion as "*the distance between a learner's current conceptual development (as measured by independent problem solving) and that learner's potential capability, as measured by what can be accomplished under guidance or in collaboration with more capable peers*" (Vygotsky, 1978, p. 86). This concept, that has become part of the theoretical mainstream in pedagogy since the translation of his work "Mind in Society" in 1978, has directly influenced the design of web-based learning environments (Mayes & Freitas, 2004, pp.18-19). The influence of this constructivist theme is showed by Peal and Wilson (2001), who described some assumptions increasingly charactering these kinds of learning settings. First of all, the coherence between the learning activities, inserted in a real or simulated activity systems, and the actual situations. Secondly, the close attention devoted to structure the interaction among participants, under the guidance by an expert. Finally, the fact that the supervision tasks gradually handed over to increasingly competent learners.

So, the above theoretical considerations increasingly influence the empirical way in which learning environments are designed. They present features more and more oriented to improve the "autopoetic unities" (Knuth & Cunningham, 1993, p. 167), instead of merely transmitting instructions and tasks. In this sense, self-organized learning can be seen as an activity in which individuals are primarily responsible for their own planning, performance, and evaluation of learning activities in order to attain specific learning goals. Consequently, the role of the learner involved in an online course has considerably changed. In the first 10 years of the World Wide Web, in fact, the learner was considered no more then a "consumer" able to browse, read and use materials, however without being ever actively engaged in the production of learning content (Schaffert & Hilzensauer, 2008). On the contrary, nowadays, the learner has become a *prosumer* (Fallows, 2006), that is to say, a producer and, at the same time, a consumer of resources. In this way, he/she is able to actively participate in content development (for example through blog postings, by contributing to Wiki pages, or taking part in discussion forums).

On these grounds, it is clear that has become imperative the ability to design the so called PLEs, or Personal Learning Environments (Tosh, 2005), which, making use of multiple technologies, are capable to intercept and capitalize learner's competences and abilities (Mourshed et al., 2002). In this way, PLEs are fundamental in realizing training paths specifically conforming to learners' needs. Consequently, there is a tendency to adapt contents and tools to learners' personal characteristics (such as cultural background, technical expertise, technological knowledge, physical/cognitive abilities) and situations in which users are directly involved (Koper & Oliveir, 2006).

To reach this goal, the peculiarities of these environments, pointed out by recent studies as the learning environments of the future (Cross, 2006; Wilson, 2008), typically reflect user-centred design assumptions (Quintana et al., 2001; Ardito et al., 2006). It becomes more and more important to promote reliance on active, rather than passive, learning, as well as to emphasize in-depth learning and understanding, students' greater responsibility and accountability and an increased sense of autonomy in learners themselves (O'Neill & McMahon, 2005). Harasim, Hiltz, Teles and Turoff (1995) talks about network learning, that means the use of computers in teaching and learning, as an authentic student-centred environment, because, in a context mediated by computers, students have greater control on teaching and learning processes.

In this way, learning becomes an active and constructive process in which students strategically manage the available training resources to create new knowledge by establishing an active cooperation with the medium rather than merely receiving instructions from it (Kozma, 1991). Recently, McCombs and Vakili have defined the learner-centred approach as "*the perspective that couples a focus on individual learners – their he-*

*redity, experiences, needs – with a focus on learning – the best available knowledge about learning and how it occurs and about teaching practices that are most effective in promoting the highest levels of motivation, learning, and achievement for all learners*" (2005, p.1564). Moore (1983), perhaps overemphasizing the growing need to personalize the training path as well as the user-centred design assumptions, has developed the *independent learning theory*, which combines two dimensions, transactional distance and learner's autonomy. Dialogue and structure, the two variables that describe "transactional distance", are classic definitions in distance education. Dialogue is described as "*the extent to which, in any educational program, the learner, the program, and the educator are able to respond to one another*". Structure, the second variable, is "*the measure of an educational program's responsiveness to learner individual needs*" (1983, p.157). Learner's independence, according to Moore's theory, is a positive quality, or attribute, in the separation between teacher and learner.

Therefore, to go beyond the mere transmission purpose of distance training, it is necessary to introduce contextual elements in the training process (Wiley, 2000). So, the quality of an online course will be increasingly evaluated considering its capability to integrate in specific situations where learners can face real problems (Alvino & Sarti, 2006). For this reason, the notion of "practice fields" proposed by Barab and Duffy (2000) takes increasing relevance, as it becomes more and more important to propose students as little as possible abstract tasks and activities. It is instead very important to let them approach actual reality as much as possible, in order to make the learning activities authentic, that is to say, consistent with the social context in which skill or knowledge are normally embedded and incorporated. So, in the design of online learning environments, we can note a growing use of theoretical approaches inspiring to practice fields, such as learning based on problem solving (Savery & Duffy, 1995) and cognitive apprenticeship (Collins, Brown & Newman, 1989), focused on the relationship between the nature of learning tasks in an educational or training environment and their characteristics when they are put into practice.

In particular, this is a very important element in online courses addressed to adult subjects because, as suggested by andragogy (Knowles, 1984), only the activity related to a specific kind of knowledge (especially its application) is the most effective drive to acquire that knowledge. For example, it is necessary that an adult learner may have the sensation to control his/her training path by selecting the most appropriate kind of knowledge allowing him/her to maintain and develop his/her personality structure and independence. This happens especially in informal contexts, during everyday activities, in which the subjects – through their work activity – can develop their own human and professional culture. Therefore, increasing efforts should be made for using educational contents and tools within an educational strategy aimed at building personalized training paths, but a personalized fruition cannot disregard the possibility to find the right content at the right time (Masie, 2003). This approach closely reflects the guidelines laid down in the UK Government's Green Paper on lifelong learning (1998) foreseeing that, in future, learners will not be tied to particular locations, being able to study at home, at work, or everywhere else through the use of broadcast media and on-line access. This is accomplished by helping people to learn wherever they choose and supporting them in assessing how they are doing and where they want to go next. In this way, the basic premise of lifelong learning is that it is not feasible to equip learners at school, college or university with all the knowledge and skills they need to prosper throughout their lifetimes. Therefore, people will need continually to enhance their knowledge and skills, in order to address immediate problems and to participate in a process of continuous vocational and professional development. This approach reflects flexible learning assumptions, for example, the theoretical position expressed by Holmberg (2006), when reflecting on a model where the technical support should combine with sufficient flexibility and adaptability of studying materials and studying methods. Flexible learning can be characterized by several factors, such as more flexible curricula, forms of study, study tempo, examination forms, different learning styles, geographical independence, and variation in communication forms between student and teacher, and in student-to-student ones. So, basing on specific pedagogical and technical requirements, the aim is to allow each learner to become able to individually adapt his/her training path and to give him/her the possibility to choose among different educational contents and online tools. This choice would depend on his/her own conditions, abilities, achieved knowledge and training needs (Koper & Oliveir, 2006). In other words, the new educational imperative is to empower people to manage their own learning in a variety of contexts throughout their lifetimes (Bentley, 1998). This implies the awareness that effective learning is related to the competency of accessing significant knowledge, as well as of being able to control, recover and elaborate the knowledge, wherever it is collocated (Perkins, 1993).

## ICTS AND LIFELONG LEARNING: EUROPEAN AND ITALIAN OBJECTIVES

Among the goals set by the Lisbon Treaty, Information and Communication Technologies (ICTs) have a strategic role in improving lifelong learning and in ensuring access to permanent education and training to all. In 2000, the European Council called upon National Governments to promote a quick development and spreading of ICTs for the purpose to adopt the necessary training and information levels for the European Society of the Third Millennium. In 2001, the European Commission, through the initiative "The *e*Learning Action Plan-Designing tomorrow's education" (CEC, 2001), invited all Member States to "*persist in the efforts towards the effective integration of ICTs in education and training systems*" and to "*fully exploit the potentialities of internet, multimedia environments and virtual learning for better and faster lifelong learning experiences*". Other European initiatives, such as the "e- Europe Action Plan 2005" (CEC, 2002), point out e-learning as a priority action, considering it an effective answer to the demand for labour force re-qualification in Europe. Within this frame, the "E-learning 2004-2006 Program" (European Parliament, 2003) represented the premise for the formulation of the "Lifelong Learning program 2007-2013" (European Parliament, 2006), in which ICTs, together with political cooperation, innovation and languages, are one of the three transversal priorities. Finally, the initiative called "2010- Taking part in Information Society" identifies e-learning as the most effective answer in the area of lifelong learning and for the promotion of an active and egalitarian participation for everyone.

These issues, resulting from the Lisbon European Council, were adopted by the Italian Government through Directive "Training and development of Public Administration staff" (Dec. 13, 2001) and the subsequent Directive "E-learning training projects in Public Administration" (Aug. 8, 2004). Its guidelines contain some elements to be included in the planning and design of a distance-training course in the Public Administration related to educational content typologies, their organization and use. First of all, the educational contents should turn into materials to be included in the platform, and should guarantee both multimedia and interactive use modalities (hypertext, audio-video, simulations, virtual laboratories, exercises). Secondly, in organizing the educational contents, and in choosing the approaches and educational tools to be used, it is necessary to consider the individual content typologies and the purpose of the training course. Finally, regarding the use of the educational contents, a blend of different (synchronous online, asynchronous online, offline) supply channels and the creation of virtual classes should be taken into account to develop continuous interactivity. In addition, it is important to make the training path tracking possible, in order to allow both tutors and learners controlling the learning levels throughout the different stages of the course.

These recommendations find concrete application in the PuntoEdu ATA Project, which is the main topic discussed in the following pages.

## THE PUNTOEDU PROJECT

"PuntoEdu ATA" is a blended learning application planned by the National Agency for School Autonomy Development in cooperation with the Public Education Department. It is specifically aimed at developing a virtual community among the Italian school support staff, combining the training process with an exchange of practices and interests. This Project is extremely innovative, because it is the first blended-learning experience carried out on a national scale addressed to the Administrative, Technical and Auxiliary Staff (also briefly called ATA staff) employed in all Italian schools. These heterogeneous profiles (such as Administrative and Technical Assistants, Cloakroom attendants, Cooks, Gardeners, School Co-operators, Nurses) are generally not skilled in using computers and online tools. PuntoEdu ATA is the first step in the construction of a permanent professional training system aimed at upgrading, through the use of the new technologies as learning and teaching tools, the whole Italian School System and finalized to improve existing individual expertises and skills.

For all these reasons, this Project seems to perfectly reflect both the Lisbon's objectives - as it represents an application of ICTs in the area of lifelong learning - and the Italian Government's intentions, being explicitly addressed to the Public Administration Staff.

We shall hereafter describe the general organization pattern of the course and the main characteristics of the platform, by investigating whether, and in which ways, this Project represents an effective application of the theoretical aspects described in the previous pages. Particular attention has been paid to the increasing need to guarantee training path personalization, bearing in mind the difficulties to attain this goal due to the great heterogeneity of learners in terms of professional and computer-related skills.

From an organizational point of view, PuntoEdu ATA has adopted a blended-learning approach combining face-to-face training modules with distance training modules. It has been implemented basing on a three-stage cyclic process through: (a) face-to-face meetings (meant as opportunities for participants to collectively share the learning contents under the guidance of tutors as learning facilitators); (b) assisted independent learning, supported by an online tutor, which makes use of offline and online learning materials specifically tailored to the needs of each professional profile; (c) online collaboration activities, through an e-learning platform (devoted to forum discussions, chat, assisted distance exercises, and virtual classes). The training path has been based on a credit system, so that each learner has to reach a total amount of 72 credits to complete the course: 48 credits for online activities (equivalent to 24 hours online, one hour corresponding to 2 credits) and 24 credits for face-to-face meetings/lessons (equivalent to 12 classroom hours). The project has been organized in a modular way, which ensures freedom of choice to all students through the credit system. In this way, each learner is able to decide how to reach the total number of credits by selecting his/her preferred online activities (by sending a homework at the end of each proposed activity, by participating in the Thematic forum, or by downloading educational materials).

Moreover, each actor involved in the course has the opportunity to monitor the training path flow: each learner, through his/her own portfolio, has the opportunity to control his/her carried out activities and acquired credits. Likewise, each tutor has the opportunity to trace out the activities of each learner and those of the whole virtual class, in order to monitor personal and collective learning levels. Blended learning is judged the most appropriate and effective educational model both considering the huge number of involved learners (over 45,000), and because, as provided for by art. 62 of the National Collective Agreement on Employment (CCNL, Jul. 24, 2003), "*it allows widespread, rather inexpensive, interactive, personalized, repeatable, up-to-datable and developable training actions*". At the same time, PuntoEdu is addressed to heterogeneous subjects, considering learners' professional profiles, their achieved knowledge and their ICT skill levels. For these reasons, it has been necessary to correctly integrate distance and in-presence training, bearing in mind the importance of learners' actual presence (in the classroom) and the relevance of tutors' support. From these elements derives the necessity of effectively improving the personalization of the training path in order to face the usually scarce technical skill levels of the participants.

Concerning the online environment, it has been necessary to adopt different procedures for supporting learners throughout their training experience and promoting cooperation among them. Regarding the first objective, the platform presents several specific functions: an area of explanatory materials (simulations, audio lessons, slides, examples); different operational proposals and exercises (performed step by step and audio-commented); various links to other resources dealing with the online proposed themes; an help desk to be contacted by e-mail; an online guide (with the basic information on the thematic areas of the training course as well guidelines for understanding the credit system); a FAQ corner, a glossary and an online page assistant. To promote the cooperation among learners, instead, the system allows each one of them to present him/herself trough a personal portfolio and to interact each other through a chat line or different types of forum. The forums were: Thematic (devoted to specific professional contents), Community (to promote participants' socializing and free discussions on topics not strictly related to the professional contents proposed in the course modules) and Virtual class forum (reserved to the members of the virtual classes). Therefore, the methodological approach adopted in PuntoEdu has tried to use all the opportunities offered by the net at their best, especially those regarding interactivity and multimedia. On the one hand, learners have been stimulated to play an active role, through the availability of several highly-interactive multimedia materials and, on the other hand, learners' activity has been placed within a social environment (virtual class), which allowed them effectively interacting with their tutor and colleagues. Another important element characterizing the PuntoEdu project consists in the so-called "accessibility": learners, located in all Italian regions, were able to complete their training since they were in possession of the necessary technology for having access to electronic format materials easy to update. Being learners who could accede the learning materials anytime, they had the opportunity to choose the time in which they could better learn to complete their coursework, and receive timely feedbacks.

## RESEARCH OBJECTIVES AND DESIGN

Our research was aimed at analyzing, basing on the evaluations made by the two main actors involved in the course - tutors and learners - whether, and how, the PuntoEdu platform and structure was capable to provide a personalized training path to the ATA staff.

To achieve this purpose, in our research we have distinguished two macro-categories of objectives.

The first category includes the objectives we have defined "general", which mostly relate to activities concerning online course evaluations. These objectives concern two dimensions. The first one is a technical dimension. It refers to the following elements: (a) the quality of contents (training aid quality, content pertinence to the target, and capability to respond to participants' training needs); (b) the platform usability (consistency of the environment structure with contents, course objectives and structure, platform accessibility and browsing ease); (c) the learning process design and the management quality (quality and recurrence of in-presence and online lessons, clear distinction of the roles and tasks of the different actors involved in the course). The second dimension, of those concerning more "general" objectives, is the training/educational one. It regards: (a) the learning process effectiveness (mastery of contents, ability to apply training contents to different contexts, improvement of problem-solving abilities, change in behaviors) and (b) the learning process efficiency and effectiveness (whose indicators are the use of available resources, return level of exercises and learners' participation in team activities).

The second macro-category of objectives in this research might instead be defined "specific", and results from PuntoEdu own peculiarities, in particular the blended-learning model and the kind of support provided by tutors to learners.

On the basis of these objectives, the questions driving our research are: how can we integrate online and face-to-face activities in a blended-learning course in order to improve the personalization level of the training path? What technological aspects (platforms, online tools, techniques) are capable to design at best a system that may prove to be accessible, intuitive, and user-friendly? Which elements should be included in the educational contents in order to allow them generating learning experiences and meeting learners' training needs? Which features make them both suitable for achieving the specific learning purposes, both appropriate to everyday work requirements? In which way is it possible to allow each learner managing what he/she has learned throughout his/her lifetime? How could the tutor improve the individual training path personalization and provide a customized support to each learner? Finally, how can technology support tutoring activities?

In order to answer to these questions, the study involved quanti-qualitative instruments in a concurrent research design (Greene & Caracelli, 1997; Cresswell, 2003). In this way the results of the two on-line questionnaire (one addressed to students, the other to tutors) has been integrated with those obtained from some on-line focus groups (separately conducted with learners and tutors). The two surveys have been managed during the course: everyone could access the questionnaires trough a link in PuntoEdu homepage from the beginning of the training activities till the end of the course (seven months). Considering the non compulsory character of these surveys, the high response rate is a clear indicator that they were considered and welcomed as an important occasion to give voice to the respondents themselves.

The on-line focus groups (some conducted with some students which had already completed the training course, others with students which were still attending it) were carried out basing on a synchronous method. This allowed participants, equipped with headphones and microphones, to simultaneously take part in the discussions from their posts. Though the statements of the 18 participants in the focus groups cannot be generalized, they are, however, significant and useful to enrich the themes dealt with in the questionnaire In fact, they could catch some specific elements and transversal problems, as well as innovative solutions and choices aimed at improving the platform and future on-line educational/training projects.

## Main Results of the Research

Before analyzing the most significant results of our evaluations, we think it would be useful to briefly describe the tutors' and learners' sample. The tutors' sample included 802 subjects (out of 1,453 total respondents) who answered an online questionnaire. Four fifth interviewed tutors are over-40 years old; there is a slightly higher prevalence of women (57%) and the most recurrent professional profiles are school managers (37,7%), executives (by 22.2% technical and by 18.7% administrative staff) and teachers (18.5%). Most tutors had already experienced online courses in the past, and in some cases, had participated in the previous editions of the PuntoEdu ATA Project. The learners' sample, composed by over 15,000 persons (out of 44,697 enrolled persons) was characterized as follows: female gender prevalence (two participants out of three were women); of ripe age, in average (70% of the sample being over-50 years old); with a long work experience (over 80% of the sample had worked in this sector for more than 20 years). The learners' professional profiles refer mainly to School Co-operators (48.4%), Administrative Assistants (38.7%) and Technical Assistants (12.5%), while the other categories (such as Cloakroom attendants, Cooks, Gardeners, Nurses) are residual.

In the following pages we present the main results of a combined analysis of the data collected through the questionnaire and the focus groups. We shall point out the strengths and weaknesses identified in the course in relation to training path personalization, that is to say, the elements in favour and those against it.

Collected data are based on a scale of values ranging from 1 (minimum satisfaction) to 6 (maximum satisfaction) and refer to the different aspects concerning the technical and training dimension of PuntoEdu ATA. As regards the first dimension, the speed of access to the platform is considered quite satisfactory1 by both respondents' groups (about 90% of the learners' sample and about 70% of the tutors' sample). The platform is considered very easy to browse by 90% learners and 79% tutors. High-satisfaction levels are expressed as regards the graphic design of the learning environment (by 73.8% learners and by 74% tutors). Finally, the easy-to-reach information in the platform obtains higher than average scores among 89.6% learners and 73.2% tutors. In addition, learners are very satisfied with the aid and support tools included in the platform (82.5% of the sample).

These evaluations confirm that PuntoEdu has been designed bearing in mind the essential characteristics pointed out by literature to increase users' personalization and satisfaction levels. It seems, in fact, *accessible* (information can be easily searched, identified and found, Longmire, 2000), *intuitive* to use (the graphic interface facilitates users while they are browsing the site, for example, by enhancing the visibility of available services) and, consequently, *user-friendly* (Karlsudd, 2001), considering that many participants in the focus group defined the site *graphics pleasant* and *captivating*.

Another element, particularly appreciated by the respondents' sample, concerns training aid quality, which is judged quite satisfactory by 90.8% learners and by 76.8% tutors. This positive evaluation (emerged also from focus groups) refers both to downloadable materials, both to those supplied by the tutors during face-to-face meetings. Not only the quality, but also the variety and clearness of the learning aids are particularly appreciated. In particular, the project is judged extremely effective in the way it tackles professional themes with an innovative learning approach that makes use of the new technologies. In fact, an outstanding element of the training aid stressed by learners consists in its usefulness also in everyday work activities, so that the course is perceived as an effective contribution to the qualitative increase of lifelong learning. All professional profiles has revealed as the most appreciated characteristics the "support to students with disabilities" (18.5%), the "medical aid" (17.5), the "safety" (14.9%), the "human resource management" (12.2%) and the aspects related to "administration and accounting" (10.3%). All of these elements are transversal topics considered very useful to face everyday tasks within the school environment. Therefore, to summarize the main characteristics of PuntoEdu training aid, we may use the following adjectives: *educational* (capable to generate learning experiences), *independent* and *autonomous* (serving to the specific purposes it was created for, Longmire, 2000), *persistent* (allowing to manage students' learning throughout their lifetime, so that their personal stock of resources and knowledge may be immediately accessible despite changes in technology) and *useful* (meeting everyday communication, work and learning needs, Sharples, 2000). We must however point out also a few negative aspects underlined by learners about the training materials. First of all, their content does not always fully meet the target requirements. Secondly, they are judged too vague and general and not completely responding to the specific training needs of each professional profile. Thirdly, even though the learning material is generally considered complete and varied, its contents are not always updated in compliance with the latest regulations in force. In addition, the three most represented profiles of the sample underline that several themes learners would welcome are not included and dealt with in the course. In particular, the administrative assistants complain about the lack of issues related to pensions, career reconstruction, tax payment and ATA staff rights and duties. The topics the school co-operators would welcome refer to computer literacy, regulations on leaves, work permits and job flexibility, hygiene and sanitary measures and juvenile uneasiness. Finally, the subjects indicated by the technical assistants are related to the communication and cooperation with professors and colleagues, daily work planning, privacy and personal data handling and English language courses.

Concerning the training/educational dimension, important elements useful to evaluate the effectiveness of PuntoEdu design in providing learners with high personalization levels and in conforming to their specific training needs, can be drawn from learners' opinions about the blended-learning model. An analysis of the survey data reveals that most learners declare that online training is more flexible (in 46.6% cases) and requires less time (62.3%) than in-presence training. The focus groups allowed us deepening this evaluation: several participants declared that the flexibility of online training, as well as the opportunity to have access to the platform at any time, gave them the opportunity to choose when (in which days and hours) performing online activities depending on their personal needs. It is interesting to note, in fact, that 22.4% of the learners' sample (corresponding to 3,437 respondents) declared they used to accede the platform, in order to complete online activities, also "during the weekend", 35.6% "at home", subtracting time to their personal engagements, and 508 learners answered even "during the night". This gave all learners, also those who are usually very busy, the possibility to complete their training path. In this way, the system flexibility has weighted positively on the high rates of learners who successfully completed the course (nine learners out of ten). These data are confirmed by the focus groups, showing that the most appreciated aspect of online training consists in its anywhere availableness and its allowance in communicating with teachers, experts and peers (Sharples, 2000). In this way, the online learning environment permitted all learners to study interactively in the context of their own workplace, as well as at home, and promoted cooperation through technology.

As regards the other component of the blended learning model, that is to say, face-to-face training, most learners declare that this traditional learning system is more interactive (85.8% respondents), more amusing (69.4%) and guarantees quick feedback (81.3%) compared to online training. By combining the questionnaire and the focus groups results we can note that the recurrence of online and in-presence learning intervals, in particular the quantity of hours devoted to each of these learning modalities, has not been uniformly appreciated by learners. Even though 34.4% of the sample considers the PuntoEdu structure adequate, 16.4% would welcome more online hours and almost 50% ask for more face-to-face meetings. In general, traditional classroom lessons are considered necessary to clarify problems related to ITCs and access to platform, but, above all, to establish personal relationships. Most learners, in fact, think it is extremely important to be able to give a face to the other learners and tutors, and recognize the importance of interaction (real, in presence, not virtual, online) as an essential factor for knowing each other. This is judged the best way to encourage future moments of sharing, both from a personal and from a professional point of view. Face-to-face meetings have allowed learners, on the one hand, to more clearly describe to their tutors the difficulties they encountered in using online tools and, on the other, to socialize with colleagues and share with them professional issues and personal interests. In this way, learners, being able to express their personal training needs, could receive from tutors precise information for solving their specific problems or difficulties. At the same time, they could find a concrete support not only in tutors, but also in other learners, thereby facilitating "peer-to-peer" knowledge transfer.

Consequently, the opportunity offered to learners to use different learning modalities, that is to say, different online tools (chat, forum) as well as different settings (real or virtual classes), allowed them choosing the most appropriate alternative on the basis of their own preferences and personalities (for example shy people generally prefer an online rather than an in-presence setting). Also the opportunity offered to learners, and not only to administrators, to include new subjects in the Thematic or Community forum is another element that helps personalizing the course. In fact, it allows students putting forward questions related to the subjects discussed in the training course, as well as professional issues, for the purpose of sharing problems or difficulties encountered during the course or in everyday work activities. This method led each learner to give his/her personal contribution to a joint construction of the learning process. Therefore, we can consider PuntoEdu a *generative system*, since it allows learners to construct contents and new objectives resulting from them, a system that can be modified, thereby increasing its potential through collaboration (Longmire, 2000). So, the innovative training model proposed has actually created real and virtual communication spaces useful both for updating activities, and for placing knowledge, information and best practices created or discovered during usual professional activities at everyone's disposal.

The general positive evaluation of the blended model expressed by learners is also connected to the effective combination of two kinds of training. The 66.6% of the sample learners declared that only through a real integration of in-presence and online lessons it is possible to attain positive learning results. Besides, most participants in the focus groups have appreciated the real continuity provided by PuntoEdu in the activities concerning these two different stages. In fact, the same themes proposed and discussed during face-to-face lessons were submitted also to the virtual class. This was done in order to examine more in depth the problems and issues that could not be thoroughly discussed in the classroom because of lack of time, or had emerged after the end of the "traditional" lesson.

## Tutors' Role

A final subject, which in some respects seems to summarize the evaluations reported in the previous pages, refers to the answers given by the interviewees about training path personalization: 87.5% learners judged it completely satisfactory, as well as 68.5% tutors. Strictly connected with this aspect is the analysis of the role played by tutors during the training experience in analyzing the ways in which they succeeded in facilitating the learning process, and in providing a support as close as possible to learners' needs and requests. In PuntoEdu, this is a very difficult task considering learners' great heterogeneity in terms of professional profiles, and, consequently, their different interests and computer skills.

We have collected in this connection some additional information drawn from two different surveys carried out on tutors and learners in order to analyze, on the one hand, the major kinds of support provided by tutors to learners, divided into in-presence and online modules, and, on the other hand, learners' appraisal of e-tutoring activities.

During online training, tutors provided first of all, an ITC support (21.5%), as well as information on training, that is to say, an orientation to the training course (19.8%). Online training included lessons on specific subjects (14.5%) and the creation of individual made-to-measure training paths (9.3%). The training tools mostly used by tutors to support learners' online work consisted in virtual classes (47.1%), e-mail messages (29.4%), and other external resources, such as platforms and forums aimed at managing the groups (6.2%). During face-to-face meetings, the tutors provided their students with technological and ITC support – guidelines on how to browse the platform and use the related tools (15.6%), ITC literacy (10.1%). The lessons did not only include standard didactic activities, that is to say, lessons focused on specific subjects (15.9%), but also more transversal and exciting group activities (role-playing, brainstorming, learners' self-presentation and discussions on real and pragmatic case-histories amounted to more than 40% total activities). In addition, a great deal of tutors' in-presence activities were devoted to establishing a positive atmosphere in the classroom, and included group management (18.3%), provision of emotional support (8.1%) and reduction of learners' sense of isolation (6.3%). These results underline the efforts made by tutors to optimize the potentialities of the blended-learning model, which tries to combine at best the opportunities offered by online tools with the traditional teaching setting. In both cases, it was interesting to note the particular attention paid by tutors to increase learners' motivation and involvement. In online environments they always tried to identify the most appropriate tools for the target, while in face-to-face meetings they chose to put into practice transversal activities specifically referred to learners' actual work experience, rather than focusing on merely abstract issues.

Learners' appraisal of tutors' activities, measured in the survey through a scale of values ranging from 1 (minimum satisfaction) to 6 (maximum satisfaction), is generally positive, the sample average score being 5.31. More than 60% of the learners' sample is close to the highest satisfaction level and almost 80% of them do favourably judge tutors' activities by attributing them an over-5 average score: response time, guidance to the use of training materials and online communication tools, timely communications, emotional support and help in the construction of a personal training path.

By combining learners' and tutors' opinions expressed in the focus groups, we can summarize the weight of the tutors' role on course personalization as follows:

- Tutors are willing and prepared to give suggestions and information in order to lead learners to solve their difficulties without imposing them a solution. They take upon themselves a guidance role, helping each learner to acquire the contents of the lessons and identifying the most appropriate learning method for each student. This is even more relevant if we consider the characteristics of PuntoEdu learners, namely adult subjects who generally need to personally and independently manage their training paths, and to actively apply achieved knowledge, rather than being submitted to it (Cercone, 2008).

- Professional background and transversal competences; in particular, when tutors belong to the learners' professional profile, they are aware of specific job-related problems. This encourages them to provide a more personalized support based on learners' peculiar training and professional requirements.
- Technical support, especially in the - *unfortunately not unusual* - case learners should show they have difficulties in using the platform due to their scarce computer literacy levels. They specified step by step - in a way tutors have often defined *elementary* - the basic procedures to follow in order to make a functional use of the platform, thereby personalizing their support on the basis of the specific needs expressed by different subjects. Moreover, during face-to-face meetings, in front of very heterogeneous classes composed by subjects with different computer literacy levels, tutors usually adopted a "peer-to-peer" knowledge-transfer method. This strategy was realized by organizing small work teams, where technically skilled students used to help those encountering difficulties in using a PC.
- Organizational management, aimed at supervising the general structure of the course, at combining face-to-face and distance training modules, and at explaining the learners who seemed disconcerted in front of a new training method what to do. Several tutors have defined themselves *facilitators* and have reported they had less difficulties to offer this kind of support during in-presence training modules than during distance ones. In the first case, in fact, face-to-face interaction gave them the opportunity to better understand learners' difficulties and give consequently more precise information for solving problems. During online activities, instead, learners' questions often seemed too vague and muddled.
- Strong encouragement to students not to drop the training course in the frequent case in which learners looked demotivated, by helping them to counter their loss of enthusiasm, and showing them the advantages their attendance to the course would capitalize from a personal and a professional point of view.

Basing on these elements, PuntoEdu design and tutors' activities seem to have been developed with a clear awareness of some implicit assumptions borrowed from the constructivist approach. This appears evident, in particular, when considering the attention paid to the existing different learning styles among learners and the effort profuse in order to encourage them to perform the tasks by themselves. These aspects confirm the assumption that the successful results, in terms of learning, depend mostly on the effective participation of students, as active actors involved in a learning process, rather then on the teachers activities (Berge and Collins, 1995). Therefore, the different kinds of support provided by tutors have increased learners' satisfaction and their appreciation for the completeness of the course.

## Major Weaknesses Identified the Design of a Personalized Blended-Learning Course

Up to now, we have pointed out the elements and peculiarities of PuntoEdu aimed at promoting training path personalization. We have however identified from learners and tutors' evaluations also a few limits in the project. Some of them refer to the low levels of computer literacy shown by most learners, while other weak points have been identified in the overall organization and design of the course itself.

Regarding the first aspect, the most evident deficiency underlined by interviewees is the lack of a preliminary course on computer use, to be held before the beginning of actual training. Considering that almost 60% of the learners' sample complains that online training demands too advanced technical skills, it emerges clearly how much a preliminary computer course would provide all learners with sufficient familiarity with the platform use. Besides, it would allow tutors managing more easily the work group, which is often formed by learners with quite different computer skills. This disparity has not allowed tutors, so far, to provide learners with a really customized support, since they had to deal with too many different requests. Their teaching role was sometimes limited to that of a guide giving advices and suggestions, in the case of technically skilled learners (Administrative and Technical assistants). In most cases, however, they were obliged to spend much time in teaching the other learners the basic elements for using a computer (as most learners were incapable to attend an online lesson, and some of them *did not even know how to switch on a PC*). Therefore, the most skilled learners were obliged to slacken their learning rate. Due to these gaps, most e-tutors have stressed the need for a more accurate learners' pre-selection based on their knowledge of the tools to be used in the platform, as well as a preliminary course aimed at teaching them how to use such tools. In this way it would be possible to set up classes with students with the same competence level. Besides, the technical difficulties, along with the general lacking of sufficient ITC and computer skills, have penalized also the general organization of the course. Quite often, in fact, the planned subjects to be discussed during in-presence meetings could not be dealt with, as most hours spent in the classroom were used for teaching learners the basic notions on computer use. Moreover, it often happened that the learners who were not accustomed to use a computer and the related communication tools seemed to be more interested in technical matters than in educational contents. This is a frequent risk in distance education: a feeling of inadequacy towards the medium leads learners to devote most of their time and energies to the solution of technical problems, or to become familiar with new programs and online functions, without taking care of the educational contents of the course (Ross, 1996). Regardless of these considerations, we would also add that the project does not take into due account a fundamental element, pointed out by literature, which would ensure the favourable outcome of a training course based on the use of new technologies, and namely, *user competence* (Karlsudd, 2001). This term implies that the user has achieved the necessary knowledge and skills required to effectively interact with a computer. Consequently, also the concept of computer system usability, or literally, its "ease of use", seems to be lacking in PuntoEdu, because, as happens in many cases, if an e-learning system is not usable, a learner spends more time to learn how to use the software rather than to learn the contents of the course.

Further weak points underlined by learners and tutors refer, instead, to the general organization and design of the course. First of all, the available time for carrying out all intended activities has been considered too short, and does not allow learners to completely assimilate the training contents, thus affecting the effectiveness of the learning process. We have often noticed a sort of *credit anxiety*, because most learners used to speed up their learning pace merely to reach the necessary credits for ending the course. Consequently, though the course dealt with an exhaustive number of themes, they could not be studied in depth. Time limits have also penalized tutors' activities, especially their ability to provide a personalized support. Often, they were not able to help each learner as needed, as they had the possibility to give only general information unsuited to answering specific needs, because there was not time enough for closely following each student. A second weak point refers to the course timetable. Both learners and tutors have expressed a negative opinion on the training path schedule, that is to say, on the fact that the course has been planned in periods of the year in which the ATA staff is in general busy with school activities (in particular, the course seems to have avoided the months in which school activities are over). The third element that seems to have affected the learning process effectiveness, preventing learners from properly taking advantage of the online environment, concerns the insufficient ITC equipment available in schools, both in quantitative and in qualitative terms. This is a very critical aspect, especially if we consider that many learners have not a private online connection to the web (35.4% of the sample). Finally, the work groups have been judged *too large* (several learners remember classes including 45 students), and this made tutors' management of the activities difficult, as it affected the learners' homework quality as well as their whole learning process in general. A limited number of students would allow tutors to more properly and accurately follow them, and learners to more effectively benefit from the lessons, because, quoting Rowntree, "*it cannot be reasonably expected that a tutor could manage effectively a virtual class more numerous than in an in presence one, unless all that we offer is only a computerized help-line or assistance to an help-help group*" (1995, p. 213).

These weaknesses show the difficulties inherent in the organization of a course capable to conform, as much as possible, to the personal training and professional requirements of each learner. At the same time, they underline how, sometimes, the efforts to adopt a student-centred design can meet with difficulties and problems. Very often, as it could be partly noticed also in PuntoEdu, this happens because, though technology has the potential to extend and improve educational and training activities, opposite results might be achieved not because it (technology) isn't effective, but because it does not adapt to the way people wanted to learn (Armenski and Gusev, 2005).

## Solutions and Recommendations

Apart from the considerations made about the (specific) case presented in this chapter, we would like to recommend some improvements that could be useful from two points of view. On the one hand, the aim of making PuntoEdu system as much as possible suited to learners and, on the other hand, the more general purpose of contributing to design, through the latest technologies, an easily accessible training path and a flexible course capable to be tailored on learners' personal needs.

To reach this goal, priority should be given to a preliminary in-depth evaluation of learners' actual training requirements, by investigating their cultural background and their computer skill levels. Only in this way, it will be possible to offer a system with the characteristics of a really personal learning environment, capable to allow learners independently managing their training/educational process. The challenge consists in finding an appropriate and balanced mix between effective and efficient use of the new technologies and attainment of pedagogical aims, in order to make the learning system individual and personal. This means to discover how to make it conforming as much as possible to learners' skills and learning methods and, at the same time, adaptable to their ever-changing skills and knowledge (Sharples, 2000). In particular, most of the weak points underlined by learners and tutors in PuntoEdu can be ascribed to the lack of an adaptive test system, that is to say, a computerized test aimed at accurately comparing the training level of each student with a short number of queries tailored to the characteristics of the individual learner (Wainer, 2000). This kind of system would permit to know learners' preferences, goals, previous educational experiences, and knowledge, and would prove beneficial for both learners and tutors. Learners would have the opportunity to test their knowledge basing on their own performances, goals and difficulties and to evaluate their real knowledge levels and weak points. Tutors would be able to better understand their learners' achievements and encountered difficulties, thus enhancing their teaching as well (Lazarinis, Green & Pearson, 2009). Focusing on the PuntoEdu project, this system would avoid, or, at least, reduce the frequent problems rising in connection with most learners' scarce IT and computer literacy levels, and would thereby emphasize the value of the user acceptance concept, which entails that users become well-disposed to the program and its functions. Even if a good user acceptance can be secured in the implementation process (Karlsudd, 2001), the experience made with PuntoEdu shows the importance to guarantee this aspect before the beginning of the course.

## FUTURE RESEARCH DIRECTIONS

On the basis of the main results achieved by our research, we think that new methods should be sought for testing the acceptability and impact degree of this particular learning system as regards its effects on students' learning experiences, and especially, its ability to provide a customized made-to-measure training path. We would also underline that, although changing technologies are key drivers in educational change (Attwell, 2007), the reality of learning and educational practice is not only a technical matter. In fact, technical problems are usually the main source of troubles for online learners. Being the available technological tools often unsatisfactory and insufficient, this could lead to problems in using the learning platforms. Therefore, the real challenge in educational practice must to take into account other fundamental matters. It consists more specifically in developing, implementing and establishing new learning approaches based on new teaching concepts, through an optimization of the potentialities of the new technologies. The question is to turn from theory into practice the assumptions on which the constructivist approach is based through the development of personal learning environments, student-centred design and flexible learning, in order to avoid a teacher-centred and passive learning approach as much as possible, and promote, instead, the learners' active role in learning and teaching processes.

To conclude, we think that our research can provide reliable information and suggestions on the improvements to be brought and the best practices to be considered in view of the future editions of PuntoEdu ATA, planned from 2010 onwards. In particular, the discussed results would be useful to develop an effective blended learning and to reach higher personalization levels, in order to avoid all identified weaknesses and to overcome the difficulties encountered in the last edition.

## CONCLUSION

Considering the characteristics of PuntoEdu we have described and the evaluations expressed by learners and tutors, the Italian blended-training course discussed in this chapter seems a positive example of methodological approaches combining with technological environments aimed at reaching an appropriate educational mix suitable to specific situations, and providing a double opportunity. The first concerns training path personalization: empirical research allows us saying that the effort to conceive the training material in a modular and personal way equals the advantages it brings, since it provides each student with the appropriate just-in-time training tools conforming to his/her needs. This is the powerful promise technology offers us: to give precise information to a particular person in the very moment it is required (Cabrera & Sànchez, 2009).

The second opportunity offered by PuntoEdu to learners consists in including the course in an organizational logic using online tools, in order to acquire them in their everyday professional practice and be able to solve professional problems in real time (Trentin, 2005). Therefore, PuntoEdu can be considered a bridge toward the establishment of a virtual learning professional community, supporting a potentially continuous training (Trentin, in press). This approach confirms that, nowadays, lifelong learning plays a key role in people's development, improvement and enhancement, as well as being considered a competitive factor. Besides, such a perspective departs from the Taylorist logic, which considers it a social harmonizer, rather than a medium aimed at increasing the value of human resources. While, until few years ago, traditional in-presence training, equal for everyone, gave rise to a serial and repetitive standardization of learning contents and processes, today the scenario is changed. There is an increasingly widespread awareness of how the new technologies can be used effectively in lifelong learning processes both to combine work activities with an upgrading of employees skills (Giorgetti and Palumbo, 2003), both to achieve higher flexibility and personalization levels.

Finally, the positive evaluation generally expressed by learners on the tutors' activity and on the blended -learning model, allows us saying that the alternation of online and face-to-face training modules can turn into an opportunity to combine high-tech with high-touch. In other words, the blend of these different training settings shows the potentialities of joining sophisticated technology with the possibility to get in touch with other people, a purpose that Naisbitt (1984) identifies as the key to distance-learning success. A similar concept was lately reaffirmed also by Spitzer (2001) who, by stating "don't forget the high-touch using the high-tech in distance learning", underlines the importance of the human factor also when, in distance education, advanced technologies are used (Trentin, 2004). In this sense blended learning can be appreciated, as PuntoEdu learners did, because *"it does not leave students completely alone"* (Maragliano, 2004, p. 72). Thanks to a real integration between face-to-face with online modules and the support provided by tutors in each of these different settings, this model succeeds in escaping the so-called "coldness of the virtual environment". In fact, whereas learners feel "protected" by the walls of a classroom where they are together with their school-fellows, in online training, students are left alone in front of a computer screen and need to be helped by benchmarks and signals to orient themselves.

## REFERENCES

Alexander, J. O. (1999). Collaborative design, constructivist learning, information technology immersion, & electronic communities: a case study. *Interpersonal Computing and Technology: An Electronic Journal for the 21st Century, 7*(1-2), October.

Alvino, S., & Sarti, L. (2006). Strumenti per la progettazione nell'e-learning. [TD]. *Tecnologie Didattiche*, *39*(3), 4–15.

Ardito, C., Costabile, M. F., De Marsico, M., Lanzilotti, R., Levialdi, S., Roselli, T., & Rossano, V. (2006). An Approach to Usability Evaluation of e-Learning Applications. *Universal Access in the Information Society International Journal*, *4*(3), 270–283. doi:10.1007/s10209-005-0008-6

Armenski, G., & Gusev, M. (2005). Infrastructure for e-Testing. *Facta Universitatis (NIS), Series. Electronics and Energetics*, *18*(2), 181–204.

Attwell, G. (2007). The Personal Learning Environments – the future of eLearning?. *eLearning Papers, 2*(1), January.

Barab, S. A., & Duffy, T. M. (2000). From Practice Fields to Communities of Practice. In Jonassen, D. H., & Land, S. M. (Eds.), *Land Theoretical Foundations of Learning Environments* (pp. 22–55). New York, NY: Erlbaum.

Bentley, T. (1998). *Learning beyond the classroom: education for a changing world.* London, UK: Routledge.

Berge, Z., & Collins, M. (Eds.). (1995). *Computer-Mediated Communication and the Online Classroom in Distance Learning*. Cresskill, NJ: Hampton Press.

British Secretary of State for Education and Employment. (1998). *The learning age: a renaissance for a new Britain*. London, UK: The Stationery Office.

Cabrera, I. M., & Sànchez, J. J. D. (2009). Development of e-learning contents by learning objects design. In L. Gómez Chova, D. Martí Belenguer, & I. Candel Torres (Ed.), *Proceedings of INTED2009 Conference* (pp. 2833-2838). Valencia: International Association of Technology, Education and Development (IATED).

CEC-Commission of the European Communities. (2001). *The eLearning Action Plan – Designing tomorrow's education*. COM (2001) 172 final, Bruxelles.

CEC-Commission of the European Communities. (2002). *e-Europe action plan 2005: An information society for all*. COM (2002) 263 final, Bruxelles.

Cercone, K. (2008). Characteristics of adult learners with implications for online learning design. *AACE Journal*, *16*(2), 137–159.

Collins, A., Brown, J. S., & Newman, S. E. (1989). Cognitive Apprenticeship: Teaching the crafts of reading, writing and mathematics. In Resnick, R. B. (Ed.), *Knowing, learning and instruction: Essays in honour of Robert Glaser* (pp. 453–494). Mahwah, NJ: Lawrence Erlbaum.

Creswell, J. W. (2003). *Research design: Qualitative, quantitative, and mixed approaches*. Thousand Oaks(California), CA: Sage Publications.

Cross, J. (2006). *Informal Learning: Rediscovering the Natural Pathways That Inspire Innovation and Performance*. San Francisco, CA: Pfeiffer & company.

European Parliament. (2003). E-learning 2004-2006 program. Decision No 2318/2003/EC, December, Bruxelles. Retrieved October 21, 2009, from http://europa.eu.int/eur-lex/pri/en/oj/dat/2003/l_345/l_34520031231en00090016.pdf

European Parliament. (2006). Life-long learning program 2007-2013. Decision No.1720/2006/EC, November, Bruxelles. Retrieved October 21, 2009, http://eur-lex.europa.eu/LexUriServ/site/it/oj/2006/l_327/l_32720061124it00450068.pdf

Fallows, J. (2006). Homo Conexus. *Technology Review*, July. Retrieved June 5, 2009, from www.technologyreview.com/read_article.aspx?id=17061&ch=infotech

Giorgetti, M. G., & Palumbo, M. (2003). Prefazione. In L. Stagi, & G. Vercelli (Ed.), *E-learning e formazione continua. Risorgeco: il trasferimento di buone pratiche attraverso la Fad* (pp. 9- 14). Milano, IT: FrancoAngeli.

Grabinger, R. S. (1996). Rich environments for active learning. In Jonassen, D. H. (Ed.), *Handbook of Research for Educational Communications and Technology* (pp. 665–692). New York, NY: Macmillan.

Greene, J. C., & Caracelli, V. J. (Eds.). (1997). *Advances in mixed-method evaluation: The challenges and benefits of integrating diverse paradigms*. San Francisco, CA: Jossey-Bass.

Harasim, L., Hiltz, S., Teles, L., & Turoff, M. (1995). *Learning Networks: a field guide to teaching and learning online*. Cambridge, UK: The MIT Press.

Holmberg, C. (2006). Flexibelt lärande – från korrespondensundervisning till öppna och fria studier. In L. Borgström, & P. Gougoulakis (Ed.), *Vuxenantologin. En grundbok om vuxnas lärande*. Stockholm, SW: Atlas akademi.

Jarvis, P. (1987). *Adult Learning in the Social Context*. London, UK: Croom Helm.

Karlsudd, P. (2001). *Att lära på tunna linor och bred(a) band. Pedagogik i utbildning basera på informations- och kommunikationsteknologi. Konstruktion av ett analysverktyg.* Kalmar, SW: Högskolan Kalmar.

Knowles, M. S. (1984). Introduction: the art and science of helping adults learn. In Knowles, M. S. (Ed.), *Andragogy in action: applying modern principles of adult learning* (pp. 1–21). San Francisco, CA: Jossey-Bass.

Knuth, R. A., & Cunningham, D. J. (1993). Tools for Constructivism. In Duffy, T. M., Lowyck, J., & Jonassen, D. H. (Eds.), *Designing Environment for Constructive Learning* (pp. 163–188). Berlin, DE: Springer.

Koper, R., & Oliveir, B. (2006). La rappresentazione del learning design di unità di apprendimento. Modellare attività e ruoli nei processi di apprendimento. [TD]. *Tecnologie Didattiche, 39*(3), 16–29.

Kozma, R. B. (1991). Learning with media. *Review of Educational Research, 61*(2), 179–211.

Lazarinis, F., Green, S., & Pearson, E. (2009). Multi-criteria adaptation in a personalized multimedia testing tool based on semantic technologies. *Interactive Learning Environments, 14*(1), 1–17. doi:10.1080/10494820902909459

Longmire, W. (2000). A Primer on learning objects. *Learning Circuits.* Retrieved September 10, 2008, from http://wwwlearningcircuits.org/mar2000/primer.html

Maragliano, R. (Ed.). (2004). *Pedagogie dell'e – learning.* Bari, IT: GLF Editori Laterza.

Masie, E. (2003). Making sense of learning specifications & standards: a decision maker's guide to their adoption (2nd edition). *The Masie Centre.* Retrieved February 20, 2006, from http://www.masie.com/standards/s3_2nd_edition.pdf

Mayes, T., & De Freitas, S. (2004). Review of e-learning theories, frameworks and models. Commissioned review report as part of the JISC-funded e-pedagogy desk study on e-learning models. Retrieved October 20, 2009, from http://www.jisc.ac.uk/uploaded_documents/Stage 2 Learning Models (Version 1).pdf

McCombs, B., & Vakili, D. (2005). A learner-centred framework for e-learning. *Teachers College Record, 107*(8), 1582–1600. doi:10.1111/j.1467-9620.2005.00534.x

Moore, M. G. (1983). The Individual Adult Learner. In Tight, M. (Ed.), *Adult Learning and Education* (pp. 153–168). London, UK: Croom Helm.

Moreno, F., & Bailly-Bailliere, M. (2002). *Diseño instructivo de la formación on-line.* Barcelona, ES: Ariel Educación.

Mourshed, M. M., Matipa, W. M., Kelliher, D., & Keane, M. (2002, November). *Towards interoperability: ICT in academic curricula for sustainable construction.* Paper presented at the 1st International Conference: creating a sustainable construction industry in developing countries, Stellenbosch, South Africa.

Naisbitt, J. (1984). *Megatrends: Ten New Directions Transforming Our Lives* (1st ed.). New York, NY: Warner Books Ltd.

O'Neill, G., & McMahon, T. (2005). Student-Centred Learning: What Does It Mean For Students and Lecturers? In G. O'Neill, T. McMahon, & M. McMullin (Ed.), *Emerging Issues in the Practice of University Learning and Teaching* (pp. 27-36). Dublin, IR: AISHE.

Peal, D., & Wilson, B. (2001). Activity theory and web-based training. In Khan, B. H. (Ed.), *Web-Based Training* (pp. 147–153). New Jersey, NJ: Educational Technology Publications.

Perkins, D. N. (1993). Person-plus: a distributed view of thinking and learning. In Salomon, G. (Ed.), *Distributed cognitions. Psychological and educational considerations* (pp. 88–110). Cambridge, UK: Cambridge University Press.

Piaget, J. (1970). *Science of education and the psychology of the child.* New York, NY: Orion.

Quintana, C., Carra, A., Krajcik, J., & Soloway, E. (2001). Learner-Centred Design: Reflections and New Directions. In Carroll, J. M. (Ed.), *Human-Computer Interaction in the New Millennium* (pp. 605–626). New York, NY: Addison-Wesley.

Ross, A. R. (1996). The influence of computer Communication skill on participation in a computer conference course. *Journal of Educational Computing Research, 15*(1), 37–52. doi:10.2190/6TYW-ADV1-W0LC-N9H0

Rossi, P. G. (2006). *Che cos'è l'e- Portaolio.* Roma, IT: Carocci.

Rowntree, D. (1995). Teaching and learning Online: A Correspondence Education for the 21st Century? *British Journal of Educational Technology, 26*(3), 205–215. doi:10.1111/j.1467-8535.1995.tb00342.x

Savery, J. R., & Duffy, T. M. (1995). Problem Based Learning: An instructional model and its constructivist framework. *Educational Technology, 35*(5), 31–38.

Schaffert, S. & Hilzensauer, W. (2008). On the way towards Personal Learning Environments: seven crucial aspects. *eLearning Papers*, 9, July.

Sharples, M. (2000). The design of personal mobile technologies for lifelong learning. *Computers & Education, 34*(3), 177–193. doi:10.1016/S0360-1315(99)00044-5

Spitzer, D. R. (2001). Don't forget the high-touch with the high-tech in distance learning. *Educational Technology, 41*(2), 51–55.

Stigmar, M., & Sundberg, D. (2001, July). *Teachers as reflective Learners.* Paper presented at the 26th international IUT-conference, Johannesburg, South Africa.

Tosh, D. (2005). A concept diagram for the Personal Learning Landscape. Retrieved June 1, 2007, from http://elgg.net/dtosh/weblog/398.html

Trentin, G. (2004). *Apprendimento in rete e condivisione delle conoscenze: ruolo, dinamiche e tecnologie delle comunità professionali online.* Milano, IT: FrancoAngeli.

Trentin, G. (2005). From formal to informal e-Learning through knowledge management and sharing. *Journal of e-Learning and Knowledge Society, 1*(2), 209-217.

Trentin, G. (in press). E-Learning and teaching quality. *International Journal of Instructional Media, 35*(1).

Vygotsky, L. S. (1978). *Mind in society: The development of higher psychological processes.* Boston: Harvard University press.

Wainer, H. (Ed.). (2000). *Computerized adaptive testing: A primer* (2nd ed.). Mahwah, NJ: Lawrence Erlbaum Associates.

Wiley, D. A. (2000). *The Instructional Use of Learning Objects.* Bloomington, MN: Association for Educational Communications and Technology.

WILSON, S. (2008). Patterns Of Personal Learning Environments. *Interactive Learning Environments, 16*(1), 17–34. doi:10.1080/10494820701772660

## KEY TERMS AND DEFINITIONS

**Accessibility:** A term generally referred to the ability of a product or a service of being accessible by as many people as possible. With particular regard to the Internet, the term is referred to the ability to access to the Web by all subjects, also by those with disabilities (physical or mental), providing the online system of specific elements in order to suit different needs. Specifically referring to distance education, web accessibility can be referred to the opportunity given to learners to access to the Web anytime and anywhere, overcoming the in presence training logistic and temporal limits, increasing the liberty of choosing the time and place they learn best.

**Blended Learning Model:** A learning model characterized by the combination ("blended") between face to face and distance training modules through the use of e-learning platform, implying the use of different online tools, both synchronous, both asynchronous ones. It can be conceptualized as a wide variety of technology/media integrated with conventional, face to face classroom activities in a planned manner. There are different aspects of a training course that can be designed in a blended modalities (time, space, technology, teaching approach) and the regarding decision depends on learners' features, learning objectives and available resources.

**Computer System Usability:** It refers to the easy with which people can use a computer system and the relative online tools in order to achieve a particular goal. It can be subdivided into hardware and software aspects.

**Flexible Learning:** A learning model that, allowing learner to adapt his/her training path individually choosing among different educational contents and online tools, is aimed to suit personal formative needs. It has been identified by a set of teaching and learning theories, methods and systems increasing the freedom of choice, convenience and personalization of learners, allowing them to adapt their learning process on the basis of specific needs as well as previous knowledge.

**Learner-Centred Approach:** It is an approach to education focused on students' needs, goals, abilities and learning styles, in order to let them play an active role in the learning process, instead of considering them as passive recipients of information.

**Lifelong Learning:** All learning activities undertaken throughout life, supported by formal and informal education systems, both within and outside the workplace. In general, it is designed for those who having a working career that also involves professional refresher courses, in order to adjust or improve professional skills, and it is an important tool in maintaining employability.

**Personal Learning Environment (PLE):** A learning system that supports the users in taking control of and managing autonomously their own learning processes, in order to reach learning's objectives. It is a set of tools and technologies, based on interoperability, giving the possibility of inter-communication, providing learners the opportunity to personalize learning environment to best suit their needs and modifying their own learning process, tools as well as materials.

## ENDNOTE

1. The percentages reported in the text have been obtained by adding the percentages of respondents who indicated both 5 and 6 answer options.

# Chapter 3
# Development of a Web-Based Educational Platform to Interact with Remote Mobile Robots

**Luis Payá**
*Miguel Hernández University, Spain*

**Oscar Reinoso**
*Miguel Hernández University, Spain*

**David Úbeda**
*Miguel Hernández University, Spain*

**Luis M. Jiménez**
*Miguel Hernández University, Spain*

**José M. Marín**
*Miguel Hernández University, Spain*

## ABSTRACT

*In this chapter the authors approach the problem that hand-on experiments may present in engineering studies and how Internet has become a powerful tool to improve the students' motivation, interaction and degree of learning. Also, the authors address some challenges that must be taken into account in order to improve the effectiveness of the remote laboratories. They have implemented an interactive tool so that students can monitor and control the evolution of a team of mobile robots through Internet. This platform is designed for a subject whose contents are computer vision and robotics, and it allows students to learn and practice the basic concepts on those fields and their relationship. In this chapter they present the architecture and basic features of the platform and the experiences collected during the use of it.*

DOI: 10.4018/978-1-61692-791-2.ch003

## INTRODUCTION

The experimental formation of the students plays a very important role in *engineering education*. It is necessary that students learn how to use real industry equipment to solve real problems. This way, the laboratories must provide all the necessary resources to put into practice the knowledge the student acquires in the theoretical study of the subjects. However, the traditional laboratory has a set of lacks that may limit the student's learning, such as the rigid scheduling, the limited number of equipments and the evaluation process. The students cannot experiment freely and sometimes they do not dispose of all the time they require to achieve the objectives of the practical lesson. Besides, the cost of the setting and maintenance of the laboratory is usually high, so the contents of the practical lessons will be strongly conditioned by the number of available equipments. This way, several students will have to share the same equipment and they can not experiment freely to improve their own knowledge. Apart from these facts, the traditional evaluation system is carried out through a report that is checked by the professor to verify if the student has reached the desired level of knowledge. However, the student does not know the result of the evaluation until the professor feedbacks to him the result and, in addition, in that moment the student can not modify the report delivered to improve the evaluation.

During the last years, the development and wide spreading of Internet has allowed the creation of new educational models (Dormido, 2004). A usual application of web-based techniques consists in the development of remote laboratories, which allow the students to train with real systems remotely and with a more flexible timetable. However, there are some challenges that must be addressed in order to improve the effectiveness of the remote laboratories, such as reliability, robustness, transparency and the implementation of a friendly user interface with a high degree of interactivity and feedback to the student.

The remote access to the laboratory through Internet to perform experiments solves the problems previously exposed. The students can access the laboratories in a free timetable, from their own house, and disposing of all the time they require to accomplish the aims of the lessons. Also, the students can access the systems individually, independently of the number of equipments available. At last, through an online evaluation system, the student can know the evaluation results in real time and the professor can take into account not only the final results but also the work the student has actually carried out to evaluate the practices. Even, several educative centres could share their equipments and so, the associated expenses (González-Castaño, Anido-Rifón, Vales-Alonso, Fernández-Iglesias, Llamas-Nistral et al, 2001). It is also interesting to highlight the fact that students are nowadays highly motivated to make use of and benefit from the resources available in remote environments through Internet (Stafford, 2005), and these systems can help us to remove barriers to science for people with disabilities (Colwell, Scanlon and Cooper, 2002).

In this chapter we address some examples of web-based laboratories that have been developed and their main features. The central topic of the chapter is the description of the platform we have developed to remotely access the robots in the laboratory. We present the philosophy we have followed during the design, the applications where it can be used and the experiences the students have felt during the use of the tool. Al last, we outline the future developments to be carried out on the tool to improve its functionality and interactivity.

## BACKGROUND

The information and communication technologies have been put into practice in recent years in the field of control systems teaching, with successful results, as (Dormido, 2004) shows. These technologies allow us to implement both virtual laboratories that simulate the behavior of some devices, and remote laboratories that permit us to use the real equipments available in the laboratory in a remote way.

The virtual laboratories simulate the behavior of some devices in a Web-based environment. As an example, the work of Candelas, Puente, Torres, Ortiz, Gil et al (2003) presents a platform that is capable of simulating a robot arm and also, students can teleoperate the equivalent real robot. Masár, Bischoff and Gerkes (2004) present a framework to develop virtual laboratories for use in distance education for control engineers including a virtual laboratory for an inverted pendulum and a virtual laboratory for mobile robot control through a web browser. Guzmán, Berenguer, Rodríguez and Dormido (2009) present an interactive tool for mobile robot motion planning to enhance full understanding of these algorithms by the students. Sánchez, Morilla, Dormido, Aranda and Ruipérez (2002) present a virtual laboratory using Java simulations for diverse Control learning topics. At last, Jara, Candelas, Torres, Dormido, Esquembre et al (2009) show how to build a collaborative environment where students can interact among them and with the teacher, in order to carry out practical lessons in a synchronized platform.

However, in some applications, it is difficult for the students to learn how to use real equipment just through simulation. Remote laboratories allow us to fill this gap as they offer the opportunity to use the real equipments available in the laboratory through Internet, providing the student with a continuous feedback of the state of the process. In this field, Borgolte (2008) exposes some considerations that must be taken into account for remote operation of a laboratory with a mobile robot, such as the collision avoidance, network time-outs and battery charging. Khamis, Pérez-Vernet and Schilling (2002) address a survey on the design and implementation of remote experiments on motor control of mobile robots, emphasizing on user interface enhancement through the use of virtual reality, and in (Khamis, Rivero, Rodríguez and Salichs, 2003) these concepts are set up in the 'Developer' architecture to teleoperate and control the B21r robot. New control platforms are being developed, as the one presented in (Marín, Nomdedeu, Wirz and Sanz, 2009), that introduces the control of several robots by using a PDA or mobile phone as input and presents some performance results. Jimenez, Puerto, Reinoso, Fernández and Ñeco, (2005) present a tool to carry out control systems training in a remote way, using Matlab/Simulink to test different kinds of controllers on a servomotor system.

Comparing to other approaches, the platform we have built permits the access to the robots available in the laboratory, in a transparent way for the user. The platform can easily be extended to different kinds of robots and there is a common graphical interface to access all of them. The students can monitor and control them in an intuitive way, without needing a deep knowledge of the architecture of the robot they are using. This way, the training is centered in the objectives of the subject and the students take more profit of the teaching and learning process. Also, it allows easy communication between the robots so the student can carry out some tasks that imply collaboration between the members of a team of robots to fulfill the task.

## DESCRIPTION OF THE WEB-BASED EDUCATIONAL PLATFORM

### Objectives of the Platform

We have developed a remote laboratory that allows the operation of the mobile robots available in our laboratory, in a transparent way for the user, from their own home, in a free timetable and with no limitations of time. It can be applicable to subjects about computer vision and robotics and permits accessing the mobile robots available in our laboratory, to monitor and control their evolution. Our main objective while designing this platform was to give access to the robots so that the students can test the algorithms they develop to control the robot so that it performs a determined task. We have tried to centre the focus of the experimentation in the goals of the subject (robot control and computer vision). This way, to use the platform, the student does not need any knowledge about the internal architecture of the robot to make the experimentation, and he can develop the algorithms in a high-level programming language, with the same methods, independently of the robot he wants to control.

The students can access the platform from any computer through Internet, independently of their operative system and with a very simple installation. Also, there is a common graphical interface to access all the robots, and the students can monitor and control them in an intuitive way. Also, these concepts could be extended to other kinds of robots so, we could add new environments or change one or more robots without necessity of modifying the architecture of the platform.

## Components of the System

In this section, the principles of the physical architecture of the system are presented. In the current implementation, three different working environments are available. Each working environment is composed of a WifiBot robot that has a wireless connection to the access point, and an IP camera, that provides us with a general view of the working environment. The availability of three working environments permits the simultaneous access of three students to carry out the practices. The basic structure of the platform is shown on Figure 1.

The robots can move freely in a 200x300 cm rectangular area, bounded by walls, and with some obstacles inside it. The web cam that monitors the environment is situated in the ceiling, at a distance of 300 cm from the floor. It provides up to 30 frames per second and offers a bird's eye view of the environment where the robots evolve. The platform has been developed with the Wifibot 4G robot. It is a flexible and low-performance robot that offers a wide variety of expansion possibilities at different levels, what make it suitable to the development of different practices. It is equipped with a pan-tilt camera onboard that takes images from the environment, from the point of view of the robot with a maximum resolution of 640x480 pixels. Also, each wheel has an encoder to measure each speed individually. These encoders allow us to estimate the position of the robot (after an odometer process). At last, two infrared sensors are situated in the front of the robot, with a detection range between 20 and 120 cm. These sensors can be used both for tasks of obstacle avoidance, as a safety measure and in tasks that imply following a mobile agent.

Apart from these hardware components, some other visual artificial landmarks have been situated along the environment with different purposes. The first one is a square mark situated on the floor, which can be viewed from the ceiling camera. It

*Figure 1. Basic architecture and components of the platform*

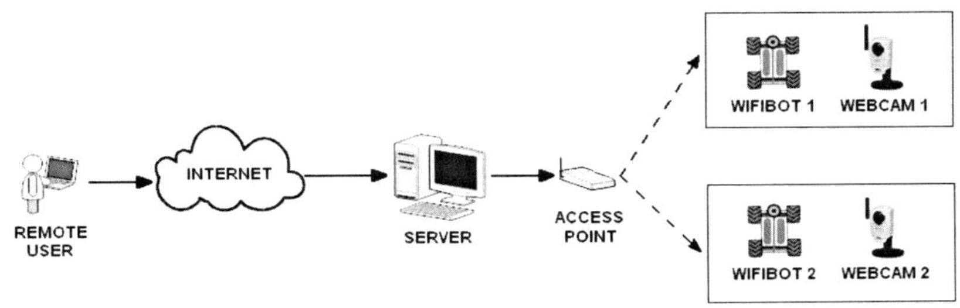

will constitute the target point where the robot has to tend in some tasks. The second mark consists in two circles with different size, situated at the top of the robot. Thanks to it, we can draw the trajectory and orientation of the robot from a set of frames captured from the ceiling camera. The last mark consists in four small circles situated at the vertexes of a square. It can be viewed from the robot camera. The students have to detect it in a practical session with a computer vision process and situate the robot at a relative position from it.

Besides, there is a PC that is connected to the network of the laboratory where some basic services run, such as the web server, where the client application is available so that the students can download and install it in their computers, the identity server, which acts as the base of the communications system we have implemented and the SQL server, used to implement several safety mechanisms such as the restriction to the access and a record of all the actions each user has carried out with each robot.

## Software Architecture

The communication needs have been solved through the use of two different communication protocols: CORBA and SSH communications.

**CORBA Communications**. The communication between the different members of the system has been implemented using the CORBA (Control Object Request Broker Architecture) reference model. CORBA (OMG, 1995) provides an object-oriented methodology defined for the implementation of distributed applications. It will constitute the reference model used in the general design of the platform. Two fundamental features of CORBA are:

- Separation between interface and implementation. The interfaces of the objects are specified in a language specially defined with this goal, IDL (Interface Definition Language), which is part of the CORBA standard. IDL isolates the interface of the object from its implementation, offering more portability and interoperability this way.
- Independence of the location. An object offers services through its operations and attributes, which are visible through its interface. The clients can require the accomplishment of certain operations over an object with independence of its location. The element that allows this transparency in the location and access to the objects is ORB (Object Request Broker).

Then, a CORBA architecture allows a client application to make operations over a CORBA object, that resides in a server. The implementations of the objects that are in the server side define the methods that implement the IDL interfaces. These objects can be implemented in different programming languages. This standard has been used in similar tasks of communication, resulting efficient to interchange information in a team of heterogeneous robots in RoboCup F2000 league (Utz, Stulp and Moeld, 2004). Also, it has demonstrated its robustness and efficiency in the implementation of other previous distributed applications (Gonzalez-Castaño et al, 2001; Payá, Juliá, Reinoso, Gil and Jiménez, 2006; Payá, Reinoso, Gil and Jiménez, 2007). The main components of the communication network are:

**Onboard Servers**. Each robot has been equipped with an onboard PC where the necessary services to access the sensors and actuators of the robots run. These services have been implemented through several CORBA interfaces. Thanks to these interfaces, the student will be able to monitor the state of all the sensors (infrared sensors and odometer data) and to control the movement of the robot (starting movement, setting up an advance/steering speed and stopping the robot). Also, an interface has been implemented to get the visual data both from the camera each robot has on it and from the ceiling camera.

**Identity Server**. This server constitutes the basis for the correct functioning of the system. It runs in a PC that is connected to the laboratory network, whose IP is the only piece of information the rest of the components of the system must know to correctly establish the communications between them. Apart from acting as a bridge between the rest of the members of the application, it has two main functions. Firstly, it is in charge of keeping a list of all the robots and the cameras that are active at each moment in the system, taking into account which environment they belong to and which services they offer. Secondly, this server carries out an access control from the client applications to the robots. This access control is carried out through a reservations system, where the student can reserve some slots of time with a determined duration. During these periods of time, the student has the right to freely access the system to make the necessary experiments. When this time finishes, if the next time slot is reserved by another student, the first one is disconnected. With this system, students have not to wait an environment to be free and the system is not monopolized by a student during a long period of time.

**Client Application**. The client application has been developed entirely using the programming language **JAVA**. Thanks to it, this application can be run on any computer, independently of its architecture and operative system. Also, java supports CORBA in a native way, what means that the client application can interact with the CORBA services developed in the laboratory side (both those offered by the robots and those offered by the cameras and the identity server). Thank to the use of CORBA, the student can access the system from any computer that has Internet access.

The appearance of the client application is a graphical interface from which the student can monitor the state of the robots and send commands to move them. The functionality of this application is explained deeply in the following section. The implementation of the client application has been carried out through Java Web Start. This technology permits starting Java applications that reside in a web server, checking first if the version of the application the client has installed is the latest one. If not, it downloads the newest version and the application will run in local mode. The starting of such applications can be carried out from a web page or through a link in the client desktop. Thanks to this technology, we can be sure that an application is always distributed with its most up to date version. The only condition the client computer has to meet to make use of the application is to dispose of the last distribution of JRE (Java Runtime Environment).

In brief, the sequence of operation is the following one; at first, it is necessary that the Identity server is running. After this, the onboard servers of the robots must be activated. When one of these servers starts, it publishes the name of the available robot and the interfaces it implements in the identity server. When a client application wants to access the services a robot offers, it first makes a request to the identity server, indicating the symbolic name of the robot and the interfaces it wants to access. If the robot is available at that moment, the Identity Server provides the client application with the references to the interfaces the robot implements. From that moment, the communication is carried out in a bidirectional way between the client application and the onboard server of the robot. In a typical mode of operation, the client application sends some requests to capture data from the sensors and movement commands to the motors.

**SSH Communications**. To solve some complicated tasks with the robots, the student has to write an algorithm (in a high-level programming language), to download it to the robot he is operating, to compile and to run it. To achieve these goals, a second level of communications, using SSH, has been developed. To integrate these communications in the client application, the Java library JSch has been used. This library allows us to integrate the functionality of the SSH protocol in the application. Basically, SSH gives support for a reliable remote access and file transfer. It can encrypt, authenticate and compress the data transmitted automatically. More specifically, we have used a JSch function to send the file that contains the source code from the user's computer to the computer in the laboratory where it will be compiled and run, and other function to run commands in a remote way. As a result, we can compile remotely the source code and show the results of the compilation to the student. If the compilation has been carried out successfully, the program can be run and otherwise, the student should correct the source code and send it again to the remote machine. Thanks to this programming methodology, the student does not need to install any library in his computer. However, the depuration of possible errors becomes a slow process due to the fact that the source code must be sent several times until all the possible errors have been solved.

## Graphical Interface

Figure 2 shows the appearance of the client application. From this graphical interface, the student is able to continuously see the images both from the ceiling camera and the robot camera. The amount of frames per second is configurable to avoid the saturation of the network. Also, both video panels have a button associated so that the student can capture snapshots and save them in JPEG format, during the development of the task. This window also provides the student with basic commands to control the movement of the robot. Through the arrow buttons, the student can make the robot go ahead, go backwards, turn left or turn right. Also the numerical current values of the advance and steering speeds and the infrared sensors are shown.

When the student starts running this application, the first task consists in getting the control of a working environment (in the case he has made a reservation or any of them is available). This option is accessible from the 'Connection' menu. It gives access to a window where the student has to introduce the login and password he has been assigned to access the system. If these data are correct, the system looks for an available environment and gives its control to the student. Once this step is completed, the student can control the robot with the basic commands in the graphical interface.

However, the basic control buttons the graphical interface puts at the student's disposal are not always enough to solve a complicated task

*Figure 2. Graphical interface for the monitoring and control of the robots*

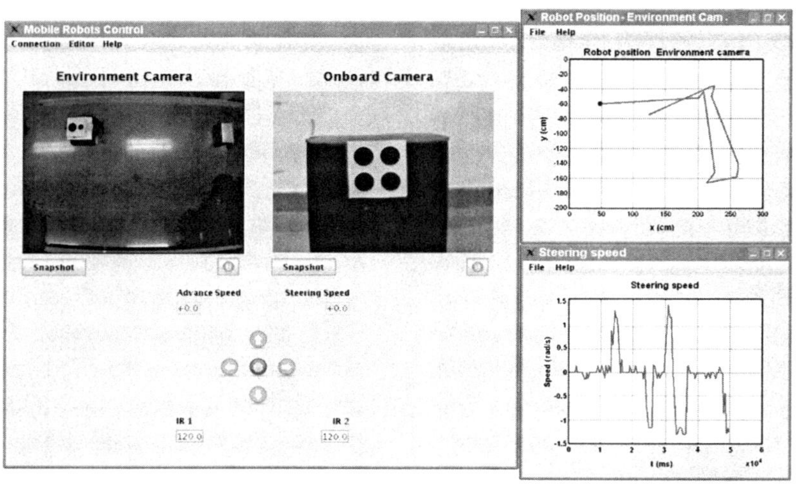

that may include both image analysis and robot control. In this case, the student has to develop a control algorithm in a high level language (C language in this case) and he has to compile and run it in the remote environment, and monitor the task. This process can be carried out through the 'Editor' menu. This option opens a window where the student can write, send, compile the program and see the error messages produced during the process. This compilation is carried out in the server.

At the end of the task, the student will usually need to plot some variables, such as the trajectory of the robot or the value of the infrared sensors. Using the top menus, the user can decide which data he wants to save while the application is running and the name of the files where these data have to be saved. Also, the application allows the user to visualize some data in real time, while the robot is performing the task, as shown on Figure 2. These options are accessible from the 'Send' menu.

Several protection measures have been implemented. First, a SQL database has been implemented to restrict the access to the application only to those users that have been previously registered in the database, through a login and a password. This verification is carried out before checking which robots are available in that moment. Secondly, this database also registers all the actions the users have carried out in the system, from the verification of the student until he leaves the system and the environment is released. Apart from this safety measure, another prevention mechanism has been implemented to avoid malfunction of the robots. To do it, an independent thread has been programmed. This thread runs concurrently with the user program and it is in charge of monitoring the advance and steering speeds of the robot, the infrared sensors and the batteries level. In case that any speed is over a threshold, or the robot has a wall or obstacle very near, this thread can stop the robot and reinitialize the algorithm. If the battery level goes under a threshold, the robot is stopped and the student is assigned a different environment to test the algorithm.

## Contents of the Practical Sessions

Several practical sessions are proposed to the students to be carried out through this platform. As exposed before, this platform is devoted to the study of computer vision, mobile robots and the relationship between them. In this section, we detail the kind of practical sessions we could develop with the platform, and the specific contents the students could learn by means of the tool. Some of these possible contents are:

**Computer Vision and Image Processing**. The students must use *OpenCv* as a tool for image processing. By means of this tool the students must acquire the references of the images to make the proposed practices. *OpenCV* is an open source computer vision library originally developed by Intel. It is free for research use under a BSD (Berkeley Software Distribution) license. The library is cross-platform, and runs on Mac OS X, Windows and Linux. It focuses mainly towards real-time image processing. Currently, this library supports some features such as: real-time capture, video file import, basic image treatment (brightness, contrast, thresholding, etc.), object detection (face, body, etc.) and blob detection.

Students make use of the *OpenCV* library to address various image processing algorithms in the practices proposed. In this way, it is necessary for students to develop and implement a set of image processing algorithms in order to tackle the practical suggested. Some of the basic processing algorithms are the following:

- **Image acquisition:** The first operation that user has to accomplish consists in acquiring the images from the camera. We provide the student with a template with the necessary code to capture an image. The student has to work on this template to make the capture and to make the necessary analysis over the image.

- **Segmentation:** The purpose of the segmentation in a digital image is to distinguish between the objects of interest and the rest of the image or background. Image segmentation is typically used to locate objects and boundaries (lines, curves, etc.) in images. The result of image segmentation is a set of objects differentiated from the rest of the image (background). Some of the more common segmentation algorithms provided by the *OpenCV* library are thresholding, edge finding and mathematical morphology.
- **Location:** Other activity the student must carry out over the image acquired by the robot consists in the localization of some features of the image in order to estimate the position of some objects in the image. *OpenCv* has implemented some utilities to accomplish the location procedure.
- **Image Features Extraction:** The concept of feature or visual landmark is used in computer vision to denote a characteristic in an image that could be extracted and it is relevant with regards to the background of the image. Features can refer to a neighborhood operation, by means of a feature extractor/detector applied to the image or by means of specific structures in the image itself such as points or edges or more complex structures. In the proposed practices the robots must recognize on the acquired images a set of features. From these features the robot must be capable to determine the location of the object or the location of the other robot that incorporates such features. So, a visual landmark may be defined as a significant point in the space that can be detected using images captured from the environment. The desired properties of a visual landmark are:
    - Invariance to viewpoint changes: That is, the same interest points should be detected from different viewing angles and distances (scale).
    - Spatial stability: When computing a relative measurement with a stereo camera, the accuracy in the detection of the point in both images highly influences in the result.
    - Independence to illumination conditions.

However, in the proposed practices it is not necessary to implement complex feature detectors due to the images acquired by the robot in the environment are very clear. Simple algorithms of feature detection can be used to extract the position of the objects in the environment: obstacles, target point or other robots. Some of these feature detectors proposed in the practices are the following:

- Harris Detector: The Harris Corner Detector (Mikolajczyk and Schmid, 1994) is probably the most widely interest point detector used, due to its strong invariance to scale, rotation, lighting variation and image noise. It is based on the following matrix *C(x; y)* which is computed over a *pxp* patch for each interest point at position *(x; y)*.

$$C(x,y) = \begin{pmatrix} \sum I_x^2 & \sum I_x I_y \\ \sum I_x I_y & \sum I_y^2 \end{pmatrix}$$

where $I_x$, $I_y$ are the image gradients in horizontal and vertical direction. Let $\lambda_1$ and $\lambda_2$ be the eigenvalues of the matrix *C(x; y)*, the auto-correlation function *R* will be sharply peaked if both of the eigenvalues are high. This means that shifts in any direction will produce a significant increase, indicating that it is a corner.

$$R = \lambda_1\lambda_2 - k\left(\lambda_1 + \lambda_2\right)$$

Some authors have used this detector with good experimental results with $k = 0.04$. This is the case of Davidson and Murray (2002) where a Harris Corner Detector with a *15x15* patch is used.

- Good Features to Track Detector. This feature detector determines which image points are sufficiently characteristic and easily recognizable to be easy to track (Shi & Tomasi, 1994). It finds corners with big eigenvalues in the image. In the first step the minimum eigenvalues for each pixel of the image source are calculated, and it performs an expansion (only the maximum remains in a local *3x3* neighborhood). The next step consists in discarding the corners whose eigenvalues take a value under a certain threshold (the minimum quality accepted for the characteristic points of the image). Finally, the function ensures that all the corners found are sufficiently different from each other, taking the two most distinctive and checking that the distance between the points is appropriate. If not, the point is discarded.

**Mobile Robotics**: In the field of *mobile robotics*, this platform allows the student to develop algorithms to get used with some concepts studied during the theoretical classes. First, students can get familiarized with some typical sensors in mobile robotics, such as encoders, infrared sensors and cameras. The first task each student should carry out consists in moving the robot with the arrow buttons, with a random movement, and get sure he can read the data from all the sensors and can interpret correctly them. A very interesting proof they can make consists in studying how they can integrate the data from the encoders to get the trajectory of the robot and how these data behave when the robot slips while it is turning. They could also make a calibration of the infrared sensors to know how they behave depending on the distance the obstacle is from the robot.

When a mobile robot has to carry out a task, from the point of view of the planning, there are several kinds of architectures to design the algorithm to control the robot. On the one side, the first type includes those architectures that try to make a strategic plan of the task, using a model of the environment with high precision. These are purely deliberative architectures that are based on a centralized planning. After reading the measures of the sensors, a sequence of actions is planned and generated. On the other side, the other type of architecture, known as reactive, is much more flexible and adaptable to new conditions in the robot or environment. This system is based on a set of rules that contains information about how the robot has to behave depending on the readings of the sensors. No internal model is present, only an appropriate action for each set of sensors readings. A third type, that situates between the two commented, is constituted by the behavior-based architectures. Those behaviors describe how the robot reacts given a value of the sensory data. The final control action depends on the concurrent running of several behaviors. The hybrid architectures offer a compromise between those purely reactive and the deliberative ones. A reactive system is used to carry out a low-level control and a planner takes decisions in a higher lever. It is usual that the reactive process is in charge of safety functions, and the high level one uses a planner to plan the action to carry out.

Also, with this tool, students can practice with the motion control of a robot. The objective of motion control is that the vehicle makes movements previously planned so that he can react in an appropriate way to the perception from the environment. This problem can be tacked from the point of view or the control theory. Taking into account the mathematical model of the vehicle, the student has to design the necessary controller to stabilize the vehicle over a working point or following a reference trajectory, while it compensates the effect of perturbations or obstacles. The platform allows making the necessary experiments to identify the model of the vehicle, to design and implement the control algorithm and to monitor the behavior of the robot while carrying out the final task.

**Visual Control of a Mobile Robot**. The third field of application is in the visual control of a robot, where the data extracted from the images of a camera are used to control the movement of the robot. In this field, the information from the ceiling cameras can be used to carry out the localization of the robot within the environment. From a sequence of images from the ceiling camera, and using some of the Image Processing algorithms previously exposed, the trajectory of the robot can be deducted. Also, the onboard camera can be used for different tasks. As an example, a database can be created with some images along the environment. These images could constitute a map where the robot could localize using the visual information it is currently capturing. The student could use two different approaches with this aim: the model-based one, based on the extraction of a set of relevant points or features from the image, or the appearance-based model, that tries to work with the images as a whole to make the necessary comparisons. Also, the onboard camera could be used in tracking tasks, in which the robot has to situate itself at a determined relative position and orientation from an object in the environment, or has to follow a mobile agent from a relative distance.

## Pedagogical Approach

The experience has been developed in the Miguel Hernandez University, Elche (Spain), with the Industrial Engineering students, in a fourth year subject about Computer Vision and Robotics, during the academic year 2007/2008. 42 students took part in the experience, and it lasted six weeks, starting the first week of May, 2008.

The experience starts from an instructional pedagogical design that combines presence theoretical classes and computer-based distance training. The steps we propose to follow during the development of the subject are:

1. Motivation and orientation of the students. Presentation of real cases of study and application as a framework to the contents of the subject.
2. Theoretical study of the most popular algorithms in computer vision and mobile robots.
3. Identification of the practical problem to solve in the laboratory while getting used with the material to use.
4. Resolution of simple cases via web.
5. Design of a complex control algorithm. Test of the performance of the system via web.
6. Feedback of the results obtained and experience collected to the lecturers.

Points 4 and 5 involve computer-based distance training. The web-based educational platform presented has been developed with the aim of covering these two points. With this aim, currently, there are three different practical sessions available.

**Session 1: Basic Control of the Robot:** The student must create a program so that the robot moves forward, describing a straight line. The robot must avoid the obstacles it finds in its way, and it must stop when it has travelled a distance of three meters. The student has to make use of the infrared sensors (to detect the presence of obstacles), of the odometer data (to compute the position of the robot and the distance it has travelled) and of the images captured by the ceiling camera (to know the position of the robot at each moment and compare it with the results computed using the odometer data). In general, the robot has to move straight, and it has to describe a 90º arc when it finds an obstacle. The robot must turn to the side where the obstacle is farthest from, and finally, it must stop when the distance it has travelled is higher than three meters. To compute this distance, the student is provided with a function that integrates the odometer data and that returns the coordinates of the robot with respect to the initial position.

This problem can be solved using several control strategies, such as reactive control, or behavior-based control. From the point of view of behaviors, the problem could be solved using a competitive coordination of two behaviours, 'Go straight' and 'Turn'. The students are advised to design a flow chart of the task before writing the program.

Once the robot has fulfilled the task, the student has to make a graphical representation of the path the robot has followed, using the odometer data. After this, the student must draw the same trajectory, but computed from the information provided by the external camera. A comparison and a critical analysis of the results is demanded. Figure 3 shows two typical graphical representations the student could make to show the development of the task: (a) Robot position, computed from an external point of view (ceiling camera) and (b) robot position, computed from an internal point of view (integration of the odometer data). The student has to comment the difference between them, and the reason why the odometer data are sometimes wrong and how the help of an external point of view is absolutely necessary to know with precision the position of the robot.

The main objective of this session is to get used to work with the robot through the platform through a quite simple application. Also, the student will empower the knowledge in robotics control. This way, we provide the students with some templates to develop the algorithm, and with some methods they can use in their programs. As an example, there is a specific function that computes the position of the robot using the information of the ceiling camera.

**Session 2: Going to a Target Point:** Taking as a basis the previous exercise, the student must make the necessary changes in the program so that the robot moves from its initial position to a target point, trying to avoid the obstacles it finds in its way. An artificial landmark on the target point indicates its situation. This landmark can be viewed from the ceiling camera so, analysing the images of this camera, its position can be inferred. As in the previous exercise, the robot must move straight to the target point, turning when it finds an obstacle. Once the obstacle has been surpassed, the robot must orientate again to the target point and move straight to reach it. This problem can also be approached from the point of view of any of the existing control strategies: deliberative,

*Figure 3. Some results after running the algorithm designed to solver the practical session 1. (a) robot trajectory, computed from the ceiling camera data and (b) robot trajectory computed through the integration of the odometer data.*

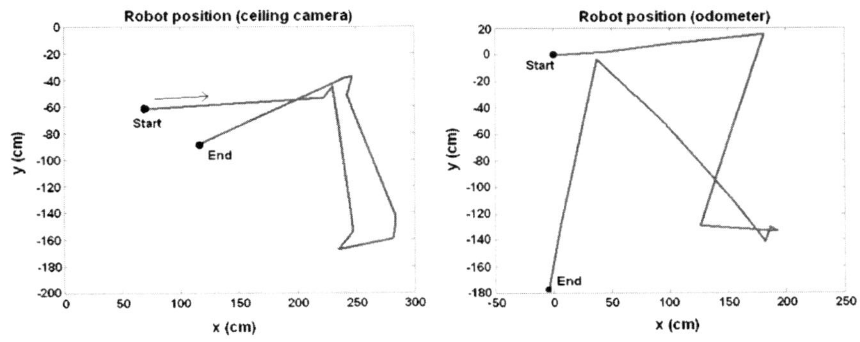

*Figure 4. Sequence of visual operations to extract the position of the target point. (a) Original colored image as captured by the ceiling camera, (b) intensity image, (c) binary image, after a thresholding process, (d) segmentation of contours on the image and (e) extraction of the target contour after a shape and area test.*

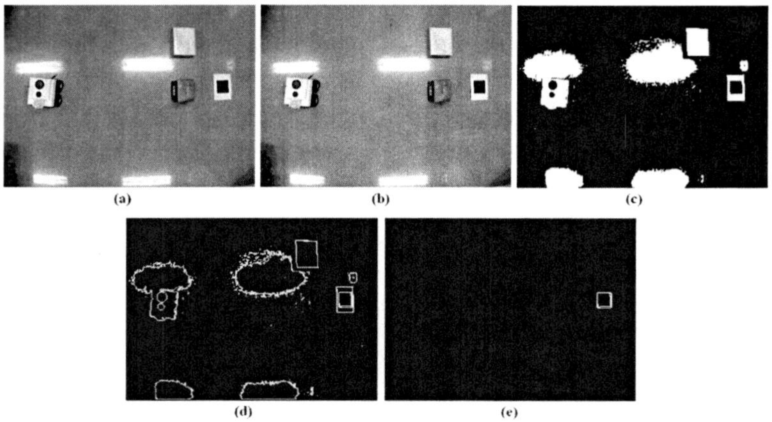


reactive or hybrid. Figure 4 shows, step by step, the image analysis each student must carry out to extract the coordinates of the target point.

**Session 3: Visual Control of the Robot:** The goal of this session is to introduce the concepts of visual control of a robot. The student has to make use of the *OpenCV* library, which includes interesting functions for image manipulation. In the working environments where the robots move, there are some visual marks that are visible from the camera each robot carries on it. Firstly, the robot must move with a random movement, trying to avoid the obstacles, until one of these marks appears in its visual field. From this moment, the robot has to try to situate at a determined distance from the mark, and it must stop when this goal is achieved. We propose the students to solve the problem using competitive coordination of the behaviours 'Random movement' and 'Go to mark'. Only one of these behaviours must be active at the same time depending on the presence of the mark in the visual field of the robot.

After the third session, the student is able to solve a complete problem that involves computer vision and mobile robots, from the first approach to the critical analysis of the results obtained and comparison between different alternatives. The student will also know a standard tool to carry out operations with images (*OpenCV*).

The evaluation method we have used in the subject is twofold. On the one side, the theoretical knowledge of the algorithms in computer vision and mobile robots is tested through a presence final written exam. On the other side, the performance during the training sessions is evaluated through a final report each student must deliver to the lecturer. In this report, the student must include the algorithm developed thoroughly commented and explained, the graphical representations necessary to understand the development of the task (robot trajectory, velocity, evolution of the infrared measures, etc.), critical comments about the results obtained and any other personal comment that could help to improve the contents of the practical sessions in future academic years. The student must deliver this report to the lecturer and also, he must expose it in some face-to-face tutorial sessions.

## Students' Experience

The experience has been developed during the academic year 2007/2008. Each practical session was open to the students during two weeks so, the entire experience lasted six weeks. The number of students who started this experience was 42. All of them completed the first and the second sessions. However, two of them didn't complete the third session so the total number of students who completed the training period of the subject was 40, i.e. 95% of the students completed it. This is a quite good result comparing with the previous year, when only 77% of the students completed all the sessions.

To analyze the experience of the students with the platform, we must take into account that, the previous year, session 1 and session 2 took three laboratory hours each and session 3 was devoted six hours. The students worked in three-people groups, and we observed that, some students, who hadn't a high degree of initiative, didn't handle the robot. With the platform, each student handles the robot individually.

Figure 5 shows the evolution of the average period of time the students devoted to each one of the designed practical sessions with the remote system. As we can observe, the average amount of time they devoted is clearly higher comparing to the time they devoted in the presence ones carried out the previous year. Students are considerably more predisposed to carry out the exercises, and they don't really care the amount of time they devote to complete the task and to fully understand it. Also, we must highlight the fact that almost all students carried out all the practical sessions. Only two students abandoned before completing session 3. In average, students have devoted 3.63 hours to session 1, 3.31 to session 2 and 7.50 to session 3.

Figure 6 shows the number of sessions each student has started to complete the task. These data put into relief that, in average, students prefer to carry out the sessions in different periods of time, instead of being connected a considerably long period, what really differs from the method used in the previous years. Obviously, these data might be distorted by the fact that when the number of request to access the systems is high. In this case the system limits the time the platform can be took up by one student.

Although it is not possible to check in the long term the advantage of carrying out the practical sessions remotely, we can observe a higher degree of predisposition in the students. Also, the periodic surveys the students fill in show their high motivation to complete their formation with this kind of remote laboratories.

After the last session, all the students who took part in this practical system filled in a questionnaire, where they expressed their general opinion about the new system. In general, students found the tool ease of use and useful to understand the theoretical concepts of the subject. They also liked the feedback information received about the

*Figure 5. Average number of hours each student has devoted to the realization of each practical session*

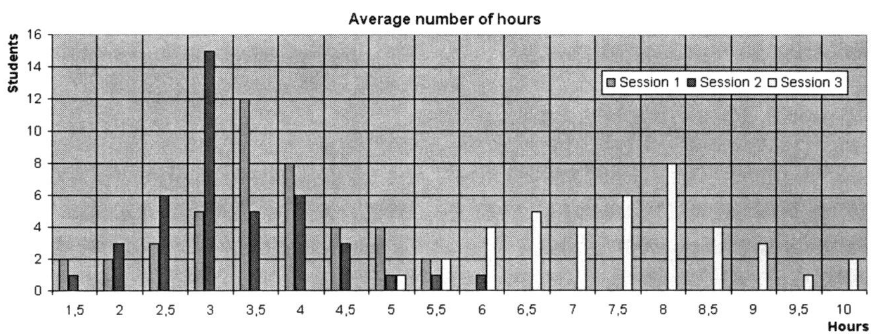

*Figure 6. Number of sessions started out by the students to complete each practical session*

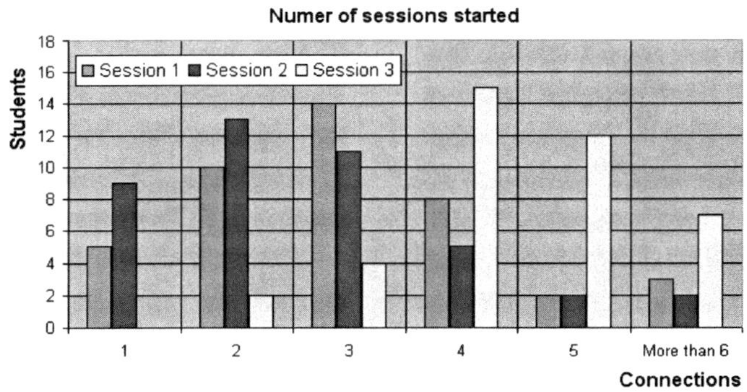


behaviour of the robot and the degree of interactivity the platform permits. Actually, they found it a quite good tool to reinforce the theoretical concepts they study in the classroom. They assessed especially well the degree of flexibility this platform offered, comparing to other practical sessions that require physical presence, and the freedom of access, that adapts to their pace of learning. On the other hand, they criticised the fact that, the days before the deadline to present the results of each session, they had problems to reserve the time slot they desired, because most of them where busy. Also, they would have preferred to have a first physical contact with the robot before starting the web sessions, to have a better knowledge of the equipments and the way they work. Sometimes, they reported some punctual problems of the system during the performance of the robot, such as battery problems, that must be solved in a future. However, in general, the experience has been satisfactory for the students.

## FUTURE RESEARCH DIRECTIONS

This chapter has presented a system to carry out practical lessons through Internet, what presents numerous advantages both from the students' and the lecturers' point of view. However, it must be taken into account the fact that, despite information and communication techniques in education are rapidly spreading, nowadays teachers and students are still mainly used to face to face methods. This way, the adaptation to new student-centered learning environments is a complex process that has to be analyzed and discussed in deep. The past experiences of the students must be definitely taken into account when setting up a web-based environment in the educational process.

Many issues have to be taken into account while designing and setting up a web-based system. Among them, interactivity and autonomy constitute two fundamental features in knowledge acquisition. They increase the depth of learning or understanding because they help learners to develop an active relationship with the material (Evans and Gibbons, 2007). The student is allowed to deepen in the concepts he considers more necessary or he is interested in particularly, at the pace his theoretical basis or previous preparation allows him. However, we must try to avoid an excessive technological complexity that would displace the focus of attention of the student. This fact has to be analyzed to know which percentage of the time the student is connected is really spent learning the objectives of the subject.

Dealing with real equipment makes the students aware of the practical application of the theoretical knowledge they have received. In short, the student gets more involved in the teaching and learning process and takes more profit of it. This degree of motivation should be compared in both situations (remote and presence), and anyway, the student must be aware of the fact that the use of the real equipment could be slightly different comparing to the remote use, basically due to the help tools we have implemented to make the tasks easier.

The model presented has proved to be a good mechanism to improve the knowledge in some concepts of computer vision and mobile robotics. From the point of view of the lecturers, it has presented a great advantage because their physical presence has not been necessary during the development of the sessions. However, during the first year, the platform has presented several technical problems that have had to be solved quickly. The general impression is that, when these small technical problems are fully debugged, it will be a very powerful system the student will be able to use without the technical support of the teacher, so, the lecturers' efforts will be centered in the contents and objectives of the subject.

The lecturers also agree in the fact that thanks to this tool, the students have shown a higher level of interest and implication in the subject. All the students work with the robots during the training, they have no pressure about the time they dispose to achieve the objectives and, at last, they generally get better marks in the final exam, comparing to previous years.

However, from the point of view of the lecturers it must be considered the fact that it may not be enough to fully understand these fields just via web. This feature should be studied and maybe, some presence support classes should be scheduled to enhance the educational process. In this sense, the adaptation to this method has been quite a hard procedure, due mainly to the fact that our students were more used to face to face classes. Other problem we have reported is the high dependence students present from the platform/interface. In this model, we also lack a more social-constructivist approach where the students could interact among them to take more profit of the experience. We are now studying how we could integrate the platform in a collaborative pedagogical model.

Anyway, the model presented has promising features that make it applicable to other fields of knowledge. It will definitely help to set up new teaching methodologies that empower the autonomy and the independency of the students.

## CONCLUSION

This chapter has presented an interactive tool we have implemented so that students can monitor and control the evolution of a team of mobile robots through Internet. With this platform, they can deepen in the knowledge of basic concepts of mobile robots, computer vision and their relationship. The practical sessions we have proposed cover the most important areas of knowledge in these fields, and allow students testing the algorithms in a real robotic platform without a deep knowledge of its architecture.

Several servers have been implemented so that the students can operate the robots in a transparent way, independently of the internal architecture of the robot. Also, these concepts could be extended to other kinds of robots so, we could add new environments or change one or more robots without necessity of modifying neither the Identity Server nor the Client Application. The student has a continuous feedback of the task to get sure it is being performed correctly. At the end of the task, he can plot the necessary data to study how the process has been developed. As CORBA constitutes an intrinsically open philosophy, the design of the laboratory admits future expansion easily, so new robots or sensors could be added just by inheriting the properties of the existing objects. This way, the use of this platform is not only limited to educational purposes but it also can be applied to other research and development activities.

The platform developed presents several benefits both for the student, for the lecturer and for the academic institution. The student benefits from the geographical, temporal and platform independence, in a system that empowers his autonomy, motivation and cooperation with other students and lecturers, and he accesses through simple and friendly interface. It also allows the lecturer putting at the disposal of the students a tool to fully understand the theoretical concepts and the academic institution takes profit of the saving that supposes the fact of not needing full equipment per each student in the laboratory.

The experience we have collected during the development of the practical sessions has been very fruitful. Students have demonstrated to be very motivated to learn in this way, as this tool allows them to establish their own learning pace and gives them autonomy to develop the proposed tasks. In general, the students have devoted more time to develop the practices and have taken more profit from them, comparing to the presence method. They have found the experience quite interesting, fruitful and they have shown their predisposition to use this kind of methods.

## REFERENCES

Borgolte, U. (2008). Considerations on a remotely operable mobile robot laboratory. Proceedings of Virtual University 2008, Bratislava, Slovakia.

Candelas, F. A., Puente, S. R., Torres, F., Ortiz, F., Gil, F., & Pomares, J. (2003). A virtual laboratory for teaching robotics. *International Journal of Engineering Education*, *19*(3), 363–370.

Colwell, C., Scanlon, E., & Cooper, M. (2002). Using remote laboratories to extend access to science and engineering. *Computers & Education*, *38*(1-3), 65–76. doi:10.1016/S0360-1315(01)00077-X

Davidson, A., & Murray, D. (2002). Simultaneous localisation and Map-Building using active vision. *IEEE Transactions on Pattern Analysis and Machine Intelligence*, *24*(7), 865–880. doi:10.1109/TPAMI.2002.1017615

Dormido, S. (2004). Control learning: present and future. *Annual Reviews in Control*, *28*(1), 115–136. doi:10.1016/j.arcontrol.2003.12.002

Evans, C., & Gibbons, N. (2007). The interactivity effect in multimedia learning. *Computers & Education*, *49*(4), 1147–1160. doi:10.1016/j.compedu.2006.01.008

González-Castaño, F. J., Anido-Rifón, L., Vales-Alonso, J., Fernández-Iglesias, M. J., Llamas-Nistal, M., Rodríguez-Hernández, P., & Pousada-Carballo, J. M. (2001). Internet access to real equipment at computer architecture laboratories using the Java/CORBA paradigm. *Computers & Education*, *36*(2), 151–170. doi:10.1016/S0360-1315(00)00056-7

Guzman, J. L., Berenguer, M., Rodriguez, F., & Dormido, S. (2009). An interactive tool for mobile robot motion planning. *Robotics and Autonomous Systems*, *56*(5), 396–409. doi:10.1016/j.robot.2007.10.001

Jara, C. A., Candelas, F. A., Torres, F., Dormido, S., Esquembre, F., & Reinoso, O. (2009). Real-time collaboration of virtual laboratories through the Internet. *Computers & Education*, *52*(1), 126–140. doi:10.1016/j.compedu.2008.07.007

Jiménez, L. M., Puerto, R., Reinoso, O., Fernández, C., & Ñeco, R. (2005). Recolab: laboratorio remoto de control utilizando Matlab y Simulink. RIAI. *Revista Iberoamericana de Automática e Informática Industrial*, *2*(2), 67–72.

Khamis, A., Pérez-Vernet, M., & Schilling, K. (2002). A remote experiment on motor control of mobile robots. Proceedings of 10th Mediterranean Conference on Control and Automation, Lisbon, Portugal.

Khamis, A., Rivero, D. M., Rodríguez, F., & Salichs, M. (2003). Pattern-based architecture for building mobile robotics remote laboratories. Proceedings of IEEE International Conference on Robotics and Automation, Taipei, Taiwan.

Marín, R., Nomdedeu, L., Wirz, R., & Sanz, P. J. (2009). Robotics Internet Tele-Lab: programming using mobile devices. Proceedings of Inernational. Conference on Multimedia and ICT in Education, Lisbon, Portugal.

Masár, I., Bischoff, A., & Gerkes, M. (2004). Remote experimentation in distance education for control engineers. Proceedings of Virtual University 2004, Bratislava, Slovakia.

Mikolajczyk, K., & Schmid, C. (2005). A performance Evaluation of Local Descriptors. *IEEE Transactions on Pattern Analysis and Machine Intelligence*, *27*(10), 1615–1630. doi:10.1109/TPAMI.2005.188

OMG, Object Management Group. Common Object Request Broker: Architecture and Specification. Revision 2.0. (1995).

Payá, L., Juliá, M., Reinoso, O., Gil, A., & Jiménez, L. M. (2006). Behaviour-based multi-robot formations using computer vision. Proceedings of 6th IASTED International Conference on Visualization, Imaging and Image Processing, Palma de Mallorca, Spain.

Payá, L., Reinoso, O., Gil, A., & Jiménez, L. M. (2007). Plataforma distribuida para la realización de prácticas de robótica móvil a través de Internet. *Información Tecnológica*, *18*(1), 27–38.

Sánchez, J., Morilla, F., Dormido, S., Aranda, J., & Ruipérez, P. (2002). Virtual control lab using Java and Matlab: A qualitative approach. *IEEE Control Systems Magazine*, *22*(2), 8–20. doi:10.1109/37.993309

Shi, J., & Tomasi, C. (1994). Good features to track. *Proceedings of Computer Vision and Pattern Recognition*, 593-600, Seattle, USA.

Stafford, R. F. (2005). Understanding motivations for Internet use in distance education. *IEEE Transactions on Education*, *49*(2), 301–306. doi:10.1109/TE.2004.842904

Utz, H., Stulp, F., & Moeld, A. (2004). Sharing belief in teams of heterogeneous robot. *Proceedings of RoboCup 2004 Symposium*, Lisbon, Portugal.

## ADDITIONAL READING

Arkin, R. (1998). *Behavior Based Robotics*. Massachusetts, PA: MIT Press.

Berger, K. A., & Topol, M. T. (2001). Technology to enhance learning. Use of a web site platform in traditional classes and distance learning. *Marketing Education Review*, *11*(1), 15–26.

Candelas, F.A., Puente, S.T., Torres, F., Segarra, V., & Navarrete, J. (2005). *Flexible system for simulating and tele-operating robots through the Internet, 22*(3), 157-166.

Carusi, F., Casini, M., Prattichizzo, D., & Vicino, A. (2004, Sep). *Remote control of a Lego mobile robot through the web.* Paper presented at the Workshop of Internet Based Control Education, France.

Casini, M., Prattichizzo, D., & Vicino, A. (2003). The automatic control telelab: a user-friendly interface for distance learning. *IEEE Transactions on Education*, *46*(2), 252–257. doi:10.1109/TE.2002.808224

Das, A., Fierro, R., Kumar, V., Ostrowski, J., Spletzer, J., & Taylor, C. (2001). A framework for vision based formation control. *IEEE Transactions on Robotics and Automation*, *18*(1), 82–95.

Demitriou, A. G., & Lambert, A. H. (2006). Virtual environments for robotics education: an extensible object-orientation platform. *IEEE Transactions on Robotics and Automation*, *12*(4), 75–91.

Gonzalez, R. C., & Woods, E. (1993). *Digital Image Processing*. Reading, MA: Addison Wesley.

Guimaraes, E., Maffeis, A., Pereira, J., Russo, B., Cardozo, E., Bergerman, M., & Magalhaes, M. F. (2003). REAL: A virtual laboratory for mobile robot experiments. *IEEE Transactions on Education*, *46*(1), 37–42. doi:10.1109/TE.2002.804404

Horacek, P. (2000). Laboratory experiments for control theory courses: A survey. *Annual Reviews in Control*, *24*(1), 151–162. doi:10.1016/S1367-5788(00)00015-8

Jones, J. L., Seiger, B. A., & Flynn, A. M. (1999). *Mobile Robots. Inspiration to implementation*. Massachussets, PA: A.K. Peters.

Kao, C. P., & Tsai, C. C. (2009). Teachers' attitudes toward web-based professional development, with relation to Internet self-efficacy and beliefs about web-based learning. *Computers & Education*, *53*(1), 66–73. doi:10.1016/j.compedu.2008.12.019

Latombe, J. C. (1991). *Robot Motion Planning*. Amsterdam: Kluwer Academic Publishers.

Mahdizadeh, H., Biemans, H., & Mulder, M. (2008). Determining factors of the use of e-learning environments by university teachers. *Computers & Education*, *51*(1), 142–154. doi:10.1016/j.compedu.2007.04.004

Murphy, R. R. (2000). *An Introduction to AI Robotics (Intelligent Robotics and Autonomous Agents)*. Cambridge, MA: MIT Press.

Ojeda, L., & Borenstein, J. (2004). Methods for the reduction of odometry errors in over-constrained mobile robots. *Autonomous Robots*, *16*(3), 21–25. doi:10.1023/B:AURO.0000025791.45313.01

Pastor, R., Sánchez, J., & Dormido, S. (2003). A XMLFramework for the Development of Web-based Laboratories focused on Control Systems Education. *International Journal of Engineering Education*, *19*(3), 445–454.

Payá, L., Gil, A., Reinoso, O., Riera, L., & Jiménez, L. M. (2006, Jun). *Distributed platform for the control of the WiFiBot robot through Internet*. Paper presented at the Symposium on Advances in Control Education, Madrid, Spain.

Röhrig, C., & Jochheim, A. (2000, Dec). *Java-based framework for remote access to laboratory experiments*. Paper presented at the Symposium on Advances in Control Education, Gold Coast, Australia.

Sagiroglu, S., & Yilmaz, N. (2009). Web-based mobile robot platform for real-time exercises. *Expert Systems with Applications*, *36*(2), 3153–3166. doi:10.1016/j.eswa.2008.01.046

Salajan, F. D., Perschbacher, S., Cash, M., Ralwar, R., El-Badrawy, W., & Mount, G. J. (2009). Learning with web-based interactive objects: An investigation into student perceptions of effectiveness. *Computers & Education*, *53*(3), 632–643. doi:10.1016/j.compedu.2009.04.006

Schmid, C. (2000, Jun). *Remote experimentation techniques for teaching control engineering*. Paper presented at the International Scientific-Technical Conference Process Control, Kouty nad Desnou, Czechoslovakia.

Siegwart, R., & Nourbakhsh, I. R. (2004). *Introduction to Autonomous Mobile Robots*. Cambridge, MA: MIT Press.

Siegwart, R., & Saucy, P. (1999, May). *Interacting mobile robots on the Web*. Paper presented at the Workshop Proceedings of the IEEE International Conference on Robotics and Automation, Detroit, USA.

Thamma, R., Huang, L. H., Lou, S. J., & Diez, C. R. (2004). Controlling a robot through Internet using Java. *Journal of Information Technology*, *20*(3), 25–33.

Theophilo, A., Endler, M., & Cerqueira, R. (2005, Sep) *Evaluation of Three Approaches for CORBA Firewall/NAT Traversal*. Paper presented at the International Symposium in Distributed Objects and Applications, Cyprus.

Tzafestas, C. S., Palaiologou, N., & Alifragis, M. (2006). Virtual and remote robotic laboratory: Comparative experimental education. *IEEE Transactions on Education*, *49*(3), 360–369. doi:10.1109/TE.2006.879255

Yang, F. Y., & Tsai, C. C. (2008). Investigating university student preferences and beliefs about learning in the web-based context. *Computers & Education*, *50*(4), 1284–1303. doi:10.1016/j.compedu.2006.12.009

You, S., Wang, T., Eagleson, R., Meng, C., & Zhang, Q. (2001). A low-cost internet-based telerobotic system for access to remote laboratories. *Artificial Intelligence in Engineering*, *15*(3), 265–279. doi:10.1016/S0954-1810(01)00003-6

## KEY TERMS AND DEFINITIONS

**Autonomy:** In education it refers to the self-sufficiency of a student during the teaching and learning process.

**Distributed Platform:** System that permits the interaction between several components which are located in different spatial locations.

**Image Processing:** Process that takes an image as input and extracts relevant information from it.

**Interactivity:** In computer science, it is the ability that an application has to accept and respond to human stimuli.

**Mobile Robots:** Robot that has the capability to move around in its environment, and whose movements can be controlled.

**Remote Laboratory:** Interactive tool that permits carrying out distance practices with real equipment.

**Virtual Laboratory:** Interactive tool that simulates the behavior of some equipment to carry out distance practices.

**Visual Control:** Algorithms to control the behavior of a system (e.g. a robot) depending of some visual information from the environment.

# Chapter 4
# Evaluating and Implementing Teaching Standards:
## Providing Quality Online Teaching Strategies and Techniques Standards

**Bob Barrett**
*American Public University, USA*

## ABSTRACT

*As of the end of 2006, 38 states in the United States have established state-led online learning programs, policies regulating online learning, or both. Also, 25 states have state-led online learning programs, and 18 states are home to a total of 147 virtual charter schools serving over 65,000 students (http://www.nacol.org). This chapter will survey current online teacher training standards and trends, in terms of what is required of new online instructors. It will also focus on the use of the online learning environment as a vehicle to help instructors to prepare for online teaching in terms of current teaching strategies used – both from the live (on-ground) and online learning environments. This chapter will focus on several universities in terms of their approaches to online teacher training for experienced instructors, as well as new teaching recruits as they prepare to transition from traditional classrooms over to virtual classes.*

## INTRODUCTION

As of the end of 2006, 38 states in the United States have established state-led online learning programs, policies regulating online learning, or both. Also, 25 states have state-led online learning programs, and 18 states are home to a total of 147 virtual charter schools serving over 65,000 students (http://www.nacol.org). In 2001, 56% of traditional learning institutions offered distance learning programs. An additional 12% of the schools stated they planned on adding distance learning programs to their curriculum within the next three years (National Center for Education Statistics, 2003). Thus, more secondary- and post-secondary level teachers will need to seek additional education in order to obtain and master quality online teaching skills and strategies. As a result, more universities are offering online education courses and teacher training in order to help recruit and hire more online instructors. Thus, there is a growing need to increase the number

DOI: 10.4018/978-1-61692-791-2.ch004

of online instructors to teach at many educational institutions.

## Online Student Enrollments

As more technology has become available in many parts of the globe, a new type of student population has emerged. The traditional student image of higher learning has been somewhat limited in many countries, but given the impact of the Internet, this traditional "student body" has changed to online communities. According to Preece (2000), these online communities "consists of people who interact socially as they strive to satisfy their own needs or perform special roles; a shared purpose that provides a reason for the community; policies that guide people's interactions; and computer systems to support and mediate social interaction and facilitate a sense of togetherness" (p. 10). In the field of business and management, educators have recognized the demographical changes of the student population. In a virtual environment, the student is not the same traditional student seen in classrooms in previous years, but rather one that reflects a vast array of cultural differences and needs that require educators to help build "new learning paths" towards the creation of virtual learning communities.

The number of students taking at least one online course continues to expand at a rate far in excess of the growth of overall higher education enrollments. The most recent estimate, for fall 2007, places this number at 3.94 million online students, an increase of 12.9 percent over fall 2006. The number of online students has more than doubled in the five years since the first Sloan survey on online learning. The growth from 1.6 million students taking at least one online course in fall 2002 to the 3.94 million for fall 2007 represents a compound annual growth rate of 19.7 percent. The overall higher education student body has grown at an annual rate of around 1.6 percent during this same period (from 16.6 million in Fall 2002 to 18.0 million for fall 2007 - Projections of Education Statistics to 2017, National Center for Education Statistics). As the following table illustrates, over one-fifth of all higher education students are now taking at least one online course.

Who are these 3.9 million students? The overwhelmingly majority (over 80 percent) are studying at the undergraduate level with only 14 percent taking graduate level courses and the remainder in some other for-credit course. Using survey results and figures from the most recent federal data (Digest of Education Statistics: 2007, National Center for Education Statistics) to compare enrollment patterns shows only slight variations in the proportions of students by education type. The proportion of undergraduates in online education (83.9 percent) is slightly below that of the total population of higher education students (85.6 percent). (Allen & Seaman, 2008)

While technology has provided a powerful infrastructure, the emerging technologies have allowed educational institutions, educators, and students to provide education on a much higher playing field – in a virtual learning environment. Consequently, the business world has also worked with technology in this venture to help assist educational institutions in becoming more modern and adaptive for change. As a result, these changes only signify to the educational and learning communities that technology recognizes a need for change – but do we, as educators, recognize the need for change completely? Finally, many educational institutions, as well as the business world, are focusing on the learning process and its impact on their organizational structure and employees.

## Online Learning and the Learning Organization

While many people consider online learning to be a new academic endeavor, one must also consider the next step for college graduates – the world of work. In this regard, the corporate environment may differ from the academic setting; however, the need to learn and grow is equally important in the world of business and academia. While online learning has been focused more on the academic setting, many companies are learning that online learning has many benefits in the corporate/business environments. Thus, many companies and organizations are focusing on the "learning" element of their employees' daily work lives, as well as helping to build their knowledge management with a concentration on helping the organization learn from previous and current experiences. Thompson (1995) stated that "organizational learning involves the acquisition of new information and the ability to analyze that information creatively, learn from it, and apply that learning in useful ways." (p. 95). As organizations realize that there is a need to "capture" and "utilize" this type of learning, they also realize the need for the organization, as a whole, to concentrate on building up this learning element to include everyone in their respective organization, as well as setting up informal and formal learning center or circles.

Further, Thompson (1995) noted that in order to "become a learning organization [one] must create the conditions within the organization that lead to what Deming termed "profound knowledge" (p. 94). What is this profound knowledge? Further, Thompson (1995) described it as involving "the acquisition of new knowledge and competence, as well as the ability to transfer that understanding to others so that they come to have the same level of knowledge together with the abilit y to pass it on to others." (p. 94). What one has to consider is the differences and similarities between educational institutions and these new "learning organizations" in the corporate world. Basically, both entities have an interest in learning and its impact on the student, administration, overall organization, and society. A key difference may be the academic credit that university students may enjoy in the educational setting; however, many companies are also offering academic credits for courses taken in the many newly created "corporate universities." As a result, both of these entitles have to establish, maintain and continuously evaluate their standards for education, as well as their standards for teaching their learners. In particular, this chapter will focus on learning in the context of online learning, along with the key emphasis on teaching standards in terms of their role and function in the online learning environment.

## Learning Architecture in Online Learning

Vogt (1995) wrote about the foundation for learning in the context of organizations as being: "The building blocks of a learning context are:

- a continuous learning mindset
- an architecture of learning
- cultural and emotional support for learning" (p. 300).

Designing and developing a course is a major task, which consists of several underlying factors. First, the course designer needs to build a course based on the learning objectives. Second, the course has to be built with the use of the current or intended educational learning software. Third, the course has to be built with learning activities or some "adjustment room" for the instructor or trainer to add in additional activities or learning experiences for the adult learner. How can this be successfully accomplished? During this process, the course designer, instructor, and information technology (IT) staff need to work together to reach a final product for instructional purposes.

As the learning architecture is being built, a road map is being developed and followed by each member of the course development team. Vogt (1995) described the "learning architecture" as a road map to answer the following questions:

- Why should we learning?
- How should we learn?
- Where does learning happen? (p. 301)

The skills and abilities of each member of the online course development team are necessary and important; however, the key player working between the product, service, and customer is the instructor. What are our standards for instructors in today's online environment? Before we can look at the standards, we need to backtrack for a moment and evaluate the recruitment process. Does our current recruitment and hiring standards meet the needs of the online learning environment or are we using antiquated methods of recruitment?

## Online Instructor Recruitment and Staffing

Historically, many colleges and universities have recruited and hired online instructors based on their review of received resumes and recommendations of others. However, these two methods may not be efficient enough to accommodate the needs of educational institutions in staffing their various online teaching positions. As a result, many of these institutions are searching for better methods of recruiting and hiring personnel. While some have outsourced these human resources duties, other companies are learning how to create and implement best practices in order to seek, interview, hire, and train potential online instructors to teach their online course offerings. Jones (1993) described best practices as centered:

*... on the very essence of good management: guiding employees toward greater productivity, liberating them from the burdens of disorganization without saddling them with restrictive bureaucracy, and helping them to overcome some measure of the troublesome flaws inherent in people and processes. These are the measures of effectiveness and efficiency (p. 11).*

Therefore, we need to examine and explore how we can our best improve recruitment and hiring practices – especially in hiring the best, qualified candidates for online teaching positions? Further, as more educational institutions are beginning to offer more courses online, there is a need for a different type of educator. These online educators need to offer the same type of high-quality learning, but in a different educational format. Thus, these instructors need to possess certain characteristics that will "fit" both the needs of the online learner, as well as the educational institution. Further, with the decline of instructors, due to teacher burnout or early retirements, can online training programs help to train and educate new, non-traditional teaching professionals to enter the ranks of online teaching? Can these new types of instructors meet the ever-changing needs of educating the online student population, as well as sharing valuable life experiences in their given field or program of study?

## SUMMARY HIGHLIGHTS OF CHAPTER

This chapter will survey current online teacher training standards and trends, in terms of what is required of new online instructors. It will also focus on the use of the online learning environment as a vehicle to help current and potential online instructors to prepare for online teaching in terms of current teaching strategies used – both from the live (on-ground) environment, as well as those strategies used in the online learning environment.

This chapter will focus on several universities in terms of their approaches to online teacher training for both experienced instructors and new teaching recruits as they prepare to transition from traditional classroom environments over to virtual learning environments. While there is still a large population of graduates who have learned in the traditional learning setting (on-ground classes), there is a growing number of adult learners obtaining their degrees from online universities (with the same type of accreditation as their on-ground counterparts). As a result, both online and on-ground graduates are now seeking additional education in order to compete for online (adjunct) teaching opportunities.

Finally, this chapter will examine four major elements. First, it will provide an overview of the recruiting, hiring, and training aspects of the online teaching environment. Second, it will focus on how other educational institutions are recruiting and training their online instructors according to their established teaching criteria. Third, this chapter will examine current standards used to measure and evaluate the instructional learner's level of educational technology and their technical skills sets needed for effective online teaching. Fourth, this chapter will discuss what learning principles and concepts, which are presented and reinforced in online teacher training programs, are used to prepare non-teachers in obtaining the necessary skills sets to become certified by the given university's standards for online teaching.

## ONLINE TEACHING STANDARDS AND STRATEGIES

### Issues, Controversies, Problems

#### Overview

The purpose of this chapter is to address the growing concerns of establishing e-learning teaching standards in current online teacher/instructor training courses and programs. Many instructor training programs were originally designed to prepare instructors for teaching on-ground courses. However, with the advancement of various educational software teaching platforms, the role and function of teaching has started to change drastically– especially in the online learning environment. As a result, training programs for many colleges and universities have started to transition from on-ground class preparation/classroom management over to the online classroom environment. Therefore, the standards needs to be continuously evaluated and changes made in order to meet the growing needs for online instruction.

While traditional teachers have seen the impact of economic crises, on a global scale, many students have started to move away from traveling to and from the "physical" on-ground classroom and opting for online courses. Also, schools have seen an increase in their student populations, and they are faced with the growing dilemma of lack of physical classroom space. Thus, the need for additional online courses has risen as a result of these ever-increasing student enrollments. Further, many traditional teachers have been considering or reconsidering the option of transitioning over to the online learning environment, as opposed to limiting their career possibilities solely to the on-ground teaching experiences. Finally, many current and potential instructors are seeking training in order to obtain proper online instruction to prepare them for online teaching.

### The Global Impact on Virtual Learning

In the business world, when "a brand expands it reach around the globe, it achieves favored perceptions that are greater than the sum of its national parts" (Holt, Quelch, and Taylor, 2004, p. 191). This branding, known as global branding, relies on the input of the various stakeholders and how their cultural differences can enhance the quality and acceptance of such a brand. In the field of education, one needs to understand how these new virtual learning communities have created a new type of global branding of education in terms of linking various stakeholders throughout the world into a stronger and more diversified learning environment. Contextually, one can see a new, global branding of course management systems, which affects and supplements the needs of growing, virtual learning communities. As a result, educators need to reflect on the historical changes in distance learning in order to better understand how technology can enhance their virtual teaching – as well as helping them to adapt from their traditional "framework of teaching" into a more modern and culturally diversified way of teaching.

## Educational Delivery on the Web

The vast array of online course offerings has attracted a larger audience than ever expected. As a result, the academic community has raised several questions about the validity of online learning. Specifically, one of the key questions posed has been: "Can they (online learners) receive the same level of educational quality in the online (web) format, as traditional schools have offered over the years in terms of correspondence and live, instructional courses?" While there have been numerous positions taken by educators and writers on this topic, this paper will concentrate on examining how educators have adapted their teaching strategies to an ever-changing online learning environment.

The roots of distance learning development has been traced back to the early 1700s in the United States, however, this learning movement has been somewhat slow in its development. Despite the impact of technology in the educational arena, there have been barriers of resistance to distance learning. Drummond-Hay and Saidel (2004) commented on several barriers to knowledge sharing that could be applicable to the online learning environment.

- There is no recognition or reward for sharing knowledge.
- People are competitive and believe that their knowledge increases their power.
- There is no vehicle for storing and categorizing knowledge, or the existing vehicle is difficult to use.
- They don't know anyone would be interested in what they know.
- They don't share knowledge because they are not aware of what they know (pp. 293-295).

Given the barriers stated above, the author does note and strongly recommends a change of the status quo in order for the educational profession to move forward. While some educators may still cling to the Socratic method of teaching – teaching methods, strategies, and techniques do need to change. Also, we should learn from Socrates' example – that teaching does not have to occur inside a physical classroom – rather learning can occur in an open space (perhaps virtually). Further, rather than being focused on one way of teaching and learning, we, as educators, need to focus on our audience. Has the demographics of our student population changed over the past decade? If so, are we meeting the needs of our virtual learning communities – or just meeting the needs based on past teaching experiences? Nonetheless, in order to focus on the audience, we need to focus also on the instructor in the context of their role and function.

## The Role and Function of the Online Instructor

The main person involved in the online course execution is the instructor. The instructor is viewed as the leading subject-matter expert (SME) for the course topic and as the one that will facilitate the learning in the course. The students, as in traditional learning environments, will focus their attention on the instructor and his or her teaching style in terms of learning strategies and techniques. Carter (2009) stated that "the instructor takes on the most important role in developing the coursework materials, syllabus, and the opportunities to allow students to communicate in an effective and efficient manner. Discretion in administering distance education courses is a combination of college policies and decision making on behalf of the instructor. Both the rules and policies of the college and instructor expectations are necessary for the development of a distance education course" (p. 11). While online instruction is not for all current and potential instructors, many colleges and universities must look beyond their own faculty rosters to increase the number of qualified and skilled online instructors. In fact, there has been a growing increase in the recruitment efforts of many land and online programs. For purposes of discussion, this chapter will focus on the online programs and their needs for online instructors. While there are many instructors moving from live (face-to-face) course instruction into the realm of online instruction, some of the past and current teaching standards have been modified or adapted to meet the needs of online instruction in today's educational environ.

## Online Teaching Standards

What are teaching standards? Who should create them and why are they important? Historically, teaching standards have been established from the findings and research of numerous educational institutions and centers of learning. However, as online learning has emerged onto the academic scene – a reevaluation of current teaching standards has started to be reconsidered by colleges and universities in general. Further, most accrediting bodies approving online schools and programs' accreditation have had to refocus their approaches and strategies to this new learning environment. As a result, they have designed and develop new sets of standards to evaluate and accredit this new type of learning environment.

Besides looking at the curricula of online programs, these accrediting bodies also have had to look at another factor. How do we examine the teaching standards of an online instructor versus a live (on-ground/face-to-face) instructor? Berge and Clark (2009) noted that "the North American Council for Online Learning conducted a comprehensive literature review for standards involving online teaching. The NACOL *National Standards for Quality Online Teaching* were published in 2008, which used the SREB *Standards for Quality Online Teaching*, (SREB, 2006) with minor revisions. As noted in the NACOL publication, NACOL also added two standards from the Ohio Department of Education's *Ohio Standards for the Teaching Profession* and the Electronic Classroom of Tomorrow's *Teacher Evaluation Rubric* based on the results of the review.

This set of standards uses a rubric with a rating scale as follows:

- 0 Absent – component is missing
- 1 Unsatisfactory – needs significant improvement
- 2 Somewhat satisfactory – needs targeted improvements
- 3 Satisfactory – discretionary improvement needed
- 4 Very satisfactory – no improvement needed

The 13 categories below have several items in each to score using the rubric above.

1. The teacher meets the professional teaching standards established by a state-licensing agency or the teacher has academic credentials in the field in which he or she is teaching.
2. The teacher has the prerequisite technology skill to teach online.
3. The teacher meets the professional teaching standards established by state-licensing agency or the teacher has academic credentials in the field in which he or she is teaching. The teacher has the prerequisite technology skills to teach online.
4. The teacher provides online leadership in a manner that promotes student success through regular feedback, prompt response and clear expectations.
5. The teacher models, guides, and encourages legal, ethical, safe and healthy behavior related to technology use.
6. The teacher has experienced online learning from the perspective of a student.

7. The teacher understands and is responsive to students with special needs in the online classroom.
8. The teacher demonstrates competencies in creating and implementing assessments in online learning environments in ways that assure validity and reliability of instruments and procedures.
9. The teacher develops and delivers assessments, projects, and assignments that meet standards-based learning goals and assesses learning progress by measuring student achievement of learning goals.
10. The teacher demonstrates competencies in using data and findings from assessments and other data sources to modify instructional methods and content and to guide student learning.
11. The teacher demonstrates frequent and effective strategies that enable both teacher and students to complete self- and pre-assessments.
12. The teacher collaborates with colleagues.
13. The teacher arranges media and content to help students and teachers transfer knowledge most effectively in the online environment. (p.6).

While the above rubric categories cover many intended standards, it is the responsibility of the educational institution to accept, reject, modify or adapt the standards to meet their institutional and teaching needs. In many cases, most of these institutions will need to review, update, or modify their teaching standards. The key element in each teaching standard area is the need for the instructor to work with technology as a vehicle to help them to guide and facilitate the learning process, as well as keeping the communication process active and interactive. As each learning body accepts, modifies, adapts or creates their teaching standards, they also need to look at the best practices used by others in academia and the world of business.

## USING BEST PRACTICES TO MEET TEACHING STANDARDS

What are best practices? Do they just occur or do they just develop or evolve due to certain situations, circumstances or experiences? Since some portion of distance education can be traced back to the 1700s in the context of correspondence schools (Jeffries, 2004, ¶ 7), we can conclude that distance learning, outside of the traditional context, has been slowly evolving. However, we usually refer to our technology-based distance education in terms of the advent of audiovisual devices, which were first used in the early 1900s. Due to the invention of film, Thomas Edison noted that "our school system will be completely changed in the next ten years" (Saettler, 1968, p. 68). Actually, many educators at that time were skeptical of the use of film in the classroom, but this was not the end of the technological evolution in the classroom as we have seen over the past several decades – especially in the field of distance education.

With the increasing amount of technology used in the field of education, the distance education environment evolved from the beginning elements of the paper and pen correspondence courses to that of online (on-demand) courses. As the courses and teaching standards for online courses began to change, several colleges and universities continued to focus on offering the best of the best in terms of their course offerings – especially emphasizing their best practices (Jones, 1993). We need to keep in mind the ultimate outcome of learning – the ability to apply it to one's own personal, work, and career endeavors. Further, we need to think in terms of how current learners will carry with them their new education and/or training skills and abilities into their professional (workplace) and personal lives. Employers are ultimately affected by having either a skilled or partially-skilled workforce. Thus, education is a major consideration for workers, employers, and educational institutions.

While educational institutions and centers of learning have focused on developing their own standards and good practices, we, as researchers, need to help guide them towards the acceptance of good practices of others (whether modified or completely refashioned). What this means is that there is a need to explore and examine the current, good practices of other educational institutions, as well as establishing standards for others to identify with and perhaps implement into their own set of standards. Chickering and Gamson (1987) constructed several principles of good practice, with an emphasis on undergraduate education, which can also be focused on graduate education – especially with a concentration on establishing good practices for online teaching.

### Principle 1: Good Practice Encourages Student-Faculty Contact

**Lesson for online instruction:** Instructors should provide clear guidelines for interaction with students.

### Principle 2: Good Practice Encourages Cooperation Among Students

**Lesson for online instruction:** Well-designed discussion assignments facilitate meaningful cooperation among students.

### Principle 3: Good Practice Encourages Active Learning

**Lesson for online instruction:** Students should present course projects.

### Principle 4: Good Practice Gives Prompt Feedback

**Lesson for online instruction:** Instructors need to provide two types of feedback: information feedback and acknowledgment feedback.

### Principle 5: Good Practice Emphasizes Time on Task

**Lesson for online instruction:** Online courses need deadlines.

### Principle 6: Good Practice Communicates High Expectations

**Lesson for online instruction:** Challenging tasks, sample cases, and praise for quality work communicate high expectations.

### Principle 7: Good Practice Respects Diverse Talents and Ways of Learning

**Lesson for online instruction:** Allowing students to choose project topics incorporates diverse views into online courses. (pp. 3-7)

## TEACHING STRATEGIES

### Handling Classroom Barriers

While some teaching tools may be effective in one learning environment, they may not be as successful in another. Therefore, as each environment is unique, as well as the learners in it, the online instructor needs to assess the virtual environment and determine if changes are necessary. However, not all educators may be as flexible in their teaching methodology, and they may not be as willing to change. Thus, this leads us to another important question for examination: Do online educators incorporate different teaching strategies and techniques to meet the ever-changing needs of their virtual learners in terms of learning from their cultural differences in order to enhance the learning experiences of all?

While we may hope that all educators are continuously improving their teaching methods and strategies in the classroom, we must recognize the fact that some may not. In the traditional classroom, there has been an "expected" structure of teaching methods and strategies to be used in the classroom environment. However, in the virtual learning environment, educators have had to "unlearn" their old way of thinking in terms of teaching methodologies. In turn, online educators have had to learn new ways of implementing and nurturing the learning process for their virtual student populations. Merryfield (2003) wrote about how "online technologies diffuse triggers of difference" (p. 160). Further, she noted, "Gone are the powerful catalysts of visual and aural clues that make people want to listen, ignore, hide, or respond in a face-to-face classroom. People respond to text instead of a person's physical presence, personality, accent, or body language" (p. 160). Therefore, online instructors must learn how to strategically approach learning from different perspectives and approaches in order to achieve similar results for online students, as their counterparts (on-ground students).

As a result, the online learning environment has helped to break down a few of the barriers for learners with previous bad learning experiences, as well as for students with disabilities entering classrooms with physical barriers (i.e., lack of ramps, small doorways, steps instead of elevators, etc.). Also, this new type of learning environment has helped to "level" the playing field, in which students can act, react, and be proactive in the learning process. White (2002) noted that, "Nowhere is thinking more evident than in the textual environment of the online classroom. If writing is thinking, then online students display their thinking throughout the course, illustrating their individual styles and changing attitudes" (p. 6). Along this same line of thinking, educators can incorporate various strategies to help draw upon the experiences of all class members – rather than just a select few. This demonstrates the beauty of online learning – because online learning is a continuous process (not limited to a set time and place as a traditional course is scheduled). For example, in the live (on-ground) learning environment, the instructor may lecture on several key concepts or topics and then open the floor for questions. In the online learning environment, the instructor can publish a lecture or two for the learner to read on his or her own time. Then the online instructor can post a series of discussion questions for students to comment on during a given period of time in the course – which can quickly grow. Further, this type of learning environment may be more inviting for certain learners to participate more in this type of learning environment – rather than participating in a live classroom setting.

## Motivational Strategies for Encouraging Participation

No matter what type of learning environment is presented to students, there are still students who are shy or lack focus or motivation to learn. As a result, it is the responsibility of the instructor to work with these students to help create an environment conductive for learning. One barrier that instructors may face is showing certain students the importance of learning and how their experiences can be an important addition to the overall learning experience. McConnell (1978) illustrated the advantage of using personal history-sharing practices in a classroom in order to help draw upon experiences for all students in the following passage.

*Many students who do not identify with the dominant culture in the class are likely to need the reassurance that these kinds of anecdotes provide. The university world looks so strange and omnipotent to them that they welcome this glimpse of a fellow human being. Even when their instructors provide them with highly successful female, minority, and other role models, they assimilate the social stereotype that these instructors are "special" or unusual" but that they themselves are ordinary and could never be that successful (pp. 70-71)*

Further, Corey, Corey, and Corey (1997) also supported a similar teaching strategy to help involved all students into the learning environment, as noted:

*Using personal stories from a variety of students who have struggled and found their own way can be a source of inspiration to new students who so often claim to be lost on an impersonal campus. If students see that others like them have been able to overcome major obstacles and have been successful at turning these blocks into stepping stones, their motivational level increases and provides a direction for them to pursue (p. 1).*

With both the personal history-sharing practices and personal stories in mind, these teaching strategies can help an educator to enhance the learning environment, as well as develop a new "learning culture" in the virtual learning environment. Schein (1992) defined culture as:

*A pattern of shared basic assumptions that the group learned as it solved its problems of external adaptation and internal integration that has worked well enough to be considered valid and, therefore, to be taught to new members as the correct way to perceive, think, and feel in relation to those problems (p. 12).*

Therefore, while there may have been cross-cultural differences perceived as barriers in the past by others, instructor and members of a virtual learning community do have a unique opportunity to remove these barriers and create a change in the learning process. They have the potential for developing a "new culture" or rather a "new learning culture." This new learning culture could work as a catalyst to help change current educational thinking and perhaps make changes in the current curriculum. As instructors develop a "new culture" or "new online learning culture" for online students, the use of effective strategies and techniques are important. Further, the instructor should recognize that strategies, like standards, need to be constantly evaluated and updated in order to maintain the same level of effectiveness in all courses. Otherwise, the lack of emphasis in this area can only lead to stagnation in terms of teaching effectiveness and learning. This could, in turn, ultimately affect the overall learning experience for students.

## Assessment Issues, Problems, and Solutions

While the online instructor works with the required curriculum and course objectives by strategically planning learning activities, offering lectures/discussions, and providing evaluative measures, a major concentration needs to be place on assessment. Not all assessments may be appropriate for some courses or subject content, therefore, it is essential that the course designer and online instructor should work together in order to monitor and evaluate the effectiveness of the course, instruction, and overall learning. Walvoord (2004) commented on three steps for assessment:

1. Articulate your goals for student learning.
2. Gather evidence about how well students are meeting the goals.
3. Use the information for improvement (p. 3).

In consideration of the assessment steps listed above, one standard that should always be in place is how a course or lesson is assessed and evaluated. Another area of interest should be how assessments may need to be changed from time to time to meet the course needs, as well as the learning needs of the student population. Walvoord (2004) stated that

*"Assessment works best when it is ongoing, not episodic. Assessment is a process whose power is cumulative. Though isolated, "one-shot" assessment can be better than none, improvement is best fostered when assessment entails a linked series*

*of activities undertaken over time. This may mean tracking the progress of individual students, or of cohorts of students; it may mean collecting the same examples of student performance or using the same instrument semester after semester. The point is to monitor progress toward intended goals in a spirit of continuous improvement. Along the way, the assessment process itself should be evaluated and refined in light of emerging insights (p. 2).*

It should be noted that some courses are well designed, but errors in assessment instruments may not be realized immediately. However, when there are outliers or changes in normal assessment results, this may signify to the instructional staff that some course items may need to be adjusted or modified. Further, Walvord (2004) in "How to Build an Assessment Plan or Report" suggested the following steps for writing up an assessment report or plan.

1. Embed assessment in high-stakes and high-energy processes.
2. Consider audiences and purposes
3. Arrange oversight and resources
4. Articulate learning goals.
5. Conduct an "assessment audit" of assessment measures already in place and how the data are used for decision making.
6. Take steps to improve the assessment process.
7. Take steps to improve student learning.
8. Write the report or plan. (p. 11)

Further, the instructor should be cognizant of the need to assess and perhaps question noticeable changes in assessment results – rather than ignoring these changes. One way that course designers, department chairs, and instructors assess or measure certain written assignments, discussion postings, and final projects is through the use of rubrics.

## Rubrics as Assessment Instruments

While many colleges and universities have used various forms of rubrics, they have been considered an important measurement tool by instructors to assess student performance. Huba and Freed (2000) noted that rubrics "represent a way of evaluating student achievement that is radically different from the methods we have used in the past. However, shifting from teacher-centered courses to learner-centered courses is a change of culture that, at times, requires drastic modifications in the way fundamental activities are carried out. Making standards public facilitates a more trusting relationship between teacher and learners. No longer are grading criteria a secret that only perceptive learners can discover" (p. 166). In the online learning environment, many online programs have moved successfully from the teacher-centered approach to one as being learner-centered. Rather than just assigning specific and detailed projects, there has been an ever-growing increase in the use of group work to help build the team-building skills of today's college students. Thus, the discussion of assessment, rubrics, and standards have led the discussion in this chapter towards exploring what needs to be included in the preparation and instruction (training) of current and potential instructors for online learning programs.

## Solutions and Recommendations

Not all online teacher training programs are formally structured. Some training programs are aimed at general educational practices and online software package training. Other programs are well developed and organized and require interaction with all participants during a prescribed period of time. For purposes of discussion, let us look at some general practices offered by Woodley and Kirkwood (1998) in the context of general educational assessment practices. They suggested that administrators encourage the following general assessment practices:

- Critical commenting: create narrative summaries of the strengths and weaknesses of the instructor from administrators and peers.
- Developmental testing: during the preparation of online materials, encourage "dry runs" to test the effectiveness of techniques.
- Revision of materials in light of formative evaluation: build in a feedback mechanism for faculty to make changes based on the sum of student, peer, and administrative evaluation.
- Feedback from students: require that student evaluation of instructor performance carry significant weight in the overall assessment.
- Definition of the extent of utilization: ask instructors to list the resources absolutely necessary for the completion of essential course tasks, and review their validity and currency on a regular basis. (291-98)

While each of these practices can be applied to physical (on-ground) classes, as well as online classes, they offer valuable areas for consideration. In particular, these assessment practices are important to discuss and incorporate into a training program so that the participants can recognize the importance of testing, feedback, critical analysis and other areas of importance in the learning experience of their students.

Mujtaba and Preziosi (2005) recommended that "faculty members wishing to teach online must become online students first and learn the pedagogy of online education along with the school's electronic platform. The immersion model of training, discussed earlier, has been used to train corporate trainers and to develop faculty members in distance education. Its' practical application, success, challenges and best practices should be comprehensively explored, presented, and discussed in the development process" (p. 58). Here are some of the common learning objectives for faculty developing in this orientation-type course offering.

- Learn and understand the mechanics of the online environment.
- Collect best practices and tips for beginning online faculty members to be effective in the initial online experience.
- Discover what learning strategies work best for teaching, understanding, and learning the course material.
- Know how to best engage students, keep them interested and on track to achieve course and curriculum learning outcomes.
- Learn how to best manager your time to adequately show presence on the discussion board. The number of times faculty members should log on per day/week should be decided based upon learning outcomes.
- Find out how to best manage discussion threads with large quantities of comments. (p 58)

For the purposes of discussion of assessment and evaluation in the context of teacher training, the next few sections will focus on the training program at one leading university focused on both live (on-ground) and online course offerings.

## Franklin University Online Teaching Program

Franklin University, situated in Columbus, Ohio, offers courses for the traditional and non-traditional students in the form of live (on-ground) and online courses. While they focus on recruiting and hiring potential instructors with appropriate (selected) academic credentials, they also focus on candidates with qualified work experiences in their field of study and practice. After a potential instructional candidate has been identified and recommended for hiring, the candidate is enrolled in a teacher training program. This training program consists of six weeks of course instruction in six different training modules led by a facilitator. The facilitator's focus is on the training from the perspective of an on-ground and online class perspective. A quick review of each module of instruction is listed below:

- **Module 1 – Teaching and Learning.** This module focuses on the field of teaching and what learning is in terms of the participants' previous and current educational experiences. Students are introduced to various software applications and participate in the course from the perspective of a learner throughout the training.
- **Module 2 – Teaching Strategies.** Students are presented with a variety of teaching strategies in the context of potential learning situations and dilemmas. Further, students learn how to manage their time as students and potential faculty members.
- **Module 3 – Helping Students to Think Critically.** Students examine different learning situations and are required to prepare specific assignments to measure their critical thinking skills. Also, students are required to submit work to a software database to detect potential plagiarism or related problems. This assignment provides the participants an opportunity to learn more about the given database and how to interpret the results presented by the reporting mechanism.
- **Module 4 – Providing Feedback.** Students are given a series of several written assignments to grade with the use of a standard rubric. This particular set of grading assignments helps the teaching candidate to learn more about the grading process and how to offer constructive feedback.
- **Module 5 – Ethical Issues.** Teaching today requires instructors to be more alert about ethical situations and issues in the classroom. One key issue discussed in this particular module is plagiarism and its impact on today's student, class, and the overall university.
- **Module 6 – Teaching at Franklin.** This final module focuses on the university's mission statement and policy statements, as well as their application in the classroom.

While many traditional approaches to instructor training may be lengthy at times, the average training period for new online instructors can range from 1 to 10 weeks – depending on the training standards of the university. From the author's perspective and online training experiences, the average online training program ranges between 3-6 weeks. As an industry standard, most online training programs consist of information on teaching and learning styles, the impact of communications in the classroom, courseware/software training, ethical issues and university policies. In any event, the role and function of most online instructional training programs is to acquaint the new candidate with their potential role and function as a member of the online faculty, as well as to train them in the required and potential uses of courseware/software designated for the online learning environment. Finally, they are exposed to the key university policies and regulations and who to contact for potential questions and further information. In light of the various teaching standards used in today's classroom, there is still room for improvement. The next section will share with the reader areas for possible research and improvement.

## FUTURE RESEARCH DIRECTIONS

While many schools have established teacher training programs, these programs may not be applicable in all forms of teaching – live classroom instruction versus online classroom instruction. While distance education has been formally traced back to the early 1700s, it has evolved more quickly with the introduction of computers and ultimately with the use of the World Wide Web (WWW). Consequently, the use of assessment instructions and rubrics have been quite valuable in the traditional learning environment, but there has been a need for change and adaptation of these assessment measures in order to meet the needs of today's online learning population. Thus, what has worked in the past in the traditional classroom may not necessarily meet the needs of today's online learning environment.

During the past several decades, many colleges and universities have started to share their best practices in the areas of learning, especially with online learning best practices. These universities and their online faculty have co-authored and presented on a variety of online learning topics, as well as emphasized and discussed the need for standards. NACOL *National Standards for Quality Online Teaching* has focused on creating and maintaining standards to help ensure the quality of online teaching. Organizations, such as the United States Distance Learning Association (USDLA), have started to emerge and be recognized as educational resources for online instructors and universities. From the various publications and presentations appearing in the context of online instruction, there appears to be a growing need for more standardization of teacher qualifications and training, as well as more emphasis on quality standards for online instruction. While there has been a growing need for such changes, there appears to be need for more empirical evidence of creating better standards for online instruction and online teacher preparation.

Finally, there has been a growing interest by many educational institutions to offer online teacher training programs or contract out to other training entities to offer such instruction. The key outcome desired by colleges and universities is to find the best and most qualified candidates to teaching for their educational programs. However, when there are growing enrollments and the lack of adequate preparation time, there are some educational institutions which might rush the training progress or set it aside in order to hire and place immediate candidates into teaching positions -- due to immediate organization/educational needs. The question here is whether or not educational institutions can meet their academic and accreditation requirements if they rush or set aside their current training standards? Further, we need to assess and evaluate whether not if there should be a certifying body that monitors and approves current online teacher training programs in order to meet accreditation requirements?

## CONCLUSION

As technology has increased the possibility of more adult learners to participate in taking online courses, in light of various family, business, and personal constraints, changes still need to be done in terms of embracing diversity in education. While online learning has helped to reduce the number of barriers experienced by adult learners, there are still barriers that must be addressed and handled by educator. There are several possible suggestions that might help to prevent such barriers from appearing and remaining in the virtual learning community. First, the instructor needs to adapt and update teaching strategies to draw upon the experiences and knowledge of all learners, not just a few. Second, educators can be proactive in making appropriate changes in the curriculum to help strengthen course offerings, as well as incorporating teaching strategies and technique that meet the needs of the course objectives, as well as motivating and encouraging the adult learners to want to learn even more.

Finally, we, as educators, need to recognize that the demographics of our students are changing – and for the better. We need to embrace diversity and help nurture it along the way. Merryfield (2003) summed it up best in the following quote: "Online technologies provide opportunities for teachers to experience a more global community than is possible face to face" (p. 165). As we strive to build stronger global and virtual learning communities, we need to remember that each member of these communities have a unique gift – their personal and cultural values. These values are important to a learning community – and we, as educators, can set the example by making changes today that will reflect upon our society tomorrow. Finally, evaluating and implementing of quality teaching standards is necessary and should be an ongoing function of the instructor, as well as the educational institution.

## REFERENCES

Allen, I. E., & Seaman, J. (2008). Staying the course: Online education in the United States, 2008. *The Sloan Consortium*. Retrieved July 2, 2009, from http:www.sloan-consortium.org/publications/survey/pdf/staying_the_course.pdf.

American Association for Higher Education. (1992). *Principles of good practice for assessing student learning*. Washington, DC: AAHE.

Barnes-McConnell, P. W. (1978). Leading discussions. In Milton, O. (Ed.), *On college teaching: A guide to contemporary practices* (pp. 70–71). San Francisco: Jossey-Bass.

Berge, Z., & Clark, T. (2009). *Virtual schools: What every superintendent needs to know. Distance Learning. 6(2)* (p. 6). Charlotte, NC: USDLA.

Brookfield, S. D. (2005). *The power of critical theory: Liberating adult learning and teaching*. San Francisco: Jossey-Bass.

Carter, R. (2009). *Discretion in a distance learning environment: Ethical considerations in a virtual classroom. Distance Learning, 6(2)* (p. 11). Charlotte, NC: USDLA.

Chickering, A., & Gamson, Z. (1987). Seven principles of good practice in undergraduate education. [Washington, DC: AAHE.]. *AAHE Bulletin*, *39*, 3–7.

Corey, J., Corey, C., & Corey, H. J. (1997). Use of personal stories and small groups in class. *The Keystone* (Newsletter of the Wadsworth College Success Series), (Spring), pp. 1-2.

Drummond-Hay, P., & Saidel, B. G. (2004). Capturing ideas, creating information, and liberating knowledge. In Goldsmith, M., Morgan, H., & Ogg, A. J. (2204. San Francisco: Jossey-Bass.

Holt, D. B., Quelch, J. A., & Taylor, E. L. (2004). *Managing the global brand: A typology of consumer perceptions. The global market: Developing a strategy to managing across borders*. San Francisco: Jossey-Bass.

Huba, M. E., & Freed, J. E. (2000). *Learner-centered assessment on college campuses: Shifting the focus from teaching to learning*. Needham Heights, MA: Allyn & Bacon.

In White, K. W., & Weight, B. H. (2000). *The online teaching guide: A handbook of attitudes, strategies, and techniques for the virtual classroom*. Needham Heights, MA: Allyn & Bacon.

Jeffries, M. (2004). Research in distance education: The history of distance education. Retrieved July 20, 2005 from http://www.digitalschool.net/edu/DL_history_mJeffries.html.

Jones, T. L. (1993). *The Americans with disabilities act: A review of best practices*. New York: AMA.

Merryfield, M. (2003). Like a veil: Cross-cultural experiential learning online. *Contemporary Issues in Technology & Teacher Education*, *3*(2), 146–171.

Mezirow, J. (2000). *Learning as transformation*. San Francisco: Jossey-Bass.

Mujtaba, B. G., & Preziosi, R. C. (2005). *Adult education in academia: Recruiting and retaining extraordinary facilitators of learning!*Pompano Beach, FL: Xpress Printing and Publishing.

Preece, J. (2000). *Online communities: Designing usability, supporting sociability*. Chichester: Wiley.

Saettler, P. (1968). *History of Instructional Technology*. New York: McGraw-Hill.

Schein, E. H. (1992). *Organizational culture and Leadership* (2nd ed.). San Francisco: Jossey-Bass.

Thompson, J. W. (1995). The renaissance of learning in business. In S. Chawla and J. Renesch (1995). *Learning organizations: Developing cultures for tomorrow's workplace.* Portland, Oregon: Productivity Press.

Vogt, E. E. (1995). Learning out of context. In S. Chawla &J. Renesch (1995). *Learning organizations: Developing cultures for tomorrow's workplace.* Portland, Oregon: Productivity Press.

Walvoord, B. E. (2004). *Assessment clear and simple: A practical guide for institutions, departments, and general education.* San Francisco, CA: Jossey-Bass.

Woodley, A., & Kirkwood, A. *Evaluation in Distance Learning. Commonwealth* Co-operation in Open Learning: Background Papers. J. Jenkins, ed. London: Commonwealth Secretariat, 1998, 291-98. Rpt. as "Evaluation in Distance Learning: Course Evaluation." http://www1.worldbank.org/disted/Management/Benefits/cou-02.html. In Thomas J. Tobin (2004). Best practices for administrative evaluation of online faculty. DLA 2004 Proceedings. Retrieved on July 10, 2009, from http://www.westga.edu/~distance/ojdla/summer72/tobin72.html.

## ADDITIONAL READING

Brookfield, S. D. (2005). *The power of critical theory: Liberating adult learning and teaching.* San Francisco: Jossey-Bass.

Center for Workforce Preparation (Spring, 2003). *Rising to the challenge: Business voices on the public workforce development system.* Washington, DC.

Center for Workforce Preparation (unknown). *Disability: dispelling the myths: How people with disabilities can meet employers needs.* Washington, DC.

Cornell University Program on Employment and Disability. Why hire people with disabilities? ILR Access for All. http://www.ilr.cornell.edu/ped/accessforall/index.htm?page+whyhire&CFID=2215278&CFTOKEN=70349750. Retrieved June 2, 2003.

Discrimination, D. http://www.eeoc.gov/types/ada.html. Retrieved on July 30, 2008. Diverse Perspectives: People with Disabilities Fulfilling Your Business Goals.

*Employer Tips on Interviewing Applicants with Disabilities*. http://www.foremployers.com/index.php?page=osinterviewtips Retrieved on July 27, 2008.

*Employment Checklist for Hiring Persons with Disabilities*. http://www.dol.gov/odep/pubs/fact/diverse.htm. Retrieve July 25,2 008 http://www.dol.gov/PrinterFriendly/PrinterVersion.aspx?url=http://www.dol.gov/odep/pubs/ek96/chcklist.htm. Retrieved July 27, 2008.

Freeman, R. E. (1984). *Strategic management: A stakeholder approach*. Boston: Pitman.

Goldsby, F. (2001). In John DiMarco (2006). Web Portfolio Design and Applications(pp.607-608) Hershey, PA: Idea Group Inc. (retrieved 6/1/2008)

Goodman, P. S., & Darr, E. D. (1996). Exchanging best practices through computer-aided systems. *The Academy of Management Executive*, *10*(2), 7–18.

Greenberg (2004). In John DiMarco (2006). *Web Portfolio Design and Applications*. Idea Group Inc. pp. 607-608. (retrieved 6/1/2008)

Harris, H. (2000). *Defining the future or reliving thepast? Unions, employers, and the challenge of workplace learning*. Columbus, OH: ERIC Clearinghouse on Adult, Career, and Vocational Education, Information Series, No. 380. LDP e-Portfolio Report http://bearlink.berkeley.edu/ePortfolio/page5.html (retrieved 6/1/2008).

Sanders, M. (2000). In John DiMarco (2006). *Web Portfolio Design and Applications*. Idea Group Inc. pp. 607-608. (retrieved 6/1/2008)

The, A. D. A. Your responsibilities as an employer. http://www.eeoc.gov/facts/ada17.html. Retrieved July 15, 2008.

*The2008DiversityInc Top 10 Companies for People With Disabilities*. http://www.diversityinc.com/public/3573.cfm. Retrieved July 30, 2008.

*The Americans with Disabilities Act: A Primer for Small Business*. http://www.eeoc.gov/ada/adahandbook.html. Retrieved July 31, 2008.

*The Council for Disability Awareness*. http://www.disabilitycanhappen.org/chances_disability/disability_stat.sasp. Retrieved July 15, 2008.

U.S. Department of Labor – Bureau of Labor Statistics. *(2008)*.http://www.bls.gov/cps/home.htm. Retrieved August 4, 2008.

Washington Education Association and American Federation of Teachers – Washington. (Nov. 21, 2005). *Best employment practices for part-time faculty*. Taskforce report and recommendations. Retrieved 1/26/09 from http://www.sbtc.ctc.edu/college/_hr_bestpractices.aspx

## KEY TERMS AND DEFINITIONS

**Adult Learning:** Participants, ranging from 16 to 90 years of age, involved in the learning process whether for career, leisure or professional interests.

**Distance Education:** Educational or learning experiences enjoyed by students in non-traditional classroom settings via the use of web technologies. This type of education has been traced back to the correspondence courses of the 1700s.

**Learning Styles:** Adult learners may learn in a variety of settings and ways to achieve the final objectives of a course, workshop or training. Some learners are better with visual approaches as opposed to auditory approaches to learning. Not all adult learners learn in the same way or manner, so the instructor needs to be aware of the various learning styles of adult learners in the classroom setting.

**Online Learning:** The process of offering credit or non-credit courses via a web-delivery system to reach traditional and non-traditional students in either a synchronous or asynchronous format.

**Online Teaching:** Teaching strategies and techniques designed to address the learning needs of online students in the context of the online learning environment via the use of web technology.

**Rubric:** A criterion of standards used to measure students' learning from a given set of topical areas in order to assess the student's overall mastery of these given standards in the context of a given rating system.

**Teaching Standards:** Standards created, implemented, and evaluated by administrators and other leading educational authorities in order to measure the overall effectiveness and efficiency of instructors in the delivery of classroom instruction and the facilitation of student learning.

**Teaching Strategies:** Strategies used by instructors to help students learn from various learning activities in terms of applications, situ-

# Chapter 5
# Patterns of Interaction in Online Learning

**Kevin Downing**
*City University of Hong Kong, Hong Kong S.A.R.*

**Kristina Shin**
*Hong Kong Polytechnic University, Hong Kong S.A.R.*

**Flora Ning**
*City University of Hong Kong, Hong Kong S.A.R.*

## ABSTRACT

*This chapter describes a case study which examines detailed data related to student and tutor usage of an asynchronous discussion board as an interactive communication forum during a first semester associate degree course in applied psychology, and identifies 'what works' in relation to discussion board use. The case demonstrates how students gradually create an online community, but only if they are prompted in a timely and appropriate way by the course and assessment structure. Three distinct phases in online interaction are identified, and the case suggests these might be largely mediated by assessment tasks.*

## INTRODUCTION

Learning facilitation, using the Web as a vehicle for content dissemination and teacher-student interaction, continues to dominate debates related to online learning (Nash, 2004). However, research conducted in this area tends to focus on examining the importance of teacher-student and student-student interaction in the online learning process, and in particular the use of discussion boards to assist in creating an effective online learning environment (Downing & Chim, 2004a). Some research suggests effective ways of creating such an environment, (Chou, 2001; Gilbert & Dabbagh, 2005; Henri & Pudelko, 2003) but relatively few studies (De Laat & Lally, 2004; Yukselturk & Top, 2006) have undertaken detailed week by week analysis of tutor and student discussion board activity throughout a semester, and then used this data to make recommendations about how an effective online learning community can be established with appropriate use of online discussion board tools.

DOI: 10.4018/978-1-61692-791-2.ch005

## Online Learning: Interactivity, or Lack of Interactivity

With the exponential growth in information and communication technology, educators are presented with opportunities and challenges in terms of the use of the internet for formal educational purposes and web-based instruction (Boettcher, 1999; Downing, 2001; Mc. Naught & Lam, 2005). The development of metacognition in undergraduates is an area of focus for both traditional classroom based and online learning environments (Downing et al, 2009). For example, the impact of social and cultural factors on cognitive development has long been recognised, with even Piaget (1977) acknowledging the impact of social factors and peer interaction on cognitive development, and more recent studies have generally confirmed this view (Downing et al. 2007). Consequently, the need to cultivate and maintain interactivity within online learning environments remains a major challenge. Previous research has generated consistent concern about a perceived lack of interaction in online educational environments (Hron & Friedrich, 2003), prompted by the probably erroneous assumption that our 'traditional' classrooms are filled with the vital learning interactivity that online environments supposedly lack. For example, according to Robertson and Klotz (2002), the literature provides evidence that online courses are often configured and delivered in a style associated with independent study and that, whilst this format might work in some instances, it leaves what they call a 'missing link' in student learning. Consequently, researchers argue that students in an online learning environment lack opportunities to experience the benefits of both structured dialogue and the sense of community that can be created in the more traditional on-site classroom environment. Cook, (2000), Seabolt and Arends, (2000), and Muirhead, (2001) support this view that the interactivity of the traditional classroom is a vital, yet missing part of web-based instruction, and argue that online interaction is somehow flawed because it does not allow for the social and emotional interaction allegedly taking place in traditional classrooms. Downing and Chim, (2004b) take a very different approach, investigating the relationship between personality type, preferred learning style, and different learning environments, and demonstrating that classroom based 'introverts' behave more like 'extraverts' when involved in online discussion forums, and that students with a more reflective learning style are actually more active in online discussions than when based in the classroom. In some ways, well-designed online learning can be seen as a form of problem-based learning which requires the same facilitation or scaffolding that is evident in the latter approach (Downing et al, 2009). In fact, it is perhaps an anomaly that the criticisms directed at online learning are not often used against the problem-based approach which is often effectively online learning without being online whereby students are given problems to follow up and not always in collaboration with their peers!

## Synchronous and Asynchronous Discussions

Synchronous learning is often referred to as 'live' learning in which student-student and student-tutor interactions occur in real time. The critical difference between synchronous (real time) and asynchronous (anytime, anywhere) discussions is described by Boaz *et al.* (1999) who suggest that the growth of online 'chat' is evidence of the potential value of synchronous online discussion activity. Certain situations best lend themselves to synchronous communications, including group meetings or activities requiring group consensus or simultaneous response. Synchronous discussions are especially useful for brainstorming or replicating the face to face situation, and tend to be more successful when utilised by small groups (Conrad & Donaldson, 2004). However, one of the problems of synchronous discussion boards or chat rooms is that they do not always allow time for students to reflect and consider what they want to say, and consequently those students who are more reflective in their learning style often report feeling left out. In contrast, Downing and Chim, (2003) suggest that asynchronous discussion boards provide opportunities for a less pressured learning environment where participants can contribute to debates at a pace and time (within reasonable parameters) which suits them. They argue that this constitutes part of the added-value which can be brought to the learning experience with appropriate use of an asynchronous discussion board tool, and demonstrates that learning outcomes should normally drive the use of technology rather than the other way around.

Most providers of online courses utilise asynchronous discussion groups to generate student-to-student and student-to-instructor interaction (King, 2001; Clyde, 2004). In general, tutors facilitate online learning via the posting of open-ended, thought-provoking questions to encourage student response and discussion. In fact, a survey of online instructors conducted by Berge (1997) found that forty-one out of the forty-two respondents utilised discussion boards as a teaching method. This asynchronous model provides each learner with the time to adequately respond and reply as appropriate. It provides some flexibility for the learner to respond at his/her individual 'peak time', when he/she is at his/her best. Redmon and Burger (2004) see the asynchronous nature of discussion boards to be a distinct advantage offering the opportunity for reflection before response. In addition, the flexibility of communication in asynchronous discussion can produce greater depth of learning than the synchronous environment alone (Conrad and Donaldson, 2004). Cox and Cox (2008) found evidence that interaction between students in an asynchronous learning environment leads to a community of learners. The utilisation of a discussion board provides students with the opportunity to share their thoughts with others in the class and can help establish a collaborative learning environment which allows students to become acquainted with fellow classmates and tutors. Bourne *et al.* (1997) characterise asynchronous learning environments as capable of providing anywhere and anytime learning, but also identify a wide variety of issues which remain to be resolved in relation to the effective use of asynchronous discussion boards. These issues include the difficulties involved in encouraging early engagement, the creation of a sense of a learning community, and the sustainability of interaction. Previous studies which address these areas either focus on ways of reducing the potential social isolation of students through online exchange (Lally and Barrett, 1999), explore issues related to emergent role development and group awareness (De Laat & Lally, 2004), or concentrate on the establishment and effectiveness of forums for professional exchange and discussion amongst teachers (Selwyn, 2000).

## Critical Factors in Creating and Facilitating an Active Online Learning Community

The fostering of interaction is an intangible aspect of an online learning community and according to White (2004), group interaction is not always spontaneous. She suggests that while facilitators cannot force the growth of online interaction, careful facilitation plays a major role in cultivating student involvement. The importance of thoughtful and careful facilitation is also noted by the Australian Flexible Learning Framework who state, 'Effective facilitation (sometimes called moderation) is arguably the single biggest factor in the success of an online community' (Backroad Connections, 2003, p.3). Unlike traditional face-to-face learning environments, facilitators face unique communication challenges in establishing an active online learning environment (Coghlan in Backroad Connections, 2002, p.2). In order to facilitate effective community building activities which can help develop 'positive social dynamic and cognitive learning that is created through a variety of communication' (Woods and Ebersole, 2003), it is necessary to understand the stages in which online communities develop, the behaviours of students in the progression through these stages, and the strategies that can be used to facilitate this progression (Salmon and Giles, 1997; Wegner, 1998; Backroad Connections, 2003).

Despite the proliferation of debate, and with the possible exception of Salmon's work (2000), there remains a lack of clear information on what works in terms of setting up and sustaining a successful online learning environment using the discussion board tool. The study which forms the basis for this chapter begins to address this lack of prior research by analysing discussion board activity and content data for one semester, and consequently provides insight into the three issues raised by Bourne *et al.* (1997):

- What works in terms of encouraging early engagement with the asynchronous use of the discussion board?
- How does the sense of a learning community develop, and how can this be encouraged?
- What works in terms of sustaining online interaction?

## The Blended Learning Model

In order to identify the success factors in terms of establishing and cultivating an effective online learning community, a detailed week by week analysis of tutor and student discussion board activity, using the Blackboard learning platform, is performed on one 'blended learning' course throughout a single semester. Following the framework of Garrison and Anderson (2003) who identified the three critical components (students, teachers and content) in the formal educational context of an online discussion board, a case study design is utilised to explore the level of student-tutor and student-student interaction and the content of interaction which is defined according to its agreed purpose, using inter-rater reliability with three independent raters agreeing with each other about coding decisions.

Blended learning is generally defined as the combination of different methods, techniques and resources for effective learning. Valiathan (2002) describes this as a mix of various event-based activities, including face-to-face classrooms, online learning, and self-paced learning. In this context blended learning seeks an optimum blend of self study, teacher-led events and group collaboration which can be deployed in a blend of asynchronous or synchronous modes, depending on the intended learning outcomes. The course selected for this study is constructed of ten units of learning material with students recommended to spend approximately ten hours studying each unit. A large variety of materials including video clips, audio clips, images, animations, url links, power point presentations, and formative and summative quizzes are utilised for teaching and learning. A total of 7 hours and 40 minutes of face-to-face contact is provided via five tutorials which take place in weeks one, three, six, nine and twelve of a thirteen week semester. Each of tutorials 1, 2, 3, and 5 are 1 hour and 20 minutes in duration with tutorial 4 lasting two hours and 20 minutes to allow for students summative small-group presentations. To allow students to engage in discussion and collaboration with fellow students and the course tutor, a discussion board is provided on the Blackboard learning platform for the online component of the course. The main objective here was to encourage participation in online discussion and foster the formation of an active virtual learning community.

Most research on the application of discussion boards/forums in blended learning show that active participation only occurs when the task is a formal class requirement with contribution towards grades (Alshare, Kwun, & Grandon, 2006). Gandell *et al.* (2000) categorise the extent of Web use according to the relevance and importance of learning goals appropriately addressed, and identify five categories that represent a continuum of extent of use:

- **Minimal:** Use of the Web that is neither relevant nor necessary to achieve any explicitly stated course learning goals and therefore has no impact on course-related learning.
- **Supplemental:** Use of the Web that is relevant but not necessary to achieve a few explicitly stated course goals and therefore does not have much impact on related student learning.
- **Integral:** Use of the Web that is relevant and contributes to achieving some of the learning goals in the course, and would have a fair impact on student learning.
- **Central:** Use of the Web that is relevant and necessary to achieve most learning goals in the course, and would have a substantial impact on student learning.
- **Exclusive:** Use of the Web that is relevant and necessary to achieve all learning goals in the course, and would have a major impact on student learning.

The extent of Web use for this blended learning course is in the exclusive category where the use of the Web would have a major impact on student learning, given that the online materials (units) are both relevant and necessary to achieve all the learning and assessment outcomes.

## Case Study Background

The focus of this case study is the analysis of discussion board activity in determining what works in terms of encouraging and sustaining discussion board use in the development of an effective online learning community. Data related to asynchronous discussion board activity from both tutor and students was captured and retained by a research assistant over a seventeen week period, which began when the course was released online, precisely one week before the start of the study period, and extended three weeks beyond the thirteen weeks of the course duration. This was later analysed on a week by week basis to highlight student discussion board activity, and to relate this to tutor discussion board activity, and other prompts built into the asynchronous course materials. Content materials and assessment tasks for the whole course (ten units) were made available from the first day of the semester so that students could learn at their own pace. Of particular interest were the categories of student-student interaction and student-tutor interaction over the timescale identified above. Using these categories, data was analysed according to two broad emergent themes for student-student and student-tutor interactions:

- **Student - Student / Student - Tutor Interaction for instrumental reasons.** This category includes all postings primarily related to seeking and providing academic assistance with course materials and contents or enquiries about assignments and the structure of the course.
- **Student - Student / Student - Tutor Interaction for emotional / social reasons.** This category includes all postings primarily related to seeking and giving reassurance and assistance with social or emotional questions/issues related to studying the course.

These themes emerged as a result of identifying that the interactions on our discussion boards generally fell into two clear categories and could usefully be classified accordingly. Postings were either primarily instrumental or social/emotional in terms of their purpose (we agreed that more than 95% of the posting content had to fall within the category descriptions above). This classification was surprisingly easy to achieve with no significant disagreements amongst the three independent raters, or subsequent blind rating by the author. Interestingly, but beyond the scope of this paper to consider further, these categories also appear in research into coping strategies conducted by Carver, Scheier and Weintraub (1989).

First year associate degree programme freshmen enrolled in a blended learning applied psychology course at a university in Hong Kong form the sample in this study. All 32 students enrolled in this 'Practical Psychology for Everyday Life' course during Semester A (September to December) volunteered retrospectively (they were approached after the semester was completed) to participate in this study. All participants were of similar academic background evidenced by their successful application to study applied psychology at associate degree level. In week 17, in-depth interviews with ten participants (a convenience sample) were conducted by an independent research assistant not involved in the course teaching. The sole tutor for this course was the first author of this chapter, a chartered psychologist and lecturer with some 27 years experience as an educator.

## OBSERVATIONS

Data was analysed over the seventeen week period identified below in Figure 1 which shows a line graph of student and tutor discussion board activity. The course begins in week 1 and ends in week thirteen and the overall number of postings can be seen in the table underneath the graph. Whilst the total for each individual week is summed, a line graph is useful here to demonstrate the overall flow of discussion board postings and highlights three emergent phases (weeks 0 to 3, 4 to 9, and 10 to 16) marked with the dotted lines below.

Data was then analysed cumulatively for the full seventeen week period according to the coding categories identified for this case study. Cross-tabulations of student-student and student-tutor interaction for instrumental and social reasons were presented in Table 1 (weeks 0 to 16), Table 2(a) (weeks 0 to 3), Table 2(b) (weeks 4 to 9), and Table 2(c) (weeks 10 to 16) below following independent rating and categorising by three raters.

The graph and table in Figure 1 show the overall pattern of postings between tutor and students over the seventeen week period of this study. The most striking pattern is the degree of

*Figure 1. Table and graph to show overall distribution of discussion board postings from week 0 to week 16*

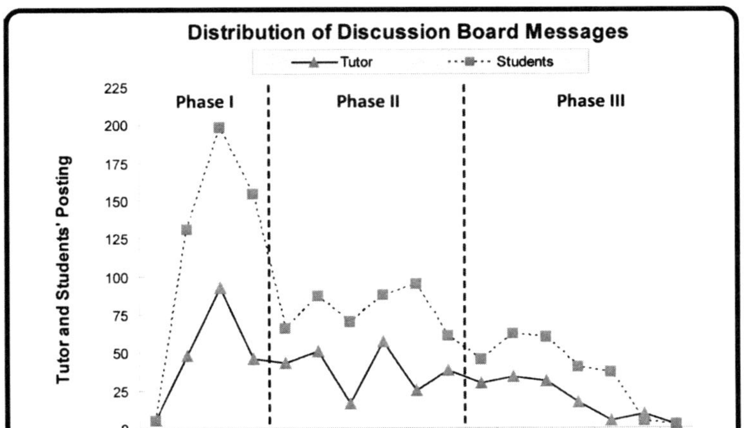


| | 0 | 1 | 2 | 3 | 4 | 5 | 6 | 7 | 8 | 9 | 10 | 11 | 12 | 13 | 14 | 15 | 16 |
|---|---|---|---|---|---|---|---|---|---|---|---|---|---|---|---|---|---|
| Tutor | 6 | 48 | 93 | 46 | 43 | 51 | 16 | 57 | 25 | 38 | 30 | 34 | 31 | 17 | 5 | 9 | 2 |
| Students | 5 | 131 | 198 | 154 | 66 | 87 | 70 | 88 | 95 | 61 | 45 | 62 | 60 | 40 | 37 | 4 | 2 |

*Table 1. Table summarising student-student and student-tutor postings for instrumental and social reasons (weeks 0 to 16).*

| | Instrumental | Social | Total |
|---|---|---|---|
| **Student-student interaction** | 269 | 564 | 833 |
| **Student-tutor interaction** | 489 | 434 | 923 |
| **Total** | 758 | 998 | **1756** |

*Table 2(a). Table summarising student-student and student-tutor postings for instrumental and social reasons (weeks 0 to 3).*

| | Instrumental | Social | Total |
|---|---|---|---|
| **Student-student interaction** | 87 | 295 | 382 |
| **Student-tutor interaction** | 144 | 155 | 299 |
| **Total** | 231 | 450 | **681** |

*Table 2(b). Table summarising student-student and student-tutor postings for instrumental and social reasons (weeks 4 to 9).*

| | Instrumental | Social | Total |
|---|---|---|---|
| **Student-student interaction** | 116 | 176 | 292 |
| **Student-tutor interaction** | 226 | 179 | 405 |
| **Total** | 342 | 355 | **697** |

*Table 2(c). Table summarising student-student and student-tutor postings for instrumental and social reasons (weeks 10 to 16).*

| | Instrumental | Social | Total |
|---|---|---|---|
| **Student-student interaction** | 66 | 93 | 159 |
| **Student-tutor interaction** | 119 | 100 | 219 |
| **Total** | 185 | 193 | **378** |

parallelism between the two lines, with an exception around week 8 which might be explained by the type and timing of the assessment tasks for this course. Assessment was divided into three broad components. The first component was participation, the extent to which the student engages with the course, which spanned the duration of the course (13 weeks) and was worth 20% of the total marks. 10% of this mark was awarded for in-class participation assessed over the five tutorials, and 10% was awarded for online discussion board participation. This assessment component provides additional motivation for students to engage in both classroom and online activities. The second assessment component required students to make a short presentation on a topic in the tutorial which took place in week 9 (40%), and the third assessment component involved submission of a 2000 word written paper (40%) by week 15.

The next most notable feature of the data in Figure 1 is the emergence of three distinct phases in terms of posting activity also identified in Tables 1 and 2, and the summary graph in Figure 2, which appear to be largely driven by the timing and nature of the formative and particularly the summative assessment tasks identified above.

## Phase One: Weeks 0 to 3 (The Socially Formative Phase)

The tutor adopted a nurturing and supportive role during the first three weeks of the course, which can be operationally defined as becoming heavily engaged (in terms of providing an encouraging and non-critical response) with students via the online discussion board, and ensuring that most tutor postings contained encouraging and supportive comment. This was intended to create a culture of high trust or what Biggs, (1999) calls an appropriate 'climate for learning'. Evidence of this can be seen in the tutor postings data in Tables 1 and 2. From week four the intention is for the tutor to gradually withdraw, increasingly

*Figure 2. Graph summarising student-student and student-tutor postings for instrumental and social reasons over the three identified phases (weeks 0 to 16)*

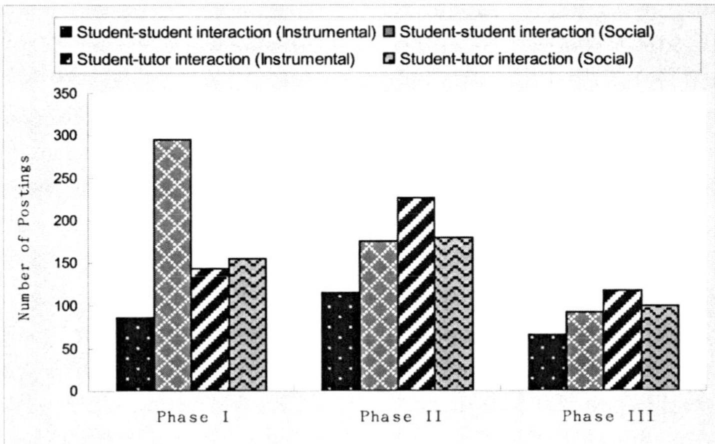


responding by acknowledging good questions and reflecting these back to the online student group to encourage them to engage in metacognitive activity (Downing & Shin, 2006; Downing et al., 2009), and to stimulate further independent discussion and peer learning activity over the remaining ten weeks of the course. A formative assessment task, due in week 3, was designed to encourage early engagement with the asynchronous use of the discussion board, and to attempt to initiate the beginnings of a sense of a supportive online learning community. This formative assignment required each student to contact a fellow student and post a short introduction to that individual on the discussion board. The number and nature of student postings during the first three weeks of the course demonstrates that this was an effective way of encouraging early engagement with both the discussion board environment and each other. In fact many of the students, who had been in online contact during this exercise, subsequently chose to sit together in classroom sessions from tutorial three until the end of the course.

Phase one is characterised by interaction which is largely social in nature, with student-student interaction for social reasons accounting for significantly more postings than the other three categories. The next highest categories are student-tutor interaction for social reasons followed by student-tutor interaction for instrumental reasons. Analysis of the content of the latter category show most postings to be related to practical course arrangements, tutorials and assignments. The final category was student-student interaction for instrumental reasons suggesting perhaps that students have not yet sufficiently developed the social relationships with their peers necessary for collaborative learning. A review of student feedback for this semester confirms this assertion with most student comments identifying the need to build some sort of relationships between each other and the tutor at this early stage. Almost all students identified the early online exercise of contacting and introducing a fellow as very effective in terms of creating a sense of belonging to a group and only one student commented that he found it 'annoying'. This finding confirms that of Brown (2001) who identifies the first stage of her three stage model as being about making friends online with whom students felt comfortable communicating. This is very similar to what happens in traditional classrooms where the creation of a safe and supportive learning environment provides an effective context for subsequent learning activity. The social role of the tutor is more clearly defined at this stage than the relationships between students, and this accounts for the significantly higher levels of student-tutor interaction in the social category during this socially formative and somewhat exploratory stage. By week three, all students said that they felt more comfortable in the online discussion board environment and this is confirmed by a notable rise in giving support to their colleagues for instrumental reasons. This is perhaps a form of social learning through modelling the tutors online social/emotional support behaviours in the manner described by Bandura (1965), and certainly set the scene for a warm and supportive learning environment both online and in the tutorials. In fact the importance of developing a sense of trust in the learning environment (McGregor, 1967; Biggs, 1999) is identified as being an even more critical success factor in online learning and working environments by Grundy (2002). This probably because the lack of intensive early face-to-face contact might be perceived by some students as quite threatening so reassurance and positive reinforcement from tutor and peers is even more critical.

The socially formative assessment task to be posted on the discussion board by week three undoubtedly contributed to student-student social interaction during this phase, and substantially assisted in the early stages of relationship building almost certainly leading to more student-student instrumental interaction in phase two, and setting the scene for a generally high level of overall discussion board activity.

## Phase Two: Weeks 4 to 9 (The Socially Instrumental Phase)

Brown (2001) typifies the second stage as one of community conferment or acceptance, occurring when students are part of a long, thoughtful, threaded discussion on a subject of importance. The interactions between weeks 4 and 9 inclusive demonstrate an increase in student-student interaction for instrumental reasons but this remains the lowest category overall. However, contrary to phase one where social interactions were paramount, this period shows a well balanced mix of both social and instrumental interaction (see Table 2(b)). The increase in the student-tutor interaction for instrumental reasons is assignment driven again, this time by the requirement to produce a group summative assignment in the form of a presentation on a selected topic in week 9. Surprisingly, in individual follow-up interviews with ten of the student participants, seven stated that they began to feel a sense of competition with other groups during this phase and therefore felt more 'comfortable' asking the tutor for help with instrumental matters than their peers/competitors. All ten interviewees said that they used private email, rather than the discussion board, to communicate with their fellow presentation group members during this phase. Most gave the reason that they did not want to give away any 'secrets' about their presentation to the other groups. They also admitted being 'careful' about how they phrased discussion board requests to the tutor for instrumental help during this phase so as not to give their 'presentation plans to other groups', and frustrated that the tutor refused to answer queries via email. The tutor refused to answer individual email queries, except of a private/personal nature throughout the course, on the basis that this might encourage more sharing and collaborative learning online. The gradual reduction in student-student interaction for instrumental reasons (see Figure 1) between week 4 and 9 is largely a result of students experiencing a sense of inter-group competition given that the presentation assignment due in week 9 was summative in nature and carried a substantial proportion (40%) of the overall marks for the course. Whilst the overall number of postings during this period is up very slightly on phase one, the distribution of postings according to the four categories is very different and suggests that Brown's (2001) second stage of community conferment or acceptance is compromised when students perceive they are in competition. In fact the highest number of postings during this phase was student-tutor interaction for instrumental reasons (see Figure 2) which is more consistent with Yuselturk and Top's (2006) 'task oriented area' classification where instrumental questions take priority over social interaction. Nonetheless, social interaction remained very slightly above instrumental interaction overall providing evidence that some sense of community prevailed during this phase.

### Phase Three: Weeks 10 to 16 (The Withdrawal Phase)

In this phase, both student-student and student-tutor interaction begins to drop away considerably, but a well-balanced mix of social and instrumental postings is maintained. The overall number of postings during this phase is 378, compared with 697 in phase two, demonstrating that some level of disengagement from the discussion board is taking place. At this stage of the course students should have completed most of the online course material and be preparing for their individual summative written assignment (40%) due in week 15. All ten students in the individual follow-up interviews reported that they 'considerably reduced' the frequency of logging on to the online course at this stage, citing final assignment production pressure. This general disengagement with the online learning materials clearly led to a general reduction in discussion board use because students were less likely to be logging into the course to study course materials. This assertion was borne out by course login statistics which also showed a steady downward trend after week ten which largely paralleled the reduction in discussion board activity. The follow-up interviews also revealed that once again many students (eight out of the ten interviewed) felt a keen sense of competition with their peers (this time on an individual basis) and preferred to just concentrate on their final written assignment believing that this would bring them more benefits than continuing to engage in the online discussion board. However, student-tutor interaction remains at phase one levels with students reporting that maintaining tutor contact to the bitter end was very important and 'might influence their grade positively'. When asked at interview about this, most students said they were grateful to the tutor for support during the course, and still had some questions to ask in relation to the final assignment so that is why they had more contact with the tutor than their peers at this stage of the course. However, when pressed four of the students admitted they thought it 'might influence their final assignment grade'. All but one student said they felt a sense of friendship or community with their fellow students but that this was tempered by the need to get a good individual grade in their final assignment. All ten of the interviewed students said they would attempt to keep in social contact with at least one of their peers after the course was complete, which suggests some adherence to Brown's (2001) third stage of camaraderie, but one which is much more complex and multi-dimensional than she suggests.

## CONCLUSION

Some insights have been gained from this case study into the questions posed by Bourne *et al.* (1997) in terms of what works in facilitating an online discussion board, and some further questions are raised about the complexity of discussion board interaction over the duration of a semester-long course.

Question 1 asked what works in terms of encouraging early engagement with the asynchronous use of the discussion board. There is little doubt from the level of online activity and interaction identified in Figure 1 and Table 1, that early engagement with an asynchronous discussion board can be greatly facilitated by the design of a simple yet appropriate socially formative assignment. By asking students to contact each other and introduce a fellow student using the discussion board medium, a great deal of early interaction was facilitated. In phase one, there were a total of 681 postings from 32 students (Table 2(a)) and these included both student-student and student-tutor interaction with the emphasis (almost twice as many) being in terms of social interaction. These high levels of interaction and support created a sense of shared purpose and group cohesion and effectively supported students to build online relationships and establish their online identity. In terms of Brown's (2001) first stage of 'making friends online with whom students felt comfortable communicating', this approach is successful. However, the established role of the tutor is clearly important in facilitating a supportive learning environment in the early weeks of establishing an online sense of community. According to Salmon (2000) the role of the facilitator during this stage is to provide support and guidance to students in navigating their way through the content as they learn to contribute (p. 4). The high level of tutor involvement in this phase appeared to be successful in encouraging active participation from the students. This provides further support for previous research which indicates that the tutor must provide regular and timely feedback to students in order for participants to value the discussion process (Woods and Ebersole, 2003; Pena-Shaff, Altman & Stephenson, 2005; 425).

Question 2 asked how does the sense of a learning community develop, and how can this be encouraged. This is the most problematic question to be answered because, whilst it might be possible to classify postings as primarily social or instrumental in nature, students will also take into account many other factors before deciding when and what to post. This is evidenced by the data in phase two, and the comments from students in the follow-up interviews, which demonstrate that students are often influenced by what they perceive, are pragmatic considerations about the competition they are involved in when required to complete summative assignments. Despite the fact that the tutor for this course made it very clear from the outset that assessment was criterion, rather than norm-referenced, and that it was therefore possible for every student to be graded 'A', there was nonetheless a clear formation of separate presentation working groups, and a subsequent reluctance to share too much online with non-group members. In retrospect, this would have been an appropriate time to create separate working groups within the discussion board, rather than continue with one group which all students had access to. This would have positively influenced the continuation of a sense of a supportive learning community established in phase one. This finding is broadly in agreement with that of Nicol *et al.* (2003) who point out that the social context of online learning is qualitatively different from more traditional modes and that both practitioners and researchers need to recognise this complexity. In this case study, the timing and handling of the group summative assessment task clearly interfered with the continued establishment of a sense of a supportive and nurturing online learning community, and that if we are to take full advantage of the power of online technologies, we must develop our understanding of their impact upon the social context for online learning.

Question 3 asked what works in terms of sustaining online interaction and this is a question which requires some analysis. The results from this study, and others (Brown, 2001; Yuselturk and Top, 2006; Hwang and Wang, 2004) suggest that online discussion activity might go through a series of stages or phases, which on the surface might not be too dissimilar to what happens in classroom based learning. In other words, there is a socially active phase, an instrumental phase and then a gradual, and perhaps natural, process of disengagement. The current study demonstrates that students take a pragmatic approach to this process, disengaging when they feel they have all the information they need to complete the summative assessment tasks they are set. To that extent it is not effective or worthwhile to attempt to sustain online interaction for the duration of the whole course. Provided students have engaged in reflective online discussion activity early on, and completed the online course materials, it might be counter productive to try to sustain involvement through to the end of the course. We should interpret sustaining online interaction in a way which adds the provision: 'as far as there is educational value in so doing'. If the question is interpreted in this way, educators are provided with much more scope in terms of how they decide to use, and how they evaluate the success or failure of online discussion forums.

Vygotsky (1978) pointed out that conceptual learning was a collaborative effort which required supportive dialogue so it is reasonable to assume that online discussion has the potential to enhance both collaboration and concept development. However, some researchers take the view that true social interaction leading to cognitive growth in an online context is rare (Son, 2002; Meyer, 2003; Wickstrom, 2003) whereas others (Poole, 2000; Grady, 2003; Schallert, Reed and D-Team, 2003) demonstrate that significant social interaction leading to effective knowledge construction does take place in online discussion forums. As Kay (2006) points out a resolution to this debate lies in both the user acceptance of the medium and the amount of structure used to guide the online discussion board. The current study suggests that the former task is perhaps more easily achieved than the latter, and that more research is needed into 'what works' in terms of engaging and sustaining online learning communities that are truly collaborative and supportive. In summary, the development of effective online learning is a complex process and many issues remain to be solved. Attention must be given to the identification of a properly constructed pedagogical structure which can motivate learner participation and generate interest towards learning.

## REFERENCES


Alshare, K., Kwun, O., & Grandon, E. E. (2006). Determinants of instructors' intentions to teach online courses: A cross-cultural perspective. *Journal of Computer Information Systems*, *46*, 87–95.

Backroad Connections Pty Ltd. (2003) *What are the conditions for and characteristics of effective online learning communities? Australian flexible learning framework: Quick guide series (Australian national Training Authority)*. Available online at: http://www.flexiblelearning.net.au (accessed 3 April 2008).

Bandura, A. (1965). Influence of model's reinforcement contingencies on the acquisition of imitative responses. *Journal of Personality and Social Psychology*, *1*, 589–595. doi:10.1037/h0022070

Berge, Z. L. (1997). Characteristics of online teaching in post-secondary, formal education. *Educational Technology*, *37*(3), 35–47.

Biggs, J. (1999). *Teaching for quality learning in university*. London: The Society for Research into Higher Education & Open University Press.

Boaz, M., Elliott, B., Foshee, D., Hardy, D., Jarmon, C., & Olcott, D. (1999). *Teaching at a distance: A handbook for instructors*. Mission Viejo, CA: League for Innovation in the Community College.

Boettcher, J. (1999). Another look at the tower of WWWebble. *Syllabus Magazine*, *13*(3), 50–52.

Bourne, J. R., McMaster, E., Reiger, J., & Campbell, J. O. (1997). Paradigms for on-line learning: A case study in the design and implementation of an asynchronous learning networks (ALN) course. *Journal of Asynchronous Learning Networks*, *1*(2), 38–56.

Brown, R. E. (2001). The process of community building in distance learning classes. *Journal of Asynchronous Learning Networks*, *5*(2), 18–35.

Carver, C. S., Scheier, M. F., & Weintraub, J. K. (1989). Assessing coping strategies: A theoretically based approach. *Journal of Personality and Social Psychology*, *56*(2), 267–283. doi:10.1037/0022-3514.56.2.267

Chou, C. C. (2001). Formative evaluation of synchronous CMC systems for a learner-centered online course. *Journal of Interactive Learning Research*, *12*(2/3), 170–188.

Clyde, L. A. (2004). Digital learning objects. *Teacher Librarian*, *31*(4), 55–57.

Conrad, R., & Donaldson, J. A. (2004). *Engaging the online learner: Activities and resources for creative instruction*. San Francisco: Jossey-Bass.

Cook, K. (2000). Computer conferencing really makes the Web interactive. In Leach, E. J. (Ed.), *A collection of practices from the league's conference on information technology*. Mission Viejo, CA: League for Innovation in the Community College.

Cox, B., & Cox, B. (2008). Developing interpersonal and group dynamics through asynchronous threaded discussions: The use of discussion board in collaborative learning. *Education*, *128*(4), 553–565.

De Laat, M., & Lally, V. (2004). It's not so easy: Researching the complexity of emergent participant roles and awareness in asynchronous networked learning discussions. *Journal of Computer Assisted Learning*, *20*, 165–171. doi:10.1111/j.1365-2729.2004.00085.x

Downing, K. (2001). Information Technology, education, and health care: Constructivism in the 21st century. *Educational Studies*, *2*(3), 229–235. doi:10.1080/03055690120076510

Downing, K., Ho, R., Shin, K., Vrijmoed, L., & Wong, E. (2007). Metacognitive Development and Moving Away. *Educational Studies*, *33*(1), 1–13. doi:10.1080/03055690600850347

Downing, K., Kwong, T., Chan, S., Lam, I., & Downing, W. K. (2009). Problem-based learning and the development of metacognition. *Higher Education*, *57*(5), 609–621. doi:10.1007/s10734-008-9165-x

Downing, K. J. a&Chim, T.M. (2003) Learning style, student satisfaction and blended learning. In G. Richards (Ed) *Proceedings of World Conference on e-learning in corporate, government, healthcare, and higher education 2003*, Phoenix, AZ, USA, 1552-1553.

Downing, K. J., & Chim, T. M. (2004a) *What are the characteristics of effective online students? Fifteenth International Conference on College Teaching and Learning,* Jacksonville, Fl., U.S.A. 29th March-2nd April 2004.

Downing, K. J., & Chim, T. M. (2004b). Reflectors as online extraverts. *Educational Studies*, *30*(3), 265–276. doi:10.1080/0305569042000224215

Downing, K. J., & Shin, K. (2006) Developing metacognition with LASSI online.*International Conference of the Asia-Pacific Educational Research Association*, Hong Kong Institute of Education, Hong Kong, November 2006.

Gandell, T., Weston, C., Finkelstein, A., & Weiner, L. (2000). Appropriate use of the web in teaching higher education. In Mann, B. L. (Ed.), *Perspectives in web course management* (pp. 61–68). Toronto: Canadian Scholar's Press.

Garrison, D. R., & Anderson, T. (2003). *E-learning in the 21st century: A framework for research and practice*. London, Routledge Falmer.

Gilbert, P. K., & Dabbagh, N. (2005). How to structure online discussions for meaningful discourse: A case study. *British Journal of Educational Technology*, *36*(1), 5–18. doi:10.1111/j.1467-8535.2005.00434.x

Grady, D. B. (2003). Mapping online discussions with lexical scores. *Journal of Interactive Learning*, *14*(2), 209–229.

Grundy, J. (2002). Flexible learning and the flexible worker. *British Telecom White Paper,* December 2002, BT, London.

Henri, F., & Pudelko, B. (2003). Understanding and analysing activity and learning in virtual communities. *Journal of Computer Assisted Learning*, *19*, 474–487. doi:10.1046/j.0266-4909.2003.00051.x

Hron, A., & Friedrich, H. F. (2003). A review of web-based collaborative learning: factors beyond technology. *Journal of Computer Assisted Learning*, *19*, 70–79. doi:10.1046/j.0266-4909.2002.00007.x

Hwang, W. Y., & Wang, C. Y. (2004). A study of learning time patterns in asynchronous learning environments. *Journal of Computer Assisted Learning*, *20*, 292–304. doi:10.1111/j.1365-2729.2004.00088.x

Kay, R. H. (2006). Developing a comprehensive metric for assessing discussion board effectiveness. *British Journal of Educational Technology*, *37*(5), 761–783. doi:10.1111/j.1467-8535.2006.00560.x

King, K. (2001). Educators revitalize the classroom "bulletin board:" a case study of the influence of online dialog on face-to-face classes from an adult learning perspective. *Journal of Research and Computing in Education*, *33*(4), 337–354.

Lally, V., & Barrett, E. (1999). Building a learning community on-line: Towards socio-academic interaction. *Research Papers in Education*, *14*(2), 147–163. doi:10.1080/0267152990140205

McGregor, D. (1967). *The professional manager*. New York: McGraw-Hill.

McNaught, C., & Lam, P. (2005). Building an evaluation culture and evidence base for e-learning in three Hong Kong universities. *British Journal of Educational Technology*, *36*(4), 599–614. doi:10.1111/j.1467-8535.2005.00538.x

Meyer, K. A. (2003). Face-to-face versus threaded discussions: The role of time and higher order thinking. *Journal of Asynchronous Learning Networks*, *7*(3), 55–65.

Muirhead, B. (2001) Enhancing social interaction in computer-mediated distance education, *United States Distance Learning Association Ed at a Distance Magazine and Ed Journal 15*(40). Available online at: www.usdla.org/html/journal/APR01_Issue/article02.html (accessed 3 April 2007).

Nash, S. S. (2004) New quality benchmarks for online courses: Meshing technology and conceptual underpinning, Selected Papers from the *Fifteenth International Conference on College Teaching and Learning.* Jacksonville, Fl., U.S.A. 29th March-2nd April 2004, 195-222.

Nicol, D. J., Minty, I., & Sinclair, C. (2003). The social dimensions of online learning. *Innovations in Education and Teaching International*, *40*(3), 270–280. doi:10.1080/1470329032000103807

Pena-Shaff, J., Altman, W., & Stephenson, H. (2005). Asynchronous online discussions as a tool for learning: Students' attitudes, expectations, and perceptions. *Journal of Interactive Learning Research*, *16*(4), 409–430.

Poole, D. M. (2000). Student participation in a discussion oriented online course: a case study. *Journal of Research on Computing in Education*, *33*(2), 162–177.

Redmon, R. J., & Burger, M. (2004). Web CT Discussion Forums: Asynchronous Group Reflection of the Student Teaching Experience. *Curriculum and Teaching Dialogue*, *6*(2), 157–166.

Robertson, T. J., & Klotz, J. (2004) How can instructors and administrators fill the missing link in online instruction, *Online Journal of Distance Learning Administration*, 5(4). Available online at: http://www.westga.edu/~dist ance/ojdl a/winter54 /roberson54.htm (accessed 3 April 2007).

Salmon, G. (2000). *eModerating: The key to teaching and learning online* (London, Routledge Falmer).

Salmon, G. K., & Giles, K. (1997). Moderating online, *Online Education Conference, Berlin*. Available online at: http://www.emoderators.com/moderators/gilly/MOD.html (accessed 12 April 2007).

Schallert, D.L., & Reed, J.H., & D-Team, T. (2003). Intellectual, motivational, textual, and cultural considerations in teaching and learning with computer-mediated discussion. *Journal of Research on Technology in Education*, *36*(2), 103–118.

Seabolt, B., & Arends, B. (2000). *Remaining real in a virtual world*. Available online at: http://www.web ct.com/service/viewcontentframe?contentID=2385 857&pageName=index.html (accessed 3 April 2007).

Selwyn, N. (2000). Creating a 'connected' community? Teachers use of an electronic discussion group. *Teachers College Record*, *102*(4), 750–778. doi:10.1111/0161-4681.00076

Son, J. (2002). Online discussion in a CALL course for distance language teachers. *CALICO Journal*, *20*(1), 127–144.

Vygotsky, L. S. (1978). *Mind in society: The development of higher psychological processes*. Cambridge, MA: Harvard University Press.

Wenger, E. (1998). *Communities of practice: Learning as a social system*. Available online at: http://www.co-i-l.com/coil/knowledge-garden/cop (accessed 12 April 2007).

White, N. (2004). *Facilitating and hosting a virtual community*. Available online at: http://www.fullcirc.com/community/definingcommunity.htm (accessed 12 April 2008).

Wickstrom, C. D. (2003). A funny thing happened on the way to the forum. *Journal of Adolescent & Adult Literacy*, *46*(5), 414–423.

Woods, R., & Ebersole, S. (2003). Becoming a "communal architect" in the online classroom – Integrating cognitive and affective learning for maximum effect in web-based learning. *Online Journal of Distance Learning Administration*, *6*(1). Valiathan, P. (2006). *Blended learning models*. Available online at: http://www.learningcircuits.org/2002/aug2002/valiathan.html (accessed 3 April 2007).

Yuselturk, E., & Top, E. (2006). Reconsidering online course discussions: A case study. *Journal of Educational Technology Systems*, *34*(3), 341–367. doi:10.2190/6GQ8-P7TX-VGMR-4NR4

## KEY TERMS AND DEFINITIONS

**Asynchronous Discussion Boards:** An online learning tool or approach which allows anytime, anywhere access to ongoing discussions not necessarily in real time.

**Blended Learning:** A continuum of a blend or mix of online and face-to-face learning.

**Extravert:** A relatively cortically underaroused individual who seeks stimulation from interaction with others to raise levels of cortical arousal to optimal levels.

**Instrumental Reasons:** Engaging in an activity in order to achieve a practical outcome.

**Introvert:** A relatively cortically over-aroused individual who avoids stimulation from interaction with others to lower levels of cortical arousal to optimal levels.

**Metacognition:** Thinking about thinking or engaging in reflection about thinking (often one's own).

**Social Reasons:** Engaging in an activity in order to achieve a social or emotional outcome.

**Synchronous Discussion Boards:** An online learning tool or approach in which 'live' learning takes place because student-student and student-tutor interactions occur in real time.

# Chapter 6
# Design and Implementation Issues of Interoperable Educational Application:
## An ICT Application for Primary School English Education in Japan

**Yasushige Ishikawa**
*Kyoto University of Foreign Studies, Japan*

**Mutsumi Kondo**
*Tezukayamagakuin University, Japan*

**Craig Smith**
*Kyoto University of Foreign Studies, Japan*

## ABSTRACT

*This chapter reports on the development of an innovative interoperable Information and Communication Technology (ICT) application for English teaching in primary schools in Japan. An investigation into the use of the ICT application during a four month period at two primary schools is also described. The results of the initial needs analysis conducted to identify appropriate means of support for effective primary school English education, the subsequent processes of the design, the development and implementation of the ICT application, the children's reflections during use of the ICT application in English lessons, and a post-course evaluation by children and by their homeroom teachers are described. Proposals are made for the future enhancement of the interoperability capacity for the ICT application.*

## INTRODUCTION

Information and Communication Technology (ICT) is viewed throughout the world today as a necessity *in* education and an opportunity *for* education (UNESCO, 2009). ICT has a wonderful potential to improve the quality and the reach of education through the information it will eventually make accessible in every classroom and through its interactive communicative capacities that can make the ways we teach and learn more effective.

DOI: 10.4018/978-1-61692-791-2.ch006

In an attempt to improve Japan's very poor standing in international comparisons of English language proficiency, the national government proposed to advance the beginning of teaching English as Foreign Language in public schools from grade seven in junior high school to grade five in primary school. The response to the policy change from the general public and from teachers was overwhelmingly pessimistic. It was claimed that there were not enough trained primary school teachers proficient in English to teach the new courses and that the impact of poor teaching would get children off to a frustrating start with English that would have a negative long-term effect on motivation.

This chapter describes an ICT project that dealt head-on with those concerns by using a newly available ICT public resource, interactive white-boards, in a way that supported the government's teaching objectives and the authorized teaching materials. This chapter outlines the development of the first stage of an ICT application that was shown, in a fully-integrated manner, to contribute to teacher training and to enhance student motivation. The integration of these two core contributions rests on three educationally-sound assumptions:

1. Blended learning, the integration of technologically-assisted learning and traditional classroom practices, may help initiate ICT educational programs (Voos, 2003).
2. Team learning, the collaborative participation of teachers and learners in configurations that blur the conventional divisions between learners and teachers (Tajino & Tajino, 2000), may help facilitate a special form of blended learning with an ICT application that allows teachers to feel comfortable in occasionally taking the role of learner in classroom learning activities.
3. The principles of Exploratory Practice (Allwright & Hanks, 2009) can provide a philosophical framework to promote team learning in ways that deal with the legitimate concern that technology can cause divisions between participants in learning and can reduce the level of their activity in learning. Exploratory Practice places a priority on achieving quality of life in the classroom for learners and for teachers by bringing them together for mutual development, and by working to understand life in the language classroom in ways that are compatible with professional teaching practices, and in ways that are continuous.

## English Education in Primary Schools: Current Views in Europe and Asia

At the Group of Eight economic summit held in Köln, Germany, 1999, education was nominated as one of the key topics and the summit joint declaration stated that "the promotion of the study of foreign languages" was indispensable "to increase the understanding of different cultures and enhance mobility in a globalized world" (G8 Information Centre, 1999). Following this declaration, various educational initiatives in foreign language education have been undertaken; a common pillar of the reform movements has been the introduction of foreign language teaching at primary schools. It is generally agreed that primary school children have special age-related capacities for foreign language acquisition and the nurturing of constructive cross-cultural understanding (e.g., Johnson & Newport, 1989; Lenneberg, 1967; Minoura, 1984; Penfield & Roberts, 1959). See Dolitsky, McCloskey & Orr (2006) for a recent case study review of EFL teaching in primary schools in a number of different countries.

In the European Union it was decided that in addition to the study of the children's native language, two foreign languages would be taught beginning at primary school. In Germany, although there are some differences between various states, foreign language education classes have been taught twice a week since 2003 and in France, once or twice a week since 2007. English has been chosen as one of the foreign languages by almost all primary schools in these two countries (National Institute for Educational Policy Research, 2004).

Comparisons between the situation in one of the European nations, Spain, and Japan are of particular interest because of Spain's longer experience with compulsory English instruction at the primary school level. In Spain, English has been a compulsory course since 1991. The learning objectives include: 1. the development of listening, speaking, reading and writing abilities 2. the encouragement of cross-cultural understanding. In addition, the primary school curriculum is usually designed to link with foreign language education programs at secondary schools as is shown in Figure 1. Although learnability issues related to phonology, orthography, and other language distance factors are beyond the scope of this chapter, it may be that in future Japan will be able to draw useful lessons from the experiences of Spain and other European nations. Even though their languages have closer relationships with English than Japanese, Chinese and Korean, a great deal may be learned from experiences in very different as well as from comparatively similar situations.

In Asia, especially in China, South Korea and Taiwan, English is now a required course. As in Spain, acquisition of the four language skills, the enhancement of cross-cultural understanding, and the creation of an educational constructive linkage between primary and secondary schools are the main aims of English education curriculum plans. In addition, in Asia the development of a positive attitude towards learning English and communicating with other people through English is a key component of the curriculum; however, this particular learning objective is not specified in primary school English education in Spain, as is shown in Figure 1. An explanation may be that in these Asian nations more care is taken with developing positive attitudes towards English language learning and use because of issues of language distance; for example, differences in the writing systems and comparatively less social contact with people who use English as a means of international communication may have to be taken into account in lesson planning in Japan and in Asian countries.

The comparisons we have summarized in Figure 1 which include three of Japan's Asian neighbors and Spain as a representative of Europe are intended to show that teaching English at primary school has been accepted by other nations and that they have years of experience in providing English lessons for young learners. This is important to keep in mind because there has been a great deal of controversy about this matter in Japan with many people believing it will interfere with children's education in their native

*Figure 1. English Education in Primary Schools in China, South Korea, Taiwan and Spain*

| Country | Inagural year | Grade | Hours of instruction per week | Average class size | Course type | Learning objectives | | | | | | | Educational linkage |
|---|---|---|---|---|---|---|---|---|---|---|---|---|---|
| | | | | | | Possitive attitude | Autonomy | Listening | Speaking | Reading | Writing | Cross-cultural understanding | |
| China | 2005 (2003 in Beijing) | 3, 4 | four 20-minute lessons | 50 | Required | O | O | O | O | O | O | O | O |
| | | 5, 6 | two 20-minute lessons + more than two 40-minute | | | | | | | | | | |
| Korea | 1997 | 3, 4 | one 45-minute lesson | 32.9 | Required | O | — | O | O | O | O | O | O |
| | | 5, 6 | two 45-minute lessons | | | | | | | | | | |
| Taiwan | 2005 (1998 in Taipei) | 3, 4, 5, 6 | two 40-minute lessons | 30 | Required | O | O | O | O | O | O | O | O |
| Spain | 1991 | 3, 4, 5, 6 | 3 hours | 25 | Required | — | — | O | O | O | O | O | O |

(National Institute for Educational Policy Research, 2004; Ministry of Education, Culture, Sports, Science and Technology, 2007a, 2007b, 2007c)

language and that starting English lessons at secondary school, as is the current practice in Japan, is sufficient. Other critics believe primary school English teaching policies will be very difficult to implement. Thus, it is important, in addition, to also note that these nations English language programs are more ambitious than Japan's plans (which are described in the next section): English lessons are begun two years earlier than in Japan, and the learning objectives in these other nations include all four language skills while Japan's approach emphasizes the spoken language and the development of positive learning attitudes.

## English Education in Primary Schools in Japan

In Japan, English education was first introduced in the academic year 2002. It was reported that children have gained some interest in English through the learning activities in the classrooms (Ministry of Education, Culture, Sports, Science and Technology, 2004). However, a wide range of English learning activities have been carried out based on the local educational environments of individual schools because neither concrete curriculum guidelines nor textbooks were issued by the Ministry of Education, Culture, Sports, Science and Technology until the academic year 2009. For this reason the number of hours of instruction per week and the content of classroom learning activities in the classrooms varied greatly from school to school. Although the Ministry of Education, Culture, Sports, Science and Technology had claimed that regular primary school homeroom teachers could effectively teach English because they have the most intimate knowledge of the children's interests and learning abilities, homeroom teachers had not been trained to teach English and so it was generally assumed that homeroom teachers would not have adequate English communication skills and furthermore, that they would have difficulty in teaching English effectively. Therefore, assistant teachers of English, who are native English speakers, English teachers at secondary schools, and instructors at English conversation schools were requested to develop curriculum guidelines and materials. In addition, they were also asked to teach English at primary schools in order to deal with the challenges related to requiring all primary school homeroom teachers to teach English.

## The New Course of Study

In 2007 the Central Council for Foreign Language Education Academic Advisory Committee of the Ministry of Education, Culture, Sports, Science and Technology issued the following guidelines:
1. English education for 5th and 6th grade primary school children should be improved in order to enhance the educational linkage between English study at primary schools and at secondary schools.
2. Since learning activities using English in the classroom have varied a great deal among primary schools, guidelines for teaching English should be proposed in order to create equal opportunity in education for all students and equality in the educational linkage between English programs at primary schools and those at secondary schools.
3. It is appropriate that thirty five credit hours in a year (one session per week) should be allotted for teaching English to 5th and 6th grade primary school children (Central Council for Foreign Language Education Academic Advisory, 2007)

On March 28, 2008, the Ministry of Education, Culture, Sports, Science and Technology announced in its curriculum guidelines, the New Course of Study, that teaching English will be made compulsory and that English will be taught once a week beginning in 2011. In April 2008, the Ministry published "English Notebook," a textbook including a CD and a teacher's manual for teaching English to 5$^{th}$ and 6$^{th}$ grade primary school children.

The overall objective of English language activities in the New Course of Study is to form a foundation for children's English communication abilities while developing an understanding of the English language and culture through various experiences, fostering a positive attitude towards communication, and familiarizing children with the sounds and basic expressions of the English language (Ministry of Education, Culture, Sports, Science and Technology, 2009).

The New Course of Study claims that English education should deepen the experiential understanding of the languages and cultures of Japan and of foreign countries. The following teaching goals were specified: 1. Children should become familiar with the sounds and rhythms of the English language to learn about differences between English and Japanese, and to become aware of the interesting aspects of the English language and its richness. 2. Children should learn about differences in ways of living, customs and events between Japan and foreign countries and become aware of various points of view and ways of thinking. 3. Children should experience communication with people of different cultures in order to deepen their understanding of culture.

The New Course of Study also suggests that homeroom teachers should create teaching programs and conduct lessons and make efforts to get more people involved in classroom lessons by inviting native speakers of English and by seeking cooperation from local people who are proficient in English. The New Course of Study also suggests that the following important teaching points should be included in lessons: 1. Letters of the alphabet and English words which are essential for the basic spoken language communication that children may experience. 2. Grammatical forms and patterns should not be emphasized. Memorizing English words and phrases mechanically should be avoided. 3. Audio-visual aids such as CDs and DVDs should be used as the main learning materials.

Moreover, the New Course of Study makes it clear that these guidelines are not intended to regulate English language activities at primary schools and that each primary school may respond flexibly to these guidelines according to local conditions.

By 2013, however, it is anticipated that Japanese homeroom teachers will have to conduct English lessons independently on their own because the number of native-speakers or bilingual Japanese assistant teachers of English will not be sufficient to provide team teaching in each class in the nation. Thus, the concern that some primary school teachers do not have adequate English spoken language skills to teach English with confidence must be dealt with in another way. In order to cope with this situation, it is expected that Japanese homeroom teachers will conduct English lessons using CDs, DVDs, ICT materials, and interactive whiteboard technology to introduce examples of authentic spoken English to their students.

## ICT Education in Japan

### E-Japan Strategy

The Information Technology (IT) Strategy, which promotes the formation of IT-centered society, has two phases in Japan: the e-Japan Strategy: 2001-2006 and the New IT Reform Strategy: 2007-2011. In the e-Japan Strategy, it was said that Japan must take revolutionary yet realistic actions promptly, without being bound by existing systems, practices and interests, in order to create a "knowledge-emergent society," where everyone can actively utilize information technology (IT) and fully enjoy its benefits (IT Strategic Headquarters, 2001). These initiatives are intended to establish an environment where the private sector, based on market forces, can exert its full potential and make Japan the world's most advanced IT nation within five years by building an ultra high-speed Internet network and providing constant Internet access at the earliest date possible, establishing rules on electronic commerce, realizing an electronic government and nurturing high-quality human resources for the new era (IT Strategic Headquarters, 2001).

## The New IT Reform Strategy

The New IT Reform Strategy has been formulated in order to help contribute to the creation of a global borderless peaceful and prosperous society with Asia as its center. The IT Strategic Headquarters declares that by FY 2010—ahead of all other nations—through the implementation of this new strategy, Japan will achieve a complete transformation of itself through the utilization of IT to achieve, sustainable development becoming an autonomous and collaborative IT society in which all citizens can proactively participate (IT Strategic Headquarters, 2006a). These two strategies include objectives for IT education at the primary and secondary education level. The objectives aim to create an advanced IT environment and to improve teachers' IT teaching skills, to promote the use of IT in the classroom, and to boost students' information literacy.

However, the White Paper on Science and Technology (2008) published by the Ministry of Education, Culture, Sports, Science and Technology revealed that in March 2007, when the e-Japan Strategy plan was completed, the achievement percentage of setting up LANS networks at schools was 56.2%. This figure is relatively low compared with that of the United States: 94%, UK: 84% and South Korea: 100% and this means that education utilizing IT in primary schools in Japan still remains far from the target levels (Ministry of Education, Culture, Sports, Science and Technology, 2008). These particular comparisons are used because it can be expected that the Japanese government may use these nations' achievements as a target to renew its efforts.

## The School New Deal Scheme

A key policy of the School New Deal action plan is to carry out the installation of state-of the-art technology in all school facilities. In the FY 2009 supplementary budget, the Ministry of Education, Culture, Sports, Science and Technology has included appropriations for the promotion of the School New Deal, a scheme intended to carry out school-improvement measures in an integrated manner, including the acceleration of the renovation of existing school facilities to improve their earthquake-resistance, to achieve a "green" renovation of school buildings (e.g., by installing solar panels), and to improve the ICT environment at schools.

Approximately 4 trillion yen will be invested to set up an interactive whiteboard, or IWB, in all 32,000 of the nation's primary schools, to increase the number of PCs in schools, and to establish school LANS. Approximately 10 billion yen will be also invested in teacher training for primary school English education. The aim of the training programs is to improve the English language skills of teachers who will mainly teach English at primary schools through the observation of model lessons, including team-teaching demonstrations, which make use of the "English Notebook." The intention is to help primary school teachers learn English language teaching methodology and also to provide opportunities for them to improve their English language skills.

## Interactive Whiteboard Technology

An interactive whiteboard is a large interactive display that is connected to a computer and a projector. The projector projects the computer's desktop onto the board's surface, where users are able to control the computer using a pen, a finger or other device. The board is typically mounted on a wall or on a floor stand. They are used in a variety of settings in classrooms at all levels of education. The functions of interactive whiteboards include: 1. the operation of any software that is loaded onto the connected PC, including web browsers and proprietary software, 2. the use of software to capture notes written on a whiteboard or whiteboard-like surface, 3. the control of the PC (click and drag), markup (annotating a program or a presentation text) and the translation of cursive writing to text (not all whiteboards). 4. In some instances the Interactive Whiteboard may be provided with an integrated Audience Response System so presenters can carry out polls and quizzes and capture the feedback on the Interactive Whiteboard.

The above functions may be useful for primary school English education for the following reasons: 1. Various media such as images and sounds can be shown simultaneously. 2. Drawings by children of things they are interested in can be displayed. 3. Audio-visual materials such as CDs and DVDs can effectively engage children in English language activities (Ministry of Education, Culture, Sports, Science and Technology, 2008). 4. Uses of Audio-visual materials such as CDs and DVDs can allow children to feel that they are engaged in real communication. 5. Children's interest in writing English letters can be stimulated by tracing English letters on the interactive whiteboard.

## Teacher Training

The Ministry of Education, Culture, Sports, Science and Technology proposed that a 30 hour teacher training program at primary schools should be conducted each year for the two years preceding 2011, when teaching English will be made compulsory and English lessons must be held once a week. The aim of the training program is to improve teachers' English teaching skills and the teachers' English language skills. The Ministry of Education, Culture, Sports, Science and Technology also suggested that the teachers who have the main responsibility for teaching English at their primary schools should receive additional specialized teaching training courses at training centers at regional education centers. It is expected that when the teachers return to their schools they will hold debriefing sessions with their colleagues as part of local faculty development programs. This is called a 'cascade' training system in which experiences at professional development events is passed on from teacher to teacher to include teachers who were not able to attend the events themselves.

However, according to a Benesse Educational Research & Development Center (2007) report, 54.9% of primary school teachers said that they did not attend teacher training sessions held at their own schools and that 62.0% of the homeroom teachers did not take part in teacher training programs held outside of their schools. The most common reason given for non-attendance indicates a flaw in the government's teacher training plans: primary school teachers are simply too busy to add events to their full schedules, even if they are held at their own schools (JTU Institute for Education and Culture, 2009). Moreover, it was claimed that is very difficult for primary school teachers who are not experts at teaching English to pass on information that they gain through external training sessions to their colleagues at their schools. In other words, it is likely that until primary school teachers have actually taught for a few years in their own classrooms by themselves they will not feel comfortable enough to pass information about English teaching methodology on to their colleagues.

A main weakness of this so-called 'cascade' training system is the dilution effect, that is, as information is passed down through various levels in a chain of communication, the information may be altered in negative ways (Asia and the Pacific Programme of Educational Innovation for Development, 1984). For cascade training to be successful, there appear to be a number of key criteria which the program should take into account: 1. The method of conducting the training must be experiential and reflective rather than transmissive 2. The training sessions must be open to reinterpretation 3. Rigid adherence to prescribed ways of working should not be expected (Hayes, 2000).

In addition, for teachers to be receptive to adopting new and different teaching methods they need to be sure that these methods will bring benefits both to themselves and to their learners. Teacher development activities should be, accordingly, classroom-centered; they should have direct relevance to teachers' everyday school situations, and be practical. Although good teaching practice is informed by theory, an understanding of theory alone is insufficient as an agent of long-term change.

## AIM OF THE STUDY

This study was designed to explore one possible model of successfully and proactively dealing with this major transition in English education in Japan, the initiation of compulsory once a week English lessons taught by primary school teachers, including many novice EFL teachers, who cannot expect support from foreign native or bilingual Japanese speakers of English. It was considered most important to support primary school English teachers by directly and practically addressing the element of the plan which is likely to be the cause of anxiety for many teachers—their possible failure to satisfy the overall objective of the New Course of Study. The overall aim, and the teachers' greatest challenge, is to provide English language activities which will form a foundation of children's English communication skills.

An opportunity exists if productive links can be established and sustained between the national IT Strategy which promotes the use of IT in the classroom, the School New Deal scheme which aims to improve the ICT environment at schools by placing interactive whiteboards in all primary schools, and the primary school English education initiative. Thus, we developed an ICT application for interactive whiteboards that is intended to help satisfy the overall objective of the English education plan while supporting primary school English teachers in their own growth as confident and competent English language communicators and skilful English teachers.

## INTEROPERABILITY: THE CREATION OF A TEAM-LEARNING ENVIRONMENT

Interoperability is defined by the Institute of Electrical and Electronic Engineers (IEEE as cited in IEEE-USA, 2005) as follows: "the ability of two or more systems or components to exchange information and to use the information that has been exchanged." In the technical sense, in our study, the ICT application allows the efficient communication of materials developed by teachers, and other materials developers, who are working in different locations and for different organizations.

Moreover, we define interoperability, from a broader educational perspective, as the capacity of the ICT application to create a single learning environment in which the human components of the educational system, i.e. primary school children and teachers in a single class, may collaborate in a team-learning enterprise in order to accomplish their separate aims; and in which teachers and materials developers at different locations may collaborate in materials development and teacher training activities.

## DEFINITION OF THE FOUNDATION OF ENGLISH COMMUNICATION ABILITIES

The new curriculum guidelines for secondary school English education state that English education should be based on the foundation of children's English communication abilities developed at the primary school level (Ministry of Education, Culture, Sports, Science and Technology, 2009). Thus, the intention to create a link has been formalized and this makes it necessary to define what exactly the foundation of English communication abilities is and how it can be laid.

The development of a foundation of children's communication abilities in primary school has been defined as having two phases (Ministry of Education, Culture, Sports, Science and Technology, 2009): 1. the nurturing of children's positive attitudes about their own potential to become good communicators in English, and 2. the provision of children with opportunities to familiarize themselves with the sound system and to learn basic expressions of the English language.

The need of support for teachers and the aims of the program were taken into account in balanced proportions during the design and implementation stages of the interactive whiteboard application as a creative force in the classroom learning environment.

## DESIGN OF THE ICT APPLICATION

### The ADDIE Model

In order to develop the ICT application, we used the ADDIE model, a practical model for the design and development of instructional materials which centers all component processes in a holistic systematic planning environment. The ADDIE model has five phases: Analysis, Design, Development, Implementation and Evaluation; each phase has an outcome that naturally leads into the subsequent step (Gagne, Wager, & Keller, 2005).

### A Needs Analysis

As the first step in the development of the ICT application, a needs analysis of primary school children and homeroom teachers was conducted in order to ground the development in an understanding of the thoughts and feelings of all of the participants in the English learning and teaching activities.

### Children's Needs

#### Participants

Ninety 6th grade children (forty girls and fifty boys) who were studying English at two primary schools in Japan participated in our study.

#### Questionnaires

A needs analysis of primary school children was conducted in order to discover what sort of learning activities primary school children would like to participate in. The following ten questions were asked:

*1. Do you like English? 2. Do you like studying English in class at school? 3. Do you want to read English in class at school? 4. Do you want to write English in class at school? 5. Do you want to listen to English in class at school? 6. Do you want to speak English in class at school? 7. Do you want to learn secondary school level English? 8. Do you want to communicate with people from other countries in English? 9. Do you want to talk about yourself and about Japan with people from other countries? 10. Do you ever study English outside of your school class?*

Points were assigned to the children's responses on a three-point scale: 3 - for Yes, I do; 2 - for Maybe, I do; 1 - for No, I don't.

In addition, one open ended question was asked: What do you want to do in your English lessons at primary school before entering secondary school?

### Analysis and Results

The children's interest in listening to, speaking, reading, and writing English (Questions No. 3-6) was, on the whole, rather high and fairly balanced among the skills as indicated by the following results: listening to English, mean - 2.7, SD - 0.46;

speaking English, mean - 2.6, SD - 0.6; reading English, mean - 2.6, SD - 0.6; and writing English, mean - 2.7, SD - 0.6.

The mean score of children's interests in listening and writing English was higher than their interest in speaking and reading English. This may indicate that 6th grade children understand that speaking is just one aspect of English communication and their interest in writing English may reflect an interest in approaching self expression in English in a more controllable mode than by speaking. In any case, more detailed surveys of children's views, which include interviews, should be conducted.

The answers to the open-ended question also revealed the children's interest in writing English. 86% of the answers were focused on writing. Sample answers were: "I want to write a simple sentence," "I want to practice writing English letters" and "I want to write English words in order to memorize them."

The children's interest in understanding cultures of foreign countries (Question No.8) was high: mean - 2.3, SD - 0.7, and their interest in talking about themselves and their own culture to people from other countries (Question No.9) was also comparatively high: mean - 2.0, SD - 0.7.

The children's interest in studying secondary level English was high: mean - 2.2, SD - 0.7. Additional evidence of this interest was found in some of the answers to the question: What do you want to do in class at school before entering secondary school?: "I want to study secondary level English hard," "I want to study English that is useful for secondary level English study" and "I want to study English so I will not have trouble studying English at secondary school." These responses indicate that children have a serious view of the benefits they expect from their primary school English lessons. They want to prepare themselves for secondary school.

## Homeroom Teachers' Needs

### Participants

One hundred and sixty eight homeroom teachers from twenty two primary schools in Japan participated in our study.

### Questionnaires

The questions were divided into four categories: Fourteen questions were about their readiness to conduct English teaching activities in their classrooms, three questions were about their views of the Course of Study, five questions were about using ICT materials for English teaching activities, and two questions were about teacher training sessions. Points were assigned to the teachers' responses on a four-point scale to get overall measures of the homeroom teachers' needs. A four-point scale was used: from 1 - not sufficient at all to 4 – completely sufficient. In addition to the fourteen questions, the teachers were asked to respond as they liked to open-ended questions about English teaching activities, materials which can be used for English teaching activities, the use of ICT materials, and teacher training sessions.

### Analysis and Results

Figure 2 below shows the results of the needs analysis given to primary school homeroom teachers about their readiness to conduct English teaching activities.

All the mean scores in the above Figure 2 are below 3.0. This figure indicates that homeroom teachers feel anxious about their readiness to teach. The teachers feel that they do not have sufficient time to develop and prepare teaching materials and they believe they do not have enough knowledge about teaching devices which can be used for listening activities. Moreover, they state that they do not know enough about ICT materi-

*Figure 2. Results of the Needs Analysis about Teachers' Readiness to Conduct English Teaching Activities*

| | MEAN | SD |
|---|---|---|
| Homeroom teachers' English ability | 2.16 | 0.76 |
| Homeroom teachers' English teaching knowledge and skills | 2.16 | 0.69 |
| Time to develop and prepare teaching materials | 1.67 | 0.64 |
| Curriculum | 2.19 | 0.76 |
| Easy-to-use teaching materials | 2.05 | 0.70 |
| Teaching devices for listening activities and ICT materials | 1.96 | 0.78 |
| Children's positive attitudes toward English learning | 2.97 | 0.63 |
| Homeroom teachers' positive attitude toward English teaching | 2.53 | 0.66 |
| Cooperation among teachers | 2.61 | 0.71 |
| Hours of English instruction | 2.59 | 0.74 |
| Training in English instruction methods | 2.11 | 0.65 |
| Budget for English instruction needs | 1.73 | 0.67 |
| Cooperation with junior high schools | 1.76 | 0.64 |
| Administrative support | 1.86 | 0.67 |

als and other easy-to-use teaching materials. The anxiety the teachers likely feel about the above matters is suggested by their beliefs that they do not have good enough English language skills. To make matters worse for the teachers, they state that they lack English teaching knowledge and skills. The teachers' views stand in sharp contrast to their children's comparatively positive attitudes.

70.3% of the participants feel that "English Notebook," a textbook including a CD and a teacher's manual for teaching English to 5th and 6th grade primary school children published by the Ministry of Education, Culture, Sports, Science and Technology lessened homeroom teachers' burden to develop original materials for English teaching activities. Nevertheless, 88.8% of the participants feel uneasy about teaching English from the academic year 2011.

Homeroom teachers feel that teacher training sessions at their own schools are not sufficient. 21.6% of the teachers have not yet received any training, 51.0% have participated in teacher training once or twice a year. This percentage is far from the target of 30 hours of training sessions proposed by the Ministry of Education, Culture, Sports, Science and Technology. Since homeroom teachers feel that they do not have enough knowledge about teaching devices for listening activities nor about how to use ICT materials, there is an urgent need to ensure that teacher training plans which include all teachers provide the information and the skills teachers need to use ICT materials and other teaching devices for listening activities.

The responses that homeroom teachers made to the open-ended questions about English teaching activities, teaching materials, the use of ICT materials, and teacher training events indicate that homeroom teachers feel very uneasy about the challenges they face. It was clear that the underlying problem was that they lack confidence in their own English. The following examples of their comments reveal the depth of their anxiety: "I have no confidence in pronouncing English sounds and teaching English," "I feel uneasy about only homeroom teachers teaching English without help." and "Since assistant teachers of English have always conducted English activities in the classroom, I am so anxious about teaching English by myself."

In the teachers' own words, the homeroom teachers are not only "novice English teachers" but also "English learners who are not good at English."

The needs analysis of primary school children and Japanese homeroom teachers revealed that primary school children's main concern was to improve their language skills, while Japanese homeroom teachers' needs differ as they are "novice English teachers" and "English learners" as well as experts at teaching various subjects other than English. In order to meet the differing needs of primary school children and their homeroom teachers, we developed an ICT application which took into account both the needs of children and teachers.

## GRAND DESIGN OF THE ICT APPLICATION

The ICT application was designed: 1. to support classroom activities using the CD distributed by the Ministry of Education, Culture, Sports, Science and Technology, 2. to support primary school children as they learn to recognize English letters and words and practice reading English aloud, 3. to establish a model for teaching English at the primary school level, 4. to establish, in future, internet links through the technology among teachers, teacher trainers, and materials developers for the purposes of teacher training and materials development as is shown in Figure 3.

## Course Design

### Curriculum

In order to create a course curriculum for teaching English at the primary school level, eight objectives were derived from the results of the needs analysis of primary school children and the homeroom teachers and from the New Course of Study, published by the Ministry of Education, Culture, Sports, Science and Technology. The eight objectives were: 1. to set clear attainment targets, 2. to reduce homeroom teachers' workload, 3. to present a model of English instruction, 4. to build English literacy, 5. to bridge primary and secondary school English education, 6. to contribute to building a foundation of children's communication abilities, 7. to establish educational linkage with other subjects and 8. to employ ICT materials. Figure 4 below is the blueprint of the course curriculum.

As it was anticipated that the teaching points proposed by the New Course of Study would not easily attain its eight aims, we included the following features in the ICT application: 1. A virtual assistant teacher of English, teaching materials and all curriculum information was installed

*Figure 3. Grand Design of the ICT Application*

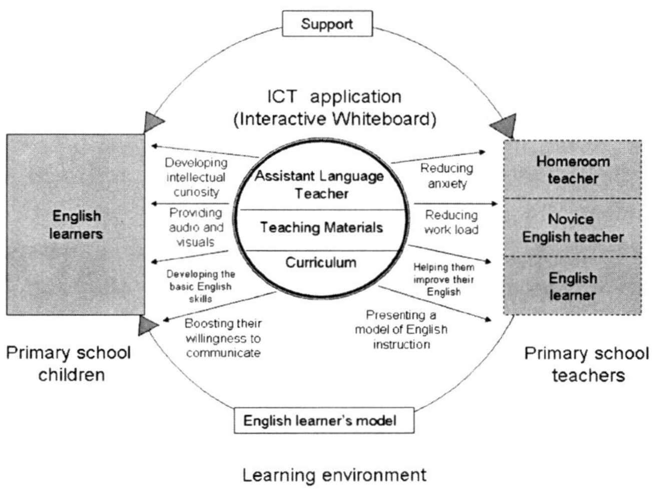

*Figure 4. Blueprint of the Course Curriculum*

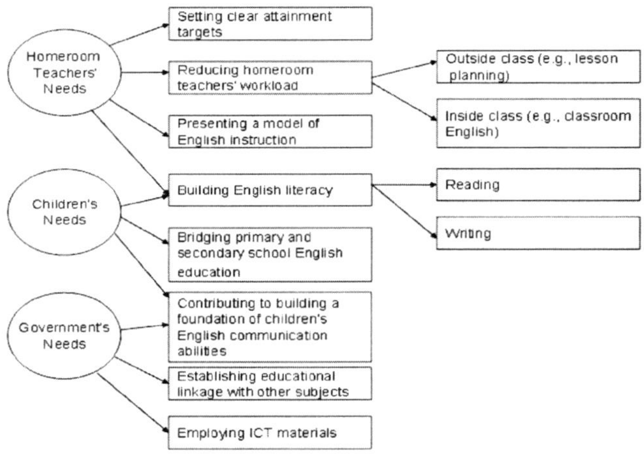


in the ICT application in order to reduce homeroom teachers' workload, to present a model of native-English instruction, and to employ the ICT materials. 2. Each lesson was composed of three components: activities with the "English Notebook," reading aloud activities and electronic penmanship tasks to build English literacy skills. 3. Homeroom teachers served as models of English learners for the children in order to reduce homeroom teachers' anxiety about their own English skills by creating a team-learning environment 4. Five lessons were organized in specific skill-building units to facilitate lesson timing and other planning logistics. 6. Letters of the alphabet and English words were presented in attractive and pedagogically principled ways. 7. Children were provided with enjoyable carefully structured writing lessons to help them make a confident transition to the English alphabet from the Japanese writing system. 8. Children were introduced to reading in English in stages which encourage successful step by step progress. 9. Lesson plans which set clear attainment targets are provided for the teachers. In a 45-minute lesson,, the first 30 minutes were set aside for activities with the "English Notebook," the next 10 minutes were for reading aloud tasks and the remaining 5 minutes were for electronic penmanship.

In order to create lesson plans for 45 minute sessions, the first 30 minutes was assigned for activities with the "English Notebook," the next 10 minutes were for reading aloud and the remaining 5 minutes were for electronic penmanship tasks. One unit was composed of 5 lessons, unlike the recommendation of 4 lessons in the teacher's manual published by the Ministry of Education, Culture, Sports, Science and Technology.

## DEVELOPMENT OF THE ICT APPLICATION

After lesson plans for the English communication activities were developed, the ICT application was created to employ lesson plans. The key points that we kept in mind as guidelines for the creation of the ICT application were the following: 1. The ICT application should provide all the materials for English communication activities in the classroom and be able to present the activities on the interactive whiteboard. 2. The ICT application should provide the same learning environment as the "English Notebook" on the interactive whiteboard, that is, all the images and the sounds used in the ICT application should be the same as those used in the "English Notebook." 3. A virtual assistant teacher of English, who is integrated in the ICT application, should give instructions to the children in the classroom in order to reduce homeroom teachers' workloads. The voice of the virtual assistant teacher of English should be recorded by the same voice actors who recorded the voices for the "English Notebook."4. In order to create opportunities for natural communication with the virtual assistant teacher, pauses should be inserted after the virtual assistant teacher's utterances. 5. The homeroom teacher should perform as a role model of an English learner who learns English together with the children. 6. A controller that can go forwards and backwards and stop screens of the ICT application should be set up in the ICT application so that the English communication activities can be conducted according to specific groups of children's learning needs. 7. The virtual assistant teacher should speak native-like English and at the tempo of native speakers of English. This helps children notice the differences between the virtual assistant teacher's utterances and their homeroom teacher's utterances as their teacher acts as a role model of an English learner in the English communication activities. 8. The letters of the alphabet should be presented on the interactive whiteboard in ways to motivate the children and facilitate their reading of the letters.

## ACTIVITIES WITH "ENGLISH NOTEBOOK": 5 STEPS TO FOSTER THE FOUNDATION OF CHILDREN'S COMMUNICATION ABILITIES

The needs analysis of primary school children revealed that children desire to practice English in order to gain knowledge which is useful for English learning at the secondary school level. A key learning objective of the activities with "English Notebook" was to allow children to gain knowledge within a framework of confidence in their own abilities in order that they may play an active part in shaping and personalizing their own communication in English.

The activities with the "English Notebook" were intended to promote language acquisition by providing opportunities for comprehensible input, up-take by students as they as manage to do a learning task, in-take as they notice and understand the key language features of the lesson, and pushed output as they actually produce language on their own. An example outline of the five lessons of one unit is shown in Figure 5. Step 1 has four components: greetings in various languages, introduction of the lessons, word-level in-take activities and communicative activities. Step 2 has five components: greetings in various languages, review of step 1, introductions of the lessons, word-level in-take activities and communicative activities. Step 3 has six components: greetings in various languages, review of step 1, review of step 2, introductions of the lessons, phrase-level in-take activities and communicative activities. Step 4 has seven components: greetings in various languages, review of step 1, review of step 2, review of step 3, self introductions, sentence-level in-take activities and communicative activities. Step 5 has three components: greetings in various languages, review of steps 1 to 4 and communicative activities. The target language of each step builds from an easy word level to a challenging sentence level presentation. Learning activities move from artificial language teaching models to authentic communication-focused models.

### Reading Aloud

This reading aloud activity was planned to create educational linkage with other subjects taught in the Japanese language, for example, with the Moral Education course. An original story was created so that the setting and the content would be familiar to the children, for example, the characters in the story were the same age as the children. An outline for the reading aloud lesson component is as follows: 1. Homeroom teachers read the story

*Figure 5. 5 Steps to Foster the Foundation of Children's Communication Abilities*

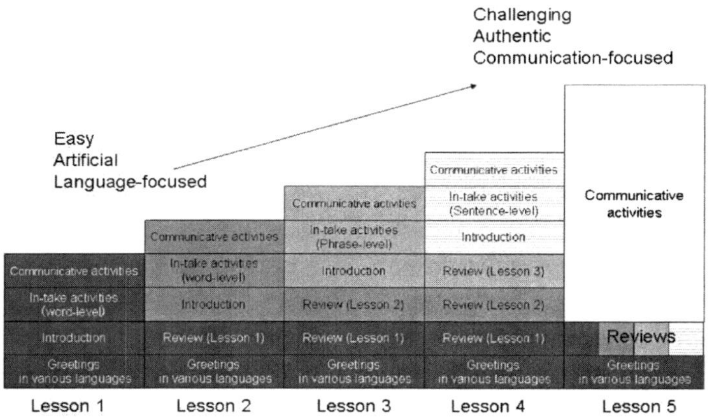


in Japanese in the Moral Education class, using pictures. 2. During an English lesson, the children read words, phrases and sentences from the same story aloud in English learning activities.

As the New Course of Study states, instructions should be given so that children become familiar with the sounds and rhythms of the English language, learn its differences from the Japanese language and become aware of the interesting aspects of the language and its richness. Thus, the characters in the story speak native-like English at the tempo of native speakers of English. Children are led to repeat the story while listening to the native-like English, imitating the tempo, rhythm, intonation. That is why we introduced "shadowing," in the ICT lessons which is "an act or a task of listening in which the learner tracks the heard speech and repeats it as exactly as possible while listening attentively to the in-coming information" (Tamai, 2003, p.3). Shadowing was developed as a method to train interpreters and this method is commonly used with senior high school and university students in Japan. Research has shown that students' pronunciation, rhythm and intonation, grammatical ability and speaking ability has improved through shadowing (e.g., Kume, 1981; Miyazaki, 2000; Someya, 1998).

## Electronic Penmanship

This electronic penmanship activity was included to enable children to trace letters of the alphabet. Through the activity, children are led to understand how writing the letters of the alphabet feels. The English words used in this electronic penmanship learning activity were from a specially created corpus-of words selected from five authorized secondary school-level English textbooks. Words which appeared in three out of the five textbooks were used in this activity and among those selected words, words which also appeared in "English Notebook" emphasized.

In this learning activity, three words were presented in the following five steps in the ICT application: 1. Children look at letters of a word, listen to the sound and look at the meaning of the word in Japanese. 2. Children repeat the sound as they listen. 3. Children come to the interactive whiteboard and touch the same word as they listen.4. Children trace the letters. 5. Children look at the word with a missing letter and then, write the missing letter in the blank.

## Implementation of the ICT Application

After the ICT application had been completed it was used in a trial run with English communication activities for ninety one 6th grade children at two primary schools in Japan from September 2008 to December 2008. Unit 3, unit 4 and Unit 5 in the "English Notebook" were used in the lessons.

[School A]
Number of children: 48
Children's Experiences of English communication activities: 6 hours, from the 5th grade
Hours of English communication activities with the ICT materials: 14 hours
Teachers:
Homeroom teacher 1 (male, experience of teaching English - 16 months)
Homeroom teacher 2 (male, experience of teaching English - 4 months)
Trainee 1 at a prefectural education center (female, experience of English teaching - 36 months)
[School B]
Number of children: 43
Children's Experiences of English communication activities: more that 50 hours, from the 1st grade
Hours of English communication activities with the ICT materials: 16 hours
Teachers:
Homeroom teacher 3 (male, experience of teaching English - 45 months)
Trainee 2 at a prefectural education center in Japan (female, experience of teaching English - 3 months)

## Course Evaluations

There following are the reasons a decision was made not to conduct objective tests to measure the children's English communication skills: 1. Our study was focused on forming a foundation of children's English communication skills, not to actually develop English communication skills. 2. Research has shown that 6th grade children's scores and their self- assessments are consistent and the rate of correlation between 6th grade children's self-assessment and assessment by friends and teachers is significant (e.g., Phillips, 1963; Nicholls, 1978).

In order to evaluate whether building a foundation of children's English communication skills was fostered by the use of our ICT application which provided all the materials for English communication activities in the classroom by presenting the activities on an interactive whiteboard, the children's reflections during use and also on a post-course evaluation were collected. A post-course evaluation was completed by the homeroom teachers.

## The Children's Evaluation of the English Lessons with the Interactive Whiteboard

### The Children's Reflections after Each Lesson

Forty two 6th grade children at School B participated in filling out a "Reflection Card," which consisted of five questions, after experiencing each one of the fourteen lessons using the ICT application with the Interactive Whiteboard.. The questions were divided into two categories: Three questions were intended to evaluate the children's interest in and their attitudes towards the English communication activities, and one question was intended to probe the children's understanding of the English communication activities. In addition to these four questions, the children were also asked to respond as they wished to an open-ended question about the English communication activities that were held on the day the evaluation was administered. Scores were assigned to the children's responses on a four-point scale: 4 - for Absolutely yes, 3 - for Yes, I do; 2 - for Maybe, I do; and 1 - for No, I don't.

**Question No. 1: Did you enjoy the English communication activities?**
The average mean score of the fourteen lessons was relatively high, 3.7. The mean score of the 1st lesson was the lowest, 3.4; and the score had gradually increased up to a high of 3.9, the

*Figure 6. Lesson plan and ICT application in Unit 5, Lesson4*

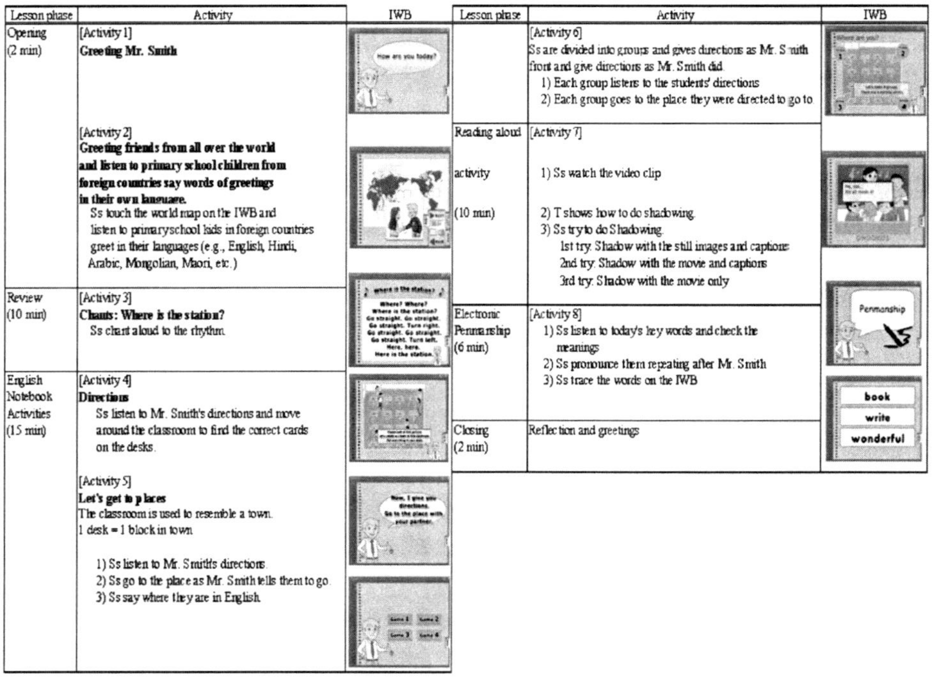

| Lesson phase | Activity | IWB |
|---|---|---|
| Opening (2 min) | [Activity 1] **Greeting Mr. Smith** | How are you today? |
| | [Activity 2] **Greeting friends from all over the world and listen to primary school children from foreign countries say words of greetings in their own language.** Ss touch the world map on the IWB and listen to primaryschool kids in foreign countries greet in their languages (e.g., English, Hindi, Arabic, Mongolian, Maori, etc.) | |
| Review (10 min) | [Activity 3] **Chants: Where is the station?** Ss chant aloud to the rhythm. | Where is the station? Where? Where? Where is the station? Go straight. Go straight. Go straight. Turn right. Go straight. Go straight. Go straight. Turn left. Here, here. Here is the station. |
| English Notebook Activities (15 min) | [Activity 4] **Directions** Ss listen to Mr. Smith's directions and move around the classroom to find the correct cards on the desks. | |
| | [Activity 5] **Let's get to places** The classroom is used to resemble a town. 1 desk = 1 block in town. 1) Ss listen to Mr. Smith's directions. 2) Ss go to the place as Mr. Smith tells them to go. 3) Ss say where they are in English. | |
| | [Activity 6] Ss are divided into groups and gives directions as Mr. Smith front and give directions as Mr. Smith did. 1) Each group listens to the students' directions 2) Each group goes to the place they were directed to go to | |
| Reading aloud activity (10 min) | [Activity 7] 1) Ss watch the video clip 2) T shows how to do shadowing. 3) Ss try to do Shadowing. 1st try: Shadow with the still images and captions 2nd try: Shadow with the movie and captions 3rd try: Shadow with the movie only | |
| Electronic Penmanship (6 min) | [Activity 8] 1) Ss listen to today's key words and check the meanings 2) Ss pronounce them repeating after Mr. Smith 3) Ss trace the words on the IWB | Penmanship; book, write, wonderful |
| Closing (2 min) | Reflection and greetings | |

score of the 14th lesson. This indicates that the number of the children who enjoyed the English communication activities had grown over time. Moreover, about 98% of the children responded either with a 4 or a 3, which makes it clear that almost the entire class had enjoyed the English communication activities. The answers to the open-ended question about the English communication activities revealed that the children's general enjoyment may have motivated them to continue to learn English. Sample responses were: "I was able to read English phrases and sentences aloud better than usual," "I'm very happy to get new knowledge," "I will keep working!" and "I enjoyed studying, talking about what I can do and what I can't do with a friend next to me in English. I will try hard next."

**Question No. 2: Were you willing to listen to the English that was spoken by your homeroom teacher and by your friends?**

The average mean score for the fourteen lessons was relatively high, 3.7. The mean score of the 1st lesson was lowest, 3.4; and the score had gradually increased up to a high of 4.0, the score of the 14th lesson. This indicates that the number of children who were willing to listen to the English that their homeroom teachers and friends spoke had increased. Moreover, more than 99% of the children responded with either a 4 or a 3. This shows that the children's incentive to listen to the non-native English spoken by their homeroom teacher and by their friends' English was high and there were no signs of frustration at gaps between the classroom English and the ICT virtual teacher's model of native English.

**Question No. 3: Were you willing to speak English yourself?**

The average mean score for the fourteen lessons was not as high, 3.5, as the scores for the first two questions. The mean score of the 1st lesson was the lowest, 2.8 and the score had gradually increased up to a high of 3.8, the score of the 14th lesson. The children's answers to the open-ended question about the English communication activities reveals that the children felt quite uneasy about speaking English at the beginning; however that as they became familiar with more English words, phrases and sentences, they gradually gained confidence in speaking English. Sample responses were: "I gradually learned to speak English, and now I can speak English and I said some English words at home," "I couldn't speak English because I felt so uneasy, but now I think I learned to speak English aloud" and "I can speak English now. I really enjoy the English communication activities."

**Question No. 4: Did you understand today's English communication activities?**

The average mean score of the fourteen lessons was high, 3.6. The mean scores of Lesson 1 in Unit 3, Unit 4 and Unit 5 were the lowest, 3.5 and the scores reached a high of 3.8, the mean score of Lesson 4 in Unit 3, Unit 4 and Unit 5. The children's answers to the open-ended question about the English communication activities indicate that the children felt that they had understood the English communication activities. Sample responses were: "I had some difficulty understanding the activities at the beginning, but in the end, I was able to understand the activities and I enjoyed them." and "Now I can speak English. I understand the meaning of English phrases and sentences."

Some of children's answers to the open-ended question about the English communication activities showed that children had set a personal learning goal that was to feel that they improved their English skills. In other words, reaching a satisfactory level of self assessment was important to the children. Sample responses included: "I don't understand how we say dates in English, so I will review it at home." and "Now I figured out what we say for April in English. I want to memorize the English words of the other months. I want to say the English words correctly." Some of children's answers to the open-ended question also showed that their experiences of not understanding the English communication activities provided an incentive and they were motivated to try harder to follow the English communication activities. The following responses showed signs of such motivation: "I can't figure out names of months in English, so I will review them at home," "I can't figure out two or three names of buildings in English, so I want to memorize them." and "My friends can read English phrases and sentences aloud very well. I have to try my best!"

The mean score of the reading aloud activity, one of the three components in each lesson, was 3.18, the lowest score among all the scores of the questions. As the sentences for the children's reading aloud varied according to the lesson, it was unlikely that the mean scores for each lesson could be usefully compared. The children's answers to the open-ended question showed that the reading aloud activity was relatively difficult for the children. Sample responses were: "The reading aloud activity was so difficult." and "The English sentences in today's activity were so long and difficult for me to read." However, some responses were more optimistic: "The reading aloud activity which was so difficult for me. Now I feel it's a bit easier. I will try my best." and "I finally learned to understand the sentences in the activity and now I realize that I can understand English." These responses revealed that their experiences in struggling to understand created incentives to learn more English.

## Children's Post Course Evaluation

Eighty nine $6^{th}$ grade children at School A and School B participated in the post course evaluation. The twenty six questions were divided into five categories: Four questions were intended to elicit information about their feelings towards the ICT English communication activities, four questions were about their interest in learning English, and two questions were about their feelings about the letters of the English alphabet. Scores were assigned to the children's responses on a four-point scale. In addition to the twenty six questions, the children were asked to respond as they liked to an open-ended question about the most and the least difficult ICT English communication activities.

## Feelings about the ICT English Communication Activities

The mean score for the question, Did you like the ICT English communication activities was 3.0 for the children at School A and 4.0 for children at School B. The mean score for the question, "Do you like English better than you did when the ICT application was not used in the classroom" at School A was 3.1 and 3.9 at School B. The mean score of the question, "Do you want to learn English using the interactive whiteboard?" at School A was 3.1 and 4.0 at School B.

## Interest in Learning English

It was revealed that more that 80% of the children at both School A and School B were interested in learning English.

## Feelings about Letters of the Alphabet

The mean score of the question: Did you try to read words that you don't know? at School B was 3.6, relatively high while 3.0 at School A. The mean score of the question: Is it easy for you to listen to and speak English with some letters of the alphabet? At School B was 3.8, rather high while 3.3 at School A.

A main objective of the Japanese government's plan is to have every child at public primary schools have experiences with English communication learning activities that will lay a foundation of positive attitudes towards learning English. It can be reasonably claimed that the ICT application described in this chapter provided English communication activities which raised children's motivation to learn more English.

## Teachers' Post Course Evaluation

Five teachers who taught the English communication activities at School A and School B as homeroom teachers and who were novice English teachers and English learners themselves participated in a post-course evaluation. Forty four questions in two categories were asked: thirty five questions were intended to evaluate the ICT English communication activities and nine questions were asked to elicit information about the teachers' feelings about the ICT application. Scores were assigned to the teachers' responses on a four-point scale: 4 - for Absolutely yes, 3 - for Yes, I do; 2 - for Maybe, I do; and 1 - for No, I don't.

The teachers felt that the ICT English communication activities were successful (Mean – 3.2) and their assessment of the children's attitudes towards participation in the activities was positive (Mean – 3.2). The teachers said that they would like to continue to conduct the ICT English communication activities. The teachers also felt that the children's English vocabulary and ability to listen to English words and phrases had improved (Mean – 3.2). Moreover, the teachers felt that the children's positive attitude towards learning English had improved (Mean – 3.2) and their interest in the cultures of foreign countries had been fostered (Mean – 3.0).

The teachers, as homeroom teachers, felt that they were able to help children learn English (Mean – 3.5), while their own lesson preparation workloads had been reduced (Mean – 3.1) and that the ICT application had helped them during the lesson (Mean – 3.3). The mean score of their feelings about learning English with the children was highest among all the scores (Mean – 3.8). This shows that the teachers enjoyed playing their roles of model learners of English.

The teachers, as novice English teachers, felt that they themselves had learned useful teacher's classroom English phrases by listening to the virtual assistant English teacher. (Mean – 3.0).

The teachers also felt that they were able to gain knowledge of English teaching skills (Mean – 3.4) and that they learned how to design English lessons (Mean – 3.6). The teachers, as model English learners, felt that they were able to learn classroom English (Mean – 3.0) and they reported that they had actually used some of the English in the classrooms (Mean – 3.0).The teachers felt that they enjoyed studying English (Mean – 3.4), which suggests that the ICT application had a good influence on teachers' attitudes towards learning English.

This shows that the teachers retained their perspective as teachers while they were playing the role of learners and that, indeed, the use of the ICT was a useful teacher training event which may be expected to help the teachers become creative and independent English teachers in future by giving them the confidence necessary to design their own original lesson plans.

## FURTHER RESEARCH DIRECTIONS

The successful use of the ICT application with interactive whiteboards is important because since schools will be provided with this technology, it is essential that full use of its educational potential be explored. For example, the ICT application has the capability to establish, in the near future, internet links among teachers, teacher trainers, and materials developers for the purposes of providing easily accessible teacher training and collaborative materials development. As for classroom teaching, because whiteboards are a traditional interface between teachers and students the use of the ICT application with whiteboards will likely remain a comfortable means for teachers to teach English. However, we anticipate new forms of the ICT application will be used in future with devices which have mobile platforms such as the iPhone3G and the Nintendo DS. Mobile ICT applications may have important roles to play in extending the teaching and learning of English beyond the walls of the classroom.

## CONCLUSION

There is some valid criticism that ICT in educational settings tends to encourage learners to adopt a passive dependent learning style and that learners tend to be isolated from one another by the technology itself. Much to the contrary, the ICT application described in this chapter seemed to encourage an active independent learning style according to the comments of the children and the teachers. A simple explanation could be that the large familiar-looking whiteboard shared by the classroom community helped create a non-threatening environment. The lesson design, in particular the anonymous safely-predictable virtual teacher, gave the children opportunities to be more than shy passive recipients of knowledge but to take part with some confidence in their own learning. With their own homeroom teacher taking the role of leading learner, the children followed along and created a team learning event.

Thus, the serendipitous combination of technological and human elements with the lesson design was crucial to success. In addition, the dynamics arising from the participants' sense of empowerment led them to anticipate success rather than failure. The needs analysis, the elicitation of their views throughout the course, and again at the end, made the children and the teachers feel that they had a voice in the project. Furthermore, the excitement of knowing that they were taking part in an exploratory study that could benefit other teachers and children empowered the homeroom teachers and their children, not individually, but as a community. A new definition of blended learning may be the use of ICT in ways that facilitate the formation of a learning community.

There is an urgent need in much of today's world, particularly in developing nations, to standardize a good quality of education for all children by giving them efficient affordable access to information and by supporting teacher training initiatives. If we can find good ways to use ICT in education, we may be in a position to share the technology and the applications with schools in developing nations. Using the internet access capacity of ICT applications we may connect students and teachers in many nations in educational enterprises. As UNESCO declares on its Communication and Information web site (2009),"Everybody should have the opportunity to acquire the skills in order to understand, participate actively in, and benefit fully from the emerging knowledge societies." The potential of interoperable educational ICT applications for teaching English in primary schools should be explored.

## REFERENCES


G8 Information Centre. (1999, June 18). Köln charter: Aims and ambitions for lifelong learning. Retrieved July 14, 2009, from http://www.g7.utoronto.ca/summit/1999koln/charter.htm

Allwright, D., & Hanks, J. (2009). *The developing learner: An introduction to exploratory practice*. Basingstoke, UK: Palgrave Macmillam.

Asia and the Pacific Programme of Educational Innovation for Development. (1984). *Training educational Personnel for integrated curriculum: Report of a seminar on further training*. Oslo, Norway: Unipub.

Benesse Educational Research & Development Center. (2007). *Daiikkai shougakkoueigo ni kansuru kihonchousa (Kyouin chousa) houkokusyo* [The 1st basic survey on English education in primary schools]. Tokyo: Benesse.

Central Council for Foreign Language Education Academic Advisory. (2007, September). *Shougakkou ni okeru eigokyouiku nitsuite* [English education in primary schools]. Paper presented at the 18th Conference of the Special Committee on Foreign Language Education. Conference material retrieved July 2, 2009, from http://www.mext.go.jp/b_menu/shingi/chukyo/chukyo3/015/siryo/ 06032708/003.pdf

Dolitsky, M., McCloskey, M. L., & Orr, J. (2006). *Teaching English as a foreign language in primary school*. Alexandria, VA: Teachers of English to Speakers of Other Languages, Inc.

ev.php-url_id=2929&url_do=do_topic&url_section=201.html

Gagne, R. M., Wager, W. W., Golas, K. C., & Keller, J. M. (2005) *Principles of instructional design (5th Ed.)*. Wadsworth: Thomson Learning.

Hayes, B. (2000). Cascade training and teachers' professional development. *ELT Journal*, *52*, 135–145. doi:10.1093/elt/54.2.135

IEEE-USA. (2005, November 11). *Interoperability for the national health information network*. Retrieved April 12, 2009, from http://www.ieeeusa.org/policy/POSITIONS/ NHINinteroperability.html#_ftnref1

Johnson, J. S., & Newport, E. L. (1989). Critical period effects in second language learning: The influence of maturational state on the acquisition of English as a second language. *Cognitive Psychology*, *21*, 60–99. doi:10.1016/0010-0285(89)90003-0

JTU Institute for Education and Culture. (2009). *Kyoushokuin roudou kokusai hikaku kenkyu iinkai houkokusho* [An International Comparative Study on the Working Conditions of School Personnel]. Retrieved July 17, 2009, from http://www.kyoiku-soken.org/official/activity/ userfiles/document/kokusaihikaku.pdf

Kume, A. (1981). Ouraru English heno apurouchi: Parallel reading no tagenteki kouka. [Approach to oral English: Pluralistic effects of parallel reading]. *Nanzan University Academia*, *30*, 159–174.

Lenneberg, E. H. (1967). *Biological foundations of language*. New York: John Wiley & Sons Inc.

Ministry of Education. Culture, Sports, Science and Technology. (2004). *Shougakkou no eigo-kyouiku ni kansuru ishikichousa houkoku* [An attitude survey towards English education in primary schools]. Retrieved July 17, 2009, from http://www.mext.go.jp/b_menu/shingi/chukyo/chukyo3/015/gijiroku/05032201/004/001.htm

Ministry of Education. Culture, Sports, Science and Technology. (2007a). *Kankoku ni okeru shougakkou eigokyouiku no genjyou to kadai* [A Current state and problems on the elementary school English education in Korea]. Paper presented at the 18th Conference of the Special Committee on Foreign Language Education. Conference material retrieved July 4, 2009, from http://www.mext.go.jp/b_menu/shingi/chukyo/chukyo3/015/siryo/05120501/s004_1.pdf

Ministry of Education. Culture, Sports, Science and Technology. (2007b). *Chugoku ni okeru shougakkou eigokyouiku no genjyou to kadai* [A Current state and problems on the elementary school English education in China]. Paper presented at the 18th Conference of the Special Committee on Foreign Language Education. Conference material retrieved July 4, 2009, from http://www.mext.go.jp/b_menu/shingi/chukyo/chukyo3/015/siryo/05120501/s004_2.pdf

Ministry of Education. Culture, Sports, Science and Technology. (2007c). *Taiwan ni okeru shougakkou eigokyouiku no genjyou to kadai* [A Current state and problems on the elementary school English education in Taiwan]. Paper presented at the 18th Conference of the Special Committee on Foreign Language Education. Conference material retrieved July 4, 2009, from http://www.mext.go.jp/b_menu/shingi/chukyo/chukyo3/015/siryo/05120501/s004_3.pdf

Ministry of Education. Culture, Sports, Science and Technology. (2008a). White paper on science and technology 2008. Retrieved July 7, 2009, from http://www.mext.go.jp/english/wp/ 1260270.htm

Ministry of Education. Culture, Sports, Science and Technology. (2008b). *Shougakkou gaikokugo-katsudou kenshu guide book* [Training guide book for foreign language activities]. Tokyo: Ohbunsha.

Ministry of Education. Culture, Sports, Science and Technology. (2009, April 21). *The course of study (Chapter4)*. Retrieved July 12, 2009, from http://www.mext.go.jp/component/a_menu/ education/micro_detail/__icsFiles/afieldfile/2009/04/21/1261037_12.pdf

Minoura, Y. (1983). *Kodomo no ibunkataiken* [Children's cross-cultural experience]. Tokyo: Shisakusha.

Miyazaki, M. (2000). Shadowing no yukousei: Listening to speech nouryoku ni kanshite [Shadowing: Effects on listening and speaking competence]. *LET Kansai Chapter Collected Papers*, *8*, 69–78.

National Institute for Educational Policy Research. (2004). *Gaikokugo no curriculum no kaizen ni kansuru kenkyu: Sshogaikoku no doukou* [A study on curriculum development of foreign languages: Recent developments in foreign countries]. Retrieved June 25, 2009, http://www.nier.go.jp/kiso/seika2/gaikokugo.pdf

Nicholls, J. G. (1978). The development of the concept of effort and ability, perception of academic attainment, and the understanding that difficult tasks require more ability. *Child Development*, *49*, 800–814. doi:10.2307/1128250

Penfield, W., & Roberts, L. (1959). *Speech and brain-mechanism*. Oxford: Oxford University Press.

Phillips, B. N. (1963). Age changes in accuracy of self-perceptions. *Child Development*, *34*, 1041–1046. doi:10.2307/1126546

Someya, Y. (1998). Prosody kyouka kunren no kouka ni kansuru action research [An action research on a prosody-strengthening exercise]. *Tsuyakurironkenkyu*, *14*, 4–21.

Strategic Headquarters, I. T. (2001, January 22). *e-Japan strategy.* Retrieved July 12, 2009, from http://www.kantei.go.jp/foreign/it/network/0122full_e.html

Strategic Headquarters, I. T. (2006a, January 19). *New IT reform strategy: Realizing ubiquitous and universal network society where everyone can enjoy the benefits of IT.* Retrieved July 12, 2009, from http://www.kantei.go.jp/foreign/policy/it/ITstrategy2006.pdf

Strategic Headquarters, I. T. (2006b, July 26). *Priority policy program 2006.* Retrieved July 15, 2009, from http://www.kantei.go.jp/foreign/policy/it/Program2006.pdf

Tajino, A., & Tajino, Y. (2000). Native and non-native: What can they offer?: lessons from team-teaching in Japan. *ELT Journal*, *54*, 3–11. doi:10.1093/elt/54.1.3

Tamai, K. (1998). Shadowing no haikeiriron to hyoukahou [Theoretical background and evaluation of shadowing]. In Simultaneous Interpretation Research Committee, Japan Association for Current English Studies, Kansai Chapter (Ed.), *Research and Practices of Shadowing* (pp. 1-19). Osaka: Japan Association for Current English Studies Kansai Chapter.

Tamai, K. (2003). Risuningu to shadowing no setten ni miru aratana shido no shiten [A new perspective on listening and shadowing techniques for English language teaching]. *Studies in English Language Teaching*, *26*, 1–19.

UNESCO. (2009). ICT in education. Retrieved July 29, 2009, from http://portal.unesco.org/ci/en/

Voos, R. (2003). Blended learning: What is it and where might it take us? *Sloan-C View*, *2*(1), 2–5.

## ADDITIONAL READING

Barber, D., Cooper, L., & Meeson, G. (2007). *Learning and teaching with interactive whiteboards: Primary and early years.* Exeter: Learning Matters.

Bruck, M., & Genesee, F. (1995). Phonological awareness in young second language learners. *Journal of Child Language*, *22*, 307–324. doi:10.1017/S0305000900009806

Butler, Y. G. (2004). What level of English proficiency do elementary school teachers need to attain to teach EFL?: Case studies from Korea, Taiwan, and Japan. *TESOL Quarterly*, *38*, 245–278. doi:10.2307/3588380

Cameron, L. (2001). *Teaching languages to young learners*. Cambridge, UK: Cambridge University Press. doi:10.1017/CBO9780511733109

Carrasquillo, A., Kucer, S., & Abrams, A. (2004). *Beyond the beginnings: Literacy interventions for upper elementary English language learners*. Clevedon: Multilingual Matters.

Council of Europe. (2001). *Common European framework of reference for languages: Learning, Teaching, Assessment*. Cambridge, UK: Cambridge University Press.

Crosse, K. (2007). *Introducing English as an additional language to young children*. London: Paul Chapman Educational Publishing.

Csikszentmihalyi, M., & Csikszentmihalyi, I. S. (Eds.). (1988). *Optimal experience: Psychological studies of flow in consciousness*. New York: Cambridge University Press.

Cummins, J., & Swain, M. (1987). *Bilingualism in education: Aspects of theory, research, and practice*. New York: Longman.

Ellis, R. (2008). *The study of second language acquisition* (2nd ed.). Oxford, UK: Oxford University Press.

Freeman, D., & Richards, J. C. (1996). *Teacher learning in language teaching*. Cambridge, UK: Cambridge University Press.

Freudenstein, R. (1979). *Teaching foreign languages to the very young: Papers from seven countries on work with 4-8 year-olds*. New York: Pergamon Press.

Genesee, F. (1994). *Educating second language children: The whole child, the whole curriculum, the whole community*. Cambridge, UK: Cambridge University Press.

Gibbons, P. (2006). Steps for Planning an Integrated Program for ESL Learners. In McKay, P. (Ed.), *Planning and Teaching Creatively within a Required Curriculum, TESOL Language Curriculum Development Series* (pp. 215–233). Virginia: Teachers of Speakers to Other Languages Inc. TESOL Association Publication.

Goto Butler, Y., & Iino, M. (2005). Current Japanese reforms in English language education: The 2003 "Action Plan". *Language Policy*, *4*, 24–45.

Graham, C. (1978). *Jazz chats: Rhythms of American English for students of English as a second language*. New York: Oxford University Press.

Honna, N. (1995). English in Japanese society: Language within language. *Journal of Multilingual and Multicultural Development*, *16*, 45–62.

Lee, M., & Betcher, C. (Eds.). (2009). *The interactive whiteboard revolution: Teaching with IWBs*. Camberwell: Australian Council Educational Research.

Lightbown, P., & Spada, N. (2006). *How language are learned* (3rd ed.). Oxford, UK: Oxford University Press.

Matthews, J. (2008). *Interactive whiteboards*. Michigan: Cherry Lake Publishing.

McKay, P. (2006). *Assessing young language learners*. Cambridge, UK: Cambridge University Press.

McKay, S. L. (2002). *Teaching English as an international language: Rethinking goals and approaches*. Oxford, UK: Oxford University Press.

Miller, D., & Glover, D. (2002). The Interactive Whiteboard as a Force for Pedagogic Change: The Experience of Five Elementary Schools in an English Education Authority. *Information Technology in Childhood Education Annual*, (1): 5–19.

Nunan, D. (2003). The impact of English as a global language on educational policies and practices in the Asia-Pacific region. *TESOL Quarterly*, *37*, 589–613. doi:10.2307/3588214

Pinter, A. (2006). *Teaching young language learners*. Oxford: Oxford University Press.

Richards, J. C., & Farrell, T. S. C. (2005). *Professional development for language teachers: Strategies for teacher learning*. Cambridge, UK: Cambridge University Press. doi:10.1017/CBO9780511667237

Slattery, M., & Willis, J. (2002). *English for primary teachers*. Oxford: Oxford University Press.

Vale, D., & Feunteun, A. (1995). *Teaching Children English: An activity based training course*. Cambridge, UK: Cambridge University Press.

## KEY TERMS AND DEFINITIONS

**The ADDIE Model:** A practical model for the design and development of instructional materials which centers all component processes in a holistic systematic planning environment: Analysis, Design, Development, Implementation, and Evaluation.

**Information and Communication Technology (ICT):** Devices which store and/or convey information and put people in communication with each other in new ways. ICT devices include land-line telephones, radios, TVs, computers, interactive whiteboards, and cell phones.

**In-Take:** If students are exposed to comprehensible input of a foreign language, they may succeed in up-taking some language feature that is new to them. If they understand the new language and it becomes part of their language knowledge, up-take has occurred.

**Interactive Whiteboard:** A classroom writing board which can display whatever appears on a connected computer screen. By touching the projected images on the whiteboard, people can perform operations.

**Interoperability:** The capacity of the ICT application to create a single learning environment in which the human components of the educational system, i.e. primary school children and teachers in a single class, may collaborate in a team-learning enterprise in order to accomplish their separate aims; and in which teachers and materials developers at different locations may collaborate in materials development and teacher training activities

**Shadowing:** Learners' repeated reading aloud of a text as they listen to a narration.

**Team Learning:** A concept that was developed in EFL education to reformulate conventional roles of teachers and students. Teachers sometimes function as teachers and at other times as learners. Learners may take the roles of learners and also that of teachers.

# Chapter 7
# Virtual Worlds:
## New Ways of Learning

**Lea Kuznik**
*University of Ljubljana, Slovenia*

## ABSTRACT

*Virtual worlds for adults (e.g. Second Life), youth (e.g. Habbo) and children (e.g. Whyville) have a great potential for learning and teaching practices for enriching wider public and engendering collective experience and collaboration. Informal learning environments such as educational virtual worlds offer children and adults various intellectual and sensory activities or "crystallized" experiences with reinforcing multiple intelligences, according to Gardner. Virtual worlds promote social interaction and offer visitors an opportunity for various interactive activities which can sometimes not be realized in real life education. Children and adults can explore and learn in a different way and from a different perspective, e.g. with educational games and simulations. Virtual worlds represent a new medium that allows people to connect in new virtual ways and offer new challenges in the educational field.*

## INTRODUCTION

Emerging technologies such as virtual worlds, serious games, wikis and social networking sites have been heralded as technologies that are powerful enough to transform learning and teaching. When we think of learning, school comes to mind first. However, many people, especially the disadvantaged, do not achieve their full potential through traditional educational approaches for a variety of reasons. A lot of valuable learning also takes place outside school, often facilitated by digital technologies, for example, through online games. Mobile technologies and internet can provide access to rich digital media content and facilitate communication with others both local and remote to provide powerful learning experiences that go well beyond the traditional classroom.

Due to new technologies new approaches to learning become possible, diversifying the range of learning experiences available, and thereby engaging with people who have not achieved their

DOI: 10.4018/978-1-61692-791-2.ch007

full potential with more traditional approaches. Many new approaches to learning and teaching are facilitated by new technologies. In addition to the real world, online world contains a whole range of virtual worlds in which we can live our second (virtual) life. Although virtual worlds for children, youth and adults differ according to their content, they offer an opportunity to learn in a virtual learning environment and have great potential for learning activities.

Virtual worlds are persistent virtual environments that allow for interaction through which people experience others as being there with them (Schroeder, 2006). These interactive online three-dimensional virtual environments are possible to visit 24 hours a day, 7 days a week (Castronova, 2005). Virtual worlds are designed for different age groups, children, youth and adults, and separated in terms of content. Some of them emphasize education (Whyville), while others focus on role play (Gaia), fashion (Stardoll), music (vSide), sports, television, movies and books (Virtual MTV), toys and games from the real world (Barbie Girls), casual games (Club Penguin), socializing (Habbo), creating the content of the virtual world (Second Life).

In all virtual worlds the player is physically represented by his/her virtual person – avatar, whose appearance is chosen and changed by each player alone (e.g. colour and length of hair, clothes, shoes, equipment…). Avatars can be people (Whyville, Barbie Girls, Second Life), house pets (Webkinz), fantasy creatures (Funkeytown), animals (Club Penguin), monsters (Moshi Monster)…

How do education keep up with virtual worlds and leisure trends? Virtual worlds are attracting interest from different organizations as platforms for learning. Also known as immersive environments, these systems can provide significant advantages over other learning strategies.

Virtual worlds are also creating opportunities for activities, which can not be realized in real life education. Above all, children can explore things and learn in a different way and from a different perspective. On this basis the paper will analyze some of learning possibilities and opportunities in educational virtual worlds for children (e.g. Whyville, Handipoints…) with millions of registered accounts. It is important to create an environment which would enable children to construct their knowledge on their own or through interaction with peers, adults, objects, learning games and other activities.

## THE CONCEPT OF EXPERIENTIAL PEDAGOGY

When designing learning activities in virtual learning environments we have to take into account some of the following theorists of learning: Dewey (1963) and his concept of experiential learning, Piaget's (1990) theory of construction of knowledge, Kolb's (1984) theory of experiential learning as a constant cyclic process and Gardner's (1991) theory of multiple intelligences. Moreover, we should also consider Vygotsky's (1978) theory which emphasizes the social component of learning, Gogala's (2005) idea of experiential pedagogy and the flow concept proposed by Csikszentmihalyi (2002).

A recent pedagogic concept which is important for designing interactive learning environments is the idea of experiential pedagogy proposed by Slovene pedagogue Stanko Gogala (2005). He claims that a successful development of child's personality requires experience - emotional exchange, a feeling that in a suitable situation enables us to become aware of the problem and work to benefit from its dismissal. However, in order to do this, we have to design encouraging environments and assure diverse experiences, considering interests of the children involved and offering possibility of choice in which children become involved in interactions with different objects, materials, peers, adults... A child is encouraged to get involved in a certain exciting activity that drags him into a circle of intense experiencing and unconventional establishment of social relations. The main factor of the experiential pedagogy is the intense situation in which a child experiences an exciting event and engages in relationships with other children and creates a more cohesive social connection and forms of child's active collaboration. And according to his/her own interests, needs, learning style helps to construct active learning environment, including different activities and social relations.

"To experience something" in the full sense of the word is not the same as "to have an experience of" something. Gogala therefore distinguishes superficial experience and peak experience. Psychology talks about superficial experiences that we call ideas, images, thoughts, emotions, and strivings. Richness of superficial experiences is enormous. The concept of peak experience, however, implies deeper mental actions as e.g. deep astonishment, experience of beautiful or suffering. We gain education via superficial experiences, whereas the upbringing is an ability to experience different cultural values growing in our psyche after we have experienced something (Gogala, 2005). Gogala views the peak experience as the very psychological base. Peak experiences are experiences that a child gains through active collaboration and encounters them in active learning environments in different interactions with materials and peers, through which a child accesses findings in explorations of the world, with his/her own actions. We can say that peak experiences are permanent collaborative interactions during which a child constructs his/her own knowledge (Kuznik 2007).

## "CRYSTALLIZED" EXPERIENCES IN VIRTUAL LEARNING ENVIRONMENTS

Gardner (1991) views peak experiences as different intellectual and sensory activities or "crystallized" experiences offered children in informal virtual learning environments such as virtual worlds. Gardner's model distinguishes among eight types of intelligence that are present in everyone but developed to a different extent. Linguistic intelligence is seen in the highly verbal person, who likes to write and read and has a good memory for detail; logical-mathematical intelligence can be traced among those who can conceptualize mathematical and logic problems quickly in their heads; spatial intelligence distinguished among those who have good visual memory and easily read maps, charts, and visual displays; musical intelligence is seen in those who play musical instruments, remember melodies, and like to work with music; bodily kinesthetic intelligence is exhibited in those who perform well in sports and crafts; interpersonal intelligence is possessed by those who have many friends, like to socialize, and enjoy group games; intrapersonal intelligence is seen in those who are independent, like to work alone, and have initiative and naturalist intelligence can be traced among those who like nature, natural phenomena and ecosystems.

It is important to design such an environment that allows a child to use any of those intelligences, and construct his/her own knowledge. Why should we encourage the development of different intelligences in virtual learning environment? Above all, in order to enhance individual intelligences, especially those that are neglected in the classroom. We have to enable children to test and experience all eight types of intelligences. But a question appears: are not all the other intelligences except for linguistic and logically-mathematical mere talents or gifts which are inborn and will appear naturally? To a certain degree this is true, however, many talents are never discovered, if some kind of experience does not trigger them. Talent is otherwise not an attribute, it is only a predisposition that must be developed through a planned engagement. If children are active in environment that offers them all kinds of intellectual and sensory stimuli, they will have, according to Gardner, "crystallized" experience. This can be an event that changes children's life because they, in such a way, discover their interests and hidden abilities which they will continue to develop throughout their entire life. Environment that offers "crystallized" experiences is important for children as well as adults.

Pedagogic concept of virtual learning environment enables: assurance of active learning environment in which children can construct their own knowledge, the choice of themes/concepts is based on children's interests, consideration of different learning styles, unforgettable experiences, active participation of children in the process of learning, inventing and discovering on their own, independent choice and decision-making, interaction with objects, participation in different activities, problem solving, expanding vocabulary while getting familiar with new objects, producing new knowledge through experience, stimulating the use of different types of intelligences, strengthening self-confidence and assuring opinion-sharing among children and adults.

## FLOW EXPERIENCES AND EDUCATIONAL GAMES

Positive psychology is the scientific study of human happiness. The history of psychology as a science shows that the field has been primarily dedicated to addressing mental illness rather than mental wellness....flow is the mental state of operation in which the person is fully immersed in what he or she is doing by a feeling of energized focus, full involvement, and success in the process of the activity (Csikszentmihalyi, 1990). Flow is experienced when perceived opportunities for action are in balance with the actor's perceived skills. Adapted from Csikszentmihalyi (2002, 1997) retaining the essential insight that perceived challenges and skills must be relative to a person's own average levels. The conditions of flow include: perceived challenges, or opportunities for action that stretch existing skills; a sense that one is engaging challenges at a level appropriate to one's capacities and clear proximal goals and immediate feedback about the progress that is being made (Csikszentmihalyi, 2002).

Flow principles have been translated into practice in a variety of contexts. Two types of intervention can be distinguished: those seeking to shape activity structures and environments so that they foster flow or obstruct it less and those attempting to assist individuals in finding flow. Several art museums, including the Getty museum in Los Angeles, have incorporated flow principles during their design of exhibits and buildings (Csikszentmihalyi, 2002). Educational settings present an opportunity to apply the results of flow research most directly. Educational game designers in virtual worlds also benefit from integration of flow principles into game play design.

In virtual worlds flow can be fostered by influencing both environment and individual. Visitors have many opportunities to actively choose and engage in activities related to their own interests and then pursue these activities without imposed demands or pacing. People select activities that challenge and stretch them. They also indentify new challenges as their capacities grow (Csikszentmihalyi, 1997). Games, sports, and other flow activities provide goal and feedback structures that make flow more likely. A given individual can find flow in almost every activity, however – working a cash register, building a house or driving a car. Similarly, under certain conditions and depending on individual's history with the activity, almost any pursuit – a museum visit, a round of golf, a game of chess – can bore or create anxiety. It is the subjective challenges and subjective skills, not objective ones, that influence the quality of a person's experience (Csikszentmihalyi, 2002).

Csikszentmihalyi developed a series of theories to help people get into their flow state. Since then, these theories have been applied to various fields for designing better human interactive experiences, e.g. games. In order to maintain a person's flow experience, the activity needs to reach a balance between the challenges of the activity and the abilities of the participant. If the challenge is higher than the ability, the activity becomes overwhelming and generates anxiety. If the challenge is lower than the ability, it provokes boredom. Fortunately, human beings have tolerance, there is a fuzzy safe zone where the activity is not too challenging or too boring, and psychic entropies like anxiety and boredom would not occur (Csikszentmihalyi, 1990).

The description of flow is identical to what a player experiences when totally immersed in a game. During this experience, the player loses track of time and forgets all external pressures. It is obvious that gamers value games based on whether or not those games can provide flow experiences (Holt, 2000). Games and simulations involve people in collaborative learning and are among the most widespread ways of learning in virtual worlds.

There are a lot of games that provide flow experiences also in educational virtual worlds for children. Some games represent active flow experience, deepened learning environments where users assemble, complete and combine information in order to solve a problem. Children engaged in educational games and simulations are interpreting, analyzing, discovering, evaluating, acting and participating in problem solving. Such educational games are, for example, the game that teaches ion engine principles, the next technology for long distance space travel in educational virtual world for children and teenagers called Whyville; the game which takes a player around the world in search of lost aliens while learning how the perceived path of the sun changes throughout the year; the game that takes a player around the world to discover rocks and fossils or the game that challenges a player to navigate altitudes and analyze vector fields to race his/her balloon.

The two interactive games for children at the Getty museum which is the first cultural institution in Whyville are designed to be fun as well as educational. Art Sets is a quick match game that teaches players about art media and subjects, sharpening their thinking skills along the way. Up to four people can play Art Sets in real time, competing to arrange artworks into sets of three based on medium (photography, paintings, or drawings) and subject (people, places, things), or by coming up with three works that make a set because they are all different.

In the Art Treasure Hunt, players are shown works of art and given clues to a historical period and place related to the object. Whyvillians are encouraged to link to the Getty web site to do research. Once they find the location and date answers, players arrange the pieces chronologically to find out which city they have to visit first. Then it is off to the Whyville airfield and the warp wagon to circumnavigate the globe to find and collect the works of art.

Successfully completing both games earns players valuable virtual currency - "clams" that they can use to buy and decorate virtual homes, use as capital to open stores, and even purchase face parts that Whyvillians use to create their online virtual persons. In addition, Art Treasure Hunt winners walk away with virtual copies, or "posters" of the artworks from the Getty Museum. Just like real art collectors, children can gradually build a collection, which they can display in their virtual homes. Whyvillians also earn clams by winning other games offered in their city, starting up virtual businesses, or by doing jobs such as writing for the Whyville newspaper. They can even run for political office.

In addition to the Getty museum's Art Sets and Art Treasure Hunt, Whyville games include ion football, where citizens play a team game to learn about electrical charges; Mimi's dance studio, where players use vector arithmetic to design a dance; and Smart Cars, where they design robot cars based on neural circuitry.

This approach to learning is much more consistent with constructivist learning where knowledge is constructed by the learners as they are actively involved in problem solving in an authentic context than with traditional instruction. Cognitive psychologists Thomas Malone and Mark Lepper studied computer games to gain insight into intrinsic motivations for learning (Malone & Lepper, 1987). Their taxonomy describes four key attributes that can be applied to educational games in virtual learning environments:

1. Challenge – players tackle a clear, fixed challenge that is relevant to them. Frequent feedback guides them towards success, clarifying both successes and failures and promoting feelings of competence.
2. Curiosity – cognitive curiosity is triggered by discrepant events and other paradoxes arising from playing the game. Sensory curiosity is triggered by multimedia elements. We have to create an environment tempting enough to attract attention and rich enough to be explored and discovered.
3. Control – players have meaningful control over their actions in the game, causing clear and powerful effect in the game universe. Contingency, choice, and power are key elements of control. The control is basically what you can do (catch, fly, run…) in the game.
4. Fantasy – the context of the game includes some degree of fantasy, which engages the emotional needs of learners while providing relevant metaphors or analogies. The very story of the game is of prime importance. It applies to emotional experience.

These attributes distinguish games from other types of learning interactions and can serve as guideposts for game developers. A game lacking in challenge, perhaps for fear of discouraging the player, will fail to motivate most players. A game that provides the player with no meaningful control, such as a role play game with one single "correct" path, will cause both motivation and learning to flag. Furthermore, a game without fantasy will appear dull and uninviting, lacking the emotional appeal to get players into the game (Edwards & Shaller, 2007).

## LEARNING POSSIBILITIES AND OPPORTUNITIES IN EDUCATIONAL VIRTUAL WORLDS

Most human learning is self-motivated, emotionally satisfying, and very personally rewarding. Researchers have found that humans are highly motivated to learn when they are in a supportive environment, engaged in meaningful activities, freed from anxiety, fear, and other negative mental states, when they have choices and control over their learning and when the challenges of the task meet their skills. When in the right context, adults as well as children, find learning fun and easy (Falk & Dierking, 2002).

Educational virtual worlds offer many possibilities and opportunities for free-choice learning which involves a strong measure of choice over what, why, where, when, and how they will learn. Here are some examples of learning activities in the educational virtual worlds that promote the use of different intelligences for children to learn about various things.

Whyville, the educational virtual world for children and teenagers is based on science and physics. It supports exploration, communication, interaction, real world problem solving, and science education as users actively participate in learning by completing science tasks and games, writing in the newspaper and researching issues confronting the community, meeting and communicating with others online, and having fun. They also develop and reinforce different kind of intelligences: Users participating in science and math activities, e.g. educational games and trading their avatar parts, are develop their logical-mathematical intelligence; users writing for the newspaper and communicating with others, whispering to a friend close by reinforce linguistic intelligence; users enjoying group games and interactions reinforce interpersonal intelligence; users changing their faces, creating their own things, designing their own avatar, and customizing their chat bubbles reinforce spatial intelligence; those using the warp wagon to quickly travel around the world and through time or virtual car to drive through the community reinforce bodily kinesthetic intelligence; users writing in the newspaper about issues they personally care about therefore share with others and reinforce intrapersonal intelligence…

Sometimes when users visit the beach, they discover that the colour of the water changed. They can take a sample of the water and visit the lab to identify which phytoplankton is in the water they collected. Then they learn the causes of phytoplankton blooms and what preventive measures are available. Next, they can hop on a boat with a special sensor and track the blooms at Whyville's beaches. Once they've analyzed enough data to find the source of the pollution that causes phytoplankton blooms, users can choose to plant marsh grass seedlings to help control future blooms.

In Getty museum users learn about art composition and travel the world and through time searching for artwork and learning about art and artists. Individuals learn about personal nutrition while participating in health science centre. An interesting project is also nutrition initiative called WhyEat. Users eat and design daily virtual breakfast, lunch and dinner menus. If they eat healthy, they move faster and chat quicker, whereas, if they do not eat healthy, their avatar begins to look sickly, they are bulimic, have a calcium deficiency and they are referred to the nutritionist. Users learn how to stay healthy.

In Whyville on nearly every activity or game, users must use critical thinking and problem-solving skills to be successful. Various activities are fostering the usage of different intelligences in each situation where users synthesize, interpret, predict and apply new knowledge. Users also learn the lessons of internet safety within the Whyville community. Abusive language is not tolerated. Users learn not to divulge personal information or passwords online.

Another educational virtual world for younger children is Handipoints which connects real life tasks with virtual world. In Handipoints parents and children together create task charts and goals. When children successfully complete activities (such as cleaning their room, taking out trash, or even brushing their teeth and eating an apple), parents grade tasks and award two types of points: the so-called handipoints that can be redeemed for real-world items, and bonus points that can be used for games, movies and clothes for their cat avatars. Parents have a special area where they can keep track of their child's tasks, goals and progress. In this virtual world children can also talk to and play with others in Handiland which is divided into rooms and distinct areas. Each destination can be reached from a map or by walking through different rooms, most of which are linked to each other. All rooms and environments are currently open to all members e.g. the burbs room, which has the following activities: post office, cartoon theatre, clothing store, furniture store, the school room where users read virtual books or play games or the neighbourhood room, which features a portal where users can access their own virtual house as well as the virtual houses of other users. Virtual world Handipoints is easily navigated, there is flexibility in the tasks, and educational facts frequently pop up during the Handiland time, but the fun of the virtual world can sometimes overshadow the tasks. Nevertheless, this virtual world encourages responsibility and healthy lifestyle.

Educational virtual world for children with activities fostering different kind of intelligences is also Mokitown. The virtual world Mokitown educates users about road and traffic safety through online collaboration, e.g. crossing the road correctly, learning about traffic lights, understanding different signals, about gestures and movements that have a set meaning and are necessary for communication. Within the world, the users move around and make decisions about road safety. When a user makes a correct decision or correctly answers road safety questions asked by "quiz bots", they earn points that they can trade in to customise their "moki" avatar. The world features an online chat environment, allowing users' collaboration and instant messaging.

The emergence of virtual worlds in pedagogical contexts tries to combine avatar-based interaction without losing out on the flexibility benefits traditional distance learning offers. For example, using Second Life for educational purposes is a relatively new phenomenon. Yet, it has received its share of publicity in the media with newspapers, network channels and websites flooding the matter with articles, insights and attention. Second Life is used as a platform for education and interactive experiences by many institutions, such as colleges, universities, libraries, government entities and corporates. There are over one hundred regions used for educational purposes covering different subjects. Educators use it for classes, research, learning and projects with their students, bringing a new dimension to learning. A series of educational institutions such as Harvard University have started to realize the pedagogical potential in Second Life and now offer online courses in this virtual reality world. Universities either rent or build their own islands in order to ensure privacy, and then set up virtual lectures in which teachers and students can communicate in real time using instant chatting or microphones. Harvard University, one of the universities that perhaps have gone the furthest when it comes to bringing education into the virtual world, now offer law courses to geographically dispersed students from all over the world (Harvard Business Review, 2006). There are also many companies in Second Life today which are putting their message out there, establishing their brands and identities, and learning to engage users with their products and ideas. However, it's suitability as a pedagogical tool has yet to be assessed to a greater extent, mainly due to its novelty.

Educational virtual world for teens is also Teen Second Life in which teens can create and customize an avatar, fly through an ever-changing 3D landscape, chat and socialize with other teens, and build anything from skyscrapers to virtual vehicles. Teen Second Life encourages teens to work together. Teen Second Life is often used by educators for classes, research, and projects with their students, bringing a new dimension to learning.

Virtual world learning experiences are fun. Classes in virtual worlds offer opportunities for visualization, simulation, enhanced social networks, and shared learning experiences. Some people learn best by listening to the course content, others by seeing and visualizing the content in context, and the rest by using a hands-on approach to demonstrate course competencies. In virtual worlds, we can leverage a mix of content and activity to support all learners: auditory, visual, and kinesthetic. Virtual worlds support these different learning styles and give students opportunities to explore, discover, and express their understanding of the subject (Calongne, 2008). Class can be held on the beach, in another country, in outer space, or in any simulated setting. Students do not need to be confined to a traditional class setting, with chairs facing forward, but can instead move within the learning environment, communicate via text or voice, offer information or ask questions whenever they like, and correspond with classmates and friends via private messaging. The learning experience is lively, engaging, and rich with social networks, interaction, and expression.

All these different possibilities for learning in virtual worlds can be organized in a framework or a model. We can use this framework to identify learning activities in our content area and connect these activities to potential applications of virtual worlds. Basically, both virtual life and real life consist of people and objects, and these can interact in three possible combinations: person-person, person-object and object-object interaction (Antonacci & Modaress, 2005). Many opportunities for learning can be categorized into these three interaction combinations.

First possibility is person-person interaction, e.g. role play. According to a scenario a child or an adult accepts the chosen role in a certain realistic situation (assuming a role of an archaeologist), takes suitable equipment, communicates with different researchers, finds out something, does something, solves something… Characteristics of person-person interaction are solving problems, group task involvement, exchange of opinions concerning certain theme, common creation… Emphasis is on the social interaction. Various games and events such as interviews, lectures, fairy telling, belong here as well.

In person-object interaction children and adults also learn how to interact with objects. This includes designing and building their own 3D objects, exploring objects by using them, organizing, dismantling and assembling objects which is how they get information concerning these objects. Children and adults can learn how to use the selected object, build a house, design contemporary and ancient jewellery, clothes, toys... We can present a problem scenario in order for children and adults to create their own virtual solutions. Different simulations involving persons (e.g. dances of different cultures) also belong here.

In object-object interaction children and adults learn how objects interact with other objects. We can use virtual worlds to illustrate and explain physical and procedural processes. For example: different simulations of cultural and natural phenomena, like a volcanic eruption, how mountains are formed when two tectonic plates collide, how hazardous chemicals get into our water supply, and how a car is built in an assembly line. A child or an adult can change different variables and influence the process with a purpose of understanding the processes or natural and cultural phenomena better.

Virtual worlds also create opportunities for activities which cannot be realized in real life education. Above all, children and adults can explore things and educational content in a different way and from a different perspective: visitor can fly, float above an object, sit on it, create his/her own, change it, jump onto or into it, break it, tie it up and explore it in a way that is not possible in real life education. Visitors can learn about e.g. museum objects and explore them in a way that is not allowed in a real museum because of different reasons (large or sensitive objects...). Because we do not have to worry about objects being damaged or stolen, we can display them in unusual or funny places: on a cloud, outside, in a park, not only in buildings. They can float in the air or they are placed on the ceiling. We can change the size of objects - make them bigger or smaller. Because of better conditions for exploration we can enlarge objects which are tiny in real life and the other way around. Virtual worlds also enable children and adults to exchange opinions with other residents of the virtual world, communication with people from all over the world, simulations that enable visitors to experience dangerous situations (e.g. feel tsunami), or take them to unreachable location (e.g. flying with spacecraft to the outer space), projection of films, slides, streaming videos.

## CONCLUSION

The capacity to learn (not just in virtual worlds) is always dependent upon prior knowledge and experience as well as upon interest, motivation, and expectations. What might someone learn by changing their race or even being an animal or a fantasy creature in virtual world? What might children and adults with physical disabilities do in virtual world which would be difficult or impossible for them in real life? Despite the open possibilities virtual worlds provide, we still remain a little bit constrained by our own real life experiences and expectations.

However, virtual worlds can introduce quality virtual learning environments with lots of peak and flow experiences and following characteristics. First of all, virtual worlds are accessible to all regardless of geographic location. By visual representation of people around us, voice communication and fully navigable and interactive 3D environment virtual worlds enable people from all over the world to feel as if they are all present in the same place together. Social experience and social collaboration with other people is the primary value of virtual worlds. Virtual worlds enable equal conditions for learning also for people with special needs, physical restraints or the handicapped. In virtual worlds individuals can express their interests, ideas and challenges. They express themselves via the character of avatar, conversations and gestures.

So what does this mean for education? Virtual worlds extend our audience to an international level, gets the users involved in the social aspects of the internet, appeals to children, youth and gamer cultures, allows user generated content (creative writing, visual art, short films…), enables collaboration, allows wandering, linking, searching activities that promote discovery, compelling technical features, enables capabilities to interface with external data sources, rich media content support and up-to-date hardware capabilities. One of the best uses of virtual worlds today are virtual events that reach people around the world. Events can allow different people to attend the same event in person and virtually. Recently, more and more emphasis is being placed on the role of information technologies in education of children, youth and adults. Internet can be accessed from the privacy of our homes, from schools where it is regularly used by teachers and students and even from kindergardens. Virtual worlds develop technological savvy, offer experiential learning as well as foster global relationships and civic responsibility.

Virtual worlds provide learning organizations a powerful, unique ability to engage and empower students in ways that accommodate their digital lifestyles, adapt to their individual learning needs and encourage collaboration. It is revolutionary, but it's not an overnight revolution. For now, the virtual worlds can be perplexing and intimidating. It is a lot like the WorldWideWeb in 1993-94: clunky and slow, but we could all see the potential. Most learning organizations are not clamoring for a place in virtual worlds yet as the notion is still new and the learning benefits are still emerging. But dismissing the importance of Web 3D technologies that millions are already using in learning strategy would be like dismissing the Internet in 1994 (Gronstedt, 2008).

Fundamentally, virtual worlds are a new communication medium that allows people to connect in new ways. An international research and analytic company Gartner Group claims that by the end of 2011, 80% of active internet users will have a "second life" in one of virtual worlds. Moreover, they predict that by the end of 2012, 3-D will become a standard practice for education and training (Gartner, 2007). It is not yet possible to switch avatars from one to another virtual world although it had already happened once accidentally (avatar from Second Life has emerged in There). Nevertheless, Google is already developing a project of universal avatars that will move through different virtual worlds (Lohr, 2008). The audience is there. The tools are available. The content is waiting. It is up to us to take the next step.

## REFERENCES


Antonacci, D., & Modaress, N. (2005). Envisioning the Educational Possibilities of User-Created Virtual Worlds. *AACE Journal*, *16*(2), 115–126.

Calongne, C. M. (2008). Educational Frontiers: Learning in a Virtual World. *Educause Review Magazine, 43*(5), September/October.

Castronova, E. (2005). *Synthetic Worlds: The Business and Culture of Online Games*. Chicago, Illinois: University of Chicago Press Publisher.

Csikszentmihalyi, M. (1990). *Flow: The Psychology of Optimal Experience*. New York: Harper and Row.

Csikszentmihalyi, M. (1997). *Finding Flow*. New York: Basic.

Dewey, J. (1963). *Experience and Education*. New York: Collier Books.

Edwards, S. E., & Schaller, D. T. (2007). The Name of the Game: Museums and Digital Learning Games. In Din, H., & Hecht, P. (Eds.), *The Digital Museum: A Think Guide* (pp. 62–68). Washington, DC: American Association of Museums.

Falk, J. H., & Dierking, L. D. (2002). *Lessons Without Limit, How Free-Chioce Learning is Transforming Education*. Walnut Creek, California: AltaMira Press.

Gardner, H. (1991). *The Unschooled Mind: How Children Think And How Schools Should Teach*. New York: Basic Books.

Gartner Inc. (2007). Retrieved November 29, 2007, from http://www.gartner.com/it/page.jsp?id=503861

Gogala, S. (2005). *Chosen Pedagogic Essays*. Ljubljana, Slovenia: Drustvo 2000.

Gronstedt, A. (2008). Making Learning Fun and Social. *E-learning Magazine*. Retrived May 10, 2009 from www.gronstedtgroup.com/pdf/ELearningMagazine.pdf

Kolb, D. (1984). *Experimental Learning (Experience as The Source of Learning and Development)*. Upper Saddle River, New Jersey: Prentice-Hall.

Kuznik, L. (2007). *Interactive Learning Environments and Children's Museums - Theoretical Model and It's Planning*. Unpublished doctoral dissertation, University of Ljubljana, Slovenia.

Lohr, S. (2008, October 15). Free the Avatars. *The New York Times*. Retrieved from http://www.nytimes.com

Malone, T. W., & Lepper, M. R. (1987). Making Learning Fun: A Taxonomy of Intrinsic Motivations for Learning. In Snow, R. E., & Farr, M. J. (Eds.), *Aptitude, Learning and Instruction III: Conative and Affective Process Analyses* (pp. 223–250). Hillsdale, New York: Lawrence Erlbaum Associates.

Montessori, M. (1990). *The Discovery of the Child*. New York, New York: Ballantine Books.

Nakamura, J., & Csikszentmihalyi, M. (2002). The concept of flow. In Snyder, C. R., & Lopez, S. J. (Eds.), *Handbook of Positive Psychology* (pp. 89–105). Oxford, UK: Oxford University Press.

Piaget, J., & Inhelder, B. (1990). *Psychology of Children*. Novi Sad, Serbia: Dobra vest.

Review, H. B. online version. (2006). *Avatar - based marketing*. Retrieved April 12, 2009 from http://harvardbusinessonline.hbsp.harvard.edu/hbsp/hbr/articles/article.jsp?articleID=R0606B

Schroeder, R. (2006). Being There and the Future of Connected Presence. *Journal of Teleoperators and Virtual Environments*, *15*(4), 438–454. doi:10.1162/pres.15.4.438

Vygotsky, L. S. (1977). *Thinking and Talking*. Belgrade, Serbia: Nolit.

## ADDITIONAL READING

Aldrich, C. (2009). *Learning Online with Games, Simulations, and Virtual Worlds: Strategies for Online Instruction*. San Francisco: Jossey-Bass.

Andersen, A., Hristov, E., & Karimi, H. (2008). *Second Life - New Opportunity for Higher Educational Institutions*. Bachelor Thesis, Business Administration, Jönköping University, Sweden.

Bartle, R. A. (2004). *Designing Virtual Worlds*. Indianapolis: New Riders Publishing.

Castronova, E. (2007). *Exodus to the Virtual World: How Online Fun is Changing Reality*. New York: Palgrave Macmillan.

Deutschmann, M., & Molkadanielsen, J. (Eds.). (2009). *Learning and Teaching in the Virtual World of Second Life*. Norway: Tapir Academic Press.

Figueiredo, A. D. (2005). *Managing Learning in Virtual Settings: The Role of Context*. Hershey, PA: Information Science Publishing.

Finkelstein, J. E. (2006). *Learning in Real Time: Synchronous Teaching and Learning*. San Francisco: Jossey-Bass.

Gee. P.J. (2007). *What Video Games Have to Teach Us About Learning and Literacy*. New York: Palgrave Macmillan.

Gronstedt, A. (2008). *Training in Virtual Worlds*. Alexandria, VA: ASTD Press.

Holt, R. (2000). *Examining Video Game Immersion as a Flow State*. Bachelor Thesis, Department of Psychology, Brock University, Canada.

Jain, L. C., Howlett, R. J., Ichalkaranje, N. S., & Tonfoni, G. (2002). *Virtual Environments for Teaching & Learning*. New Jersey: World Scientific Publishing Company. doi:10.1142/9789812776570

Meadows, M. S. (2008). *I, Avatar: The Culture and Consequences of Having a Second Life*. Berkeley, CA: New Riders Press.

Mennecke, B.E. (2008). Second Life and Other Virtual Worlds: A Roadmap for Research. *Communications of the AIS,* 20 (20).

Palloff, R. M. (2004). *Collaborating Online: Learning Together in Community*. San Francisco: Jossey-Bass.

Rothfarb, J. R., & Doherty, P. (2007). Creating Museum Content and Community in Second Life. In Trant, J., & Bearman, D. (Eds.), *Museums and the Web 2007*. Toronto, Ontario, Canada: Archives & Museum Informatics.

Shaffer, D. W. (2006). *How Computer Games Help Children Learn*. New York: Palgrave Macmillan. doi:10.1057/9780230601994

Smith, R. M. (2008). *Conquering the Content: A Step-by-Step Guide to Online Course Design*. San Francisco: Jossey-Bass.

Swain, J.J. (2001). *Power Tools for Visualization and Decision - Making, ORMS Today.* Retrieved May 7, 2009 from http://www.lionhrtpub.com/orms/surveys/Simulation/Simulation.html

## KEY TERMS AND DEFINITIONS

**Avatar:** A computer user's representation of himself/herself or alter ego, whether in the form of a three-dimensional model used in computer games. It is an "object" representing the embodiment of the user.

**Educational Games:** Games that have been specifically designed to teach people about a certain subject, expand concepts, reinforce development, understand an historical event or culture, or assist them in learning a skill as they play.

**Experiential Learning:** The process of making meaning from direct experience. Experiential learning focuses on the learning process for the individual (unlike experiential education, which focuses on the transactive process between teacher and learner). An example of experiential learning is going to the zoo and learning through observation and interaction with the zoo environment, as opposed to reading about animals from a book. Thus, one makes discoveries and experiments with knowledge firsthand, instead of hearing or reading about others' experiences.

**Flow:** The mental state of operation in which the person is fully immersed in what he or she is doing by a feeling of energized focus, full involvement, and success in the process of the activity.

**Interaction:** A kind of action that occurs as two or more objects have an effect upon one another.

**Peak Experiences:** Experiences that a child gains through active collaboration and encounters them in active learning environments in different interactions with materials, peers and adults, through which a child accesses findings in explorations of the world, with his/her own actions. In general, permanent collaborative interactions during which a child constructs his/her own knowledge.

**Virtual Learning Environment:** A software system designed to support teaching and learning in an educational setting. It works over the Internet and provides a collection of tools such as those for assessment, communication, uploading of content, return of students' work, peer assessment, administration of student groups, collecting and organizing student grades, questionnaires, tracking tools, etc. New features in these systems include wikis, blogs, RSS and 3D virtual learning spaces.

**Virtual World:** A computer-based simulated environment intended for its users to inhabit and interact via avatars.

**Whyville:** An educational virtual world geared towards teens and children. Its goal is to engage its users in learning about a broad range of topics, from science and business to art and geography.

# Chapter 8
# E-Learning Challenges in the European Knowledge-Based Society:
## Romania Case Study

**Cristina Barna**
*Spiru Haret University, Romania*

**Manuela Epure**
*Spiru Haret University, Romania*

**Ruxandra Vasilescu**
*Spiru Haret University, Romania*

## ABSTRACT

*In the context of 2009 European Year of Innovation and Creativity, this chapter focuses on ICT for innovation as a key challenge in the knowledge-based society. Today we are facing the growing complexity of the e-learning phenomenon and its role as a basic tool for high quality education and training. The authors approach the importance of e-learning in the European Lifelong Learning Program 2007 – 2013, the conceptual framework of e-learning, the characteristics of a teaching philosophy that provides stability, continuity and long-term guidance in the e-learning environment, the imperative of quality assurance and improvement in e-learning– a new paradigm in higher education systems, and the interdependencies between e-learning, e-inclusion and e-working. The Romanian case is presented as a comparative study with the EU and US standards in higher education.*

## INTRODUCTION

The chapter presents the e-learning challenges in the European knowledge-based society in the context of relaunching Lisbon growth and jobs strategy, of the European Lifelong Learning Program 2007 – 2013, and of the 2009 European Year of Innovation and Creativity. The main objectives of the chapter are the awareness of the e-learning role for the success of the European Lifelong Learning Program 2007 – 2013, and for innovation in education as a key challenge in the knowledge-based society. We deal with the

DOI: 10.4018/978-1-61692-791-2.ch008

conceptual framework for e-learning: the terms used, the broad definition of the concept, the most recent definitions such as the definition of the Commission of the European Communities 2008, the definition of Webopedia Computer Dictionary 2009, the definition of BNET Business Dictionary 2009, the definition of MSN Encarta 2009, proposing also a teaching statement philosophy adapted to the e-learning environment characteristics of teaching. The Chapter also includes discussions on the Romanian case, a case study about understanding the imperative of quality assurance in e-learning. We conclude with a research on a future paradigm: social e-learning, which means setting up a socially inclusive e-learning environment within the European Union context. An important challenge is to direct e-learning to e–inclusion and to understand the interdependencies between e-learning and e-working.

## MAIN FOCUS OF THE CHAPTER

### E-Learning: A Key Challenge in the European Lifelong Learning Program 2007-2013

The year 2009 is the European Year of Innovation and Creativity and it stays under the sign of the overall framework of several EU policy initiatives fostering Creativity and Innovation, amongst which the *European policy cooperation in Education and Training* has a leading place. It is common knowledge that the successful education and training in the knowledge-based society depend more and more on the innovative use of ICT. A remarkable progress in the use of ICT for education and training across Europe over the past few years should be pointed out: major benefits of ICT were seen in schools, but also in higher education (for distance learning, virtual mobility and ongoing professional development) and in big companies and public administrations as shown by e-learning in the workplace. ICT has played a very important role in enhancing creativity and innovation in learning.

Four years after it was relaunched in 2005, the *Lisbon growth and jobs strategy* demonstrated that it is working, but the European Union must continue the reforms in order to succeed in a knowledge-based society marked by the acceleration of the globalization phenomenon. Definitely, the "*triangle of learning" (education – research – innovation)* plays a major role for a positive trend in growth and job opportunities. But what does the *New Lisbon Strategy* involve in fact? – an increased research development and innovation, a more dynamic business environment, *investing in people*, and greening up the economy. With reference to the objective of investing in people, we must consider besides more and better jobs, *lifelong learning* as essential, therefore we understand *e-learning* as the core of the lifelong learning concept.

The European Union strategic framework of co-operation in the fields of education and training is represented by the agreements of the 10-year work program of the *European Commission*, *Education and Training 2010* which are implemented through the open method of coordination. The *Education and Training 2010 Work Program* of the European Commission has made a vital contribution towards achieving the main objectives of the Lisbon Strategy: growth and jobs working together for Europe's future. The conclusions of the Spring 2007 European Council described education and training as prerequisites for a well-functioning knowledge triangle (education - research - innovation) which plays a key role in boosting growth and jobs. In this context, of education seen as booster for growth and jobs and as the key to increasing opportunities for individuals and for creating a new Meta framework of levels in Europe, we will further analyze the e-learning phenomenon.

Developing innovative information and communications technologies solutions to promote better education and training throughout a citizen's life is a special focus of the *European Lifelong Learning Program 2007 - 2013*. This new program is in fact a single umbrella for education and training programs and replaces previous education, vocational training and e-learning programs, which ended in 2006. Information and communications technologies are seen as powerful tools for quality improvement and ease access to education and training, and because of this *ICT* is also *Key Activity 3* of the *Transversal Program of Lifelong Learning Program*. On the other hand, besides the European Lifelong Learning Program, there are other important initiatives at the European level as *European Distance and E-learning Network, eEurope Action Plan, eTEN, eContent, e-Skills for the 21st Century,* and *Learnovation Initiative 2009* which was developed with the support of the European Commission as a contribution to the European Year of Creativity and Innovation in order to make European education and lifelong learning a lever for innovation. At the present, ICT for innovation is considered to be a key challenge in the knowledge-based society. The challenge is to achieve innovative transformation of the provision of education and training, and e-learning plays a key role in achieving pedagogical innovation, technological innovation and organizational innovation. The recent trend towards post-initial, informal and non-formal learning opened the way for e-learning towards interactive learning, creative content, personalized and self-directed learning, etc. This relates more closely e-learning to the Lifelong Learning agenda and the creation of a European Lifelong Learning Area.

## E-Learning: Conceptual Framework

Today we are facing the growing complexity of e-learning and its role as a basic tool for education and training. Terms such as "digital literacy", "digital competence", "t-learning", "e-tivities", "e-maturity" and of course, "e-learning", have become part of our daily life. Generally, e-learning is a broad definition of the field of using technology to deliver learning and training programs. It is an evolving concept and an all-encompassing term typically used to describe media such as CD-ROM, Internet, Intranet, wireless and mobile learning. Some include Knowledge Management as a form of e-learning. First, in 1995 it was referred to as "Internet-based Training", later "Web-based Training" to clarify that delivery could be on the Inter- or Intra-net, then "Online Learning" and finally e-learning, adopting the in vogue use of "e-" during the dot.com boom.

The Webopedia Computer Dictionary (2009) defines e-learning as a form of education via the Internet, network, or standalone computer. Therefore, e-learning includes web-based learning, computer-based learning, virtual classrooms and digital collaboration. The BNET Business Dictionary (2009) presents e-learning as a development from computer-based training which consists of self-contained learning materials and resources that can be used at the pace and convenience of the learner. The MSN Encarta (2009) definition of e-learning is more synthetic: learning using electronic means.

The definition used for the e-learning initiative and its successive developments in Europe focuses on *the use of new multimedia technologies and the Internet to improve the quality of learning by facilitating access to resources and services as well as remote exchanges and collaboration* (Commission of the European Communities, 2008). E-learning is more than "web-based training", as it involves processes and applications including computer-based learning, web-based learning, digital collaboration. E-learning is no longer seen as the synonym of "online learning", which is only a part of technology-based learning, describing learning via the Internet, intranet and extranet.

Carliner (2002) divided the uses of e-learning in two categories: formal learning, which includes online education, online training, blended learning with classroom delivery and printed materials, and informal learning, which includes knowledge management, electronic performance support, and blended learning with related materials in other media.

We are now witnessing the impact of e-learning in school education, higher education, adult learning, learning at the workplace and also informal and self-directed learning. As for school education, we may say that schools with higher level of e-maturity show a faster increase in performance scores, and pupils, teachers and parents think that ICT has a positive impact on the learning. Also, ICT use is most widespread in higher education and this results in the growth of satisfaction among students. We should not forget that ICT has opened new learning opportunities for adults, in particular supporting informal learning, and many large companies and public sector organizations have invested in e-learning and content management systems, reporting high levels of satisfaction and significant cost reductions.

## TEACHING PHILOSOPHY IN THE E-LEARNING ENVIRONMENT

*The biggest truth in learning is that its purpose is to unlock the human mind and to develop it into an organ capable of thought - conceptual thought, analytical thought and sequential thought. (anonymous)*

Having a clear and consistent teaching philosophy is crucial when we talk about e-learning. Starting from the wider definition of teaching as "a scholarly activity which is purposeful, reflective, documented and shared in an evaluative forum" (Menges & Weimerm 1996) it is important to focus in order to articulate a single teaching philosophy that reflects the personal view on the teaching process, and to incorporate the benefits for all the parties involved: *students*, *university administration* and *teaching staff*. The teaching staff must also be aware of the fact that their teaching statement philosophy is not only a personal document but also a public one.

Gail Goodyear and Douglas Allchin (1998), in their study of the functions of a statement of teaching philosophy, identify the main purpose as follows: "In preparing a statement of teaching philosophy, professors assess and examine themselves to articulate the goals they wish to achieve in teaching.... A clear vision of a teaching philosophy provides stability, continuity, and long-term guidance.... A well-defined philosophy can help them remain focused on their teaching goals and appreciate the personal and professional rewards of teaching". Starting from this point, we will try to emphasize the specific elements of the TSP while relating it to online teaching.

When we refer to the TSP (TSP = teaching statement philosophy) adapted to the e-learning environment characteristics of teaching, we are trying to highlight from the beginning how the effectiveness of online teaching can be evaluated, as the starting point of the TSP setting. Why? Because a significant number of the Romanian teaching staff is still reluctant and distrustful when it comes to the effectiveness of online teaching, thus we need to reconsider the basic milestones when we coach them to elaborate their TSP, while incorporating their personal view concerning online teaching. We strongly believe that a well-defined TSP can help them remain focused on their teaching goals and appreciate the *professional* and *personal rewards of teaching.* It is about demonstrating the desire to grow as a professional teacher (Lyons, 1999). A professor is supposed to keep learning all of his/her life and should be seen as a role model, one who is a life-long learner and can inspire the students and those with which they interact virtually. Therefore, what exactly are the personal and professional rewards? While asking a few people in our department about it, we discovered that a large and well-defined survey must be conducted, because more information is needed on how the teaching staff perceives the drivers of online teaching: motivating factors, psychological implications of working in a virtual environment. It is also about measuring the reaction-time in terms of the individual adjustment with the new IT tools, finding your own identity as in a large virtual community, and having a real control of the teaching process, the classroom and teacher, the teacher-student interaction.

As an example, implementing an e-learning platform, such as Blackboard, in our university, has arisen a wide range of issues for the professors: changes to be made in the curricula, adapting and rewriting the traditional learning resources, acquiring new skills in order to be able to use the new learning environment at its most effective level, understanding the computer-based assessment principles and adapting the traditional assessment procedures using the new IT tools, and finally, positioning themselves as recognized professionals without face-to-face contact with the learners.

The difficulties concerning the TSP re-writing came up when the teaching staff had to define, in this new context, their learning objectives because, for example, it was important to assess and to examine themselves in order to articulate the goals they wish to achieve in online teaching.

As a teacher you need to define and to present the learning objectives, for example, while always having in mind the specificity of the new learning environment, so different than the traditional face-to-face environment. It is important to clearly describe how you will teach, the ways in which you will make decisions about the course content and teaching methodologies. The e-learning environment means that you need to reflect thoroughly about the ways in which you communicate your goals as an instructor, the corresponding actions to be taken in the virtual classroom, and also, to monitor the students' feed-back.

*To conclude: a clear vision of one's teaching philosophy provides stability, continuity, and long-term guidance.* So, the teachers need to redefine their teaching philosophy if they are to use the new e-learning facilities. How will they define the stability? The usage of the new technologies, the new tools is a must but while keeping the same course content. Is it possible? Is it relevant? Should we be more careful about the rhythm of changes? And how often must we revise our course content? So, we suggest keeping as milestones the basic principles, concepts, definitions and methods of the science that mean stability in terms of building the framework, and adapting these basics to the new ICT reality, giving samples, making study cases available, renewing the applications and of course, making them appealing in order to keep the online students connected in the classroom. Some professors are saying that it is far more difficult to keep their online audience focused than the traditional classroom audience. So, it is important to find your own ways to present the course content and maintain the stability at the same time. For us it is crucial to create the possibility of sharing good practices inside the university and not only there, but also inside the e-learning community, while using the same e-learning platform.

What about continuity when we address different target groups of students, located all over the world?

Having online students in different locations all over the country and abroad requires a precise schedule of the online activities, enabling free access for each student any time. Continuity, also means that the teacher should consider the possibility to get feedback from students, to maintain a close contact through available communication tools such as: e-mail, discussion forum, to guide them to achieve performance in their self-study activity.

Can we still provide long-term guidance, and what about defining the "long-term" concept in this new framework of e-learning? Nevertheless, the traditional teacher faces a lot of new challenges: the course content presentation is no longer just an oral presentation, but it is also supposed to be on the topic of using the appropriate computer tools: power-point presentations, pdf files, short case studies as movies, building schemes and figures and a lot of other new "wired" e-tools. It is not so easy to adjust to this and to teach yourself how to adapt to this new environment.

In this part of the chapter we intend to explain the developments in the teaching philosophy related to the e-learning environment and to explore how teachers must shift the new tools available in their new environment. The teacher-student relation is no longer a direct, face-to-face one, because the e-learning environment implies that the computer interferes between these two "actors", making teachers rethink the ways to turn teaching effective, to measure the outcomes and the design and to conduct the assessment process while giving the appropriate feedback to the students.

Implementing the e-learning system is really a considerable challenge for everyone: for the teachers because they feel ignored and less involved – the computer mediates the link between students and professors; for the students because they feel alone and without guidance or supervision in their learning effort; for the organizations because they need to adapt and incorporate the new ICT technologies, much more efficient and easy to use. Despite of all these difficulties, the basic questions concerning the TSP are the same: why do I teach in the online environment? What motivates me to do this? What are the opportunities and constraints? What do I expect to be the outcomes of my online teaching? What is the student-teacher relationship I strive to achieve and with what kind of mutual benefits? How do I know when I have taught successfully? What code of ethics should guide me? Having in mind all these questions, I think that every teacher who explores the possibility to expend his activity in online teaching, must give answers first to himself and when all becomes clear to share his new TSP with the rest of the academic community and with the stakeholders.

There are many ways of working online, there are so many tools to play with, but the main focus is always on the students or the community members and meeting their needs. We are talking about the personalized learning, as follows:

a. developing a new pedagogy – from linear to multi-threaded, from static to dynamic, from content to experience, from demonstration to inference and, last but not least, from objectives to goals and from uniformity to diversity;
b. making good choices about tools and processes – assure the information exchange, create the climate for idea creation, decision-making and social/group building experience;
c. evaluating accessibility: level of students and professors skills required, the interaction level inside the learning environment, leading to a synchronous or asynchronous activity.

In our TSP you must refer to the above-mentioned issues, because your students are waiting for it and because this means that you have personalized your TSP to the new learning environment and according to the knowledge society general requirements.

And finally, we may say that *academic autonomy* allows professors, within the limits of the law, to impart selected social, political, economic and cultural views into the e-learning environment. A TSP must be a thoughtful presentation of selected and prioritized values (Goodyear & Allchin, 1998).

What should we do in the future in order to improve the general public's and authorities' perception of e-learning teaching?

We intend to develop a study among our teaching staff and students (during the academic year 2009-2010), based on our experience of implementing the Blackboard e-learning system at *Spiru Haret* University, the biggest university in Europe in term of number of distance-learning students. Why? We are committed to do it because a lot of traditionalists are contesting the efficiency of using e-learning in higher education. What for? The survey will provide us with information to be shared with others, to disseminate good practices in all the e-learning community using the same ICT tools. The goals and objectives of the study, the methodology and the data processing have, as a starting point, the study developed by Mills, Yanes, Casebeer at the University of Texas in 2008.

The findings of the research will be used in order to develop a long-term strategy of distance-learning teaching in our university and perhaps in our country if the society, the main stakeholders (employers) will agree to be involved in.

## QUALITY ASSURANCE IN EDUCATION: A FRAMEWORK FOR E-LEARNING IN ROMANIA, AT SPIRU HARET UNIVERSITY

Quality development and assurance is currently of growing interest and a difficult matter to handle. In spite of the different approaches, depending on regional and local points of view, it is widely considered important worldwide. Quality standards and guidelines are used everywhere in Europe, though more in the Anglo-Saxon and Benelux countries (82%) and less in the new EU Member States (58%), according to a report on quality in e-learning in the countries of Europe (Quality in E-learning, Report 2005). But while it is generally agreed that quality is very important, it is very differently implemented in practice because of the different views on the quality of the provided products in Europe. As it is common knowledge that no learning or assessment method is ideal and the only way to go, there is no single way to approach and deliver quality in e-Learning either. It depends on local traditions and particular features on the one hand, and on each and every institution on the other hand. The formulation of quality assurance systems for technology-based education, while most frequently regulated at a regional or national level, has in recent years been driven by international developments. The global reach of the Internet and the lack of ways to regulate transnational commercial activities allow fraudulent operators to spring up. So, it is crucial to have a firm quality framework and strong principles based on local and international expertise.

Most of the European countries have issued quality assurance guidelines, starting rather from the concept of quality than from quality as a technique, 'so its implementation is very much dependent on the type of organization or process at hand (Gilmore and Hunt, 1995). But Deming (1994) says that 94% of quality problems result from a faulty system. But, who has actually sufficient expertise to determine which system is faulty and which is not? The education providers should be supervised in point of quality by experts, but the inspection should refer to what criteria as long as every institution has selected and implemented a specific strategy that best suited its own views? A lot of confusion or unfair judgments may occur from this special circumstance: experts may not agree to a particular quality system adopted by an education provider. *General and specific approaches* should enjoy unbiased consideration.

The effectiveness of any quality improvement is as much a function of the ability to foster agreement around common goals as of any substantive input or process adjustments attempted by an institution. In many circles, the term 'quality' is understood as shorthand for Total Quality Management (TQM), or its close cousin, Continuous Quality Improvement (CQI). 'Quality assurance' is an activity based on the generic concept of TQM. The quality framework is a tool for continuously improving online programs in higher education. Based on recommendations of the higher education community, the quality framework provides ways of demonstrating institutional quality. As institutions continuously improve pedagogy, and as technology evolves, the framework itself is a work in progress, designed to facilitate the sharing of effective practices among institutions.

Romanian Government issued the Quality Assurance in Education framework under the form of a Government Ordinance in 2005, as a material need deriving from a needs assessment process, before Romania's integration to the EU (2007). It is a general framework, having no particular reference to e-Learning. The methodology of quality assurance in education is based on the learning outcomes concept, and has included the following components:

a. criteria – a fundamental aspect of the education provider organization and operation
b. standards and reference standards – description of the requirements expressed under the form of rules or outcomes, defining the minimum mandatory level of performance of a task
c. performance indicators – a measurement tool of the extent of achievement of an activity carried on by an education provider in relation with the standards
d. qualifications – the learning outcome obtained on completion of a program of studies.

The following processes are deemed as providing quality in education:

a. effective planning and attainment of expected learning outcomes
b. outcome monitoring
c. internal assessment of outcomes
d. external assessment of outcomes
e. continuous improvement of learning outcomes

The quality assurance system refers to the following areas and criteria:

1. *institutional capacity* – resulting from the internal organization, the available infrastructure, as defined by the institutional, administrative and managerial structures
2. *educational effectiveness* – mobilization of the proper resources to obtain the expected learning outcomes
3. *quality management* – materialized in: quality assurance strategies and procedures, objective and transparent strategies of assessment of the learning outcomes, procedures of periodical assessment of the teaching staff, access to the learning resources, systematically updated database related to internal quality assurance, transparence of public information in relation with the programs of studies, the certificates and diplomas issued
4. *functionality of the quality assurance structures*.

The same ordinance sets forth the need for a special authority in charge with monitoring quality assurance in education and having special assignments and qualified staff, mostly deriving from the teaching staff.

At the institutional level, *Spiru Haret* University, a private university fostering technology-based education, has developed its own quality assurance system, starting from the general national framework and from international expertise in the field and adding its own views, in line with its own objectives. Starting from Gilbert definition of quality assurance (1992, p. 32) as 'the assembly of all functions and activities that bear upon the quality of a product or service so that all are treated equally, planned, controlled and implemented in a systematic manner', the university has developed its own activities, based on its own Manual providing its specific methodology, criteria and procedures and internal authorities to monitor the proper observation of its own guidelines. The Manual's mission statement sets forth that Quality Assurance as seen by the university is a sub-function of Total Quality Management, applied at the level of the institution to show that quality is a managed outcome.

The main goal focuses on the efforts of all the participants in the university community so that the students – future graduates – should acquire the knowledge that they need in a knowledge-based society, which will be a starting point for higher performance on the labour market and society. The Manual does not deal only with the theoretical issues of quality assurance and culture of quality, but also explains methodologies and rules of quality implementation and improvement within the basic units, departments, divisions, faculties and University and sets forth the legislation related to quality assurance in education.

By conveying a pragmatic nature to the manner of structuring and handling the quality issues, it has been a landmark for the Manual of Quality Assurance Procedures. In view of the significance that the cycles I, II and III have in the general structure of the University learning system, this manual has made a central point in discussing the methodologies, criteria, standards and performance markers for the above cycles. The idea of presenting the aforementioned was to provide models for the departments that shall consequently adopt and adjust and, thus, they may implement the requirements of these models into their own activity of analysis and assessment of the educational process quality that these units are accountable for.

As a rule, the means of quality assurance and culture of quality have been issued to be applied mainly to the full-time classes, but also to the part-time and distance learning (e-Learning) depending on their specificity.

The Manual focuses on the analysis of the quality issues in the cycle I of undergraduate studies – criteria, markers, standards, rules for implementation and evaluation of the education quality that may be implemented into various components of the educational process – programmes of study (curricula, syllabuses), programming and development of the teaching activity (courses, seminars, practical works), self-evaluation and peer assessment of the teaching staff, specialty practice and teaching practice and the university documents.

Since all the faculties have assumed as a mission the organization and development of the educational process and also the carrying out of scientific research, the Research Management Division analyses and presents herein the "technology" of improving quality of scientific research in its various applications: the structure and operation of research at *Spiru Haret* University and how the research strategy is seen within the departments and faculties. It is worth mentioning the importance of the internal procedure of hierarchical place of the faculties within *Spiru Haret* University in terms of their objectives, markers and scores for the scientific research analysis.

The Manual was published in 2007 and its content is still to be acknowledged by part of the teaching staff, by the students – who are still unaware of the institutional quality assurance authorities and procedures – and by the stakeholders. Should the content of the *Manual of Quality Assurance Procedures* be assimilated by the teaching staff and students and the efforts for quality be enhanced, this shall undoubtedly be beneficial to all the members of the university community, firstly to the students – the beneficiaries and participants in improving quality in education, and to the teachers who act as promoters of this quality assurance process. The constitution of the *quality assurance structures* plays an essential role in the good practices of quality implementation. The establishment of a category of *professionals in quality assurance* is an issue more and more present in universities worldwide, who should cooperate with the university staff to reach this common goal. The university has established *Quality Assurance Commissions,* a valuable solution in the process of quality implementation and assessment, while the *Quality Assurance Department* is responsible for the support of the quality assessment process and the achievement of the required improvement measures. The Quality Assurance Commissions are established both at the institutional level and for each faculty or department.

The quality assurance is *outcome-based,* the knowledge, abilities and skills acquired upon completion of a program of study. Within the quality assurance process, *three fundamental areas* are emphasized, in line with national regulations: *institutional capacity*, expressing the coherence of its own communication and administration system, the adequate nature of the material and financial resources required for a stable, long-term operation and of the human resources required for the achievement of its mission and objectives; *educational effectiveness*, explicitly expressed in how the teaching, learning and research processes develop, the techniques and methods being used, how the students and the teaching staff are recruited, so that the institution obtains the desired results in learning and research; *quality management*, focused on those strategies, structures, techniques and operations that allow high performances in the education quality assurance and improvement. In a nutshell, management concentrates on how the institution manages the quality of its activities.

For the purpose of organizing and achieving the quality assurance process, the institution employs the relations that are being established among the following components: domains, criteria, procedures, standards and performance markers.

They stand for the reference data in the education quality management, also providing the best framework for the database and information that the institution turns to for the internal monitoring that helps build the files for the quality external assessment.

To the purposes of the Manual, *procedure* means the „know-how" for carrying on a certain activity, the stages to go through in a given order so that a quality activity be achieved (teaching, seminar work, lab) or to elaborate a certain specific product (syllabus, curriculum, list of assessment of the staff performance, etc), as well as the tools being used to reach the desired objective.

*Criteria* are specific to any of the above domains and assume a fundamental role of organization and operation of a quality providing institution. In Romania, the first mentioned domain – institutional capacity – equals with the criterion of *institutional, administrative and managerial structures* and the criterion of *material resources*.

The second, *educational effectiveness*, includes criteria such as: the content of the program of study, the scientific research activity and the financial activity of the organization. The third domain, *quality management*, includes criteria such as: strategies and enforcement of quality assurance, assessment procedures of the learning results; periodical assessment of the teaching staff; the accessibility of the learning-fit resources; the database, constantly updated, which regards the internal quality assurance; the transparency of the public interest information related to the program of study, certificates, diplomas and qualifications; the functionality of quality assurance in education.

The *standards* correspond to each criterion. The *standard* means the description of the requirements that are formulated in terms of regulations or results, addressed to a mandatory minimum level of an Act of Education.

The *reference standards* describe the prerequisites that define an optimum level of achieving an activity by a quality providing institution, based on the good practices that are currently used nationally and internationally.

*Performance markers* serve as a level estimation, a measure of how an activity is achieved in an institution, compared to the standards and the reference standards in use.

As an example, at least two standards (*mission, objective and academic integrity* and *leadership and administration*) are incumbent upon the first criterion above, the institutional capacity, i.e. the institutional, managerial and administrative structures. In its turn, the former standard – mission, objectives and academic integrity – is measured by the markers such as mission and objectives, academic integrity, liability and public responsibility. The same applies to the correlations among criteria, standards and markers for the domains 2 and 3 above.

The enforcement of its own quality assurance system is still at the beginning; the university has a powerful e-Learning platform, Blackboard, an essential tool in providing e-Learning services.

The learning outcomes are yet to come, since no Cycle I has ended so far in order to be analysed. But the efforts taken in regulating quality assurance are in good faith and in line with national and international framework.

A special mention should be made in the national quality assurance guidelines related to the selection of the quality assurance experts, which is an essential issue; quality assurance reviewers should not be selected at random but based on previous solid training in the line of quality assurance! The experts should not necessarily be teachers – because of a potential conflict of interests when reviewing a competitive education provider, but rather unbiased experts in education. An unbiased view may only be acquired by the joint efforts of the experts on the one hand and of the students and stakeholders on the other hand.

While defining general quality assurance principles, criteria and procedures is a pre-requisite and essential for any education system, a special mention should be made to e-Learning, as sometimes their application may be technologically difficult and different from the traditional modes of teaching and learning; specific e-Learning solutions should be issued for the design, development and implementation of the e-Learning offering. Quality assurance frameworks should be reviewed from time to time; an annual revision might not be useless under the circumstances of the fast growth, expansion and alteration brought by technology.

An e-learning quality assessment was conducted at Spiru Haret University, in 2008-2009, and the aim of this evaluation was to establish to what extent our e-learning activities meet the QA standards at the national, European and US level. The study has identified the main quality criteria accepted in all tree above-mentioned areas, we also selected the most important standards for each criterion and the position held by the Spiru Haret University e-learning system was measured with an appropriate scale.

Spiru Haret University positioning – additional comments:

- Spiru Haret University started e-learning implementation in the academic year 2006-2007 just for testing and only with a limited number of online courses; major progress were made between 2007-2008. Still a lot of work to do;
- over 2.5 mil. EUR were invested in IT communication facilities & e-learning platform last academic year: the Blackboard e-learning platform and our own servers to run the application for over 50,000 concurent users;
- state-of-the-art computers, over 10,000, providing easy access to all our students not matter if they have an PC at home or not ;
- a new organizational structure was created - DL/E-learning Department- having competencies in the coordination, supervision and improvement of the educational process, administrative duties – supervising in cooperation with IT the operation of all 44 distance learning labs, located all over the country and abroad;
- the teaching staff and administrative staff was included in short one-on-one tutorials for the use of Bb tools, is needed to have a long-run CPD (continuing professional development) programme oriented not only to professional updating, but also to the usage of the new ITC tools;
- there are no relevant research projects oriented to e-learning effectiveness, improvement and delivery. Some small researcher teams are exploring the field, with insignificant results so far.
- a modern and flexible infrastructure was build, able to assure easy access to Blackborad e-learning platform, good connectivity to the Internet, with 3 different providers, a large number of IT labs all over the country and abroad, established as student support centers;

*Table 1. A synthetic table of the study results:*

| **Quality criteria & standards** (*selected after a wide literature reviewing –mostly from USA*) | **QA standards and actual status of the E-learning system at Spiru Haret University** **) | **National QA Requirements for e-learning** | **European QA Requirements ENQA*****) (*no specific standards yet elaborated*) | **ISO/IEC 19796-1:2005 quality standard** (*our university didn't ask ISO certification yet*) |
|---|---|---|---|---|
| **Institutional commitment***, *meaning:*<br>Financial<br>Organizational<br>Faculty & staff development<br>Research | **Yes, *very good***<br>**Yes, *good*,***needs improvement*<br>**Yes, satisfactory to good,***own CPD-program for staff; staff evaluation*<br>**Yes**, *Unsatisfactory* | Not specified<br>Existence of a DL Department<br>General provisions, no details<br>Not specified | **The existence of policies and procedure** for QA at institutional level<br>**Approval, monitoring and periodic review** of programs and awards<br>**Quality assurance of teachig staff**: need to have qualified and competent teaching staff | General conditions *(101 criteria and 32 descriptive criteria)* |
| **Technology**<br>Infrastructure<br>Accessibility<br>Synchronous interaction<br>Instructional materials | Yes, ***very good***<br>*Yes,**very good***<br>*Yes,**good***<br>***Acceptable***,*Own QA procedures and evaluation* | PC + Internet<br>Easy access using different communication networks<br>Yes, no detailed description<br>General framework | Information system: the institutions should collect, analyse and use relevant information for the effective management of their programs of study | Technical aspects *(103 criteria and 23 descriptive criteria)*<br>Data storage and data processing *(37criteria and 14 descriptive criteria)* |
| **Student services**<br>Before entrance in the V-classroom<br>During the learning experience<br>Continued connection after programme graduation | Yes, through a specific website<br>*Good*, Blackboard (eg LCM system) + on campus<br>*Not yet implemented (project phase)* | Yes, public information available, testing options<br>Yes, detailed<br>Not specified | **Public information**: should be published up to date, impartial and objective information about the programs of study<br>Learning resources and **student support**: available resources should be adequate and appropriate for each program offered | Functionalities *(69 criteria and 29 descriptives)*<br>Encoding of information *(59 criteria and 3 descriptive criteria)* |
| **Instructional Design and Course Development** | *Yes, acceptable* (own procedures, methodology & standards) | Yes, just a description of the procedures | **Learning resources** and student support: available resources should be adequate and appropriate for each program offered<br>**Assessment of students** = the process should be open, using published criteria, procedures and it should be applied consistently | Theoretical aspects *(80 criteria and 17 descriptive criteria)* |

*continues on following page*

- multimedia outstanding facilities, such as Educational broadcasting channel- TVRM;
- good services for students - large administrative staff with flexible office hours, available on the desk, telephone and email;
- an alumni organisation should be encouraged to be active in order to provide continuity in students communication and to enable the evaluation of the postgraduates' insertion on the job market;

*Table 1. continued*

| **Quality criteria & standards** *(selected after a wide literature reviewing –mostly from USA)* | **QA standards and actual status of the E-learning system at Spiru Haret University **)** | **National QA Requirements for e-learning** | **European QA Requirements ENQA***)** *(no specific standards yet elaborated)* | **ISO/IEC 19796-1:2005 quality standard** *(our university didn't ask ISO certification yet)* |
|---|---|---|---|---|
| **Instruction process and Instructors** | *Needed to be improved,* low feed-back from learners, solitaire learning, Instructors should improved their interaction with students *Good assessment activities*, small rate of complains | Yes, Support for instructors –guide Special training for instructors – e-learning platform familiarization Instructor's activity must be periodically assessed by students | **Quality assurance of teachig staff**: need for qualified and competent teaching staff | |
| **Financial sustainability** | *Very good* Affordable fees for different social categories due to our social-oriented strategy for knowledge transfer | Not specified | | |
| **Evaluation** | *Yes, own procedures for periodical evaluation- content, delivery, assessment,student services* | Self-evaluation Periodical evaluation from a local or external QA body | | |

*) The Western Interstate Commission for Higher Education (USA) presents nine aspects of the domain of"commitment"-WICHE 2001such as: financial commitment, physical plant, articulation, technical support etc. and Institute for Higher Education Policy emphasizes technological aspects of institutional support in term of having plan, security, redundancy in delivery structure and systems for maintenance of the technological infrastructure (IHEP,2000).

**) Note: The self-assessment, about the extent of Spiru Haret University (USH) e-learning system meeting the QA criteria/standards, used a 5 level-scale: ***very good***, ***good*** (needs slight improvements), ***acceptable*** (needs improvments), ***satisfactory*** (needs major improvments), ***unsatisfactory*** (major improvement +changes in the institutional strategy + major changes in organizational structure)

***) European Association for Quality Assurance in Higher Education (ENQA) elaborated a set of general standards and guidelines for quality assurance, no specific distinction was made for e-learning. ENQA has Recently organized a worshop on Quality Assurance in E-learning, discussing the aspects and criteria of e-learning evaluation in higher education (7-8 oct.2009, Sigtuna, Sweden). Sweden National Agency for Higher Education performed a study in nine countries across Europe and one conclusion was that quality is not an issue for many, especially for the quality assurance agencies. The worshop supposed to answer at a few relevant questions: Which new aspects and criteria specific for e-learning do we have to consider? How can we integrate e-learning criteria in the national evaluation program? How can we built up cooperation/knowledge exchange at a European level between national assurance/accreditation organizations and organizations with experience in e-learning quality such as EADTU, EFQUEL and JISC? In our opinion, QA in e-learning is an ongoing process in EU and we need to have an adaptive approach, identify our national specificity and tom develop our own set of standards and criteria using the knowledge and good practices of other univerities, no matter where they are located.

- our own e-learning specific procedures and methodologies help us to have an efficent management of the learning content and delivery methods. It is still room for improvement and designing more atractive courses for the students, knowing that the learning process is self-oriented, independent learning process in the absence of face-to-face interaction between teachers and learners;
- our Quality Assurance Department has its own program of evaluation and periodical review of e-learning process and a report is published annually.

Final remarks: the QA for e-learning is far from a final standardization in EU and Romania, but our university is commited to improve and promote the new learning environment along with traditional classroom teaching process.

## INTERDEPENDENCIES: E-LEARNING, E-INCLUSION, E-WORKING

We can speak about a future paradigm: social e-learning, which means setting up a socially inclusive e-learning environment within the European Union context. A key challenge is to direct e-learning to e–inclusion. In Digital and Social Inclusion Chart, Barcelona (2004) are stated the following key areas which are good starting points for both implementation and further research: social solutions to social problems, community and awareness, towards the transparent PC, problem solving methodology for e-learning, and Internet for everybody. The imperative of addressing the "digital divide" comes along with the strong growth in the use of ICT by enterprises and households. This is the reason for what Riga Ministerial Declaration (2006) drew attention to the broad importance of e-inclusion. E-inclusion would increase equity, create new opportunities for work and entrepreneurship, strengthen culture and encourage civic participation. As stated by the Riga Ministerial Declaration (2006), e-inclusion means both inclusive ICT and the use of ICT to achieve wider inclusion objectives. It focuses on participation of all individuals and communities in all aspects of the information society. E-inclusion policy, therefore, aims at reducing gaps in ICT usage and promoting the use of ICT to overcome exclusion, and improve economic performance, employment opportunities, quality of life, social participation and cohesion. In line with *i2010 - a European information society for growth and employment*, e-inclusion policy addresses issues in the fields of active ageing, geographical digital divide, accessibility, digital literacy and competences, cultural diversity and inclusive eGovernment.

Another important connection is between e-learning and e-working. Seretta (2005) considers that the learning habits of today's students will have a great impact on tomorrow's workers. Nowadays young people are so familiar with the computer and network technology that they will expect a similar virtual working environment. All of these have significant implications on higher education institutions and the work place. As always, today's youth culture gets incorporated into tomorrow's global culture. He thinks we should learn a lot from the next generation today. For example, adults have a difficult time working in teams in a face-to-face environment, they want to be let alone trying to do it online. Today's youth are using Internet-based multi-user games and Voice over IP to form virtual teams with people they may not know, carry on and complete a task and then disband. In effect, they are forming small, temporary learning communities. We can build this into future work and learning environments knowing that there will be much less resistance to using technology to communicate and work in a virtual environment. This is why it is imperative to address also the e-working concept. EU (2009) defines e-working as any normal business activity carried out from a remote location by using modern computing and communication technology. Statistical Indicators Benchmarking the Information Society research distinguishes between home-based eWork, mobile eWork and eWork by self-employed who work from small offices in their home. Terms very frequently used are the following: telecommute, telework, e-work, e-work centre, virtual office, remote worker and mobile worker. We can identify a lot of benefits to the e-worker and the organization: better work, increased job satisfaction, increase in motivation, reduced stress levels, reduced absenteeism, improved time management, improved productivity etc. Also, the e-working solution has major benefits to society such as access to more opportunities for people with disabilities, encourages greater diversity in the workforce and creates opportunities for e-workers to use extra time for the benefit of their community. E-working is closely linked to the development of the European knowledge-based society. The knowledge society opens new perspectives for the quality of work and e-working as a new working method could be considered a major one.

## FUTURE RESEARCH DIRECTIONS

We intend to continue our research work in the following directions:

- analyzing the future trend of including Knowledge Management as a form of e-learning;
- analyzing the future trend of Second Life Universities in 3D cyberspace and the possibility of Second Life cyberspace to become an useful tool for distance learning and also an interdisciplinary research space;
- developing in the academic year 2009 – 2010 a survey among the teaching staff and students of *Spiru Haret* University - Romania, regarding the experience of implementing Blackboard e-learning platform; the survey will provide us information to be shared with others and to be used for developing an e-learning strategy adapted to Romania's realities.

## CONCLUSION

At least every professor and maybe many students are thinking about the shifting determined by the e-learning phenomenon in education and the training systems. And if we consider e-learning as the core of life-long learning, there are other stakeholders interested in this evolving issue, too. European knowledge-based society is facing today the growing complexity of e-learning, new terms as "digital literacy" or "digital competence" in daily life, and new challenges: the imperative of a clear vision of a new teaching philosophy in the e-learning environment which would provide stability, continuity, long-term guidance and high quality, the shifting towards a social e-learning and e-inclusion with focus on participation of all the individuals and communities in all aspects of the information society, the imperative of addressing the e-working concept as a main consequence of e-learning expansion and even a reflexive question: Second Life Universities – on the edge?

## REFERENCES

American Association of Higher Education. (2000). *Implementing the Seven Principles: Technology as a lever*. Washington, DC: AAHE.

American Federation of Teachers. (2000). *Distance Education: Guidelines for good practice*. Washington DC: AFT(AFL-CIO)

ARACIS. (2009). *Guide for evaluating the by distance education*. Vth Part. Retrieved from http://www.aracis.ro

Business Dictionary, B. N. E. T. (2009). *Business Definition for: E-learning*. Retrieved 23.06.2009 from http://dictionary.bnet.com/definition/E-learning.html

Carliner, S. (2002). *Designing E-learning*. American Society for Training and Development.

Commission of the European Communities. (2008). The use of ICT to support innovation and lifelong learning for all – A report on progress. *Commission Staff Working Document*. Brussels, 09/10/2008, SEC(2008) 2629 final

Encarta Dictionary, M. S. N. (2009). E-learning. Retrieved 23.06.2009 from http://encarta.msn.com/dictionary_701705852/e-learning.html

Frydenberg, J. (2002). Quality Standards in e-Learning: a matrix of analysis. *International Review of Research in Open and Distance Learning, 3*(2).

Gilbert, J. (1992). *A slice by slice guide tot total quality management*. Great Britain: Tudor.

Gilmour, P., & Hunt, R. (1995). *Total Quality Management*. Australia: Longman.

Goodyear, G., & Allchin, D. (1998). Statement of Teaching Philosophy. In M. Kaplan (Ed.), *To improve the academy*, 17 103-122. Stillwater, OK: New Forums Press.

Government of Romania (1995). *Government Ordinance 75/12 July 2005*

Menges, R. J., & Weimer, M. (1996). *Teaching on solid ground: Using scholarship to improve practice*. San Francisco: Josey Bass Publishers.

Mills, Sh.J., Yanes M.J., Casebeer, C.M. (2009)- Perception of distance learning among faculty of a college of education. *MERLOT Journal of Online Learning and Teaching,5*(1), march 2009

Ministerial Declaration Riga. *Latvia* (2006). Retrieved 29.06.2009 from http://ec.europa.eu/information_society/events/ict_riga_2006/doc/declaration_riga.pdf

*More and better jobs in a knoewledge-based economy* (2009). Retrieved 29.06.2009 from http://ec.europa.eu/information_society/tl/ecowor/ework/index_en.html.

Pawlowski, J. M. (2007), *The new Quality standard for e-learning: Enabling Global Quality Development*.Retrieved from from http://www.initiatives.ref.org./Initiatives-2005/document.php?id=337

Seretta, B. (2005). Virtual companies. Net – learning and net – working will be common. *CHECK point e-learning newsletter*. Retrieved 2005 from http://www.checkpointelearning.com/index.php?co=8&aID=963

Spiru Haret University. (2007). *Manual of Quality Assurance Procedures*. Romania: Publishing House Fundatia Romania de Maine.

Webopedia Computer Dictionary. (2009). E-learning. Retrieved 23.06.2009 from http://www.webopedia.com/TERM/E/e_learning.html

## ADDITIONAL READING

Danish Technological Institute (Ed.). (2008). *Compendium of Good Practice. Cases of e-learning*. Education and Culture DG.

e-learning Industry Group (2005). *i2010: Fostering European e-learning Content to Make Lisbon Target a Reality*. Retrieved from www.elig.org/downloads/i2010%20Fostering%20European%20eLearning%20Content.PDF

ECOTEC. (2008). *Evaluation of the eLearning Program*. Retrieved from http://ec.europa.eu/dgs/education_culture/evalreports/training/2007/joint/elearning_en.pdf

European Commission. (2007). *European i2010 initiative on eInclusion and Web Accessibility – 'To be part of the information society'*. Retrieved from http://ec.europa.eu/information_society/activities/einclusion/docs/i2010_initiative/comm_native_com_2007_0694_f_en_acte.pdf

European Commission. (2007). i2010 – Annual. *The Information Society, 2007*, Retrieved from http://eur-lex.europa.eu/LexUriServ/LexUriServ.do?uri=COM:2007:0146:FIN:EN:PDF.

Gardiola, C. (2008). *Studies in Second Life, University affairs*, December 1, 2008, www.universityaffairs.ca

Hadad, W., & Draxler, A. (2002). *Technologies for education. Potentials, parameters and prospects, UNESCO, Paris*. Washington, DC: AED.

Sauciu, C., Castello, V., Dell'Aiuto, V., & Di Genova, D. (2009). T-learning for social inclusion. *eLearning Papers*, www.elearningpapers.eu N. 12 February 2009

Science Daily. (2007). Distance learning moves into Second Life-virtual classroom, *Science Daily. Realease.* Retrieved from www.sciencedaily.com/releases/2007

Shepherd, J. (2007). It's a world of possibilities. *The Guardian.*

TIME Center. (2007). *Results of the eLearning Initiative.* Grenoble School of Management. Retrieved from http://ec.europa.eu/education/more-information/moreinformation139_en.htm

## KEY TERMS AND DEFINITIONS

**E-Inclusion:** A socially inclusive e-learning which increases equity.

**E-Learning:** A new form of education which uses technology to deliver learning and training programs.

**E-Working:** A new working method; any business activity carried out from a remote location by using ICT.

**Quality Assurance (QA):** A set of activities aimed at ensuring a product suitable for the intended purpose, providing confidence in the product.

**Teaching Statement Philosophy (TSP):** A short reflective essay, a statement of beliefs and attitudes relative to purpose of education and role of teacher, definition of teaching, the nature of pedagogy, student learning and assessment of knowledge, skills and dispositions, classroom atmosphere.

**Total Quality Management (TQA):** A management strategy aimed at rising quality awareness and based on the principle of elimination of any potential mistake.

# Chapter 9
# Online Learning Management and Learners' Behavior:
## A Case Study of Online Learning in Japan

**Minoru Nakayama**
*Tokyo Institute of Technology, Japan*

**Hiroh Yamamoto**
*Tokyo Institute of Technology, Japan*

**Rowena Santiago**
*California State University - San Bernardino, USA*

## ABSTRACT

*Online learning has been playing a major role in university teaching across the world. For three consecutive years, the authors have surveyed bachelors and masters students who were enrolled in online courses at a Japanese university, in order to study learners' behavior while they are engaged in online courses. It was also their goal in this study to identify learning strategies and instructional design techniques that can contribute to the development of e-learning standards and can be applied to online course design and management. This book chapter will discuss how these issues were addressed using the survey data collected over three years, and based on the results of data analyses, provide a discussion of some guiding principles for the design and implementation of online learning.*

## INTRODUCTION

The blended learning environment is becoming a familiar style of university instruction, in spite of challenges related to the effective design and management of this type of classroom learning environment. Blended or hybrid courses, which are a combination of face-to-face and online teaching components, are usually preferred because these courses provide opportunities to review and extend students' learning opportunities. Numerous case studies about this type of learning environment have been reported (Diaz & Cartnal, 1999; Terrell & Dringus, 2000; Birch, 2002 ; Pintrich & Schunk, 2002 ; Koen 2005). To promote this learning style, the course design and the kind of learning support for students, including mentoring and tutoring support, are important issues (Wojciechowski & Palmer 2005).

DOI: 10.4018/978-1-61692-791-2.ch009

The role of learner characteristics as an influencing factor in one's learning performance has been studied since the 1970s. Learning performance has been reported to depend on learner attitudes and learning styles, as in the case of visual learners who benefit more when learning with visual-aid materials, or how learning with text-based materials could be an advantage for language dominant learners. This phenomenon is well-known as ATI or attitude-treatment interaction (Cronbach and Snow, 1977). Because of the effects of learners' attitude on learning performance, it has always been recommended that the effects of ATI be considered in multi-media learning environments. While learner attitude is usually taken into account as part of systematic design of instruction, there is limited report on its role and effect in online learning environments.

The purpose of this research is to investigate any existing relationship between learner characteristics and one's learning behavior, and to explore the possibility of developing a management strategy for blended or hybrid courses where learner characteristics are also taken into account.

For three consecutive years, the authors surveyed bachelor and masters students who were enrolled in blended courses at a Japanese university, in order to collect data on the behavior of students while engaged in blended courses (Nakayama et al. 2006, Nakayama et al. 2007a, Nakayama et al. 2007b, Nakayama et al. 2008).

Online assessment is also addressed in this research. One of the learning goals of university instruction is to develop students' logical thinking and writing (Biggs, 1999) and this is true even with online courses which are, as mentioned earlier, gaining popularity in higher education and taught as blended or fully online courses. E-learning, however, has its restrictions on how learning performance is assessed. Online testing is usually conducted through multiple-choice questions, without using any essay type of learning assessment. Major reasons for employing multiple-choice testing in e-learning include ease of implementation and ease of managing learner responses.

Conventional face-to-face classes, on the other hand, often employ essay-type examinations for the purpose of assessing learners' meta-cognitive understanding and ability to build logical structures beyond the understanding of basic knowledge (Biggs, 1999; Brown and Knight, 1994). Recently, various types of natural language processing systems have been developed, and this case study will also look at how these techniques may be applied to online assessment using essay-type testing.

## BACKGROUND

In Japan, e-learning (including distance learning) has been used mainly as a supplementary learning activity in combination with, or based on, regular face-to-face instruction, because only synchronous face-to-face courses are accredited in Japanese universities. Therefore the role of online courses was limited to supporting extended learning or for self-study. Asynchronous learning, in particular, has not been encouraged until 2000 when the Japanese University Council of the Ministry of Education Culture, Sports, Science and Technology (MEXT) approved the use of online courses as an accredited way of teaching and learning in higher education (Japanese University Council, 2000). To date, the use of online courses is gradually becoming integrated in university teaching.

As a result of these new policies, a new fully online Japanese graduate course was established in 2001 at the national university where this study was conducted (SUGSI, 2009). All classes in this program were made available asynchronously for students who want to earn master's and doctor's degrees in information engineering. The first enrollments took place in April of 2002. Most courses are delivered using the course website, and students can seek advice from a professor or research adviser using Internet video conferencing or other communication methods. Therefore, it is not necessary to be on-campus for courses or for advising. As with the traditional graduate programs, a masteral or doctoral thesis is still required to earn a degree.

Fully online courses are now recognized in Japan as one mode of instructional delivery, but the number of students who take these courses is still limited. Because most Japanese university courses are organized as face-to-face sessions, the best opportunity for students to use online materials is to be part of a blended or hybrid learning environment, which consists of both face-to-face lecture sessions and online learning activities.

One basic version of blended or hybrid courses is when students mainly learn in a face-to-face session, and then this learning is enhanced by providing additional information, such as study notes, that is stored in an online server. Open courseware, or OCW, (Abelson, 2008) is an example of this blended or hybrid version. In Japan, some universities have started forming OCW consortia since 2005 after universities began to introduce blended learning environments in their curriculum (Japan OCW, 2009).

In Japan, half of high school graduates attend university before getting jobs. Therefore, the range and distribution of university students' age is narrow and university education is an extended form of K-12 education. Recently, however, student characteristics are becoming diverse, thus making a more personalized style of education necessary, if not required. Online learning seems to be a suitable learning support system for addressing this situation.

According to the growing trend in the use of information communications technology or ICT, these online learning systems often include some form of learning assessment feature, and in most cases, they include a testing function, such as multiple-choice testing. The effectiveness of online testing with multiple-choice questions has been reported to accurately evaluate learner's ability, as in the case of Computerized Adaptive Testing or CAT (Linn, 1989). This form of assessment is also a growing trend in the area of licensing exams, e.g., English proficiency tests (CASEC, 2001).

In spite of the availability of multiple-choice testing features in online learning systems, there is still a preference, if not a demand, for essay-type assessment in online environments. For reasons indicated earlier in this chapter, essay-type tests are often given to students, usually as assigned written reports on a given topic related to course content. And in an online learning environment, these essay tests are usually posted by students as document files via email or web. When essay-test is used for assessment of learning, there is an increase in instructor's paperwork. To reduce the instructor's workload systematically, peer review is sometimes introduced (Ueno, 2008), where one student reviews another student's essay. When students are asked to peer review several essays, this could bring additional benefits to learners, e.g., peer exchange of feedback or opinion, but students need to be given additional time, and even some form of in-class training, to be able to do a successful peer review.

When high level of accuracy is required in the assessment of essay-testing, a review system that is based on a computerized system can be applied (Burstein et al. 2004). But since this type of system needs natural language processing capability, and only a few systems capable of processing Japanese documents are available. Among them is the prototype system that was developed by Ishioka and Kameda (2003) and was used in this study.

The issue of cultural differences is often considered when a person's performance is influenced by one's cultural background and country of origin. In this chapter, all subjects are Japanese, so on the outset, there are limitations on the generalizability of results which should be taken into consideration. Moreover, being able to identify common Japanese characteristics can still pose difficult challenges. During the development of the instruments for this study, even the survey results were dependent upon and were limited by the pilot group's characteristics. Therefore, the results of this survey are to be considered as a case report. For personality measures, while the authors were able to use a Japanese version of IPIP, Japanese psychologists agree that there is still a need for personality inventories designed specifically for Japanese subjects (Wada, 1996; Murakami and Murakami, 2001).

A study on motivation by Itoh (1995) noted the following as a typical Japanese characteristic: most Japanese put emphasis on effort as competence, so many carry the belief that effort provides good results and that effort is a virtue. Therefore the number of school days attended by a student can be considered and evaluated, for instance, as an index of that student's effort for learning. Our previous survey showed that conscientiousness is often a major factor in learning. (Nakayama et al., 2006, 2007a, 2007b).

Matumura and Hiruma (2000) surveyed Japanese university students using Sternberg's thinking style inventories, and they suggest that there are significant differences between groups. Those groups are categorized by gender (male vs. female) and by areas of discipline (science, humanities and arts). In Japanese universities, individual aptitude is often associated with a student's choice of major discipline (science and technology vs. humanities). Therefore, a student's discipline area was also considered in this survey.

## ONLINE LEARNING ISSUES IN JAPAN

Although the survey results from each previous year were analyzed and discussed, no overall three-year analysis and discussion have been made. Further, within the past three years, the contextual issues for students and for the instructors who taught the courses may have changed dramatically. Thus, the ability to determine what those changes are will make a significant contribution to the improvement of blended learning.

The aim of this chapter, therefore, is to show the quantitative differences in the causal relationship between characteristics and behavior across student levels (bachelors vs. masters) and between the survey years.

To address the limitation of online learning regarding the use of essay-tests for assessment, this study also investigated the use of an automated assessment system as a natural language processing tool for conducting essay-type tests in online learning. The use of this evaluation software for scoring Japanese essay tests was compared with experts' assessment and scoring of essay tests.

## METHODOLOGY

### Survey Group

The survey was conducted using two-unit bachelor or master courses, which were taught by the same professor as 15-week blended courses at a Japanese national university during 2005, 2006 and 2007. These two-credit courses were offered each Spring Term. The first course was "Information Society and Careers", a bachelor-level class for university freshman, and the other was "Advanced Information Industry Studies", a master's course for students in their first year of graduate work. Most of the students were majoring in Engineering.

Students attended face-to-face classes, and were also able to access the course content online outside of class. The total number of students with valid survey data was 201 (91 bachelors; 110 masters).

### Online Course Material

The e-learning components were originally designed for a fully online course. The modules include video clips of the instructor and the lecture for that session, plus the presentation slides which were used in the face-to-face lecture. Most tests were conducted in the multiple-choice format.

Learners can assess their responses and view their individual scores after completing the test. They are given as many opportunities as needed to retry and answer each question until they are satisfied with their own scores. This in turn motivated them to learn the course content well, using the accompanying video clips and presentation slides. But more importantly, the online learning materials were designed to encourage students to catch-up with what they had missed in class, and to maximize their learning experience.

To encourage maximum participation in e-learning, the following benefit was explicitly provided to students: online test scores for modules would count towards their final grades in the course. Also, students can make up for class absences by taking and passing online tests that correspond to the face-to-face class session that was missed. This encouraged students to do online modules and tests because missing a regular face-to-face class session often affected their final test scores and the evaluation of their learning experience. It is common among Japanese students to pay particular attention to what affects their learning performance and their final grades.

## Survey Instruments

To extract learner characteristics among Japanese students, five constructs were surveyed, using the same constructs and questionnaires in previous studies conducted in 2006 and 2007 (Nakayama et al., 2006, 2007a, 2007b). These constructs were: motivation (Kaufman and Agars, 2005), personality (Goldberg, 1999; IPIP, 2004), thinking styles (Sternberg, 1997), information literacy (Fujii, 2007) and self-assessment of online learning experience. In this chapter, the relationship between essay tests and two of these constructs (information literacy and learning experience) were also investigated. Further descriptions of these two metrics are given in the following sections.

### Motivation

The motivation inventory used in this study was developed by Kaufman and Agars (2005), and provided scores for "Intrinsic Motivation" and "Extrinsic Motivation" (Kaufman 2004).

### Personality

For the second construct (personality), the International Personality Item Pool (IPIP) inventory was used. Goldberg (1999) lists five personality factors and for this construct, there were five component scores: "Extraversion", "Agreeableness", "Conscientiousness", "Neuroticism" and "Openness to Experience".

### Thinking Styles

Sternberg's Thinking Styles had three components: "Legislative Style", "Executive Style" and "Judicial Style" (Sternberg, 1997; Matsumura & Hiruma, 2000). Their scores were also measured.

### Information Literacy

Information literacy is made up of various abilities, such as operational skills in information communication technology, and, knowledge of information science. Fujii (2007) defined and developed inventories for measuring information literacy. For this construct, the survey had 32 question items, and 8 factors were extracted: interest and motivation, fundamental operation ability, information collecting ability, mathematical thinking ability, information control ability, applied operation ability, attitude, and knowledge and understanding. The total mean of factor scores was used to indicate each student's information literacy level. This inventory was originally developed to measure information literacy among high school students across international countries. It can also be used to measure the information literacy level of university students (Fujii, 2007).

Secondary factor analysis was conducted on the above ten-factor scores for information literacy, and as a result, two secondary factors were extracted (Nakayama et al. 2008). The first secondary factor (IL-SF1) consists of "operational confidence and knowledge understanding"; the second one (IL-SF2) consists of "attitude issues".

### Learning Experience

Students' online learning experiences were measured using a 10-item Likert-type questionnaire. This questionnaire was administered twice: during the second week of the term and at the end of the course. As in previous studies, three factors were extracted from this instrument: Factor 1 (F1): overall evaluation of e-learning experience, Factor 2 (F2): learning habits, and, Factor 3 (F3): learning strategies (Nakayama et al, 2006, 2007a, 2007b).

### Learning Performance

The students' final grade for the course was based on various learning activities, which included their final test scores, their learning attitude (as indicated by the number of class days attended), and their online course learning experience with modules and tests. Three indices were identified and used as indicators of learning performance: the number of days attended (NDA), the number of completed modules (NCM), and online test scores (OTS). In particular, the number of days attended (NDA) is considered by most Japanese university students as the key factor that affects their final grade. Therefore, most students are very particular about their total class attendance. In the surveyed courses, both the number of completed modules (NCM) and the online test scores (OTS) were considered as important as the NDA and survey participants had to pay attention to all indices: NDA, NCM and OTS.

### Final Test for the Courses

For bachelor students, the final test was conducted by a proctor during the scheduled finals week at the university. All students gathered in a lecture room, and answered four questions -- two questions included some multiple-choice tasks and the other two questions were essay-tests.

For masters students, the final test was a written report based on their research work on two self-selected topics chosen out of a given set of five themes.

## RESULTS (1): IMPACT OF LEARNER CHARACTERISTICS, ONLINE LEARNING EXPERIENCE, AND INFORMATION LITERACY

Common indices for learner characteristics and learning experience were extracted using factor analysis. While these factors were often defined independently for each year of analysis, they were not necessarily stable. Therefore, a factor analysis of the surveyed data sets, which included additional but same-format data from the extended surveys, was conducted. In total, there were 558 learner characteristic samples and 456 learning experience samples.

### Factors of Learner Characteristics

Learner characteristics were measured using the three constructs in this study, and altogether they consisted of the following 10 factors.

- Motivation: Intrinsic motivation and Extrinsic motivation
- Personality (IPIP: International Personality Item Pool): Extraversion, Agreeableness, Conscientiousness, Neuroticism, Openness to Experience

*Table 1. Factor loading matrix for learner characteristics and correlation matrix among factors.*

| | Legislative/ Judicial Style | Motivation | Positive Emotionality | Conscien-tiousness Executive Style |
|---|---|---|---|---|
| | LJ | MOTIV | EA | CONSC |
| Intrinsic motivation | 0.13 | 0.67 | 0.10 | -.09 |
| Extrinsic motivation | -.09 | 0.73 | -.03 | 0.08 |
| Extraversion | 0.05 | 0.03 | 0.60 | -.11 |
| Agreeableness | -.02 | 0.00 | 0.64 | 0.18 |
| Conscientiousness | -.03 | -.04 | 0.18 | 0.49 |
| Legislative Style | 0.70 | 0.02 | -.01 | 0.03 |
| Executive Style | 0.17 | 0.08 | -.18 | 0.46 |
| Judicial Style | 0.70 | -.03 | 0.06 | 0.02 |
| F1: LJ | 1.0 | | | |
| F2: MOTIV | -.37 | 1.0 | | |
| F3: EA | -.18 | -.25 | 1.0 | |
| F4: CONSC | .35 | -.15 | 0.14 | 1.0 |
| Contribution ratio by each factor ignoring other factors | 0.20 | 0.19 | 0.14 | 0.11 |
| Total | | 0.44 | | |

LJ: Legislative Style and Judicial Style
EA: Extraversion and Agreeableness
MOTIV: Extrinsic and Intrinsic motivation
CONSC: Conscientiousness and Executive Style

- Thinking Style: Legislative style, Executive Style, Judicial Style

Within the initial set of data, the number of factors was too large, so a secondary factor analysis was conducted to extract common factors and to reduce the number of factors from the 558 data responses. As a result, four secondary factors were extracted and are summarized in Table 1. The first factor (LJ) consists of two thinking styles (legislative and judicia)l, the second factor (MOTIV) consists of Intrinsic and Extrinsic motivation, the third factor (EA) consists of Extraversion and Agreeableness, and the fourth factor (CONSC) consists of Conscientiousness and Executive thinking style.

These factor patterns were extracted using promax rotation, then factor axes were correlated with each other. The correlation matrix of factor axes is also summarized in Table 1. The rest of the factors, including Neuroticism and Openness to Experience were excluded from the common factors. Originally, the five factors of personality characteristics were independent of each other, and Extraversion and Agreeableness were often expressed collectively as Positive Emotionality (Five-Factor Model, 1991). According to the independent characteristics of the five factors, the correlation coefficient between EA and CONSC is not great. Therefore, the extracted factors seem to be reasonable. In any event, the number of factors for learner characteristics was reduced to 6 factors (4 secondary factors and 2 other factors).

Additionally, second factor scores, which are defined as the mean of the combined scores, were compared between bachelor and masters students

(N=201), and there were no significant differences. This result confirms that among students, similar learner characteristics did exist.

## Factors of Learning Experiences

Based on our previous analysis of learning experience survey items, three factors can be extracted from 10 question items (Nakayama et al., 2006). To determine the structure of question items for learning experiences, factor analysis was conducted using data from 456 responses.

As a result, the following factor loading matrix is summarized in Table 2, and the same three factors that were extracted are as follows: overall evaluation of e-learning experience (to be referred to as "e-learning evaluation" from here on), learning habits, and learning strategies. The factor patterns were also extracted using promax rotation, then the second factor (learning habits) axis was negatively correlated with axes for both factors of e-learning evaluation and learning strategies. The correlation coefficient between e-learning evaluation and learning strategies was relatively small.

Factor scores are summarized in Figure 1. In the comparison of factor scores between bachelor and masters students across three years (N=201), there was a significant difference in the third factor, learning strategies ($F_{(1,195)}=48.8$, $p<0.01$). There was no significant difference between bachelors and masters in any of the three factors when compared to each other across the three years of the survey ($F_{(2,195)}=1.0$, $p=0.35$) and also for the interaction between student's group and years ($F_{(2,195)}=0.2$, $p=0.79$). This result has remained consistent since the first survey study was conducted (Nakayama et al., 2006).

## Causal Analysis

To create the causal paths from learner characteristics to learning performance, correlation coefficients were calculated from the learners' metrics. Correlation analysis was conducted using metrics which were based on causal paths: learner

*Table 2. Factor loading matrix for learning experience and correlation matrix among factors*

| | L1 | L2 | L3 |
|---|---|---|---|
| Q1. E-learning is easy to follow and understand | 0.70 | -.03 | 0.10 |
| Q2. I learn better in online course | 0.48 | 0.20 | -.08 |
| Q3. Online materials are useful to me | 0.61 | 0.10 | -.10 |
| Q4. It is easy to schedule online learning time | 0.57 | -.16 | 0.18 |
| Q5. Online course content is interesting | 0.68 | 0.11 | -.05 |
| Q6. Overall, online course is a favorable learning experience | 0.82 | -.07 | -.02 |
| Q7. I'm a conscientious student | -.04 | 0.51 | 0.07 |
| Q8. It is my habit to do learning preparation and review | 0.11 | 0.49 | 0.08 |
| Q9. I have my own method and way of learning | -.01 | 0.18 | 0.62 |
| Q10. I have my own strategies on how to pass a course | 0.01 | -.01 | 0.65 |
| Correlation among factor axes L1 | 1.0 | | |
| L2 | -.35 | 1.0 | |
| L3 | -.07 | -.34 | 1.0 |
| Contribution ratio by each factor ignoring other factors | 0.28 | 0.14 | 0.12 |
| Total contribution | | 0.43 | |

L1: e-Learning evaluation; L2: Learning habit; L3: Learning strategies

*Figure 1. Comparison in factor scores of learning experience between bachelors and masters*

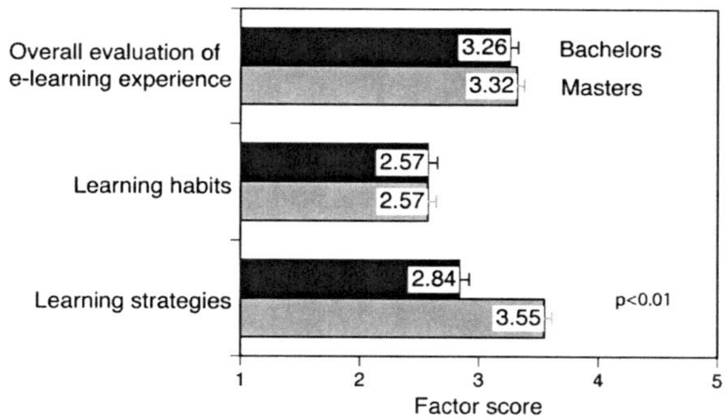


characteristics, learning experience and learning performance. Using the values of correlation coefficients between the metrics and prior proposed path models (Nakayama et al., 2006, Nakayama et al., 2007b), a causal analysis was conducted.

The variables selected were Thinking Style (Legislative & Judicial), Motivation (Intrinsic & Extrinsic Motivations), and Conscientiousness (Conscientiousness & Executive thinking style). The causal analysis was conducted using multiple-sample path analysis using structural equation modeling technique (Toyoda, 2007; Kline, 2005). The multiple-samples are bachelors vs. masters, and each year of the three years of the survey.

## Comparison Between Bachelors and Masters

A causal path, which is based on groups of bachelor and masters students for all three years, is illustrated in Figure 2. In the figure, boxes show the variables, single arrowhead lines show the paths and the two arrowhead arcs show the correlation relationships. Both path and correlation coefficients are indicated for each arrow line.

In referring to the degree of fitness for the model structure as a GFI (Goodness-of-Fit index; GFI=0.91), the causal diagrams for both bachelors and masters are significant. To make the differences between bachelors and masters obvious, these path coefficients were compared using

*Figure 2. Causal path diagram (bachelors and masters)*

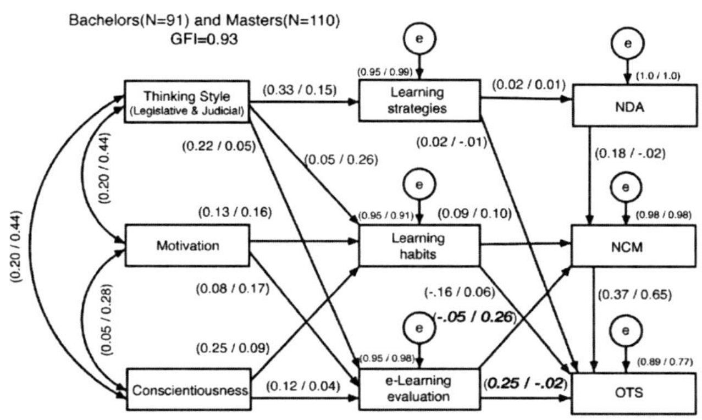


NDA: Number of day attended, NCM: Number of complete modules, OTS: Online test scores
Coefficients in bold italics are significantly different.

statistical tests to check their consistency (Toyoda, 2007).

In the results, two path coefficients, which are illustrated in bold italic characters, are significantly different: the path from "e-Learning evaluation" to "NCM (Number of complete modules)", and the path from "e-Learning evaluation" to "OTS (Online test scores)". To determine the validity of the results, the GFI was compared with a controlled model which was constrained to be equal to the path coefficients. The GFI for a model without constraints is larger than for one with constraints, so the differences in these path coefficients was determined (Toyoda, 2007).

Bachelors prefer e-learning to obtain better online test scores, but masters prefer to complete as many modules as possible in order to learn more, and their e-learning evaluation is not related to their online test scores. There are no significant differences between the two groups except for these two points.

The results of this analysis and of previous analyses continue to suggest that results of e-learning evaluation differ between bachelors and masters.

## Comparison across Three Years

To determine the differences in path coefficients for both bachelors and masters across three years, a statistical analysis using the SEM technique was conducted, applying the same procedures that were used in the statistical tests for Figure 2. The resulting path diagram is summarized in Figure 3. The format is the same as in Figure 2, and the significant differences in coefficients are illustrated with bold-italic characters.

According to changes in coefficients for each path, the coefficients for indices of learning performance increased slightly from year to year, and other coefficients for e-learning evaluation and learning strategies also fluctuated somewhat from year to year. In comparing the results between bachelors (Figure 4) and masters (Figure 5) from year to year, the path coefficient between e-learning evaluation and online test scores (OTS) shows a gradual decrease across the years for both groups. When the online learning environment was new, students found a benefit in obtaining higher online test scores. After online learning had become a familiar environment, the degree of relationship between e-learning evaluation and the online test scores (OTS) decreased. The relationship between e-learning evaluation and the number of completed modules (NCM) varied between bachelors and masters. The correlation decreased for masters (0.91/0.50/-0.12), but it increased for bachelors (-0.35/0.12/0.17). This indicates that bachelor students may have better

*Figure 3. Causal path diagram (across three years)*

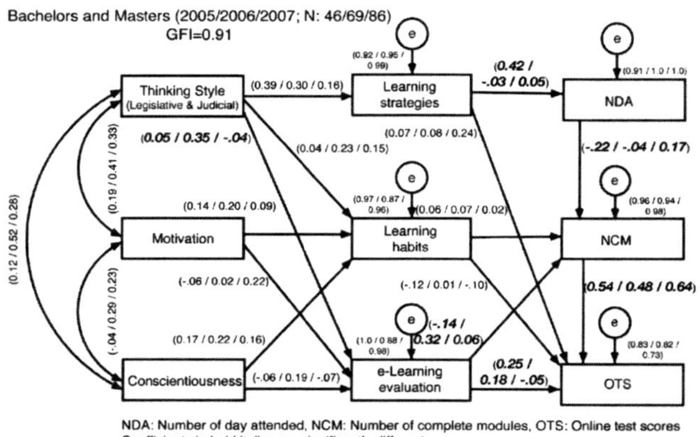


NDA: Number of day attended, NCM: Number of complete modules, OTS: Online test scores
Coefficients in bold italics are significantly different.

*Figure 4. Causal path diagram for bachelor students (across three years)*

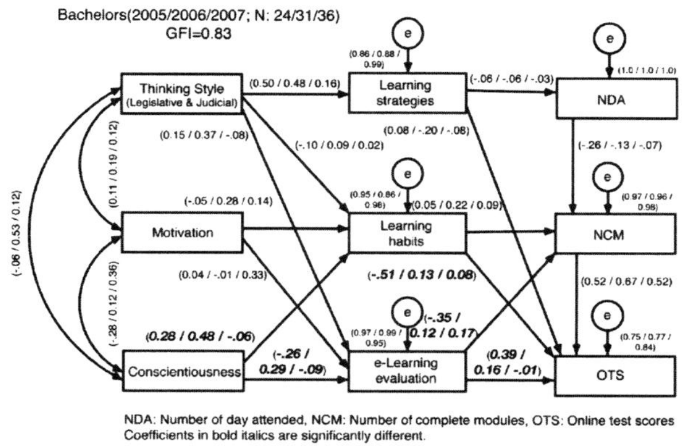


*Figure 5. Causal path diagram for masters students (across three years)*

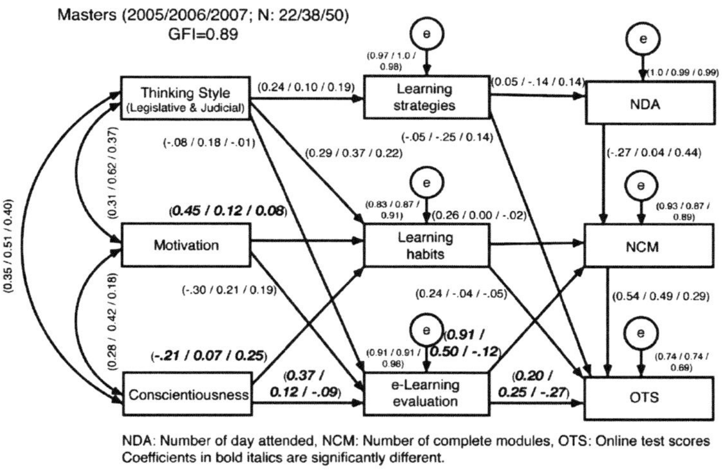


understood the benefits of content learning in online courses.

Coefficients between conscientiousness and learning habits also changed across groups and years. For masters, it gradually increased with each year, but for bachelors it gradually decreased. Although masters students demonstrated learning habits that closely related to the personality trait of conscientiousness, bachelors eventually become more lenient with their learning habits.

Those points should be discussed within the context of other learning environment issues, and they will be subject of our further study.

## Relationship with Information Literacy

Students' information literacy (Fujii 2007) was measured during one particular year, and its preliminary relationship with other factors has been reported previously (Nakayama et al., 2008). For this paper, common factors were extracted in a new manner, and the relationship between common factors for 86 students responses was analyzed (bachelors=36, masters=50) using the SEM technique. The causal path is summarized in Figure 6. In comparing the causal paths between bachelor and masters students, the impact

*Figure 6. Causal path diagram for information literacy between bachelors and masters*

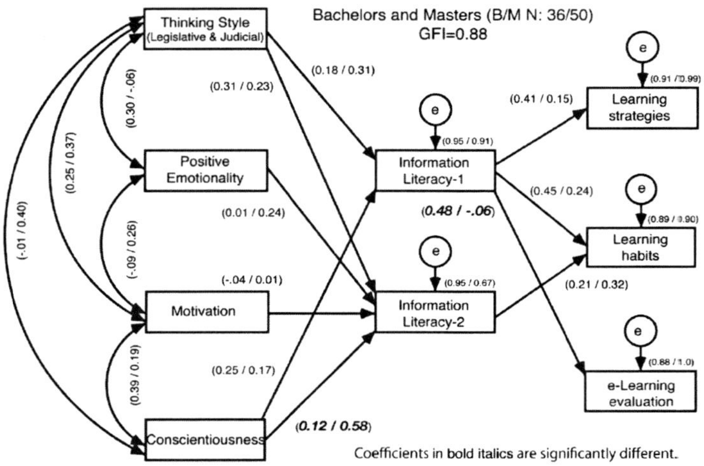


of conscientiousness and information literacy on operational confidence and knowledge understanding was significantly different. For the path from conscientiousness to attitude of information literacy, the coefficient for masters is higher than bachelors (B=0.12; M=0.58). For the path from information literacy for operational confidence and knowledge understanding to e-learning evaluation, the coefficient for bachelors is higher than masters (B=0.48; M=-0.06).

This suggests once again that major areas of information literacy are different between bachelors and masters, and that the impact of information literacy on operational confidence and on knowledge and understanding is different for bachelor and master students.

## RESULTS (2): ASSESSMENT OF LEARNING PERFORMANCE ON ONLINE COURSES

An additional third course, which was offered in the Spring and Autumn terms of 2006-2007, was also selected for this survey. The third course title was "Information Society and Careers", a 2-unit bachelor-level class for university freshmen, which was offered as a fully online course. Students could choose to attend either the blended or the fully online course, in accordance to their preference.

All students took part in the final test which included two essay-tests at the end of the course, and received the appropriate credit units. Learner characteristics were also measured using the five constructs mentioned earlier.

For this analysis, student enrollment in these courses is as follows: blended learning course at the bachelor level had 47 participants, fully online course at the bachelor level had 39 participants, and blended learning course at the masters level had 78 participants.

### Essay-Test Assessment

Although there was a little variation in how essay testing was given to bachelors and masters students, this same type of assessment was conducted in both levels.

The essay-tests were reviewed by two outside experts and were found to be sufficient for course completion. Before the assessment, these two experts independently evaluated the essays using a 3-point scale (0-2) that was applied to each of the

*Table 3. Mean of expert's assessment and their correlation coefficients.*

| Mean(SD) | Expert 1 | Expert 2 | r |
|---|---|---|---|
| Essay test 1 (N=398) | 7.7(1.4) | 6.6(1.6) | 0.56 |
| Essay test 2 (N=398) | 7.5(1.5) | 6.1(1.8) | 0.63 |
| Total | 15.3(2.4) | 13.1(2.7) | 0.67 |

five aspects of the essay test, namely: certainty, fitness for learning content, argument, various aspects and figuring. For this study, all usable data were used for this analysis.

Assessment scores from the two experts who evaluated the two essay questions are summarized in Table 1. Here, scores for the two essays (Essay 1 and Essay 2) at the master's level were used based on the two essay reports that the students wrote. The ratings that the experts gave for these two sets of essay tasks were very close and almost similar. Correlation coefficients are also summarized in Table 3. Overall, assessment scores from each of the two essays strongly correlated with each other (r=0.67), therefore they could be merged to form a single score.

For the automated Japanese essay assessment, an automated scoring system (Ishioka and Kameda, 2003) was used. It is possible to use this system via web site. As a result, another set of scores was generated using the assessment software and these scores measured three factors: "rhetoric", "logical structure" and "content fitness".

The relationship between experts' assessment score and the automated assessment score were examined. Correlation coefficients (r) are summarized in Table 4. Table 4 shows that experts' assessment significantly correlates with the factor of "logical structure" on the essay for all courses (r=0.30). There are no significant relationship between experts' assessment and "rhetoric" or "content fitness" of the automated essay-scores.

This suggests that expert evaluation of the essay is focused mainly on "logical structure" rather than other factors.

## Performance in Essay-Testing Between Blended and Fully Online Courses

The university credit courses used in this study can serve as examples of courses where essay-tests are conducted in both blended and fully online settings. Therefore, it would be very interesting to find out whether the essay-test performances of students in these two online learning settings are equivalent or not.

Experts' assessments for the three groups, namely bachelor-blended, bachelor-fully online, and masters-level, are compared in Figure 7. As the figure illustrates, assessment scores are almost of the same level across all three groups. Experts evaluated these essay-tests using standard criteria, so that it is possible to compare the scores. The task style was different between bachelors and masters, however, these results did not mean that bachelor students and master students had the same level of performance when it comes to essay-writing.

When comparing the experts' assessment scores between blended learning and fully online courses at the bachelors level, no significant differences were found ($t_{(73)}$=0.47, p=.64). This indicates that in fully online courses, as well as in blended courses, learning performance can be measured using essay tests without the need to

*Table 4. Correlation between experts' assessment scores and automated assessment scores.*

| N=209 | Expert 1 | Expert 2 | Total |
|---|---|---|---|
| Rhetoric | (-.02) | (-.12) | (-.07) |
| Logical structure | 0.16 | 0.39 | 0.30 |
| Content fitness | (-.05) | (-.07) | -0.01 |
| Total | 0.16 | 0.46 | 0.35 |

*Figure 7. Expert's assessment scores*

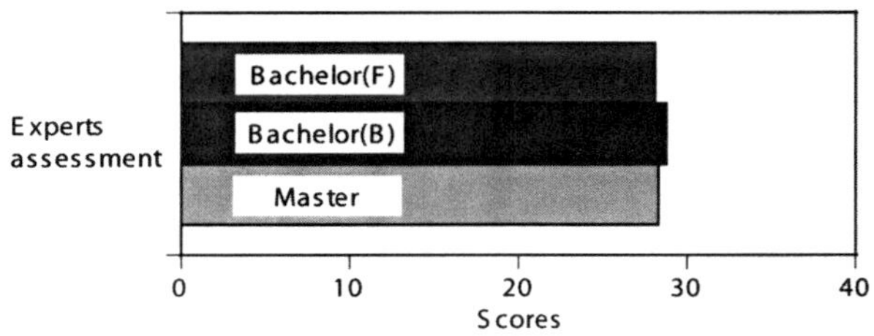


be in a face-to-face session to conduct this type of assessment.

## Automated Essay Assessment

Assessment scores for essay-testing using the automated assessment system are illustrated in Figure 8. In this figure, performance scores in the three groups are compared. It was not possible to analyze the difference between all bachelors and masters scores because testing styles were totally different, but scores for the master group are higher than scores for bachelor groups on two factors -- "logical structure" and "content fitness". This system automatically adjusts some scores in relation to other factors in the given situation using a minus-points system (Ishioka and Kameda, 2003), with the result that the total score does not simply reflect the sum of three factor scores. Among all the total scores, the score for masters is the highest. This suggests that the points deducted for masters is smaller than the ones for bachelors, so that the result based on total scores seems reasonable.

## Multiple Choice Test and Essay-Test

As explained in the introduction, most online testing consists of multiple-choice tasks. For the bachelor students' final paper-and-pencil test, both multiple-choice tasks and essay tests were included. According to the comparison of scores for multiple-choice tasks between the two groups, the scores in the blended courses are significantly higher than scores in fully online courses ($t(73)=5.1, p<0.01$). This could mean that bachelor students in blended courses have a better understanding and knowledge of the learning content in weekly face-to-face sessions. On the other hand, students in fully online course who may possess some previous knowledge of information technology which was the main content of the course (Nakayama et al., 2008) seem to have the ability to summarize this previous knowledge

*Figure 8. Assessment scores for the essay-test using the automated assessment system*

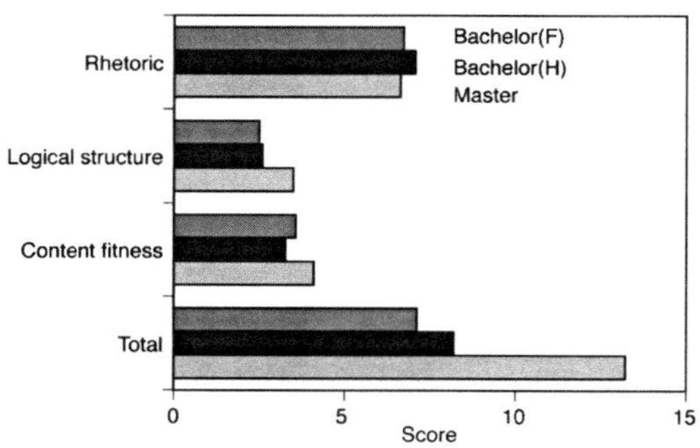

*Table 5. Correlation coefficients between multiple-choice test scores and essay test scores.*

| | B(Blended) | B(Fully) |
|---|---|---|
| | N=45 | N=30 |
| Reviewers | (-.06) | (-.09) |
| Rhetoric | 0.37 | (0.28) |
| Logical structure | (-.17) | (-.12) |
| Content fitness | (-.15) | 0.54 |
| Total | (-.01) | -0.36 |

for an essay test. Thus, it is possible that there is no significant difference in the scores of between essay-tests in blended courses and essay-tests in fully online courses.

To determine the effect of performance in multiple-choice tasks on scores for essay-tests, correlation coefficients in scores between multiple-choice tasks and essay-test were extracted and summarized in Table 5.

The correlation coefficients between scores for the multiple-choice tests and experts or automated assessments for blended and fully online courses are summarized in Table 5. Almost all coefficients are not significant, and this result confirms that essay-tests measure different aspects of learner performance than multiple-choice tasks.

## Relationship with Learner's Metrics

The conventional metrics which relate to learner characteristics may affect the essay-test scores as measures of learning performance, thus, a correlation analysis was conducted. The correlation coefficients are summarized in Table 6.

As results indicate, additional interesting correlations were observed: essay-test scores negatively correlated with "e-learning evaluation" scores (r=-.41); and, the information literacy factor scores of "operational confidence and knowledge" (r=-.47) in blended learning and essay-test scores correlated with "the number of days attended" (r=0.40) in blended learning for masters students.

As discussed in earlier sections, the possible reason may depend on the learning content and learning environment. Therefore, these findings could be related with the content of the courses. Other learner characteristics did not affect students' essay-test scores. Further detailed analysis

*Table 6. Correlation coefficients between expert's assessment and survey metrics.*

| | Masters | Bachelors | |
|---|---|---|---|
| | | blended | fully online |
| | N=76 | N=45 | N=30 |
| Information literacy | | | |
| Operational confidence and knowledge | (0.08) | -.47 | (0.03) |
| Attitude | (-.13) | 0.00 | (0.01) |
| Learning experience | | | |
| E-learning evaluation | (-.04) | -.41 | (-.21) |
| Learning habit | (-.01) | (-.16) | (0.26) |
| Learning strategy | (-.11) | (-.01) | (0.12) |
| Behavioral data | | | |
| Number of days attended | 0.40 | (0.02) | - |
| Number of completed modules | (0.22) | (0.05) | (0.00) |
| Online test scores | (0.22) | (-.03) | (0.25) |

of these factors will be investigated in our next study.

## FUTURE RESEARCH DIRECTIONS

According to the above analyses, four common factors for learner characteristics and three common factors for e-learning experience were extracted using the accumulated data. These results coincided with almost all of our previous results which were based on each annual survey, thus establishing the validity of this series of data analyses. In particular, results indicate that there is no significant difference in learner characteristics and that there is no difference in e-learning experiences between bachelors and masters students except for learning strategies. This implies that designing a blended course for bachelors and masters students will not vary much and that regardless of the level (graduate or undergraduate), the e-learning experience will end up being similar for both groups. What could vary will be the individual strategies that students will apply towards learning the course content and how to pass the course.

Causal analyses were also conducted to analyze the relationship between learner characteristics and learning performance. The result of the overall analyses suggests that there is a difference between bachelors and masters students. This difference can be found in the few numbers of affecting paths between observed variables, indicating a significant difference between the two groups. Figure 2 shows only two differences: the path coefficient between e-learning evaluation and online test scores for bachelor students is larger than the one for masters, and, the path coefficient between e-learning evaluation and the number of completed modules for masters is larger than the one for bachelors. These results indicate that bachelor students seek efficiency, while master students seek to maximize the learning opportunity. Bachelor students availed of the incentives that were provided in this course (e.g., online test scores can be used to make up for class attendance in face-to-face class sessions) because they have not yet acquired the sufficient e-learning skills at this level. On the other hand, the course incentives were not as attractive to master students who were more focused on learning the class content and online materials, since they have already acquired the necessary learning skills and attitudes for university study. The implication of these results on the instructional design of blended courses is to provide more learning activities and materials in blended courses for graduate students, while for undergraduate students, more structure and scaffolding towards the development of learning skills, along with course content, should be provided.

The results of information literacy analysis also suggest that there is a difference between bachelor and masters students (see Figure 6). Bachelor students, who have operational confidence and knowledge of information literacy, prefer to learn with the online learning materials. For master students, it is their conscientiousness that affects their attitude towards information literacy.

These results are based on surveys of Japanese students, so their distinctiveness and limitations should be carefully taken into consideration. Nevertheless, the results suggest that the online course developer or instructional designer will have to address the learner's background which includes learning experience, learning skills and attitudes towards university learning. For example, incentives to promote online learning should be chosen carefully, because some incentives (such as compensation for their learning evaluation) may lead to non-relevant learning behaviors. Masters students, who are more matured learners, are more capable of ignoring the influences of such incentives. The instructional designer for blended courses needs to be aware of the fact that bachelor students' learning behaviors can be easily stimulated by integrating simple course design features, such as incentives for learning operational skills. For masters students, the instructional designer has to consider more closely the learning styles they have already acquired.

Although these factors were observed since the early stages of introducing online learning and throughout the three years, it was also noted that some of their effects declined during this time period. This decline is indicated by results shown in Figure 3-5. This implies that the influence of learner's maturity on learning behavior can change as online learning gains wider acceptance and popularity in the university learning environment.

The management of online learning environments in university settings will be the subject for our future study.

In analyzing the role of essay-test in online courses, it became evident that the students' ability in essay writing may be involved with various learner competencies, including learners' experience. Therefore, it can be inferred that the learning environment (e.g., online) which is part of the learning experience, could influence learner's performance in essay writing. According to survey results, there is no significant difference between fully online and blended courses and the score of multiple-choice tests did not correlate with the score of essay-tests.

These results confirm that performance in essay-testing is different from performance in multiple-choice testing and this depends on learner's readiness. In this survey, only three courses were selected as cohort. Both bachelors and masters students, having been enrolled in various courses, usually write many reports and essays during those courses. Even freshman students are trained to write essays structurally and logically. This means that their readiness for essay writing has been affected by many aspects of their learning. Therefore, the relationship between their writing literacy and essay-test performance should be examined using various survey methods.

The use of an automated assessment system for essay-testing was also investigated and it was found that the accuracy of the automated system is comparable to expert assessment. This supports the use of automated assessment system for essay-testing in an online learning environment. For multiple-choice testing, a computer-adaptive testing system was developed using IRT (Item Response Theory), and this system was applied to the online learning environment. When using this system, the item pool of questions should be prepared in advance.

It is important that various results from experimental trials and significant evidences regarding the use of automated assessment systems in an online learning environment be consolidated and summarized. This topic could be the subject of further studies.

## CONCLUSION

In this chapter, quantitative differences in the causal relationship between learner characteristics and learning behavior across student levels (bachelors vs. masters) and the survey years were shown, and two types of analysis were conducted. To create common indices for learner characteristics and learning experience, a factor analysis of all data was conducted. As a result, revised factors were extracted, namely, four factors for characteristics: thinking style (legislative and judicial), positive emotionality, motivation, and conscientiousness, and three factors for learning experience: overall evaluation of e-learning experience, learning habits, and learning strategies. To determine the relationship between these factors, a causal analysis was conducted using the Structural Equation Modeling technique, and the parameters of each group were compared using statistical tests.

When comparing the results between bachelor and master students, the impact of overall evaluation of e-learning experience was significantly different. Differences in the impact of overall evaluation of e-learning experience and "number of days attended" were also detected across the three years of the surveys. For bachelor students, the impact of conscientiousness, overall evaluation of e-learning experience and learning habits were significantly different across the three years, and for master students the impact of motivation, conscientiousness, and overall evaluation of e-learning experience were significantly different. The relationship between students' information literacy and common factors was also analyzed and the differences between bachelors and masters were confirmed once again.

These results provide evidence that there are some key points regarding learner characteristics that need to be considered, and which could help in the design of effective blended learning environments.

To measure students' learning performance in online learning activities, essay-tests were introduced and examined as assessment tools for blended and fully online courses in the bachelor level and for blended courses in the master's level.

Also, to investigate the effects of using an automated assessment system for essay-tests, a prototype system was introduced and results were discussed. As the results indicate, a common assessment factor, "logical structure", was used by both experts and automated system. There is little difference in scores resulting from the use of essay test as an assessment tool in blended and fully online courses at the bachelor level. However, there is a significant difference in scores for multiple-choice tasks. Though most of these results may depend on learning content and environment, it is possible to assess learning through the use of essay-tests in either blended or fully online courses.

## ACKNOWLEDGMENT

This research was partially supported by the Japan Society for the Promotion of Science (JSPS), Grant-in-Aid for Scientific Research (B-19300274: 2007-2009).

## REFERENCES

Abelson, H. (2008). The Creation of Open CourseWare at MIT. *Journal of Science Education and Technology*, *17*(2), 164–174. doi:10.1007/s10956-007-9060-8

Biggs, J. (1999). *Teaching for Quality Learning at University*. Buckingham, UK: SRHE and Open University Press.

Birch, P. D. (2002). E-learner competencies,*Learning Circuits – ASTD Online Magazine*. Retrieved 11 January, 2006 from http://www.learningcircuits.org/2002/jul2002/birch.html

Brown, S., & Knight, P. (1994). *Assessing Learners in Higher Education*. Kogan Page.

Burstein, J., Chodorow, M., & Leacock, C. (2004). Automated Essay Evaluation: The Citation Online Writing Service. *AI Magazine, 25*, (3), 27-36, American Association for Artificial Intelligence *CASEC: Computerized Assessment System for English Communication*. Retrieved 1st July 2009, from http://www.nextet.net/c/jiem/index.html

Cronbach, L. J. & Snow, R., E. (1977). *Aptitude and instructional methods: A handbook for research on interactions*. Oxford, England: Irvington

Diaz, D. P., & Cartnal, R. B. (1999). Students' learning styles in two classes: Online distance learning and equivalent on-campus. *College Teaching*, *47*(4), 130–135. doi:10.1080/87567559909595802

Five-Factor Model. (1991), Retrieved 15 December, 2005 from http://www.personalityresearch.org/bigfive.html

Fujii, Y. (2007). Development of a Scale to Evaluate the Information Literacy Level of Young People -Comparison of Junior High School Students in Japan and Northern Europe. *Japan Journal of Educational Technology*, *30*(4), 387–395.

Goldberg, L. R. (1999). A Broad-Bandwidth, Public Domain, Personality Inventory Measuring the Lower-Level Facets of Several Five-Factor Models. In Mervielde, I., Deary, I., De Fruyt, F., & Ostendorf, F. (Eds.), *Personality Psychology in Europe, 7* (pp. 7–28). The Netherlands: Tilburg University Press.

International Personality Item Pool. (2001). *A Scientific Collaboratory for the Development of Advanced Measures of Personality Traits and Other Individual Differences*. Retrieved 27 October, 2004 from http://ipip.ori.org/.

Ishioka, T., & Kameda, M. (2003). JESS: An Automated Japanese Essay Scoring System. *Bulletin of the Computational Statistics of Japan, 16*(1), 3–19.

*Japan Open Courseware Consortium*, Retrieved 1st July 2009, from http://www.jocw.jp

Japanese University Council, Ministry of Education, Culture, Sports, Science and Technology (MEXT). "Requirements of Higher Education System in Global Age" (in Japanese). Retrieved 1st July 2009, from http://www.mext.go.jp/b_menu/shingi/12/daigaku/toushin/001101.htm

Kaufman, J. C. (Personal communication, September 26, 2004).

Kaufman, J. C. & Agars, M. D., *Kaufman-Agars Motivation Scale*.Unpublished instrument (2005).

Kaufman J. C. & Agars M. D. (2005).*Kaufman-Agars Motivation Scale*. Unpublished instrument.

Kline, R. B. (2005). *Principles and Practice of Structural Equational Modeling*. New York: The Guilford Press.

Linn, R. L. (Ed.). Educational Measurement, 3rd Ed., (1989). (Japanese translation by Ikeda, H., Fujita, K., Yanai, H., Shigemasu, K., The Center for the Study of Learning, Yokohama, Japan 1992)

Matsumura, N., & Hiruma, F. Shikou Sutairu (2000). *Thinking Styles* (translation of Sternberg (1997) "Thinking Style" and author's review). Shinyousha, Tokyo, Japan.

Murakami, Y., & Murakami, C. Big Five Handbook (in Japanese), Gakugeitosyo, Tokyo (2001). Itoh T.,(1995). Zisonshin No Izi To Kouyou (Maintainance and Development of Self-respect), in Miyamoto & Nasu (Ed.), *Theory and Development of Achievement Motivation*, Kanekoshobo, Tokyo.

Nakayama, M., Yamamoto, H., & Santiago, R. (2006). Investigating the Impact of Learner Characteristics on Blended Learning among Japanese Students. In [Academic Conferences.]. *Proceedings of ICEL, 2006*, 361–370.

Nakayama, M., Yamamoto, H., & Santiago, R. (2007a). Relationship between Learner Characteristics and Learning Performance in Hybrid Courses among Japanese Students.In [Academic Conferences.]. *Proceedings of ICEL, 2007*, 341–349.

Nakayama, M., Yamamoto, H. & Santiago, R. (2007b). The Impact of Learner Characteristics on Learning Performance in Hybrid Courses among Japanese Students. *The Electronic Journal of e-Learning, 5*, (3), 195-206.

Nakayama, M., Yamamoto, H., & Santiago, R. (2008). The Impact of Information Literacy and Learner Characteristics on Learning Behavior of Japanese Students in Online Courses. *International Journal of Case Method Research & Application, XX*(4), 403–415.

Sternberg, R. J. (1997). *Thinking Styles*. Cambridge, UK: Cambridge University Press. doi:10.1017/CBO9780511584152

SUGSI. Shinshu University, Graduate School on the Internet, Retrieved 1st July 2009, from http://cai1.cs.shinshu-u.ac.jp/xoops/

Terrell, S., & Dringus, L. (1999). An investigation of the effects of learning style on student success in an online learning environment. *Journal of Educational Technology Systems*, *28*(3), 231–238.

Ueno, M., Songmuang, P., Okamoto, T., Nagaoka, K. (2008). Item Response Theory with Assessors' parameters of Peer Assessment. *IEICE TRANSACTIONS on Information and Systems*, J91-D, (2), 377-388.

Wada, S. (1996). Construction of the Big Five Scales of Personality Trait Terms and Concurrent Validity with NPI. *Japanese Journal of Phycology*, *67*(1), 61–67.

Wojciechowski, A., & Palmer, L. B. (Summer 2005) Individual student characteristics: Can any be predictors of success in online classes? *Online Journal of Distance Learning Administration, 8,* (2). Retrieved 27 January, 2006 from http://www.westga.edu/~distance/ojdla/summer82/wojciechowski82.htm

## ADDITIONAL READING

Baylen, D. M., Santiago, R., & Nakayama, M. (2009). How Do We Foster the Quality of Hybrid Courses in Teacher Education? *Proceedings of Society for Information Technology & Teacher Education Conference*, *2009*, 1732–1737.

Nakayama, M., & Santiago, R. (2004). Two categories of E-Learning in Japan. *Educational Technology Research and Development*, *52*(3), 100–111. doi:10.1007/BF02504680

Minoru Nakayama, Hiroh Yamamoto, Rowena Santiago (2007). The Impact of Learner Characteristics on Learning Performance in Hybrid Courses among Japanese Students. *The Electronic Journal of e-Learning, 5.* (3), 195-206.

Nakayama, M., Yamamoto, H., & Santiago, R. (2008). Impact of Information Literacy and Learner Characteristics on Learning Behavior of Japanese Students in Online Courses. *International Journal of Case Method Research & Application. WACRA*, *XX*(4), 403–415.

Santiago, R., & Nakayama, M. (2006). Understanding E-Learners' Characteristics and Performance in Online Courses.In R.Mizoguchi et al. (Eds), International Conference on Computer Education (ICCE). *Learning by Effective Utilization of Technologies: Facilitating Intercultural Understanding (pp.521-524)*, Amsterdam: IOS Press.

# Chapter 10
# E-Learning Methodologies in Higher Education: The Case of Accounting

**Alicia Mateos-Ronco**
*Universidad Politécnica de Valencia, Spain*

**Mª del Mar Marín-Sánchez**
*Universidad Politécnica de Valencia, Spain*

## ABSTRACT

*The Spanish educational system will require certain changes in order to achieve the Bologna objectives for the European Higher Education Area, including with new activities and roles for both students and teachers, who must assume new skills that will affect concepts and attitudes related to the teaching and learning processes. This chapter describes the authors' experience in designing E-learning methodologies for the teaching of accountancy in the Business Administration Degree Course at the Polytechnic University of Valencia. The chapter's methodology designed for teaching accounting, is based on PBL (Problem Based Learning), compiled with Internet based technologies. The authors analyze its use and evolution in two accounting subjects in the first and the fourth year of the degree. The conclusions obtained from the statistical treatment of the results show that there is a direct correlation between the use of an active E-learning model and obtaining satisfactory exam results in the subject.*

## INTRODUCTION AND OBJECTIVES

The Declarations of the Sorbonne (1998) and Bologna (1999) established a starting point for the harmonisation program of the different *European higher education systems.* The process called for the adoption of a single European degree system to improve the employment prospects of graduates and to make the European higher education system more *competitive* internationally. Harmonisation of the European Higher Education Area (EHEA) is expected to be complete in 2010. In Spain, the Organic Law of Universities passed in 2001 foresaw the complete integration of Spanish higher education into the EHEA and since then radical changes have taken place in the structures of Spanish undergraduate and postgraduate degree courses.

DOI: 10.4018/978-1-61692-791-2.ch010

In this context, achieving the Bologna objectives and establishing the high standards of the European Higher Education Area requires the *reform* of the educational system, the development of a professional profile and roles and activities different from the traditional ones for both teachers and students (Monereo, Pozo, 2003). The latter will have to take on *new competencies* that will influence their concepts and attitudes on teaching and learning within the framework of learning projects (Zabalza, 2003). Students will also have to take a leading role in the educational process by adopting significant and cooperative autonomous learning methods.

The process will doubtless require a *profound change* in the mindset of the dominant culture of both students and teachers, with a higher degree of cooperation between both, aimed at improving learning results. Teachers will have to select the appropriate *methodologies* to achieve the required results, using as a reference the professional academic profile and the characteristics of training in skills (Argüelles, 1997; Cañibano, 2008), as well as the structural and organisational settings in which they will be carried out (class size, space, educational organization, etc.).

This paper describes the *teaching experience* acquired by the authors in designing *E-learning methodologies* for application to one of the social sciences (Ballestero, 1980), i.e. *Accountancy*, in the Business Administration degree course at the Polytechnic University of Valencia.

The teaching methodology is based on *Problem Based Learning* (PBL) and intensive use of *Information and Communication Technology* (ICT) provided by the computer-based Educational Platform of the University. The experience involved *two accounting subjects* considered to be among the most important in the first and second cycles, respectively, of the degree course, involving a large number of students. In both cases, students were free to design their own individual learning systems.

The fundamental *objective* of this work is therefore to *evaluate the results* obtained from the teaching-learning process in the subject of accountancy in the Business Administration degree course by the application of *ICT-based teaching methodologies*. The analysis of the results obtained shows that there is a direct correlation between the students who opt for an active learning model from the teaching methodology described here and those who achieve satisfactory results in the subject.

This general objective has been divided into two specific parts:

- A description of the *innovation in teaching* the subject of Accountancy by the use of ICT.
- An evaluation of the *level of acceptance* of the teaching method by students of the first and second cycle, respectively.
- An evaluation of the *suitability of the proposed teaching method* according to the results obtained by students and the cycle involved.

The work consists of three different sections: the first describes the *methodology* designed by the authors *to teach* the subject, its evolution throughout the academic years in which it was put into practice and details of its implantation.

The second gives the *results obtained* in each of the years for each of the subjects considered, distinguishing between students who adopted the proposed method and those who followed the traditional study method. The *statistical treatment* of the results, together with a discussion and the conclusions are contained in the final section.

Finally, the *analysis of the conclusions* will serve as a basis for the evaluation of the suitability of the proposed method and for any necessary changes to adapt it to the characteristics, conditions and limitations of the teaching-learning process.

## BACKGROUND

An empirical study carried out in 2002 (Celestino, Echegaray, & Guenaga, 2002) demonstrated the generally *low level of incorporation of Webs* and their contents for support in the important subjects of Financial Management and Computer Applications for Management in Business Faculties in other Spanish universities.

In the case of the UPV, the new technologies are widely used by both teachers and students. In the academic year 2002/03 a *web-based educational platform* was put into operation to facilitate and stimulate new work strategies by means of forums, chat rooms and new ways of evaluating students' performance. It proved to be so successful that it inspired us to begin the present work in order to verify to what extent results were improved in the subject both in the first and second cycles.

The present study was carried out in the context of the degree course in Business Administration at the Polytechnic University of Valencia.

The course consists of 327 credits throughout the five years of the course. Students can choose to specialise in one of three sectors: industry, services or construction, a feature which distinguishes it from Business Studies courses in other Spanish universities.

Subjects included are, as previously commented, are the two main subjects of the first (*Financial Accounting*) and second (*General and Analytical Accounting*) cycles. It is considered that students must successfully pass the first of these in order to be able to deal with the second.

Table 1 gives a list of the competencies in which students receive training throughout the business degree course.

In accordance with the White Paper on Business Management and Administration, the specific competencies in which students receive training in the *subject of Accounting* are as follows:

- Analysis of financial information for use as a management and decision-making tool.
- Use of accounts for the correct understanding of financial information and decision making. The analysis of information is practically impossible without an understanding of this subject.
- Capacity to put theoretical knowledge into practice in solving problems, with examples taken from the real business world of the type which the student is likely to have to deal with in his professional career.
- Capacity to explain economic questions. An understanding of the subject is necessary to explain to others economic factors affecting the company.
- Use of accounting for an understanding of the present and future impact of financial operations on company capital and assets.

Competence management presents many problems (Levy-Leboyer, 1997), however, *new ICT based teaching methods* should provide a stimulus to teachers (Clares, 2005; Guenaga, Celestino, & Echegaray, 2003). It should also be pointed out that traditionally both subjects have involved *high failure rates* and repeated years for many students. This situation means that teachers

*Table 1. Competencies included in the Business Administration course.*

| **Specific** | **Generic/Transversal** |
|---|---|
| *Technical*<br>• Accounting<br>• Finance<br>• Marketing<br>• Organization/ Human Resources<br>*Environment*<br>• Economics<br>• Law<br>• Sociology<br>• History<br>*Instrumental*<br>• Math/Statistics<br>• Computer Systems | • Foreign Languages<br>• Oral and written expression<br>• Creativity and innovation<br>• Communication capability<br>• International environment<br>• Critical thinking<br>• Adapting to change<br>• Working in group/under pressure<br>• Time management<br>• Ethical values<br>**Transferable**<br>• Internships<br>• Real environment simulation |

Source: Cañibano, 2008.

are continually trying new approaches with the aim of improving exam results.

It should also be pointed out that this course is given in a Polytechnic University in which the new technologies are widely used by both teachers and students (Paredes, & Estebanell, 2005). For example, the university has an Intranet on which students have access to notes, support material, scientific articles, etc., which many other universities still do not have.

A study carried out by the Basque Country University in 2003 (Clares, 2005) concluded that the new technologies could become the key to making a decisive contribution to the quality of training by improving individual, group and team work and the incorporation of new evaluation methods.

In the case of the UPV, in the academic year 2002/03 a *web-based educational platform* was put into operation to facilitate and stimulate new work strategies by means of forums, chat rooms and new ways of evaluating students' performance. It proved to be so successful that it inspired us to begin the present work in order to verify to what extent results were improved in the subject both in the first and second cycles.

## E-LEARNNING METHODOLOGY

The description of the E-learning methodology applied to these two important subjects will assist us in reaching the first objective of this study, which consists of describing the innovation project in the use of ICT devices in Accounting. Each of the subjects will be described separately in the following sub-paragraphs.

The subject of Financial Accounting has a total of 7.5 credits and is taught in only one semester of the first year. In 07/08, the last year analysed, there were 339 students enrolled in the subject. General and Analytical Accounting, with 9 credits, is taught in the fourth year and there were 303 students enrolled in the subject in 07/08.

### E-Learning Methodology Applied to the Subject of Financial Accounting

The subject is divided into three parts:

1. Lectures in the theory of the main contents of the subject, worth a total of 2.75 credits.
2. Practical classes, also worth 2.75 credits, in which students do exercises individually or under supervision.

Both of the above aspects are evaluated in the final exam of the subject.

3. Practical Problem Based Learning (PBL) classes (2 credits) in which intensive use is made of ICT systems. Our attention will be focussed mainly on the teaching of these classes and the exams associated with them.

*Table 2. Teaching program of subjects analysed: Business Studies Degree Course - PUV*

| | | | | | | |
|---|---|---|---|---|---|---|
| **1st Semester** | Business Law | Basic Mathematics | Optional | Microeconomics | Introduction to Business Sectors | |
| **2nd Semester** | Financial Accounting | Introduction to Statistics | Economy of Business I | | | |
| **7th S** | General and Analytical Accounting | Econometrics | Quality Control | Integrated Business Computer Systems | Specialisation | Optional |
| **8th S** | Business Management | Production Management and Logistics | Cost Management | Import and Export Management | Languages II | Optional |

Source: Compiled by the authors.

It is important to remember that participation in the practical PBL and ICT based classes in (3) above is *voluntary*. For those who opt to participate, the final subject mark is calculated as the weighted average of different scores, of which practical classes are given a specific weight of 30% and the others 70%. For those who do not participate in the practical classes, the final mark is made up of 100% of the other scores.

PBL sessions are given in computer-equipped classrooms and intensive use is made of new technologies. In a 2-hour session, using *Contaplús* software, students must solve a problem consisting of 15 accounting entries without assistance similar to those previously practiced in class. The use of the software program is explained in the first session and practice is provided in its use. The problems increase in complexity with time and are related to the contents of the other two-thirds of the subject.

After the third session, students master the *Contaplús* program and regard it as a useful problem-solving tool. The aim is to achieve by PBL the specific skills required for accounting, while at the same time being aware of their many limitations (Barnett, 2001).

ICT systems also come into play since the problems to be solved are often conveyed to students via the university's own educational platform. In the last 20 minutes of the session, students can also use this medium to carry out *self-evaluations* consisting of 10 multiple-choice questions randomly selected from a total of 50, so that the exam is different for each student. Both students and teachers agree that the using the Intranet platform makes this work much easier.

## E-Learning Methodology Applied to the Subject of General and Analytical Accounting

The teaching methods used in this subject are practically identical to those described above, allowing for the fact that students at this stage are expected to have greater knowledge and experience. The subject is divided into the following parts:

1. Lectures in theory, worth 4 credits.
2. Practical classes, with 3.5 credits, in which the theory is put into practice. Students are given the problems to solve previous to these classes.
3. PBL-based sessions, with intensive use of ICT systems, worth 1.5 credits.

Students are evaluated in the subject according to the system they opt for, since attendance at the practical classes is not compulsory. If they participate in the practical sessions, which are designed to improve their knowledge and skills in the subject, the final mark is composed of a weighted average of all the student's exams. They may also choose to take only the final exam, whose score will constitute 100% of their final mark in the subject.

Practical classes based on PBL and ICT are given in computer-equipped classrooms. Students are divided into groups of three to analyse the final accounts of a business company they have chosen themselves. They work as a *team* in three-hour sessions under the supervision of a teacher. Each team is expected to design its *own computer tools* for the financial analysis using Excel software. In the final session, each team delivers a report to the teacher on the situation of the company and recommendations for further action, as well as an oral synthesis of their conclusions.

The students' final scores for the practical sessions are composed of a weighted average of the score given for the final report and analysis (60%), the score for the Excel application designed for the calculations (10%) and the oral exegesis of the conclusions (30%).

The use of this methodology initiates students in the habit of working as part of a team (Katzenbach, 2000) and trains them in problem solving and the use of new technologies. Besides the training they receive in accounting, it also improves their oral and written expression skills.

## RESULTS

The results obtained by students who studied this course between 2002/03 and 2007/08 will be used to determine whether the objectives proposed in this study have been reached. Students' acceptance of the methodology will be evaluated as well as its suitability for use in teaching the subject according to the results obtained by students and the study cycle to which they belong. The results are presented in the figures below.

### Results Obtained in Financial Accounting

We included the number of students that took part in the six years under study from 2002/03 to 2007/08 together with their characteristics in Table 3. The average number of students in the six years is 330, of which 192 opted to take part in the practical classes using PBL and ICT systems. Of these, 118 managed to obtain a pass in the practice sessions and 66.5% of these also obtained a pass in the subject, while 33.5% did not, as can be seen from Figure 1.

Figure 2 shows the results for the average number of students divided into four groups as follows:

1. Students who passed the subject having participated in practical PBL classes
2. Students who passed without participating in practical classes
3. Students who failed having participated in practical classes
4. Students who failed after not having participated in practical classes

*Table 3. Numbers of students per year who take exams, pass and fail in relation to participation in practical classes.*

| Years | 02/03 | 03/04 | 04/05 | 05/06 | 06/07 | 07/08 | Average |
|---|---|---|---|---|---|---|---|
| Total Students | 334 | 319 | 322 | 338 | 328 | 339 | 330 |
| Students examined | 247 | 215 | 213 | 239 | 167 | 181 | 210 |
| Students who took part in practice | 241 | 249 | 157 | 168 | 194 | 143 | 192 |
| Students who obtained passes in practical work | 174 | 125 | 65 | 99 | 119 | 128 | 118 |
| Students who obtained passes in the subject | 132 | 102 | 53 | 86 | 73 | 89 | 89 |
| Students who passed WITH practice | 87 | 71 | 31 | 41 | 39 | 68 | 56 |
| Students who passed WITH-OUT practice | 3 | 4 | 9 | 10 | 3 | 3 | 5 |
| Students who passed the subject and failed practice | 8 | 23 | 13 | 10 | 4 | 4 | 10 |
| Students who failed subject and passed practice | 32 | 53 | 34 | 49 | 60 | 42 | 45 |

Source: Compiled by the authors

*Figure 1. Average percentage of students who pass and fail the subject after obtaining passes in practice carried out with PBL and ICT*

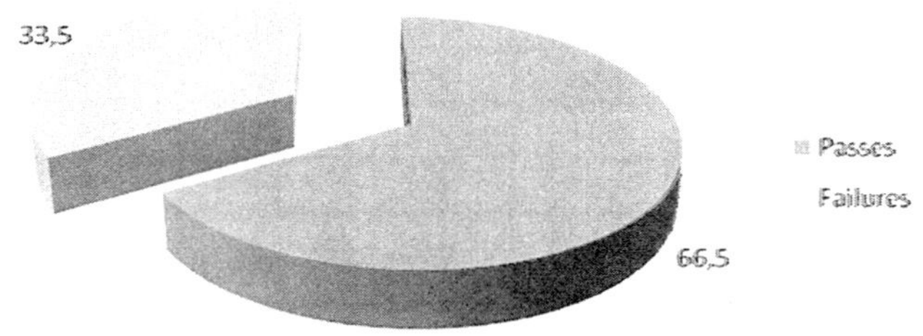


*Figure 2. Average percentage of students who passed and failed Financial Accounting from 2002/03 to 2007/08 in relation to whether or not they participated in practical PBL classes*

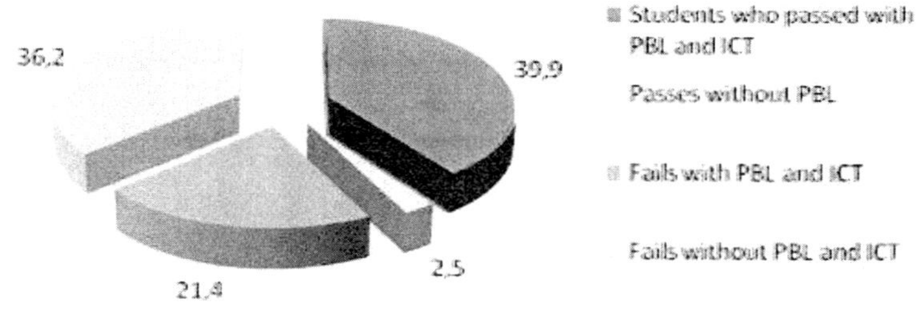


## Results Obtained in General and Analytical Accounting

Using the same methodology applied previously, Table 4 shows the evolution of the number of students and the study methods used by them from 2002/03 to 2007/08 (and average numbers for the whole period) in the fourth year subject General and Analytical Accounting.

The figures show that a significant percentage (56%) of the average number of 277 students took the active learning option (86% of those who sat the final exam). Of those who passed, 85% took part in practice classes (see Figure 3), while no student who obtained a negative mark in practice managed to pass the final exam in the subject.

## Analysis of the Results

The results obtained in this study show a remarkable *correlation* between the pass rates of students and whether or not they participated in practical classes, demonstrating that those who did participate achieved much higher pass rates.

However, the results also show that the relationship between practical classes and success rate cannot be demonstrated for a part of the student sample. This is probably due to the lack of sufficient computer terminals in the classrooms, since students have to share computers with classmates, thus giving the less motivated the opportunity to take advantage of the work of their more highly motivated classmates. We foresee improvements in future teaching methods to overcome this problem.

We have also noted that the students who become accustomed to active PBL and ICT based learning methods in the first two years continue to use them throughout the remainder of their university career, with a high participation rate in active E-learning methods (see Figure 5).

*Table 4. Numbers of students per year who took, passed and failed the exam in the subject in relation to whether or not they took part in practical classes.*

| Year | 02/03 | 03/04 | 04/05 | 05/06 | 06/07 | 07/08 | Average |
|---|---|---|---|---|---|---|---|
| Total students | 187 | 254 | 289 | 310 | 320 | 303 | **277** |
| Students examined | 119 | 179 | 204 | 202 | 206 | 175 | **181** |
| Students who took part in practice | 140 | 177 | 179 | 145 | 115 | 173 | **155** |
| Students who obtained passes in practical work | 125 | 167 | 173 | 145 | 115 | 171 | **149** |
| Students who obtained passes in the subject | 46 | 76 | 83 | 110 | 89 | 76 | **80** |
| Students who passed WITH practice | 41 | 75 | 76 | 86 | 66 | 66 | **68** |
| Students who passed WITHOUT practice | 5 | 1 | 7 | 24 | 23 | 10 | **12** |
| Students who passed the subject and failed practice | 0 | 0 | 1 | 0 | 0 | 0 | **0** |
| Students who failed subject and passed practice | 63 | 76 | 85 | 35 | 37 | 66 | **60** |

Source: Compiled by the authors.

*Figure 3. Average percentage of students who used active learning methods and also achieved a pass in the subject General and Analytical Accounting in the years 2002/03 to 2007/08 (Source: Compiled by the authors)*

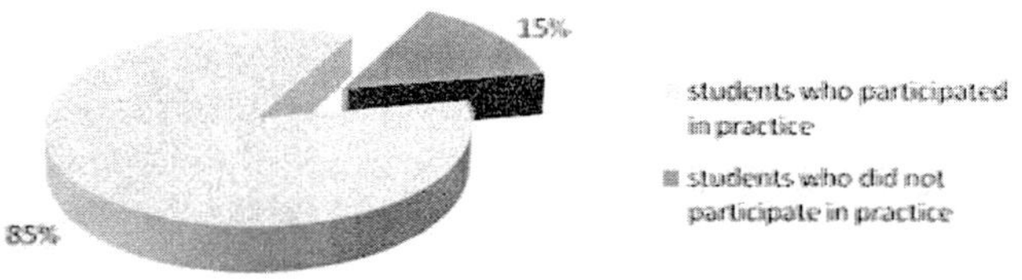


*Figure 4. Average of passes and failures in General and Analytical Accounting in relation to learning method for the years 2002/02 to 2007/08 (Source: Compiled by the authors)*

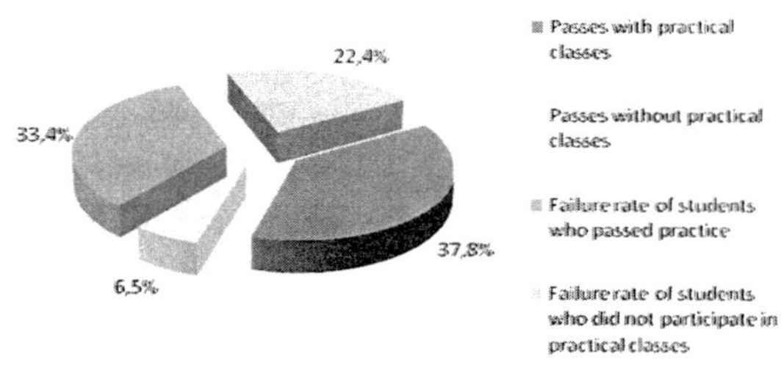

*Figure 5. Average percentage of students who voluntarily used PBL with ICT in General and Analytical Accounting from 2002/03 to 2007/08 (Source: Compiled by the authors)*

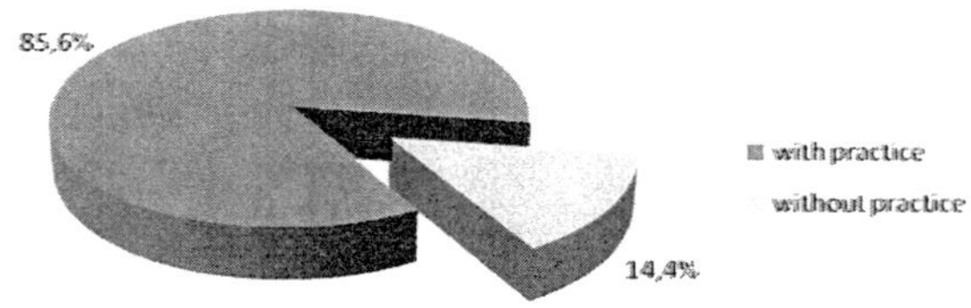


## FUTURE RESEARCH DIRECTIONS

The application of the E-learning methodologies in accounting subjects would be the solution to some student´s problems to reach the assigned competences, like we have seen in our paper. We know foreign Business Administration degree where they apply this kind of methodologies, so we are going to compare these experiences with ours in order to improve our system. We can study which percentage of e-learning methodologies apply another degrees, in accounting subjects, comparing with our rates. This will be our next work.

Another important future research line is to study the results of the Erasmus students. The UPV has a high number of foreign students, so we can compare their results in accounting subjects with the Spanish ones.

## CONCLUSION

The application of E-learning methods in the first years of the university degree course with an average number of 120 students per group (300 in total) is regarded with certain apprehension by many lecturers, and even more so in important subjects considered to be difficult with high failure and dropout rates. We therefore regard the results of this study as important for the following reasons:

1. Exam results improved significantly among the sampled students who actively followed E-learning methods coupled with the use of ICT technology, which encourages us to continue with the task of expanding their use.
2. An analysis of the evolution of the students throughout their degree course in Business Administration and Management attempts to correlate the first year exam results in the subject with those from the fourth year, when students are supposed to have greater knowledge of the subject. This evolution had never been systematically dealt with prior to our study. The conclusions reached, which point to the higher *success rate* among those who participate in ICT-based methods, support our conviction that the use of such methods should be encouraged.
3. Finally, the present study is an analysis of the situation in regard to the teaching of the two subjects involved and describes quantitatively and systematically the results obtained. We consider that they amply demonstrate that they are suitable for use in subjects with similar contents at higher levels. We also consider this aspect to be of special importance in the present context of change which Spanish universities are currently experiencing, involving changes to degree structures in order to harmonise with the European Higher Education Area.

These conclusions reinforce our commitment to these methods and have encouraged us to continue the work of improving them and sharing the results with other universities and teachers working in similar conditions.

## REFERENCES


Argüelles, A. (1997). *Formación basada en competencias laborales*. Méjico: Limusa.

Ballestero, E. (1980). *El encuentro de las ciencias sociales. Un ensayo de metodología*. Madrid, Spain: Alianza Universidad.

Barnett, R. (2001). *Los límites de la competencia. El conocimiento, la educación superior y la sociedad*. Barcelona, Spain: Gedisa.

Cañibano, L. (2008, May). *Higher Education in 'Business Administration' in Spain: Adapting to the European Area of Higher Education*. Paper presented at the I Convegno Nazionale of SIDREA: 'La Ragioneria e l'economia aziendale: dinamiche evolutive e prospettive di Cambiamento', Siena, Italy.

Celestino, A., & Echegaray, O. Guenaga, G. (2002). *Evaluación de la incorporación de las Nuevas Tecnologías en la estrategia docente del ámbito de las Ciencias Empresariales*. Paper presented at the Conferencia Internacional de Tecnologías de Información y Comunicación en Educación, ICTE, Badajoz, Spain.

Clares, J. (2005): El uso de las TIC en educación superior. In Universidad de La Laguna (Ed.), *Actas del XII Congreso Nacional de Modelos de Investigación Educativa: investigación e innovación educativa* (pp. 243-250). Tenerife: Servicio de Publicaciones Universidad de La Laguna.

Guenaga, G., Celestino, A., & Echegaray, O. (2003). Integración de las TIC en la educación superior. *Pixel-Bit Revista de Medios y Educación*, *21*, 21–28.

Katzenbach, J. R. (2000). *El trabajo en equipo*. Barcelona, Spain: Granica.

Levy-Leboyer, C. (1997). *Gestión de las competencias*. Barcelona, Spain. *Gestion*, 2000.

Monereo, C., & Pozo, J. L. (2003). *La Universidad ante la nueva cultura educativa. Enseñar y aprender para la autonomía*. Barcelona, Spain: Síntesis.

Paredes, J., & Estebanell, M. (2005). Actitudes y necesidades de formación de los profesores ante las TIC y la introducción del crédito europeo: un nuevo desafío para la educación superior. *Revista de Educación*, *337*, 125–148.

Zabalza, M. A. (2003). *Competencias docentes del profesorado universitario*. Madrid, Spain: Narcea.


## ADDITIONAL READING


Alves, P., Pires, J., Amaral, L., Cordeiro, J., Shishkov, B., Verbraeck, A., & Helfert, M. (2009). The role of learning styles in intelligent tutoring systems. In Cordeiro, J.; Shishkov, B.; Verbraeck, A.; Helfert, M. (Ed.), *CSEDU 2009: Proceedings of the First International Conference on Computer Supported Education: Vol. I* (pp. 315-320). Lisbon: Portugal.

Andreu, H. B., & Nussbaum, M. (2009). An experimental study of the inclusion of technology in Higher Education. *Computer Applications in Engineering Education*, *17*(1), 100–107. doi:10.1002/cae.20188

Birch, D., & Burnett, B. (2009). Bringing academics ob board: encouraging institution-wide diffusion of e-learning environments. *Australasian Journal of Educational Technology*, *25*(1), 117–134.

Bobbio, A., Cantore, L., Miranda, N., & Zollo, A. (2007). New tools for scientific learning in the EduSeis Project: the e-learning experiment. *Annals of Geophysics*, *50*, 283–290.

Fernando, M. S. D., & Dahanayake, A. N. W. KhosrowPour, M. (2004). E-learning and quality university environment: a better mix of technology based learning and administration with traditional university setting. *Innovations Through Information Technology, Vols. 1 and 2* (pp. 1426-1428). New Orleans, LA.

García, M. A., & Vico, A. (2004). *La formación universitaria en Administración y Dirección de Empresas: análisis de su adaptación al mercado de trabajo y propuesta de Plan de Estudios*. Madrid, Spain: AECA.

González, C. (2009). Degree in International Business and a major in accounting and finance: a proposal from the University of Valencia. *Spanish Journal of Finance and Accounting, 38*(142), 311–330.

González, J., & Wagenaar, R. (Eds.). (2003). *Tuning Educational Structures in Europe*. Bilbao, Spain: Universidad de Deusto.

Hyde, R., Jefferies, A., Williams, R., & Remenyi, D. (2008, November). *Listening to the Learner's Voices in HE. How do students reflect on their use of technology for learning?* Paper presented at the 7th European Conference on E-Learning. Agia Napa: Cyprus.

Luic, L., & Kalpic, D. (2008). The role of ERP in management on higher education financing. In Cordeiro, J.; Shishkov, B.; Ranchordas, A.; Helfert, M. (Ed.), *ICSOFT 2008: Proceedings of the Third International Conference on Software and Data Technologies: Vol. ISDM/ABF* (pp. 339-347). Oporto: Portugal.

Mandinach, E. B. (2005). The development of effective evaluation methods for e-learning: a concept paper and action plan. *Teachers College Record, 107*(8), 1814–1835. doi:10.1111/j.1467-9620.2005.00543.x

Paredes, J., & Estebanell, M. (2005). Actitudes y necesidades de formación de los profesores ante las TIC y la introducción del crédito europeo. Un nuevo desafío para la educación superior. *Revista de Educación, 37*, 125–148.

Penalba, O., García-Tejedor, A. J., Cerezo, Y., & Álvarez, J. A. (2009). A tool for time management in the new European Higher Education System. In Cordeiro, J.; Shishkov, B.; Verbraeck, A.; Helfert, M. (Ed.), *CSEDU 2009: Proceedings of the First International Conference on Computer Supported Education: Vol. I* (pp. 291-296). Lisbon: Portugal.

Pérez, B. E., & Cardoso, S. M. J. (2009). The implementation of a degree in the context of the European Space for Higher Education: the University of Seville case. *Spanish Journal of Finance and Accounting, 38*(142), 293–310.

Ramonet, M. C., Rada, V. L., Vila, M. N., Bernado, B. S., Penamaria, A. S., Williams, R., & Remenyi, D. (2008, November). *Syllabus Flexibility and adaptation to the new European Higher Education Area through the inclusion of the e-Learning.* Paper presented at the 7th European Conference on E-Learning. Agia Napa: Cyprus.

Regueras, L. M., Verdú, E., Muñoz, M. F., Pérez, M. A., de Castro, J. P., & Verdú, M. J. (2009). Effects of competitive E-Learning tools on Higher Education Students: a case study. *IEEE Transactions on Education, 52*(2), 279–285. doi:10.1109/TE.2008.928198

Salas-Morera, L., Berral-Yeron, J., Serrano-Gómez, I., & Martínez-Jiménez, P. (2009). An assessment of the ECTS in Software Engineering: a teaching experience. *IEEE Transactions on Education, 52*(1), 177–184. doi:10.1109/TE.2008.921801

Salinas, J. (2004). Educación superior y tecnología digital. In Martínez, F., & Prendes, M. (Eds.), *Nuevas tecnologías y educación* (pp. 113–118). Madrid, Spain: Pearson.

Sánchez-Franco, M. J., Martínez-López, F. J., & Martín-Velicia, F. A. (2009). Exploring the impact of individualism and uncertainty avoidance in Web-based electronic learning: an empirical analysis in European Higher Education. *Computers & Education*, *52*(3), 588–598. doi:10.1016/j.compedu.2008.11.006

Selwyn, N., Marriott, N., & Marriott, P. (2002). Home computers & university ICT use. *Journal of Computer Assisted Learning*, *18*(1), 44. doi:10.1046/j.0266-4909.2001.00206.x

Sulcic, V., & Lesjak, D. (2009). E-Learning and study effectiveness. *Journal of Computer Information Systems*, *49*(3), 40–47.

Totter, A., Grund, S., Grote, G., Cantoni, L., & McLoughlin, C. (2004, June). *A methodological approach to the evaluation of e-learning technologies.* Paper presented at ED-MEDIA 2004: World Conference on Educational Multimedia, Hypermedia & Telecommunications. Lugano: Switzerland.

Trentin, G. (2006). The Xanadu project: training faculty in the use of information and communication technology for university teaching. *Journal of Computer Assisted Learning*, *22*(3), 182–196. doi:10.1111/j.1365-2729.2006.00168.x

Vadillo, M. A., & Matute, H. (2009). Learning in virtual environments: some discrepancies between laboratory and Internet-based research on associative learning. *Computers in Human Behavior*, *25*(2), 402–406. doi:10.1016/j.chb.2008.08.009

Westera, W. (2004). On strategies of educational innovation: between substitution and transformation. *Higher Education*, *47*(4), 501–518. doi:10.1023/B:HIGH.0000020875.72943.a7

Woods, R., Baker, J., & Hopper, D. (2004). Hybrid structures: faculty use and perception of web-based courseware as a supplement to face-to-face instruction. *The Internet and Higher Education*, *7*(4), 281–298. doi:10.1016/j.iheduc.2004.09.002

Yunker, J. A. (2005). The dubious utility of the value-added concept in higher education: the case of accounting. *Economics of Education Review*, *24*(3), 355–367. doi:10.1016/j.econedurev.2004.06.003

## KEY TERMS AND DEFINITIONS

**Accounting:** The system of recording and summarizing business and financial transactions and analyzing, verifying and reporting the results.

**Competences:** The knowledge and ability that enable a person to do something.

**E-Learning Methodologies:** Knowledge or skill acquired by instruction or study using electronic procedures.

**European Higher Education Area (EHEA):** The objective of the Bologna process to create more comparable, compatible and coherent systems of higher education in Europe.

**Higher Education:** Education beyond the secondary level provided by a college or university.

**Information and Communication Technology (ICT):** All types of advanced technology used to manipulate and communicate information.

**Problem Based Learning (PBL):** An educative proposal that is developed on the basis of small work groups which go through a cooperative learning process, in order to search for a track to solve a complex problem, proposed by the teacher.

# Chapter 11
# Learning Methods in Entrepreneurial and Managerial Training

**Mario G.R. Pagliacci**
*Università degli Studi di Perugia, Italy*

## ABSTRACT

*Knowledge Society changes enterprises, and big emphasis is given to persons and human capital. Enterprise becomes a learning organization based on scientific-technical transfer, on human and cybernetic intelligence, on information and communication technologies. Role of entrepreneurs and managers is exalted in this context; they are asked to look, to promote, to exploit, to run all spaces and subjects are able to carry knowledge. As consequence, targets, contents and methodologies of entrepreneurial and managerial training need to be revised; either in scholastic institutions - first university - or in other public and private educational organizations. The distinctive competence of entrepreneurs and managers asks that their training is focalized on relations; as consequence, inter-active teaching methods have to be adopted: learning by doing, by playing and dramatization.*

## INTRODUCTION

Knowledge Society changes style of life and work of individuals and organizations.

Role of traditional factors of production is revised in economic context: big emphasis is given to human capital, as the main factor able to better the efficiency of enterprise and achieve useful conditions for innovation. As consequence, business systems and processes are changing, in order to satisfy three kind of exigencies (Ricketts, 2002):

a. facing continuous changes in external and internal context;
b. governing transactions connected to opportunistic behaviors;
c. generating new knowledge.

Nowadays enterprise is asked to become a *learning organization*, and *knowledge* is essential for processes, products, services, in order to satisfy

DOI: 10.4018/978-1-61692-791-2.ch011

consumer's need, to better the competitiveness of markets, to increase the profitability. In "White Paper on Growth, Competitiveness, Employment: The challenges and ways forward into the 21st century" is written:

*The key elements in competitiveness....include in particular the quality of education and training, the efficiency of industrial organization, the capacity to make continuous improvements in production processes, the intensity of R&D and its industrial exploitation, the fluidity of the conditions under which markets operate, the availability of competitive service infrastructures, product quality and the way in which corporate strategies take account of the consequences of changes in society, such as improved environmental protection.....*

*(European Commission, 1993, Chapter 2)*

Role of entrepreneurs and managers is exalted in this context; they are asked to run and increase enterprise knowledge and to assure structural and functional conditions for enterprise solidity and development.

In order to pursue these targets, technicalities are not so important; nevertheless courses of study in commercial schools and universities are based on specialist subjects and traditional methods of teaching. It is important that entrepreneurial and managerial training is revised, according to Schumpeter (1942) who suggested reinforcement of high schools, as an important asset in capitalistic system.

About *didactic subjects*, it is necessary to enlarge inter-disciplinary vision, in order to train pupils in transversal approach to problems.

About *modalities and processes of teaching*, e-learning methodologies can integrate entrepreneurial and managerial training, but they are not so good in developing relational and inter-personal skills. This purpose is achieved by learning by doing methodologies: they offer to pupils useful relational experiences, on engaging them in real entrepreneurial contexts. Nevertheless these methodologies are not so compatible with institutional practices in school and university.

Better integration in institutional teaching is allowed by learning by playing methodologies, when they are based on virtual reality.

In order to reach a good equilibrium among different needs and/or constraints, I consider really useful the experiences of dramatization.

This paper analyzes the new exigencies in entrepreneurial/managerial life, and evaluates some training methodologies that are adopted in European school and university. The purpose is in demonstrating that traditional methodologies in teaching entrepreneurial and managerial disciplines, have to be integrated by new methodologies, able to increase relational feeling and capacities.

## KNOWLEDGE ECONOMY

Peter Drucker was the first Author (1933) who introduced the concepts of *Knowledge Society* and *Knowledge Economy*: he thought a society where the fundamental resource is knowledge generated by persons, instead of tangible assets.

In Europe, the most authoritative declaration in favor of Knowledge Society was inspired by Jacques Delors: in "White Paper on Growth, Competitiveness and Employment" was underlined the central role of:

*Investment in education and training: knowledge and know how throughout life...... Preparation for life in tomorrow's world cannot be satisfied by a once-and-for-all acquisition of knowledge and know-how...... Tomorrow's trades will require the ability to make diagnoses and propose improvements at all levels, and the autonomy and independence of spirit and analytical ability which come of knowledge. Hence the need to adapt the content of training and to be able to improve one's training (knowledge and know-how) whenever necessary...... Lifelong education is therefore the overall objective to which the national educational communities can make their own contributions.*

*(European Commission, 1993, Chapter 2)*

*Knowledge Era* concerns all areas of human life and expands in all sectors of the economic system; products and services progressively become the results of knowledge and the inter-sector contamination makes inadequate the classification of technological sectors.

Global markets and immaterial economy generate and increase new cultural and know-how experiences, as well as new "hybrid" products and services. Enterprises have to change competitive strategies, entrepreneurial formula, managerial procedures. Traditional production factors are less important and knowledge of generative individuals becomes the most important factor. As consequence, labor market is changing: the most satisfying jobs are reserved to people skilled in digital technologies and interactive communication networks, able to enrich and renew own competences, on using either professional and social experiences as lifelong learning.

Nowadays, successful enterprise is a *knowledge-based organization*; it is characterized by the fundamental role of knowledge generated by internal ideas and experiences as well as by learning from "others" (Nonaka&Takeuchi,1997); enterprise becomes a *learning organization* where external people - clients, suppliers, banks and so on - are not only "partners in business" but "bearers of knowledge" also. Accumulation and organization of knowledge becomes the *intellectual capital* (Sveiby, 2001) used by enterprise for pursuing its own competitive advantage.

"Intellectual capital" is a concept that John K. Galbraith used first time on addressing a letter to Michael Kalecki; but Thomas Stewart (1999) is the first Author giving the idea of intellectual capital as "collective brainpower" useful for creating richness. Centrality of individual, introduced by Stewart, was developed by Sveiby, Sullivan, D'Egidio; they extended the interest towards the clients and the whole social system which is related to enterprise (see Figure 1).

In my opinion, Andriessen&Stam (2004) gave a complete evidence of the fundamental aspects of intellectual capital:

- *intangible resources* are in all organizations, but their mix is variable according to technological, territorial, temporal characteristics;
- in *knowledge-based organizations*, intangible assets prevail on tangible ones; they

*Figure 1. Composition and role of Intellectual Capital*

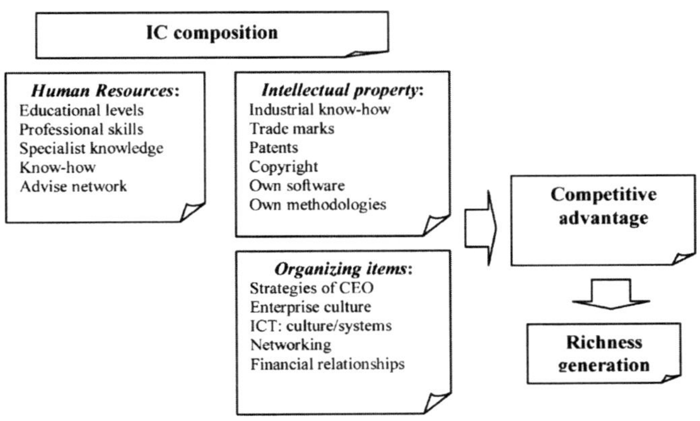

increase the value when knowledge increase, but they can lose the value as time passes;

- *intellectual capital* gives competitive advantage, especially when organization chooses to abandon its own business and create a new one;
- *competitive advantage* increases the capacity of enterprise in generating medium-long term profitability.

## CHARACTERISTICS OF KNOWLEDGE-BASED ENTERPRISES

All enterprises have some intangible resources; nevertheless some enterprises - especially in advanced services, but in other sectors also - have a high capacity in generating new knowledge, in diffusing into organization, in incorporating into processes, products, services (Nonaka&Takeuchi, 1997). In these knowledge-based enterprises role of intellectual capital is prevalent, and its highest manifestation is the *Human Capital*, because it can develop either *Organizing (or Structural) Capital* (i.e.: procedures, proceeds, know-how) as *Relational Capital* (all relationships generated by business life) (see Figure 2).

### Human Capital

Stewart writes (1991) that Human Capital is the fundamental component of Intellectual Capital, "*source of innovation and renovation*" (p. 124). It concerns knowledge, competence, ability and motivation that the single person brings from outside or generates into the organization. Stewart underlines that not all human resources can be considered as Human Capital. According to Sveiby&Lloyd (1992) four categories of employees exist:

1. *managers:* they are able to conduct a team and to manage business, but they have not the specific know-how of professionals;
2. *clerks*: they support professionals and managers, but have no power to decide;
3. *professionals*: they are "knowledge workers", aiming to develop own abilities without links; they are not able to coordinate people;
4. *leaders:* they are the strength of "knowledge organization" and it is very difficult to replace them; they are the creators of the enterprise often, and they play a role of arbitrators.

Among these categories, it is possible to discover some individuals able to bring exclusive and strategic competences and to increase knowledge capital of enterprise: they are the Human Capital.

Especially knowledge-based enterprises are interested in carrying on effective policies, in order

*Figure 2. Interconnections among elements of Intellectual Capital*

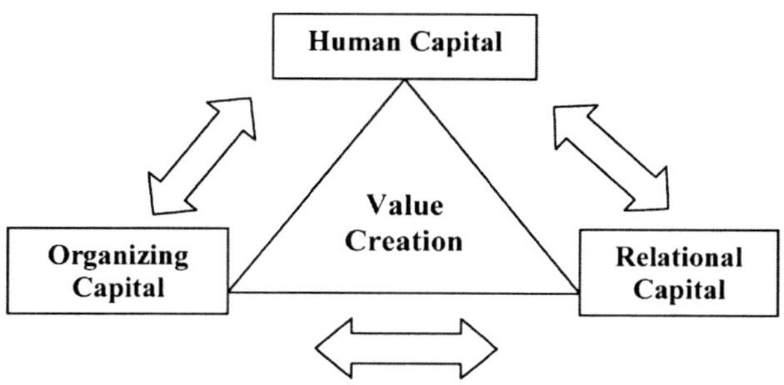

to preserve and increase Human Capital. This is one of the most important role of entrepreneurs and top managers.

## Organizing Capital

Organizing (or Structural) Capital is the knowledge that any individual transfers to the enterprise in form of reports, documents, handbooks and similar. It concerns intangible assets above all (i.e.: specialist know-how, procedures, etc.), but intellectual property also (i.e.: patents, trade-marks, trade-secrets, know-how, copyright) which enjoys the protection of the law.

Organizing Capital represents the "adhesive" charged to link the components of Intellectual Capital: without it, Human Capital would coincide with Intellectual Capital, and Relational Capital did not exist (Bontis, 1998).

Peter Drucker writes in *The Age of Social Transformation* (1994) that organization can assure the stability needed by knowledge workers; organization is able to transform specialist know-how in profitability. Nevertheless it is important to underline that not all the organizing structures are good in developing Intellectual Capital: a structure based on concepts of top-down management, specialization, planning, seems inadequate; on the contrary, a reticular structure, based on concepts of middle-up-down management, attraction of resources, integration, flexibility, seems ideal.

It is the task of entrepreneurs and top-managers to organize enterprise in such a way for developing and exploiting knowledge.

## Relational Capital

The third type of Intellectual Capital concerns all the relationships that organization generates among the people working into enterprise, as well as outside people related with enterprise.

Internal relationships concern exchanging of information among individuals, in order to support their learning and the improvement in knowledge and expertise. They can be generated by social abilities (leadership, self-esteem), interpersonal relationships (confidence) and sharing of social identity (common style and values). The most useful tools are internal communication and information technology, able in reinforcing links among persons and supporting the flow of ideas.

External relationships concern a lot of different single subjects and groups that are involved - directly or indirectly - with the life and the fortune of enterprise. Among these, it is important to underline *customer capital*; it represents the value of relationships that enterprise manages with commercial partners: clients and suppliers.

Table 1 shows the complexity of internal and external actors interacting in the system where enterprise moves and operates (Cantino&Devalle, 2004).

In order to increase Relational Capital, it is very important to create, develop and maintain the conditions of reciprocity (bilateral exchange) and confidence (psychological link); this is an important task for entrepreneurs and top-managers.

*Table 1. Internal and external subjects*

| Actors directly involved | Subjects in interaction |
|---|---|
| Entrepreneur | Market system |
| Shareholders and Partners | Technological system |
| Managers | Socio-cultural system |
| Financiers and banks | Legislative system |
| Employees and self-employed workers | Banking system |
| Suppliers | Local communities |
| Customers | Consumer groups |
| Competitors | Environmental groups<br>Political groups<br>Ethnic groups<br>Trade Unions organizations<br>Public administration |

## NEW SKILLS FOR ENTREPRENEURS AND MANAGERS

Entrepreneurial reinforcement and quality of managerial skills are common targets in all countries:

- developed countries have to assure the renewal of "entrepreneurial park" and the change of managerial models towards high-tech and innovation economy;
- less developed countries have to enlarge entrepreneurial basis and reinforce strategic technological sectors.

In all countries, Knowledge Society and Economy emphasize the role of Intellectual Capital in enterprises and other social organizations. Nevertheless, it must be underlined that entrepreneurial and managerial high-quality is a rare resource, especially in innovation field. In another paper I wrote (Pagliacci, 2009) that only few entrepreneurs and managers are really motivated in accessing to innovation, and their ability is in organizing enterprise in such a way to attract useful competences wherever they are - in the internal or external of enterprise - and to utilize them according to the Figure 3.

First Penrose (1959) emphasized role of individual and collective knowledge. Individual skills are used in day-to-day operations and become

*Figure 3. Flow towards competitive advantage*

COMPETENCE
⇩
ORGANIZATIONAL ROUTINE
⇩
ORGANIZATIONAL KNOWLEDGE
⇩
ORGANIZATIONAL COMPETENCE
⇩
CORE COMPETENCE
⇩
COMPETITIVE ADVANTAGE

organizational routines and rules, but successful rules only become organizational knowledge. To gain competitive advantage, enterprise must manage and continuously generate new experiential knowledge to be used to create new operating systems that are able to generate new competences. Such competences constitute a superior source of competitive advantage, because they are rare, valuable and difficult to imitate (Teece, 1997).

Sveiby writes (2001) that *knowledge management* is able to transform enterprise in *knowledge organization*: this is the role of *knowledge workers*; but entrepreneurs and top managers only can create the best conditions of equilibrium between stimulation of individual abilities and governance of multiplicity, in order to pursue business targets.

### Entrepreneurial Models are Changing

Knowledge Society and Economy change style and models in running enterprises, so that entrepreneurs and top managers are asked to have "transversal" competences and to express particular character and behavior skills:

- ability in identifying risks and running them in order to take all opportunities;
- receptiveness in taking decisions in conditions of uncertainty;
- attitude to change either interpretative models as organizing and relational structures;
- disposition to delegate actions, still assuming responsibility in results.

These skills do not need technical and specialist competences, rather ability to interpret internal and external context, in order to pick out and run menaces and opportunities. Nothing different of the ancient Chinese wisdom, where efficiency and efficacy of public administration was assured by Mandarins; their training was not specialist and the final exam was a kind of cultural test, finalized to understand if the candidate was a gentleman (Weber, 1976).

Actually, this approach seems to be in the mind of young: Pagliacci et alii, (2006) made a research on a sample of students attending the Faculty of Economics in Università degli Studi di Perugia (Italy) and pointed out that "*....entrepreneurs cannot be short of ability in organizing, in putting forth ideas...and in willing to do*" (p. 91). Once again it is underlined that entrepreneurs (and top managers) are not asked in specialist role, rather in choosing winning strategies and organizing enterprises in flexible way, in order to allow quick corrections according to any kind of external and/or internal change. According to Charles Darwin, surviving species are not the strongest ones, neither the most intelligent, but the most prompt in changing. In case of business survival, that means a double ability:

- on one hand it is asked *rationality* in order to keep good decisions in the interest of enterprise;
- on the other hand relational skills (let me propose a neologism: "*relationality*") are necessary, in order to balance and integrate different actors towards synergic results.

The concepts of r*ationality* and *relationality* have to be revised and integrated.

Traditional "*homo oeconomicus*" who takes decisions according to "rational utility" only, is an artificial and unreal concept, just a memory of the past.

Adam Smith wrote:

*Everybody continuously tries to look for the best investment of his own capital. Actually everybody looks for his own advantage, and not for the advantage of the community. But the research of his own advantage, naturally and necessary gets to prefer the investment that is more favorable for the community. (Smith,1975, p.581).*

Nowadays the advantage of community cannot be as an indirect consequence of private business, so that modern entrepreneur must integrate his business activity into a "cobweb" of reciprocal relationships, mutually advantageous, taking in account social dimension (ethic, ecology, and so on). According to World Commission on Environment and Development (1987) goal is "*the satisfaction of present needs without compromising the capacity of future generations to satisfy their needs*".

It is not easy to make compatible private business interest with social conditions. Nowadays entrepreneur is asked to have conscience of his social role and a strong confidence in himself. He must recover the enormous deficit of imaginary (Boia,1998) caused by the classic concept of rationality, and to accept the way of the unknowable, as an authentic visionary (Delattre, 2003). According to Coste&Roche (2004), entrepreneurs have to change their point of view and to work according a creative approach. The alternative condition is well described by Andrea Sartori:

*The comic and, in the same time, tragic condition of entrepreneur and creative manager, is like son who has not solved his problem with father, who has not reached a correct social integration, crushed under the weight of impossible responsibilities, of too much indeterminate duties. (Sartori, 2009, p. 115).*

## HAVE TO CHANGE TARGETS AND METHODS OF ENTREPRENEURIAL/ MANAGERIAL TRAINING

Purpose of safeguard and development of entrepreneurial patrimony is pursued by countries in different way, but all are addressed to young people especially, according to two fundamental guide-lines:

- stimulating young generation towards entrepreneurship, either on continuing existing firms - especially family ones - as on starting-up new business;

- inculcating the culture of risk linked with relational culture, as two factors that are essential for taking the best opportunities offered by globalization and knowledge-era.

European Commission is strongly engaged on this matter. In addition to general programs in favor of entrepreneurship, it is to remind the new program named "Erasmus for Young Entrepreneurs"; it was designed according the scheme of "Erasmus", one of the major components of the Union's Lifelong Learning Program: until now, almost 2 million students had part of their education in an European university, having the opportunity to live and study in different culture and educational system.

"Erasmus for Young Entrepreneurs" is open to people that aim starting-up a new enterprise or just started their own company within the past three years. New and aspiring entrepreneur can spend working time (as little as a month or as long as six months) with an experienced entrepreneur in another EU Member State, having the opportunity to know how another enterprise is run, how the boss takes decisions, how managers/owners deal with suppliers and customers, the style of human relationships and so on. This experience can be useful for the host entrepreneur, so that both parties gain the opportunity to learn about the other's national market, business culture, and possibly get access to innovative ideas. In addition, any party has the possibility to enter in an enlarged network of relationships that can be maintained and increased thanks internet tools.

Long distance tools are a sensational opportunity to create contacts with and among entrepreneurs in order to exchange experiences. Only as an example, European Union creates "The Entrepreneurship Video Awards" by which European businesspeople have the chance to express their own ideas on business, to show something of their experiences, and to be creative on film. The entrepreneurs were invited to submit short videos on one of three topics: the entrepreneurial spirit, innovative entrepreneurship, responsible entrepreneurship; the purpose is to identify and show what makes the entrepreneur tick, and which can inspire others to follow through on their ideas.

Another example of entrepreneurial training using digital tools is offered by the exhibition "The SME Experience" that run in may 2009 in Brussels.

This interactive exhibition was able:

*to show visitors how it feels to be an entrepreneur. They will glimpse the various sensations, hopes and fears, and challenges and rewards experienced by entrepreneurs at the different stages in their company's life...... how does an entrepreneur develop and evaluate business ideas, how do they deal with stress, how do they manage risk, what does the freedom to be 'your own boss' bring, how do they find customers, how do they overcome red tape, how do they negotiate with suppliers, how do they ensure sufficient cash flow... (Enterprise Industry Magazine, 2009, p. 6).*

In spite of special programs - as European Commission ones - training in economic and managerial areas is generally entrusted to school institutions (especially public economic high schools and faculties of economics); in addition, public and private entrepreneurial organizations play a role of integration and reinforcement, especially in Lifelong Learning.

I consider that it is necessary to analyze the contents and the methods of teaching, in order to understand whether they are really useful to develop the distinctive competences of entrepreneurs and managers in knowledge-era.

In the course, this paper intends to analyze the contribution of University - especially Faculty of Economics - in stimulating and training entrepreneurial/managerial abilities of students.

The guide-lines of the analysis concern:

- *question of diffusion*;
- *question of contents;*
- *question of methods.*

## Question of Diffusion

All countries are interested in reinforcement of entrepreneurial park, either under quantitative/ qualitative point of view as in its renewal and updating.

School system might be the principal agent in young's incitement towards entrepreneurship, so that basically economics and entrepreneurial culture have to concern all students, from primary school to university. On the contrary, in European Countries economic and managerial culture is thought in commercial and economic school classes only; in addition, these classes are focused on specialist disciplines (i.e.: accounting, finance, marketing and so on) rather in entrepreneurial skills, able to stimulate characteristics of risk management, relationship, creativity and innovation pulsing.

In the same time the economic system asks more and better entrepreneurs, school system is able to train - in the best hypothesis - good specialist managers. As consequence, it is observed an opening out between the two systems, and this reflects on a kind of delusion of student's expectations.

This gap must be filled by several actions; one of these can be the different approach of school system towards entrepreneurial training, taking in account the criteria of knowledge economy.

## Question of Contents

Best literature agrees that training based on specific disciplines and technical subjects can be useful for middle managers and professionals, but is not suitable for entrepreneurs and top managers. Their role asks a distinctive competence focalized on relations: in the external of the firm, in order to keep the opportunities of growth by adequate policies of alliance; in the internal of the firm with the purpose to exercise leadership towards human resources, founded on the lever of motivation rather than on control.

On the contrary, philosophy orienting teaching in the Faculties of Economics is based on the principle of rational utility of *homo oeconomicus*; as an inevitable consequence, the knowledge of technicalities and its regulating mechanisms is assumed as necessary and sufficient.

Recent research of Daniel Kanheman (Nobel 2002 in economics) - together his colleague and friend Amos Tversky - refutes the principle that rational decision would be influenced by content of the problem only. Kanheman demonstrated (1994) that choices are influenced by context (framing effect) and emotional factors. This new approach about the dynamic of economic decisions, was developed by Pietroni&Rumiati (2008) under the point of view of economic relationships and negotiations, which are so important for economic operators, especially entrepreneurs and managers.

Nevertheless, I presume that a long time will be necessary before these studies become as institutional contents in European Faculties of Economics. For the moment, European studies in Economics are characterized by strong presence of macro/microeconomic and specialist business disciplines, organized according to a multi-disciplinary logic, where the integration among different teachings/teachers (typical of inter-disciplinary logic) is very low. In substance, Faculties of Economics are usually structured for the purpose to "produce" middle managers and professionals to be employed by big firms; not for training new generation of entrepreneurs and "whole-managers", destined to small and medium firms. This approach is extremely incoherent in comparison with European business structure, where SMEs are more than 95%.

Entrepreneurs and whole managers need to be trained for analyzing complex situations and taking decisions in uncertainness and risky conditions; they need to be rapid in decisions and ready to diagnose mistakes and to decide corrective actions. These abilities can be developed if students are trained to analyze problems under different points of view, even if they are divaricating. It is necessary a high horizontal integration among disciplines, as well as it happens in real running of enterprises.

In another paper I wrote:

*Entrepreneurial and innovating spirit cannot be taught, but it can be stimulated; it is necessary to put the question if and how the characteristics for entrepreneurial success are stimulated - or checked - by university courses. Knowledge Society and Economy are changing the models in working and making business; as consequence are asked new competences: i.e. problem solving, communication, risk management, self-organisation. University also has to take part in this process and to adopt new educational and training parameters: no longer imperative and assertive transfer of knowledge from professor to student, but a new style of teaching focused on the relative and evolutive value of knowledge, on the comparison of different perspectives of knowledge (Pagliacci et alii, 2008).*

University learning has big merits in enlargement and transmission of culture, but it suffers of big limits in accompanying students towards autonomous and creative thinking, free of pre-existing schemes and models, of standardized formula and solutions. These are essential characteristics for successful entrepreneur in knowledge-era.

## Question of Methods

Teaching methods in universities are characterized by low dialectic among disciplines, strong tendency to assertion, absence of critical spirit. It is necessary to admit that these limits concern teaching style of professors.

Famous writer Gabriel G. Marquez remembers that lectures of his professor at university were monotonous monologues like, and the monotony of his voice had the hypnotic effect of a snake-charmer.

I wrote diffusely about this question in another paper (Pagliacci, 2004), and concluded: "Teachers have a strong inclination in presenting their own doctrine as the unique valid thinking line; they induce students towards any forms of intellectual obedience" (pp. 93-94).

An alternative experimentation is proposed by the "Ecole de Management de Grenoble" (France), where figurative arts practice for students was adopted since six years, in order to allow students:

- to develop their own intuitions;
- to have an experience of real innovation and to accept in working out of known fields;
- to better understand reality and the link between the artist and the world;
- to increase their ability in communication towards others;
- to optimize their creative resources.

Coste and Roche (2004) - Authors of the experimentation - clarify that the purpose consists:

*in giving to students the awareness of their sentiments, a medley of restlessness and excitement. When students are aware of these sentiments, we can fortify their self-confidence so that they "authorize" themselves to be spontaneous in creating a sound, a word, a sensation, in the receptiveness of listening their wishes... (Coste&Roche, 2004, p. 43)*

Apart some innovating experimentations, the aliened style of teaching is prevalent, and it let's imagine student's state of mind about professors! An indirect evidence is given by an Italian-French research (Boissin, Casagrande, Montrone, Pagliacci, 2009) about the question of young entrepreneurship. We verified that decision of Italian students about the possible starting-up of their own enterprise, is influenced by family at first, secondly by friends, and marginally by professors. It is important to underline that the investigated sample was composed by students in economics, so that opinion of their professors - experts in economic and managerial matters - could be relevant !

This is an additional demonstration that students can recognize professors as experts in their own discipline, but they are taken in low account as educators.

My conclusion is that model of teaching, like a soloist snake-charmer, have to be replaced by a new model where professor is like a conductor, so able in valorizing abilities of singles and the whole orchestra. In this way, university can recuperate its fundamental role in educational process: instilling self-confidence and self-thinking in students, with the purpose to able them in free expression of their abilities.

## METHODOLOGIES AND PROCEDURES INTEGRATING TRADITIONAL TEACHING

It is time that traditional learning practices and procedures are invigorate by new style in teaching - especially in public school and university; nevertheless change must be gradual and respect two basic principles:

1. *compatibility to budget and procedures*;
2. *integration with traditional teaching.*

### E-Learning and Simulation Models

Previous first principle receives a successful answer by e-learning methodologies; they progressively increased the field of application, as far as to substitute - rather than integrate - some traditional teaching areas. In my opinion, the best application of e-learning concerns people not allowed to go to traditional classes, owing to various reasons:

- psycho-physical problems, enabling to be present in institutional educational places (i.e.: physical or mental handicapped, old people…..);
- occupational or legal impediments, that are incompatible with timing and/or places of traditional classes (i.e.: sailings, workers operating in oil rig or platforms, prisoners…..);
- motivational or opportunistic choices (i.e.: entrepreneurs and top managers do not like to confront *de visu* with others on professional topics).

Apart special situations, my opinion is that e-learning methods are very useful when are used for integrating traditional teaching. For instance, in teaching foreign languages in Faculty of Economics.

It is well known the importance for economic operators (entrepreneurs and managers too) to have a very good command of several foreign languages (English plays the dominant role); nevertheless didactic plans of faculty are unable to offer to students the necessary training. Time and effort that can be devoted to practicing writing, speaking and listening foreign languages are absolutely insufficient. According to Figure 4, mastering business foreign language concerns either knowledge-area as communication area.

According to experts (Ellis, Johnson and Brieger) teachers must balance between knowledge area and communication area; on the contrary, time and tools do not give the possibility to practice communication area, taking in account the different knowledge levels and personal skills of students. In this exemplary situation, e-learning methods can integrate teacher's activity, supporting students - singly or in small groups - to complete and increase their training.

*Figure 4. Business language areas*

| **LANGUAGE KNOWLEDGE** | **COMMUNICATION SKILLS** |
|---|---|
| ⇩ | ⇩ |
| **General Language**<br>• grammar<br>• vocabulary | **General Communication**<br>• discussion and social<br>• listening |
| **Specialist Language**<br>• marketing<br>• finance<br>• human resources | **Professional Communication**<br>• presentation<br>• telephoning<br>• negotiation |

An important group of learning methods concerns *virtual reality*; informatics and digital technologies get increasing applications, according to three typologies:

- non-immersive approach: it allows control on virtual environment, without participating;
- immersive approach: it enables to participate to virtual dynamics;
- augmented reality: it is possible to enrich reality with virtual elements.

Several software are well-known about simulation, and they are diffusely used at school and university: *what if applications* and *business games* can engage students in refined problems of business management and economic choices, on giving the feed-back and the evaluation of the adopted solutions.

Additional educational applications can be offered by several *social network*, which allow a relational approach. A kind of *second life environment*, specialized in entrepreneurial and managerial training, could offer students the opportunity to virtually meet well experienced entrepreneurs and managers, in order to put questions and exchange ideas; in the same time, entrepreneurs and managers could utilize this virtual environment - where the real identity is covered - in order to debate any situations and problems they do not like to put in discussion in real life.

E-learning methods are - more or less - able to respect the condition of *compatibility to budget and procedures* of school and university; nevertheless they are lacking in satisfying the second condition of *integration with traditional teaching*, especially under inter-active and emotional profile.

I just underlined that professors - especially at university - adopt monologue style in lectures, so that the best integration is in emphasizing relational approach. On the contrary, e-learning applications offer to students a virtual inter-action only, so depriving them of relational added value and associated emotions.

This conclusion could be extended to professional training also. In the course of a research on a panel of entrepreneurs and managers, Pagliacci et. alii investigated about the tools that are considered useful for reinforcing the innovative culture of employees. The result is the following hierarchy of tools:

1st : Seminar : average mark 4,2
2nd: Informatics : average mark 3,6
3rd: Lecture : average mark 3,5
4th: E-learning : average mark 3,3
5th: Book : average mark 3,2
6th : Learning by playing : average mark 2,7
(Legenda: min=1;max=5)

It is not casual that all non-interactive tools (book, conference, informatics, e-learning) received similar average marks (between 3,2 and 3,6); on the contrary, seminar received the average mark of 4,2: the only tool which is able to create an interactive relationship among participants.

In our paper we wrote:

*seminar is considered the most efficacious tool for training in innovation field (78% of interviewees gave the evaluation mark of 4 or more) because it is able to offer either technical knowledge... as involving methodology. Interviewees...prefer that fundamental contents are communicated by a direct process involving individuals and their personal relationships. The word "seminar" recalls the action "to seed" and the inter-active process of continuous re-interpretation and re-elaboration operated by individuals...(Pagliacci et alii, 2010).*

In our opinion better results can be obtained by methods based on playing; nevertheless interviewee assigned low average mark (2,7); it is possible that this approach is not well known yet.

About these methods, in next paragraphs.

## LEARNING BY DOING

Learning by doing methodologies in entrepreneurial/managerial training have the purpose to give a real experience in starting-up and running business activities.

In Europe, first programs in favor of students were in Great Britain around the second half of 20th century; nowadays a lot of Countries are associated in Young Enterprise Network; it promotes and supports learning by doing methodologies in high school and university.

The most interesting programs give to students - organized in small groups - the chance to develop an entrepreneurial process: from entrepreneurial idea, to enterprise start-up, until the engineering of products or services and their marketing. The entire process develops as well as a real enterprise; nevertheless the young enterprise runs in "protected condition" and it cannot fail. In fact the central network is engaged in supporting start-up with small money and in protecting young enterprise by possible risks, first of all financial insolvency. On the other hand, role of the school institution is like an "incubator" in supplying some real services: place, tools, and tutoring of specialized teachers.

My personal experience as a tutor of several young enterprises promoted in my Faculty, convinced me that this methodology is really effective for plunging students in entrepreneurial atmosphere, in this way on motivating and encouraging them to put into practice knowledge they received by professor's lectures. Students demonstrate high participation, so confirming the idea of Hawken that a good school is able to transform learning in playing.

As usual, the opposite face of coin exists: it is very difficult to make compatible these projects with budget, procedures and time of institutional teaching; in addition it is necessary to consider the barriers posed by traditional and conservative people, influencing educational and didactic guide-lines either in the internal (professors and administrative employees) as in the external (parents, local and central stakeholders). It is the case of the habitude of many professors in using written tests for the assessment of students, in order to reduce time and efforts. In my opinion, it is necessary to develop new paradigms and innovative researches in order to experiment original guide-lines for assessing relational and creative abilities of students.

In synthesis, learning by doing methodologies are the optimal final target in entrepreneurial and managerial training; but they have to be adopted step by step, on studying progressive intermediate solutions. It is the case of learning by playing methodologies, able to satisfy Hawken idea (to transform learning in playing), without breaking too much rituals and procedures of institutional didactics.

## Learning by Playing: Dramatization

A kind of balancing between *compatibility to budget and procedures* and *integration with traditional teaching*, can be assured on adopting the way of learning by playing, as integrating part of a curricular discipline. Methodologies of dramatization - where business experiences are lived in reality, even if in virtual way - are based on active participation of persons in training: they are asked - singly or in small groups - to perform a role in competitive business games or in discussing a controversial business question, in order to keep the most convenient decision, taking in account the constraints of the context and the human dynamics of other players, having different roles and emotional behaviors.

Dramatization in business training is able to simulate the continuous sequence of decisions-actions-reactions characterizing the dynamic of enterprise, where the results are not strictly connected to the objective value of the single decision-action, rather to the subjective evaluation and reaction of people are involved in. It is a kind of training based on *relationality*, because players (as students as professionals) utilize theoretical knowledge in order to develop and optimize the inter-active process.

I experimented dramatization in communicating to students the dynamics of negotiation in commercial and financial, domestic and international context; i.e.: assessment of enterprises and risk of credit rating, import-export contracts, factoring agreements, claims management, constitution of joint ventures. According to my experience, this kind of approach is really useful in order to give a practical idea of the connection among *knowledge-to know doing-to know negotiating* and the relational feed-back of negotiation. In addition, dramatization performances are welcome as by students either by young entrepreneurs and managers; this is attested by following opinion of Giuseppe Di Cesare, a student of mines:

*few professors only create a contact with reality, like a link with external context. It is important a balancing between practice and theory. ... simulation of cases is useful in order to understand reality: theory about enterprise and business world shows an orderly and polite environment, but practice is different! For instance business meetings are characterized by strong quarrels sometime, owing to interest conflicts among participants. ... Another interesting case we simulated concerns a trading negotiation...it let us understand that it is not easy to conclude an agreement in presence of divaricated interests. ...These experiences gave us the opportunity to actively participate as individually as in group...It is possible to learn by making mistakes also ...If all courses would be based on this methods...students have the best conditions to reach a good educational and managerial training.... (Di Cesare, 2009, unpublished report)*

Unfortunately, dramatization methods excite a kind of perplexity in traditionalist professors, because of they are afraid to lose their centrality in educational process. This is not truth; on the contrary teacher passes from the condition of soloist in his monologue to the role of stage-manager in dramatization; he has the responsibility to:

- analyze real business cases, in order to extract problems and situations that are didactically useful, in coherence with the level of learning and the maturity of students;
- arrange the didactic context and the business plot, without prefiguring dynamics and results of "drama", because of the scenario is freely created according to the different roles of players;
- give fluidity to the "scenic action" in case of stops or useless deviations;

- end of the didactic activity of dramatization, on proposing to students the evaluation of results in the light of disciplines and researches.

It is understandable that dramatization reaches its best effects when more professors are involved in; in fact this is the right way for pursuing the target of inter-disciplinary logic in entrepreneurial and managerial training.

## CONCLUSION

Experts agree that entrepreneurial and managerial training in Knowledge Society and Economy have to be based on relational skills rather than to specialized abilities. Nevertheless didactic methods in school and university are not coherent with, either for budget and organizing reasons as for hostility of traditionalist professors.

Enlargement of e-learning methodologies helps teaching modernization and receptiveness of professors, but these methods are not really useful for developing the fundamental entrepreneurial and managerial skills; their competence can be synthesized as "rationality in decisions associated to *relationality* in actions".

In addition, traditional courses are based on multi-disciplinary logic, not coherent with reality of business running.

My opinion is in favor of diffuse experimentation in school and university of learning by doing and by playing methodologies: the only methods that are able to train a new generation of knowledge-based entrepreneurs and managers.

In order to increase effectiveness of these methods, efficiency of their technicalities and to optimize costs, new researches, applications and experiments are necessary; nevertheless, this is the right way for reducing asymmetries in budgeting and organizing school and university.

In the same time, it is necessary to start an "educational program" for teachers - university professors, particularly – finalized to let them understand what is their fundamental role in utilizing real and virtual simulation methodologies, especially in entrepreneurial and managerial training.

## REFERENCES

Boia, L. (1998). *Pour une histoire de l'imaginaire*. Paris, France: Les Belles Lettres.

Boissin, J.P., Casagrande, A.,Montrone, A. & Pagliacci,M. (2009). Gli studenti universitari e l'imprenditorialità. Uno studio comparativo Italia-Francia. *AUR&S*, 1-2.

Coste, D., & Roche, L. (2004). La place de l'art plastique dans une école de management. *Humanisme & Entreprise*, 04-266.

Drucker, P. (1993). *Post Capitalism Society*. New York: Harper Collins.

European Commission. (1993). White Paper on growth, competitiveness, and employment: The challenges and ways forward into the 21st century, *Part A, COM (93) 700 final*.

European Commission. (2009)... *Enterprise Industry Magazine*, *4*, 1–2009.

Kahneman, D. (2007). *Economia della felicità*. Milano, Italy: Il Sole 24 Ore.

Nonaka, I., & Takeuchi, H. (1997). *The Knowlegde-Creating Company*. Milano, Italy: Guerini e Associati.

Pagliacci, M. (2004). L'apprentissage par le jeu (Learning by playing). In Lodziensis, U. (Ed.), *Formation et développement des compétences manageriales dans l'Europe élargie* (pp. 93–103). Lodz, Poland: Wydawnictwo Uniwersytetu Lodzkiego.

Pagliacci, M. (2009). Towards a systemic assessment and evaluation of SMEs.*Cahiers du CEREN*. 27(2009).

Pagliacci, M. (2006). *Orientation entrepreneuriale des étudiants et role de l'Universitè*. Grenoble, France: Réseau PGV Editions.

Pagliacci, M., et al. (2008, October). *Esprit entrepreneurial et innovant des étudiants universitaires*. Paper presented at the meeting *Les cultures étudiantes* of Université Pierre Mendès-France, Grenoble, France.

Pagliacci, M., et al. (2010). Il potenziale creativo negli studenti e il fabbisogno innovativo nelle imprese *AUR&S*.3-4/10

Pietroni, D., & Rumiati, R. (2008). *La mente che negozia*. Milano, Italy: Il Sole 24 Ore.

Sartori, S. (2009). Quale creatività nella crisi? *Il Ponte*, LXV-4.

Smith, A. (1975). *La ricchezza delle nazioni*. Torino, Italy: UTET.

Stewart, T. A. (1999). *Il capitale intellettuale. La nuova ricchezza*. Milano,Italy: Ponte alle Grazie.

Weber, M. (1976). *Sociologia delle religioni. Confucianesimo e taoismo*. Torino, Italy: UTET.

## KEY TERMS AND DEFINITIONS

**"Hybrid" Products/Services:** Advanced products/services that are obtained by utilizing a mixture of different technologies, generally supplied by several technological sectors.

**Knowledge Society:** Social-economic system, where knowledge of individuals and groups is the fundamental asset for increasing welfare.

**Knowledge-Based Enterprise:** Enterprise founding its success on intangible assets represented by intellectual capital (human, structural and relational capital).

**Learning by Doing Methodologies:** In entrepreneurial/managerial training these methodologies have the purpose to give a real experience in starting-up and running business activities: from entrepreneurial idea, to enterprise start-up, until the engineering of products or services and their marketing.

**Learning by Playing Methodologies:** They operate in virtual reality. Special case of dramatization emphasizes the active participation of persons in training: they are asked - singly or in small groups - to perform a role in competitive business games or in discussing a controversial business question.

**Learning Organization:** In Knowledge Society and Economy, enterprises and other organizations have to invest in learning of employees, in order to maintain and increase competitiveness.

**"Relationality":** I propose this neologism in order to underline role of relational skills in comparison and combine to role of rational skills (rationality).

# Chapter 12
# Including Nomadic People in Collaborative E-Learning: Experiences in Research Projects

**Ugo Barchetti**
*University of Salento, Italy*

**Alberto Bucciero**
*University of Salento, Italy*

**Luca Mainetti**
*University of Salento, Italy*

## ABSTRACT

*The focus of this chapter is the design of a solution for Computer-Supported Cooperative Learning (CSCL) that is able to connect both stationary and mobile users in live shared-learning sessions. The authors started from experiences that were mainly technology-driven to arrive at the development of two subsystems, OpenWebTalk and MobileWebTalk, that build, flexibly and simply, mixed reality environments in which users cooperate to perform the same learning task. From these experiences, the authors argue that heterogeneous learning environments (stationary and mobile) can only be really effective if they are designed from a unique abstract model. Therefore the challenge is to derive a conceptual model to describe a collaborative learning session that can be deployed in different devices.*

## INTRODUCTION

Traditionally, collaborative work and learning have been supported by groupware tools called Computer-Supported Cooperative Work (CSCW).

The term CSCW was first coined by Irene Greif from MIT and Paul M. Cashman from DEC in 1984, at a workshop attended by individuals interested in using technology to support people in their work.

According to Baecker, Grudin, Buxton and Greenberg (1995, p. 141), Computer-Supported Cooperative Work or CSCW is computer-assisted coordinated activity carried out by groups of collaborating individuals.

Examples of CSCW are: communication between instructors and trainees (simulation and training applications), data sharing (for visually

DOI: 10.4018/978-1-61692-791-2.ch012

supported discussion by scientists or decision-makers), support for innovative teaching and learning, and support for collaborative learning.

One of the commonest ways of conceptualizing CSCW systems is to consider the context of a system's use. One such conceptualization is the CSCW Matrix, first introduced in 1988 by Johansen and also appearing in Shen and Dewan (1992). The matrix considers work contexts along two dimensions: first, whether collaboration is co-located or geographically distributed, and second, whether individuals collaborate synchronously (at the same time) or asynchronously (not dependent on others being around at the same time).

In this matrix, Collaborative Virtual Environments (CVE) systems are listed as Virtual Worlds in the *Remote Interactions* section.

In fact, CVE can be seen as the result of the convergence of interests and research studies in both virtual reality and Computer Supported Cooperative Work fields. CVEs are applications that (re)create a multi-user virtual world, according to Damer (1997), as two- or three-dimensional graphical environments inhabited by users (represented by digital actors called "avatars") that share with other users time, space and actions, cooperating together for a common goal.

The classification provided in Figure 1 tends to give a general homogeneity of devices used in the interactions. In other words, it is supposed that all the people involved in the cooperation use the same technical environment and devices, the same software user interface and interact in the same way with the software system.

On the other hand, mobile technologies are increasingly offering new opportunities for "anytime, anywhere" computing, allowing users to access information, and collaborate with colleagues far from their desktop station. This emergence of mobile devices and new forms of connectivity allows new forms of collaboration, not limited to the traditional stationary workstation but tailored to the capabilities of these new devices supporting ubiquitous cooperation.

In this context, the previous matrix should be modified by the addition of one more dimension, "user interface interaction," that differentiates the homogeneous collaboration forms from those characterized by the use of different devices (multi-device) or different forms of presentation and interaction with the user (multi-modality).

We believe that properly designed shared workspace applications can be as useful in supporting mobile users as they are for non-mobile

*Figure 1. Time and Space Groupware Matrix*

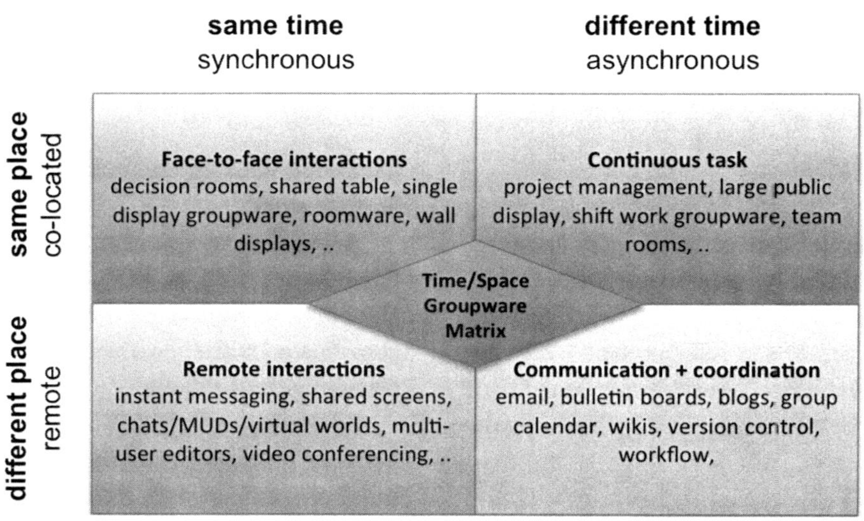

ones. Furthermore we think that a heterogeneous workspace, made up of mobile and stationary users, could be much more effective than a traditional one. This is because the "anytime, anywhere" access to group information for the mobile users allows the development of shared workspace with support for contextualized communication (real-world information) for the same mobile users and the non-mobile ones that can experience multi-sensorial, on-field information that they could never get from their traditional virtual environment. On the other hand, stationary users, having more powerful devices than the mobile ones, can more easily access complex information, allocating vastly different cognitive resources to a display (i.e. the computer monitor) than a person in the field who needs to pay attention to the external environment, e.g. traffic (Kahneman, 1971).

In this chapter we focus our attention on the description of past experiences acquired from different research projects about learning. We show how the applications developed for these projects are based on the same conceptual and implementative framework, also giving support to the mobile learning environment, and how they can be used jointly with the traditional CSCW systems, in particular with the CVE system for learning.

We present on the one hand a framework to support stationary people through the generation of 3D collaborative experiences, and on the other an extension of this framework to support in a flexible way both stationary and mobile systems through a collaborative mixed environment for representing and mapping information from one platform to a second one with different display and computing capabilities. We explore the use of heterogeneous collaboration (especially for educational purposes) thought the creation of a software architecture, running also on mobile devices. This architecture is based on an overall framework that can configure its own user view and environmental interactions according to an XML-based configuration description in order to represent workspace and interaction rules shared with the 3D stationary users.

The framework for stationary people is developed with macromedia technologies and is named Webtalk, whereas OpenWebTalk is the same framework developed with open source language and technologies.

The framework for people on the move represents an extension of the WebTalk/OpenWebTalk system, both designed and developed by GSALab (Graphics and Software Architectures Lab) at the University of Salento.

The chapter is organized in the following sections. First a review of the most relevant CVE and LMS (learning management systems) is presented. The second section describes our experiences and the projects in which we have been involved, and the third describes our views on CVE and e-learning, and the use of awareness in mixed reality applications to enhance the involvement of users. The fourth section describes the reference framework used in the projects and its evolution in support of awareness. The fifth section shows the obtained results as educational benefits. Finally, we present our future research directions and a conclusion.

## A SURVEY OF CVE AND LMS

Technologies designed with the purpose of supporting virtual learning environments are not neutral. They reflect a certain understanding of communication and a certain understanding of learning, which are represented and incorporated in the functionality of the system, in the system architecture and in the interface design. The system's developers, however, rarely provide an explicit definition of the underlying pedagogy of their system and therefore it is difficult to choose an appropriate technology when designing and organizing learning environments. Therefore the need arises to define the methodological bases for the creation and evaluation of technological solutions to support problem-oriented project-based learning (POPP) (Illeris, 1981; Dirckinck-Holmfeld, 1990).

These methodological bases must take into account two different aspects: on the one hand, learning design based on pedagogical best practices, and, on the other, Multi-user Virtual Environments (MUSEs) development based on the current techniques of computer graphics.

Learning design provides a vocabulary for describing teaching and learning processes, and is itself pedagogically neutral (Koper & Olivier, 2003). The design becomes explicit and can be reflected upon by the designers themselves or by others who may further refine the design and share it within a community (Koper &Tattersall, 2005). Instructional Management System Learning Design (IMS LD) has emerged as the standard. It allows the expression of lesson plans as formally expressed Units of Learning (UoL). Learning designs with this specification are expressed in Extensible Markup Language (XML), making them machine-readable, i.e. learning designs can be run using IMS LD compatible software such as CopperCore or.LRN (which can be embedded within a learning management system), rendering the delivery and management of courses more economical (Koper &Tattersall, 2005; Burgos, Tattersall & Koper, 2005).

IMS LD is based on the Educational Modelling Language (EML) created by Rob Koper and his team at the Open University of the Netherlands (Burgos, Tattersall & Koper, 2005). It is defined as "a semantic information model and binding, describing the content and process within a 'unit of learning' from a pedagogical perspective in order to support reuse and interoperability" (Koper, Rodrígues-Artacho, Lefrere, Rawlings & Rosmalen, 2002). Building on this language, IMS LD was designed to provide a containment framework of elements that describe any design of a teaching-learning process in a formal way.

A Multi-User Virtual Environment (MUVE) is a computer-, server- or internet-based virtual environment that allows participants to move around and use various forms of communication (text chat, voice chat or instant messaging). It allows participants to create a virtual identity which persists beyond the initial session (Maher, 1999; Ritzema & Harris, 2008). The term was coined by Chip Morningstar and F. Randall Farmer in 1990 (Morningstar & Farmer, 1991) and is often used interchangeably with "Virtual World" (VW) (Castranova, 2001). Second Life is one of the most well-known MUVEs, in part owing to the intense media scrutiny it has attracted, but predominantly because the content is created almost exclusively by users. At the time of writing, it boasts nearly sixteen million user accounts, one and a quarter million residents having logged in during the previous sixty days (LindenLabs, 2009). Though Massively Multiplayer Online Role-Playing Games (MMORPGs) such as World of Warcraft resemble MUVEs in many ways, including users sharing the same virtual space, they differ in important ways, too. In MUVEs there are no "levels" to be worked through or embedded fiction that directs the activities of participants; instead the experiences are shaped by users (Ondrejka, 2008).

MUVEs and MMORPGs are populated by motional "avatars"; the term is derived from Sanskrit and used in Hindu mythology to denote the earthly form adopted by a deity, commonly Vis,n,u (Leeming, 2001). In MUVEs and MMORPGs, this term denotes the representation of a character, controlled either by an individual or a software agent in the case of a "bot", which acts somewhat like a virtual automaton (Duridanov & Simoff, 2007). The choice of avatar can reflect a player's personality, gender or ethnicity. It is also possible for a participant to assume a completely different identity which in itself may constitute a significant learning experience, particularly important in role-playing scenarios. In addition, they are able to communicate with large groups of avatars (via voice- or text-chat or asynchronously with podcasting or inworld, text-based documents called notecards) or communicate more intimately with a single avatar (using instant messaging) (Tashner, Riedl & Bronack, 2005). Avatars are able to interact with and modify the virtual environment and are even able to interact beyond the confines of the MUVE if objects are linked to web pages (called "web on a prim" in Second Life) (Tashner et al., 2005).

## OUR PREVIOUS EXPERIENCES

Our first approach to multi-user 3D virtual environments was in 1998 with the reconstruction of the "National Science and Technology Museum" of Milan (Paolini et al., 1999; Barbieri, 2000; Barbieri & Paolini, 2001) designed and implemented in the HOC Laboratory at the Polytechnic of Milan: a 3D virtual exhibition on the machines "invented" by Leonardo da Vinci, or, more precisely, of wooden machines built according to the drawings left by Leonardo. The original aim of this project was to build a virtual museum where several visitors could "go together". The application, an award winner at the Museum & Web Conference (New Orleans 1999), allowed the exploration of a building vaguely representing the actual museum. A "guide" playing the role of "Leonardo" had the task of guiding visitors through the virtual rooms.

### SEE – Shrine Educational Experience

A collaborative project was begun in 2001 with the HOC laboratory at the Polytechnic of Milan and the Israel Museum, Jerusalem to develop a virtual 3D application presenting the Shrine of the Book: a wing of the Museum preserving the Dead Sea Scrolls, ancient Hebrew manuscripts containing the earliest known version of the Bible and the writings of a religious community that lived in Qumran, near the Dead Sea, between the second century BC and 68 AD. The project had strong educational goals and targeted an international audience. It was decided to design a learning experience, targeting middle and high school students potentially from all over the world. The cultural goal focused on encouraging students to compare the culture of the Qumran community with their own and that of other participants. The virtual experience had to be educational, but also engaging: it thus included both cultural discussions and games. Students were organized in two teams (two classes against two, from four different geographical areas) that engaged in a playful competition based on cultural quizzes and assignments. The 3D environment had to reproduce the actual museum building of the Shrine of the Book, because its architecture embodies a number of important symbolic meanings.

SEE involved 20 classes of middle and high school students from Italy, Israel and Belgium and again results were very satisfactory. Detailed accounts of both evaluation phases can be found in Di Blas, Paolini and Poggi (2005). Although the SEE experience was discontinued (for a number of organizational reasons), two new projects started in 2004 following its success: Stori@Lombardia (funded by the Regional Government of Lombardy, Italy) and Learning@Europe (developed in collaboration with Accenture International Foundation and Fondazione Italiana Accenture).

### Stori@Lombardia

Stori@Lombardia was intended to promote local cultures and identities within the Italian region of Lombardy (around Milan). It was again targeted at middle and high school students, but only in Lombardy schools. What might students from towns no more than a few miles apart have to tell each other? What unique perspectives would each of them be able to contribute? In fact, every town of medium-large size in Lombardy was a city-state in the Middle Ages: different towns belonged to different leagues of communes and fought against each other, allied with the German Emperor or rebelling against him. Therefore, it is interesting for citizens of Milan to meet online students from Como to discuss medieval history: by researching their local sources, they will find, for example, that Emperor Frederick I was a merciless enemy of Milan and a hero of Como, builder of its city walls and important local monuments.

This project involved the creation of a new set of documents in Italian (again in the form of interviews with experts plus maps, chronologies, and summaries) for background knowledge about each town's medieval history, and an ad hoc virtual environment representing the court and dungeons of a medieval castle; the games took place in a labyrinth shaped like a medieval village and in the field outside the castle's walls.

## Learning@Europe

Learning@Europe (Di Blas, Poggi & Torrebruno, 2006) is a collaborative web application fully developed using WebTalk framework developed jointly by GSALab (Graphics and Software Architectures Laboratory) at the University of Salento and the Hoc Laboratory (Hypermedia Open Center) at the Polytechnic of Milan, and has been tested for three years with more than 2000 users. L@E is structured on a six- to seven-week experience: four classes of students, aged fifteen to nineteen, from different European countries, take part in a cultural competition (two classes against two). Students meet together four times on a shared online 3D environment accessible over the Internet: the four cooperative sessions are distributed across about two months, each session lasting about one hour. Two students per class are represented in the 3D world by "avatars" (see Figure 2). The environment's advanced features foster interaction and cooperation among students. Meetings are devoted to cooperative activities, such as discussions (Figure 2) and games. Students meet their peers from different geographical areas, discuss relevant cultural matters with them, and play with them in the virtual world, divided into two teams; all games are based on cultural riddles requiring an accurate knowledge of the subject matter; competition is a powerful motivator, adding excitement to the experience. Students are also encouraged to work together with their remote team members, strengthening ties with them.

To achieve in-depth comprehension of the cultural themes proposed, further educational activities are performed in the intervals between a session in the virtual world and the following:

*Figure 2. Avatars presenting their countries*

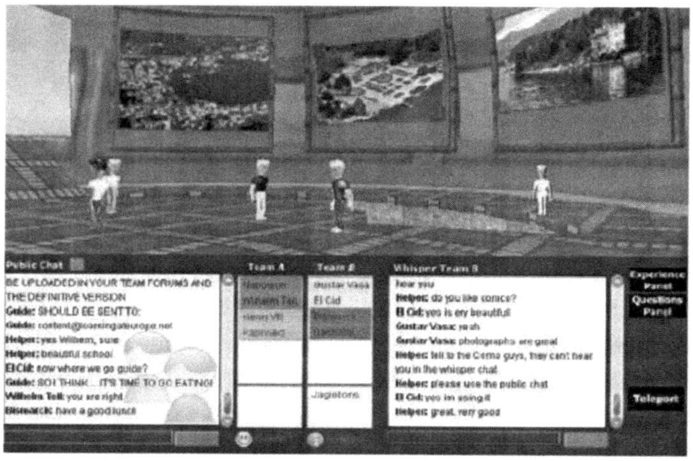

students are asked to study a set of contents – in the format of interviews with international experts – and to prepare homework in collaboration with their team members by doing some research; for example, they may have to relate a significant historical issue to its present consequences and analyze the traces left in their local context; comparing their research with the works of the other students, they should gain an interesting picture of how differently the same process is regarded from different European perspectives.

### Learning@SocialSports

In 2006 a new collaboration started with Fondazione Italiana Accenture and Verde Sport (of the Benetton group) within a Master's in Sport Business Strategies. The aim of the new project, Learning@SocialSport, was to bring together young athletes (aged thirteen to nineteen) from different sports clubs around Italy to reflect on the social value of sport. Among the less explicit goals was the intention to educate their trainers and parents through the young participants, promoting dialog and raising awareness about the benefits and dangers of sports in terms of personality development, ethical issues, social integration, and "healthy" attitudes of families, trainers, and institutions towards young people practicing sports. The setting for this new 3D-world experience – sport clubs, gyms and sport associations – differs from schools in many important ways: the time available is even shorter, because participants meet for practice only a few hours a week and the time used for the project cannot be considered – as it is in schools – an equally effective alternative to regular practice. L@SS involved in its first edition (January-March 2007) approximately 90 young athletes aged thirteen to eighteen, from eight sports associations in Italy. The format has again proved highly engaging and capable of stimulating reflection and changing attitudes about the topics discussed (Poggi & Torrebruno 2007). The 2008 edition is currently under evaluation.

## CONSIDERATIONS

The format for each project in which we have participated was based on a storyboard taking into account the learner feedbacks and the acquired experiences. The initial format of SEE - Shrine Educational Experience - was based on the experience acquired with Virtual Leonardo: testing showed that users enjoyed meeting other users and chatting with them; they spent an average of 55 minutes in the 3D environment if they met someone else, as opposed to an average of five minutes when they did not meet anyone (Barbieri & Paolini, 2000). They rarely engaged, however, in in-depth cultural discussions about virtual objects on display: conversations were generally shallow and not focused on cultural content. This brought significant innovations in SEE: users had to read contents before meeting and the activities in each cooperative session were carefully planned in advance. Being aimed at schools, SEE was designed with four main educational goals: providing high-quality content, favoring cross-cultural exchange, motivating students through interaction with remote peers, and improving their technological skills. After preliminary tests in seven schools in 2002, a first version of the storyboard was defined in spring 2003 (Figure 3). Observations conducted in every school led to a number of refinements implemented in the subsequent phase, in spring 2004, then inherited by L@E (Figure 3). The main innovations included a Virtual Gym for students to train before the sessions, collaboration via email with team partners to produce the final homework, and a preliminary collaborative task: the Team Presentation. Evaluation helped with identifying additional educational benefits: improvements of English and skills for group work, increased motivation at school, exploration of new learning methods, improved attitude at school.

The two new projects which started in 2004, L@E and S@L, were based on the SEE storyboard, with two new features: an additional chat panel without 3D graphics, to tackle contents in more

*Figure 3. Storyboard evolution over the years*

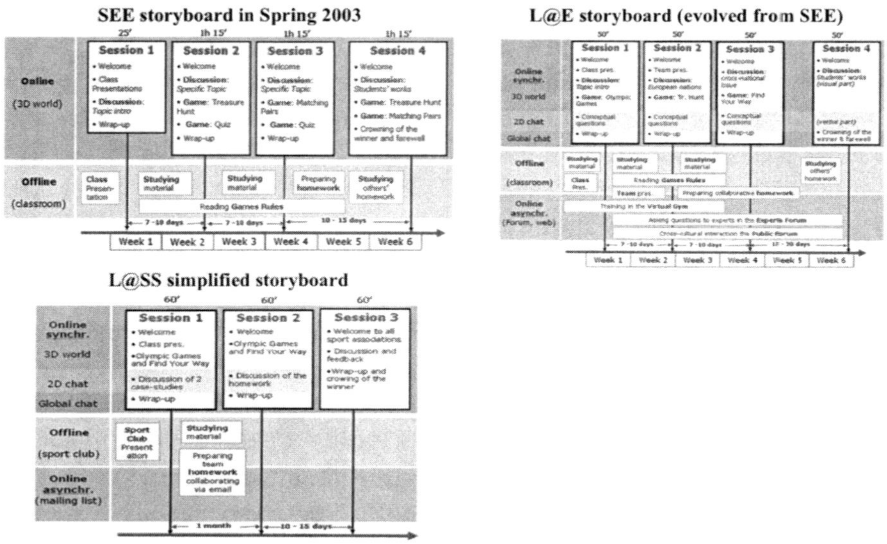


depth with open-ended conceptual questions and to involve more users hands-on, and a set of forums, to collaborate with remote team partners and ask questions of the authors of the contents. As explained above, the storyboard of L@SS was simplified in many respects (Figure 3).

## The Key Aspect: Awareness

All the previous applications were developed using the Webtalk/OpenWebTalk framework which provided a proper support for the pedagogic format in the projects. Our first aim was to define an XML-based declarative framework managing the 3D e-learning collaboration through a language able to support the elementary rules for creation of collaborative games and to generate, through a fast prototype system, a large number of collaborative experiences.

Moreover, traditional (standalone and web-based) collaborative learning systems do not fully engage the users (especially undergraduate students), since they cannot discover activities of peers until they sit in front of the computer and connect to the Internet. That is, a student who issues a learning activity cannot be certain that their peers are aware of the activity. Students can only interact with and affect the workspace, which is virtually connected on the Internet. This lack of awareness may lead to doubt and inefficient interaction among students. As the lack of complete engagement may prevent positive interdependence and promotive interaction, many web-based collaborative learning environments are unlikely to have the same quality of service as a face-to-face learning environment.

The unawareness of collaborative activity can be eliminated by informing students of the context of collaborative activity in the Internet workspace, regardless of whether students are connected to the Internet. Context information is defined as any information for characterizing an entity that is considered relevant to the interaction between a user and an application. Many applications, such as mobile context-aware tour guides (Abowd et al., 1997), have demonstrated the utility of context-awareness. Therefore, in a web-based collaborative learning activity, students should be given the contextual information to make them aware of learning activity on the Internet. Moreover, web-based collaborative learning systems must consider the high mobility of students to enhance the learning activity awareness throughout the system.

Thus, "Awareness" plays an important role in CSCW systems. According to Greenberg, Gutwin and Cockbum (1995), there are four different kinds of "awareness" in CSCW traditional systems:

- *Workspace awareness* is about who is present in the workspace, where they are, and what they are doing;
- *Informal awareness* means the general sense of who is around and what they are depending on;
- *Social awareness* is the information that a person maintains about others in a social or conversational context;
- *Group-structured awareness* involves knowledge about such things as people's roles and responsibilities, their positions on an issue, their status, and group process.

The main aspect in a collaborative work is the *workspace awareness,* that is, the instantaneous perception to interact within a shared workspace with one or more users. The basic meaning of awareness in traditional collaborative systems is to know who the collaborators are, what they are doing, what they have done and what they want to do. In other words, in WYSIWIS (What You See Is What I See) CVE systems, awareness is achieved by sharing the same conception of space (the shared stage where users move) and the same notion of time, that is, the instantaneous event propagations within the virtual world (avatars' movements, environment reactions to each action performed, etc.).

The WYSIWIS approach, intrinsically emphasizing that collaboration requires commonalities among the collaborators, does not suit all situations characterized by considerable technological differences, above all if the collaboration has to be achieved when users use different communication and work devices (i.e. desktop computer vs. mobile devices) and different space-temporal notions (real world for mobile users vs virtual world for stationary users).

Personalized groupware should offer a system that conforms to the individual need of participants and groups. Chang and colleagues (1995) mentioned a WYSINWIS (What You See Is NOT What I See) style in their collaborative writing tool for the user's own viewing spaces. In line with Haibin Zhu (2004), we suggest the terminology WYSINWIS to emphasize the differences among peoples' requirement for different inputs and outputs.

We think that an effective collaboration can be achieved even between heterogeneous (technologically different) sub-environments, if users can share similar notions of space and time:

- *time*: some of the events in one of the sub-environments can be propagated in all other sub-environments, thus giving a sense of time synchronicity between them;
- *space*: the sense of mutual position given in a generic 3D CVE by the avatar's virtual world coordinates can be associated and translated into the real-world position for mobile users.

In other words, mobile users while moving could be provided with a geo-position tracker (i.e. a simple GPS receiver), which gathers data about their geo-referred position; this information is then forwarded to the central communication system, which takes care of the maintenance and the consistency of the shared state. In this way also the 3D sub-environment could be aware of the *presence* of mobile users, for example, having a 2D map of their position added to the CVE. On the other hand, mobile users can be kept informed of 3D CVE virtual users in a huge number of ways, mainly depending on the device capabilities and the degree of connectivity and bandwidth available (flat or dial up, broadband UMTS or simply GPRS).

Moreover, most of the products, commercial or research-derived, that were used in the collaboration in a mixed environment were mere applications rather than flexible frameworks: they required extensive reprogramming for use in different situations and for different purposes, being also inherently oriented towards code construction in a *code-centered* fashion.

We wanted, instead, to create a "format" that could be used over and over, designing our application in a declarative way and using simple authoring tools, thus using a declarative approach since the environment can be automatically generated from these declarative descriptions.

Our next main goals were to:

- design a *flexible collaborative framework* able to integrate different devices making multiple heterogeneous users collaborate together.
- define and implement a mobile learning experience (UbiCrossWords) in order to test the above framework.
- define a language for an abstract representation (a modeling language) of a generic learning experience.

Then we developed an extension of the WebTalk/OpenWebtalk Framework in order to support the collaboration among mobile people. This framework was called MobileWebTalk and it was our first attempt to support awareness in the CSCW systems.

## THE REFERENCE FRAMEWORK: OPENWEBTALK/MOBILEWEBTALK

As we said before, over the years our research group has developed some 3D multi-user applications that have evolved towards different applicative platforms like OpenWebTalk and MobileWebTalk, characterized by:

- flexibility: they can be used in several applicative domains (simulation, learning, training, etc.).
- ease of configuration: they can be customized by simply editing a sort of scene graph.
- support and task integration for both stationary and mobile users.

OpenWebTalk and MobileWebtalk are based on the same paradigms:

- *Interaction Control Model* to drive the collaboration between users and the virtual world.
- *XML formal description* of either the static properties or the dynamic ones of the virtual environment.

The development of these systems sprang from the need to create 3D collaborative learning experiences with significant differences (in terms of world geometries, interactive objects, textures, collaboration features, etc). For each different application different versions were needed (e.g. different content and different quizzes for different groups of users) to prepare specific experiences. Flexibility and configurability were revealed, therefore, to be crucial requirements. Moreover, in order to expand the number of users, we needed to improve both performance and reliability whilst decreasing, if possible, requirements on the connection bandwidth.

To endow our virtual environment with a strong sense of virtual presence, in addition to the full graphic-driven paradigm, the overall application provides a set of interaction features to drive collaboration among users in the specific way the designer intends it to do so. Our frameworks propose a declarative format to reduce the need for programming for non-expert designers of collaborative experiences. For this reason we examined the major issues concerned in the formal description of a collaborative virtual environment from both a static point of view, in terms of what the virtual world is like when it is generated, and from a dynamic point of view, in terms of how it can evolve during the collaborative sessions through a declarative description of the Event Conditioned Actions (ECA) that can be performed in it. We also manage "collaborative metaphors" that we can define as a set of basic rules which describe different modalities of interaction between users and between the users and the environment. These rules encompass various aspects, such as the way users can gather in groups, the possible ways of chatting to each other, how to navigate in the virtual space, how to visualize the world and objects, etc. Taking decisions on all these aspects shapes a collaborative situation.

The architectural levels that all WebTalk applications share (i.e. OpenWebTak and MobileWebTalk) are composed of:

- **scene graph and behavior schema**: coded through XML-Schema it represents the structure of a valid WebTalk application compliant XML-instance, where the elements composing XML-instances, hierarchical rules between elements and supported data types, have been defined.
- **scene graph and behavior prototype**: an XML document representing the skeleton of a WebTalk collaborative session where the designer has already fixed geometries forming the virtual environment as well as the main user interaction rules.
- **scene graph and behavior instance**: the final WebTalk XML-instance completed with all information and content depending on the specific context (specific users involved, specific target of the experience, particular topics given).

When an XML instance is generated, the system is ready to start a collaborative session. The XML file is sent (at run time) to the clients' runtime environment, which interprets the declarations and provides the instance with the right components taken from a library (on the one hand, it instances the right 3D models in the world, and on the other, it sets up the collaboration rules that will govern the shared experience).

## The Framework for Stationary People: OpenWebTalk

OpenWebTalk is a framework to support high performance and high-resolution 3D real-time collaborative experiences. The OpenWebTalk architecture is based on a client/server paradigm and exploits an application server hosting a Web Server for static and dynamic contents and a server-side daemon (the OpenWebTalk server communication manager) for sharing data in co-operative and distributed applications. Whereas the server is listening to client connections and distributing events between the participants, maintaining a centralized state repository, the client side is composed of an application which runs both the rendering and the collaboration modules. The collaboration logic, via the event and behavior manager, detects every event generated in the 3D interface and forwards them, through the OpenWebTalk Communication Protocol, to the server. Likewise, any other events generated at the same moment by other clients connected to the same environment are distributed by the Server Communication Manager to the Client's Communication Manager on the client side, which manages them by running the right action. Users can thus see each other's avatars and objects moving and operating in response to the events and to the 3D world solicitation, collaborating with each other during the online sessions. The whole system architecture has been developed using C++.NET 2005, built up around the MVC (Model View Controller) design pattern in which the model represents the shared world state, the view represents each client application, and the controller is the programming logic that creates and regulates each end-user GUI (Graphical User Interface) as well as the shared environment.

Our framework is based on features and functionalities that optimize rendering performance through the customization of the G3D rendering module, an open source 3D engine (http://g3d-cpp.sourceforge.net). In the render module we introduced optimization that can be grouped into two different classes:

- image quality optimizations.
- performances optimizations.

In the image quality optimization class, we grouped all the optimizations that concern the rendered-frame quality from a qualitative perspective: the render module dynamically selects the right mix of optimizations to dynamically balance quality with performance. Our renderer module uses bump mapping, and per-pixel and per-vertex rendering optimization.

Level of detail and Frustum culling optimization are used during the performance optimizations to improve the rendering speed (measured in frames per second [FPS]). Another important feature of our framework is the ability to manage physics. It is obtained by the OWT physics engine that is based on an open-source module that calculates mechanics and collision inside the environments. This module is by Newton Dynamics (http://www.newtondynamics.com). Newton Game Dynamics is an integrated solution for real-time simulation of physics environments. It offers API that provides scene management, collision detection and dynamic behavior. The last functionality that characterizes our framework is the 3D positional audio feature. This feature manages the audio rendering into the 3D collaborative environments. The 3D audio is very important for improving the "virtual presence" during the sessions. Every sound source is rendered in its "real" position inside the virtual world, reproducing the sound that a real user would have heard in the real world.

## The Framework for Mobile People: MobileWebTalk (MoWeT)

While designing the extension to WebTalk framework for the support of heterogeneous users we wanted to keep the high degree of configurability that characterized OpenWebTalk in order to accomplish the highly flexible manner in which collaboration among real people happens. In fact, different groups require different functionalities according to their domain of collaboration, their culture of collaboration, the group processes they use, etc. It is therefore highly desirable that a groupware platform can be tailored to the specific groups using it. Flexibility in *MobileWebTalk* is achieved through a tailorable collaboration model based on a *collaborative metaphors* concept which is the basis of the WebTalk framework, as previously explained.

OpenWebTalk architecture offers a huge support for collaborative metaphors: we can set up in the XML world configuration file a set of specific behaviors that can be applied to a specific metaphor. Therefore we can select what behavior is applied to a specific shared object at a particular moment. When the specific collaborative metaphor is activated, the corresponding set of interaction rules takes effect, and every object uses the right behavior to interact with the "shared world". Thanks to the Collaborative Metaphor paradigm, we are able to manage complex interactions between entities in a virtual shared environment, specifying the current set of collaboration rules governing every aspect of the virtual world. Obviously, by defining a huge number of metaphors and melting them together, we can govern the collaborative environment, recreating the exact collaborative situation we want. We wanted to have the same flexibility in configuration of the mobile sub-environment, so we devised a collaboration model made of entities, actions and events that could have sense in real-world usage as they had in the CVE usage.

## MoWeT Platform

The MoWeT platform is designed to provide a flexible and configurable solution that implements integration between RFID and GPS localization technologies, allowing users to share the same experience in a collaborative environment. The collaboration is reached through a client/server architecture: the client application is conceived in a modular way, in order to separate the specific tasks into different classes; it manages map visualization, connections (GPS, RFID, Internet) and event/action interactions; the server, instead, keeps track of the user's movements and sends this information to other users.

On the client side we have two types of localization technologies, GPS for outdoor environments and RFID for indoor environments.

The application interacts with an RFID reader, usually Compact Flash (CF), and a GPS receiver, integrated or externally connected via USB or Bluetooth, to obtain geographic lat/lon coordinates. In the absence of GPS coverage, "position" can be detected through an RFID tag. Each tag, identified by its id, is associated with a pair of pre-calculated lat/lon coordinates. When MoWeT receives a signal from a tag, it identifies the user position and represents it on their own PDA. GPS has priority over RFID when both signals are detected; however, RFID technology can also be used in combination with GPS to increase accuracy in detecting the current position of the users.

In the first situation, MoWeT receives GPS data and loads (from Google Maps service) the right portion of the satellite-image, centering it in the device display according to the user position.

When a user moves in an indoor environment (i.e. a building), MoWeT automatically switches to the new coordinates associated with RFID tags and loads the map of the corresponding building. MoWeT detects the presence of the tag with the strongest signal and initiates the corresponding action, for example, displaying the user or a POI position on the map.

POIs can be either the specific points of interest related to the specific domain (i.e. e-learning scenario) or users themselves. Moreover they are often used like "hotspots" that the user, while moving, must find or achieve; in this case, MoWeT shows the users question forms, information forms, web pages, movies or multimedia contents. In this way, every hotspot has an associated *behavior*, or set of *events/actions*, for example, to display the route to the next POI in the guided tour.

The server-side aspect of the platform manages the mutual sharing of users' session state. For example, in the presence of connectivity like WiFi, GPRS, UMTS, etc., it is possible for users to view updated positions not only of themselves or POIs, but also of other users participating in the same navigation session. This information is shared through a server that handles receiving and forwarding of messages that signal the change of state and insure the consistency of the system.

## Platform Architecture Overview

The MoWeT core was conceived after the design pattern *Model View Controller* (MVC). In this way the management of interfaces (*View*) has been separated from the methods for the listening and management of events and actions (*Controller*) and from the business logic of the system (*Model*).

View and Controller carry out the management of screen and user interfaces, allowing, in particular, resources, interfaces and outputs from the model to be shown and listening to the events initiated or/and data entered by the user.

The main module is *Core Client* (see Figure 4), which incorporates the entire management and communication with View (Map Handler) /Controller (Object Handler) and hides other modules of the Model. Localization Manager switches between in-door (RF-Id) and out-door (GPS) localization systems. XML Handler load session declarative description and parse it, calling methods of Map Handler that are responsible for rendering the scene over the display.

*Figure 4. MoWeT engine modules*

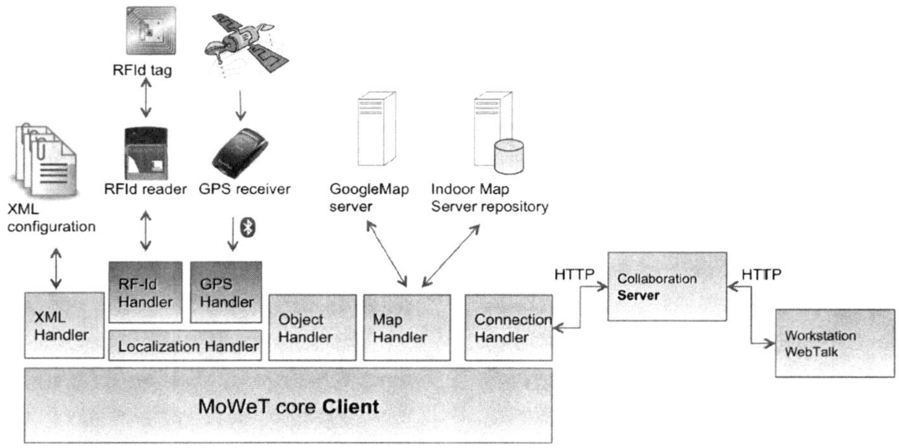


## Platform Customization

The customization of the platform for each specific domain is obtained through a generalization of the paradigm *Interaction Control Model* of OpenWebTalk (Barchetti, Bucciero, Mainetti & Santo Sabato, 2008). In fact it allows a set of "behaviors" to be applied that are made up of events and actions (the achievement of a hotspot and its effects are special cases of this) that drive and control the user interaction with both the environment and the PDA.

During a "navigation session" the user may trigger one or more events, such as *proximity* (*OnProximity*) or *leaving from* a hotspot (*OnDistance*), or be in the *presence of* an RfID tag (*OnPresence*). "Reengage radius" feature or "threshold handling" are techniques to avoid duplicate reads of the same event owing to signal instability.

The customization of MoWeT is obtained by using a formal declarative description stored in an XML configuration file. The XML file defines behaviors used in a session (actions that specify the rules to be used, events to handle, position of POIs, resources). The system is implemented in such a way as to allow users to choose different tours and different profiles (e.g. intermediate, expert, child and so on). According to tour type and user profile, a specific XML file is used by the system.

## RESULTS

The WebTalk/OpenWebTalk framework was used for the previously reviewed projects that involved only stationary students. Data collected over six years consistently show that the educational experiences structured according to the format previously presented are extremely engaging, educationally effective (on a wide range of educational benefits), and very versatile. Figure 5 summarizes data on participants in the four 3D-based educational programs since 2002.

### Education Benefits for Stationary People

Although large amounts of quantitative and qualitative data have been collected every year (through surveys of students and teachers, session reports by online tutors, focus groups with teachers, collection of chat logs, forum posts, and students' work, etc.), we present here only the evaluation of the global educational impact given by teachers after the last session, in order to offer

*Figure 5. Participants in educational programs based on shared 3D worlds since 2002*

| | Shrine Educational Nov. 2002 - May 2004 | Stori@Lombardia Nov. 2004 - June 06 | Learning@Europe Mar. 2005 – Feb. 2008 | Learning@SocialSport 25 Jan. - 12 Mar. 2007 | TOTAL |
|---|---|---|---|---|---|
| **Teachers** | **80** | **62** | **354** | **9** (trainers) | **505** |
| **Students** | **1480** (12-19 years old) | **1116** (12-19 years old) | **6130** (15-19 years old) | **90** (athletes 12-19 years old) | **8816** |
| **Classes** | **69** | **60** | **292** | **16** (groups of 6 athletes) | **437** |
| **Schools** | **38** | **42** | **188** | **8** (sport associations) | **276** |
| **Towns** | **23** | **29** | **173** | **7** | **232** |
| **Countries** | **3** (Italy, Israel, Belgium) | **1** (Italy) | **19** (1) | **1** (Italy) | **20** |
| **Sessions** | **71** | **60** | **296** | **17** | **444** |
| **Experiences** | **17** | **15** | **74** | **4** | **110** |

an overview of each program's results across the years. Data presented in other works (Di Blas et al., 2005; Di Blas et al., 2006) offer details of the benefits achieved: deeper understanding of the subject, high engagement, improved attitudes, development of skills in technologies and English, group work, etc. Although each teacher may find one aspect more important than the rest, all find the experience valuable in that it provides a wide range of benefits through one set of activities. Negative ratings are rarely given by more than 5% of teachers and instructors (see graphs below), whereas satisfied and extremely satisfied educators are usually in the 60 to 70% range, but can be anything from 50 to 90%. On the basis of the evaluations consistently given by teachers over the years (and often discussed and ratified by focus groups of teachers at the end of each year), we conclude that the educational format presented in this paper is pedagogically effective.

## A Testing Scenario for Mobile People

The MobileWebtalk framework that involved stationary and mobile people was evaluated in a user test at the University of Salento (Italy) in 2006; rooms used for the indoor test were covered by a good wireless LAN signal.

### Participants

A total of 36 students volunteered to participate in three different test sessions. They were divided in two different teams composed of six students (two in the desktop 3D environment, two playing as chat users, two with the mobile device). They were aged between nineteen and 24 years old. They were all experienced computer users. The game topic was university life.

### The Game

The game consisted in compiling a collaborative crossword puzzle and finding the definitions in different ways:

- the users with the 3D desktop, to gain their definitions, participated in a treasure hunt to find the hidden objects in the virtual environment representing some of the rooms of the Innovation Engineering Dept.;
- chat users were asked to answer a set of questions related to the university's courses (such as computer science questions);
- mobile users (each user had a mobile device connected through the wireless connection to the shared environment) were asked to perform a list of tasks, each one consisting of a location they had to find and a related question.

*Figure 6. Overall results of the interviews about the learning projects*

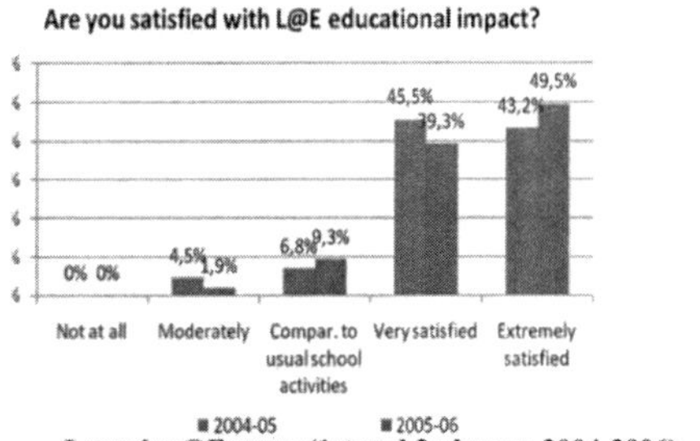


**Learning@Europe (1st and 2nd year: 2004-2006)**
**2004-05:** 44 responses, representing 91.7% of teachers
Average score: 4.27 out of 5
**2005-06:** 107 responses, representing 68.6% of teachers
Average score: 4.36 out of 5

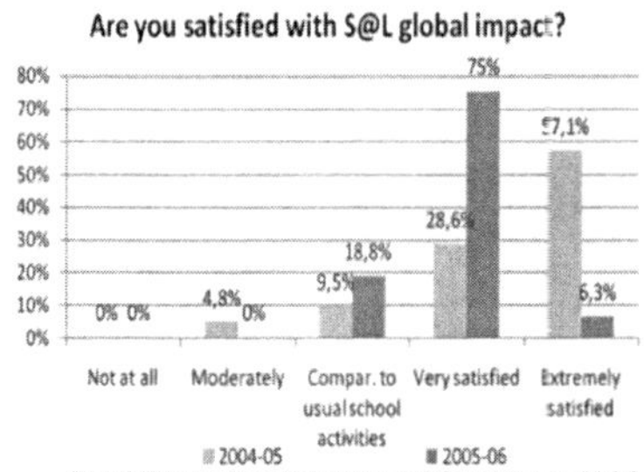


**Stori@Lombardia (1st and 2nd year: 2004-2006)**
**2004-05:** 21 responses, representing 58.3% of teachers
Average score: 4.38 out of 5
**2005-06:** 16 responses, representing 66.7% of teachers
Average score: 3.87 out of 5

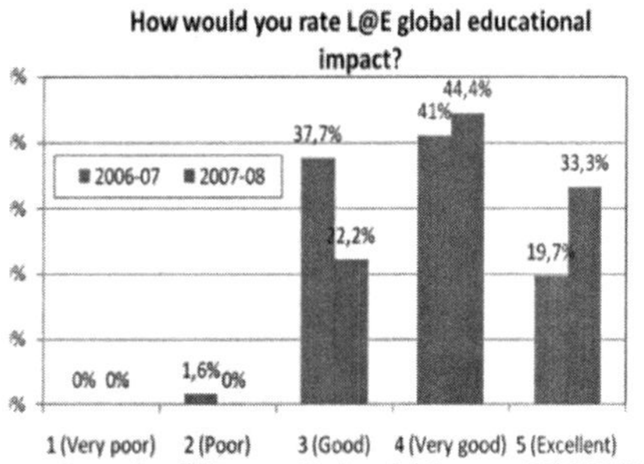


**Learning@Europe (3rd and 4th year: 2006-2008)**
**2006-07:** 61 responses, representing 76.3% of teachers
Average score: 3.79 out of 5
**2007-08:** 9 responses, representing 87.5% of teachers
Average score: 4.11 out of 5

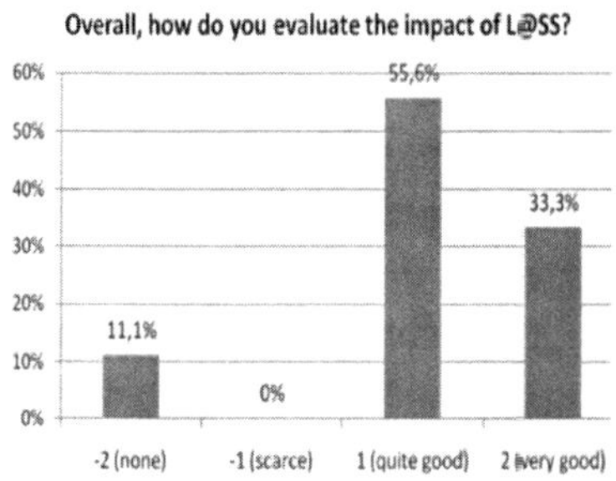


**Learning@SocialSport (1st year: 2006-07)**
9 responses, representing 100% of trainers
Average score: +1 (range: -2 to +2)

All the users involved in the game could communicate with others using the chat. The game lasted approximately 60 min. During this time, the students had the opportunity to answer the questions and to chat with other students in their team. At the end of each game, each player was given a questionnaire.

The questionnaire contained fifteen questions that could be clustered into three sections: the first section asked the students how satisfied they were with their introduction to the game; the second section collected data on the motivational aspects of the game; the third section focused on the usability of individual functions.

All the game phases were governed by expert super-users (guides) who took care to keep interest and action alive and provide some help to participants.

## Discussion Framework

The scenario describes the global rules. Each player has to solve the tasks (actions, questions, etc.) and ultimately learn. The real-time collaborative framework gives direct feedback on the current status in the game and on the outcome achieved so far. Conflicts and competition are realized through the opportunity to gain points (by solving tasks or catching others) against the opponent team. Playing in groups means there is interaction in the game. This effect is additionally supported by the chat function. The representation is realized through implementation of the WYSINWIS paradigm: the orientation is achieved for 3D online users through the 3D virtual model in which they play, for mobile users through the digital map; there are no orientation issues for mere chat users. These structural elements characterized our game and should engage the player.

### Results

We asked the participants whether it was fun to play the game. Most of the students (ten of the twelve) indicated that they liked it and would play it again any time. Two participants liked it, but thought playing it once was enough. Nobody chose the option "It was a waste of time". Enthusiastic comments in the open questions support these findings. Therefore the game is entertaining and students like to play it. Then the students were asked to vote for the three most significant game key issues from a technical point of view. They could select up to three answers. The figure below shows the results.

## FUTURE RESEARCH DIRECTIONS

Traditionally, experiences in the CVE field have been the result of several iterations based on the implementation aspects of the system without a structured approach. Such approach would be useful in driving the user (although not expert in a specific applicative domain) in the definition of key points, such as general goals of the collaboration, organizational issues, pedagogical strategies, etc. before discussion of a development phase.

Moreover, the need for a structured approach to CVE design and implementation is a necessary condition when there are different stakeholder types involved (users, experience designers, 3D designers, software architects), different potential devices (smartphones, net-books, notebooks, wearable computers, workstation PC, PDAs, etc.) and the virtual environment can be easily customized for different application domains such as e-learning, collaborative games and so on. The structured approach to CVE design is useful if we think of a virtual environment generation engine that allows us to obtain different CVE customizations to automatically configure different devices.

This structured approach is the result of an abstraction process of several previous experiences in the CVE field, a conceptual modeling as base for the definition of a language able to define a generic collaborative session. The language must allow us to obtain, in a simple and intuitive way, the virtual environment for the selected user type and device, by using the sort of interpreter that understands the conceptual model generated.

The abstraction process must be driven by two main requirements:

- the language must be easy to learn and to teach to non-technical users.

*Figure 7. Most important positive and negative aspects of the experience*

| *Most important positive aspects (maximum three choices)* | | *Most important negative aspects (maximum three choices)* | |
|---|---|---|---|
| The position tracking on a map is a significant value added during the game. | 12 | The difficult typing of text on a mobile device has effectively hindered me in sending chat messages | 2 |
| This game is more interesting than a static game. | 8 | The mobile screen could not be read in e conditions | 2 |
| The opportunity to explore independently the collaborative world is a value added | 6 | I had great difficulty in keeping an overview of different visualizations | 1 |
| The user interface was friendly and helped the play | 3 | The difficult typing of text on a mobile device has effectively hindered me in sending chat messages | 2 |

- the language must represent all the aspects of a heterogeneous collaborative virtual environment that allows collaboration using different devices and is easy to use for the specific application domain.

In answer to the first requirement it is important to identify a suitable metaphor and this means translating concepts that characterize virtual environment into concepts more understandable by the users of the language. It is important to have a clear idea of the concepts useful for describing a collaborative virtual session and how these concepts are related. Briefly, it is useful to design a conceptual map with its main goal being CVE description.

Given the several aspects that define a virtual environment, the language will be based on different abstraction levels; each of them pays attention to a specific aspect of the virtual collaborative session. It is important, for example, to separate the static and dynamic aspects. Static aspects are useful for representing the environment and all its components that do not change during collaboration between users. Dynamic aspects may be influenced by several other aspects during the collaboration between users.

In this way, it should be possible to define a structure made up of a set of core components that will be the languages' primitives to be used to define a specific virtual environment description oriented to the specific goal and to the specific device.

The CVE conceptual map that has been derived is shown in Figure 8.

In the picture two different types of concepts are represented: static (blue) and dynamic (orange). There is the concept of "time", which defines the start and end time and the concept of the people (main element of the conceptual map).

At this point (and this is one of our future works) it is possible to define a set of stencils to be associated with each element of the conceptual map: providing a set of stencils for the conceptual map allows the use of the language to be simplified.

The conceptual map needs a refinement step to define the properties of each element. These properties, when we define a specific collaborative

*Figure 8. CVE conceptual map*

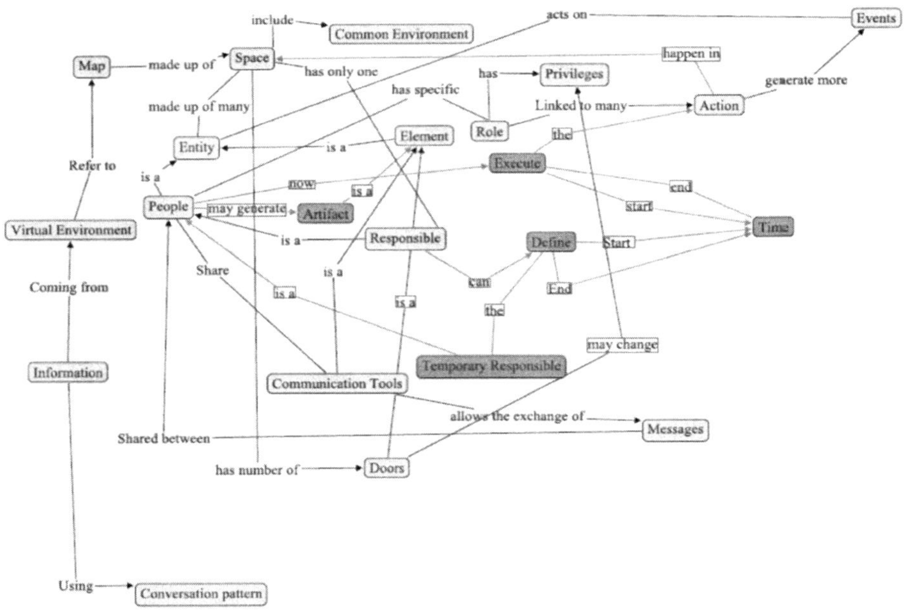

virtual environment using the conceptual map, will be filled by different types of users.

There are two different types of properties:

- domain experts, who define the most important aspects of the CVE such as the people of the environment, the communication tools and so on.
- technical user experts in the implementation of CVE, who will add details such as data about the definition of the communication systems and so on. These aspects may change depending on the device used for the CVE.

The real importance of the language lies in the possibility of making the design decisions machine-readable. A language is not useful if it is not related to a tool that helps the user in the modeling of a session and makes it machine-readable and thus understandable by the engine that will generate the virtual environment designed.

To do this, the starting-point should be the definition of a meta-model that represents a 1:1 mapping with the language primitives (coming from the conceptual model). The design of the specific collaborative session will be a specific instance of the generated meta-model.

For the complexity of the conceptual model and the language that comes from it, an ontological language seems to be the best choice.

Starting from these considerations, our future work will be to define in detail both a language and a tool that cover the complexity of the language and that allow us to obtain a machine-readable version of the design.

## CONCLUSION

In this chapter we described the experiences we gained during the years we spent developing a lot of 3D collaborative applications for education purposes. These experiences have shown the need to take into account not only the pedagogical and educational aspects related to the specific experience, but also the conceptual, design and implementative aspects of a generic experience that can involve stationary and mobile people.

In sum, our main research goals addressed:

- fast prototyping of contents through a flexible and configurable framework;
- collaboration management through the support of the definition of a complex set of rules (collaborative metaphors);
- definition of an architecture able to support different deployment configuration (p2p, publish/subscribe, client-server);
- giving support to different fruition devices;
- giving support to different technology infrastructure.

Analyzing these goals we realized that a language was necessary, a language able to provide the proper support for all involved specialists during the definition, design and implementation of a 3D collaborative e-learning experience.

In the past, we dealt with some of these aspects, providing an answer to the fast prototyping of contents and collaboration management with the OpenWebTalk framework. The support for different devices has been resolved with MobileWebTalk and its experimentation. Finally, the language and a tool that covers the complexity of the language supporting different deployment configuration, are subjects of further research.

The next step will be to evolve the platform to support extended interaction modalities, fully realizing the scenario of ubiquitous collaboration. The most challenging future work, starting from the lessons learned from the study of the similarities between these mobile and stationary systems, will be to define a methodology of abstract representation (a modeling language) of a generic "learning session", intended as a set of "core components".

This abstract description should be able to describe every learning session in terms of organizational situation and pedagogic paradigm, supplying a formal and machine-readable description to the technological platforms that will deliver it, thus finally arriving at the definition of a "learning session" description meta-model.

## ACKNOWLEDGMENT

We would like to thank HOC (Hypermedia Open Center) laboratory, Israel Museum, Lombardia Region, Accenture Fondation, Fondazione Italiana Accenture and MIUR (Ministero dell'Istruzione, dell'Università e della Ricerca) that have contributed in different ways to the success of each project described.

## REFERENCES

Abowd, G. D., Atkeson, C. G., Hong, J., Long, S., Kooper, R., & Pinkerton, M. (1997). Cyberguide A mobile context-aware tour guide. *ACM Wireless Networks*, *5*(3), 421–433. doi:10.1023/A:1019194325861

Baecker, R. M., Grudin, J., Buxton, W. A. S., & Greenberg, S. (1995). *Readings in human-computer interaction: Towards the year 2000* (2nd ed.). San Francisco: Morgan Kaufmann.

Barbieri, T. (2000). *Networked virtual environments for the web: The WebTalk-I and WebTalk-II architectures.* Paper presented at the IEEE for Computer Multimedia & Expo 2000 (ICME), New York(pp. 179-182).

Barbieri, T., & Paolini, P. (2000). Cooperative visits to WWW museum sites a year later: Evaluating the effect. In Bearman, D., & Trant, J. (Eds.), *Museums and the Web 2000* (pp. 173–178). Pittsburgh, PA: Archives & Museum Informatics.

Barbieri, T., & Paolini, P. (2001). *Broadcast and on-line cultural heritage: Reconstructing Leonardo's ideal city - from handwritten codexes to webtalk-II: a 3D collaborative virtual environment system.* Paper presented at the 2001 Conference on Virtual Reality, Archeology, and Cultural Heritage, Glyfada, Greece, (pp. 61-66).

Barchetti, U., Bucciero, A., Mainetti, L., & Santo Sabato, S. (2008). *OpenWebTalk: A framework to support high performances and high resolution 3D collaborative experiences.* Paper presented at INTED 2008 International Technology, Education and Development Conference, Valencia, Spain, (p. 112).

Burgos, D., Tattersall, C., & Koper, R. (2005). Repurposing existing generic games and simulations for e-learning. *Computers in Human Behavior*, *23*(6), 2656–2667. doi:10.1016/j.chb.2006.08.002

Castranova, E. (2001). *Virtual worlds: A first-hand account of market and society on the Cyberian frontier*. CESifo Working Paper Series No. 618. Available at SSRN: http://ssrn.com/abstract=2948

Chang, K. H., Gong, Y., Dollar, T., Gajiwala, S., Lee, B., & Wear, A. W. (1995). *On computer supported collaborative writing tools for distributed environments*. Paper presented at the ACM 23rd Conference on Computer Science, (pp. 222-229).

Damer, B. (1997). *Avatars! Exploring and building virtual worlds on the internet*. Berkeley, California: PeachPit Press.

Di Blas, N., Paolini, P., & Poggi, C. (2005). A virtual museum where students can learn. In Tan, L., & Subramaniam, R. (Eds.), *E-learning and Virtual Science Centers* (pp. 308–326). Hershey, PA: Idea Group.

Di Blas, N., Poggi, C., & Torrebruno, A. (2006). Collaboration and playful competition in a 3D educational virtual world: The Learning@Europe experience. In E. Pearson & P. Bohman (Eds.), *Proceedings of World Conference on Educational Multimedia, Hypermedia and Telecommunications 2006* (pp. 1191-1198).

Dirckinck-Holmfeld, L. (1990). *Kommunikation på trods og på tværs. Projektpædagogik og datamatkonferencer I fjernundervisning, Picnic–news no. 9*. Aalborg University.

Duridanov, L., & Simoff, S. (2007). 'Inner listening' as a basic principle for developing immersive virtual worlds. *Heidelberg Journal of Religions on the Internet*, 3(1).

Greenberg, S., Gutwin, C., & Cockbum, A. (1995). *Sharing fisheye views in relaxed-WYSIWIS groupware applications*. Paper presented at *Gruphics Inleface*, Toronto, Canada (pp. 28-38).

Haibin, Z. (2004). *From WYSIWIS to WISINWIS: role-based collaboration*. Paper presented at the 2004 IEEE International Conference on Systems, Man and Cybernetics, (pp. 5441-5446).

Illeris, K. (1981). *Modkvalificeringens pædagogik*. Denmark: Unge Pædagoger.

Johansen, R. (1988). *Groupware: Computer support for business teams*. New York: The Free Press.

Kahneman, D. (1971). *Attention and effort*. Englewood Cliffs, NJ: Prentice-Hall.

Koper, R., & Olivier, B. (2003). Representing the learning design of units of learning. *Journal of Educational Technology & Society*, *7*(3), 97–111. Retrieved from http://dspace.ou.nl/bitstream/1820/19/2/IMSLD-article%20v1p07-final.pdf.

Koper, R., Rodrígues-Artacho, M., Lefrere, P., Rawlings, A., & Rosmalen, P. (2002). *Survey of educational modelling languages (EMLs)*. Technical report, 1-79. Retrieved April 2009, from http://dspace.ou.nl/dspace/handle/1820/227.

Koper, R., & Tattersall, C. (2005). Preface to learning design: A handbook on modelling and delivering networked education and training. *Journal of Interactive Media in Education, 18*, 1–7.

Leeming, D. (2001). *A dictionary of Asian mythology* (Online, O. R., Ed.). London: Oxford University Press.

LindenLabs. (2009, 28 July 2009). *Economic Statistics*. Retrieved October 5, 2008, from http://secondlife.com/whatis/economy_stats.php.

Maher, M. L. (1999). Designing the virtual campus. *Design Studies*, *20*(4), 319–342. doi:10.1016/S0142-694X(98)00043-X

Morningstar, C., & Farmer, F. R. (1991). The lessons of Lucasfilm's Habitat. In Benedikt, M. (Ed.), *Cyberspace: First Steps*. Cambridge, MA: MIT Press.

Ondrejka, C. (2008). Education unleashed: Participatory culture, education, and innovation in second life. In Salen, K. (Ed.), *The ecology of games: Connecting youth, games, and learning* (pp. 229–252). Cambridge, MA: The MIT Press.

Paolini, P., Barbieri, T., Loiudice, P., Alonzo, F., Zanti, M., & Gaia, G. (1999). *Visiting a museum together: how to share a visit to a virtual world*. Paper presented at Museums&Web '99, New Orleans (USA), (pp. 27).

Poggi, C., & Torrebruno, A. (2007). From the Dead Sea scrolls to social sports, passing through European history: an effective pedagogical format based on 3D worlds. [Chesapeake, VA: AACE.]. *Proceedings of ED-Media*, *07*, 4240–4248.

Ritzema, T., & Harris, B. (2008). the use of second life for distance education. *Journal of Computing Sciences in Colleges*, *23*(6), 110–116.

Shen, H. H., & Dewan, P. (1992). *Access control for collaborative environments*. Paper presented at the 1992 ACM conference on Computer-supported Cooperative Work (pp. 51-58). New York: ACM Press.

Tashner, J. H., Riedl, R. E., & Bronack, S. C. (2005). *Virtual worlds: Further development of web-based teaching*. Paper presented at the Hawaii International Conference on Education, Honolulu, Hawaii, (pp. 4579-4588).

## KEY TERMS AND DEFINITIONS

**3D Collaborative Learning Experiences:** A scheduling of learning sessions that identify a learning experience. Any session is based on a storyboard. Any storyboard describes 3D collaborative environments where the users meet together and learn well-defined topics cooperating each other.

**3D Multi-User Applications:** Applications that provide a navigation of 3D environments supporting multi-user interaction.

**Awareness:** Awareness is the state or ability to perceive, to feel, or to be conscious of events, or objects. In our context (Heterogeneous Learning Environments), awareness regards the capability of each user to perceive the reality through different perspectives (i.e. 3D o mobile views).

**Collaborative Learning Systems:** learning systems that teach different topics involving users with different profile (i.e. learner, guide, Helper, teacher) in the same environment at the same moment.

**Collaborative Metaphor Paradigm:** A paradigm that helps to describe a set of rules regarding 3D users involved in a collaborative virtual environment. These sets of rules are named collaborative metaphor.

**Collaborative Virtual Environments:** Virtual environments where people meet (in a virtual way, of course) together and interact each other.

**Games:** Interactive experience among users where the main goal is to win according to well-defined rules.

**Heterogeneous Learning Environments:** learning environments for stationary and nomadic people.

**Stationary People:** Users that interact each other by PC and an Internet connection, without moving from own PC.

**Virtual Museum:** A 3D reconstruction of Museum with all objects that characterize the museum. A high resolution rendering of this reconstruction provides most fidelity and awareness during the navigation.

**Virtual Worlds:** 3D environments, users and objects that represents virtually different worlds.

# Chapter 13
# Usability of Interoperable Educational Tools in Language Teacher Education:
## The Nigerian Context

**A. N. Maduekwe**
*University of Lagos, Nigeria*

**A. O. Adeosun**
*University of Lagos, Nigeria*

## ABSTRACT

*This chapter presents a survey aimed at identifying the level of usability and applicability of interoperable educational tools in Nigeria language teacher education. The background summarizes the benefits of e-technologies in learning process. It then explores the different types of interoperable tools and e-competencies required by pre-service teachers in a second language context. Utilising one Nigerian University as a case study, the survey sampled one hundred teacher trainees selected from 300 level English Education students' of the Department of Arts and Social Science Education, University of Lagos, Nigeria. Two research questions were posited while two instruments- the Internet Application Competence Assignment (IACA) and the Internet Literacy Competency Questionnaire (ILCQ) were used in data sourcing. Analysis of data involved descriptive and inferential statistics. On the whole, findings show that 39% of the pre-service teachers operated within low level Internet skills, 49% were able to operate within higher competency level while the consolidated level skills posed the most difficult area of competency in usability of interoperable educational tools in language teacher education. The chapter ends with proposed solutions and recommendations for futuristic research directions within the context of global e-learning support.*

DOI: 10.4018/978-1-61692-791-2.ch013

## INTRODUCTION

The development and emergence of e-learning standards and interoperability frameworks have become a global phenomenon of great importance while the imperatives of the new technologies are increasingly manifest in pedagogical and andragogical - related issues. This thrust aligns with school restructuring efforts in countries like United States, India, France, Malaysia, Brazil, Egypt, Ivory Coast, Kenya, United Kingdom, Finland, New Zealand, Australia, Uganda, South Africa, Mali and Nigeria etc. All these countries have recently launched e-learning educational initiatives. Technologies and research on interoperability of e-learning tools have gone beyond mere rhetoric to being the pivot for problem solving, thinking, communication skills and learning standards. Learners use e-learning application tools to explore, analyse, exchange and present information responsibly and creatively. The potential classroom application of e-applications has constituted vital consideration in planning and provision of numerous opportunities for the masses, bringing people closer to each other than ever before, through inexpensive and instantaneous mode of communication. No serious nation can embrace the shift to global information-based education without aligning learning strategies with e-learning.

Numerous studies (Schwab, 1999; Owhotu, 2006; Ajelabi, 2006) have advocated that pre-service teachers should appreciate the potentials of technology as a cognitive instructional tool and endeavor to enter the teaching field ready to use technology to enhance language learning. In this context, the Nigerian National Policy on Education clearly acknowledges the need to establish its priorities in teacher education and e-technologies when it expressly affirms that the purpose of teacher education should be to "provide teacher trainees with the intellectual and professional background adequate for their assignment and make them adaptable to changing situations" (see 6 (d) p. 33). It further states that education shall continue to be highly rated in national development plans because education is the most important instrument of change. Underlying this policy is the core mission of inculcating in teachers the right values, the knowledge, attitudes, behaviours, skills and competence required by the individual for national survival, understanding the world around us and for the acquisition of mental, physical, social and technological skills needed to perform their tasks effectively. Any fundamental change in technological outlook of any society has to be preceded by an educational revolution (Maduekwe, 2006).

The aim of this chapter therefore is to determine the usability of interoperable educational tools in language teacher education with a view to highlighting specific problem areas that need to be addressed in English as second language (ESL) Nigeria context. The chapter is structured as follows:

- Background. This outlines and incorporates views of others into the topic.
- Profile of e-learning in Nigeria Education Context.
- Interoperable tools: Types.
- E-learning Competencies/Skill Required by Teacher Trainees.
- Methodology.
- Result.
- Discussion of the Main Points.
- Solutions and Recommendations.
- Future Research Directions
- Conclusion

## BACKGROUND

Researchers (Warshauer, 1995a; Scrimshaw, 1998; Luke, 2000; Durrant & Beavis, 2001; Akudolu, 2003; Isu, 2004; Maduekwe, 2005) indicate that the use of e- technologies in teaching and learning may improve student achievement in language study while others argue that technology use does not produce differences in students' test scores. (Kinzer & Risco; 1998 ; Odogwu, 2000) demonstrated that the collaborative, student-centred environment that the internet creates leads to more active learning. In order to ensure that the exciting opportunities afforded by computers and mediated communications provide meaningful experiences, teacher trainees must be aware of and must be actively involved in making the best possible use of what is available in their environment. Furthermore, researches into language classroom applications of electronic communication suggest positive impact on learning results (Leask & Pachler, 1999; Goodwyn, 2000; Leu & Kinzer, 2000, Abbot, 2001). They have also shown that for language learners, it is the communicative facilities of the Internet rather than the resources offered that are actively tapped by teachers and learners. For example (Nelson, 2001) compared the impact of Internet resources and CD-ROM in promoting student-centred active language learning. He stated that technology provided 'crucial support' to the students in several ways, such as creating authentic tasks, opening communication and collaboration avenues with experienced teachers and showing students' work to a larger audience by posting writing assignments on a class web page.

(Pratt & Sullivan's, 1994) study of the effects of computer networking on teaching English as second language (ESL) writing at the University of Puerto Rico revealed strong differences in participation patterns. 50% of the students participated once during oral discussion as compared to 100% students' participation in electronic discussion. Holistic rating in pre and post writing samples also showed marked improvement in the writing of students in the computer-networked classroom compared to those in the traditional classroom with oral discussion. (Rewinking & Rickman, 1998) examined students' vocabulary achievement when they read electronic texts that provided meanings of difficult words. They found that those students using the computer generated texts scored higher on follow-up tests than their peers who read print-based texts and used print based dictionaries and glossaries. Likewise, in a study of high school students, (Anderson & Horney, 1998) found that at risk readers who took advantage of electronic resources available on electronic texts, such as digitized pronunciation and digital pictures, scored higher on reading comprehension than their peers who did not use electronic textual aids. (Drucker,1994) study with the internet indicated that students' language showed a wider variety of discourse functions and a more sophisticated range of morph syntactic features, in addition to stimulating students' interests in one another which contributed to peer learning and decreased reliance on the teacher. He recommended that electronic discussions precede oral discussions as this allows focus on the ideas at hand without undue anxiety over articulation and delivery of ideas discussed.

Similar position effects were seen in studies across cultures. (Tella, 1992) studied the mail exchanges between Finnish and British youths. The research yielded the following results:

- Improved quality writing with a real purpose and international audience
- More versatile modes of writing from personal, expressive to argumentative genres
- Opportunity to practise language in open ended linguistic situations.
- More public and collaborative reading in addition to the use of different reading styles.
- A switch from teacher-centred large-group sponsored teaching to a more individualized and learner-centred working environments

According to (Haddad & Jurich, 2002) evidence from large studies and meta-analysis suggests the use of ICTs, particularly e-technologies, is correlated to positive academic outcomes, including higher test scores, better attitude towards schools and better understanding of concepts. They reported that in a longitudinal study of a state wide experiment with computers in language classroom, the low achieving students made the most gain.

From another perspective, (Hernes, 2002; Idowu, Adagunodo, & Idowu, 2004) examined the issue of equity in the utilization of e- learning tools in higher education. They observed that though schools are increasingly well equipped and connected to the Internet, considerable differences exist in the standards of usage along levels, type and gender lines. They confirmed that several studies document that boys are more active than girls in using the new technical tools. The same trend, they assert applies to teacher training and skills. Other researches (Kenning & Kenning, 1983; Collins, 1991; Eastman, 1996; Warshauer, 1996; Bates, 2001; Leu & Kinzer, 2000) have called for a shift away from the traditional framework for explaining the nature of language learning motivation to increased emphasis on the need for equity and refinement that bring the utilization of interoperable support tools to traditional teaching.

## Profile of E-Learning in Nigeria Education Context

There is, no doubt, that there are problems encountered in profiling e-learning progress in Nigeria's education context. Researches (Bassey, Umoren, Akuegwu, Ndida & Ntukidem 2007) have noted that there are a wide variety of different e-learning tools and practices in Nigeria. They stressed that the early exposure came 1987 with the launching of the National Policy on Computer literacy and Education 'so that Nigerian children at various levels of education must be brought in contact with the new and modern tool. What were obtainable then, they posited, was only aspects of ICT such as print, audio/video tapes and digital radios (World Bank, 2002). In February (2007) the Federal Ministry of Education created ICT department (Wiki Education, 2007). Support for expanding use and equity of media technologies in Nigeria education was brought to limelight by the launching of a National Policy on Information and Communication technology in 2001, followed by the creation of the National Information Technology Agency (NITDA) (Asogwa 2006, Olibie and Akudolu 2008).

Also, studies (Odunsaya 2002; Effie 2003; Shettima 2005; Maduekwe 2006; Busari 2006; Salawudeen 2006; Asoqwo 2006; Buganje, 2007) have dealt extensively with issues concerning the access and utility of interoperable tools in education in Nigeria's higher education. (Salawudeen, 2006) for instance, contended that e-learning techniques mostly adopted by Nigerian institutions are in prepared lectures on CD-ROM. He concluded that mostly the students took the challenge upon themselves to go to the public internet cafes where there exist diverse attentions because of people with diverse interest on the net at the same time. The bandwidth shared on various systems at the cafes is very low hence; a multimedia interactive lecture is not obtainable because of low bandwidth. The population of students is enormous and the facilities inadequate. Though most of the institutions of higher learning in Nigeria have started building their ICT centres, the focus is mainly to put up an internet facility alone without considering other components that make up e-learning centres.

(Bassey, Umoren, Akuegwu, Udida and Ntukiden 2007) pointed out that significant investment is being made in computer technologies to support functions such as the extension of programmes to distant sites, teaching, learning, research and other management functions. They lamented that the government has in recent past evolved and funded e-policy programmes aimed at providing e-learning facilities in higher education in Nigeria. This bold step they observed was not sustained and as such, further development of e-learning technology has attracted a not-so-good attention.

(Buganje, 2007) lamented that e-learning is very minimal in our language curriculum.

According to him, Internet connectivity in our institutions still rely on small cafes owned by private individuals. For e-learning to succeed in a developing country like Nigeria, it needs to build on the existence of infrastructure, along with some degree of connectivity (Gunawardana, 2006; Adeya, Oyelara- Oyeyinka, 2006). Additionally, (Owhotu, 2009) indicated that the major constraints to harnessing Nigeria's e-tool potential are the lack of energy infrastructure and alternative technologies. Poor infrastructure in teacher training institutions he observed negates the demands of information and knowledge societies in terms of employment and entrepreneurship among the post basic, secondary and tertiary level graduates.

In the same view (Uwadia, 2000) asserted that the problems encountered by Internet usage in teacher education include, slow access speed, poor internet connection, poor power supply, difficulty in finding relevant information and time available for internet use. (Ushie, Beshel, Asanya, & Inyang, 2008) examined the use of internet services by academic staff in Federal Colleges of Education in Nigeria. Results showed that the World Wide Web and e-mail were the most popular e-tools used by academic staff. He noted that academic staff uses Internet services mainly to write academic articles and publications for promotions. Also, the results confirmed that academic staffs were faced with many constraints such as lack of Internet services and inadequate knowledge of the use of the Internet.

(Maduekwe, 2004; 2006) asserted that the globalizing economy of the 21$^{st}$ century demands that language teacher trainees should be engaged with a variety of multimedia materials to improve academic learning. She further claimed that it is in this particular area that the use of the Internet in the teaching and learning process constitutes a major breakthrough that is becoming even more critical for teacher training.

(Busari, 2006) submited that an average trainee hose access to computer is very limited will surely be limited in intensity, scope and innovation. Educational technology centres must create the awareness of their roles and offer opportunities to students. The archaic gadgets, fillings and slides must be modernised creatively to meet the current needs of teacher education programmes. In the same vein, (Uwadie, 2000) warned that without adequate utilisation of technological tools, teachers will find it extremely difficult to deliver appropriate education and training to their students at all levels. She further asserted that if the situation does not change, schools will be graduating illiterates. The current technological revolution in education demands strong teacher training to implement new technology programmes (Perelman, 1990). If urgent measures are not taken to solve the problem of lack of teacher expertise, digital technology will have no impact on teaching / learning process (Bonnet, 1997). (Siegel, 1994) cited in (Akudolu, 2000a) supports this notion when he noted that teachers do not only need to know how to use e-learning materials, they need in addition to learn how to integrate them seamlessly into the curriculum.

According to (Effie, 2003), the need for teachers to acquire e- knowledge presents the rationale for life long learning. She argues that in a technological society we are no longer unfamiliar with words such as online banking, e-shopping; telemedicine and virtual learning as new words are added to our vocabulary on continual basis. Teachers must keep up with technological development to respond to the changing needs that are brought by it. As she put it: e-learning English as a second / foreign language in the new millennium could be a fascinating journey of discovery of self and of construction of knowledge.

In conclusion, there is no doubt that e-learning tools and application have come a long way. The conditions under which these technologies thrive in Nigeria are diverse and sometimes very harsh in nature. While some institutions such as University of Lagos, University of Ibadan, Obafemi Awolowo University have the facilities for e-learning, others are still developmental because of remoteness in location, funding and infrastructure in terms of ICT. Though e-learning has gained ground, much of the school projects, notably the pilot scheme in 56 schools between 1987 and 2000 failed (Owhotu, 2009a). The focus was mainly to put up the internet facility and virtual libraries without considering other components that make up e-learning centre. In the words of (Warshauer 1995a) e-learning environment needs to be intimate, interactive and investigative.

## Interoperable Tools: Types

This section focuses on technological tools which are mostly available for education but hold tremendous promise globally in both developed and developing nations. Before discussing the survey in details, the section explores the types of interoperable tools, definition, roles and accessibility. The aim is to consider what current resources can be fully incorporated into Nigeria educational context. The term "Interoperable tools" is associated with quite a range of diverse systems, characteristics and capabilities seen in an e- learning environment. Interoperable refer to a range of equipment which are used in learning context. These technologies might include: personal computers, laptops, notebooks, mobile phones, iPods, the web, blogs, e-books, e-assessment and a whole range of electronics. In this paper, the interoperable technology tools are not viewed as single technologies. Rather, they are adopted as combinations of hardware and software, media and delivery systems. They evolve and converge rapidly, as seen in PCs, laptops, notebooks, and digital cameras that are both video and single-image, local area networking, the World Wide Web, CD-ROMs DVDs, application software such as word processing, spreadsheets and simulations, e-mail, digital libraries, computer mediated conferencing, videoconferencing and virtual reality. Decisions on the choice of utilising these technologies in developing nations remain subject to many considerations and constraints, ranging from constancy of power supply to availability of skilled technical and managerial support to maintaining the technological infrastructure.

## The Internet

The Internet (The Net) is an extensive resource and communication network linking other computer networks across the world. Pedagogically, the Internet has changed the definition of literacy by introducing readers and writers to electronic texts that incorporate features not typically found in traditional written prose (Behrmann, 1988; Bolter, 2000; Kerchmer, 2000). Thus, the ability to communicate through animated graphics, video, digitalised pronunciations, hyperlinks and other information resources necessitate the development and creation of new opportunities for language instruction. Language is generally agreed to be a powerful index of culture and identity with universal appeal. The size, geographical spread and the speed of transfer and reception of information offered by the Internet are rapidly revolutionalizing the way information is received and transmitted. Several researchers (Leu, 2000; Haddad & Jurich, 2002) have argued that the characteristics of the texts redefine literacy by introducing new ways of reading and writing.

*Digital forms of expression are increasingly replacing printed forms and there is a widespread consensus, at least intuitively, that this shift has consequences for the way we communicate and disseminate information, how we approach the task of reading and writing and how we think about helping people to become literate. (Behrmann, 1988 p. 102).*

The benefits of the Internet are of significant importance in effective education delivery systems and language programme enhancement. Some of these are:

- Internet can be used to support a range of communication strategies, especially easy asynchronous communication between educator and learner, and amongst learners. Where appropriate, this communication can be extended to include groups of people rather than just individuals. A major component of this strength is the capacity to support many requirements for communication to ensure effective management and administration of the system.
- Combining the above, Internet can provide educators with a range of very interesting opportunities for creating resources that allow learners different levels of interactivity. This can lead to the creation of interesting and exciting interaction of learners with educational resources.
- The electronic-based texts in the net are fixed whereas electronic texts are interactive and malleable.
- The uses of electronic enhancement such as digitized pronunciations, graphics and video are examples of how reading material can be manipulated and modified on the computer. Such texts offer learners the ability to access multiple resources connected to networked environments. When readers engage in print-texts they are confined to the limits of what is written on the paper in front of them.
- Students who work with projects presented and carefully adapted by teachers on sites, inevitably come in touch with elements of various cultures. This will in turn have an impact on the way they face the world and at the same time helping to create a global village.

## The World Wide Web

The World Wide Web is currently the most popular method of accessing the internet. It contains millions of electronic pages, graphics, photographs and video clips which provide immediate access to a worldwide database of information. It provides teachers and students with not only repository of resources but also an opportunity to publish and share their own work. The range, authentic and topicality of the resources are invaluable to teachers and learners. According to (Burbules & Callister, 2000) the web, given its ease of use and accessibility, will continue to grow in importance in English language teaching. Additionally, it is fast becoming a gateway to other internet sources developing from a set of static resources to something more interactive and dynamic. Although the web serves as a useful repository of resources, there is need, however, for teachers to be aware that there are materials currently available on the web, which may not be useful in content. Much of what exists presently tends to "represent a triumph of form over content" (Sullivan, 1993). Sites for English Language teaching sometimes may feature sparse content and limited or restricted skills. Hence providing students with the access to retrieve unlimited resources is not enough. (Postman, 1993) has warned that "schools must be sure it is the right content which must be customarily and persistently scrutinized, criticized and modified" (p. 185). Teachers must also prepare students to use the information effectively.

## Electronic Mail (E-Mail)

In most language classroom issues, the e-mail is more widely used than other services on the Internet. It has become an important supplement to classroom teaching. (Waschauer's, 1995b) study of how the Net is used in language teaching revealed that over 50% of the 125 cases were devoted to e-mail activities. Email enables communication using computer networks and telephone lines. The speed, efficiency, environmental friendly, paperless and cost effective way of sending messages has much to offer the language teacher. It provides authentic natural communication using the target language in a real setting, which is motivating in itself. In addition to encouraging independent learning, the practice of communication and sharing of resources, materials and ideas through e-mail offers opportunities for experimentation, for pushing the boundaries of research among students and teachers. E-mail correspondence makes easy storage and manipulation of messages. Communication via e-mail can take the form of electronic dialogue, journals with teachers' response to students' entries through questions, answers and feedback transmitted electronically. Writing conferences in a computer-networked environment promote collaborative work among students and revision of drafts based on electronically transmitted comments. However, e-mail correspondence eliminates the richness of face-to-face discussions.

## Presentational Software

PowerPoint and similar programs are already common place among academics and other professionals. While a single slide presentation requires skill to develop, the increasing sophisticated level of such a presentation requires high level training.

## Discussion Lists

E-mail discussion lists provide language teachers with the means to collaborate with each other to obtain information, material and resources that will help in teaching. These are services, which received contributions from subscribers and automatically mail them out to everyone who has subscribed to the discussion list. Each list has its own purpose, scope and potential of connecting people with similar interests. Queries, viewpoints, announcement and other information of interest are sent automatically to members on the list with the result of replies received almost instantaneously. The speed, simplicity, cost-effectiveness and accessibility of discussion lists are a useful resource for teachers.

## Multimedia, CD-ROM, DVD

Multimedia, CD-ROMs and DVDs are very exciting learning tools in language classroom. The development cost are usually high especially those that carry large quantities of data in a variety of formats like audio and video clips, Internet connections to other databases, large amount of information and built- in simulations and other enrichments. Putting all these together for content application requires expert handling. It is advisable that the utilization of this medium is considered only when enrolments justify the cost, especially in a developing economy.

## Newsgroups

Newsgroups offer easy, fast and inexpensive sharing of resources and ideas among people all over the world. The newsgroups cover a wide range of topics listed by content. Newsgroups lend themselves readily to working with pupils as they encourage and stimulate discussion and debate on up-to-date issues. They are, however, not entirely free from irrelevant and trivial materials.

In sum, interoperable learning tools can be used for either one or two purposes, or, in some cases, for both purposes simultaneously. The first purpose is to enhance the richness and quality of education in the classroom. The second is to distribute campus developed knowledge products off-campus through distance education and open flexible learning. Using tools such as e-mail, the Web, audio, video, computer-conferencing, both synchronously and asynchronously, a very rich interactive and individualised environment can be created that allows learners to dictate their pace of learning, place of learning and the company they wish to keep or not keep while learning. Under the right conditions and used properly, the technologies can be highly effective as both teaching and learning tools. The challenge for institutions is to develop the pre-service teachers' knowledge and skills to exploit the technologies' full potential. (Dharnarajan, 2002).

## THE NATURE OF E-LEARNING SKILLS/COMPETENCY REQUIRED BY LANGUAGE TEACHER TRAINEES

Teacher trainees need constant and continuous renewal to be effective, motivated and up to date in their competency and skills. (Cajkler, 1993; Higham & Macaro, 1993) noted that all trainees should have opportunity to experience the following skills as a normal and inescapable part of their training. These skills are:

A. Lower Level Skills
   - Having basic knowledge of computer skill involves the ability to use a computer operating system including basic hardware (e.g. mouse, monitor, keyboard etc.) and the understanding of basic terminology and concepts (e.g. boot, log in, inbox, download, log out, icons etc).
   - Navigating the extensive resources available requires familiarity with search engines and online tools to obtain the necessary information from the Internet.
   - Acquiring skills in electronic communication involves knowing how to access electronic mail accounts and other related facilities and familiarizing oneself with the specific register of electronic complex communication.

B. Higher Level Skills
   - Downloading resources and participating or contribution in sharing resources involves the ability to access different related facilities and familiarize oneself with the specific register of electronic communication.
   - Selecting, evaluating and integrating of existing resources on the Internet into the curriculum requires an awareness of the aims and objectives of the school's instructional programme and students learning needs to tailor the use of computer resources planned in lessons to meet those needs.
   - Setting up and using interactive multimedia for instructional purposes involving the integration of various stimuli such as text, sound, photographs, pictures and video into an interactive learning system, such as creating and setting up one's own websites.

C. Consolidated Skills
   - A reasonable knowledge of existing web editing tools.
   - A basic knowledge of Hyper Text mark-up language (HTML is used to write 'pages' on the web).
   - An ability to make advanced web pages containing tables and forms.
   - Skills in handling graphic, sound and video films in HTML documents.
   - An understanding of the dynamic nature of hypertext files.

In support of these skills, (Owhotu, 2006) rightly asserted that:

*If language teacher education programmes are to meet their responsibility to prepare teachers for the 21$^{st}$ century, then we have a responsibility to help teachers employ technology in support of integration. (Owhotu, 2006, pp. 9 - 21)*

The teacher trainer is not only expected to become empowered in the use of desktop applications but also in the use of technologies in general with the intent of improving classroom teaching and learning (Akudolu, 2004). Teacher trainees therefore need what Fowowe and Gbadegesin citing (Lawal 2006) refer to as techno-pedagogical ability which is essential in integrating the technologies involved in computer education and virtual education in their teaching practice.

## Statement of the Problem

The quality of teachers' competence remains the cornerstone of any educational system. Numerous studies (Okebukola, 2000; Akudolu 2004; Isu, 2004; Maduekwe, 2007) advocate that pre-service teachers must appreciate the potential of e-technologies as an instructional tool in language classroom and must enter the teaching field with skills and competence ready for students' learning. Yet, teacher education institutions in Nigeria have not effectively responded to the need to integrate e-technologies throughout teacher preparation programme. Most teacher training institutions in Nigeria lack interoperable e-tools for training purposes. Reports, thus, indicate that many pre-service teachers have limited knowledge of how to operate in a technology-enriched classroom or how to use e- technologies in their professional practice (Sotunwa, 1998; Tiamiyu, 2000; Maduekwe, 2004). The critical question is: what is the level of usability and applicability of interoperable tools in Nigeria language teacher education especially in this era of globalization and open courseware programme? In this regard, White (1998) has warned that:

*Without providing teachers with e- competencies with which to develop their profession skills and judgement, then teaching will be reduced to the level of craft which will not provide a sound basis for quality in teacher education and language education in general (White, 1998, pp.125-127).*

## Purpose of the Study

The study aims to:

1. Determine the extent to which language teacher trainees are equipped in operational skills competencies in the use of the Internet.
2. Determine whether gender will pose a militating factor in the competency skills of teacher trainees.

## Research Questions

1. To what extent are language teacher trainees equipped with the interoperable skills of the internet at the lower, higher and consolidated levels of competencies?
2. To what extent will gender pose a militating factor in the competency skills of teacher trainees?

## Hypothesis

1. There will be no significant difference in the level of competency of operating the Internet at the lower, higher and consolidated levels of competencies and language teacher trainees' performance in the Internet application competence assignment.
2. Gender will not be a militating factor of teacher trainees' internet operational skill competency.

## Significance of the Study

This study is worthwhile in effective education delivery system and language programme enhancement because: Internet can be used to support a range of communication strategies, especially easy asynchronous communication between educator and learner, and amongst learners. This study will provide educators with a range of very interesting opportunities for creating resources that allow learners different levels of interactivity. This can lead to the creation of interesting and exciting interaction of learners with educational resources. Students who work with projects presented and carefully adapted by teachers on web sites, inevitably come in touch with elements of various cultures. This will in turn have an impact on the way they face the world and at the same time helping to create a global village.

## METHODOLOGY

### Design of the Study

This study was conducted using a qualitative research methodology in the form of informal observation, and administration of course assignments and questionnaires. Qualitative research methodology was chosen for this study because it allowed the researchers not only to collect firsthand accounts of participants' experiences, but also it allowed them to delve more deeply into those experiences with the participants.

### Population of the Study

This comprised English Language teacher-trainees of the Department of Arts and Social Sciences Education of the University of Lagos, who at the end of their four-year degree programmes are awarded B.A Ed. (Hons.) English and are certified to teach English Language at the Secondary School level.

### Sample and Sampling Technique

The subjects for the study are one hundred students of 300 level Language Education in the Department of Arts and Social Sciences Education of the University of Lagos. They consisted of fifty-four males and forty-six females. Sixty-one of them were admitted through Joint Matriculation Entry (JME) while the remaining thirty-eight came in through Direct Entry admissions. The group was chosen because they have been exposed to courses in computer appreciation in their lower levels (100 & 200 levels). They have also been exposed to some Internet concepts & skills through course assignments that frequently refer them to the Internet.

### Research Instruments

There are two principal instruments used for the study:

- Internet Application Competence Assignment (IACA).
- Internet Literacy Competence Questionnaire (ILCQ)

The Internet Application Competence Assignment was aimed at determining students' versatility with the use of various computer packages as well as their familiarity with the World Wide Web. The assignments were six titles derived from the course outline and subjects were required to use them, read about them, make notes and prepare ahead for the lectures. The Internet Literacy Competence Questionnaire was administered to them at the completion of the course assignments. The questionnaire has three sections: Section A dealt with the subjects' bio-data such as age, gender, level & mode of entry, while section B contained ten close-ended items constructed to determine the low level e- competence possessed by the subjects. Section C also contained ten open-ended questions constructed to determine the higher level e- competence of the students and also to have a clearer understanding of the options chosen in section B.

### Validity and Reliability of the Instruments

To ascertain the validity of the instruments, the questionnaire was subjected to opinions of experienced lecturers in the Faculty of Education whose suggestions were used to modify the instrument before it was trial tested on thirty selected subjects of comparable status to the subjects. The questionnaire was validated using Cronbach Coefficient formula: Cronbach's Alpha (CATPCA algorithms) Cronbach's Alpha per dimension (S = $1,\ldots,_p$): as = $m_w$ ($\lambda_s$ ½ - 1) 1 (λs ½ ($m_w$ - 1) Total

Cronbach's Alpha is $a = m_w (\sum_s \lambda_s^{½} - 1)\ 1 \sum_s \lambda_s$ $½ (m_w - 1)$ with $\lambda_s$ the sth diagonal element of $\Lambda$ as computed in the Orthonormalization step during lasiteration. Source: (SPSS version 17). The internal consistency reliability of the instrument was found to be 0.78 and 0.82.

## Procedures

The assignments were given during the course of teaching ASE 305 titled Teaching English Language at the Senior Secondary School Level. The course required a 4-hour lecture per week which was split into twice in a week. At the beginning of the course, students were intimated of their participation in the research. The use of Instructional materials, of which the Internet plays a prominent role, was part of the course outline. The researchers, who were also the course lecturers, decided to expose the students to the practical demonstrations of this aspect. At the middle of the course, students were given series of assignments related to the course outline and were required to source the internet to locate the information/solutions to the assignment, do a write up on the topics, locate and cite web sources where the information could be found and send the reports through e-mail. They were also required to use various office packages- Microsoft Word, PowerPoint, Excel, Adobe PageMaker and PDF to send in their reports. A total of twelve assignments, spanning six weeks were submitted through e-mail. At the end of the assignment, students were administered with the questionnaire through e-mail which they downloaded, filled and submitted to the researchers.

## Analysis of Data

The results of the assignment and the responses from the questionnaires were analysed using both descriptive and inferential statistics such as frequencies, mean, t-test and chi-square. To determine the levels of skill competencies, the subjects were divided according to the ranking discussed in the literature review- lower, higher and consolidated levels. However, to set the statistical ranges, the reading proficiency assessment by Widdowson (1978) was used. According to him, reading proficiency is determined at three levels- independent (60 and above), dependent (40-59) and frustration (less than 40). The same range was used to determine the level of internet skill competencies.

## RESULT

The results are presented according to the research questions and hypotheses.

***RQ1:*** To what extent are teacher trainees equipped with the interoperable skills of the Internet at the lower, higher and consolidated levels of skill competencies?

The results on Table 1(a) indicate that the majority of the subjects operated below the expected level of Internet skill/competency and application. While the expected level is 33, the highest level they could attain was a higher skill level with a frequency of 46. The lower skill level closely followed with a frequency of 39. The consolidated level has the lowest frequency of 15.

*Table 1(a). Chi-Square frequencies of levels of internet skill/competency*

| | Observed frequency | Expected Frequency | Residual | Chi-square | Df |
|---|---|---|---|---|---|
| Lower skill level (less than 40) | 39 | 33.3 | 5.7 | 5.229 | 2 |
| Higher skill level (between 40-59) | 46 | 33.3 | 12.7 | | |
| Consolidated skill level (60 & above) | 15 | 33.3 | -18.3 | | |

*Table 1(b). Teacher trainees perceived e-literacy*

| | Yes | No |
|---|---|---|
| Computer literacy | 89% | 11% |
| Internet usage | 86% | 14% |
| Web design | 28% | 72% |

Results in Table 1(b) showed the teacher trainees perceived e-literacy level. Majority of the subjects 89% are computer literate; 86% are familiar with internet use, while 28% are familiar with web design. However, there is no regularity in the claim to use the Internet to access their mails when it is required.

Results in Table (1c) above showed that the majority ofsubjects acquired internet/computer skills rather informally, i.e. through self efforts (58%) and reliance on friends/ relatives (27%). However, only 36% of the subjects claimed to have acquired some competence by attending computer training courses.

Table 1(d) above showed that majority of the respondents claimed the frequency of Internet use Internet (70%), access mails (64%), discussion list (50%) and require assistance (73%).

***Ho1*** There will be no significant difference in the level of competency of operating the Internet at the lower, higher and consolidated levels of competencies and teacher trainees' performance in the Internet application competence assignment.
***Ho2*** Gender will not be a militating factor of teacher trainees' interoperable skill competency.

Results on Table 2 indicate that the total mean score of interoperable competence is 34.70 as against that of tool application which is 53.01. This indicates that the subjects performed better in the Internet Application Competence Assignment (IACA) than the e- Literacy Competence Questionnaire (ILCQ), hence the null hypothesis is rejected. Furthermore, Table 2 above showed that the male students performed better in ILCQ (36.6) as against female students by 32.4. The mean score of the males is also higher than the total mean score. The male students also performed better in IACA with a mean score of 53.3 as against the female students 52.7 and the total of 53.01, though the difference is not significant. The F-ratio showed a significant value 0f 1.49 for ILCQ but 0.9 for IACA. This result lends supports to several studies suggesting that boys are more active than girls in

*Table 1(c). Sources of training experience*

| | Computer/internet Training course | University courses | Friends/relatives/ cyber café attendants | Self efforts |
|---|---|---|---|---|
| Source of computer literacy acquisition | 36% | 10% | 27% | 27% |
| Source of internet experience | 14% | 3% | 25% | 58% |
| Source of web design experience | 9% | 3% | 8% | 10% |

*Table 1(d). Frequency of internet use*

| | Everyday/often | Once a week | Fortnightly | When required |
|---|---|---|---|---|
| Frequency of internet use | 11% | 14% | 5% | 70% |
| Frequency of mail access | 9% | 20% | 6% | 64% |
| Frequency of assistance required | 6% | 10% | 11% | 73% |
| Frequency of internet discussion | 1% | 3% | 43% | 50% |

*Table 2.One-Way analysis of variance of ICT competence and application by competency and gender*

| Skills | Gender | Frequency | Mean | Standard deviation | f-ratio |
|---|---|---|---|---|---|
| Computer literacy competence | Male | 54 | 36.63 | 19.25 | 1.49* |
| | Female | 46 | 32.43 | 15.24 | |
| | Total | 100 | 34.70 | 17.56 | |
| Competence in computer application | Male | 54 | 53.26 | 21.21 | .90 |
| | Female | 46 | 52.72 | 23.70 | |
| | Total | 100 | 53.01 | 22.28 | |

using technical tools (see Hernes, 2002; Idowu, Adagunodo, & Idowu, 2004). On the other hand, the result however ignites serious considerations as girls are expected to perform better because of their motivation and skill for secretarial related courses (Maduekwe, 2006b) thus poor input factor may have been responsible for the differences in performance observed. It further emphasized the need to restructure the programme of instruction in ICT use and application in higher education and encourage further research in futuristic gender/ ICT related areas.

## DISCUSSION

This study has clearly demonstrated that the majority of the teacher trainees in Nigeria ESL context have already acquired some level of usability regarding interoperable tool competence, while others showed outright ignorance of expected effective e-skills utilization especially in their study schedules. The results also support the idea that poor training accounted for the lack of consolidated Internet skills/ competency manifested by teacher trainees in their assignments. This finding is in consonance with the earlier studies of (Kwache, 2007) who confirmed the low level computer and the internet skills of both University undergraduate students and lecturers. With the high awareness on of e- tools on ground, it is disheartening that the majority of the students could not define e- learning terms. Most of the subjects could not define simple computer/Internet terms such as inbox, download, icons, menus, log-in and log-out. These justified claims of acquiring computer/internet training through self effort (58%) as shown on Table 1(c). Learning through self effort as depicted above in Table 1(c) is by trial and error and there is often no theoretical foundation for experiences acquired. The works of (Leask & Pachler, 1991; Strudler, 1991; Waschauer, 1995b) support the need for integration of teachers.

Also, observations from the Internet Application Competence assignment showed that 78% have e-mail addresses from which their reports were sent. This study is in line with the findings of (Ushie, Beshel, Asanga, & Inyang, 2008) who established from their study with internet usage, that majority of the undergraduates in Federal Colleges of Education were popular with using e-mails. While 22% of the subjects used friends, colleagues or relatives' e-mail accounts, about 12% could not locate the web addresses for their reports indicating difficulty in the use of search engines. On the whole, 39% of the subjects were able to operate within lower level Internet skill; 46% were able to operate within the higher competency level which is the highest level attained by the majority of the subjects (see Table 2).

It is also important to note that most of the subjects could not handle the skills required for the consolidated level, which has the lowest frequency of 15. The Internet Application Competence Assignment feedback showed that 83% mailed their reports within the hypertext page, while 17% sent the reports as attachments. However, 5% of the attached reports were blank indicating error in the attachment/mailing process. Also, while majority of the subjects 88% were able to download their reports as well as locate the web addresses for their assignments, the consolidated level posed the most difficult area of competency in Internet use and application. This study corroborates (Olibie and Akudolu, 2008) findings that there was a low extent of undergraduate competence in utilizing digital technologies. By indicating lack of competence in using e-tools, language teacher trainees cannot be meaningfully involved in the information society. This can further limit and negate these students from becoming part of global communication network as well as encouraging quality in Nigeria education. This is manifested in their inabilities to properly attach documents to their mails, locate specific web addresses for their assignments, and design web pages.

This finding may not be unconnected with the fact that Internet services are still relatively new in the Nigerian society especially at the tertiary levels such that most trainees take the Internet for granted. This may also not be unconnected with the low Internet skills of teacher trainers. Other problems noted included lack of knowledge of relevant search engines as well as the lack of understanding of the existence and use of multimedia on the Internet. This justified the claim to heavy reliance on cybercafé attendants and others- friends, colleagues, cybercafé attendants- that assisted them in tackling the assignments most of the time. We can therefore logically attribute this low-level competence to their poor computer/internet training, experience, and/or frequency of use as confirmed in Table 1(c). It must therefore, be admitted that not much in terms of usability interoperable educational tools in language teacher education has been achieved.

## SOLUTIONS AND RECOMMENDATIONS

Against the backdrop of the issues and challenges we have highlighted in this paper, it is recommended that:

1. There is the need to consider how best to integrate specific objectives and resources into the teacher education programme. As e-learning becomes an important part of education and as literacy is redefined by the new technology, it becomes mandatory that teacher- trainees are inducted into the utilization of interoperable educational tools in daily instruction and curriculum.
2. Teacher trainees need training and empowerment on the use of technological tools. They are expected to apply their collaborative, communicative, acquisition and problem-solving skills in the use of the Internet in their curriculum. This situation emphasizes how important it is then for teacher preparation and staff development programme to be put in place to prepare teacher trainers on how to integrate technology with English Language curriculum.

## FUTURE RESEARCH DIRECTIONS

The implications of the low usability of interoperable educational tools in language teacher education become germane in the light of the results of this study. The emerging trends in the frequency of use of these tools which was mostly "when required" as indicated in Table 1(d) showed that trainees are yet to see the internet as a component part of their everyday life. The overall picture of the future that emerged portends serious danger for teacher education programmes and the society at large in this era of globalization. Nonetheless, one shares the hope with (Olubamise and Awe,

2007) cited in (Owhotu, 2009b) that the future is bright for e-educational tools in Nigeria, but (that) the building blocks are not yet in place and (that) the time to start is now. There is therefore the need for critical pedagogy which requires a continuous quest for the use and application of e-learning tools on both immediate and long –term basis to enable trainees attain the required level of competence in their everyday learning experience. Towards this end, (Odogwu, 2000) warned that "a domesticated consciousness in the use of the Internet and mediated technologies in Nigeria will not be averted until educators (teachers and learners alike) are regarded as intellectuals who can create and recreate knowledge" (p.34) Implicitly, the workforce of the future language teacher education will need a whole spectrum of awareness, knowledge and skills to deal with technology and the globalization society. Hopefully, the answers for many of the infrastructural challenges identified may lie in higher institutions embracing a holistic approach to education, investing concurrently on pedagogy, skill training, practice and interoperable learning tools.

## CONCLUSION

In conclusion, there is no doubt that e-learning tools and utilization have come a long way in Nigeria's higher education. The conditions under which these technologies thrive in Nigeria are diverse and sometimes harsh in nature. Though e-learning has gained ground, the focus is mainly to put up the Internet facility and virtual libraries without considering other training standards that make up e-learning applicability. No language programme can function adequately without proper integration. Effectiveness, access, collaboration and sustainability in practice are the intertwined issues which must be addressed when considering the overall impact of the use of e- learning tools. It is the involvement not the tool that stimulates communication in the target language. Whatever the case, (Burbles, 2001) aptly warned that "language learning with and on the web is not just about information access, retrieval or even critical hyper-reading and writing. They should also not be seen to replace the support and motivation provided by the teacher, nor should they be regarded as the be-all and the end-all of instruction" (p.23). What they offer language teachers is, as (Warshauer, 1995) puts it "a powerful new tool that can help implement good pedagogy, not a magic wand that once replaces previous pedagogy" (p220). In the final analysis, the real issue is on how to harvest the sustainable and beneficial power of technologies to meet the challenges of the twenty- first century and make language teacher education more relevant, more responsive and more effective on life long basis.

## REFERENCES

Abbot, C. (2001). *ICT: changing education.* London: Routledge Publishers.

Adegoke, K. A. (2000, November). *Towards the enhancement of teacher education in the new millennium.* Lead paper presented at the 2nd Biennial National Conference on Teacher Education at Adeniran Ogunsanya College of Education, Otta/ Ijanikin, Lagos State, Lagos.

Adeya, C. N., & Oyelaran-Oyeyinka, B. (2002). *The internet in African Universities: Case studies from Kenya and Nigeria.* Retrieved October, 11, 2002, from URL http:// www.intech.unu.edu

Ajelabi, A. O. (2006). Computers in humanities education. In V.B. Owhotu (Ed.), *An Introduction to Information and Communication Technologies in Education* (pp. 87 – 90). Lagos: Sibon Books Ltd.

Akudolu, Lillian – Rita. I. (2000). *Restructuring Nigerian Secondary Education system through Information & Communication Technology (ICT) – Driven Curriculum.* Paper Presented at the third Conference of the World Council for Curriculum and Instruction(WCCI)Nigeria Chapter, Abuja.

Akudolu, Lillian – Rita. I. (2004). Evaluation of primary school teachers' use of information and communications technology (ICT) for curriculum integration. *Journal of Curriculum Organisation of Nigeria (CON).* 2, (1), 112-117.

Anderson, I., & Horney, M. A. (1998). Transforming text for at-risk readers. In D. Reinking,M. &McKenna (Eds), *Handbook of Literacy and Technology Transformation in Post Typographic World.*

Asoqwo, U. D. (2006). *E-learning: A panacea for access, equity and quality higher Education in Nigeria.* Paper presented at the 30th annual conference of the Nigerian

Association for Educational Administration and Planning (NAEAP) held at the Faculty of Education Hall, Enugu State University, Enugu.

Bassey, U. U., Umoren, G. U., Akuegwu, B. A., Udida, L. A., & Ntukidem, E. P. (2007, September). *Nigerian graduating students' access to e-learning technology: Implications for Higher Education Management.* Paper presented at the sixth International Internet Education Conference held in Egypt, Cairo.

Bates, T. (2001). *National strategies for e- learning in post secondary education and training.* Paris: UNESCO, 11EP

Behrmann, M. (1988). *Integrating computer into the curriculum: A handbook for special educators* (pp. 25–32). Boston: College Press.

Bolter, J. D. (2000). *Remediation: Understanding new media.* Cambridge, MA: MIT Press.

Bonnet, M. (1997). Computers in the classroom: some value issues. In McFarlane (Ed). *Information Technology and Authentic Learning.* (pp. 145-159)

Bugaje, I. (2007). *Nigeria: Education reform and muslims.* Retrieved from file http://www.all africa. com 18/4/2007.

Burbules, N. (2001). The web as a theoretical place . In Snyder, I. (Ed.), *Silicon Literacy: Communication, Innovation and Education in Electronic Age.* New York: Routledge.

Burbules, N., & Callister, T. (2000). Knowledge at cross roads: some alternate futures of hypertext learning environments. *Educational Theory, 40*(1), pp23–pp50.

Busari, T. O. (2006). Information and communication technology in science and technology education. In V.B. Owhotu (Ed.), *An Introduction to Information and Communication Technologies in Education.* (pp146 – 162). Lagos: Sibon Books Ltd.

Cajkler, W. (1993). The official perspective – modern languages & IT in the 1990s . In Higham, J., & Macaro, E. (Eds.), *Information Technology in Initial Teacher Education: The modern languages perspectives* (pp. 5–34). York, UK: University of York.

Collins, A. (1991). The role of computer in restructuring schools . *Phi Delta Kappan, 73,* 28–36.

D. & Draxter. A (Eds.), *Technologies for education: Potentials, Parameters and Prospects.* (pp.58). Washington: AED.

Dhanarajan, G. (2002). *Objectives and strategies for effective use of ICTs.* In Haddad, W.

Drucker, P. F. (1994). *The age of social transformation.* Manchester, UK: Atlantic Publisher.

Durrant, C., & Beavis, C. (2001). *(ICT) Use of English: Teachers, learners and technology.* Melbourne: Wakefold Press.

Eastman, D. (1996). *The internet and ELT: The impact of the internet on English language teaching*. Britain: British Council.

Effie, D. (2003). E-learning ESL: Bringing the world together. *In Global Peace through the Internet. TESL Journal. 10.*

Fowowe, S. S., & Gbadegesin, S. S. (2008). Computer instruction: Apedagogicla approach that facilitates learning systems in the 21st century. In Nwabuko, N. C. & Akinpelu, Biobun (Eds.), *Shifting Paradigms in the Teaching Function in ICT Era* (pp.57-60) Lagos: Nigerian Association for Educational Media and Technology (NAEMT) Publisher.

Goodwyn, A. (2000). *English in the digital age: Information and communication technology and the teaching of English*. London: Cassell.

Gunawardana, K. D. (2006). An empirical study of the potential challenges and benefits of implementing e-learning in Sir Lanka. *Special issue of the International Journal of Computer, the Internet and Management,* 33, 1-8.

Haddad, W. D., & Draxter, A. (Eds.), *Technologies for education: Potential, Parameter and Prospect* (p. 24). Washington: AED.

Haddad, W. D., & Jurich, S. (2002). ICT for education: potential, and potency . In Haddad, W. D., & Draxter, A. (Eds.), *Technologies for education: Potentials, Parameters and Prospects* (pp. 28–39). Washington: AED.

Hernes, G. (2002). *Emerging trends in ICT and challenges to educational planning.*

Higham, J., & Macaro, E. (Eds.). (1993). *Information technology in initial teacher education: the modern language perspective* (pp. 5–34). York: University of York.

Hoffman, J., & Person, P. P. (2000). Reading education in the next millennium: What your grandmother's teacher didn't know that your grand daughter's teacher should? *Reading Research Quarterly*, *35*(1). doi:10.1598/RRQ.35.1.3

Idowu, B., Adagunodo, R., & Idowu, B. (2004). Gender differences in computer literacy among Nigerian undergraduate students. *The African Symposuim: An Online Educational Research Journal*, *4*(3), 1–7.

Isu, C. O. (2004). Information and communication technology (ICT) as a veritable tool of business education for human resource development. [Con]. *Journal of Curriculum Organisation of Nigeria*, *11*(2).

Kenning, M. J., & Kenning, M. M. (1983). *An introduction to computer assisted language learning*. Oxford: Oxford University Press.

Kerchmer, R. A. (2000). Understanding teachers' perspectives of internet use in the classroom. Implications for teacher education and staff development. *Reading & Writing Quarterly*, *16*(2).

Kerr, R. (1993). *Restructuring classroom. Interaction with networked computer: Effects on quantity and characteristics of language production*. Paper presented at the meeting of the American Council of Teachers of Foreign Languages San Antonio.

Kinzer, C., & Risco, V. (1998). Multimedia and enhanced learning: Transforming pre-service education . In Reinking, D., McKanna, M., Labbo, L., & Kieffer, R. (Eds.), *Handbook of Technology and Literacy: Transformations in a Post-typographic world* (pp. 182–202). Hillsdale, NJ: Erlbaum.

Kwache, P. Z. (2007). The imperatives of information and communication technology for teachers in Nigeria higher education. *Merlot Journal of Online Learning and Teaching*, *1*(1), 24–32.

Leask, M., & Bachler, N. (Eds.). (1999). *Learning and Teaching Using ICT in the Secondary School* (pp. 112–116). London: Routledge Publishers. doi:10.4324/9780203212301

Leu, D. J. (2000). Continuously changing technologies and environments for literacy: deitic consequences for literary education in an information age . In Kamil, M. (Ed.), *Handbook of Reading Research, (3)* (pp. 743–777).

Leu, D. J., & Kinzer, C. K. (2000). The convergence of literacy instruction with networked technologies for information and communication. *Reading Research Quarterly*, (35): 108–127.

Luke, C. (2000). Cyber –schooling and technological change: Multiliteracies for new times . In Cope, B., & Kalantzis, M. (Eds.), *Multiliteracies: Literacy Learning and the Design of Social Features* (pp. 69–91). New York: Routledge.

Maduekwe, A. N. (2004, September). *A new learning experience: Language teachers' perception of Information, Communication Technologies (ICT) in Nigeria ESL context.* Paper Presented at the West African Linguistics Society Conference, University of Ibadan, Nigeria.

Maduekwe, A. N. (2006a). ICT in the world of work and Nigerian schools. In V.B. Owhotu (Ed.), *An Introduction to Information and Communication Technologies in Education.* (pp.146 – 162). Lagos: Sibon Books Ltd.

Maduekwe, A. N. (2006b.) Perspective on teacher education & ICT in the language classroom. In V.B. Owhotu (Ed), *An Introduction to Information and Communication Technologies in Education.* (pp182 – 202). Lagos: Sibon Books Ltd.

Maduekwe, A. N (2007). *Principles and practice of teaching English as a second language.* Lagos, Lagos State: Vitaman Books.

Nelson, C. (2001). *ICT: Changing education.* London: Routledge.

Odogwu, H. N. (2000). Survey of computer education in secondary schools. *ASUU-UNILAG Journal of Comtemporary Issues*, *1*(1), 33–51.

Odusanya, O. O., & Bamgbala, O. A. (2002). Computing and information technology skills for final year medical and dental students at the college of medicine University of Lagos, Nigeria. *The Nigerian Postgraduate Medical Journal*, *9*(4), 190–193.

Okebukola, P. (2000) Teachers advised to acquire computer education. *The Guardian Newspaper.* Thursday, August 14, p. 35.

Olibie, E. I., & Akudolu, Lilian- Rita. I (2008, August). *Digital empowerment of students in universities in South –East zone of Nigeria.* Paper presented at a conference on Higher Education Research and Policy Network (HERPNET). Ibadan: Nigeria.

Olorundare, S. (2006, October). *Utilization of ICT in curriculum development, implementation and evaluation.* Paper presented at the National Conference on Information and Communication and Technology. Institute of Education, University of Nigeria, Nsukka

Owhotu, V. B. (2006). The social dimensions of technological innovation and revolution. In V. B. Owhotu (Ed), An *introduction to Information Technologies in education.* (pp.9 – 22). Lagos: Sibon Books Ltd.

Owhotu, V. B. (2009a). ICTs in basic and post-basic education: A comparative overview and lessons for Nigeria. *WCCI Chapter Journal of Curriculum and Instruction*, *7*(3), 31.

Owhotu, V. B. (2009b, February). *African Asian dialogue: Promoting a self reliant approach to basic education development through research and dialogue.* Paper presented at the Round table/ Launch of the Africa-Asia project, Faculty of Education, University of Lagos.

Perelman, L. J. (1990). Education in the information age: a new learning enterprise. *The Technology Education Comes to Education*. 12ED-19ED.

Postman, N. (1993). *Technology: The surrender of culture to technology* (p. 185). New York: Vintage Books.

Pratt, E., & Sullivan, N. (1994, September). *Comparison of ESL writers in networked and regular classrooms*. Paper Presented at the 28th Annual TESOL Convention Baltimore.

Reinking, D., & Rickman, P. (1998). *Handbook of literacy and technology. Transformation in a post-typographic world*. Oxford: Oxford University Press.

Salawudeen, O. S. (2006, October). E-learning technologies: The Nigerian experience. *Paper presented at the XXIII Fig conference*, Munch Germany.

Schwab, R. L. (1999). *Technology and the changing roles in teacher education. In log-in or lose-out: technology in the 21st century education* (pp. 151–155). American Association of Colleges for Teacher Education.

Scrimshaw, P. (1998). Cooperative writing with computers in Scrimshaw, (ed), *Language classroom and computers*. London: Routledge.

Shettima, A. K. (2005). *Nigeria university education in the 21st century*. Retrieved February 20, 2005, from http://www.mac found.org/site/c/.html

Siegel, J. (1994). Teach your teachers well. *Electronic Learning* April, 34

Sotunwa, O. O. (1998). Integrating computer technology into the teaching of Nigerian languages. In Nwabuko, N. C. & Akinpelu, Biobun (Eds.), *Shifting Paradigms in the Teaching Function in ICT Era* (pp.17-22) Lagos: Nigerian Association for Educational Media and Technology (NAEMT) Publisher

Sullivan, N. (1993). Teaching writing on a computer network. *TESOL Journal*, *3*(1), 19–23.

Tella, S. (1992). *Boys, Girls and e-mail: A case study in Finnish senior secondary schools*. Helsinki: University of Helsinki, Department of Teacher education

Tiamiyu, M. A. (2000). Availability, accessibility and use of information technologies in Nigeria federal agencies: *A Preliminary Survey*. Nigeria. 105.

Ushie, A., Beshel, C., Asanga, D., & Iyang, J. (2008). Academic staff use of internet services Federal colleges of education in Middle Belt of Nigeria. In Nwabuko, N. C. & Akinpelu, Biobun (Eds.), *Shifting Paradigms in the Teaching Function in ICT Era* (pp.47-49) Lagos: Nigerian Association for Educational Media and Technology (NAEMT) Publisher.

Uwadia, C. O. (2000). Information and communication technology in Nigeria: A survey, critique and projections. *ASUU-UNILAG Journal of Contemporary Issues*, *1*(1), 33–51.

Uwadia, C. O. (2000). Information and communication technology in Nigeria: a survey, critic and projections. *ASUU-UNILAG Journal of Contemporary Issues*, *1*(1), 33–51.

Warshauer, A. (1995a). Virtual connections: online activities and projects for networking language learners. University of Hawaii. *Second Language Teaching Curriculum Centre,* 220-225

Warshauer, (1995b). Computer – mediated collaborative learning: Theory and practice *Modern Language Journal, 154-156.*

White, R. V. (1998). *The ELT curriculum design, innovation and management*. Oxford: Oxford University Press.

World Bank. (2000). *Information and communication technology: A World Bank group strategy*. Washington, D C: The World Bank Group.

Yusuf, M., & Onasanya, J. (2004). Information and communication technology and education: Analyzing the Nigerian national policy for information technology. *International Education Journal*, *6*(3), 316–321.

## KEY TERMS AND DEFINITIONS

**Competence:** Refers to one's underlying knowledge of a system, event or fact. It is a non observable, idealised ability to do something. It is not possible to lay claim to technological competence without a mastery of the skills involved.

**E-Learning:** A construct that involves the integration of technology, knowledge acquisition and idiosyncratic human interpretations. It involves working proficiencies in e-mail use, familiarity with CD-ROMs, DVDs, PCs, laptops, notebooks, and digital cameras that are both video and single-image, local area networking, the World Wide Web, application software such as word processing, spreadsheets and simulations, digital libraries, computer mediated conferencing, videoconferencing and virtual reality.

**Interoperable:** Refers to a range of which are used in learning context. These technologies might include: personal computers, laptops, notebooks, mobile phones, iPods, the web, blogs, e-books, e-assessment and a whole range of electronics.

**Language:** Is seen as the most sophisticated communication tool of life and what it means to be human. It is that distinctive human reality which serves as the means and end of behaviour ordered and achieved within any given community, society or nation at large. The mastery of language skills is a prerequisite to overall academic success at every stage of development.

**Nigerian Context:** In Nigeria context English is used as a second language. Learning English is therefore based on the conviction that language is a process which can only be achieved effectively by using the target language for the purpose of communication.

**Skill:** It is an ability to do something well, especially because one has learned and practiced it

**Teacher Education:** Commonly referred to as teacher training, is the art and science of institutionally providing pre-service or in-service training to education students in the theoretical basis, specialized knowledge and the acquisition of practical and applied skills in the teaching profession, with adequate attitudes and orientation. Teacher education involves the systematic integrated formal professional training in teaching and other teaching support services for different levels of educational system (Adegoke, 2000). Teacher education is central to both quality of education and development in any nation and is expected to provide student teachers with the intellectual and professional background adequate for their assignment and make them adaptable to changing situations.

**Usability:** Refers to the use and integration of digital technologies with the intent of improving classroom teaching and learning.

# Chapter 14
# Myth, Magic & Method: Using Subphenomenology to Analyse Weblog Data

**Jocene Vallack**
*CQ University, Australia*

## ABSTRACT

*Researchers from all disciplines are increasingly inclined to acknowledge intuition and reflective practice as a valid ways of knowing. But in technology and areas other than the arts, this thinking is still new, and few strategic frameworks are available to assist researchers to approach intuitive research with rigor. In this chapter, Subphenomenology is laid out as a methodology for analysing weblog writing, as data for research. As a template for other first-person research, the framework showcases the author's own experiences as a novice Web 2.0 user. Starting with the research question, "Why do I resist learning with technology?" I show how candid blogs are analysed to reveal an archetypal image of Echo and Narcissus in response to the research question. This chapter formulates how Subphenomenology uses intuition to access unconscious knowing, and reveal an archetypal image of the research in question. The case studied, like all case studies, may not be applicable to every learner who, in the described sample, shies away from technology. But it may provide profound insight to those who self-identify with the given universal myth. Subphenomenology is a formula, which can be applied to any weblog data, or indeed any creative work, to enable researchers to understand more about the universal implications of their most subjective reflections.*

DOI: 10.4018/978-1-61692-791-2.ch014

## INTRODUCTION

A famous psychologist once said:

*And it is very important for a person to know their unconscious is smarter than they are.... So you build your technique around instructions that allow the conscious mind to withdraw from the task and leave it all up to the unconscious (Erickson in Neville, 1989, p.68).*

Such a technique is Subphenomenology. The method of free-association data collection lifts the lid of the unconscious so that images and forms may appear to the conscious mind through dream and meditation.

C. Q. University, in Australia, has a current research project that is seeking to better understand the nature of web-based Personal Learning Environments (PLEs) and the consequential implications of these PLEs for teaching and learning. The proverbial elephant in the lounge room however, is that many otherwise capable academics, still resist technology. As a Research Fellow with this project, and oddly, a self-confessed (but now evangelised) technophobe, I used my blog data to map and analyse the learning curve resulting from my new and frequent encounters with Web 2.0 technology. Using an arts-based, qualitative methodology that I had developed and published earlier, I analysed the blog entries to gain insights into this phenomenon of academic 'end-user' resistance to technology. The methodology is called Subtextual Phenomenology (Vallack, 2005a), indicating subliminal meaning behind the language used to describe the phenomenoa. For the sake of eloquence, and possibly because I have now served time in the technologists' den of acronyms, where everything can seem abbreviated to the point of obscurity, I will hence-forth refer to the methodology as Subphenomenology. This chapter is about the structure of Subphenomenology, and it demonstrates an approach to using blog data for research. Firstly I will set out a brief description of the current research context in which I am using Subphenomenology, along with the research results. Then I will present the structure of this methodology and argue for its philosophical rigor. Finally I will illustrate the methodology with the outcome of our current research and demonstrate the potential of Subphenomenology as a template for further blog analysis.

So what is the outcome of the PLE inquiry into academic technophobia? Using Subphenomenology, it became evident that the relationship between a recalcitrant technologist and the technology itself may be akin to that of Echo and Narcissus. Here is the story of Echo and Narcissus:

*Echo was a beautiful nymph, fond of the woods and hills, where she devoted herself to woodland sports. She was a favorite of Diana, and attended her in the chase. But Echo had one failing; she was fond of talking, and whether in chat or argument would have the last word. One day Juno was seeking her husband, who, she had reason to fear, was amusing himself among the nymphs. Echo by her talk contrived to detain the goddess till the nymphs made their escape. When Juno discovered it, she passed sentence upon Echo in these words: "You shall forfeit the use of that tongue with which you have cheated me, except for that one purpose you are so fond of REPLY. You shall still have the last word, but no power to speak first."*

*This nymph saw Narcissus, a beautiful youth, as he pursued the chase upon the mountains. She loved him, and followed his footsteps. Oh, how she longed to address him in the softest accents, and win him to converse, but it was not in her power. She waited with impatience for him to speak first, and had her answer ready. One day the youth, being separated from his companions, shouted aloud, "Who's here?" Echo replied, "Here." Narcissus looked around, but seeing no one, called out, "Come." Echo answered, "Come." As no one came, Narcissus called again, "Why do you shun me?" Echo asked the same question. "Let us join one another," said the youth. The maid answered with all her heart in the same words, and hastened to the spot, ready to throw her arms about his neck. He started back, exclaiming, "Hands off! I would rather die than you should have me." "Have me," said she; but it was all in vain. He left her, and she went to hide her blushes in the recesses of the woods. From that time forth she lived in caves and among mountain cliffs. Her form faded with grief, till at last all her flesh shrank away. Her bones were changed into rocks, and there was nothing left of her but her voice. With that she is still ready to reply to anyone who calls her, and keeps up her old habit of having the last word.*

*Narcissus was cruel not in this case alone. He shunned all the rest of the nymphs as he had done poor Echo. One day a maiden, who had in vain endeavored to attract him, uttered a prayer that he might some time or other feel what it was to love and meet no return of affection. The avenging goddess heard and granted the prayer.*

*There was a clear fountain, with water like silver, to which the shepherds never drove their flocks. Nor did the mountain goats resort to it, nor any of the beasts of the forest; neither was it defaced with fallen leaves or branches; but the grass grew fresh around it, and the rocks sheltered it from the sun. Hither came one day the youth fatigued with hunting, heated and thirsty. He stooped down to drink, and saw his own image in the water; he thought it was some beautiful water=spirit living in the fountain. He stood gazing with admiration at those bright eyes, those locks curled like the locks of Bacchus or Apollo, the rounded cheeks, the ivory neck, the parted lips, and the glow of health and exercise over all. He fell in love with himself. He brought his lips near to take a kiss; he plunged his arms in to embrace the beloved object. It fled at the touch, but returned again after a moment and renewed the fascination. He could not tear himself away; he lost all thought of food or rest, while he hovered over the brink of the fountain gazing upon his own image. He talked with the supposed spirit: "Why, beautiful being, do you shun me? Surely my face is not one to repel you. The nymphs love me, and you yourself look not indifferent upon me. When I stretch forth my arms you do the same; and you smile upon me and answer my beckonings with the like." His tears fell into the water and disturbed the image. As he saw it depart, he exclaimed, "Stay, I entreat you! Let me at least gaze upon you, if I may not touch you." With this, and much more of the same kind, he cherished the flame that consumed him, so that by degrees he lost his color, his vigor, and the beauty which formerly had so charmed the nymph Echo. She kept near him, however, and when he exclaimed, "Alas! Alas!" she answered him with the same words. He pined away and died; and when his shade passed the Stygian river, it leaned over the boat to catch a look of itself in the waters. The nymphs mourned for him, especially the water-nymphs; and when they smote their breasts, Echo smote hers also. They prepared a funeral pile, and would have burned the body, but it was nowhere to be found; but in its place a flower, purple within, and surrounded with white leaves, which bears the name and preserves the memory of Narcissus. (Jalic & Inc., 2009)*

Like Echo, the reluctant technologist feels dumb and inarticulate amidst an onslaught of ever changing acronyms and terminologies. And like Narcissus, the technology is self-contained and completely without empathy. Like Echo, the novice end-user is alone with her anxiety for technology, which rises with her increasing inability to communicate her anxiety. In this chapter I will discuss the methods that led to such insight. But let us start with a brief look at the research context from which the archetypes of Echo and Narcissus emerged.

## BACKGROUND: THE PLE RESEARCH CONTEXT FOR APPLYING SUBPHENOMENOLOGY TO WEBLOGS

CQUniversity has been working on a project that explores the idea of Personal Learning Environments (PLEs@CQUni) created through portable, Web 2.0 technology such as Google, Twitter, You-Tube, Flickr, Delicious and more. In the context of this research, the notion of personal learning environments is limited to places that are accessed via a computer, that is, we are referring to online PLEs rather than life-world spaces. The list of online learning spaces grows daily, of course. Our PLEs@CQUni project, developed initially through the forward thinking of David Jones, set out to explore "mechanisms to support learner autonomy and self-regulation within a personalised learning space" (Jones, Vallack, & Fitzgerald-Hood, 2008) beyond the scope of the organisation's Learning Management System.

Popular debate in this area frequently compares personal learning environments (PLEs) with learning management systems (LMSs). So the next logical question might be:

*...and do we now really need an LMS such as Blackboard, Moodle and Sakai?*

This attracts further debate. Cann (2009) says that " A VLE/LMS is all about controlling how you learn. A PLE is about giving you control over how you learn." (Cann, 2009). Beer and Jones (2008) put it this way:

*Learning Management Systems give value to organisations by providing a means to sequence content and create a manageable structure for instructors and administrators (Siemens 2004). This is valid from a management and control standpoint but it can be argued that the fundamental purpose of universities and therefore learning management systems is to provide an environment for a learner to learn. The use of ICT within tertiary education has impacted more on administrative services than on fundamentals of learning and teaching (Beer & Jones, 2008, p.66)*

This will be a debate driven by politics and enterprise, as so much money has been invested into university management systems, and personal empires come into question. This debate is outside of the scope of this chapter, but it is relevant insomuch that Subphenomenology provides the scaffolding for learners to gain inner knowing and thereby take greater responsibility for their own learning. A lecturer will not be able to predict what a student will learn through Subphenomenology.

So to be clear, what exactly *is* a personal learning environment (PLE)?

I consider Atwell's succinct definition to be representative of the general 'insiders' view:

*The idea of a Personal Learning Environment recognises that learning is ongoing and seeks to provide tools to support that learning. It also recognises the role of the individual in organising his or her own learning. Moreover, the pressures for a PLE are based on the idea that learning will take place in different contexts and situations and will not be provided by a single learning provider. Linked to this is an increasing recognition of the importance of informal learning (Atwell, 2007)*

Similarly, Alan Cann says that a PLE is:

*...a system that helps learners take control of and manage their own learning. This includes providing support for learners to set their own learning goals, manage their learning, manage both content and process, and communicate with others in the process of learning (Cann, 2009)*

## THE ACTION RESEARCH CYCLE AND THE REFLECTIVE WEBLOG JOURNAL

The Action Research process, was conceived by Lewin as an applied social science. Whitehead and McNiff (2006) explain:

*Kurt Lewin, one of its acknowledged founding fathers...saw action research as a procedure that would allow workers to have a greater say in their work contexts. He promoted action research on the basis that workers 'greater involvement would probably improve their productivity. "(Whitehead & McNiff, 2006, p.21).*

Reason and Bradbury (2006) describe it as,

*working towards practical outcomes, and also about creating new forms of understanding, since action without reflection and understanding is blind... "((Reason & Bradbury, 2006 p.2).*

The Plan-Act-Reflect spiral continues in an aim to improve the research situation, until the project is (for whatever reason) terminated. The PLEs@CQUni project has adopted such an Action Research approach. Initially, three researchers met on a regular basis, brainstormed and planned and acted on those plans, as was agreed to be appropriate. It is the reflective phase, however, that is the domain for Subphenomenology. I embarked on the reflective phase with a series of weblog entries describing my early encounters with Web 2.0 tools, from my perspective as a Web 2.0 novice. Using the sub-phenomenological methods, I wrote my way to the *archetypal* explanation for my inter-subjective situation. I wrote until the myth of Echo and Narcissus manifested.

### The Position of Subphenomenology in the PLEs@CQUni Research Context

Figures 1 and 2, adapted from earlier work (Vallack, 2009) show the evolution of Subphenomenology as a methodology for reflecting on one's personal practice.

The PLEs@CQUni project saw me working with gifted and experienced technicians, who were telling me that they had forgotten what it was like *not* to have a comprehensive knowledge of all things computed. Therefore, I was the one in the position to identify with the elephant in the pantry – the academic who resists technological advancement in the workplace, when all about is assuming compliance. Like me, these academics are slow to learn and overwhelmed by the mere proximity of technological challenge.

At first, when I started blogging, it became as annoying as it was apparent that every time I forgot a password or username, it was my fault that the THING wouldn't let me in. I decided then that Technology is no gentleman. It is, in fact, most ungracious in its denial of any shared responsibility for error. It lacks all emotional intelligence (Goleman, 1997). If there is error, there is always an excruciatingly logical explanation. But unlike some otherwise gifted professionals who have been driven to early retirement by a machine, I have opted now for a relationship of convenience with technology, because of the advantages it affords me. But I know that it doesn't love me- it just is – take it or leave it. And this is why some of us, who relate emotionally to the world and anthropomorphically to the things in it, hit the un-empathetic, un-expressive brick wall that is the personality of this machinery; this Narcissus. My frustration with the computer's lack of compassion became evident in the early weblogs. At that time, I was not aware of any pattern emerging. I did not consciously seek connections at that stage. I just let my irritation flow into free association – like this:

***(Secret and password protected) Diary of a Web 2 Novice (Jocene Vallack, 2008a)***

***October 8th, 2008***

*Gee you spend a lot of time for nothing in front of a computer screen. I have wasted hours this*

*Figure 1. The action research methodology of the PLEs@CQUi project, showing the reflective phase, which is the focus for sub-phenomenology methodology*

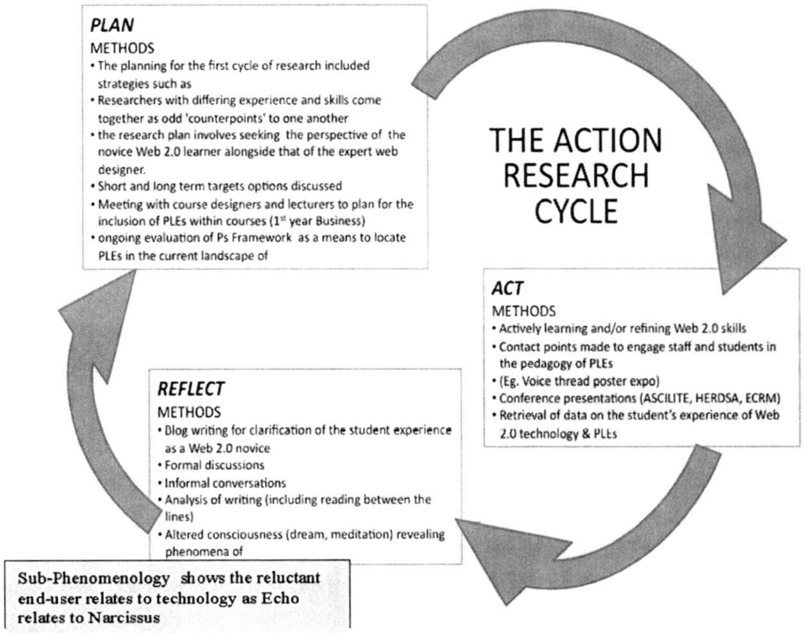


*Figure 2. The methodological framework for sub-phenomenology*

***Sub-Phenomenology***

| | |
|---|---|
| EPISTEMOLOGY | OBJECTIVISM |
| THEORETICAL PERSPECTIVE | TRANSCENDENTALPHENOMENOLOGY |
| METHODOLOGY | SUB-PHENOMENOLOGY |
| METHODS | |

- FREE ASSOCIATION WEBLOG DRAFTS
- REWRITE DRAFT MAINTAINING ESSENTIAL MEANING
- THROUGH ALTERED STATES OF CONSCIOUSNESS, ALLOW MAGICAL IMAGES AND MYTHICAL EXPLANATIONS TO EMERGE
- USE MENTAL CONSCIOUSNES TO ANALYSE ARCHETYPAL FORM THAT HAS EMERGED IN RESPONSE TO RESEARCH QUESTION

*week trying every password I've ever used to get back into this weblog (for some reason I prefer the full name of the thing. The abbreviation sounds obscene.). Anyway, Edublog has been closed for renovations, but, of course, I just thought it was me. When it asked me if I had forgotten my password, I affirmed that this was the case and put in a request for a new one to be sent to my email. Unfortunately, when I set up this blog, I had to use my home email, and to get into that from work required me to send for another password from Bigpond. This line of obscurity is now prominently in my work diary, for there is no way I could remember it, and I am afraid to change it to something else that, clearly, is forgettable. I try to use the same password, but then some machine demands that I embellish it by adding a lot of B*##y!I style characters. So then, like it* *not, I have another password to contend with. Another password that will ensure that no-one can break in to see what I am about to publish on my PUBLIC WEBLOG!*

*I don't know what all this security is about – it's just a nuisance. Anyway, I work with a shop load of super-geeks (all gorgeous) who could break into anything I construct (if they really wanted to be bored out of their brains!).*

*So the thought for the day is – just because you've hit another "invalid username", doesn't mean that it's not because the system isn't down! (Love all those triple negatives when I'm feeling like the martyr.*

*Which reminds me - I still haven't been able to access my car radio since they took out the battery! (Vallack, 2008 weblog: http://jocene.edublogs.org/2008/10/20/velocity-ubiquity/)*

As I switch my role from that of author to analyst, I see my/the novice's frustration with the uncompassionate system. When I first started to write the blogs, I had not imagined that it would become research data, and I did not attempt to analyse it. That is how it should be with Subphenomenology. Better not to at this stage, lest it ushers in self-conscious censorship. Better to just allow the image to emerge from the unconscious in good time.

Jung explains the significance of this phenomenon:

*Image and meaning are identical: and as the first takes shape, so the latter becomes clear. Actually the pattern needs no interpretation; it portrays its own meaning (Jung in Neville, 1989 p.81).*

Neville (1998) colours this with an explanation of the archetypal psychology for which Jung is famous. He elucidates the significance of the myth:

*Archetypal psychology as a contemporary way of thinking about culture and behaviour is largely based on the work of Carl Jung. Jung devoted himself to documenting the patterns he found in human behaviour, both individual and collective. When it came to explaining these patterns, he fell back on Plato's notion of archetype. Following Plato, he was inclined to understand archetypes as pre-existent forms which are replicated again and again in nature and in our experience. He wrote of archetypes as "instinctual patterns of behaviour", which are genetically inherited, as "structures of the collective unconscious" and as "modes of apprehension" which shape our encounter with reality.... We can learn something of the nature of these patterns in the "old stories" or myths of ancient cultures (Neville, 1989, p.22).*

In our PLE research, the archetypal patterns of behaviour are embodied in the mythical forms of Echo and Narcissus. Subphenomenology, as we have discussed, is the methodology that looks underneath the rhetoric to glimpse the unconscious, collective forms that story-board our lives. The creative blogging process is the platform on which the forms materialise, It will lead the artist and researcher to the mythical form, which is the image for that particular research question.

Subjective, autoethnographic (Boucher & Ellis, 2002) data is useful to the researcher so long as it is candid. It comes more easily to some. Other researchers, with more sense that intuition (Myer-Briggs, 2009) will probably prefer to measure the research in some concrete way. And that's good too. But some of us just know more that we can say (Polanyi, 1967), and this approach is for those inclined to trust the tacit dimension of knowledge. From a young age, at various acting schools, I learned to use my vulnerabilities and shortcomings, because therein lie the nuggets of humanity that hook the audience with truth. If the researcher can write blogs (or paint, or photograph, or play) in ways that are uncensored and unguarded, the data will be useful (and intriguing). If not, it might be better for that researcher to use another approach, because only authentic data will unveil the unpredictable. Contrived writing will become cliched and artificial. Writing authentically is potentially humiliating, but I try to take pride in my bravery, when in the name of research I show the shadow of myself.

***Velocity & Ubiquity?(Jocene Vallack, 2008b)***

***October 20th, 2008***

*"About this time last year I delivered a talk to students on Plagiarism. This was the standard student orientation delivery, warning students of the evils of coveting someone else's intellectual property. Now please remember that I am a novice to Web 2.0, and that I generally struggle to be bothered with a lot of technological tricks (that promise all sorts of nerdy fun then fail to deliver because of memory, or gremlins or some boring crash). Add to that my technologically-unlikely personality profile (self-centred extrovert who needs a real audience on a daily basis, and defensive, glory-hogging new PhD graduate who needs recognition for anything resembling original thought) and you may start to appreciate the perplexive nature of my encounter with Web 2.0 anonymity. Now, hear me me me ask - How do we reconcile the idea of shared intellectual property within a western academic environment wherein plagiarism is the ultimate misdemeanour? Does an embrace of Web 2.0 mean that that I am to be both intellectually and ethically challenged, to take on all this new information AND become more gracious to boot. I may as well turn Buddhist. But when Stephen Downes (2005) talks about it, it doesn't sound too bad. I wonder how he views Buddhism?" (Vallack, 2008, Weblog: http://jocene.edublogs.org/2008/10/20/velocity-ubiquity/)*

Clearly I am also trying hard to be amusing, in a self-debasing way. I think this is forgivable, as I attempt to cover naked embarrassment with comedy.

## ISSUES AND CONTROVERSIES: IS THIS RESEARCH SCIENTIFIC?

No – and deliberately so. Much has been written now in favour of post-positivism, although for some disciplines, no urgent need to confront the inadequacy of positivist methods has arisen to necessitate invention of other frameworks. Positivist methods are inadequate for this research, because the results we need are not quantifiable. Let us take a moment to be satisfied that there are valid alternatives to modernist science.

Tarnas (1993) informs us that the foundations of modernism were established somewhere between the fifteenth and sixteenth centuries. It was during this time that science took precedence over mysticism, and the early supremacy of the "transcendent" over the "material" was now "largely inverted". This mind-set typified Husserl's intellectual climate, one hundred years ago, when he was writing about transcendental phenomenology. Little wonder that when he set out his philosophical phenomenology, well ahead of its time, he was dismissed as off-course and esoteric.

Tarnas (1993) sums up modernism thus:

*This emergence of the modern mind, rooted in the rebellion against the medieval Church and the ancient authorities...took the three distinct dialectically related forms of the Renaissance, the Reformation, and the Scientific Revolution. These collectively ended the cultural hegemony of the Catholic Church in Europe and established the more individualistic, sceptical, and secular spirit of the modern age. Out of that profound cultural transformation, science emerged as the West's new faith (Tarnas, 1993, p.282).*

Jean Gebser (1986) suggests that human awareness has evolved through various stages. Remnants of each stage may remain to integrate with one's present mode of consciousness. I would like to explore Gebser's theory as a possible explanation of the *mechanics* of Subphenomenology. Firstly, I shall borrow a useful summary of Gebser's theory of consciousness as an overview and starting point.

Mahood (1996) writes:

*The focus here has been Gebser's approach to understanding the unfoldment of human consciousness. The first part dealt exclusively with the model examining each of Gebser's structures of consciousness in turn; The Archaic, Magical, Mythical, Mental, and Integral. We saw the Archaic structure could best be described as a zero-dimensional, non-perspectival world which could be likened to a state of deep sleep. It was characterized by non-differentiation and the total absence of any sense of separation from the environment. This was a world of identity between self and surroundings; not a world in which we could speak of consciousness in any terms that would be meaningful to our modern understanding of the term. By contrast, the magical structure was characterized by a certain separateness, but not a total separation by any means. Dimensionally this could be described as one-dimensional, a pre-perspectival state of timelessness and spacelessness. It was likened to a state of sleep. Magic man was much apart of his environment, to be sure, and felt secure only within his group, his tribe or clan. It was the transition from the Archaic to Magic structure of consciousness that has probably been mythologically captured in the story of the "Fall of Man". The clothing of knowledge in myth is what characterized the transition to the mythical structure of consciousness, the two-dimensional, unperspectival state of consciousness that can best be likened to a dream. Imagination and attunement with natural rhythms became important factors in man's life. The separation begun in the Magic structure reaches a tensional climax in the Mythical. This structure is superseded by the mental structure, whose appearance coincides with the rise of Greek civilisation. In this regard, it can be seen that modern thought disregards a good deal of mankind's history ....By comparison, the Mental structure of consciousness is a three-dimensional, perspectival world that we described with the term wakefulness. The polar tensions of mythology are replaced by the analytical separation of duality and opposition. Thinking is primary, and in its latter stage, rational thinking is primary. But this structure, too, is yielding to a mutation which Gebser identifies as the Intregral structure of consciousness. This is described as a four-dimensional, aperspectival world of transparency. This is a time-free, space-free, subject and object free world of verition (Mahood, 1996, p.15-6).*

How then, might Gebser's stages of consciousness inform the process of Subphenomenology and its role in deciphering weblog data?

I have put it that as a methodology, Subphenomenology sets out a series of research methods through which transcendental forms, from the unconscious mind of the subject/researcher, may present themselves. But what actually happens in the mind? How do these archetypal images rise to the surface of consciousness? From where do they come? The mechanics of such manifestations, and possible answers to these questions are more elusive than the forms themselves. At the end of the chapter, I have attempted to describe the phenomenon of intuition though an anecdote that I journalled some years ago, for preservation of the experience. It is my best attempt to put into words what is probably known clairsentiently. Perhaps the healthy skeptic will find Gebser's terminology more convincing and less esoteric. Allow me to parallel the two frameworks:

I have been using terms like *intuition*and *instinct* to describe the *tacit* aspects of the various methods essential to the methodology. This methodology depends on trusting a hunch – very magical? Perhaps. If, as a Subphenomenologist, I embark on an academic thesis with blind faith, and a thought that something might be revealed to me, in Gebser's terms, I am drawing on the remnants of magical consciousness. If my consciousness receives archetypal images, which I know only through some irrational consciousness, is that not mythical consciousness? When my rational consciousness takes these images and intellectualises them into a structured methodology, which I argue is valid research, is that not mental consciousness? Perhaps too, the incorporation of the various levels of consciousness suggests that the thinking is also moving beyond mental consciousness, which according to Gebser, will not tolerate any form of thinking other than its own?

If one accepts Gebser's idea that we retain scraps of consciousness from our mutating past, and if our previous levels of consciousness are, indeed, *ever present (Gebser, 1985)*, then it might explain the eclectic nature of contemporary methodology, which collaborates equally well with hunch, image and rational thought. These combine, or *integrate*, to form the process of Subtextual Phenomenology.

To illustrate this point in a more spatial way, I summarised, in table form, the possible links between Gebser's levels of consciousness and aspects of Subtextual Phenomenology (Vallack, 2005):

A key point of Gebser's thesis is that each structure of consciousness is held "ever-present" within us. Moving to the next level of consciousness does not mean the redundancy of the prior structure. The currently dominant mental structure, endorsed through scientific method and positivist perspectives, cannot tolerate other kinds of know-

*Figure 3. Gebser's structures of consciousness aligned with & sub-phenomenlogy*

| Gebser's STRUCTURES OF CONSCIOUSNESS | Characteristics of this level of consciousness | Aspect of Sub-Phenomenology which relates to this level of consciousness |
|---|---|---|
| ARCHAIC | Presentiment | The EPOCHE (But to be accurate, I am still wondering about this) ? |
| MAGIC | Space-timelessness. No individuality. United with everything. Gebser says: **"When the ...wakeful consciousness is sufficiently depressed so that the surroundings are no longer present ...where even the psychic reality of dream and image vanish, his individuality is obliterated in the magic realm."..(Gebser, 1985, p.163). and: "...when the suppliant re-emerges from the depths of meditation and returns to his rational, wakeful consciousness, he brings along from the magic depths his recovery and health. (Gebser, 1985,p.164).** | MEDITATION |
| MYTHICAL | Archetypes. Animated, primal images, which Gebser says are: **"...reflections of the inner, dark and unfathomable forces in man which we call the powers of the soul or psyche." (Gebser, 1985, p.165).** | DREAMS<br><br>TRANSCENDENTAL (ARCHETYPAL) FORMS |
| MENTAL | The discovery of causality. Method replaces mystery. Abstraction and philosophising. Reason & synthesis | DATA ANALYSIS & COGNITIVE ASPECTS OF WEBLOG WRITING PROCESS<br><br>Reason & synthesis |
| INTEGRAL | The culmination of all previous levels of consciousness, plus a forth dimension created by a freedom from time. **"Without freedom from time an effectual supersession of the spatial confinement of three-dimensional reality is not possible....Time must first become concrete and conscious in all its forms; something can be superseded and integrated only when consretized."(Gebser, 1985, p. 355)**<br><br>Integration and transcendence | Writing in the academic or creative genres engages the sub-phenomenological researcher in varying modes of consciousness. The writing becomes inter-subjective as the universal form is manifest in all like situations. the archetype itself is the inter-subjective product of the collective unconscious (Jung)<br>We *suspend disbelief* and accept as present reality the story and characters as they present themselves (magical). We engage in the quest (mythical). At times we reflect critically (mental). And what about that vague stirring that goes almost unnoticed (archaic)?<br>The research process draws on various modes of consciousness to produce and analyse data. |

ing and so sanctions the notion of each mode of consciousness replacing the previous one. Postmodern eclecticism is a predictable reaction to it. Modernism is the dualistic, either/or way of viewing a world. The methods of Subphenomenology embrace postmodernist notions such as intuitive research, (Braud & Anderson, 1998), writing as a method of research (Richardson, 1994) and performance text in the "seventh moment of inquiry" (Denzin, 2003). But like Gebser, it moves beyond the fragments of postmodernism to the big picture. Gebser suggests that as each new phase mutates, it adds to the expansive whole. Rather than make the past structure superfluous, it incorporates and enhances that which has gone before.

Image and story are powerful communication tools. These are the weapons of our dreams. Here is a story version of the philosophical process of Subphenomenology:

*Phenomena Lost*

or

*The Story of Art*

As you would know, there are three planes of existence. There is the physical, life-world from which we now speak, which is the first and lowest plane. Secondly, there is the transcendental plane where artists sometimes go, and where Plato discovered his 'forms', having peered into the third plane, which is of course, the plane of the gods.

As it happened, a small god, known only by the generic term, "Phenomena", once descended to earth via magic. He was unable to understand any of the languages spoken in this life-world, but he knew that in order to re-ascend to his rightful place in the kingdom of the gods, he would need to establish his true identity; that is, his element. Aphrodite had once smiled upon him and shown him the element of beauty, and this had inspired him to seek the essence of his own existence. It had, in fact, inspired him in every way. When he would seek to catch a glimpse of beauty, he would sometimes see Aphrodite in strange and unexpected places. There was occasional talk of beauty in the life-world, but since the small god could not understand talk, he would look underneath the language for clues; he sought knowledge subtextually. And he hoped with all his objectivism that his own element might become as clear as beauty.

Phenomena, as he was vaguely known, had found himself amidst a busy and forbidding life-world plane. He became confused. At first there were no signs of his role-model, Aphrodite, but as he became accustomed to the harsh physicality of the place, he would see specks of light here and there which he knew to be fallen droplets from her eyes.

This regained sense of Aphrodite gave him confidence. He explored the plane, wandering here and there without any purpose that was apparent to him. He explored the world experientially, but he could not talk about it, because he did not understand talk. This meant that he could not categorise his thoughts by using language as a clustering mechanism. His thoughts were becoming many and untidy – lying about on the floor of his mind – in the very place that was to be kept special for thoughts of Aphrodite! The more he experienced, the more the mess piled up. The more it piled up, the more pressure it put on his mind, until one day it happened that he decided to take a good look at the items that had accrued in his mind. And as he clambered over all the stuff, he got higher and higher until his head was sticking up into the transcendental pane. From there he lost sight of his actual experiences, but he could just manage to see them reflected in a large lake, next to which he had been residing. He gazed at his reflected experiences. He was too high to see any of them in watery detail, but to his astonishment he saw that the many and varied items had fallen into a pattern. The colours had balanced, as if arranged by a painter, and there was texture and movement in the design. Like Narcissus he became transfixed with an image of himself – his form, his element. He wondered if he should name it in order to take it back to earth. Then suddenly it was gone. The reality of the life-world dissolved the image, as a drop of blood from a terrorist's weapon fell from the sky to implode the aqua vision.

This loss of insight impacted upon the little god. Having been sucked rudely back down to earth through a tunnel of reality, he decided to pursue his element by safer, scientific means. He learned language so that when he caught glimpses of his true identity, he could borrow words and clichés to capture and hold them. He gathered themes to trap his insights. He sought to find and name his element through rigor and existential phenomenology. And he took lessons in piano and mathematics to appease his status anxiety.

He forgot about the transcendental plane, which had shown him patterns. There was too much to do – too much to label, for now he was in the real world of passion and survival, and this talk of other dimensions of thought did not sound compliant with current academic terminology

It seemed that he would never find his true element, so instead he gave himself a name. He called himself Persephone. As he became accustomed to this lowly plane, he developed fear and doubt and depression. And when he thought he could smell the perfume of Aphrodite on the breeze, he dismissed it as a brain tumour.

Then one day as he sat at his piano, and all hope of finding his purpose and identity had passed, he drifted into a daydream. And as he dreamed, he began to play, and the music evoked patterns. They were the same patterns that he had glimpsed in the transcendental plane, but now they shook with sound. And he cried out, "I am Art!" Just like that!

He was Art. For it is art that transcends the lifeworld to reveal universal patterns, and Art who is the go-between for heaven and earth. Of course Art needs an instrument through which to express himself, so he did not know who he was until he spoke through his language of music (Vallack, 2005b, p.100.).

## SOLUTIONS AND RECOMMENDATIONS: SUBPHENOMENOLOGY HARNESSES INTUITION FOR RESEARCH RIGOR

Subphenomenology is a methodologically valid approach to using authentic phenomenology in the Husserlian sense. Because it challenges scientific positivism on some levels, I have argued extensively (Vallack 2005a) for the philosophical consistency within the theoretical framework of this methodology. It will appeal to the strengths of artists, blog writers and researchers with high creativity, because it scaffolds circumstances through which intuition can work as the medium for the delivery of the phenomenological research object: the archetype from the unconscious mind. As the story of the little god might suggest, Transcendental Phenomenology, through which one may glimpse the big picture, cannot be reached with the language and life-world descriptions of common qualitative methodologies. It involves uncovering the universal, intersubjective archetype. The archetype, at first a product of the research, can then be used to further inform the inquiry. Having established, for example, that my relationship with technology is embodied in the myth of Echo and Narcissus, I might then ask how the details in the story – her dumb ineloquence, his vain attrition - further enlighten the research. For example, it was after the manifestation of the myth that I became consciously aware of my humiliating inability to talk the technological talk. I am not good with acronyms, possibly due to a mild dyslexia.

I will now review my contention that Subphenomenology is a methodology that is informed by a consistent and rigorous theoretical structure. Weerakkody (2009) correctly points out that each researcher needs to be clear about the assumptions s/he brings to an inquiry. I think the difference between arts-based research and art for its own sake, is that the first must show context and methodological sense, whereas the second can show or not show anything at all. The researcher must be able to speak for the research, but art can speak for itself.

Weerakkody (2009) asserts:

*Research epistemologies decide how we conduct research. Therefore it is necessary to identify the epistemology and the theoretical perspective one hopes to use when examining a research question or phenomenon, which in turn helps the researcher to choose the most suitable methodology and data collection methods....Each epistemology has its own assumptions, which need to be clear to the researcher....Qualitative and quantitative research vary at the level of methods, but not at the level of epistemology or theoretical perspectives. Each has specific strengths and purposes, which must be considered when deciding on which method/s will suit one's research question/s and inquiry. The two methods are just different and have no hierarchical standing (Weerakkody, 2009, p16).*

The last point about potential hierarchical status of methods is interesting. During the twentieth century, when mental consciousness (Gebser, 1985) reigned, quantitative methodology tended to be viewed as more rigorous than qualitative methods. In some areas, including educational technology, I think this inclination endures. Certainties are preferred, perhaps? But primarily, one must ask if the methods for providing answers to the research questions are appropriate. A poorly worded survey will yield a load of meaningless statistics, just as surely as an uncommitted pretense at intuitive inquiry will produce unauthentic, predictable clichés. The beauty of Subphenomenology is that the answers lie hidden from the consciousness until they are evoked to appear – fresh and unexpected. The research question, unlike the research hypothesis, allows us to discover what we don't yet know.

## The Four Elements of Research Design: Epistemology, Theoretical Perspective; Methodology and Methods

I am perplexed by the conglomeration of terminologies that are sometimes undefined and misused in academic research. We need to be clear about what we do and ensure that others understand the connotations we attach, often thoughtlessly, to language. I include myself as one such tardy perpetrator. We need to make amends. I hope that the glossary of terms at the end of this chapter will go some way towards that.

Crotty (1998) agrees. He says that often the four process elements of Epistemology, Theoretical Perspective, Methodology and Methods are:

*thrown together in a grab-bag style as if they were all comparable terms. it is not uncommon to find, say, symbolic interactionism, ethnography and constructionism simply set side by side as 'methodologies', 'approaches', 'perspectives', or something similar....Lumping them together without distinction is a bit like talking about putting tomato sauce, condiments and groceries in one basket....Tomato sauce is one of many forms of condiment and all condiments are groceries.... Similarly one may feel urged to do some sorting out when confronted by items like symbolic interactionism, ethnography and constructionism all slung together (Crotty, 1998, p.3).*

The following figure, adapted from Crotty (1998, p.5), categorises some common methodological concepts under the four elements of methodological structure.

Subphenomenology carefully sets out its structure under the headings of these four elements that are shown in Figure 4.

*Figure 4. Categories of methodological concepts for orderly research*

| EPISTEMOLOGY | THEORETICAL PERSPECTIVE | METHODOLOGY | METHODS |
|---|---|---|---|
| Objectivism | Positivism | Subphenomenology | Interview |
| Constructionism | Post-positivism | Ethnography | Questionnaire |
| Subjectivism | Interpretivism | Grounded Theory | Survey |
| | Symbolic Interactionism | Heuristic Inquiry | Observation – participant/ nonparticipant |
| | Transcendental Phenomenology | Action Research | Case Study |
| | Existential Phenomenology | etc | Statistical analysis |
| | Hermeneutics | | Visual ethnographic methods |
| | Postmodernism | | Blog writing first- person data |
| | etc | | etc |

## Epistemology

Epistemology is about the way we know what we know. The research will be set into a belief, which underpins the knowledge perspective. Typically, knowledge will come from one of these three viewpoints: Objectivism, Constructionism or Subjectivism.

Subphenomenology, is (paradoxically) like Scientific Method, and based on Objectivism. This means that unlike most forms of emergent, qualitative inquiry, it assumes the existence of objects, outside of the research situation and outside of the researcher's own mind. In the case of Subphenomenology, these objects are the metaphysical archetypes (or Platonic Forms, or inter-subjective archetypes, or mythical metaphors, for the reader should be aware that I am using these terms interchangeably to describe the forms that present themselves to researchers through Subphenomenology.). It is assumed that these *a priori* objects exist, whether or not the researcher actually finds them.

## Theoretical Perspective

This is the philosophical context of the research design. Subphenomenology is informed by Husserl's theory of Transcendetal Phenomenology. Through transcendence of the life-world, one can encounter the mythical forms, the archetypes that embody the research.

## Methodology

This methodology accommodates the objectivist position that those images have been there all along, waiting to be discovered, and are therefore intersubjective, that is, common to humankind, in the same sense as Plato's Gods are representative of human forces..

Informed by its theoretical perspective, this methodology is based on the study of experiences, lifeworld & transcendental, not on language. Despite the initial blogging, this is not hermeneutic research in the way that most existential phenomenology is language-based and interpretive. It focuses on the *subtext*. The unconscious forms lurking between the lines are sought. It is defined by its methods of magic and myth, which make conscious these forms. In the PLEs research, Subphenomenology presented Echo and Narcissus. A different myth may represent each research inquiry.

After the archetypal object appears, language becomes a means of communicating the phenomenon, and making explicit that which has been implicit. It is used to synthesise fragments of phenomena that have presented themselves during the transcendental phase.

## Methods

### 1. Working Solo as Researcher and Research Subject

It is essential to Transcendental Phenomenology, that the researcher exceeds mundane subjectivity through intersubjectivity. This occurs though one's solo journey into the epoche, beyond which lie the eternal forms of existence. Husserl says,

*Subjectivism can only be overcome by the most all-embracing and consistent subjectivism (the transcendental). In this (latter) form it is at the same time objectivism (of a deeper sort)... " (Husserl,1927, p.34).*

*Weblogging is initially a solo activity.*

### 2. Free Association

Data inspired by the research topic, is freely voiced or written in blog drafts without censorship or judgment. It is important to disengage judgment at this stage.Initially, the data is not transcribed or analysed. It is left to float between the conscious and the unconscious, later to be gathered as image rather than language. Parts of it may drift into an unconscious synthesising activity, which takes place prior to the presentation of archetypal image.

This idea of free association belongs to Sigmund Freud, but there is little wonder that Husserl also used it. There are connections between the *free-association* concept of Freud and the Transcendental Phenomenology of Husserl. Both scholars had been writing about the same time, and both had studied under Brentano. Little wonder, then, that their thinking might be in tune. Koestenbaum's (1964) observation sheds light on the link between free-association and the epoche essential to Transcendental Phenomenology:

*Not only did both Freud and Husserl live at approximately the same time (Freud lived from 1865 to 1939, Husserl from 1859 to 1938), study under Franz Bretano, and write important works at the turn of the century (Freud's Interpretation of Dreams was published in 1900, and Husserl's Logical Investigations appeared in 1900 and 1901), but above all there are important affinities between Husserl's phenomenological epoche and Freud's basic rule (free-association). The process of psychotherapy is a systematic and repeated application of the kind of honesty and distancing that is characteristic of the epoche. It can be argued that psychotherapy is the epoche applied to one's personal life (Koestenbaum, 1964* **in** *Husserl p.LXX111).*

My reading of Speigelberg (1972), suggests that Husserl might have endorsed a system of accessing an unconscious object by firstly preparing a pathway through free-associated ramblings, inspired by, but not necessarily apparently relevant to the chosen topic:

*As to Husserl, there is again no evidence of serious interest in psychoanalysis until very late in his life. But this late evidence is sufficient to show that his conception of phenomenology as a science of pure consciousness by no means involved the denial of the unconscious or permanent disinterest in it. (Spiegelberg,1972, p.135-6).*

### 3. Experiencing the Epoche

The topic of inquiry is always with the researcher, and meanings are unconsciously formed in terms of the researcher's experience of the research phenomena. Dreams and meditations provide images that are not yet acknowledged as forms. This is the transcendental stage when the form may appear, but it might be unrecognised by the researcher until it reappears through the blog writing, or other such art-making processes.

This method in the Subphenomenology process has similarities to Heuristic Inquiry (Moustakas, 1990) in that they both are informed by Transcendental Phenomenology. Moustakas uses visions, images and dreams to engage with his inquiry. Whereas for Subphenomenology it is a means to an end, for Moustakas it becomes a satisfying end in itself, hence as Moustakas (1990) points out, Heuristic Inquiry differs from phenomenology.

*In heuristic investigations, I may be entranced by visions, images and dreams that connect me to my quest. I may come into touch with new regions of myself, and discover revealing connections with others....Emphasis on the investigator's internal frame of reference, self-searching, intuition, and indwelling lies at the heart of the heuristic inquiry.... Essentially, in the heuristic process, I am creating a story that portrays the qualities, meanings, and essences of universally unique experiences. Through an unwavering and steady inward gaze and inner freedom to explore and accept what is, I am reaching into deeper and deeper regions of a human problem or experience and coming to know and understand its underlying dynamics and constituents more and more fully. The initial "data" is within me; the challenge is to discover and explicate its nature. In the process, I am not only lifting out the essential meanings of an experience, but I am actively awakening and transforming my own self. Self-understanding and self-growth occur simultaneously in heuristic discovery (Moustakas, 1990, pp11-13).*

My own research through blogging was thus driven. The theoretical framework and outcomes of Subphenomenology are different, but the spirit of the subjective and reflective process is akin to Heuristic Inquiry. Moustakas (1990) says, "Intuition makes possible the perceiving of things as wholes". This sounds so much like Husserl's explanation of apodictic truths, as they form during the transcendental phases, to produce transcendental intersubjectivity. Moustakas (1990) explains it more easily than do the translated Husserlian texts:

*For example, one can view a tree from many angles, sides, front, and back; but one cannot see a whole tree. The whole tree must be intuited from the clues that are provided by careful observation, experience, and connecting the parts and subtleties of the tree into patterns and relationships that ultimately enable an intuitive knowing of the tree as a whole. Every act of achieving integration, unity or wholeness of anything requires intuition (Moustakas, 1990, p.23).*

Some researchers will not wait patiently for elusive intuition, and will prefer other methods. They should then seek them out. Initial uncertainty is part of this methodology, because the research cannot be controlled by the conscious mind. It waits for the unconscious to yield up the essential image to seal the research and justify all that time spent in the dark, wondering if the whole research project will be meaningless. Some personality types cope with the uncertainty better than others. This method, at the core of Subphenomenology, is for those who don't always need to think too much. The image cannot be calculated or consciously controlled.

### 4. Writing about the Blogging to Analyse the Object

When the mythical object has become apparent to the researcher's consciousness, s/he can critically and objectively analyse the research. In Gebser's terms, "mental Consciousness" comes in to play. Now I might write about Echo and Narcissus and the parallels that I see between that myth and my own relationship with technology. Another way of viewing this process might be to consider the complimentary perspectives of the left and right brain hemispheres. Writing rationally about the fruits of the unconscious is a kind of psychological triangulation. It completes the *whole brain* data analysis. Guillaume (2005) explains qualities that each brain hemisphere can bring to our daily functioning, and therefore, it would seem, to our research:

*Our human brain has a right and left hemisphere, and these hemispheres function very differently in their ability to process information. Our left hemisphere is analytical, logical, and linear. Our right hemisphere is "highly specialized to manage complex relationships, patterns, configurations and structures". While our left brain is likely to miss the forest for the trees, our right brain can get lost in abstract thought and have difficulty getting down to specifics. We integrate both ways of processing information to help us navigate in our daily lives. While it may be true that an artist relies more heavily on right brain thought processes to create, he will need left brain analytical thought processes to determine what methods and materials will be most useful in bringing his creation to life (Guillaume, 2005).*

In the end, Subphenomenology engages the conscious to articulate the thousand words painted by the unconscious image. It brings together the rational and the intuitive aspects of knowing. And it also moves beyond the intensely subjective, personal research to scrutiny of the shared, intersubjective research object. The same art which revealed the research outcome can then be showcased on a public platform to enable other to comment on, or remake in another genre, or recreate the research results.

**5. Showcasing the Work for Input by Others**

Most of this methodology is about the internal phenomenon of intuition; that is, right-brain work (Guillaume, 2005). As a kind of research triangulation, I presented the Echo and Narcissus mythical research outcome to an audience for feedback. This was an opportunity to see if others would identify with the mythical nymph, as my research predicts. Anecdotally, they did. I was then able to make a rational judgment about the results and processes. Neville (1989) supports the idea:

*The mythology of the artist or creative thinker tends to overlook the significance of verification.... When Jung took to painting as a means of dealing with his inner conflict after his break with Freud, he found himself tempted to view his productions as great art, because to him the process of painting them in emotional intensity felt like great art. Fortunately he was clever enough to recognise what was happening to him – a phenomenon which he called 'inflation by the anima'.... Only conscious and unconscious working in cooperation can produce a truly worthwhile 'creative' product. That cooperation involves the conscious mind's ability to evaluate (Neville, 1989, p.179).*

Verification is useful for the Subphenomenologist because the feedback from others allows one to determine not only, as Neville points out, if the audience has been moved by "great art", or at least, great insight, but also if the research object might be seized intersubjectively. Did the audience relate to the analogy of Echo and Narcissus the same way as me? Did it make sense to them? Could anyone else identify with it? These questions have been answered for me informally. A more thorough investigation might be stuff for further research.

## FUTURE RESEARCH DIRECTIONS: WRITING FROM THE ALTERED STATES OF CONSCIOUSNESS

Years ago when I was teaching English to Secondary school students, we played a game to overcome the infectious strain of writers' block that sometimes plagues the classroom. We played "5 minute essays", which involved writing as many words as possible in the time, without regard for sense or cohesion. The next step was the best, as we read them aloud with humorous affect. For some it resulted in a lot of stream-of-consciousness writing, emanating from a sort of semi-trance. A few students were so inspired by their own resonating ramblings that they redrafted them into a cohesive product. Subphenomenology, in its early phases, works with altered states like that. Apparently some great writers also work like it. It's a documented phenomenon, and one worthy of further investigation. I think now, with so much interest in spirituality in education and attention to emotional intelligence, we are ready to embark on this sort of elusive research 'Brigadoon'. Frameworks, like Subphenomenology, Heuristic Inquiry, Autoethnography, Narrative Inquiry – and more - are now emerging to offer some rigor and guidelines to intuitive research. It is time.

Neville documents the passive, trance-like creativity of the novelist, Aldous Huxley:

*Aldous Huxley... used to go into what he called "deep reflection". This was a sort of meditation in which he became very relaxed, oblivious to everything around him and narrowly focussed on the problem occupying him. He did not think in this state, but simply let ideas happen to him. He was able to write in this state, if he desired, just as Brahms could in his self-induced trance (Neville, 1989, p.167).*

For Moustakas, creative writing and its prerequisite period of *indwelling*, is a "conscious and deliberate" activity:

*It involves a willingness to go with unwavering attention and concentration into some facet of human experience in order to understand its constituent qualities and its wholeness. To understand something fully, one dwells inside the subsidiary and focal factors to draw from them every possible nuance, texture, fact, and meaning. The indwelling process is conscious and deliberate, yet it is not lineal or logical. It follows clues wherever they appear; one dwells inside them...Indwelling requires practice to enable the researcher to tap into intuitive awakenings and tacit mysteries as well as the explicit dimensions which can be observed, reported, and described (Moustakas, 1990, p.23).*

By contrast, the draft phase of the blog writing method in Subphenomenology takes the passive form, like a day-dream, or indeed, a night dream. In my experience, it is during this altered, dreamy state of consciousness, that the "whole" forms, to which Moustakas refers, seem to materialise. Later, before I publish my blogs, I consciously check details, engaging mental consciousness and left-brain activity. But the interesting phase comes first, when the mind runs free with the Gods.

## CONCLUSION: MAGIC, MYTH AND SOUL IN 21ST CENTURY EDUCATION

The soul of research is drawn to truth. Last century, traditional methodologies were safely impersonal, Web technology was neatly contained and controlled in a central management system, and scientific hypothesis ensured that we were safe from unexpected research results. This is changing. Narcissus is dead. The daffodils grow wild in his place. The interactivity of Web 2.0 technology may draw Echo near again, and persuade her to try again. When the pendulum swings, it swings wide of its balanced resting place. Qualitative researchers, bored by modernism and propelled towards the outer perimeter of post-modernism, now celebrate the possibilities of embracing emotion, image and metaphor in research. This is where technology now ventures, through Skype, Second Life, Facebook and so much more. Avens (2002), whose own interest is in storytelling as research, an approach not unlike the narrative characteristic of blogging, highlights our new quest for intuitive and authentic inquiry. He says that soul and metaphor are essential to arts-based research:

*Academic psychology, in its eagerness to be as scientific as physics, has devoted all its energies not to understand but to explain the soul (psyche) from the viewpoint of natural sciences. In this way the soul has been exorcised from the only field which is traditionally dedicated to its study: it has been explained away, reductivised (Avens, 2001, p.81).*

My early experiences with learning technology were awful because they seemed to incorporate a lot of aggressive rote learning. If Beer and Jones (2008) are right about central learning management systems being more about control than learning, then not meeting the demands for technological literacy might be seen as subversive. Many academics will know the hostile undercurrent that exists towards those who won't learn to independently learn the system. For some reason, even in an otherwise pedagogically enlightened and supportive learning institution, an inability to keep up with technology may still viewed as sloth.

Now as I interact and experiment with machinimas and other inventions from the internet, I learn surprisingly quickly. I don't think I was motivated before now. Now I am becoming independent with technology, and it's narcissistic ways don't intimidate me anymore. I am finding a voice. I am encouraged to be creative. The technology becomes my enabler, not my disabler. I am not just an Echo at the back of the class crying 'F-what? Why do I press F8? Why?'.

## FINALLY: APPLYING SUBPHENOMENOLOGY IN REFLECTIVE PRACTICE

There is currently a lot of talk about *reflective practice* in research. Subphenomenology is a type of reflective and reflexive practice that is informed by Transcendental Phenomenology. My everyday work in *Action Research* demands pedantic attention to the going-over-things in my mind. I hear the term, *reflective practice* bandied about willy-nilly, but like *phenomenology*, there appears around it a plethora of connotations and understandings. Subphenomenology aims to provide scaffolding on which to build an approach to phenomenological, transcendental, reflective practice. Transcendental Phenomenology is the *theory* about phenomenological, reflective practice. Subphenomenology is the methodology I used to realise this theory. I hope that others may find the framework useful, and creatively tune it to suit their own aesthetic inclinations.

I am also aware that some readers will be frustrated by the elusive nature of what I am calling intuition. It's hard to explain. Intuition is something that is felt. I will leave you with this anecdote to account for it as best I can:

## ANECDOTE

Last night I played cards again with two of my friends. Over the years, the card game setting has hosted a ritualistic context for friendship. The game routine has become so automatic that we don't need to think much about the strategies and responses to play. This means that we can concentrate on the conversation. We tend to play the same music, sit in the same places and consume the same sorts of refreshments each time. We have become boldly unimaginative, and we draw comfort from the familiarity of the routine. One horrific night, about ten years ago, they rang me at 2.00am to tell me their son had collapsed and died, and to bring my cigarettes for a card game. I'm not trying to be funny about this. I am mindful of the function of social tradition and ritual in our otherwise chaotic and sometimes tragic lives.

Our card games see three players, each of whom perform with a different problem-solving approach. Over the years, each of us has probably won and lost to about the same measure. Anne's style is task oriented. Her play is consistent. She has learned the best responses to the card patterns, and she plays her own cards accordingly. Allan has the uncanny ability to count cards. He can remember which cards have been discarded. Usually he's too busy talking or listening to do much with this potentially unfair advantage. Occasionally he puts his mind to the game, and would almost be unbeatable except for one factor, which works in my favour – his lack of defence against irrationality. Allan has the skills to predict the play of a logical opponent, but my play is often erratic. I never remember what has been thrown out because I'm more focussed on conversation or I am simply daydreaming. I frequently discard that which I should keep because I don't look properly. I occasionally concentrate and I seem to be naturally lucky. Allan will say things like, "How can you not have that card? You must have had it or you wouldn't have..." The no-strategy strategy can work against the rational opponent.

Anyway, last night, for no apparent reason, I sensed a card that Allan was holding. His finger moved over it for a moment, and I asked him if that card was a seven. Of course he would not tell me at first, but I held back sevens and won the round. Afterwards, he looked quizzically at me and confirmed that my guess had been correct. I don't know how that sort of thing happens, but I will try to describe the sensation. It is the sort of hunch. It does not seem to have much to do with clear thinking. To the contrary, in fact, it is preceded by a mental void, an absence of mind. It is how I understand the epoche.

I see the card. I see the tip of the finger brush the card. My mind goes blank. I empathise with the contact between fingertip and card. I know it through touch. It is a seven. When it happens like this – unprovoked by any urgent sense of greed, need or public pressure, it's right. If I try to do this by engaging consciousness, no message is received. If I guess it, it's wrong. This is like my way of knowing Husserl's phenomenology.

When I look to the card, I intend the object.

When my consciousness recedes and I am inside the moment of contact between card and hand, I am inside the epoche.

As I am withdrawing from the epoche back into consciousness, I ask myself what I encountered, and the phenomenon of Seven follows me out of the epoche and trails into my consciousness. The word "seven", is constituted in my consciousness.

In the epoche, I do not see the card. I do not hear "seven". I touch it through a kind of projection, and constitute that knowing through language as I re-enter the conscious life-world.

My transcendental Seven is not the life-world seven, which Allan is holding in his hand. Mine is the universal Seven. If I needed to determine whether that which he holds is the seven of hearts, or perhaps the seven of clubs, I would again need to touch the epoche – hearts or clubs? – and open to know if the answer has again followed my consciousness, magnetised, to again be absorbed into my porous, lifeworld consciousness. Unfortunately, if I put my mind to such a task, it fails. It is therefore an unreliable method for cheating at cards (Vallack, 2005a).

## REFERENCES

Atwell, G. (2007). Personal learning environments - the future of eLearning? *Journal*, *2*(1). Retrieved from http://www.elearningpapers.eu/index.php?page=doc&vol=2&doc_id=8553&doclng=6.

(2001). Avens . InReason, P., & Bradbury, H. (Eds.), *Handbook of Action Research.*

Beer, C., & Jones, D. (2008). *Learning Networks: Harnessing the Power of Online Communities for Discipline and Lifelong Learning.* Paper presented at the Lifelong Learning Conference, CQUniversity, Queensland.

Boucher, E., & Ellis, C. (2002). *Ethnographically Speaking:Autoethnography, Literature and Aesthetics*. California: Altimira Walnut Creek.

Braud, W., & Anderson, R. (1998). *Intuitive Inquiry*. London: Sage.

Cann, A. (2009). *What the heck is a PLE and why would I want one?* 2009, from http://www.microbiologybytes.com/tutorials/ple/

Crotty, M. (1998). *The Foundations of Social Research: Meaning and Perspective in the Research Process*. Sydney: Allen & Unwin.

Denzin, N. (2003). *Performance Ethnography: Critical Pedagogy and the Politics of Culture*. London: Sage.

Downes, S. (2005, 14 September, 2005). *What e-learning 2.0 means to you*. Presentation at the Transitions in Advanced Learning Conference, Ottawa. Retrieved 15 October, 2005, from http://www.downes.ca/cgi-bin/page.cgi?post=21521

Gebser, J. (1985). *The Ever-Present Origin*. Athens: Ohio University Press.

Goleman, D. (1997). *Emotional Intelligence: Why it can Matter more than IQ*. New York: Bantam.

Guillaume, P. (2005). *Myth, Metaphor and Magic*. 2005, from www.ourworld.compuserve.com

Husserl, E. (Ed.). (1927). *Britannica*. Great Britain: Harvester.

Jalic, & Inc. (2009). *Greek and Roman Mythology> Echo and Narcissus*. Retrieved 7th August, 2009, from http://www.online-mythology.com/echo_narcissus/

Jones, D., Vallack, J., & Fitzgerald-Hood, N. (2008). *The Ps Framework: Mapping the Landscape for the PLEs@CQUni Project*. Paper presented at the Hello! Where are you in the Landscape of Educational Technology? ASCILITE 2008, Melbourne.

Koestenbaum, P. (1964). Introduction to the Paris Lectures . In *The Paris Lecturers*. The Hague: Martinus Nijhoff.

Mahood, E. (1996). The Primordial Leap and the Present: The Ever-Present Origin- an overview of the work of Jean Gebser. *Journal*. Retrieved from www.grailwerk.com/docs/synairetic.htm

Moustakas, C. (1990). *Heuristic Research: Design, Methodology and its Applications*. London: Sage.

Neville, B. (1989). *Educating Psyche*. Melbourne, Australia: Collins Dove.

Polanyi, M. (1967). *The Tacit Dimension*. London: Routeledge & Kegan Paul Ltd.

Reason, P., & Bradbury, H. (2006). *Handbook of Action Research*. London: Sage.

Richardson, L. (1994). Writing: A Method of Inquiry . In Denzin, N., & Lincoln, E. (Eds.), *Handbook of Qualitative Research*. Thousand Oaks, CA: Sage.

Spiegelberg, H. (1972). *Phenomenology in Psychology and Psychiatry: A Historical Introduction*. Evanston, USA: Northwestern University Press.

Tarnas, R. (1993). *Passion of the Western Mind*. San Francisco: Random House.

Vallack, J. (2005a). *Death of an Author: Subtextual Phenomenology: A Radical Methodology Towards the Transcendental Object*. Unpublished PhD Thesis. La Trobe University, Australia.

Vallack, J. (2008a). The (Secret and Password-Protected) Diary of a Web 2.0 Novice. *Journal*. Retrieved 4th November, 2009 from http://jocene.edublogs.org/2008/10/08/secret-and-password-protected-diary-of-a-web-2-novice/

Vallack, J. (2008b). Velocity & Ubiquity. Weblog *Journal*. Retrieved 4th November, 2009 from http://jocene.edublogs.org/2008/10/20/velocity-ubiquity/

Vallack, J. (2009). *The (Secret and Password Protected) Diary of a Web 2.0 Novice doing Subtextual Phenomenology*. European Conference of Research Methodologies (ECRM 2009) Conference Proceedings, Valletta, Malta http://www.academic-conferences.org/ecrm/ecrm2009/ecrm09-proceedings.htm

Vallack, J. M. (2005b). I Know What I Like! *Qualitative Research Journal*, *5*(2), 99–111.

Weerakkody, N. (2009). *Research Methods for Media and Communication*. New York: Oxford University Press.

Whitehead, J., & McNiff, J. (2006). *Action Research Living Theory*. London: Sage.

## ADDITIONAL READING

Atwell, G. Personal Learning Environments. Webpage: http://project.bazaar.org/2006/06/01/personal-learning-environments/

Braud, W., & Anderson, R. (1998). *Intuitive Inquiry*. London: Sage.

Crotty, M. (1996). *Phenomenology in Nursing Research*. Melbourne, Australia: Churchill Livingstone.

Downes, S. (2007) Web 2.0 and your own Learning and Development. (Video) http://video.google.com/videoplay?docid=-5431152345344515009

elearn space (2009) http://www.elearnspace.org/Articles/connectivism.htm

Gebser, J. (1984). *The Ever-Present Origin*. Athens, OH: Ohio University Press.

Goleman, D. (1997). *Emotional Intelligence: Why it can Matter more than IQ*. New York: Bantam.

Heywood, P., McCann, T., Neville, B., & Willis, P. (Ed's) (2005) *Towards Re-enchantment: Education, Imagination and the Getting of Wisdom*. Queensland, Australia: Post Pressed Publishers. http://people.bath.ac.uk/mnspwr/Thoughtpieces/ARspiritualpractice.htm

Husserl, E. (1964). *The Paris Lecturers*. The Hague: Martinus Nijhoff.

Jones, D. (2009) *The Weblog of a David Jones* http://davidtjones.wordpress.com/

Jones, D., Vallack, J., & Fitzgerald-Hood, N. (2008). *The Ps Framework: Mapping the Landscape for the PLEs@CQUni Project.* Paper presented at the Hello! Where are you in the Landscape of Educational Technology? ASCILITE 2008, Melbourne.

Moustakas, C. (1990). *Heuristic Research: Design, Methodology and its Applications*. London: Sage.

Public Library of Charlotte and Mecklenburg County. (August 2006) Website: Learning 2.0: 23 Things. http://plcmcl2-things.blogspot.com/

Reason, P. (2000) Action Research as Spiritual Practice.

Spiegelberg, H. (1982). *The Phenomenological Movement: A Historical Introduction* (3rd ed.). Boston: Martinus-Nijhoff.

Vallack, J. (2002). Phenomenology - Michael Crotty's Euphemism for Nonphenomenology. *Qualitative Research Journal*, *2*(1), 18–24.

## KEY TERMS AND DEFINITIONS

**Apophantic Domain:** Used in Phenomenology, this term refers to that of the senses and propositions. In contrast to this is the ontological domain that of life-world things- relationships, business, politics

**A Priori:** Eternal and timeless structure. Constructed in the mind and not based on experience. Not empirical.

**Essence:** Element: A mandatory feature, fundamental to a given phenomenon. In Transcendental

Phenomenology, I use this word as a simile for universal object.

**Existential Phenomenology:** (arguably) originating from the work of Heidegger, it fixes on an ontological, psychological phenomenology, as opposed to Husserl's philosophical and epistemological phenomenology, that is, Transcendental Phenomenology. The author argues that Existential Phenomenology alone produces only life-world *themes*, not the universal *objects* of true phenomenological reduction.

**Intuition:** Knowledge which is not based on perception, memory or introspection. A hunch. A sixth-sense.

**Intuit Essences:** To allow the essential features of a phenomenon to just occur, as opposed to consciously trying to work it out.

**Lifeworld:** The everyday world. Not the transcendental or apophantic domain.

**Phenomology:** A methodology and a philosophy based on the work of Edmund Husserl. It's about getting to the core of an inquiry. The results are often images and metaphors rather than descriptions. In popular use, it is informed by an epistemology of either objectivism or constructionism. Pure phenomenology, such as that cited in this paper, embraces Husserl's notion of the transcendental object, and is objectivist. Phenomenology is a process of inquiry through which universal objects are presented.

**Radical Fundamental:** Subtextual Phenomenology is radical in that it is informed by the essential and original phenomenology of Edmund Husserl

**Subtextual Phenomenology:** I created Subtextual Phenomenology with my PhD research in 2005. (J. Vallack, 2005) More recently, the name of this methodoogy has been modified, as a matter of linguistic convenience, to *Subphenomenology.* Here it offers a set of methods, non-sequential steps, for the application of Transcendental Phenomenology to blog-based research data.

# Chapter 15

# E-Learning:
## A Management-Oriented Fourfold Strategy in Some East African Universities

**Peter Neema-Abooki**
*Makerere University, Uganda*

**Alfred Kitawi**
*Strathmore University, Kenya*

## ABSTRACT

*Electronic learning (E-learning) strategies require a realization of the changes in both the demand and supply of e-learning resources. The conceptualization of e-learning, a precedent stage in any e-learning strategy development, affects the deployment and use of e-leaning. Since the development of e-learning strategies corresponds to different models available, this chapter aims at highlighting on and proposing an e-learning fourfold strategy in the management of universities. The strategies to this effect are:* **:** *Ideological, Methodological, Output, and Ecological. The chapter heretofore rationalises that the Ecological strategies have an impact on the other three. Universities are therefore called to develop a clear e-learning strategy framework that is commensurate with the existential needs; hence, a strategy that reflects and actuates the mission and vision of a university within a specific context. The chapter therefore analyses the impact of the fourfold strategy with particular reference to Africa-based universities.*

## INTRODUCTION

Technology can be conceived as an art, a process or a product. In the case of Information Technology (IT), it can refer to computers, telecommunications equipment and other technologies associated with automation. It has an impact on individuals, organisations and society (French 1992, p. 518). These technologies have to support the creation, maintenance, manipulation and storage of information. It has its respective methods and applications. An Information Communication Technology (ICT) system can include: hardware, software, data and procedures. The Internet and World Wide Web (WWW) offer educators an opportunity to provide learners with innovative and new virtual environments that can eventually stimulate and enhance the learning process (Brown, 2002).

The transformation of the education sector generally, and the e-learning sector specifically, is

DOI: 10.4018/978-1-61692-791-2.ch015

being driven by a number of broad economic, technological, and social trends that have accelerated in recent years. One key aspect is the significant increase in the demand for higher education in both developed and developing countries. According to one estimate, overall demand for higher education is expected to grow from 48 million enrolments in 1990 to 159 million in 2025—an annual growth rate of 3.5 percent (LaRocque & Latham, 2003).

Different colleges and universities have endeavoured to develop their own ICT strategies to be competitive and deliver their functions efficiently and effectively. For instance, Makerere University in Uganda asserts with Stiles and York (2003) that ICT enables the Lecturer to equip the learner towards the achievement of goals. Strathmore University in Kenya follows suit and propagates e-learning as an indispensable means in the provision of alternative forms of learning.

Electronic learning (E-learning) is defined as the use of any of the new technologies or applications in the service of learning or learner support (Laurillard, 2006). It is learning/training that is prepared, delivered, or managed using a variety of learning technologies. E-learning includes the delivery of content via Internet, intranet/extranet (Local Area Networks/Wide Area Networks), audio- and videotape, satellite broadcast, interactive TV, CD-ROM (Boon, Rusman, Van der Klink, & Tattersall, 2005, p. 206). The Internet, computer based multimedia, and World-Wide Web are the underlying technologies of e-learning. E-learning is an off-shot of information technology 'cyperbole'.

E-learning technologies can be used in three main ways in universities and colleges: i) technology enhanced classroom teaching; ii) distance education or distance learning; iii) distributed learning (a mix of deliberately reduced face to face teaching and online learning also called 'the mixed mode' or ' flexible learning'). In technology enhanced classroom teaching, the teacher or lecturer acts as a guide to help the student explore the maze-work of information provided through different technological devices. The student thus becomes more of an explorer in the intricate web of resources provided. The students are at times able to extract 'new' information to the classroom experience, from time to time unknown to the teacher. Distance education or distance learning is learning experience provided from another remote location. The geographical limit can span from few kilometres to thousands of kilometres. Distance learning is achieved through different networking devices and software applications in a bid to create a dialogue.

Some educationists emphasize on the need for any learning process to be a dialogue. E-learning can help to encourage dialogues and learner centeredness. Web, Jones, Barker & Van Schaik (2004) cite Kolb's model, typifying learner centeredness, which involved an approach similar to action research. The approach was geared towards four elements: active experimentation (planning of learning experience), concrete experience (participation in a learning episode), reflective observation (an introspection of what has been learnt) and abstract conceptualization (an internalization of the learning as an integral entity of previous learning). In recent studies done, it appears that those social science subject areas that fall towards the harder end of the disciplines (Psychology, Economics and Geography) definitely use ICTs more successfully(Louw, Brown, Muller, & Soudien, 2009).

In many countries, there has been greater demand for e-learning because of the craze towards Knowledge Based Economies (KBEs) and consequently the need for life long learning. This means that such economies are ready to access and to pay considerable sums of money to get relevant content delivered conveniently and flexibly (Bates, 2001, p. 25). E-learning has -as corresponding to it – aims, strategies, structures, standards, content delivery and pedagogy. There is increased use of e-learning in many educational institutions especially in universities. While universities – as the zenith of learning – should act as pace-setters in the creation, adoption, adaptation and deployment of e-learning technologies, the focus of this chapter is on e-learning strategies within a particular context; namely, universities.

E-learning strategies require a realization of the changes in both the demand for and supply of e-learning resources. Developing an e-learning strategy is essential in setting a course that will enable a university, faculty or department, to achieve predetermined goals (Engelbrecht, 2003, p. 38). Indeed, before a university adopts any e-learning strategy, an analysis of the impact on: mission, the organisational structure; decision making; decentralisation of power; social and cultural structure; involvement of members of staff; revenue and expenditure; existing processes; weaknesses and threats; and, of course, strengths and opportunities needs to be placed under careful scrutiny. It should be about: providing a solution; a return on expectation; enabling learning and driving performance; motivating learners and encouraging organisations; ensuring that it becomes interwoven into the fabric of the entire organisation and that it becomes invisible (Dublin, 2004, p. 294).

The conceptualization of e-learning, a precedent stage in any e-learning strategy development, affects the deployment, use, and success of e-learning. E-learning is directly influenced by ontological perceptions. The ontological perception of an institution will influence the principles, epistemology, methodology and the way e-learning is implemented to produce results. A positivistic approach, which views reality in quantifiable terms, will affect the formulation and implementation of an e-learning strategy commensurate to it. The ontological perceptions of an organization, for instance, a 'blue-sky' oriented university, a research based university or a teaching focused university, affects its e-strategy formulation. Jefferies, Carstern-Stahl & McRobb (2007, p. 120) express the same view and emphasise that the use of virtual learning tools (emails, tutorials, quizzes, web pages and Power Point) can all be related to a positivistic pedagogy, while the use of discussion boards foster andragogic social constructivist pedagogy.

Different instructional designers, analysts, programmers and users agree on learner centeredness being the hub of e-learning (Blass & Davis, 2003, p. 1; Sharpe, Benfield, & Francis, 2006, p. 137). The electronic equipment is not a replacement of the teachers or instructors, but a tool to enable the educators achieve their objectives. E-learning therefore creates a discourse in the learning process.

The development of e-learning strategies corresponds to different models available. One of the models was developed by Marshall and Mitchell (2004, p. 187). It involves a pent-stage framework consisting of an initial stage (ad-hoc processes), a planned stage (clear and measurable objectives for e-learning projects), a defined stage (defined process for development and support of e-Learning), managed staged (ensuring quality of e-learning resources and student outcomes) and optimising stage (continual improvement in all aspects of the e-learning process). The other model, developed by Sharpe et al.(2006, p. 139), incorporates three modes: Mode 1 is the baseline course administration and learner support; Mode 2 blends learning leading to significant enhancements to learning and teaching process; Mode 3 is an online course module. Salmon (2005, p. 203) builds his prototype according to the nature of universities. The first model is built on the traditional brick and mortar university, and in addition, integrates online components as 'add-ons' or in a blended mode; the second is built on multi-mode results from the need to address the desire of younger undergraduates to attend on campus while also increasing flexibility and value through multimedia and online provision. Meanwhile, the last mode consists in learning through distance education.

The last model has undergone a number of changes from the first generation – characterised by only the print media – to the fifth generation which uses interactive multi-media, campus portal and automated response systems. An example of such a university is the University of Southern Queensland (USQ). USQ was conceptualised in terms of: e-information repositories, a variety of e-applications and an e-interface.

Blass and Davis (2003) provide a framework for eight generic areas which can be used as basis of both design parameters and evaluation tools for e-learning. These eight generic areas are merged into four higher order groupings or categories. The first broad category is the appropriateness criterion which seeks to establish appropriateness and sustainability of staff and content, market and students. Design criterion focuses on the target population and the 'look' and 'feel' of e-learning. The parameters used are learning aspirations and cognitive ergonomics. The interaction criterion focuses on faculty-student interaction and student-student interaction as its guiding principles. The fourth criterion is evaluation. Its principles are reinforcement strategies and achievement of purpose. Its central concerns are effectiveness of student learning and product effectiveness.

Engelbrecht (2003, pp. 41-43) gives a number of e-learning models. The first is the content, service and technology model which emphasized on the delivery of traditional content via the internet. The demand driven model highlighted on technology being a support or tool to achieve desired outcome in a cost effective way. Its stress was on ICT infrastructure. The other model was the instructional design model which focussed on pedagogy, learning models, and delivery and development strategies.

When the different models available for e-learning strategy formulation are integrated, a general model which typifies features present in all models include: ideological strategies, methodological strategies, output strategies and ecological strategies, hence the objectives of this Chapter, and as shown in Figure 1. Explanations of the proposed generalized framework with the specific sub-characteristics/frameworks of each stage are hereby addressed.

## GENERALIZED E-LEARNING STRATEGY FRAMEWORK

### Ideological Strategies

The core capabilities that are obvious or are most enjoyed or admired within a university may not

*Figure 1. E-learning strategy in the management of universities: A synthesis of perspectives*

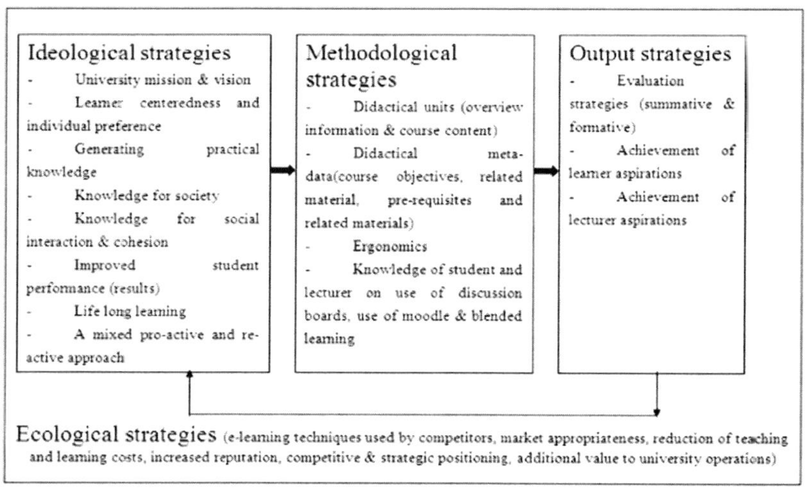

be strategically relevant. Instead, they need to be those that a wide range of 'stakeholders' (students, clients, partners, funding bodies) both perceive and value (Salmon, 2005, p. 209). Before strategy building is effected, an analysis of the strengths, weaknesses, opportunities and threats (SWOT) needs to be undertaken in terms of financial, physical, human and environmental capital. Ideological strategies deal with the actual conceptualisation of e-learning in line with a university's mission and vision and its statement. The sub-issues that emerge in this strategy include: A university's mission and vision, the need to encourage learner centeredness and individual preferences, the urge to foster life-long learning, building a pro-active and reactive approach to issues and thereby generating knowledge, ensuring that knowledge generated is for the society and increases social interaction and cohesion.

Vorley & Nelles (2008, p. 2) define the functions or mission of a university as teaching and learning, research and a third mission, which is to realize their broader socio-economic potential through knowledge exchange and partnerships. Martin and Etzkowitz (2000, p. 13) echo the same by explicating that in addition to the two traditional roles of teaching and research, a third mission is important- contribution to the economy. We can therefore, using the functionary approach, state that universities are characterised by three essential features: teaching, research and community service (serving the socio-economic needs). The researchers define quality extramural to these substantive features. Some authors see some of these features as dialectical. Liu (2005) observes that the academics inherent in universities and the more diverse demands in society are in a dialectic unity. Survival lies in service, and development in contribution. This survival is promoted through a healthy engagement in teaching, research and providing practical solutions to society. If engagement is really to be beneficial to all concerned stakeholders, timely and relevant information and knowledge within and without the academy needs to be provided, and e-learning provides one of these opportunities.

Once the vision has been agreed upon, the next step is to generate a mission statement to shape the actions needed to achieve the vision (Engelbrecht, 2003, p. 39). A *Mission statement* is a brief description of a company's fundamental purpose. It answers the question: "Why do we exist?" The mission statement therefore articulates the company's purpose both for those in the organisation and for the public (New York Times, 2009). The actions deal with the formulation and formalisation of knowledge principles. If a university conceptualizes itself as an entrepreneurial university, its principles will be different from one which conceives itself as a traditional brick and mortar university or adaptive-reactive university.

An entrepreneurial university will be geared towards knowledge for action, pragmatism and in certain cases, constructivism. The use of e-learning is therefore approached in a participatory way. The learners are encouraged to be part of the learning process. Previous knowledge acquired by the learner becomes crucial in developing new knowledge which is practical and useful. A traditional brick and mortar university may put more emphasis on knowledge for knowledge's sake, and as such it will follow a more idealistic and realistic approach. In such a situation, the use of e-learning in terms of generation and transmission of knowledge will in most cases be uni-directional. Positivist approaches are perhaps epitomized in education by the classical behaviourist view of learning as conditioned response. This states that the world out there has to be rigorously tested using scientific methods and later described objectively. The epistemology of e-learning therefore concentrates on the measurement of the world out there independent of what the learner understands apriori. Constructivist approaches, on the other hand, hold that reality is a construct that cannot be determined independently of the observer. This group of theories cannot be seen as a single, coherent approach, since their antecedents are to be found among widely divergent sources from various disciplines, for example psychologists like Vygotsky (1978), Wittgenstein (1953), Barthes (1988) and, perhaps most clearly, Berger and Luckmann (1966) could be classified under constructivism (Jefferies et al., 2007). All these ontological perceptions adopted within the different university models will inevitably affect the understanding, use and results obtained through e-learning.

Ideological strategies are also influenced by the need to improve student performance and learner centeredness. These ideological strategies affect methodological and consequently output strategies. For instance, a critical pedagogy which is impregnated with the emancipatory approach, emphasize that current educational practices underpin and maintain oppression and exploitation (Clegg, Hudson, & Steel, 2003, p. 50). The methodological strategies therefore will focus on how to provide an antithesis to the whole situation. Meanwhile, Blass & Davis (2003, pp. 231-233) cite ideological strategies in the appropriateness criteria with an emphasis on nature, context and desired outcomes as its sub-issues. As regards nature and context, subjects that are heavily dependent on text and reading can be put into an e-learning format but care needs to be taken in considering whether it should. The following questions become pertinent: Is there an appropriate technical platform to support e-learning? ; Does a university have the necessary technical expertise to support the platform? ; Does the university have the necessary funding to support the technical platform?; What are the outputs needed from the platform?

Other questions like the type of knowledge generated – for instance, knowledge for action, for understanding, for policy making or for social interaction – will determine the ecological, methodological and output strategies. A research oriented university might be more geared towards knowledge for action and change. Its focus will be to ensure that intellectual property generated is useful to both the immediate and remote environment. It will therefore tend to use e-learning methods that foster the generation of knowledge like online discussion boards, case studies, reflective tools, simulation and heuristics. A teaching oriented university will tend to use e-learning to transmit knowledge through uploading course materials using software like Moodle or WebCT. The emphasis, irrespective of a university's mission, should be to make knowledge as pragmatic as possible in a bid to create life-long learners. The learners have to understand learning and become independent learners, understand knowledge and become competent in constructing knowledge within their disciplines (Wingate, 2007).

The learner should be both pro-active and reactive in the process. Pro-active because the learner has to be able to judge what is valuable or relevant; and reactive because most of these value judgments are as a result of many intrinsic and extrinsic variables, some of which the learner is aware of only during the learning process. This means that users of e-learning need to be given the necessary critical thinking, reading and writing skills in order to be co-creators of knowledge to enhance social interaction and cohesion.

## Methodological Strategies

Criteriology, that is, the relationship between knowledge and knower, will influence the methodological/pedagogical strategies. The knower in a university is not a uniform entity but is sourced from different backgrounds (from the economic, social and political perspectives), enters the university system at different levels (e.g. diploma, mature and direct entry), and has different expectations (in terms of process, structure and outcome). Consequently, e-learning methodological strategies have to address the different types of relationships and needs between the knowledge and the knower. Some of these strategies are focussed on didactical meta-data, didactical units, ergonomics and knowledge on the use of different technologies. High impact, high performance, and high sample engagement of new learners facilitates a lasting impression. Training in communication skills in relation to online teaching has a very low priority even though research has shown that online communication skills constitute a critical parameter for the quality of online teaching (Levinsen, 2007).

The e-learners need knowledge on how to use different technologies, that is the ability to be e-learners (Elliott, 2002). Knowledge has both '*homo-centric*' and '*techno-centric*' perspectives. Homo-centric, because drawing of consistent patterns from information and to present it logically to produce knowledge and truth is a human attribute. Techno-centric since when information communication technologies are used in expert and decision support systems, the knowledge cannot be dissociated from hardware and software components (e.g. database management systems, analytical systems). Knowledge has to be packaged, presented, and communicated in a meaningful way. It should be used to serve as a basis of further knowledge-development.

A methodological framework developed by Sharpe et al (2006, p. 139) includes four modes of e-learning. The modes are:

1. Baseline course administration and learner support (*this includes assessment criteria, past exam questions, timetabling announcements, reading lists, tutor contact details, course evaluation tools, frequently asked questions and additional web resources)*
2. Blended learning leading to significant enhancements to learning and teaching processes (*it focuses on communication in terms of entities, technology and the media involved, form of assessment, collaboration platform and learning content deployment)*
3. Online course module (*it includes presentation of course materials, communication between tutor and students, self-assessment and monitoring of progress)* gives an approach to structure methodological strategies through different e-conceptualisation modes and didactical concepts.

The ability to model didactical concepts has changed the development paradigm from content orientation towards activity-process-orientation. The trend has been to create software modules with a capacity of reusing a component, object, or activity within a learning scenario (Pawlowski & Bick, 2006, p. 85). The assumption is that these critical components can be replicated in a number of similar scenarios. The components should be dynamic in terms of pedagogical models. Didactical units include an overview of the course and course content. They implement the instructional design of the learning unit. These units are ordered sequentially within a learning unit (Weitl, Süß, Kammerl, & Freitag, 2002, p. 3). In addition, the pedagogy can be packaged using an instructional design model like ADDIE (Analysis, Design, Development, Implementation, Evaluation (Kitawi & Neema-Abooki, 2007) which – according to Conlan, Wade, Bruen, & Gargan, 2002, p. 110) – pools experiences from learners and lecturers and ensures the achievement of course objectives and adaptive hypermedia systems (AHS). In the selfsame words of Cloete (2000, p. 171), AHS encourages the reuse of content; as the content does not embed the logic used to produce personalized courses but a narrative model or an Electronic Education System model (EES).

Kitawi & Neema-Abooki (2007) explain that the Systemic Design of Instruction, which is part of the methodological strategies, entails: analysis-which is assessing how educational technology affects individual/group efforts and objectives; design that emphasises the identification of the required resources to complete the tasks and implement the chosen solution in analysis; development-a process of creating and testing learning experiences; the solution is implemented in the fourth phase namely, implementation. Emphasis is on the presentation of learning experiences to the participants using appropriate media for on-campus and distance learning; the last phase is Evaluation with the aim of bridging the gap between student knowledge and the lecturer. It focuses at both formative and summative evaluations.

An instructional design model offers the developer an opportunity to create a sense of understanding, in the broadest sense of the word. Instructional design delineates a process to follow, through which a conception and understanding of the complex problem is derived. From this model other models within the realm of methodological strategies like the eternal, synergistic design model I by Crawford (2004) were developed. Its focus is more on the symbolic nature of continuous design and development which is never ending. The critical features of this model includes the design and development phase which are in a continuous state of motion, surrounding and revolving around the evaluation and feedback stages of formative evaluation.

A methodological strategy suitable for blended learning is the 6P/FB model. The 6P/FB model provides a design scheme for selecting adequate content and forms of feedback in blended learning courses. It is structured around six phases (or steps), that aim to support: definition of concrete functions of feedback; determination of a desirable course of action when providing feedback; consideration of various situational aspects that need to be considered; application of important principles and practical guidelines; selection of possible forms and organisation of feedback; answering of some of the leading questions involved. It is important to note that in both models, eternal synergistic design model I and 6P/FB model, the integration and re-integration of evaluation and its feedback is implicit. Mechanisms like measurement, diagnosis and intervention are conceived to take place to control the (learning) system (Hummel, 2006).

In addition to the above, it is crucial to ensure that course content meets didactical meta-data. Didactical metadata contains helpful information about a learning unit to support the learner in finding the appropriate learning unit, getting started with learning and navigate efficiently through the presented material according to individual objectives (Weitl et al., 2002, p. 3). Didactical metadata includes course objectives, course pre-requisites and any other related materials. The clear identification of course pre-requisites, including a decision on how the content will be relayed, for instance the use of moodle would ensure that adequate measures are undertaken to equip the student and lecturers with specific e-learning skills. Questions like:

*What are the educational objectives for the e-learning intervention (deep or surface learning, education or edutainment)? ; Who is going to structure the path through the e-learning environment (do the learners want as much information as possible to browse or is structure and sequence more important)?; How is enquiry and problem solving to be managed (is the student experience to be mainly passive or active)?; What alternatives are to be built in to overcome blocks to achievement and how will time be managed? (Blass & Davis (2003, p. 238)).*

Ergonomics is basically concerned with how well the product meets the needs of the end-user. Questions like: will the end-user be able to use the product easily? ; will the end-user be able to get help easily? ; does the 'look and feel' serve the purpose? ; become critical concerns in ergonomics. Appropriate ergonomics also ensure intensive engagement in the learning process. Issues of the end-users cognitive, psychomotor and affective domain become critical. A university, due to its conceptualization, can decide to foster the cognitive and psychomotor domain, and as such, collaboration tools and application sharing become important. In cases where the psychomotor domain also become important use of interactive tools, question and answers questions, multiple choice questions become important components in e-learning. Furthermore, issues like whether videos or sound files are to be incorporated into the presentation affects the 'look and feel' and consequently the achievement of course objectives. The language used in the presentation of content should be able to communicate effectively the information to the audience or target group.

An important aspect of methodological strategies becomes the knowledge of student and lecturer on the use of discussion boards and other tools for blended learning. A university can conceptualize itself clearly, but if the academia within is not equipped to use the e-learning tools provided, the achievement of the intended objectives become difficult or even impossible.

## Output Strategies

These strategies focus on the object of the e-learning process. Materially, this can be the achievement of positive results from summative and formative evaluations expressed through the methodological strategies. These results feed into the output strategies. Formally, it can be the actual change that occurs in the learner. It is the knowledge differential before the ideological and methodological strategies are effected, in comparison to after a student has undergone an e-learning process. Secondarily, it includes the achievement of learner and lecturer aspirations.

Some of the formative evaluation strategies can be a continuous development of an e-portfolio in text, audio or picture formats (Nossek, Peterson, Logar, & Zwiauer, 2008, p. 24) produced through methodological strategies. Portfolios are personal reflection instruments to enrich traditional school work and university lectures (Dorninger & Schrack, 2008, p. 12). The e-portfolio enables various actors. The actors include: lecturers (whose role becomes that of coach, rather than an instructor, focusing on helping the students construct their own knowledge-active learning); students (who are able to assess the learning process through time); business community (which is interested either with students' progress as prospective employees or forming a value-added judgment) and parents/guardians.

Summative evaluations should gauge the achievement of course objectives. Due to the nature of different disciplines, the instructional designer, developer, lecturer and student need to be informed and skilled to use different techniques available. Some techniques are more e-learning intensive than others. In the teaching of language, the use of language laboratories can be employed or even simulate engineering scenarios from remote locations through the use of remote experimentation (Callaghan, Harkin, McColgan, McGinnity, & Maguire, 2007, p. 1295). On the other hand, disciplines which require more human interactions need output strategies inclined towards synchronous and real time transmission. Adeptness to the various forms of summative evaluation through multiple choice questions (MCQs), essays, aptitude tests, proficiency tests, enable the measurement of different domains, the psychomotor, affective and cognitive to ensure holistic learning.

Effective and efficient feedback should be part of the output strategies. The feedback relayed should be specific, measurable, accurate, reliable and timely (SMART) for the achievement of learner aspirations. The output strategies should integrate as much as possible, the aspirations of the lecturer and learner.

In the case of learner centeredness, one could argue that learners are both the efficient and final cause in a university. Efficient cause because, through the use of participatory and emergent approaches, they become the creators of their own learning experience. They also decide what they want to learn and how they want to learn using e-learning. Universities which are entrepreneurially inclined will have the aforementioned influence on and from learners. The final cause is also the learner(s) because they are the end of the learning experience after the affecting methodological strategies. Learner centeredness ensures that they are equipped to survive in a dynamic and turbulent environment in a bid to become life-long learners.

The achievement of lecturers' aspirations is another important sub-issue. It can be conceived at two levels: the macro level of what the organisation expects from the lecturer (typified in ideological and methodological strategies); at a micro level of what the lecturer expects from the students (exemplified through direct didactical experience). This means that the lecturer becomes an important component in the designing and realization of learners' experience. Their own intrinsic and extrinsic motivation becomes vital in the survival and achievement of previous e-strategies.

## Ecological Strategies

The term ecology can be used in two senses. The first meaning is an environment which offers student opportunities to receive learning through methods and models that best support their needs, interests and personal situations (Richardson, 2002, p. 48). The second meaning of ecology refers to the environment or surroundings in which a university exists. An aspect of ecology is the market. Some scholars have developed e-learning strategies whose central concern is the market. Pope (2002) conceptualizes e-learning strategies according to Michael Porter's five market forces. The questions crucial in formulating strategies include: What is the bargaining power of suppliers (i.e. how can e-learning reduce our suppliers' costs and our transaction costs)? When it comes to content creation, the best actors will be employees who can transfer their intellectual capital to the larger repository. What is the bargaining power of buyers (i.e. how can e-learning improve customer (student) relations, add value to their operations, and effectively increase switching costs)? What are the possible threats from new entrants (i.e. can e-learning technology improve our organisations profitability and strategic position to reduce the threat of new entrants encroaching on our market and reduce margin)?

The level of a university's business intelligence will be a key determinant. The following questions are important in gathering intelligence: What are the threats from substitute products? (i. e. how will e-learning technology provide a tool that reduces substitute products in terms of courses offered, mode of delivery and content?) What is the rivalry from existing firms? (i.e. can e-learning technology improve organisational efficiency to allow the university to be one step ahead of the competition?) Some subjects which are more personal in nature will necessitate synchronous e-learning modes for example psychology, sociology and anthropology.

A university's competitor e-learning strategy is likely to influence the techniques adopted. If for instance in a particular location, most universities use WebCT, then a university might be forced to adopt WebCT or a similar e-learning software like Moodle. Furthermore, in a race to be competitive, a university might decide to position itself strategically depending on the market niche, for instance one which offers blended learning or one whose conceptualisation is purely distance learning. These strategies will affect the packaging, deployment and standards developed for pedagogy. The framework applies mostly in universities which adopt an entrepreneurial model or an adaptive-reactive model. It will therefore be less applicable to the traditional on Campus University.

E-learning strategies are to be conceptualised using both views, an enabling environment and the physical environment which includes the market. These strategies take into consideration the e-learning techniques employed by other universities, the market appropriateness of the e-learning technology, competitive and strategic positioning, add-on value to university operations, increased reputation (intangible) and reduction of teaching and learning costs. Ecological strategies have an impact on the ideological strategies, methodological strategies, and subsequently output strategies. It should enable active and collaborative learning.

Typically it becomes a synthesis of '*nurture*' and '*nature*'.

The ecology offers a very learner-centred experience in which students locate, select, and access instructional strategies and models that address unique and specific learning needs. For any given topic, the learning ecology will present students a variety of learning options in the studying, teaching, exercises, and projects (Richardson, 2002, p. 50).

## IMPACT OF THE FOUR-FOLD MANAGEMENT STRATEGY IN EAST AFRICA

In East Africa, like elsewhere in Africa and in any other developing world, tertiary education systems continue to be elitist as regards access and the socio-economic composition of the student body. Financial resources have been insufficient to sustain growth of enrolment and improvement of quality (World Bank, 2002). The gross enrolment ration in tertiary institutions in Sub-Saharan Africa in 2006 was at 5%, the lowest compared to other regions in the world. East African countries like Kenya, Tanzania and Uganda by 2006 had absolute numbers of student enrolled at 103,000, 55,000 and 88,000 respectively (UNESCO, 2008). This means that in terms of access, a big proportion of the population is still unable to enter or access tertiary institutions. In terms of funding, these East African countries have adopted various funding mechanisms to ensure that many students gain admission to their tertiary institutions. In terms of physical infrastructure, some of the resources provided by many universities are still inadequate. The foregoing scenario is a truism also to other countries like Rwanda and Burundi. The duo is now part of the Pentanation East African community.

The Authors argue that using the three models previously mentioned, that is, technology enhanced classroom teaching, distance education or distance learning and distributed learning, access to different programs will be improved. Thus the formulation of a universities e-learning strategy becomes essential for the survival and development of an institution.

Without prejudice to the foregoing, this Chapter has proposed a model that is totally new. The proposed model is not a disadvantage but is a potential complement to other reputable models like those of Marshall and Mitchell, Sharpe and co-authors, or Paulk and co-authors. For, although models necessarily differ in SPOT (Strengths, Possible improvement, Opportunities, and Threats) Analysis, no model has a legitimate claim of being the best. As Oliver and Dempster (2003) presuppose, there appears no ready model that ensures e-learning will be embedded but the relevant operations within the existential situation. In a similar vein Stiles (2004) calls organisations, including educational institutions, to undertake an honest analysis in terms of strengths and weaknesses, and this Chapter adds opportunities and threats, viewed against strategic goals. Equidistantly, Stiles and Yorke (2003) rule that the implemented design should be more learner-centred. Bonks and Dennen (2002) hold that the reason why some people choose to implement some form of electronic learning is incumbent on the provision of alternative forms of learning.

The immediate foregoing observation underscores the opinion that ICT would enable the instructor to achieve learner goals leading to increased learning; which is one of the objectives asserted by institutions like Makerere University (Kitawi & Neema-Abooki, 2007). Suffice to reiterate that new models are always needed. For, while some universities might have embraced e-learning in a more substantive way, many others might perhaps be still shopping around for a model that will best ensure their integral development. A perennial caution however is the imperative to taking recourse of a blend of several models for optimum success.

This Chapter propagates that East African Universities, and other African educational institutions, should take a leaf from the foregoing. In the selfsame words of Gibbs (1999), institutions need to concentrate on how strategy is developed, over and above all what it says. Sharpe et al. (2006, p. 141) accordingly recommend that each school should develop, publish and maintain their own e-learning strategy.

## Impact of Ideological Strategies on universities within Eastern Africa

Some notable universities like Makerere University, Strathmore University, University of Nairobi, University of Dar-es-Salaam, and National University of Rwanda, among others, are trying to harness the full potential provided by ICTs. Recently, East Africa was joined with/to the world's undersea fibre network and it's the hope of many, within the academy and business community, that this stance will greatly improve their core businesses. This will contribute a great deal to the problem identified by Hollow (2009) thus:

*The third most common response, from 18% of the respondents, was that of bandwidth as the top priority for improving eLearning. Again, another 40% considered this to be either second or third most significant priority area. Responses focussed around the prohibitive cost of bandwidth and identified it as the primary barrier for using eLearning with one respondent stating that 'the high cost of bandwidth in Africa just defeats the whole purpose of eLearning'. The recurring monthly expense meant that people are careful in their usage and are forced to limit the amount of content that is downloaded. Associated with the cost of bandwidth is the difficulty of accessing required content due to the slow connection speed. These factors hinder the progress of eLearning activities for both students and teachers and mean that certain tools are not accessible. As communicated by one respondent, 'the limited connection prevents us from using Moodle and getting OERs from the web'.*

An assertion is that administrators in different universities should be trained on the 'what' or ontology of e-strategy formulation. Most, if not all universities within Eastern Africa, operate within different philosophies, and as such, crafting of e-learning strategies in line with the mission and vision becomes essential. Due to the lack of philosophical disciplines, or rather disciplines which train the mind to think critically in some of these universities, the researchers argue that these universities should employ experts to enable them develop strategies in-line with their raison d'être. In addition, academicians within these universities should be trained on learner centeredness through the use of technology. With the shift to knowledge based economies, suitable conceptual mechanisms within all universities in these countries should be set-up to ensure that these institutions become a hub for knowledge generation and transmission, as opposed to being only knowledge consumers. A 'garbage-can' methodology of implementing ICTs without due regard to their usefulness can only be prevented if an institution conceptualizes itself clearly. This will ensure that the students become pro-active and are engaged in the learning process. An understanding of the different philosophical paradigms used together with information technology can ensure that these organisations adopt the right paradigm in line with their creed.

## Impact of Methodological Strategies on Universities within Eastern Africa

As noted in Kitawi & Neema-Abooki (2007), using a case example of Makerere University, methodological strategies should ensure that students are involved from the analysis stage of instruction to the actual design, development, implementation and evaluation to ensure that there is no sub-optimisation of goals by curriculum designers. This will guarantee that the final consumer (i.e.

student) is contented through provision of an effective learning environment. An inter-disciplinary co-operation between education and information technology ensures that the curriculum designers and system developers of e-learning software actually develop useful and pragmatic electronic-tools (e-tools). It was also envisaged by Unwin (2008) that most institutions within Africa, and in particular Botswana, were still at an infancy stage of e-learning development because of a lack of consensus of a suitable platform for content development and learner management. The use of open source (which are readily available and inexpensive) should be encouraged in-line with the customisation of software to suit an institution needs. The interrelation between students, lecturers, curriculum designers (with knowledge on learning principles and theories) and system designers will ensure that appropriate ergonomics are employed. Knowledge on content management systems, didactical and meta-data units will ensure development of the right components. In addition, the development of proprietary systems will ensure that e-learning is not only used for learning and teaching purposes, but also for management to learn about the progress of the core of an academic institution.

Nor should it be taken for granted that users of eLearning tools are conversant with the tools. A thorough training on how and when to use eLearning tools will help a great deal in eliminating any fear or mistrust in the use of ICT. In addition, suitable institutional mechanisms like appropriate funding should be availed to enable lecturers and instruction designers to use and acquire the tools. This is an important pre-requisite in methodological strategies.

In terms of capacity building, universities should ensure that skilled and appropriate manpower is developed to ensure that the right collaborative learning tools are developed. This will also eliminate the possibility of importing certain skills which a university might not be able to sustain in the long run.

## Impact of Output Strategies on Universities within Eastern Africa

It is a common feature in most academic institutions within Africa not to assess the level of contentment of both lecturer and student. The experience, at least in most institutions, is to be part of the system without any feedback. In this light, it is imperative for all stakeholders within African universities to provide useful information to improve learner's experience. This means that e-strategies built by different universities should have as part of it, a method to evaluate the use and usefulness of e-learning tools. A mechanism which adjudicates the evaluation stage of methodological strategies should also be set up. A re-evaluation of strategies can ensure that a digital divide within an academic institution is eliminated which can be a consequence of full scale adoption of ICTs without appropriate control mechanisms.

## Impact of Ecological Strategies on Universities within Eastern Africa

There is need to develop ecological e-learning strategies which fits each academic institution according to its competitors, students, governments and private and public companies. The way forward for most universities is to be able to detect and react to the environment through the use of ICT. Ecological e-learning strategies have an impact on the ideological, methodological and output strategies and thus its importance cannot be underscored.

The changing role of government in education and implementation of Public Private Partnerships (PPPs) place new demands and require much different skills and knowledge to implement than traditional methods if they are to be done right (LaRocque & Latham, 2003). Most universities need to know and be convinced of the benefits of e-learning tools on organisational operations. Universities also need to develop a clear e-learning strategy framework that is commensurate with its needs.

University managers and administrators need to be trained on how to assess and access convenient suppliers electronic tools (through various contractual agreements), be equipped with the 'know-what' of e-Learning, 'know-who' are the competitors and the tools they use, and understand the 'know-why' of eLearning in a bid to make their economies more knowledge based. They should be able to judge how content, culture, process and organisation, regulation and ICT infrastructure fit into the overall institutional model and strategy.

There is need for universities to act as vanguards in ICT adoption and implementation. If any economies are to be self sufficient, the different universities need to ensure that the products can actually compete equally both within and outside their respective countries. In order to achieve this, they need to harness the full potential of ICT offered through e-Learning (Neema-Abooki & Kitawi, 2009).

Future research focus, in line with the domain of the foregoing, could investigate into the impact of the various components (strategies) on overall university performance in terms of its mission and vision, or otherwise, within African/East African Universities.

## CONCLUDING REMARKS

The Chapter has essayed to propose a symbiosis of perspectives on strategies to managing a university from her mission statement to deliverable e-learning. The challenge is one of developing an e-learning strategy that reflects a university's mission and vision within a specific context (ecology). The strategy has as its critical elements the identification of the target group, the cognitive, affective or psychomotor domain to be addressed, the learning situation of the group, instruction models, learning unit development, content development-adaptation-adoption and deployment, organisation of content, actual learning and evaluation of the learning outcome towards the achievement of a university's objective. This can be achieved, sequentially and clearly through the modelling of e-learning strategies into ideological, methodological, output and ecological strategies with its own sub-frameworks. These sub-frameworks pre-suppose their own parameters and indicators which should be clear to all stakeholders to ensure that the e-learning strategies are beneficial and of substantive quality.

## REFERENCES

Bates, T. (2001). *National strategies for e-learning in post secondary education and training*. Retrieved November 24, 2008, from http://www.unesco.org//iiep.

Blass, E., & Davis, A. (2003). Building on solid foundations: establishing criteria for e-learning development. *Journal of Further and Higher Education*, *27*(3), 227–245. doi:10.1080/0309877032000098662

Bonks, C. J., & Dennen, V. P. (2002). *Evaluating online learning: frame works and perspectives.* Workshop held 17th February 2002, United States.

Boon, J., Rusman, E., Van der Klink, M., & Tattersall, C. (2005). Developing a critical view on e-learning trend reports: trend watching or trend setting? *International Journal of Training and Development*, *9*(3), 205–211. doi:10.1111/j.1468-2419.2005.00229.x

Brown, T. J. (2002). Individual and Technological Factors Affecting Perceived Ease of Use of Web-based Learning Technologies in a Developing Country. *Electronic Journal of Information Systems in Developing Countries*, *9*(5), 1–15.

Callaghan, M., J., Harkin, J., McColgan, E., McGinnity, T., M., & Maguire, L., P. (2007). Client-server architecture for collaborative experimentation. *Journal of Network and Computer Applications*, *30*, 1295–1308. doi:10.1016/j.jnca.2006.09.006

Clegg, S., Hudson, A., & Steel, J. (2003). The Emperor's New Clothes: globalisation and e-learning in Higher Education. *British Journal of Sociology of Education*.

Cloete, E. (2000). Electronic education system model. *Computers & Education*, *36*(1), 171–182.

Conlan, O., Wade, V., Bruen, C., & Gargan, M. (2002). *Multi-model, Metadata Driven Approach to Adaptive Hypermedia Services for Personalized eLearning*. Springer-Verlag Berlin Heidelberg.

Crawford, C. (2004). Non-linear instructional design model: eternal synergistic and design development. *British Journal of Educational Technology*, *35*(4), 413–420. doi:10.1111/j.0007-1013.2004.00400.x

Dorninger, C., & Schrack, C. (2008). Future Learning Strategy and ePortfolios in Education. *iJET, 3*(1), 11-14.

Dublin, L. (2004). The nine myths of e-learning implementation: ensuring the real return on your e-learning investment. *Emerald*, *36*(7), 291–294.

Elliott, M. (2002). Creating a Culture of Learning. *E-learning*, *3*(2), 42–43.*E-learning*

Engelbrecht, E. (2003). *A look at e-learning models: investigating their value for developing an e-learning strategy*. Bureau for Learning Development, Unisa.

French, C. S. (1992). *Computer Science* (IV ed.). London: DP Publications Ltd.

Gibbs, G. (1999). *Institutional learning and teaching strategies: A guide to good practice. Circular 99/55*. Higher Education Funding Council for England.

Hollow, D. (2009). *ELearning in Africa: Challenges, priorities and future direction* (Electronic Version) from www.gg.rhul.ac.uk/ict4d/workingpapers/Hollowelearning.pdf.

Hummel, H. (2006). Feedback Model to Support Designers of Blended-Learning Courses. *International Review of Research in Open and Distance Learning*, *7*(3).

Jefferies, P., Carsten-Stahl, B., & McRobb, S. (2007). Exploring the relationships between pedagogy, ethics and technology: building a framework for strategy development. *Technology, Pedagogy and Education*, *16*(1), 111–126. doi:10.1080/14759390601168122

Kitawi, A. K., & Neema-Abooki, P. (2007). *Systemic design of instruction on achieving the goals of undergraduate level education in universities: A case study of Makerere University*. Paper presented at the CISSE Conference.

LaRocque, N., & Latham, M. (2003). The promise of e-learning in Africa: The potential for public-private partnerships. *E-government series* (January, 2003).

Laurillard, D. (2006). E-Learning in Higher Education. In Ashwin, P. (Ed.), *Changing Higher Education: The Development of Learning and Teaching*. London: Routledge.

Levinsen, T. K. (2007). Qualifying online teachers—Communicative skills and their impact on e-learning quality (Electronic Version). *Education and Information Technologies*, *12*, 41–51. doi:10.1007/s10639-006-9025-1

Liu, Z. (2005). Mission of Modern Universities and Development of Modern Society. US-China Education Review, 4.

Louw, J., Brown, C., Muller, J., & Soudien, C. (2009). Instructional technologies in social science instruction in South Africa. *Computers & Education*, *53*, 234–242. doi:10.1016/j.compedu.2009.02.001

Marshall, S., & Mitchell, G. (2004). *Applying SPICE to e-Learning: An e-Learning Maturity Model?* Paper Presented at the Sixth Australasian Computing Education Conference (ACE2004).

Martin, B., R., & Etzkowitz, H. (2000). The Origin and Evolution of the University. *vest-journal, 11*(3-4), 9-34.

Neema-Abooki, P., & Kitawi, A. (2009). *Knowledge Based Economies in Selected Universities in Uganda.* Paper presented at the INTED 2009 conference.

New York Times. (2009). Retrieved July 29, 2009, from http://sbinfocanada.about.com/od / businessplanning /g /missionstatemen.htm

Nossek, B., R., Peterson, B., Logar, S., & Zwiauer, C. (2008). ePortfolio at the University of Vienna – Framework and Pilot Projects. *IJET, 3*(1), 21-26.

Oliver, M., & Dempster, J. (2003). Embedding e-learning practices. In Blackwell, R., & Blackmore, P. (Eds.), *Towards strategic staff development in higher education, 142–153.* Buckingham: SRHE and Open University Press.

Pawlowski, J., & Bick, M. (2006). Managing & re-using didactical expertise: The Didactical Object Model. *Journal of Educational Technology & Society*, *9*(1), 84–96.

Pope, S. (2002). Form a successful strategy (Electronic Version) (from www.elearningmag.com). *E-learning*, 34–37. Retrieved November 21, 2008.

Richardson, A. (2002). *An ecology of learning and the role of elearning in the learning environment.* Paper presented at the Global Summit 2002.

Salmon, G. (2005). Flying not flapping: a strategic framework for e-learning and pedagogical innovation in higher education institutions. *ALT-J. Research in Learning Technology*, *13*(3), 201–218.

Sharpe, R., Benfield, G., & Francis, R. (2006). Implementing a university e-learning strategy: levers for change within academic schools. *ALT-J. Research in Learning Technology*, *14*(2), 135–151.

Stiles, M. (2004). Is an eLearning strategy enough? *Educational Developments*, *5*(1), 13–15.

Stiles, M., & Yorke, J. (2003) Designing and implementing learning technology projects—a planned approach, workshop paper presented for the *EFFECTS—Embedding Learning Technologies Seminar,* University College London, 8 April. Retrieved October 15, 2009, from http://www.jiscinfonet.ac.uk/ Resources/external-resources/eltfinal.doc/view.

UNESCO. (2008). EFA Global Monitoring Report 2009: Overcoming inequality-why governance matters.

Unwin, T. (2008). Survey of e-learning in Africa (Electronic Version).

Vorley, T., & Nelles, J. (2008). (Re)Conceptualising the Academy: Institutional Development of and beyond the Third Mission. *Higher Education Management and Policy, 20* (3).

Web, E., Jones, A., Barker, P., & Van Schaik, P. (2004). Using e-learning dialogues in higher education. *Innovations in Education and Teaching International*, *41*(1), 93–103. doi:10.1080/1470329032000172748

Weitl, F., Süß, C., Kammerl, R., & Freitag, B. (2002). *Presenting Complex e-Learning Content on the Web: A Didactical Reference Model.* Paper presented at the E-Learn 2002 world conference on E-Learning in Corporate, Government, Healthcare, & Higher Education.

Wingate, U. (2007). A Framework for Transition: Supporting 'Learning to Learn' in Higher Education. *Higher Education Quarterly*, *61*(3), 391–405. doi:10.1111/j.1468-2273.2007.00361.x

World Bank. (2002). *Constructing knowledge societies: new challenges for tertiary education.* Retrieved October 25, 2005 from www.worldbank.org

## KEY TERMS AND DEFINITIONS

**E-Learning:** Utilization of learning technologies in generating and transmitting knowledge to students; be it in a classroom setting or online.

**Epistemology:** The 'intellectual condition' and output of an academic community not only in terms of teaching but also in tandem with the requisite and profound influence exerted onto the populace.

**Methodology:** Implementation methods utilized in engendering e-learning to the educands.

**Mission:** Special assignment being undertaken by an institution with a view of meeting the needs of the clientele and the society.

**Ontology:** The rationale of a particular institution's existence and the distinctive mandate that makes it stand out in the society.

**University:** An all-embracing multi-disciplinary institution of higher learning.

**Vision:** The ultimate future of the business. The ideal of focus in an enterprise.

# Compilation of References


Abbot, C. (2001). *ICT: changing education*. London: Routledge Publishers.

Abelson, H. (2008). The Creation of Open CourseWare at MIT. *Journal of Science Education and Technology*, *17*(2), 164–174. doi:10.1007/s10956-007-9060-8

Abowd, G. D., Atkeson, C. G., Hong, J., Long, S., Kooper, R., & Pinkerton, M. (1997). Cyberguide A mobile context-aware tour guide. *ACM Wireless Networks*, *5*(3), 421–433. doi:10.1023/A:1019194325861

Acquaviva, M., & Benini, M. (2004). VICE: E-Learning nell'era del Semantic Web. *Proceedings Nat. Conf. EXPO E-learning 04*.

Adegoke, K. A. (2000, November). *Towards the enhancement of teacher education in the new millennium.* Lead paper presented at the 2nd Biennial National Conference on Teacher Education at Adeniran Ogunsanya College of Education, Otta/ Ijanikin, Lagos State, Lagos.

Adeya, C. N., & Oyelaran-Oyeyinka, B. (2002). *The internet in African Universities: Case studies from Kenya and Nigeria.* Retrieved October, 11, 2002, from URL http:// www.intech.unu.edu

Adorni, G., Coccoli, M., Vercelli, G. & Vivant, G. (2008). Un modello semantico di progettazione di contenuti didattici in ambienti di e-learning. *Atti del V convegno SieL*.

Ajelabi, A. O. (2006). Computers in humanities education. In V.B. Owhotu (Ed.), *An Introduction to Information and Communication Technologies in Education* (pp. 87 – 90). Lagos: Sibon Books Ltd.

Akudolu, Lillian – Rita. I. (2000). *Restructuring Nigerian Secondary Education system through Information & Communication Technology (ICT) – Driven Curriculum.* Paper Presented at the third Conference of the World Council for Curriculum and Instruction(WCCI)Nigeria Chapter, Abuja.

Akudolu, Lillian – Rita. I. (2004). Evaluation of primary school teachers' use of information and communications technology (ICT) for curriculum integration. *Journal of Curriculum Organisation of Nigeria (CON).* 2, (1), 112-117.

Alexander, J. O. (1999). Collaborative design, constructivist learning, information technology immersion, & electronic communities: a case study. *Interpersonal Computing and Technology: An Electronic Journal for the 21st Century, 7*(1-2), October.

Allen, I. E., & Seaman, J. (2008). Staying the course: Online education in the United States, 2008. *The Sloan Consortium.* Retrieved July 2, 2009, from http:www.sloan-consortium.org/publications/survey/pdf/staying_the_course.pdf.

Allwright, D., & Hanks, J. (2009). *The developing learner: An introduction to exploratory practice.* Basingstoke, UK: Palgrave Macmillam.

Alshare, K., Kwun, O., & Grandon, E. E. (2006). Determinants of instructors' intentions to teach online courses: A cross-cultural perspective. *Journal of Computer Information Systems*, *46*, 87–95.

Alvino, S., & Sarti, L. (2006). Strumenti per la progettazione nell'e-learning. [TD]. *Tecnologie Didattiche*, *39*(3), 4–15.

American Association for Higher Education. (1992). *Principles of good practice for assessing student learning*. Washington, DC: AAHE.

American Association of Higher Education. (2000). *Implementing the Seven Principles: Technology as a lever*. Washington, DC: AAHE.

American Federation of Teachers. (2000). *Distance Education:Guidelines for good practice*. Washington DC: AFT(AFL-CIO)

Anderson, I., & Horney, M. A. (1998). Transforming text for at-risk readers. In D. Reinking,M. &McKenna (Eds), *Handbook of Literacy and Technology Transformation in Post Typographic World.*

Anderson, P. (2006). What is Web 2.0? Ideas, technologies and implications for education. *JISC*. Retrieved May 12, 2007 from http://www.ukoln.ac.uk/terminolgy/JISC-review2006.html.

Annacontini, G. (2007). Adulti in rete: tecnologie didattiche e formazione universitaria. In A. Alberici (Ed.), *Adulti e Università. Sfide ed innovazioni nella formazione universitaria e continua*. Milano: Franco Angeli

Antonacci, D., & Modaress, N. (2005). Envisioning the Educational Possibilities of User-Created Virtual Worlds. *AACE Journal*, *16*(2), 115–126.

ARACIS. (2009). *Guide for evaluating the by distance education*. Vth Part. Retrieved from http://www.aracis.ro

Ardito, C., Costabile, M. F., De Marsico, M., Lanzilotti, R., Levialdi, S., Roselli, T., & Rossano, V. (2006). An Approach to Usability Evaluation of e-Learning Applications. *Universal Access in the Information Society International Journal*, *4*(3), 270–283. doi:10.1007/s10209-005-0008-6

Argüelles, A. (1997). *Formación basada en competencias laborales.* Méjico: Limusa.

Armenski, G., & Gusev, M. (2005). Infrastructure for e-Testing. *Facta Universitatis (NIS), Series. Electronics and Energetics*, *18*(2), 181–204.

Asia and the Pacific Programme of Educational Innovation for Development. (1984). *Training educational Personnel for integrated curriculum: Report of a seminar on further training*. Oslo, Norway: Unipub.

Asoqwo, U. D. (2006). *E-learning: A panacea for access, equity and quality higher Education in Nigeria.* Paper presented at the 30th annual conference of the Nigerian

Association for Educational Administration and Planning (NAEAP) held at the Faculty of Education Hall, Enugu State University, Enugu.

Attwell, G. (2006). Personal Learning Environments. *The Wales Wide Web*. Retrieved June 30, 2008 from http://www.knownet.com/writing/weblogs/Graham_Attwell/entries/6521819364.

Attwell, G. (2007). The Personal Learning Environments – the future of eLearning?. *eLearning Papers, 2*(1), January.

Atwell, G. (2007). Personal learning environments - the future of eLearning? *Journal*, *2*(1). Retrieved from http://www.elearningpapers.eu/index.php?page=doc&vol=2&doc_id=8553&doclng=6.

Backroad Connections Pty Ltd. (2003) *What are the conditions for and characteristics of effective online learning communities? Australian flexible learning framework: Quick guide series (Australian national Training Authority)*. Available online at: http://www.flexiblelearning.net.au (accessed 3 April 2008).

Baecker, R. M., Grudin, J., Buxton, W. A. S., & Greenberg, S. (1995). *Readings in human-computer interaction: Towards the year 2000* (2nd ed.). San Francisco: Morgan Kaufmann.

Ballestero, E. (1980). *El encuentro de las ciencias sociales. Un ensayo de metodología*. Madrid, Spain: Alianza Universidad.

Bandura, A. (1965). Influence of model's reinforcement contingencies on the acquisition of imitative responses. *Journal of Personality and Social Psychology, 1*, 589–595. doi:10.1037/h0022070

Barab, S. A., & Duffy, T. M. (2000). From Practice Fields to Communities of Practice. In Jonassen, D. H., & Land, S. M. (Eds.), *Land Theoretical Foundations of Learning Environments* (pp. 22–55). New York, NY: Erlbaum.

Barbieri, T., & Paolini, P. (2000). Cooperative visits to WWW museum sites a year later: Evaluating the effect. In Bearman, D., & Trant, J. (Eds.), *Museums and the Web 2000* (pp. 173–178). Pittsburgh, PA: Archives & Museum Informatics.

Barbieri, T. (2000). *Networked virtual environments for the web: The WebTalk-I and WebTalk-II architectures.* Paper presented at the IEEE for Computer Multimedia & Expo 2000 (ICME), New York(pp. 179-182).

Barbieri, T., & Paolini, P. (2001). *Broadcast and on-line cultural heritage: Reconstructing Leonardo's ideal city - from handwritten codexes to webtalk-II: a 3D collaborative virtual environment system.* Paper presented at the 2001 Conference on Virtual Reality, Archeology, and Cultural Heritage, Glyfada, Greece, (pp. 61-66).

Barchetti, U., Bucciero, A., Mainetti, L., & Santo Sabato, S. (2008). *OpenWebTalk: A framework to support high performances and high resolution 3D collaborative experiences.* Paper presented at INTED 2008 International Technology, Education and Development Conference, Valencia, Spain, (p. 112).

Barnes-McConnell, P. W. (1978). Leading discussions. In Milton, O. (Ed.), *On college teaching: A guide to contemporary practices* (pp. 70–71). San Francisco: Jossey-Bass.

Barnett, R. (2001). *Los límites de la competencia. El conocimiento, la educación superior y la sociedad.* Barcelona, Spain: Gedisa.

Barr, R., & Tagg, J. (1995). From Teaching to Learning: A New Paradigm for Undergraduate Education. *Change Magazine, 2*(12), 8-12. Retrieved January 11, 2008 from www.cic.uiuc.edu/resources/deo/paradigm.html

Bassey, U. U., Umoren, G. U., Akuegwu, B. A., Udida, L. A., & Ntukidem, E. P. (2007, September). *Nigerian graduating students' access to e-learning technology: Implications for Higher Education Management.* Paper presented at the sixth International Internet Education Conference held in Egypt, Cairo.

Bates, T. (2001). *National strategies for e-learning in post secondary education and training.* Retrieved November 24, 2008, from http://www.unesco.org//iiep.

Beer, C., & Jones, D. (2008). *Learning Networks: Harnessing the Power of Online Communities for Discipline and Lifelong Learning.* Paper presented at the Lifelong Learning Conference, CQUniversity, Queensland.

Behrmann, M. (1988). *Integrating computer into the curriculum: A handbook for special educators* (pp. 25–32). Boston: College Press.

Benesse Educational Research & Development Center. (2007). *Daiikkai shougakkoueigo ni kansuru kihonchousa (Kyouin chousa) houkokusyo* [The 1st basic survey on English education in primary schools]. Tokyo: Benesse.

Benford, S., & Fahlén, L. (1993). A spatial model of interaction in large virtual environments. *Proc, of ECSCW '93*, pp. 107-132, Milano: Kluwer.

Bentley, T. (1998). *Learning beyond the classroom: education for a changing world.* London, UK: Routledge.

Berge, Z., & Collins, M. (Eds.). (1995). *Computer-Mediated Communication and the Online Classroom in Distance Learning.* Cresskill, NJ: Hampton Press.

Berge, Z., & Clark, T. (2009). *Virtual schools: What every superintendent needs to know. Distance Learning. 6(2)* (p. 6). Charlotte, NC: USDLA.

Berge, Z. L. (1997). Characteristics of online teaching in post-secondary, formal education. *Educational Technology, 37*(3), 35–47.

Berners-Lee, T., Handler, J., & Lassila, O. (2001). The Semantic Web. *Scientific American*. Retrieved September 23, 2008 from http://www.ryerson.ca/~dgrimsha/courses/cps720_02/resources/Scientific%20American%20 The%20Semantic%20Web.htm

Biggs, J. (1999). *Teaching for quality learning in university*. London: The Society for Research into Higher Education & Open University Press.

Birch, P. D. (2002). E-learner competencies,*Learning Circuits – ASTD Online Magazine*. Retrieved 11 January, 2006 from http://www.learningcircuits.org/2002/jul2002/birch.html

Blass, E., & Davis, A. (2003). Building on solid foundations: establishing criteria for e-learning development. *Journal of Further and Higher Education*, *27*(3), 227–245. doi:10.1080/0309877032000098662

Bly, S. (1993). Media spaces: bringing people together in a video, audio, and computing environment. *Communications of the ACM*, *36*(1), 28–46. doi:10.1145/151233.151235

Boaz, M., Elliott, B., Foshee, D., Hardy, D., Jarmon, C., & Olcott, D. (1999). *Teaching at a distance: A handbook for instructors*. Mission Viejo, CA: League for Innovation in the Community College.

Boettcher, J. (1999). Another look at the tower of WW-Webble. *Syllabus Magazine*, *13*(3), 50–52.

Boia, L. (1998). *Pour une histoire de l'imaginaire*. Paris, France: Les Belles Lettres.

Boissin, J.P., Casagrande, A., Montrone, A. & Pagliacci, M. (2009). Gli studenti universitari e l'imprenditorialità. Uno studio comparativo Italia-Francia. *AUR&S*, 1-2.

Bolter, J. D. (2000). *Remediation: Understanding new media*. Cambridge, MA: MIT Press.

Bonaiuti, G. (2007). I learning object nella prospettiva dell'eLearning 2.0. In *Atti del IV congresso Sie-l*. Macerata: EUM.

Bonks, C. J., & Dennen, V. P. (2002). *Evaluating online learning: frame works and perspectives*. Workshop held 17th February 2002, United States.

Bonnet, M. (1997). Computers in the classroom: some value issues. In McFarlane (Ed). *Information Technology and Authentic Learning*. (pp. 145-159)

Boon, J., Rusman, E., Van der Klink, M., & Tattersall, C. (2005). Developing a critical view on e-learning trend reports: trend watching or trend setting? *International Journal of Training and Development*, *9*(3), 205–211. doi:10.1111/j.1468-2419.2005.00229.x

Borgolte, U. (2008). Considerations on a remotely operable mobile robot laboratory. Proceedings of Virtual University 2008, Bratislava, Slovakia.

Boucher, E., & Ellis, C. (2002). *Ethnographically Speaking: Autoethnography, Literature and Aesthetics*. California: Altimira Walnut Creek.

Bourne, J. R., McMaster, E., Reiger, J., & Campbell, J. O. (1997). Paradigms for on-line learning: A case study in the design and implementation of an asynchronous learning networks (ALN) course. *Journal of Asynchronous Learning Networks*, *1*(2), 38–56.

Braud, W., & Anderson, R. (1998). *Intuitive Inquiry*. London: Sage.

British Secretary of State for Education and Employment. (1998). *The learning age: a renaissance for a new Britain*. London, UK: The Stationery Office.

Brookfield, S. D. (2005). *The power of critical theory: Liberating adult learning and teaching*. San Francisco: Jossey-Bass.

Brown, R. E. (2001). The process of community building in distance learning classes. *Journal of Asynchronous Learning Networks*, *5*(2), 18–35.

Brown, S., & Knight, P. (1994). *Assessing Learners in Higher Education*. Kogan Page.

Brown, T. J. (2002). Individual and Technological Factors Affecting Perceived Ease of Use of Web-based Learning Technologies in a Developing Country. *Electronic Journal of Information Systems in Developing Countries*, *9*(5), 1–15.

Bugaje, I. (2007). *Nigeria: Education reform and muslims*. Retrieved from file http://www.all africa.com 18/4/2007.

Burbules, N., & Callister, T. (2000). Knowledge at cross roads: some alternate futures of hypertext learning environments. *Educational Theory*, *40*(1), pp23–pp50.

Burbules, N. (2001). The web as a theoretical place. In Snyder, I. (Ed.), *Silicon Literacy: Communication, Innovation and Education in Electronic Age*. New York: Routledge.

Burgos, D., Tattersall, C., & Koper, R. (2005). Repurposing existing generic games and simulations for e-learning. *Computers in Human Behavior*, *23*(6), 2656–2667. doi:10.1016/j.chb.2006.08.002

Burstein, J., Chodorow, M., & Leacock, C. (2004). Automated Essay Evaluation: The Citation Online Writing Service. *AI Magazine, 25*, (3), 27-36, American Association for Artificial Intelligence *CASEC: Computerized Assessment System for English Communication*. Retrieved 1st July 2009, from http://www.nextet.net/c/jiem/index.html

Busari, T. O. (2006). Information and communication technology in science and technology education. In V.B. Owhotu (Ed.), *An Introduction to Information and Communication Technologies in Education.* (pp146 – 162). Lagos: Sibon Books Ltd.

Business Dictionary, B. N. E. T. (2009). *Business Definition for: E-learning*. Retrieved 23.06.2009 from http://dictionary.bnet.com/definition/E-learning.html

Cabrera, I. M., & Sànchez, J. J. D. (2009). Development of e-learning contents by learning objects design. In L. Gómez Chova, D. Martí Belenguer, & I. Candel Torres (Ed.), *Proceedings of INTED2009 Conference* (pp. 2833-2838). Valencia: International Association of Technology, Education and Development (IATED).

Cajkler, W. (1993). The official perspective – modern languages & IT in the 1990s. In Higham, J., & Macaro, E. (Eds.), *Information Technology in Initial Teacher Education: The modern languages perspectives* (pp. 5–34). York, UK: University of York.

Callaghan, M., J., Harkin, J., McColgan, E., McGinnity, T., M., & Maguire, L., P. (2007). Client-server architecture for collaborative experimentation. *Journal of Network and Computer Applications*, *30*, 1295–1308. doi:10.1016/j.jnca.2006.09.006

Calongne, C. M. (2008). Educational Frontiers: Learning in a Virtual World. *Educause Review Magazine, 43*(5), September/October.

Calvani, A. (2006). *Rete, comunità e conoscenza. Costruire e gestire dinamiche collaborative*. Trento: Erickson.

Calvani, A., Buonaiuti, G., Fini, A., & Ranieri, M. (2007). I Personal Learning Environment: una chiave di volta per il Lifelong Learning? *Atti del IV congresso* Sie-l. Macerata: EUM.

Candelas, F. A., Puente, S. R., Torres, F., Ortiz, F., Gil, F., & Pomares, J. (2003). A virtual laboratory for teaching robotics. *International Journal of Engineering Education*, *19*(3), 363–370.

Cañibano, L. (2008, May). *Higher Education in 'Business Administration' in Spain: Adapting to the European Area of Higher Education.* Paper presented at the I Convegno Nazionale of SIDREA: 'La Ragioneria e l'economia aziendale: dinamiche evolutive e prospettive di Cambiamento', Siena, Italy.

Cann, A. (2009). *What the heck is a PLE and why would I want one?* 2009, from http://www.microbiologybytes.com/tutorials/ple/

Carliner, S. (2002). *Designing E-learning*. American Society for Training and Development.

Carter, R. (2009). *Discretion in a distance learning environment: Ethical considerations in a virtual classroom. Distance Learning, 6(2)* (p. 11). Charlotte, NC: USDLA.

Carver, C. S., Scheier, M. F., & Weintraub, J. K. (1989). Assessing coping strategies: A theoretically based approach. *Journal of Personality and Social Psychology*, *56*(2), 267–283. doi:10.1037/0022-3514.56.2.267

Castranova, E. (2001). *Virtual worlds: A first-hand account of market and society on the Cyberian frontier*. CESifo Working Paper Series No. 618. Available at SSRN: http://ssrn.com/abstract=2948

Castronova, E. (2005). *Synthetic Worlds: The Business and Culture of Online Games*. Chicago, Illinois: University of Chicago Press Publisher.

Catarsi, C. (2007). La formazione di terza generazione: necessaria rifinitura di un paradigma", in A. Alberici (Ed.), *Adulti e Università. Sfide ed innovazioni nella formazione universitaria e continua*. Milano: Franco Angeli

CEC-Commission of the European Communities. (2001). *The eLearning Action Plan – Designing tomorrow's education*. COM (2001) 172 final, Bruxelles.

CEC-Commission of the European Communities. (2002). *e-Europe action plan 2005: An information society for all*. COM (2002) 263 final, Bruxelles.

Celestino, A., & Echegaray, O. Guenaga, G. (2002). *Evaluación de la incorporación de las Nuevas Tecnologías en la estrategia docente del ámbito de las Ciencias Empresariales*. Paper presented at the Conferencia Internacional de Tecnologías de Información y Comunicación en Educación, ICTE, Badajoz, Spain.

Central Council for Foreign Language Education Academic Advisory. (2007, September). *Shougakkou ni okeru eigokyouiku nitsuite* [English education in primary schools]. Paper presented at the 18th Conference of the Special Committee on Foreign Language Education. Conference material retrieved July 2, 2009, from http://www.mext.go.jp/b_menu/shingi/chukyo/chukyo3/015/siryo/ 06032708/003.pdf

Cercone, K. (2008). Characteristics of adult learners with implications for online learning design. *AACE Journal*, *16*(2), 137–159.

Chang, K. H., Gong, Y., Dollar, T., Gajiwala, S., Lee, B., & Wear, A. W. (1995). *On computer supported collaborative writing tools for distributed environments*. Paper presented at the ACM 23rd Conference on Computer Science, (pp. 222-229).

Chickering, A., & Gamson, Z. (1987). Seven principles of good practice in undergraduate education. [Washington, DC: AAHE.]. *AAHE Bulletin*, *39*, 3–7.

Chou, C. C. (2001). Formative evaluation of synchronous CMC systems for a learner-centered online course. *Journal of Interactive Learning Research*, *12*(2/3), 170–188.

Clares, J. (2005): El uso de las TIC en educación superior. In Universidad de La Laguna (Ed.), *Actas del XII Congreso Nacional de Modelos de Investigación Educativa: investigación e innovación educativa* (pp. 243-250). Tenerife: Servicio de Publicaciones Universidad de La Laguna.

Clegg, S., Hudson, A., & Steel, J. (2003). The Emperor's New Clothes: globalisation and e-learning in Higher Education. *British Journal of Sociology of Education*.

Cloete, E. (2000). Electronic education system model. *Computers & Education*, *36*(1), 171–182.

Clyde, L. A. (2004). Digital learning objects. *Teacher Librarian*, *31*(4), 55–57.

Collins, A. (1991). The role of computer in restructuring schools. *Phi Delta Kappan*, *73*, 28–36.

Collins, A., Brown, J. S., & Newman, S. E. (1989). Cognitive Apprenticeship: Teaching the crafts of reading, writing and mathematics. In Resnick, R. B. (Ed.), *Knowing, learning and instruction: Essays in honour of Robert Glaser* (pp. 453–494). Mahwah, NJ: Lawrence Erlbaum.

Colwell, C., Scanlon, E., & Cooper, M. (2002). Using remote laboratories to extend access to science and engineering. *Computers & Education*, *38*(1-3), 65–76. doi:10.1016/S0360-1315(01)00077-X

Commission of the European Communities. (2008). The use of ICT to support innovation and lifelong learning for all – A report on progress. *Commission Staff Working Document*. Brussels, 09/10/2008, SEC(2008) 2629 final

Conlan, O., Wade, V., Bruen, C., & Gargan, M. (2002). *Multi-model, Metadata Driven Approach to Adaptive Hypermedia Services for Personalized eLearning*. Springer-Verlag Berlin Heidelberg.

Conole, G. (2008a). Stepping over the edge: the implications of new technologies for education. In Lee, M. J. W., & McLoughlin, C. (Eds.), *Web 2.0-Based E-Learning: Applying Social Informatics for Tertiary Teaching*. Hershey, PA: IGI Global.

Conole, G. (2008b). New Schemas for Mapping Pedagogies and Technologies. In *Ariadne* Issue 56. Retrieved June, 13 2009 from http://www.ariadne.ac.uk/issue56/conole/

Conrad, R., & Donaldson, J. A. (2004). *Engaging the online learner: Activities and resources for creative instruction*. San Francisco: Jossey-Bass.

Cook, K. (2000). Computer conferencing really makes the Web interactive. In Leach, E. J. (Ed.), *A collection of practices from the league's conference on information technology*. Mission Viejo, CA: League for Innovation in the Community College.

Corey, J., Corey, C., & Corey, H. J. (1997). Use of personal stories and small groups in class. *The Keystone* (Newsletter of the Wadsworth College Success Series), (Spring), pp. 1-2.

Cormier, D. (2008). Rhizomatic knowledge communities: Edtechtalk, Webcast Academy. *Dave's Educational Blog*. Retrieved May, 27 2009 from http://davecormier.com/edblog/2008/02/29/rhizomatic-knowledge-communities-edtechtalk-webcast-academy/.

Coste, D., & Roche, L. (2004). La place de l'art plastique dans une école de management. *Humanisme & Entreprise*, 04-266.

Cox, B., & Cox, B. (2008). Developing interpersonal and group dynamics through asynchronous threaded discussions: The use of discussion board in collaborative learning. *Education*, *128*(4), 553–565.

Crabtree, A., & Rodden, T. (2008). Hybrid Ecologies: Understanding Cooperative Interaction in Emerging Physical-Digital Environments. In *Personal and Ubiquitous Computing, 12* (7) 481-493. Retrieved June, 15 2009 from http://www.mrl.nott.ac.uk/~axc/DReSS_Outputs/PUC_2007.pdf

Crawford, C. (2004). Non-linear instructional design model: eternal synergistic and design development. *British Journal of Educational Technology*, *35*(4), 413–420. doi:10.1111/j.0007-1013.2004.00400.x

Creswell, J. W. (2003). *Research design: Qualitative, quantitative, and mixed approaches*. Thousand Oaks(California), CA: Sage Publications.

Cronbach, L. J. & Snow, R., E. (1977). *Aptitude and instructional methods: A handbook for research on interactions*. Oxford, England: Irvington

Cross, J. (2006). *Informal Learning: Rediscovering the Natural Pathways That Inspire Innovation and Performance*. San Francisco, CA: Pfeiffer & company.

Crotty, M. (1998). *The Foundations of Social Research: Meaning and Perspective in the Research Process*. Sydney: Allen & Unwin.

Csikszentmihalyi, M. (1990). *Flow: The Psychology of Optimal Experience*. New York: Harper and Row.

Csikszentmihalyi, M. (1997). *Finding Flow*. New York: Basic.

D. & Draxter. A (Eds.), *Technologies for education: Potentials, Parameters and Prospects*. (pp.58). Washington: AED.

Damer, B. (1997). *Avatars! Exploring and building virtual worlds on the internet*. Berkeley, California: PeachPit Press.

Davidson, A., & Murray, D. (2002). Simultaneous localisation and Map-Building using active vision. *IEEE Transactions on Pattern Analysis and Machine Intelligence*, *24*(7), 865–880. doi:10.1109/TPAMI.2002.1017615

De Laat, M., & Lally, V. (2004). It's not so easy: Researching the complexity of emergent participant roles and awareness in asynchronous networked learning discussions. *Journal of Computer Assisted Learning*, *20*, 165–171. doi:10.1111/j.1365-2729.2004.00085.x

Demetrio, D. (2002). Cittadini in formazione. In Baratelli, M. (Eds.), *F.A.Re. Formazione con gli adulti. Esperienze a confronto*. Milano: Franco Angeli.

Denzin, N. (2003). *Performance Ethnography: Critical Pedagogy and the Politics of Culture*. London: Sage.

Dewey, J. (1963). *Experience and Education*. New York: Collier Books.

Dhanarajan, G. (2002). *Objectives and strategies for effective use of ICTs*. In Haddad, W.

Di Blas, N., Paolini, P., & Poggi, C. (2005). A virtual museum where students can learn. In Tan, L., & Subramaniam, R. (Eds.), *E-learning and Virtual Science Centers* (pp. 308–326). Hershey, PA: Idea Group.

Di Blas, N., Poggi, C., & Torrebruno, A. (2006). Collaboration and playful competition in a 3D educational virtual world: The Learning@Europe experience. In E. Pearson & P. Bohman (Eds.), *Proceedings of World Conference on Educational Multimedia, Hypermedia and Telecommunications 2006* (pp. 1191-1198).

Diaz, D. P., & Cartnal, R. B. (1999). Students' learning styles in two classes: Online distance learning and equivalent on-campus. *College Teaching*, *47*(4), 130–135. doi:10.1080/87567559909595802

Dirckinck-Holmfeld, L. (1990). *Kommunikation på trods og på tværs. Projektpædagogik og datamatkonferencer I fjernundervisning, Picnic−news no. 9*. Aalborg University.

Dolitsky, M., McCloskey, M. L., & Orr, J. (2006). *Teaching English as a foreign language in primary school*. Alexandria, VA: Teachers of English to Speakers of Other Languages, Inc.

Dormido, S. (2004). Control learning: present and future. *Annual Reviews in Control*, *28*(1), 115–136. doi:10.1016/j.arcontrol.2003.12.002

Dorninger, C., & Schrack, C. (2008). Future Learning Strategy and ePortfolios in Education. *iJET, 3*(1), 11-14.

Downes, S. (2005, 14 September, 2005). *What e-learning 2.0 means to you*. Presentation at the Transitions in Advanced Learning Conference, Ottawa. Retrieved 15 October, 2005, from http://www.downes.ca/cgi-bin/page.cgi?post=21521

Downes, S. (2005, December 12). *An introduction to connective knowledge*. Retrieved November 12, 2006 from http://www.downes.ca/cgi-bin/page.cgi?post=33034

Downes, S. (2005, October 16). *E-Learning 2.0 in eLearn Magazine October 16, 2005*. Retrieved January 20, 2009 from http://www.downes.ca/post/31741

Downes, S. (2006). *Learning networks and connective knowledge*. Retrieved November 12, 2006 from http://it.coe.uga.edu/itforum/paper92/paper92.html

Downes, S. (2008). *The future of learning 10 years on*. Retrieved August 1, 2008 from http://www.downes.ca/presentation/193

Downing, K. (2001). Information Technology, education, and health care: Constructivism in the 21st century. *Educational Studies*, *2*(3), 229–235. doi:10.1080/03055690120076510

Downing, K., Ho, R., Shin, K., Vrijmoed, L., & Wong, E. (2007). Metacognitive Development and Moving Away. *Educational Studies*, *33*(1), 1–13. doi:10.1080/03055690600850347

Downing, K., Kwong, T., Chan, S., Lam, I., & Downing, W. K. (2009). Problem-based learning and the development of metacognition. *Higher Education*, *57*(5), 609–621. doi:10.1007/s10734-008-9165-x

Downing, K. J., & Chim, T. M. (2004b). Reflectors as online extraverts. *Educational Studies*, *30*(3), 265–276. doi:10.1080/0305569042000224215

Downing, K. J. a&Chim, T.M. (2003) Learning style, student satisfaction and blended learning. In G. Richards (Ed) *Proceedings of World Conference on e-learning in corporate, government, healthcare, and higher education 2003*, Phoenix, AZ, USA, 1552-1553.

Downing, K. J., & Chim, T. M. (2004a) *What are the characteristics of effective online students? Fifteenth International Conference on College Teaching and Learning,* Jacksonville, Fl., U.S.A. 29th March-2nd April 2004.

Downing, K. J., & Shin, K. (2006) Developing metacognition with LASSI online.*International Conference of the Asia-Pacific Educational Research Association*, Hong Kong Institute of Education, Hong Kong, November 2006.

Drucker, P. (1993). *Post Capitalism Society*. New York: Harper Collins.

Drucker, P. F. (1994). *The age of social transformation.* Manchester, UK: Atlantic Publisher.

Drummond-Hay, P., & Saidel, B. G. (2004). Capturing ideas, creating information, and liberating knowledge. In Goldsmith, M., Morgan, H., & Ogg, A. J. (2204. San Francisco: Jossey-Bass.

Dublin, L. (2004). The nine myths of e-learning implementation: ensuring the real return on your e-learning investment. *Emerald*, *36*(7), 291–294.

Duridanov, L., & Simoff, S. (2007). 'Inner listening' as a basic principle for developing immersive virtual worlds. *Heidelberg Journal of Religions on the Internet*, 3(1).

Durrant, C., & Beavis, C. (2001). *(ICT) Use of English: Teachers, learners and technology*. Melbourne: Wakefold Press.

Eastman, D. (1996). *The internet and ELT: The impact of the internet on English language teaching*. Britain: British Council.

Edwards, S. E., & Schaller, D. T. (2007). The Name of the Game: Museums and Digital Learning Games. In Din, H., & Hecht, P. (Eds.), *The Digital Museum: A Think Guide* (pp. 62–68). Washington, DC: American Association of Museums.

Effie, D. (2003). E-learning ESL: Bringing the world together. *In Global Peace through the Internet. TESL Journal. 10.*

Elliott, M. (2002). Creating a Culture of Learning. *E-learning*, *3*(2), 42–43.*E-learning*

Encarta Dictionary, M. S. N. (2009). E-learning. Retrieved 23.06.2009 from http://encarta.msn.com/dictionary_701705852/e-learning.html

Engelbrecht, E. (2003). *A look at e-learning models: investigating their value for developing an e-learning strategy*. Bureau for Learning Development, Unisa.

European Commission. (2002). *European Report on Quality Indicators of Lifelong Learning*. Brussels: European Commission.

European Commission. (2009)... *Enterprise Industry Magazine*, *4*, 1–2009.

European Commission. (1993). White Paper on growth, competitiveness, and employment: The challenges and ways forward into the 21st century, *Part A, COM (93) 700 final*.

European Parliament. (2003). E-learning 2004-2006 program. Decision No 2318/2003/EC, December, Bruxelles. Retrieved October 21, 2009, from http://europa.eu.int/eur-lex/pri/en/oj/dat/2003/l_345/l_34520031231en00090016.pdf

European Parliament. (2006). Life-long learning program 2007-2013. Decision No.1720/2006/EC, November, Bruxelles. Retrieved October 21, 2009, http://eur-lex.europa.eu/LexUriServ/site/it/oj/2006/l_327/l_32720061124it00450068.pdf

Evans, C., & Gibbons, N. (2007). The interactivity effect in multimedia learning. *Computers & Education*, *49*(4), 1147–1160. doi:10.1016/j.compedu.2006.01.008

Fagioli, M. (2005). Learning Object: dal dire al fare. Retrieved June, 20 2009 from http://www.indire.it/content/index.php?action=read&id=1183

Falk, J. H., & Dierking, L. D. (2002). *Lessons Without Limit, How Free-Chioce Learning is Transforming Education*. Walnut Creek, California: AltaMira Press.

Fallows, J. (2006). Homo Conexus. *Technology Review*, July. Retrieved June 5, 2009, from www.technologyreview.com/read_article.aspx?id=17061&ch=infotech

Fini, A. (2008). 2.0. A case study on a growing community. In *Journal of e-Learning and Knowledge Society, 4, (3), September 2008* (pp. 167–175). E-Learning.

Fini, A., & Vanni, L. (2004). *Learning Objects e metadati. I quaderni di Form@re, n. 2*. Trento: Erickson.

Fini, A. (2005). Dai Learning Object al Learning Design. In *Journal of e-Learning and Knowledge Society*.

Fisher, C. (2008). *Networks and Studios*. Retrieved June, 16 2009 from http://learning2cn.ning.com/profile/ClarenceFisher

Five-Factor Model. (1991), Retrieved 15 December, 2005 from http://www.personalityresearch.org/bigfive.html

Fowowe, S. S., & Gbadegesin, S. S. (2008). Computer instruction: Apedagogicla approach that facilitates learning systems in the 21st century. In Nwabuko, N. C. & Akinpelu, Biobun (Eds.), *Shifting Paradigms in the Teaching Function in ICT Era* (pp.57-60) Lagos: Nigerian Association for Educational Media and Technology (NAEMT) Publisher.

French, C. S. (1992). *Computer Science* (IV ed.). London: DP Publications Ltd.

Frydenberg, J. (2002). Quality Standards in e-Learning: a matrix of analysis. *International Review of Research in Open and Distance Learning*, *3*(2).

Fujii, Y. (2007). Development of a Scale to Evaluate the Information Literacy Level of Young People -Comparison of Junior High School Students in Japan and Northern Europe. *Japan Journal of Educational Technology*, *30*(4), 387–395.

G8 Information Centre. (1999, June 18). Köln charter: Aims and ambitions for lifelong learning. Retrieved July 14, 2009, from http://www.g7.utoronto.ca/summit/1999koln/charter.htm

Gagne, R. M., Wager, W. W., Golas, K. C., & Keller, J. M. (2005) *Principles of instructional design (5th Ed.)*. Wadsworth: Thomson Learning.

Gandell, T., Weston, C., Finkelstein, A., & Weiner, L. (2000). Appropriate use of the web in teaching higher education. In Mann, B. L. (Ed.), *Perspectives in web course management* (pp. 61–68). Toronto: Canadian Scholar's Press.

Gardner, H. (1991). *The Unschooled Mind: How Children Think And How Schools Should Teach*. New York: Basic Books.

Garrison, D. R., & Anderson, T. (2003). [*st century: A framework for research and practice*] [London, Routledge Falmer]. *E-learning*, 21.

Gartner Inc. (2007). Retrieved November 29, 2007, from http://www.gartner.com/it/page.jsp?id=503861

Gebser, J. (1985). *The Ever-Present Origin*. Athens: Ohio University Press.

Ghislandi, P., Mattei, A., Paolino, D., Pedroni, A., & Franceschini, D. (2008). Progettare una comunità di apprendimento online per un insegnamento accademico: potenzialità e limiti di Moodle. *Atti del convegno "SIeL-Società Italiana eLearning"*. Trento, 8-11 ottobre 2008. Retrieved May, 2 2009 from http://siel08.cs.unitn.it/Atti/index.html.

Gibbs, G. (1999). *Institutional learning and teaching strategies: A guide to good practice. Circular 99/55*. Higher Education Funding Council for England.

Gilbert, P. K., & Dabbagh, N. (2005). How to structure online discussions for meaningful discourse: A case study. *British Journal of Educational Technology*, *36*(1), 5–18. doi:10.1111/j.1467-8535.2005.00434.x

Gilbert, J. (1992). *A slice by slice guide tot total quality management*. Great Britain: Tudor.

Gilmour, P., & Hunt, R. (1995). *Total Quality Management*. Australia: Longman.

Giorgetti, M. G., & Palumbo, M. (2003). Prefazione. In L. Stagi, & G. Vercelli (Ed.), *E-learning e formazione continua. Risorgeco: il trasferimento di buone pratiche attraverso la Fad* (pp. 9- 14). Milano, IT: FrancoAngeli.

Giovannella, C. (2008). Learning 2.0? *Atti del V congresso* Sie-l. Macerata: EUM.

Gogala, S. (2005). *Chosen Pedagogic Essays*. Ljubljana, Slovenia: Drustvo 2000.

Goldberg, L. R. (1999). A Broad-Bandwidth, Public Domain, Personality Inventory Measuring the Lower-Level Facets of Several Five-Factor Models. In Mervielde, I., Deary, I., De Fruyt, F., & Ostendorf, F. (Eds.), *Personality Psychology in Europe, 7* (pp. 7–28). The Netherlands: Tilburg University Press.

Goleman, D. (1997). *Emotional Intelligence: Why it can Matter more than IQ*. New York: Bantam.

González-Castaño, F. J., Anido-Rifón, L., Vales-Alonso, J., Fernández-Iglesias, M. J., Llamas-Nistal, M., Rodríguez-Hernández, P., & Pousada-Carballo, J. M. (2001). Internet access to real equipment at computer architecture laboratories using the Java/CORBA paradigm. *Computers & Education, 36*(2), 151–170. doi:10.1016/S0360-1315(00)00056-7

Goodwyn, A. (2000). *English in the digital age: Information and communication technology and the teaching of English*. London: Cassell.

Goodyear, G., & Allchin, D. (1998). Statement of Teaching Philosophy. In M. Kaplan (Ed.), *To improve the academy*, 17 103-122. Stillwater, OK: New Forums Press.

Government of Romania (1995). *Government Ordinance 75/12 July 2005*

Grabinger, R. S. (1996). Rich environments for active learning. In Jonassen, D. H. (Ed.), *Handbook of Research for Educational Communications and Technology* (pp. 665–692). New York, NY: Macmillan.

Grady, D. B. (2003). Mapping online discussions with lexical scores. *Journal of Interactive Learning, 14*(2), 209–229.

Greenberg, S., Gutwin, C., & Cockbum, A. (1995). *Sharing fisheye views in relaxed-WYSIWIS groupware applications*. Paper presented at *Gruphics Inleface*, Toronto, Canada (pp. 28-38).

Greene, J. C., & Caracelli, V. J. (Eds.). (1997). *Advances in mixed-method evaluation: The challenges and benefits of integrating diverse paradigms*. San Francisco, CA: Jossey-Bass.

GridWise. (2007). *GridWise Architecture Council Interoperability Context-Setting Framework Draft* (January 2007). Retrieved June, 28 2009 from http://www.gridwiseac.org/pdfs/interopframework_v05%20070129.pdf

Gronstedt, A. (2008). Making Learning Fun and Social. *E-learning Magazine*. Retrived May 10, 2009 from www.gronstedtgroup.com/pdf/ELearningMagazine.pdf

Grundy, J. (2002). Flexible learning and the flexible worker. *British Telecom White Paper,* December 2002, BT, London.

Guenaga, G., Celestino, A., & Echegaray, O. (2003). Integración de las TIC en la educación superior. *Pixel-Bit Revista de Medios y Educación, 21*, 21–28.

Guillaume, P. (2005). *Myth, Metaphor and Magic*. 2005, from www.ourworld.compuserve.com

Gunawardana, K. D. (2006). An empirical study of the potential challenges and benefits of implementing e-learning in Sir Lanka. *Special issue of the International Journal of Computer, the Internet and Management,* 33, 1-8.

Guzman, J. L., Berenguer, M., Rodriguez, F., & Dormido, S. (2009). An interactive tool for mobile robot motion planning. *Robotics and Autonomous Systems, 56*(5), 396–409. doi:10.1016/j.robot.2007.10.001

Haddad, W. D., & Draxter, A. (Eds.), *Technologies for education: Potential, Parameter and Prospect* (p. 24). Washington: AED.

Haddad, W. D., & Jurich, S. (2002). ICT for education: potential, and potency. In Haddad, W. D., & Draxter, A. (Eds.), *Technologies for education: Potentials, Parameters and Prospects* (pp. 28–39). Washington: AED.

Haibin, Z. (2004). *From WYSIWIS to WISINWIS: role-based collaboration*. Paper presented at the 2004 IEEE International Conference on Systems, Man and Cybernetics, (pp. 5441-5446).

Hannon, J. (2009). Breaking down online teaching: Innovation and resistance. *Australasian Journal of Educational Technology, 25*(1), 14-29. Retrieved May, 10 2009 from http://www.ascilite.org.au/ajet/ajet25/hannon.html

Harasim, L., Hiltz, S., Teles, L., & Turoff, M. (1995). *Learning Networks: a field guide to teaching and learning online*. Cambridge, UK: The MIT Press.

Hayes, B. (2000). Cascade training and teachers' professional development. *ELT Journal, 52*, 135–145. doi:10.1093/elt/54.2.135

Henri, F., & Pudelko, B. (2003). Understanding and analysing activity and learning in virtual communities. *Journal of Computer Assisted Learning, 19*, 474–487. doi:10.1046/j.0266-4909.2003.00051.x

Hernes, G. (2002). *Emerging trends in ICT and challenges to educational planning.*

Higham, J., & Macaro, E. (Eds.). (1993). *Information technology in initial teacher education: the modern language perspective* (pp. 5–34). York: University of York.

Hoffman, J., & Person, P. P. (2000). Reading education in the next millennium: What your grandmother's teacher didn't know that your grand daughter's teacher should? *Reading Research Quarterly, 35*(1). doi:10.1598/RRQ.35.1.3

Hollow, D. (2009). *ELearning in Africa: Challenges, priorities and future direction* [Electronic Version] from www.gg.rhul.ac.uk/ict4d/workingpapers/Hollowelearning.pdf.

Holmberg, C. (2006). Flexibelt lärande – från korrespondensundervisning till öppna och fria studier. In L. Borgström, & P. Gougoulakis (Ed.), *Vuxenantologin. En grundbok om vuxnas lärande*. Stockholm, SW: Atlas akademi.

Holt, D. B., Quelch, J. A., & Taylor, E. L. (2004). *Managing the global brand: A typology of consumer perceptions. The global market: Developing a strategy to managing across borders*. San Francisco: Jossey-Bass.

Hron, A., & Friedrich, H. F. (2003). A review of web-based collaborative learning: factors beyond technology. *Journal of Computer Assisted Learning, 19*, 70–79. doi:10.1046/j.0266-4909.2002.00007.x

Huba, M. E., & Freed, J. E. (2000). *Learner-centered assessment on college campuses: Shifting the focus from teaching to learning*. Needham Heights, MA: Allyn & Bacon.

Hummel, H. (2006). Feedback Model to Support Designers of Blended-Learning Courses. *International Review of Research in Open and Distance Learning, 7*(3).

Husserl, E. (Ed.). (1927). *Britannica*. Great Britain: Harvester.

Hwang, W. Y., & Wang, C. Y. (2004). A study of learning time patterns in asynchronous learning environments. *Journal of Computer Assisted Learning, 20*, 292–304. doi:10.1111/j.1365-2729.2004.00088.x

Idowu, B., Adagunodo, R., & Idowu, B. (2004). Gender differences in computer literacy among Nigerian undergraduate students. *The African Symposuim: An Online Educational Research Journal, 4*(3), 1–7.

IEEE-USA. (2005, November 11). *Interoperability for the national health information network.* Retrieved April 12, 2009, from http://www.ieeeusa.org/policy/POSITIONS/NHINinteroperability.html#_ftnref1

Illeris, K. (1981). *Modkvalificeringens pædagogik*. Denmark: Unge Pædagoger.

In White, K. W., & Weight, B. H. (2000). *The online teaching guide: A handbook of attitudes, strategies, and techniques for the virtual classroom*. Needham Heights, MA: Allyn & Bacon.

International Personality Item Pool. (2001). *A Scientific Collaboratory for the Development of Advanced Measures of Personality Traits and Other Individual Differences*. Retrieved 27 October, 2004 from http://ipip.ori.org/.

Ishioka, T., & Kameda, M. (2003). JESS: An Automated Japanese Essay Scoring System. *Bulletin of the Computational Statistics of Japan*, *16*(1), 3–19.

Isu, C. O. (2004). Information and communication technology (ICT) as a veritable tool of business education for human resource development. [Con]. *Journal of Curriculum Organisation of Nigeria*, *11*(2).

Jalic, & Inc. (2009). *Greek and Roman Mythology> Echo and Narcissus*. Retrieved 7th August, 2009, from http://www.online-mythology.com/echo_narcissus/

*Japan Open Courseware Consortium*, Retrieved 1st July 2009, from http://www.jocw.jp

Japanese University Council, Ministry of Education, Culture, Sports, Science and Technology (MEXT). "Requirements of Higher Education System in Global Age" (in Japanese). Retrieved 1st July 2009, from http://www.mext.go.jp/b_menu/shingi/12/daigaku/toushin/001101.htm

Jara, C. A., Candelas, F. A., Torres, F., Dormido, S., Esquembre, F., & Reinoso, O. (2009). Real-time collaboration of virtual laboratories through the Internet. *Computers & Education*, *52*(1), 126–140. doi:10.1016/j.compedu.2008.07.007

Jarche, H. (2005). *Learning is Conversation*. Retrieved June 10, 2009 from http://www.jarche.com/2005/12/OLD651/

Jarvis, P. (1987). *Adult Learning in the Social Context*. London, UK: Croom Helm.

Jefferies, P., Carsten-Stahl, B., & McRobb, S. (2007). Exploring the relationships between pedagogy, ethics and technology: building a framework for strategy development. *Technology, Pedagogy and Education*, *16*(1), 111–126. doi:10.1080/14759390601168122

Jeffries, M. (2004). Research in distance education: The history of distance education. Retrieved July 20, 2005 from http://www.digitalschool.net/edu/DL_history_mJeffries.html.

Jiménez, L. M., Puerto, R., Reinoso, O., Fernández, C., & Ñeco, R. (2005). Recolab: laboratorio remoto de control utilizando Matlab y Simulink. RIAI. *Revista Iberoamericana de Automática e Informática Industrial*, *2*(2), 67–72.

Johansen, R. (1988). *Groupware: Computer support for business teams*. New York: The Free Press.

Johnson, J. S., & Newport, E. L. (1989). Critical period effects in second language learning: The influence of maturational state on the acquisition of English as a second language. *Cognitive Psychology*, *21*, 60–99. doi:10.1016/0010-0285(89)90003-0

Jonassen, D. H., & Land, S. M. (2000). *Theoretical Foundations of Learning Environment*. New Jersey: Lawrence Erlbaum Associates.

Jones, T. L. (1993). *The Americans with disabilities act: A review of best practices*. New York: AMA.

Jones, D., Vallack, J., & Fitzgerald-Hood, N. (2008). *The Ps Framework: Mapping the Landscape for the PLEs@CQUni Project*. Paper presented at the Hello! Where are you in the Landscape of Educational Technology? ASCILITE 2008, Melbourne.

JTU Institute for Education and Culture. (2009). *Kyoushokuin roudou kokusai hikaku kenkyu iinkai houkokusho* [An International Comparative Study on the Working Conditions of School Personnel]. Retrieved July 17, 2009, from http://www.kyoiku-soken.org/official/activity/userfiles/document/kokusaihikaku.pdf

Kahneman, D. (1971). *Attention and effort*. Englewood Cliffs, NJ: Prentice-Hall.

Kahneman, D. (2007). *Economia della felicità.* Milano, Italy: Il Sole 24 Ore.

Karlsudd, P. (2001). *Att lära på tunna linor och bred(a) band. Pedagogik i utbildning basera på informations- och kommunikationsteknologi. Konstruktion av ett analysverktyg.* Kalmar, SW: Högskolan Kalmar.

Katzenbach, J. R. (2000). *El trabajo en equipo.* Barcelona, Spain: Granica.

Kaufman J. C. & Agars M. D. (2005).*Kaufman-Agars Motivation Scale.* Unpublished instrument.

Kaufman, J. C. & Agars, M. D., *Kaufman-Agars Motivation Scale.*Unpublished instrument (2005).

Kay, R. H. (2006). Developing a comprehensive metric for assessing discussion board effectiveness. *British Journal of Educational Technology, 37*(5), 761–783. doi:10.1111/j.1467-8535.2006.00560.x

Kenning, M. J., & Kenning, M. M. (1983). *An introduction to computer assisted language learning.* Oxford: Oxford University Press.

Kerchmer, R. A. (2000). Understanding teachers' perspectives of internet use in the classroom. Implications for teacher education and staff development. *Reading & Writing Quarterly, 16*(2).

Kerr, R. (1993). *Restructuring classroom. Interaction with networked computer: Effects on quantity and characteristics of language production.* Paper presented at the meeting of the American Council of Teachers of Foreign Languages San Antonio.

Khamis, A., Pérez-Vernet, M., & Schilling, K. (2002). A remote experiment on motor control of mobile robots. Proceedings of 10th Mediterranean Conference on Control and Automation, Lisbon, Portugal.

Khamis, A., Rivero, D. M., Rodríguez, F., & Salichs, M. (2003). Pattern-based architecture for building mobile robotics remote laboratories. Proceedings of IEEE International Conference on Robotics and Automation, Taipei, Taiwan.

King, K. (2001). Educators revitalize the classroom "bulletin board:" a case study of the influence of online dialog on face-to-face classes from an adult learning perspective. *Journal of Research and Computing in Education, 33*(4), 337–354.

Kinzer, C., & Risco, V. (1998). Multimedia and enhanced learning: Transforming pre-service education. In Reinking, D., McKanna, M., Labbo, L., & Kieffer, R. (Eds.), *Handbook of Technology and Literacy: Transformations in a Post-typographic world* (pp. 182–202). Hillsdale, NJ: Erlbaum.

Kirk, D., et al. (2005). Ways of the hands. *Proc. of ECSCW '05*, pp. 1-21. Paris: Springer.

Kitawi, A. K., & Neema-Abooki, P. (2007). *Systemic design of instruction on achieving the goals of undergraduate level education in universities: A case study of Makerere University.* Paper presented at the CISSE Conference.

Kline, R. B. (2005). *Principles and Practice of Structural Equational Modeling.* New York: The Guilford Press.

Knowles, M. S. (1984). Introduction: the art and science of helping adults learn. In Knowles, M. S. (Ed.), *Andragogy in action: applying modern principles of adult learning* (pp. 1–21). San Francisco, CA: Jossey-Bass.

Knuth, R. A., & Cunningham, D. J. (1993). Tools for Constructivism. In Duffy, T. M., Lowyck, J., & Jonassen, D. H. (Eds.), *Designing Environment for Constructive Learning* (pp. 163–188). Berlin, DE: Springer.

Koestenbaum, P. (1964). Introduction to the Paris Lectures. In *The Paris Lecturers.* The Hague: Martinus Nijhoff.

Kolb, D. (1984). *Experimental Learning (Experience as The Source of Learning and Development).* Upper Saddle River, New Jersey: Prentice-Hall.

Koleva, B. (2000). Traversable interfaces between real and virtual worlds. [The Hague: ACM.]. *Proc. Of CHI, 00*, 233–240.

Koper, R. (2001). *Modelling units of study from a pedagogical perspective. The pedagogical meta-model behind.* EML Educational Technology Expertise Centre, Open University of the Netherlands.

Koper, R., & Oliveir, B. (2006). La rappresentazione del learning design di unità di apprendimento. Modellare attività e ruoli nei processi di apprendimento. [TD]. *Tecnologie Didattiche, 39*(3), 16–29.

Koper, R., & Olivier, B. (2003). Representing the learning design of units of learning. *Journal of Educational Technology & Society, 7*(3), 97–111. Retrieved from http://dspace.ou.nl/bitstream/1820/19/2/IMSLD-article%20v1p07-final.pdf.

Koper, R., & Tattersall, C. (2005). Preface to learning design: A handbook on modelling and delivering networked education and training. *Journal of Interactive Media in Education, 18*, 1–7.

Koper, R., Rodrígues-Artacho, M., Lefrere, P., Rawlings, A., & Rosmalen, P. (2002). *Survey of educational modelling languages (EMLs)*. Technical report, 1-79. Retrieved April 2009, from http://dspace.ou.nl/dspace/handle/1820/227.

Kozma, R. B. (1991). Learning with media. *Review of Educational Research, 61*(2), 179–211.

Kume, A. (1981). Ouraru English heno apurouchi: Parallel reading no tagenteki kouka. [Approach to oral English: Pluralistic effects of parallel reading]. *Nanzan University Academia, 30*, 159–174.

Kuznik, L. (2007). *Interactive Learning Environments and Children's Museums - Theoretical Model and It's Planning*. Unpublished doctoral dissertation, University of Ljubljana, Slovenia.

Kuzouka, H., et al. (2004). Mediating dual ecologies. *Proc. of CSCW '04*, p. 477-486. Chicago: ACM. IEEE, (2000). *IEEE 100 – 2000. The Authoritative Dictionary of IEEE Standards Terms, Seventh Edition.* New York.

Kwache, P. Z. (2007). The imperatives of information and communication technology for teachers in Nigeria higher education. *Merlot Journal of Online Learning and Teaching, 1*(1), 24–32.

Lally, V., & Barrett, E. (1999). Building a learning community on-line: Towards socio-academic interaction. *Research Papers in Education, 14*(2), 147–163. doi:10.1080/0267152990140205

LaRocque, N., & Latham, M. (2003). The promise of e-learning in Africa: The potential for public-private partnerships. *E-government series* (January, 2003).

Laurillard, D. (2006). E-Learning in Higher Education. In Ashwin, P. (Ed.), *Changing Higher Education: The Development of Learning and Teaching*. London: Routledge.

Lazarinis, F., Green, S., & Pearson, E. (2009). Multi-criteria adaptation in a personalized multimedia testing tool based on semantic technologies. *Interactive Learning Environments, 14*(1), 1–17. doi:10.1080/10494820902909459

Leask, M., & Bachler, N. (Eds.). (1999). *Learning and Teaching Using ICT in the Secondary School* (pp. 112–116). London: Routledge Publishers. doi:10.4324/9780203212301

Leeming, D. (2001). *A dictionary of Asian mythology* (Online, O. R., Ed.). London: Oxford University Press.

Lenneberg, E. H. (1967). *Biological foundations of language*. New York: John Wiley & Sons Inc.

Leone, S. (2009). PLE: a brick in the construction of a lifelong learning society. In O'Donoghue, J. (Ed.), *Technology Supported Environment for Personalised Learning: Methods and Case Studies*. Hershey, PA: IGI-Publisher.

Leone, S. (2008a). The use of new technologies in advanced Italian classes. In I. Olney, G. Lefoe, J. Mantei, & J. Herrington (Eds.), *Proceedings of the Second Emerging Technologies Conference 2008* (pp. 120-129). Wollongong: University of Wollongong.

Leu, D. J., & Kinzer, C. K. (2000). The convergence of literacy instruction with networked technologies for information and communication. *Reading Research Quarterly*, (35): 108–127.

Leu, D. J. (2000). Continuously changing technologies and environments for literacy: deitic consequences for literary education in an information age. In Kamil, M. (Ed.), *Handbook of Reading Research, (3)* (pp. 743–777).

Levine, R., Locke, C., Searls, D., Weinberger, D., & McKee, J. (2009). *The Cluetrain Manifesto: 10th Anniversary Edition.* New York: Perseus Publishing. Retrieved June, 26 2009, from http://www.cluetrain.com/

Levinsen, T. K. (2007). Qualifying online teachers—Communicative skills and their impact on e-learning quality [Electronic Version]. *Education and Information Technologies, 12*, 41–51. doi:10.1007/s10639-006-9025-1

Levy-Leboyer, C. (1997). *Gestión de las competencias.* Barcelona, Spain. *Gestion*, 2000.

LindenLabs. (2009, 28 July 2009). *Economic Statistics.* Retrieved October 5, 2008, from http://secondlife.com/whatis/economy_stats.php.

Linn, R. L. (Ed.). Educational Measurement, 3rd Ed., (1989). (Japanese translation by Ikeda, H., Fujita, K., Yanai, H., Shigemasu, K., The Center for the Study of Learning, Yokohama, Japan 1992)

Liu, Z. (2005). Mission of Modern Universities and Development of Modern Society. US-China Education Review, 4.

Lohr, S. (2008, October 15). Free the Avatars. *The New York Times.* Retrieved from http://www.nytimes.com

Longmire, W. (2000). A Primer on learning objects. *Learning Circuits.* Retrieved September 10, 2008, from http://wwwlearningcircuits.org/mar2000/primer.html

Louw, J., Brown, C., Muller, J., & Soudien, C. (2009). Instructional technologies in social science instruction in South Africa. *Computers & Education, 53*, 234–242. doi:10.1016/j.compedu.2009.02.001

Lubesky, R. (2006). *The present and future of Personal Learning Environments (PLE). Optusnet.* Retrieved June 14, 2008 from http://members.optusnet.com.au/rlubensky/2006/12/present-and-future-ofpersonal-learning.html

Luke, C. (2000). Cyber –schooling and technological change: Multiliteracies for new times. In Cope, B., & Kalantzis, M. (Eds.), *Multiliteracies: Literacy Learning and the Design of Social Features* (pp. 69–91). New York: Routledge.

Maduekwe, A. N (2007). *Principles and practice of teaching English as a second language.* Lagos, Lagos State: Vitaman Books.

Maduekwe, A. N. (2004, September). *A new learning experience: Language teachers' perception of Information, Communication Technologies (ICT) in Nigeria ESL context.* Paper Presented at the West African Linguistics Society Conference, University of Ibadan, Nigeria.

Maduekwe, A. N. (2006a). ICT in the world of work and Nigerian schools. In V.B. Owhotu (Ed.), *An Introduction to Information and Communication Technologies in Education.* (pp.146 – 162). Lagos: Sibon Books Ltd.

Maduekwe, A. N. (2006b.) Perspective on teacher education & ICT in the language classroom. In V.B. Owhotu (Ed), *An Introduction to Information and Communication Technologies in Education.* (pp182 – 202). Lagos: Sibon Books Ltd.

Maffesoli, M. (2004). *Il tempo delle tribù. Il declino dell'individualismo nelle società postmoderne.* Milano: Guerini e Associati.

Maher, M. L. (1999). Designing the virtual campus. *Design Studies, 20*(4), 319–342. doi:10.1016/S0142-694X(98)00043-X

Mahood, E. (1996). The Primordial Leap and the Present: The Ever-Present Origin- an overview of the work of Jean Gebser. *Journal.* Retrieved from www.grailwerk.com/docs/synairetic.htm

Malone, T. W., & Lepper, M. R. (1987). Making Learning Fun: A Taxonomy of Intrinsic Motivations for Learning. In Snow, R. E., & Farr, M. J. (Eds.), *Aptitude, Learning and Instruction III: Conative and Affective Process Analyses* (pp. 223–250). Hillsdale, New York: Lawrence Erlbaum Associates.

Mapelli, M., & Margiotta, U. (Eds.). (2009). *Dai blog ai social network. Arti della connessione nel virtuale.* Milano: Mimesis.

Maragliano, R. (Ed.). (2004). *Pedagogie dell'e–learning.* Bari, IT: GLF Editori Laterza.

Marconato, G. (2003). Oltre l'e-learning. *Sviluppo & Organizzazione*, *200*(12), 7–11.

Marín, R., Nomdedeu, L., Wirz, R., & Sanz, P. J. (2009). Robotics Internet Tele-Lab: programming using mobile devices. Proceedings of Inernational. Conference on Multimedia and ICT in Education, Lisbon, Portugal.

Marshall, S., & Mitchell, G. (2004). *Applying SPICE to e-Learning: An e-Learning Maturity Model?* Paper Presented at the Sixth Australasian Computing Education Conference (ACE2004).

Martin, B., R., & Etzkowitz, H. (2000). The Origin and Evolution of the University. *vest-journal, 11*(3-4), 9-34.

Masár, I., Bischoff, A., & Gerkes, M. (2004). Remote experimentation in distance education for control engineers. Proceedings of Virtual University 2004, Bratislava, Slovakia.

Masie, E. (2003). Making sense of learning specifications & standards: a decision maker's guide to their adoption (2nd edition). *The Masie Centre.* Retrieved February 20, 2006, from http://www.masie.com/standards/s3_2nd_edition.pdf

Matsumura, N., & Hiruma, F. Shikou Sutairu (2000). *Thinking Styles* (translation of Sternberg (1997) "Thinking Style" and author's review). Shinyousha, Tokyo, Japan.

Mayes, T., & De Freitas, S. (2004). Review of e-learning theories, frameworks and models. Commissioned review report as part of the JISC-funded e-pedagogy desk study on e-learning models. Retrieved October 20, 2009, from http://www.jisc.ac.uk/uploaded_documents/Stage 2 Learning Models (Version 1).pdf

McCombs, B., & Vakili, D. (2005). A learner-centred framework for e-learning. *Teachers College Record*, *107*(8), 1582–1600. doi:10.1111/j.1467-9620.2005.00534.x

McGregor, D. (1967). *The professional manager*. New York: McGraw-Hill.

McNaught, C., & Lam, P. (2005). Building an evaluation culture and evidence base for e-learning in three Hong Kong universities. *British Journal of Educational Technology*, *36*(4), 599–614. doi:10.1111/j.1467-8535.2005.00538.x

Menges, R. J., & Weimer, M. (1996). *Teaching on solid ground: Using scholarship to improve practice*. San Francisco: Josey Bass Publishers.

Merriman, J. (2008). *Redefining Interoperability (or why the IEEE and Oxford English Dictionary have it Wrong)*. Retrieved July, 10 2009 from http://www.okiproject.org/view/html/site/oki/node/2872

Merryfield, M. (2003). Like a veil: Cross-cultural experiential learning online. *Contemporary Issues in Technology & Teacher Education*, *3*(2), 146–171.

Meyer, K. A. (2003). Face-to-face versus threaded discussions: The role of time and higher order thinking. *Journal of Asynchronous Learning Networks*, *7*(3), 55–65.

Mezirow, J. (2000). *Learning as transformation*. San Francisco: Jossey-Bass.

Mikolajczyk, K., & Schmid, C. (2005). A performance Evaluation of Local Descriptors. *IEEE Transactions on Pattern Analysis and Machine Intelligence*, *27*(10), 1615–1630. doi:10.1109/TPAMI.2005.188

Mills, Sh.J., Yanes M.J., Casebeer, C.M. (2009)- Perception of distance learning among faculty of a college of education. *MERLOT Journal of Online Learning and Teaching,5*(1), march 2009

Ministerial Declaration Riga. *Latvia* (2006). Retrieved 29.06.2009 from http://ec.europa.eu/information_society/events/ict_riga_2006/doc/declaration_riga.pdf

Ministry of Education. Culture, Sports, Science and Technology. (2004). *Shougakkou no eigokyouiku ni kansuru ishikichousa houkoku* [An attitude survey towards English education in primary schools]. Retrieved July 17, 2009, from http://www.mext.go.jp/b_menu/shingi/chukyo/ chukyo3/015/gijiroku/05032201/004/001.htm

Ministry of Education. Culture, Sports, Science and Technology. (2007a). *Kankoku ni okeru shougakkou eigokyouiku no genjyou to kadai* [A Current state and problems on the elementary school English education in Korea]. Paper presented at the 18th Conference of the Special Committee on Foreign Language Education. Conference material retrieved July 4, 2009, from http://www.mext.go.jp/b_menu/shingi/chukyo/chukyo3/015/siryo/05120501/s004_1.pdf

Ministry of Education. Culture, Sports, Science and Technology. (2007b). *Chugoku ni okeru shougakkou eigokyouiku no genjyou to kadai* [A Current state and problems on the elementary school English education in China]. Paper presented at the 18th Conference of the Special Committee on Foreign Language Education. Conference material retrieved July 4, 2009, from http://www.mext.go.jp/b_menu/shingi/chukyo/chukyo3/015/siryo/05120501/s004_2.pdf

Ministry of Education. Culture, Sports, Science and Technology. (2007c). *Taiwan ni okeru shougakkou eigokyouiku no genjyou to kadai* [A Current state and problems on the elementary school English education in Taiwan]. Paper presented at the 18th Conference of the Special Committee on Foreign Language Education. Conference material retrieved July 4, 2009, from http://www.mext.go.jp/b_menu/shingi/chukyo/chukyo3/015/siryo/05120501/s004_3.pdf

Ministry of Education. Culture, Sports, Science and Technology. (2008a). White paper on science and technology 2008. Retrieved July 7, 2009, from http://www.mext.go.jp/english/wp/ 1260270.htm

Ministry of Education. Culture, Sports, Science and Technology. (2008b). *Shougakkou gaikokugokatsudou kenshu guide book* [Training guide book for foreign language activities]. Tokyo: Ohbunsha.

Ministry of Education. Culture, Sports, Science and Technology. (2009, April 21). *The course of study (Chapter4)*. Retrieved July 12, 2009, from http://www.mext.go.jp/component/a_menu/ education/micro_detail/__icsFiles/afieldfile/2009/04/21/1261037_12.pdf

Minoura, Y. (1983). *Kodomo no ibunkataiken* [Children's cross-cultural experience]. Tokyo: Shisakusha.

Miyazaki, M. (2000). Shadowing no yukousei: Listening to speech nouryoku ni kanshite [Shadowing: Effects on listening and speaking competence]. *LET Kansai Chapter Collected Papers*, *8*, 69–78.

Monereo, C., & Pozo, J. L. (2003). *La Universidad ante la nueva cultura educativa. Enseñar y aprender para la autonomía*. Barcelona, Spain: Síntesis.

Montessori, M. (1990). *The Discovery of the Child.* New York, New York: Ballantine Books.

Moore, M. G. (1983). The Individual Adult Learner. In Tight, M. (Ed.), *Adult Learning and Education* (pp. 153–168). London, UK: Croom Helm.

*More and better jobs in a knoewledge-based economy* (2009). Retrieved 29.06.2009 from http://ec.europa.eu/information_society/tl/ecowor/ework/index_en.html.

Moreno, F., & Bailly-Bailliere, M. (2002). *Diseño instructivo de la formación on-line*. Barcelona, ES: Ariel Educación.

Morin, E. (1999). *Seven Complex lessons in Education for the Future*. Paris: United Nations Educational, Scientific and Cultural Organization.

Morin, E. (2008). *La Méthode. Opus*. Paris: Le Seuil.

Morningstar, C., & Farmer, F. R. (1991). The lessons of Lucasfilm's Habitat. In Benedikt, M. (Ed.), *Cyberspace: First Steps*. Cambridge, MA: MIT Press.

Motschnig-Pitrik, R., & Mallich, K. (2004). Effects of Person-Centered Attitudes on Professional and Social Competence in a Blended Learning Paradigm. *Journal of Educational Technology & Society*, *7*(4), 176–192.

Mourshed, M. M., Matipa, W. M., Kelliher, D., & Keane, M. (2002, November). *Towards interoperability: ICT in academic curricula for sustainable construction*. Paper presented at the 1st International Conference: creating a sustainable construction industry in developing countries, Stellenbosch, South Africa.

Moustakas, C. (1990). *Heuristic Research: Design, Methodology and its Applications*. London: Sage.

Muirhead, B. (2001) Enhancing social interaction in computer-mediated distance education, *United States Distance Learning Association Ed at a Distance Magazine and Ed Journal 15*(40). Available online at: www.usdla.org/html/journal/APR01_Issue/article02.html (accessed 3 April 2007).

Mujtaba, B. G., & Preziosi, R. C. (2005). *Adult education in academia: Recruiting and retaining extraordinary facilitators of learning!*Pompano Beach, FL: Xpress Printing and Publishing.

Murakami, Y., & Murakami, C. Big Five Handbook (in Japanese), Gakugeitosyo, Tokyo (2001). Itoh T.,(1995). Zisonshin No Izi To Kouyou (Maintainance and Development of Self-respect), in Miyamoto & Nasu (Ed.), *Theory and Development of Achievement Motivation*, Kanekoshobo, Tokyo.

Naisbitt, J. (1984). *Megatrends: Ten New Directions Transforming Our Lives* (1st ed.). New York, NY: Warner Books Ltd.

Nakamura, J., & Csikszentmihalyi, M. (2002). The concept of flow. In Snyder, C. R., & Lopez, S. J. (Eds.), *Handbook of Positive Psychology* (pp. 89–105). Oxford, UK: Oxford University Press.

Nakayama, M., Yamamoto, H., & Santiago, R. (2006). Investigating the Impact of Learner Characteristics on Blended Learning among Japanese Students. In [Academic Conferences.]. *Proceedings of ICEL, 2006*, 361–370.

Nakayama, M., Yamamoto, H., & Santiago, R. (2007a). Relationship between Learner Characteristics and Learning Performance in Hybrid Courses among Japanese Students.In [Academic Conferences.]. *Proceedings of ICEL, 2007*, 341–349.

Nakayama, M., Yamamoto, H., & Santiago, R. (2008). The Impact of Information Literacy and Learner Characteristics on Learning Behavior of Japanese Students in Online Courses. *International Journal of Case Method Research & Application*, *XX*(4), 403–415.

Nakayama, M., Yamamoto, H. & Santiago, R. (2007b). The Impact of Learner Characteristics on Learning Performance in Hybrid Courses among Japanese Students. *The Electronic Journal of e-Learning, 5*, (3), 195-206.

Nash, S. S. (2004) New quality benchmarks for online courses: Meshing technology and conceptual underpinning, Selected Papers from the *Fifteenth International Conference on College Teaching and Learning*. Jacksonville, Fl., U.S.A. 29th March-2nd April 2004, 195-222.

National Institute for Educational Policy Research. (2004). *Gaikokugo no curriculum no kaizen ni kansuru kenkyu: Sshogaikoku no doukou* [A study on curriculum development of foreign languages: Recent developments in foreign countries]. Retrieved June 25, 2009, http://www.nier.go.jp/kiso/seika2/gaikokugo.pdf

Neema-Abooki, P., & Kitawi, A. (2009). *Knowledge Based Economies in Selected Universities in Uganda*. Paper presented at the INTED 2009 conference.

Nelson, J., & Kerr, D. (2006). *Active citizenship in INCA countries: definitions, policies, practices and outcomes. Final report.* Retrieved June, 30 2009 from http://www.inca.org.uk/pdf/Active_Citizenship_Report.pdf

Neville, B. (1989). *Educating Psyche*. Melbourne, Australia: Collins Dove.

Nicholls, J. G. (1978). The development of the concept of effort and ability, perception of academic attainment, and the understanding that difficult tasks require more ability. *Child Development*, *49*, 800–814. doi:10.2307/1128250

Nicol, D. J., Minty, I., & Sinclair, C. (2003). The social dimensions of online learning. *Innovations in Education and Teaching International*, *40*(3), 270–280. doi:10.1080/1470329032000103807

Nonaka, I., & Takeuchi, H. (1997). *The Knowlegde-Creating Company*. Milano, Italy: Guerini e Associati.

Nossek, B., R., Peterson, B., Logar, S., & Zwiauer, C. (2008). ePortfolio at the University of Vienna – Framework and Pilot Projects. *IJET*, *3*(1), 21-26.

O'Neill, G., & McMahon, T. (2005). Student-Centred Learning: What Does It Mean For Students and Lecturers? In G. O'Neill, T. McMahon, & M. McMullin (Ed.), *Emerging Issues in the Practice of University Learning and Teaching* (pp. 27-36). Dublin, IR: AISHE.

Odogwu, H. N. (2000). Survey of computer education in secondary schools. *ASUU-UNILAG Journal of Comtemporary Issues*, *1*(1), 33–51.

Odusanya, O. O., & Bamgbala, O. A. (2002). Computing and information technology skills for final year medical and dental students at the college of medicine University of Lagos, Nigeria. *The Nigerian Postgraduate Medical Journal*, *9*(4), 190–193.

Okebukola, P. (2000) Teachers advised to acquire computer education. *The Guardian Newspaper*. Thursday, August 14, p. 35.

Olibie, E. I., & Akudolu, Lilian- Rita. I (2008, August). *Digital empowerment of students in universities in South –East zone of Nigeria.* Paper presented at a conference on Higher Education Research and Policy Network (HERPNET). Ibadan: Nigeria.

Oliver, M., & Dempster, J. (2003). Embedding e-learning practices. In Blackwell, R., & Blackmore, P. (Eds.), *Towards strategic staff development in higher education, 142 –153*. Buckingham: SRHE and Open University Press.

Olorundare, S. (2006, October). *Utilization of ICT in curriculum development, implementation and evaluation.* Paper presented at the National Conference on Information and Communication and Technology. Institute of Education, University of Nigeria, Nsukka

OMG, Object Management Group. Common Object Request Broker: Architecture and Specification. Revision 2.0. (1995).

Ondrejka, C. (2008). Education unleashed: Participatory culture, education, and innovation in second life. In Salen, K. (Ed.), *The ecology of games: Connecting youth, games, and learning* (pp. 229–252). Cambridge, MA: The MIT Press.

Owhotu, V. B. (2009a). ICTs in basic and post-basic education: A comparative overview and lessons for Nigeria. *WCCI Chapter Journal of Curriculum and Instruction*, *7*(3), 31.

Owhotu, V. B. (2006). The social dimensions of technological innovation and revolution. In V. B. Owhotu (Ed), An *introduction to Information Technologies in education.* (pp.9 – 22). Lagos: Sibon Books Ltd.

Owhotu, V. B. (2009b, February). *African Asian dialogue: Promoting a self reliant approach to basic education development through research and dialogue.* Paper presented at the Round table/ Launch of the Africa-Asia project, Faculty of Education, University of Lagos.

Pagliacci, M. (2006). *Orientation entrepreneuriale des étudiants et role de l'Universitè*. Grenoble, France: Réseau PGV Editions.

Pagliacci, M. (2004). L'apprentissage par le jeu (Learning by playing). In Lodziensis, U. (Ed.), *Formation et développement des compétences manageriales dans l'Europe élargie* (pp. 93–103). Lodz, Poland: Wydawnictwo Uniwersytetu Lodzkiego.

Pagliacci, M. (2009). Towards a systemic assessment and evaluation of SMEs.*Cahiers du CEREN.* 27(2009).

Pagliacci, M., et al. (2008, October). *Esprit entrepreneurial et innovant des étudiants universitaires.* Paper presented at the meeting *Les cultures étudiantes* of Université Pierre Mendès-France, Grenoble, France.

Pagliacci, M., et al. (2010). Il potenziale creativo negli studenti e il fabbisogno innovativo nelle imprese *AUR&S*.3-4/10

Paolini, P., Barbieri, T., Loiudice, P., Alonzo, F., Zanti, M., & Gaia, G. (1999). *Visiting a museum together: how to share a visit to a virtual world.* Paper presented at Museums&Web '99, New Orleans (USA), (pp. 27).

Paredes, J., & Estebanell, M. (2005). Actitudes y necesidades de formación de los profesores ante las TIC y la introducción del crédito europeo: un nuevo desafío para la educación superior. *Revista de Educación, 337*, 125–148.

Pawlowski, J., & Bick, M. (2006). Managing & re-using didactical expertise: The Didactical Object Model. *Journal of Educational Technology & Society, 9*(1), 84–96.

Pawlowski, J. M. (2007), *The new Quality standard for e-learning: Enabling Global Quality Development.* Retrieved from from http://www.initiatives.ref.org./Initiatives-2005/document.php?id=337

Payá, L., Reinoso, O., Gil, A., & Jiménez, L. M. (2007). Plataforma distribuida para la realización de prácticas de robótica móvil a través de Internet. *Información Tecnológica, 18*(1), 27–38.

Payá, L., Juliá, M., Reinoso, O., Gil, A., & Jiménez, L. M. (2006). Behaviour-based multi-robot formations using computer vision. Proceedings of 6th IASTED International Conference on Visualization, Imaging and Image Processing, Palma de Mallorca, Spain.

Peal, D., & Wilson, B. (2001). Activity theory and web-based training. In Khan, B. H. (Ed.), *Web-Based Training* (pp. 147–153). New Jersey, NJ: Educational Technology Publications.

Pena-Shaff, J., Altman, W., & Stephenson, H. (2005). Asynchronous online discussions as a tool for learning: Students' attitudes, expectations, and perceptions. *Journal of Interactive Learning Research, 16*(4), 409–430.

Penfield, W., & Roberts, L. (1959). *Speech and brain-mechanism.* Oxford: Oxford University Press.

Perelman, L. J. (1990). Education in the information age: a new learning enterprise. *The Technology Education Comes to Education.* 12ED-19ED.

Perkins, D. N. (1993). Person-plus: a distributed view of thinking and learning. In Salomon, G. (Ed.), *Distributed cognitions. Psychological and educational considerations* (pp. 88–110). Cambridge, UK: Cambridge University Press.

Phillips, B. N. (1963). Age changes in accuracy of self-perceptions. *Child Development, 34*, 1041–1046. doi:10.2307/1126546

Piaget, J. (1970). *Science of education and the psychology of the child.* New York, NY: Orion.

Piaget, J., & Inhelder, B. (1990). *Psychology of Children.* Novi Sad, Serbia: Dobra vest.

Pietroni, D., & Rumiati, R. (2008). *La mente che negozia.* Milano, Italy: Il Sole 24 Ore.

Poggi, C., & Torrebruno, A. (2007). From the Dead Sea scrolls to social sports, passing through European history: an effective pedagogical format based on 3D worlds. [Chesapeake, VA: AACE.]. *Proceedings of ED-Media, 07*, 4240–4248.

Polanyi, M. (1967). *The Tacit Dimension.* London: Routeledge & Kegan Paul Ltd.

Poole, D. M. (2000). Student participation in a discussion oriented online course: a case study. *Journal of Research on Computing in Education, 33*(2), 162–177.

Pope, S. (2002). Form a successful strategy [Electronic Version] [from www.elearningmag.com]. *E-learning*, 34–37. Retrieved November 21, 2008.

Postman, N. (1993). *Technology: The surrender of culture to technology* (p. 185). New York: Vintage Books.

Pratt, E., & Sullivan, N. (1994, September). *Comparison of ESL writers in networked and regular classrooms.* Paper Presented at the 28th Annual TESOL Convention Baltimore.

Preece, J. (2000). *Online communities: Designing usability, supporting sociability*. Chichester: Wiley.

Quintana, C., Carra, A., Krajcik, J., & Soloway, E. (2001). Learner-Centred Design: Reflections and New Directions. In Carroll, J. M. (Ed.), *Human-Computer Interaction in the New Millennium* (pp. 605–626). New York, NY: Addison-Wesley.

Ranieri, M. (2005). *E-learning: modelli e strategie didattiche*. Trento: Erickson.

Reason, P., & Bradbury, H. (2006). *Handbook of Action Research*. London: Sage.

Recchioni, M., Castello, V., Dell'Aiuto, V. & Sancin, C. (2008). Strumenti collaborativi, intermodalità e life long learning. dove vanno le innovazioni? *Atti del V convegno SieL*. Macerata: EUM.

Redmon, R. J., & Burger, M. (2004). Web CT Discussion Forums: Asynchronous Group Reflection of the Student Teaching Experience. *Curriculum and Teaching Dialogue*, *6*(2), 157–166.

Reinking, D., & Rickman, P. (1998). *Handbook of literacy and technology. Transformation in a post-typographic world*. Oxford: Oxford University Press.

Review, H. B. online version. (2006). *Avatar - based marketing*. Retrieved April 12, 2009 from http://harvardbusinessonline.hbsp.harvard.edu/hbsp/hbr/articles/article.jsp?articleID=R0606B

Richardson, L. (1994). Writing: A Method of Inquiry. In Denzin, N., & Lincoln, E. (Eds.), *Handbook of Qualitative Research*. Thousand Oaks, CA: Sage.

Richardson, A. (2002). *An ecology of learning and the role of elearning in the learning environment*. Paper presented at the Global Summit 2002.

Rigutti, S., Paletti, G., & Morandini, A. (2008). Lifelong Learning e e-learning 2.0: il contributo degli studi sull'usabilità. *Je-LKS - Journal of e-Learning and Knowledge Society,* 4 (1), 91-100.

Ritzema, T., & Harris, B. (2008). the use of second life for distance education. *Journal of Computing Sciences in Colleges*, *23*(6), 110–116.

Robertson, T. J., & Klotz, J. (2004) How can instructors and administrators fill the missing link in online instruction, *Online Journal of Distance Learning Administration*, 5(4). Available online at: http://www.westga.edu/~dist ance/ojdl a/winter54 /roberson54.htm (accessed 3 April 2007).

Rogers, C. R. (1983). *Freedom to Learn for the 80's*. Columbus, OH: Charles E. Merrill Publishing.

Ross, A. R. (1996). The influence of computer Communication skill on participation in a computer conference course. *Journal of Educational Computing Research*, *15*(1), 37–52. doi:10.2190/6TYW-ADV1-W0LC-N9H0

Rossi, P. G. (2006). *Che cos'è l'e- Portaolio*. Roma, IT: Carocci.

Rowntree, D. (1995). Teaching and learning Online: A Correspondence Education for the 21st Century? *British Journal of Educational Technology*, *26*(3), 205–215. doi:10.1111/j.1467-8535.1995.tb00342.x

Saettler, P. (1968). *History of Instructional Technology*. New York: McGraw-Hill.

Salawudeen, O. S. (2006, October). E-learning technologies: The Nigerian experience. *Paper presented at the XXIII Fig conference*, Munch Germany.

Salmon, G. (2005). Flying not flapping: a strategic framework for e-learning and pedagogical innovation in higher education institutions. *ALT-J. Research in Learning Technology*, *13*(3), 201–218.

Salmon, G. (2000). *eModerating: The key to teaching and learning online* (London, Routledge Falmer).

Salmon, G. K., & Giles, K. (1997). Moderating online, *Online Education Conference, Berlin*. Available online at: http://www.emoderators.com/moderators/gilly/MOD.html (accessed 12 April 2007).

Sánchez, J., Morilla, F., Dormido, S., Aranda, J., & Ruipérez, P. (2002). Virtual control lab using Java and Matlab: A qualitative approach. *IEEE Control Systems Magazine*, *22*(2), 8–20. doi:10.1109/37.993309

Sartori, S. (2009). Quale creatività nella crisi? *Il Ponte*, LXV-4.

Savery, J. R., & Duffy, T. M. (1995). Problem Based Learning: An instructional model and its constructivist framework. *Educational Technology*, *35*(5), 31–38.

Sawyer, P., & Mariani, J. (1995). Database systems: challenges and opportunities for graphical HCI. *Interacting with Computers*, *7*(1), 273–303. doi:10.1016/0953-5438(95)93605-5

Schaffert, S. & Hilzensauer, W. (2008). On the way towards Personal Learning Environments: seven crucial aspects. *eLearning Papers*, 9, July.

Schallert, D.L., & Reed, J.H., & D-Team, T. (2003). Intellectual, motivational, textual, and cultural considerations in teaching and learning with computer-mediated discussion. *Journal of Research on Technology in Education*, *36*(2), 103–118.

Schein, E. H. (1992). *Organizational culture and Leadership* (2nd ed.). San Francisco: Jossey-Bass.

Schroeder, R. (2006). Being There and the Future of Connected Presence. *Journal of Teleoperators and Virtual Environments*, *15*(4), 438–454. doi:10.1162/pres.15.4.438

Schwab, R. L. (1999). *Technology and the changing roles in teacher education. In log-in or lose-out: technology in the 21st century education* (pp. 151–155). American Association of Colleges for Teacher Education.

Sclater, N. (2008). *Web 2.0, Personal Learning Environments, and the Future of Learning Management Systems* (Research Bulletin, Issue 13). Boulder, CO: EDUCAUSE Center for Applied Research. Retrieved June, 23 2008 from http://www.educause.edu/ecar.

Scrimshaw, P. (1998). Cooperative writing with computers in Scrimshaw, (ed), *Language classroom and computers*. London: Routledge.

Seabolt, B., & Arends, B. (2000). *Remaining real in a virtual world*. Available online at: http://www.web ct.com/service/viewcontentframe?contentID=2385 857&pageName=index.html (accessed 3 April 2007).

Seely-Brown, J. (1999). Learning, Working and Playing in the Digital Age. *AAHE Conference on Higher Education*, March 1999. Retrieved June, 15 2009 from http://serendip.brynmawr.edu/sci_edu/seelybrown/

Seely-Brown, J. (2009). Learning in the Digital Age (Indiana University, April 2009) Retrieved June, 15 2009 from http://www.johnseelybrown.com/

Selwyn, N. (2000). Creating a 'connected' community? Teachers use of an electronic discussion group. *Teachers College Record*, *102*(4), 750–778. doi:10.1111/0161-4681.00076

Seretta, B. (2005). Virtual companies. Net – learning and net – working will be common. *CHECK point e-learning newsletter*. Retrieved 2005 from http://www.checkpointelearning.com/index.php?co=8&aID=963

Sharpe, R., Benfield, G., & Francis, R. (2006). Implementing a university e-learning strategy: levers for change within academic schools. *ALT-J. Research in Learning Technology*, *14*(2), 135–151.

Sharples, M. (2000). The design of personal mobile technologies for lifelong learning. *Computers & Education*, *34*(3), 177–193. doi:10.1016/S0360-1315(99)00044-5

Shen, H. H., & Dewan, P. (1992). *Access control for collaborative environments*. Paper presented at the 1992 ACM conference on Computer-supported Cooperative Work (pp. 51-58). New York: ACM Press.

Shettima, A. K. (2005). *Nigeria university education in the 21st century*. Retrieved February 20, 2005, from http://www.mac found.org/site/c/.html

Shi, J., & Tomasi, C. (1994). Good features to track. *Proceedings of Computer Vision and Pattern Recognition*, 593-600, Seattle, USA.

Siegel, J. (1994). Teach your teachers well. *Electronic Learning* April, 34

Siemens, G. (2006). *Connectivism: Learning Theory or Pastime of the Self-Amused?* Retrieved June, 6, 2009 from http://www.elearnspace.org/Articles/connectivism_self-amused.htm

Siemens, G., & Tittenberger, P. (2009). *Handbook of Emerging Technologies for Learning*. Retrieved April, 20 2009 from http://www.umanitoba.ca/learning_technologies/cetl/HETL.pdf

Smith, A. (1975). *La ricchezza delle nazioni*. Torino, Italy: UTET.

Someya, Y. (1998). Prosody kyouka kunren no kouka ni kansuru action research [An action research on a prosody-strengthening exercise]. *Tsuyakurironkenkyu*, *14*, 4–21.

Son, J. (2002). Online discussion in a CALL course for distance language teachers. *CALICO Journal*, *20*(1), 127–144.

Sotunwa, O. O. (1998). Integrating computer technology into the teaching of Nigerian languages. In Nwabuko, N. C. & Akinpelu, Biobun (Eds.), *Shifting Paradigms in the Teaching Function in ICT Era* (pp.17-22) Lagos: Nigerian Association for Educational Media and Technology (NAEMT) Publisher

Spiegelberg, H. (1972). *Phenomenology in Psychology and Psychiatry: A Historical Introduction*. Evanston, USA: Northwestern University Press.

Spiru Haret University. (2007). *Manual of Quality Assurance Procedures*. Romania: Publishing House Fundatia Romania de Maine.

Spitzer, D. R. (2001). Don't forget the high-touch with the high-tech in distance learning. *Educational Technology*, *41*(2), 51–55.

Stafford, R. F. (2005). Understanding motivations for Internet use in distance education. *IEEE Transactions on Education*, *49*(2), 301–306. doi:10.1109/TE.2004.842904

Sternberg, R. J. (1997). *Thinking Styles*. Cambridge, UK: Cambridge University Press. doi:10.1017/CBO9780511584152

Stewart, T. A. (1999). *Il capitale intellettuale. La nuova ricchezza*. Milano,Italy: Ponte alle Grazie.

Stigmar, M., & Sundberg, D. (2001, July). *Teachers as reflective Learners*. Paper presented at the 26th international IUT-conference, Johannesburg, South Africa.

Stiles, M. (2004). Is an eLearning strategy enough? *Educational Developments*, *5*(1), 13–15.

Stiles, M., & Yorke, J. (2003) Designing and implementing learning technology projects—a planned approach, workshop paper presented for the *EFFECTS—Embedding Learning Technologies Seminar,* University College London, 8 April. Retrieved October 15, 2009, from http://www.jiscinfonet.ac.uk/ Resources/external-resources/eltfinal.doc/view.

Stojanovic, N., & Handschuh, S. (2002). *A framework for knowledge management on the semantic web*. Retrieved February, 28 2008, from http://www2002.org/CDROM/poster/130.pdf

Strategic Headquarters, I. T. (2001, January 22). *e-Japan strategy.* Retrieved July 12, 2009, from http://www.kantei.go.jp/foreign/it/network/0122full_e.html

Strategic Headquarters, I. T. (2006a, January 19). *New IT reform strategy: Realizing ubiquitous and universal network society where everyone can enjoy the benefits of IT.* Retrieved July 12, 2009, from http://www.kantei.go.jp/foreign/policy/it/ITstrategy2006.pdf

Strategic Headquarters, I. T. (2006b, July 26). *Priority policy program 2006.* Retrieved July 15, 2009, from http://www.kantei.go.jp/foreign/policy/it/Program2006.pdf

SUGSI. Shinshu University, Graduate School on the Internet, Retrieved 1st July 2009, from http://cai1.cs.shinshu-u.ac.jp/xoops/

Sullivan, N. (1993). Teaching writing on a computer network. *TESOL Journal*, *3*(1), 19–23.

Tajino, A., & Tajino, Y. (2000). Native and non-native: What can they offer?: lessons from team-teaching in Japan. *ELT Journal*, *54*, 3–11. doi:10.1093/elt/54.1.3

Tamai, K. (2003). Risuningu to shadowing no setten ni miru aratana shido no shiten [A new perspective on listening and shadowing techniques for English language teaching]. *Studies in English Language Teaching*, *26*, 1–19.

Tamai, K. (1998). Shadowing no haikeiriron to hyoukahou [Theoretical background and evaluation of shadowing]. In Simultaneous Interpretation Research Committee, Japan Association for Current English Studies, Kansai Chapter (Ed.), *Research and Practices of Shadowing* (pp. 1-19). Osaka: Japan Association for Current English Studies Kansai Chapter.

Tarnas, R. (1993). *Passion of the Western Mind*. San Francisco: Random House.

Tashner, J. H., Riedl, R. E., & Bronack, S. C. (2005). *Virtual worlds: Further development of web-based teaching*. Paper presented at the Hawaii International Conference on Education, Honolulu, Hawaii, (pp. 4579-4588).

Tella, S. (1992). *Boys, Girls and e-mail: A case study in Finnish senior secondary schools*. Helsinki: University of Helsinki, Department of Teacher education

Terrell, S., & Dringus, L. (1999). An investigation of the effects of learning style on student success in an online learning environment. *Journal of Educational Technology Systems*, *28*(3), 231–238.

Thompson, J. W. (1995). The renaissance of learning in business. In S. Chawla and J. Renesch (1995). *Learning organizations: Developing cultures for tomorrow's workplace*. Portland, Oregon: Productivity Press.

Tiamiyu, M. A. (2000). Availability, accessibility and use of information technologies in Nigeria federal agencies: *A Preliminary Survey*. Nigeria. 105.

Tosh, D. (2005). A concept diagram for the Personal Learning Landscape. Retrieved June 1, 2007, from http://elgg.net/dtosh/weblog/398.html

Tosh, D., & Werdmuller, B. (2004). *Creation of a learning landscape: weblogging and social networking in the context of e-portfolios*. Retrieved September 24, 2008 from http://elgg.net/bwerdmuller/files/61/179/Learning_landscape.pdf

Trentin, G. (2001). *Dalla formazione a distanza all'apprendimento in rete*. Milano: Franco Angeli.

Trentin, G. (2004). *Apprendimento in rete e condivisione delle conoscenze: ruolo, dinamiche e tecnologie delle comunità professionali online*. Milano: Franco Angeli.

Trentin, G. (2005). From "formal" to "informal" e-Learning through knowledge management and sharing. *Journal of e-Learning and Knowledge Society*, 1(2), 209-217.

Trentin, G. (in press). E-Learning and teaching quality. *International Journal of Instructional Media, 35*(1).

Ueno, M., Songmuang, P., Okamoto, T., Nagaoka, K. (2008). Item Response Theory with Assessors' parameters of Peer Assessment. *IEICE TRANSACTIONS on Information and Systems*, J91-D, (2), 377-388.

UNESCO. (1996). *Learning: The Treasure Within. International Commission on Education for 21st Century*. Paris: UNESCO.

UNESCO. (1999). *The World Declaration on Higher Education for the Twenty-first Century: Vision and Action*. Paris: UNESCO.

UNESCO. (2008). EFA Global Monitoring Report 2009: Overcoming inequality-why governance matters.

UNESCO. (2009). ICT in education. Retrieved July 29, 2009, from http://portal.unesco.org/ci/en/

Unwin, T. (2008). Survey of e-learning in Africa [Electronic Version].

Ushie, A., Beshel, C., Asanga, D., & Iyang, J. (2008). Academic staff use of internet services Federal colleges of education in Middle Belt of Nigeria. In Nwabuko, N. C. & Akinpelu, Biobun (Eds.), *Shifting Paradigms in the Teaching Function in ICT Era* (pp.47-49) Lagos: Nigerian Association for Educational Media and Technology (NAEMT) Publisher.

Utz, H., Stulp, F., & Moeld, A. (2004). Sharing belief in teams of heterogeneous robot. *Proceedings of RoboCup 2004 Symposium*, Lisbon, Portugal.

Uwadia, C. O. (2000). Information and communication technology in Nigeria: A survey, critique and projections. *ASUU-UNILAG Journal of Contemporary Issues*, *1*(1), 33–51.

Vallack, J. M. (2005b). I Know What I Like! *Qualitative Research Journal*, *5*(2), 99–111.

Vallack, J. (2005a). *Death of an Author: Subtextual Phenomenology: A Radical Methodology Towards the Transcendental Object*. Unpublished PhD Thesis. La Trobe University, Australia.

Vallack, J. (2008a). The (Secret and Password-Protected) Diary of a Web 2.0 Novice. *Journal*. Retrieved 4th November, 2009 from http://jocene.edublogs.org/2008/10/08/secret-and-password-protected-diary-of-a-web-2-novice/

Vallack, J. (2008b). Velocity & Ubiquity. Weblog *Journal*. Retrieved 4th November, 2009 from http://jocene.edublogs.org/2008/10/20/velocity-ubiquity/

Vallack, J. (2009). *The (Secret and Password Protected) Diary of a Web 2.0 Novice doing Subtextual Phenomenology*. European Conference of Research Methodologies (ECRM 2009) Conference Proceedings, Valletta, Malta http://www.academic-conferences.org/ecrm/ecrm2009/ecrm09-proceedings.htm

Varisco, B. M. (2002). *Costruttivismo socio-culturale. Genesi filosofiche, sviluppi psico-pedagogici, applicazioni didattiche*. Roma: Carocci.

Varlamis, I. & Apostolakis, I. (2007). The Present and Future of Standards for E-Learning Technologies. *Interdisciplinary Journal of Knowledge and Learning Objects*, Volume 2.

Venkatesh, R. (2008, October 23). *The Cloudworker's Creed.* Retrieved October 28, 2008 from Ribbonfarm: http://www.ribbonfarm.com/2008/10/23/the-cloudworkers-creed/

Vogt, E. E. (1995). Learning out of context. In S. Chawla &J. Renesch (1995). *Learning organizations: Developing cultures for tomorrow's workplace*. Portland, Oregon: Productivity Press.

Von Glasersfeld, E. (1998). *Il costruttivismo radicale. Una via per conoscere ed apprendere*. Roma: Società Stampa Sportiva.

Voos, R. (2003). Blended learning: What is it and where might it take us? *Sloan-C View*, *2*(1), 2–5.

Vorley, T., & Nelles, J. (2008). (Re)Conceptualising the Academy: Institutional Development of and beyond the Third Mission. *Higher Education Management and Policy, 20* (3).

Vygotsky, L. S. (1986). *Thought and Language*. Cambridge, MA: MIT Press.

Vygotsky, L. S. (1978). *Mind in society: The development of higher psychological processes*. Boston: Harvard University press.

Vygotsky, L. S. (1977). *Thinking and Talking*. Belgrade, Serbia: Nolit.

Wada, S. (1996). Construction of the Big Five Scales of Personality Trait Terms and Concurrent Validity with NPI. *Japanese Journal of Phycology*, *67*(1), 61–67.

Wainer, H. (Ed.). (2000). *Computerized adaptive testing: A primer* (2nd ed.). Mahwah, NJ: Lawrence Erlbaum Associates.

Walvoord, B. E. (2004). *Assessment clear and simple: A practical guide for institutions, departments, and general education*. San Francisco, CA: Jossey-Bass.

Warshauer, (1995b). Computer – mediated collaborative learning: Theory and practice *Modern Language Journal, 154-156.*

Warshauer, A. (1995a). Virtual connections: online activities and projects for networking language learners. University of Hawaii. *Second Language Teaching Curriculum Centre,* 220-225

Wasson, B. (2007). Design and Use of Collaborative Network Learning Scenarios: The DoCTA Experience. *Journal of Educational Technology & Society*, *10*(4), 3–16.

Web, E., Jones, A., Barker, P., & Van Schaik, P. (2004). Using e-learning dialogues in higher education. *Innovations in Education and Teaching International*, *41*(1), 93–103. doi:10.1080/1470329032000172748

Weber, M. (1976). *Sociologia delle religioni. Confucianesimo e taoismo*. Torino, Italy: UTET.

Webopedia Computer Dictionary. (2009). E-learning. Retrieved 23.06.2009 from http://www.webopedia.com/TERM/E/e_learning.html

Weerakkody, N. (2009). *Research Methods for Media and Communication*. New York: Oxford University Press.

Weinberger, D. (2005, June 27). *The new shape of knowledge*. Retrieved on June, 26 2009 from http://www.hyperorg.com/blogger/mtarchive/004153.html

Weitl, F., Süß, C., Kammerl, R., & Freitag, B. (2002). *Presenting Complex e-Learning Content on the Web: A Didactical Reference Model*. Paper presented at the E-Learn 2002 world conference on E-Learning in Corporate, Government, Healthcare, & Higher Education.

Wenger, E. (1998). *Communities of practice: Learning as a social system*. Available online at: http://www.co-i-l.com/coil/knowledge-garden/cop (accessed 12 April 2007).

Wenger, E., McDermott, R., & Snyder, W. M. (2007). *Coltivare comunità di pratica*. Milano: Guerini e Associati S.p.A.

White, R. V. (1998). *The ELT curriculum design, innovation and management*. Oxford: Oxford University Press.

White, N. (2004). *Facilitating and hosting a virtual community*. Available online at: http://www.fullcirc.com/community/definingcommunity.htm (accessed 12 April 2008).

Whitehead, J., & McNiff, J. (2006). *Action Research Living Theory*. London: Sage.

Wickstrom, C. D. (2003). A funny thing happened on the way to the forum. *Journal of Adolescent & Adult Literacy*, *46*(5), 414–423.

Wiley, D. A. (2000). *The Instructional Use of Learning Objects*. Bloomington, MN: Association for Educational Communications and Technology.

Wiley, D. A. (2000). *Learning object design and sequencing theory*. Unpublished doctoral dissertation, Brigham Young University. Retrieved August 11, 2003 from: http://davidwiley.com/papers/dissertation/dissertation.pdf

Wilson, S. (2008). Patterns of Personal Learning Environments. *Interactive Learning Environments*, *16*(1), 17–34. doi:10.1080/10494820701772660

Wilson, S. (2005). *Future VLE – The Visual Vision*. Retrieved September 18, 2008 from http://www.cetis.ac.uk/members/scott/blogview?entry=20050125170206.

Wingate, U. (2007). A Framework for Transition: Supporting 'Learning to Learn' in Higher Education. *Higher Education Quarterly*, *61*(3), 391–405. doi:10.1111/j.1468-2273.2007.00361.x

Wojciechowski, A., & Palmer, L. B. (Summer 2005) Individual student characteristics: Can any be predictors of success in online classes? *Online Journal of Distance Learning Administration, 8,* (2). Retrieved 27 January, 2006 from http://www.westga.edu/~distance/ojdla/summer82/wojciechowski82.htm

Woodley, A., & Kirkwood, A. *Evaluation in Distance Learning. Commonwealth* Co-operation in Open Learning: Background Papers. J. Jenkins, ed. London: Commonwealth Secretariat, 1998, 291-98. Rpt. as "Evaluation in Distance Learning: Course Evaluation." http://www1.worldbank.org/disted/Management/Benefits/cou-02.html. In Thomas J. Tobin (2004). Best practices for administrative evaluation of online faculty. DLA 2004 Proceedings. Retrieved on July 10, 2009, from http://www.westga.edu/~distance/ojdla/summer72/tobin72.html.

Woods, R., & Ebersole, S. (2003). Becoming a "communal architect" in the online classroom – Integrating cognitive and affective learning for maximum effect in web-based learning. *Online Journal of Distance Learning Administration, 6*(1). Valiathan, P. (2006). *Blended learning models*. Available online at: http://www.learningcircuits.org/2002/aug2002/valiathan.html (accessed 3 April 2007).

World Bank. (2000). *Information and communication technology: A World Bank group strategy*. Washington, D C: The World Bank Group.

World Bank. (2002). *Constructing knowledge societies: new challenges for tertiary education*. Retrieved October 25, 2005 from www.worldbank.org

Yang, S. J. H. (2006). Context Aware Ubiquitous Learning Environments for Peer-to-Peer Collaborative Learning. *Journal of Educational Technology & Society*, *9*(1), 188–201.

Yuselturk, E., & Top, E. (2006). Reconsidering online course discussions: A case study. *Journal of Educational Technology Systems*, *34*(3), 341–367. doi:10.2190/6GQ8-P7TX-VGMR-4NR4

Yusuf, M., & Onasanya, J. (2004). Information and communication technology and education: Analyzing the Nigerian national policy for information technology. *International Education Journal*, *6*(3), 316–321.

Zabalza, M. A. (2003). *Competencias docentes del profesorado universitario*. Madrid, Spain: Narcea.

# About the Contributors

**Fotis Lazarinis** holds a PhD in Educational Technology with an emphasis on adaptive testing tools and on the use of e-learning standards for representing and managing testing data. He is a visiting lecturer in the Department of Cultural Heritage and New Technologies at the University of Western Greece. He has authored over 50 refereed papers in international or national conferences, journals and research handbooks. He has also published several Computer Science educational books in Greek and served as a review member for conferences and workshops.

**Steve Green** is currently Director of Undergraduate Programmes in the School of Computing at Teesside University, UK. He is a founder-member of both ARC (the Accessibility Research Centre) and DFI (the Digital Futures Institute) at Teesside and has considerable research and commercial expertise in e-learning, accessibility, open systems architectures and open publishing. He has been a project manager and technical director of a number of research and enterprise projects in the areas of learning technologies and digital media. He has published extensively on adaptability, inclusion, personal or distributed learning environments and e-learning standards.

**Elaine Pearson** is Director of the Accessibility Research Centre and a member of the Digital Futures Institute at Teesside University, UK. Her research and consultancy expertise lies in the use of digital media design and technology to support the needs and preferences of disabled people. This research has been supported by grants from British and European funding bodies including the Leverhulme Trust, Higher Education Funding Council (HEFCE), and European Social Fund (ESF) EQUAL initiative. She has published extensively on accessibility and adaptability issues and been invited to present in the UK, Ireland, Spain and Australia. Dr Pearson is also Director of Post Graduate Programmes in the School of Computing. Her teaching interests as a Principal Lecturer lie in aspects of web and mobile design for accessibility and adaptaibility.

* * *

**Oyenike A. Adeosun** holds M.ED and Ph.D degrees in Language Education from the University of Ibadan, Nigeria. She teaches English Language and Literature pedagogy and curriculum in the Department of Arts & Social Sciences Education, Faculty of Education, University of Lagos, Nigeria. A member of a number of professional associations and education networks, her research interest focuses on literacy development, basic education development, ICT integration in teacher education and Teacher Professional Development. She is currently a visiting research scholar at the Centre for the Study of International Cooperation in Education (CICE), Hiroshima University, Japan.

In 2002 **Ugo Barchetti** graduated in Computer Engineering from University of Salento. In 2007 he gained PhD in Information Engineering at Department of Engineering for Innovation, University of Salento. He is a research fellow at Department of Engineering for Innovation. His research activities include the collaboration in virtual environments in order to analyze and explore optimization techniques in heterogeneous workspaces. His studies aim to use CVEs for e-learning benefits. He took part in several projects regarding the production of e-learning collaborative virtual experiences. He acquired experience in a range of activities including the design and development of Service Oriented Architecture and middleware tools in order to support B2B and Supply Chain Management. Currently, he is contract teacher in the course of "Software Engineering I" and tutor of the course of "Computer Graphics" at the Faculty of Computer Engineering at the University of Salento.

**Cristina Barna** is an Associate Professor Ph D in Economics Department, Faculty of Marketing and International Business, Spiru Haret University, Romania. Coordinator of Online Master Programmes, using e-learning platform Blackboard. In 2004 – 2006 Responsible for the Professional Training Programme in two Leonardo da Vinci projects connected with e-learning issues: 'Preparing Trainers in the Spirit of a High Quality Educational System' and 'Training Young People for E-Market'. In 2006 – 2008 Local Senior Short Term Expert and Expert Trainer in four EU Phare projects. From 2008 member in the Management Committee in COST Action ISO701 – Comparative Analysis of Enterprise Data: Industry Dynamics, Firm Performance and Worker Outcomes, research action coordinated by Central European University of Budapest, and from 2005 member in the Romanian Working Group for COST Action 34 - Gender and Well – Being: Work, Family and Public Policies, research action coordinated by University of Barcelona. Scientific publications: author and co – author of 20 books and academic courses, 50 articles in economic reviews, 20 studies published in volumes of international symposia, 4 studies published in volumes of national symposia.

**Bob Barrett** is a professor for the School of Business at the American Public University in Charles Town, West Virginia, USA. He lectures both nationally and internationally on the topics of Electronic Portfolios (e-Portfolios), Virtual Teams/Management, and Using Online Learning as a Strategic Tool for Students with Disabilities. As a seasoned online instructor, he has created and implemented online courses for several leading universities and colleges. In addition to teaching, he has worked as a trainer to help new instructors transition from face-to-face (F2F) teaching to the growing field of online learning. Finally, his key research areas are disability in the workplace/education, as well as the impact of Human Resource Development/Human Resource Management in the creation and management of virtual teams in today's global market.

**Alberto Bucciero**, in December of 2006, gained the PhD in "Computer Engineering" at the Department of Engineering for Innovation of the University of Salento; his research activity has focussed on the design of service oriented architectures and collaborative virtual environments with particular interest in virtual collaborative learning management systems. At the beginning of his career he carried out his research in SET-Lab (Software Engineering & Telemedia Laboratory) strictly collaborating with HOC (Hypermedia Open Center) of the Electronic and Information Department of the Polytechnics of Milan. During the period of collaboration with the Faculty of Engineering of the University of Salento, he has actively participated to many projects. He is contract teacher in the course of "Management of Business Information" at the Faculty of Management Engineering at the University of Salento since

2006/07, coordination teacher of the course of "Software Engineering" in the laurea degree course in Computer Engineer (Diploma Online).

**Kevin Downing** is Senior Coordinator Academic Planning and Convenor of the Institutional Analysis Group at City University of Hong Kong. He has a substantial publication record in the fields of psychology and education, and is current editor of *International Health Abstracts*, also serving as a member of the editorial boards of *Educational Studies, and the British Journal of Community Justice.* He has experience of teaching throughout Europe and Asia, is a Chartered Psychologist, Chartered Scientist, and Associate Fellow of the British Psychological Society. Dr. Downing was awarded the City University of Hong Kong Teaching Excellence Award in 2005 for contributions to the development of "blended learning" with innovative use of technology. He successfully developed learning environments that promote active student engagement. He is also the recipient of the prestigious International Award for Innovative use of Technology in Teaching and Learning conferred in the USA in April 2004.

**Manuela Epure** is a Professor of Marketing Research in the Department of Marketing and International Business, with 17 years of academic career, becoming in 2007 a full member of Chartered Institute of Marketing, UK, and a full member of Academy of Marketing, UK. Starting with 2005, becomes responsible with the implementation of the Blackboard e-learning system in Spiru Haret University, mainly for the master courses students. E-learning quality assurance and exploring the benefits of using IT tools in the learning process are the main research topics starting with 2006. Initiator and president of the organizing committee of the international symposium "Quality management in higher education", held in Bucharest. Author and co-author of 9 textbooks, 6 distance learning course materials and more then 20 articles in Romanian and foreign revues, getting involved in two EU COST research network, A34 and ISO701, being rewarded in 2004 with the second prize for special merits in education by the Romanian President.

**Giuliana Guazzaroni** is a PhD student in e-Learning at the Faculty of Engineering of the Università Politecnica delle Marche, Ancona, Italy. Her research interests are in e-Learning, New Technologies, e-Moderating, Social Networking, Personal Learning Networks, Ubiquitous Learning, Liquid Learning Places, challenging Technologies, rethinking Pedagogy, being Design inspired. Since 2002, she has been involved in e-moderating different online courses (General Pedagogy and Theories of Education; Experimental Pedagogy; Psychology of Education; Processes and methods of Teaching; Educational Technologies; Policies, Legislation and Organization of Teaching; Methods and Techniques of Evaluation; School Legislation for Students with Different Abilities) for training teachers at the Università Ca' Foscari ("Scuola Interateneo di Specializzazione per la Formazione degli insegnati della scuola secondaria del Veneto"), Venice. She has been involved in e-moderating e-Learning courses at the Università Politecnica delle Marche and at the Università di Camerino. She has been involved in European and International projects as an Instructional designer and a teacher (FSE, Equal, Marco Polo, etc.). She has been teaching English and Italian Language in different organisations. She has a degree in Foreign Languages (1998, Università di Macerata) and a master degree in Technologies and Methodologies of e-Learning (2003, Università di Verona).

**Yasushige Ishikawa** is Professor of English Education at Kyoto University of Foreign Studies, Japan. His research interests include CALL, corpus linguistics and speech processing. He has developed multimedia dual-language (English-Spanish and English-Portuguese) CALL team teaching aids for Japanese university students, a Spanish pronunciation and vocabulary teaching aid for Japanese university students, and an EFL CALL teaching aid for self-directed learning using the AmiVoice® speech recognition system with automatic scoring of the fluency of learners' utterances. He has also designed and implemented an innovative methodology for a CALL blended-learning approach to EFL spoken language teaching in ESP courses for students preparing for careers in the hotel industry.

**Luis M. Jimenez** was born in Avila (Spain) in 1967. He received his M.Sc. degree in Industrial Engineering in 1992 from the Polytechnical University of Madrid (Spain). His current position is as Assistant Professor of Automatic Control (1998-), Miguel Hernández University of Elche, teaching subjects in the area of control engineering. From 1995 to 1998 he worked as assistant professor at University of Alicante. His research interests include Robotics control, real-time systems, advanced control systems and engineering education.

**Alfred Kirigha Kitawi** holds a Masters in Educational Management from Makerere University and is currently pursuing a Doctor of Business Administration in Higher Education Management at the University of Bath. He is currently an assistant lecturer at Strathmore University, Nairobi, Kenya. He has a higher diploma in the Management of Information Systems from the Institute for the Management of Information Systems (IMIS). The lectured in Critical Thinking, Development Studies and Ethics in Education at Strathmore University. He developed a training program at Makerere University, Faculty of Information Technology to train students on hardware, software and networking issues. His scholarly research has investigated the Impact of Commission of Higher Education on Kenyan Universities, Systemic Approach to Instruction on achieving goals of Universities and Knowledge Based Economies within the African context. He was an associate editor for Journal No 2-Journal of the World Universities Forum, 2009. On the national scene, he represents his institution in the Information Technology, Learning, Education and Training national mirror committee.

**Mutsumi Kondo** is a lecturer in the Faculty of Liberal Arts at Tezukayama Gakuin University, Japan. Her field of expertise is EFL education and second language acquisition. She received her master's degree in TESOL from the Monterey Institute of International Studies and her second master's degree in Foreign Language Education from Kansai University. Her research interests are EFL learners' psychology, autonomy, and learning strategies. She is a PhD candidate at Kansai University. She has been involved in designing English courses and classroom tasks for Japanese university students to foster self-regulation in English learning.

**Lea Kuznik** Born in 1975 in Ljubljana, Slovenia. Graduated in 1999, master`s degree in 2004 and doctor`s degree in 2007 at University of Ljubljana, Faculty of Arts, Department of Ethnology and Cultural Anthropology. She is an assistant for Slovene Ethnology. She has been taking interests on museology, children's museums and interactive learning environments, pedagogical and psychological theories of learning and play and developmental theories of children for years. Her doctoral thesis "Interactive Learning Environments and Children's Museums: Theoretical Model and It's Planning" presents first scientific research on children's museums in Slovenia. Her research is focused on up-to date technologies, virtual worlds, virtual museums, and possibilities for learning in virtual learning environments especially in educational virtual worlds. Her recent research project was designing an interactive learning environment for families in a shopping centre.

**Sabrina Leone** is a PhD student in E-learning at the Faculty of Engineering of the Università Politecnica delle Marche, Ancona, Italy. Her research interests are in lifelong learning, new technologies in tertiary teaching and learning, e-learning, cooperative learning, PLE. She was an Italian Government Lecturer in Italian Studies at the Faculty of Arts of the University of Wollongong, Australia, in 2006-2008. Her career started in 1992 and has developed in the fields of education (secondary and tertiary teacher and consultant), business consultancy (quality systems designer and manager) and linguistic mediation.She has been involved in European special projects (Socrates programmes with Sweden, The Netherlands, Great Britain, Germany, Bulgaria, Lithuania, Estonia) and Italian ones (IG students, Business Laboratory for Italian University and Secondary School students). She has studied and worked abroad (Great Britain, France, Ireland, United States, Australia). She has a honours degree in Foreign Languages (1988, I.U.L.M, Milan), one in Business Management (1998, University of Campobasso) and one in Sciences of Linguistic Mediation (2004, Scuola Superiore per Mediatori Linguistici, Florence).

**Anthonia N. Maduekwe** holds a doctorate degree in Teaching English as a Second Language (TESL) from the University of Lagos, Akoka, where she is currently an Associate Professor in the Department of Arts and Social Sciences Education. She is a teacher, an English language educator; a researcher and practitioner. Dr. Maduekwe is an outstanding scholar who has to her credit over forty-five publications in learned journals. Her research interest focuses on ICT integration in Teacher Education, Teacher Professional Development, Curriculum and Instruction and English for Academic Purposes. She is an active member of professional bodies such as World Council for Curriculum and Instruction (WCCI), International Association of Teachers of English as a Foreign Language (IATEFL), Reading Association of Nigeria (RAN), and Nigerian Association of Professional Educators (NAPE) etc. She also consults in various capacity building and teacher training for development oriented organisations including UNESCO, UNICEF, RAN, LSUBEB, etc. She is married and blessed with children and grand children.

**Luca Mainetti** is an associate professor of Software Engineering and Computer Graphics in the Department of Innovation Engineering at the University of Salento (Italy). His research interests include web design methodologies, notations and tools, services oriented architectures and applications, collaborative computer graphics. He is co-author of the methodologies for web applications design HDM (Hypermedia Design Model), W2000, and IDM (Interactive Dialogue Model). He is scientific coordinator of the GSA Lab - Graphics and Software Architectures Lab (since 2007) and the IDA Lab - ID-Automation Lab (since 2008) of the Department of Innovation Engineering at the University of Salento. He is member of the scientific council of the CRIT center – Center of Research on the enabling technologies the Internet of Things of the Department of Innovation Engineering at the University of Salento (since 2007). He is Rector's delegate to Information and Communication Technology (since 2007).

**José María Marín** received a degree in Mechanical Engineering from Universidad Nacional de Educacion a Distancia (U.N.E.D.), Madrid (Spain) in 2000, and the PhD degree in Mechanical Engineering from Carlos III University, Madrid (Spain), in 2009. Since 2001, he is a lecturer and researcher at the Miguel Hernandez University, Elche (Spain), where he teaches Theory of Mechanisms. His main researching activities have been developed in the area of mechanical vibrations, working with ball bearing, roller bearing and gears. Currently, he is working on the development of mechanical structures and robots' joints.

**Mª del Mar Marín-Sánchez,** holds a PhD in Agricultural Engineering and Master in Co-operatives Administration, from Universidad Politécnica de Valencia, Spain. She is Professor of Accounting and Tax Management at the Economic and Social Sciences Department of the Faculty of Business Administration, Universidad Politécnica de Valencia, Spain. She has taught in more than 30 Master Programmes and post-graduate courses. In addition she is responsible of the Accounting and Tax Management Area at the Centre for Research in Business Management (CEGEA), at this University. She is specialised in Accounting Management, Methodologies in Higher Education, Tax Management, Co-operative Enterprises and Agribusiness Management. She has published more than 35 scientific publications: articles in indexed reviews, books, chapters in collective books, papers. She has carried out several Research and Development Projects with public funding. She is member of several Scientific Associations: *Spanish Association of Accounting and Business Administration* (AECA), *Spanish Association of Agricultural Economy* (AEEA), among others.

**Alicia Mateos-Ronco,** holds a PhD in Agricultural Engineering and Master in Agribusiness Marketing and Administration, from Universidad Politécnica de Valencia, Spain. She is Professor of Accounting and Financial Analysis at the Economic and Social Sciences Department of the Faculty of Business Administration, Universidad Politécnica de Valencia, Spain. She has taught in more than 30 Master Programmes and post-graduate courses. In addition she is responsible of the Production and Cost Management Area at the Centre for Research in Business Management (CEGEA), at this University. She is specialised in Accounting Management, Methodologies in Higher Education, Cost Management Systems, Cooperative Enterprises and Agribusiness Management. She has carried out more than 10 Research and Development Projects with public funding. She has published more than 30 scientific publications: articles in indexed reviews, books, chapters in collective books, papers. She is member of several Scientific Associations: *Spanish Association of Accounting and Business Administration* (AECA). *Spanish Association of Accounting Lecturers* (ASEPUC), among others.

**Minoru Nakayama** graduated from Tokyo Gakugei University in 1983 and earned his Masters of Education degree in 1985. He received his Doctor of Engineering degree from Tokyo Institute of Technology in 1989, and is currently an associate professor at the Center for Research and Development of Educational Technology (CRADLE) and Department of Human System Science in the Graduate School of Decision Science and Technology, Tokyo Institute of Technology. His research interests in educational technology include learning assessment, human behavioral science, visual perception and development of learning support systems. He is an associate editor of Japan Society for Educational Technology's Educational Technology Research Journal and the IEICE Transactions on Information Systems.

**Peter Neema-Abooki** holds various academic credentials in both philosophical and theological disciplines besides a Post Graduate Diploma in Education, a Masters and a Doctor of Philosophy – both degrees in Educational Management. He is currently a Senior Lecturer of Educational Management and Administration, Human Resource Management, Educational Policy and Planning, and Educational Foundations at the East African Institute of Higher Education Studies and Development (EAIHESD) at Makerere University. Earlier on he lectured in Educational Foundations, Educational Administration, and Educational Planning and Management at Kampala University, Kisubi Brothers' Centre for Uganda Martyrs University, and Kyambogo University. He doubles as External Examiner in several Universities. His scholarly research has delved into issues that encompass not only managerial, with specific focus on Quality Assurance (QA), but also theological and socio-anthropological disciplines. On the International scene Peter is a member of, inter alia, Profiles International Uganda (The Assessment Company), Golden Neo-Life Dynamite (GNLD) International, St. James Parish-Family, Glendale, ARIZONA, U. S. A, Scientific and Technical Committee on Humanities and Social Sciences (WASET), International Academy of African Business and Development (IAABD), The Future(s) of Education Project, Oxford Abstracts, and Quest International.

**Flora Ning** is a Research Fellow in the Institutional Analysis Group at City University of Hong Kong. She is a senior statistician with research interests and publications in the fields of statistics, education and metacognition. Dr Ning was educated at the universities of Cambridge and Oxford where she studied statistics, and has a lead role as an institutional statistician and researcher at City University of Hong Kong.

**Mario G.R. Pagliacci** had a long experience as a manager in big and small private enterprises located in Italy and abroad. Nowadays he is a member of the Board of Directors or the Expert Committee in several enterprises. After 1995 he teaches "Financial Management" at the Faculty of Economics of Università degli Studi di Perugia (Italy). He is the Scientific Coordinator of "Laboratorio Athena" for researches and projects in business area, in cooperation with Italian and European organizations. He is a member of the Scientific Committee of an European Association of Economists named "Réseau PGV" (Headquarter in Grenoble-France), and he is engaged in several scientific programs in cooperation with Eastern and Western European Universities. For the account of Romanian and Bulgarian Governmental Organizations, he plays the role of expert in evaluation of research and teaching projects.

**Valeria Pandolfini** is a P.h.D. in Research Methodology in Human Sciences at the University of Genoa, Faculty of Science of Education and assistant for the chairs of Sociology of Education, Methodology of Social Research and Sociology of Labour. She submitted her DPhil on online learning communities and distance education, on the basis of an evaluative study of an adult blended course. Currently is Research Fellow at Di.S.A., Department of Anthropological Sciences, University of Genoa and the main topics of her research are generally connected to the methodological aspects of social research, with particular regard to the link between new technologies and education, impacts of new media on human interaction, blended learning in higher education and labour market studies. She has published several articles and has given numerous presentations at national and international professional conferences.

**Luis Payá** was born in Alicante (Spain) in 1979. He received his M. Eng. degree in Industrial Engineering from Miguel Hernandez University (Elche, Spain, 2002), receiving an award from the Spanish ministry of education for his student record. Since 2003, he is a lecturer and researcher at the Miguel Hernandez University, where he teaches Electricity, Control and Systems Engineering. He is currently working on his PhD thesis. His current research interests include mobile robotics and visual navigation using appearance-based techniques, map creation and robots localization. He is also interested in the application of information and communication technologies to engineering education.

**Oscar Reinoso** received the industrial engineer and PhD degrees from Polytechnic University of Madrid (UPM) in 1991 and 1996 respectively. From 1994 to 1997 he works in the Research & Development department of Protos Desarrollo in a visual inspection system. Since 1997, he has been at the Miguel Hernández University, as professor in control, robotics and computer vision. His research interests include robotics, teleoperated robots, climbing robots, visual servoing, visual inspection systems. He is author of several books, papers and communications in the cited topics. Prof. Reinoso is a member of the CEA-IFAC and IEEE

**Rowena Santiago** is a tenured professor at California State University San Bernardino and is the founding director of the Teaching Resource Center (TRC). As TRC Director, she develops and implements faculty development programs that support faculty in their teaching innovations and enhancement of teaching skills. She earned her Doctor of Education degree (Instructional Technology) from The University of Georgia (1990), her Masters in Education degree from Tokyo Gakugei University (1985), and her bachelor's degree in Elementary Education from the Philippine Normal University (1970). Her research activities include faculty readiness for online teaching, use of technology for course transformation, and the role of learner characteristics in e-learning among students in the US and Japan

**Kristina Shin** was educated in Korea, the USA and the UK and has over 10 years experience in higher education. Prior to joining the Hong Kong Polytechnic University, Dr. Shin worked for Triumph International Overseas Ltd., one of the world's leading lingerie brands, as a designer. Her interests include design and education.Dr. Shin is holder of the 2004 International Award for Innovative Excellence in Teaching, Learning, and Technology and is founding editor for the International Journal of Fashion Design, Technology and Education. She has taught extensively in both the USA and Hong Kong.

**Craig Smith** is the Chair of the Department of Global Affairs at Kyoto University of Foreign Studies, Japan. He teaches language skills and peace studies courses. He has a Primary School Teacher's Certificate and seven year's teaching experience at elementary schools in Canada, New Zealand, and Japan. His current research interests include vocabulary teaching and learning, blended-learning curriculum development, and two-language team teaching. He is involved in extracurricular experiential learning projects with his students which include a number of international community work projects and international student conferences.

**David Úbeda** was born in Elche (Spain) in 1979. He received his Eng. Degree in Telecommunications from Miguel Hernández University (Elche, Spain, 2005). Since 2007, he is a lecturer and researcher at the Miguel Hernández University, where he teaches Engineering Applied Informatics. He is currently dealing post-graduate courses. His current research interests include mobile robotics and human-robot interaction. He is also interested in the application of information and communication technologies to engineering education.

**Ruxandra Vasilescu** is an Associate Professor PhD in the LSP Department, Faculty of Foreign Languages and Literature, Spiru Haret University, Romania. Coordinator of Online Master Programmes, using e-learning platform Blackboard. Coordinator of the research projects (2009-2011) *Optimization of translations implementation in the Romanian public sphere* and *Terminological database in the legal field (in Romanian, English and French).* Scientific publications: author and co – author of 3 books and academic courses, 2 explanatory dictionaries, 2 novels and an essay translated and published by Romanian publishing houses, 10 articles in Romanian reviews, 1 study published in a French and an Irish volume

**Hiroh Yamamoto** received his Bachelor's degree in Communication Engineering from Shinshu University, Nagano, Japan in 1966. He earned his Doctor of Engineering degree from Tokyo Institute of Technology in 1999. From 1966 to 2002, he worked at Hitachi Electronics Services Co., Ltd., where he served as director of the company. He joined Shinshu University in 2002, where he held the position of Professor at the Research Center for Education Programs. He is currently a professor emeritus at the same institution and serves as a research fellow at the Center for Research and Development of Educational Technology (CRADLE), Tokyo Institute of Technology. His research interests include e-Learning and assessment. He is a member of Japan's Institute of Electronics, Information and Communication Engineers (IEICE) and the Japan Society for Educational Technology (JSET).

# Index

## L

Breinigsville, PA USA
13 October 2010
247145BV00002BD/5/P